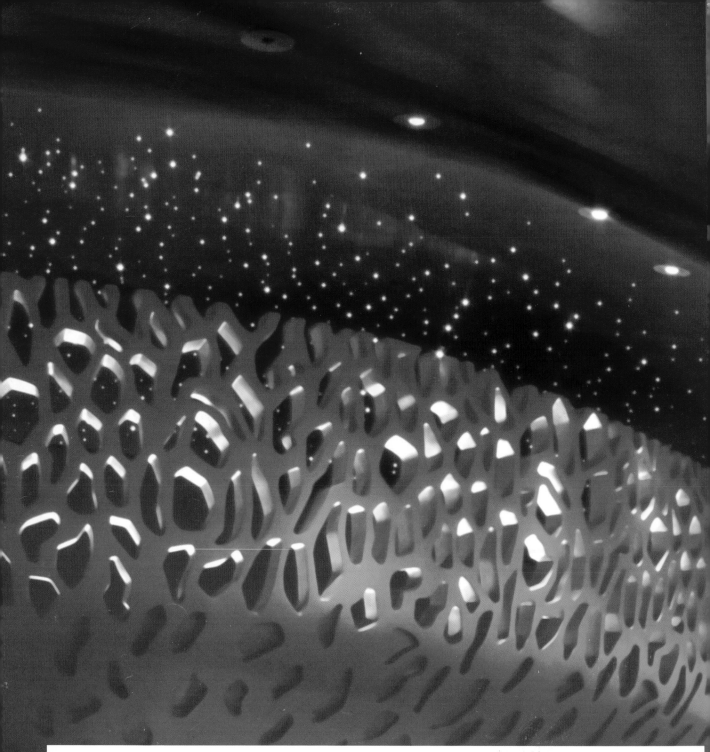

IMPRINT

PROJECT MANAGEMENT
Florian Kobler, Cologne

COLLABORATION
Barbara Huttrop, Cologne
Sonja Altmeppen, Berlin

PRODUCTION
Thomas Grell, Cologne

DESIGN
Sense/Net, Andy Disl
and Birgit Reber, Cologne

GERMAN TRANSLATION
Caroline Behlen, Berlin;
pp.22-35
Christiane Court,
Frankfurt

FRENCH TRANSLATION
Jacques Bosser, Paris

© VG Bild-Kunst, Bonn
2006, for the works by
Frank Stella

PRINTED IN ITALY
ISBN 3–8228–3989–2

© 2006 TASCHEN GMBH
Hohenzollernring 53
D – 50672 Cologne
www.taschen.com

ARCHITECTURE NOW!

Architektur heute / L'architecture d'aujourd'hui
Philip Jodidio

TASCHEN

KÖLN LONDON LOS ANGELES MADRID PARIS TOKYO

CONTENTS

CONTENTS

INTRODUCTION

OUT OF THE BOX

Architecture has broken out of the box, literally and figuratively. New technologies in design and construction have at last begun to utterly transform the built environment. In part because of these developments, boundaries that have separated architecture from art and design are also falling. The very idea of space and how it is manipulated has evolved through the understanding provided by a number of artists whose expression necessarily involves the third dimension. All of this curiously does not mean that Modernism is dead. It is just that there are so many new possibilities offered to architects that even minimalist forms are emerging from different points of view. The object is surely not just to reproduce what came before, but also to rethink architecture. This book is by no means an exhaustive selection of the architecture of the past three or five years, but it does represent a subjective overview of numerous building types and trends on an international basis. It is no accident that most of the architects featured in this book have not been in previous volumes of *Architecture Now*. Gehry, Koolhaas or Herzog & de Meuron are here, but so are Patrick Jouin, Philippe Rahm and Klein Dytham. Jouin is a designer whose efforts have taken him into the realm of architecture, in particular with his client the star-chef Alain Ducasse. Rahm (formerly of Décosterd & Rahm) is exploring the frontiers between physiology and architecture, while Astrid Klein and Mark Dytham are shaking up the Tokyo scene with everything from a 274-meter construction screen (Green Green Screen, Omotesando) to their SuperDeluxe space, described by them as "a place of fun and experimentation. A gallery, a bar, a kitchen, a jazz club, and a film studio. A cinema. A library, a school, a concert hall, and a theater." Set aside your preconceived ideas. This is Architecture Now!

GIMME SHELTER

Once upon a time, architecture served only to give shelter from the elements and an occasional wolf. A "roof above one's head" is still a primary concern, even if architects strive to make the house more and more remarkable. The Casa Equis, located in Cañete, Peru is the surprising effort by the fortyish architects Jean-Pierre Crousse and Sandra Barclay to "create the intimacy or domesticity necessary in order to live in the desert where the house is located, without denying or falsifying the situation." A picture of a child swimming in the glass pool of the Casa Equis, suspended far above a wild beach, made the rounds of the world's architecture magazines, as though a recipe for true weightlessness had finally been discovered. The problem faced by David Chipperfield in his House in Galicia was somewhat different. The 210 m² residence had to fit not only in with natural rocks, but also with an existing band of heterogeneous houses. The architect's capacity to introduce a real, varied modernity in these circumstances is a testimony to a mastery that speaks of a real change that has occurred. The progressive improvement of communications, information and trade that goes by the name of "globalization" has given rise to a new breed of architect, as much at home in Cañete, Peru as in Corrubedo, Spain. Their goal is not to create a pastiche of local architecture, nor to impose an obviously foreign vision, but to react to circumstances in an intelligent and coherent way. Today's modernity is no longer about the geometry of Euclidean boxes, even if an architect like Chipperfield is characterized by a minimalist esthetic. It is about using sensibility and technology to respond to a client's desires. This was certainly the case when the inventive Japanese architect Shuhei Endo was faced with a steeply inclined 20-meter long triangular lot, whose depth varies between 4 and just 1.5 meters. His Rooftecture S house demonstrates that extreme conditions can generate unusual, esthetically challenging solutions. The urban crowding of Japan, particularly along its east coast, often gives architects an obligation to deal with small or oddly shaped sites. The young architects of Eastern Design built their Slit House on a lot 50 meters deep and 7.5 meters wide. Though almost three times larger than the Rooftecture S site, this narrow lot inspired a remarkable design that has no less than 60 14 cm-wide slits and no actual windows. The Japanese consider the play of light within architecture to be a manifestation of nature, where green spaces may be few and far between. Though it is a concrete rectangle, the Slit House uses this traditional sensitivity to light to experiment with the elimination of traditional windows.

An Eastern esthetic is also present in the unlikely location of Hasselt, Belgium. The Villa C designed for Frédéric Chaillet, a senior partner of the architecture firm Groep Delta, contrasts an entrance marked by a massive almost blind 26-meter-long wall made of Waimes stone with a fully glazed garden façade. The use of a reflecting pool with seven stepping-stones near the dining room is related to the owner's interest in Asia, in part because of the shimmering play of light that it generates inside of the house. Made with strong contrasts, fashioned from stone, steel, glass and wood, the Villa C is an excellent example of the kind of stylistic freedom that reigns in contemporary architecture. The H House in Corsica, designed by the Paris architects Jakob + MacFarlane, has not yet been built, but its design is indicative of one strong trend in recent designs – the use of sophisticated computer technology to create forms that seem to spring from the earth itself. Where early Modernism sought most often to sit lightly on the earth, often lifting buildings up on *pilotis* for example, today's architects are more likely to dig or to inspire themselves directly from the topography of a site.

BED AND BOARD

Although hotels have to meet stringent functional requirements, it has definitely become fashionable to call on well-known designers in a bid to bring in more clients. Ian Schrager's style of hotel business, with interiors by figures like Philippe Starck, has caught on in many cities. The young architects of GRAFT recently designed Q!, a Berlin hotel with an inventive approach despite a relatively modest budget. The red wrap-around bar and restaurant brings to mind the work of Neil Denari, while integrated furniture and décor in the rooms succeeds in giving a decided flair to the establishment. In what might be called the ultimate design hotel, the large Spanish chain Silken asked no fewer than nineteen internationally recognized architects and designers to decorate the 342 rooms of the new Hotel Puerta América in Madrid. With an exterior by Jean Nouvel, the Puerta América has floors conceived by Zaha Hadid, David Chipperfield, Mark Newson, Ron Arad, Arata Isozaki and John Pawson. This mixture of architects and designers might seem surprising but there has been something of a blurring of lines between the two disciplines, with designers more and more often seeking to build. The question of where "good" design ends and big business starts is posed by the Hotel Puerta América, since creating rooms or hallways for a chain establishment is a daunting challenge even for the most talented creators.

One intelligent young designer who certainly has the ambition to break into the field of architecture is the Frenchman Patrick Jouin. Jouin has made a name for himself by creating restaurants for the celebrity chef Alain Ducasse. It was for Ducasse that Jouin created Chlösterli in the upscale Swiss ski resort of Gstaad. Fashioned inside a large wooden chalet built around 1700 by the monks of Rougemont Abbey, Chlösterli includes two restaurants, a bar and a discotheque. Furniture created by Jouin, sometimes with tongue-in-cheek farm themes, graces the restaurants. Despite the complex and rather dark interiors of the old building, Jouin has affirmed an emerging style in Gstaad, one that sets aside cool minimalism in favor of a more varied, or more heavily ornate décor. Though Jouin is not the only designer to be heading in this direction, he is one of the most prominent. His Mix restaurant in the Mandalay Bay Hotel in Las Vegas is intended to live up to the city's reputation for extravagance. Calling on volcanic imagery, he did not hesitate to design a Murano chandelier with 15 000 hand-blown glass bubbles.

Nor are well-designed hotels confined to major cities anymore. Two examples published in this volume are in fact located in some of the most remote areas of the world. The ESO Hotel in Cerro Paranal, Chile, was built by the German architects Auer+Weber at an altitude of 2 400 meters in the mountainous northern area of the Atacama desert. Built to serve users of the Very Large Telescope (VLT) perched there, the ESO Hotel does an excellent job taking the site into account while providing guests with an unexpected degree of comfort. Destined mostly to less scientifically inclined tourists, Longitude 131° is an extension to the Yulara Tourist Resort complex designed by the architect Philip Cox. Although nearby Ayers Rock is a familiar symbol of Australia, this region is rather inhospitable, with temperatures often above 40°. Longitude 131° respects its spectacular natural setting, sitting above the earth on steel piles. As both of these hotels demonstrate, the idea that "good" architecture is of interest only to the *cognoscenti* is no longer valid. Perhaps because of the public success of a certain number of signature "architect's buildings," and also because chains like Aman Resorts have imposed a high standard of design, efforts like the Hotel Puerta América or these remote facilities have become more and more common.

Though the practical side of hotels does often prohibit them from being pure expressions of architectural thought, computer-driven design and manufacturing are soon going to make inroads even in this area. The Rotterdam firm ONL [Oosterhuis_Lénárd] have designed a very unusual hotel for Dubai, called the Flyotel. Evoking a bird about to take off, the 600-room five star Flyotel would be the first example of the application of "non-standard" architectural design to such a large project. Organized at the Pompidou Center in Paris in early 2004, the Non-Standard Architecture exhibition featured ONL as well as eleven other firms including UN Studio, R&Sie (François Roche), Greg Lynn, and Asymptote. The aim of the exhibition, according to curator Fréderic Migayrou, was "not merely to present examples of digital or virtual architecture which deal with questions of representation (such as virtuality and hyperspace), but rather to highlight current modifications to the industrialization of architecture. The widespread use of application programs based on algorithmic systems presupposes changes in design and production tools. "Non-Standard Architecture" is a reflection on the language of architecture and its field of application, based on the exploitation of digital elements. Traditional construction methods can now be contrasted with production based on the prototyping of prefabricated architectural elements." More clearly put, Migayrou and some of the architects involved in the show are convinced that a "file to factory" system that allows unique shapes to be created at the same costs as "standard" or repetitive ones, is about to sweep the world. Kas Oosterhuis confirms that the Flyotel, made to allow seaplanes to dock in its internal berth, will cost "only 10% more than a standard highrise structure."

SPACE MAKES ART

Museums have long been the object of particular attention from architects. Frank Lloyd Wright's Guggenheim in New York and many others showed that unusual or intriguing architecture can have an impact on the success of an institution, sometimes even creating a public demand even when the art collection concerned is not formidable (Guggenheim Bilbao). The adventures of Thomas Krens, the dynamic director of the Guggenheim appeared set to continue as he launched one project after another in distant parts of the globe, but Krens was abruptly replaced by his second in charge, Lisa Dennison in 2005. While it appears that Jean Nouvel's Guggenheim Rio is not about to be built, Krens helped organize a competition for a new museum in Guadalajara, Mexico in 2004–05. Won by Enrique Norten, the competition elicited other interesting proposals, such as that of Asymptote. Perching their design on the city's canyon edge, the New Yorkers let their imagination and their computers run free, creating a sculptural, almost liquid form that would have called on the same "non-standard" technologies as ONL's Flyotel. Another museum that will remain virtual is François Roche's Green Gorgon, a competition entry for Lausanne's new museum of contemporary art. Inspired by nature and protean in form, the Green Gorgon sprang from the Frenchman's insistence that architecture must tell a story, that it should be enriched by "fiction." In this instance the collaboration between Charles Perrault (1628–1703), author of the classic fairy tale book *Histoires ou contes du temps passé* (1697), and the garden designer André Le Nôtre (1613–1700) of the labyrinth at Versailles was the starting point for the proposal of R&Sie. As Roche says, Le Nôtre and Perrault did not so much create a mathematical design as they attempted to develop a place where visitors would accept to "lose themselves." "It is precisely that heterotypic dimension that conditions our proposal," concludes Roche.

It might be said that Yoshio Taniguchi, the Japanese author of the recent transformation of New York's Museum of Modern Art, incarnates the opposite end of the theoretical spectrum, as far as museum design is concerned. Working in collaboration with the New York architects KPF and in particular Steven Rustow, Taniguchi succeeded in bringing some of the wonderful subtlety of his Japanese museums to the Big Apple. There is however a gap between the very size of spaces like the second floor atrium and the atmosphere of intimacy that had nurtured MoMA's role as the preeminent place of display for the art of modernity. It may be that the curators simply have to come to grips with the new space and select works that inhabit it with more force and legitimacy. For the moment, Barnett Newman's *Broken Obelisk*, described by one critic as a "mediocre sculpture by a good painter," vies unsuccessfully for attention in the atrium's oversized volume. Urban in its scale and in its rapport with neighboring buildings, Taniguchi's MoMA is also the fruit of curatorial and trustee decisions rendered possible by a very successful fund-raising campaign. Large exhibition galleries have been designed specifically to accept the weight and volume of some of Richard Serra's heaviest sculptures, but it may be fair to ask if MoMA is really the best place for contemporary art. It was and remains a temple of modernity, in its 20th century incarnation. MoMA is in good part responsible for the successful transition of modern art from revolutionary struggle to accepted norm. Events in contemporary art and indeed in recent architecture have gone in new directions to which both Taniguchi and the institution itself may not be well suited. Perhaps new expressions spring from a grittier, more hostile environment than the polished floors and white expanses of MoMA.

Herzog & de Meuron have taken a different approach in the Walker Art Center expansion in Minneapolis. The Swiss architects have created an asymmetrical stamped aluminum mesh box, but the external appearance of the architecture may be less the point than the attempt to create a place where different art forms can interact in "entirely unexpected and innovative ways." A glance at the Walker's program shows that the slogan "Where art meets life" is appropriate both to the museum itself and to its new architecture: dance, performance art, film, painting, music or theater are all part of the mix. Might it be that a more traditional version of the grand white box (MoMA) just doesn't fit anymore with the explosion of multi-disciplinary forms that is invading the arts? This would actually be less of a commentary on the success of MoMA (obviously great) than it would be about the occurrence of a real sea change in art. Where Taniguchi reveled in the creation of a temple for 20th century art, Herzog & de Meuron have leapt whole-heartedly into the 21st century at the Walker.

Not all new museums represent an attempt to redefine art and architecture. The Museum of Natural Science at Matsunoyama in Japan by Tezuka Architects seeks nonetheless to break new ground. Consisting essentially of a 111-meter-long Corten steel tube with a 34-meter-high observation tower attached, the facility is intended for viewing life beneath the surface of the abundant local snowfalls. Although dealing with snow loads that can reach 2000 tons naturally imposes technical restrictions on any building, Tezuka Architects have turned an apparent constraint into a source of invention. Like a great submarine, their design makes light of most existing museums. In form and function their steel tube is at once part of its site, and yet must sit lightly on it due to the 20 cm expansion of the structure in summer. It would be difficult to classify this work as part of any specific trend, even if it was shown at the last Venice Architecture Biennale as representative of the tendency to relate architecture to the earth. It is neither minimalist nor "non-standard," and yet it is very contemporary. Here as elsewhere, style seems to exist in the eye of the beholder more than in the design itself.

ART MAKES SPACE

The rapport between art and architecture is one that stretches back to the earliest recorded buildings, even if the definition of art has evolved substantially since it was considered a decorative part of churches or palaces. It can be said that art gave up some of its natural connection to the "real" world when paintings were hung on museum walls and sculptures placed on pedestals. A part of the real conquest of contemporary art has been to reclaim the space outside of the museum, to again invest a "real" environment. The painter Anselm Kiefer has long been known for his interest in space, whether in his paintings or in his metal (often lead) sculptures. More than many contemporary painters, he has created his own labyrinthine world in art, one where oblique references to myth or historic fact make up a kind of sedimentary history. Adding hay or sunflower seeds to paintings, as well as an often remarkably thick impasto, he frequently challenges the idea of depth or perspective with pieces that evoke a lost and future world. In this context, it might be surprising that Kiefer has for the past 13 years been working on his 35-hectare studio grounds located in Barjac, in the Cévennes area of France. Certainly not an atelier in the traditional sense, *La Ribaute* is rather a sedimentary accumulation of spaces, above and below ground. As is the case in many of his paintings, *La Ribaute* gives a feeling of having come from another time, or of being the remnant of some imperfectly understood civilization. There is no answer to the question of why he has erected bright greenhouses and dark worlds made of lead and water except that this architecture is the expression of his art, indeed of himself and his times. These built forms might bear witness to an esoteric knowledge whose meaning is lost in time, or to the terrible secret of a time too close for comfort. It is said that the difference between art and architecture is that the latter serves a purpose. And what if its purpose is to create art? The esthetic impulse and *raison d'être* behind Kiefer's "architecture" is his art, his inner world. True, visionary architects like Constant have sometimes imagined new worlds, and eccentric figures like Simon Rodia, who built the Watts Towers, have given architectural form to their own esthetic sensibility. It might well be that more conventional architects could learn from looking at examples like that of Anselm Kiefer.

Actually defining architecture may be as complex as defining art. Many different types of expression are covered by these catchall words, even if the criterion of function haunts built form. One of the recurring thoughts in contemporary architecture may have best been expressed by the words of Hamlet: "O! that this too too solid flesh would melt, Thaw, and resolve itself into a dew." The Blur Building designed by Diller + Scofidio for the Expo 02 Swiss national exhibition at Yverdon tried rather convincingly to look like a cloud hovering over the lake. Others speak of creating architecture that will react to its visitors, almost like a living creature, while some would apparently content themselves with the purely virtual. Toyo Ito's *Tower of the Winds* (Yokohama, Kanagawa, 1986) stands as a reminder that a reactive architecture, situated at the frontier to art, can indeed mark its time and raise the question of just what a form can signify. Imagine, for a moment, that art too can invest space and give it meaning, often in a more ephemeral way than architecture, but the Blur Building or the temporary pavilions at London's Serpentine Gallery show that durability is no longer a necessity for some. The American video artist Bill Viola has frequently imagined his works in an architectural setting, and indeed their scale and nature is such that they most often demand, and indeed transform space. Viola's recent collaboration with opera/theater director Peter Sellars and conductor Esa-Pekka Salonen on a 4-hour video/film to accompany Richard Wagner's opera *Tristan und Isolde* and a staging in Paris address the issues of image, space and representation that exist most powerfully at the frontier between art and architecture. "I wanted to create an image world that existed in parallel to the action on the stage," says Viola, "in the same way that a more subtle poetic voice narrates the hidden dimensions of our inner lives. The images are intended to function as symbolic, inner representations that become, to echo the words of Seyyed Hossein Nasr, "reflections of the spiritual world in the mirror of the material and the temporal." Viola writes of "the infinite ocean of an invisible immaterial world" in evoking the first act of Tristan, and gives an image of fire and light to the third act: "Act III," he explains, "describes The Dissolution of the Self in the stages of dying, the delicate and excruciating process of the separation and disintegration of the physical, perceptual and conceptual components of conscious awareness. We are plunged into the agony and delirium of death and suffering, replete with visions, dreams and hallucinatory revelations that play across the surface of a dying man's mind. When the flames of passion and fever finally engulf the mind's eye, and desire's body can never be met, the reflecting surface is shattered and collapses into undulating wave patterns of pure light." This is not to suggest that Viola's images of fire, water and light are an expression of architecture in the same sense even as Kiefer's studio. Viola uses art, and in this instance, the space of a stage, to evoke issues of life and death. Nor is architecture condemned only to the numbing exercise of budgetary restraint and placement of fire exits. Architecture at the edge dissolves the box into fire and light to become a virtual image only, but this edge is where the thought is occurring, where the built forms of tomorrow will take shape. Artists like Kiefer and Viola can help to show the way in both esthetic and intellectual terms.

BIG AND SEXY

Well-known architects often start their careers with small projects. Frank O. Gehry made himself a name with bits of chain link fence and tarmac on his kitchen floor. Big projects are another kettle of fish, as Gehry found when he designed the Disney Concert Hall in Los Angeles. Other architects write books and do drawings as Rem Koolhaas and Zaha Hadid did before they hit the big time. It just takes a while until a client with enough money will trust an innovative architect with a major building. The largest and most politically sensitive project of the brilliant Catalan architect Enric Miralles was completed only after his untimely death. But many are still not convinced by his Scottish Parliament in Edinburgh (completed by his former partner and wife Benedetta Tagliabue of EMBT and the local firm RMJM Scotland Ltd). The complexities of the project led to an official inquiry into the work, that concluded that there had been insufficient communication between EMBT and RMJM and too little control of expenses. Since expense overruns are thought to be typical of inventive architect, this example does little to shore up the reputation of the profession. Perhaps overly complicated, the Scottish Parliament was not as much the victim of an architect's hubris as it was of bureaucratic delay and indecision. In the official report on the project Lord Fraser of Carmyllie submitted to the Scottish Parliament on June 24, 2004, it is written that "Tempting as it is to lay all the blame at the door of a deceased wayward Spanish architectural genius, his stylized fashion of working and the strained relationship between his widow and RMJM in Edinburgh, the analysis of the Auditor General is unimpeachable. Costs rose because the client (first the Secretary of State and latterly the Parliament) wanted increases and changes or at least approved of them in one manifestation or another."[1]

It may be that private clients stimulate the efficiency of famous architects more than public ones. Then again, it may indeed be difficult for talented architects who are used to small projects to suddenly take on large ones. Massimiliano Fuksas is used to fairly large jobs, but none on the scale of his Fiera Milano, the new fair site of the Italian city. Essentially completed in a record time of 27 months, the complex measures no less than 1.4 million square meters in floor area and features a 1.5 kilometer-long central walkway whose artful ebb and flow seems to have been the product of a sophisticated computer program. In fact, Fuksas, based in Rome and Paris, does not actually use computers for his own designs. Naturally his office staff makes abundant use of the latest technology, but the architect prefers to draw or even to paint his buildings before turning them into digital wonders. In this case, he was inspired by storms or even tornadoes for the walkway's signature covering. Although much is made of the virtues of the computer, it is apparent in Milan that using relatively traditional means, Fuksas has been able to create a very contemporary form in an efficient and timely way. This success eluded EMBT in Edinburgh with the attenuating circumstances already described.

Rem Koolhaas/OMA may well be the highest profile architect of the moment, in good part because of his books, from *Delirious New York* to *S, M, L, XL*, and in part because of his own distinctive personality. Though OMA is much talked about, their buildings have only recently begun to keep pace with their public relations. Koolhaas is justifiably proud of the new Central Library in Seattle. As is typical of the firm, an effort was made not only to provide an appropriate envelope for the library, but also to innovate in both structure and function. Intended to be "transparent and open" unlike most libraries, the structure is largely sheathed in glass allowing views from within and without of the activities. Its angled shape is not so much an esthetic whim as it is a calculated effort to control the type and quality of light reaching interior spaces. A system of "floating platforms" and a diagonal grid intended to protect against earthquakes or wind damage are amongst the structural innovations. Within the library, a unique "Books Spiral" penetrates four levels of the stacks and contains the entire nonfiction collection, allowing for increased capacity and easier expansion of the number of books in the future. While structural innovation might well be expected of such a well-known architect, it is surely more significant that Koolhaas/OMA have dared to shake up as conservative a milieu as that of librarians, accustomed to nothing other than neatly arranged linear kilometers of stacks. The approach to the public and its use of the building is also inventive.

[1] www.scottish.parliament.uk/vli/holyrood/inquiry/sp205–00.htm

Zaha Hadid, a former partner of OMA, has also begun to build at a sustained pace, after years of trend-setting graphic work. Identified in the ground-breaking 1988 exhibition at MoMA as one of the founders of *Deconstructivist Architecture* along with Koolhaas, her current work assumes much more fluidity than the angular compositions of the Russians might have implied. Described as the "nerve center of the whole factory complex" her BMW Central Building in Leipzig tackles as staid an area for architectural innovation as a typical library. Speaking of using the architecture to create an "overall transparency of the internal organization," but also to mix functions "to avoid the traditional segregation of status groups," Hadid makes it clear that like Koolhaas, she aims at nothing less than a revision of staid methods. In the fluidity of her design she challenges the cut and dry alignments that made Henry Ford able to promise a Model T to his clients in any color, as long as it was black. Hadid also challenges the modernist precept of strict geometric plans, favoring a more organic and continual flow of movements. What is intriguing in the case of both Seattle and Leipzig is that the natural design preferences of the architects seem to truly be in tune with the better interests of the clients. Where famous architects have often sought to impose their esthetic signature in inappropriate circumstances, Koolhaas and Hadid are taking steps to truly broaden the appeal of what can be called "intelligent" architecture. Of course it is a battle for an architect to convince clients as firmly established as the Seattle Central Library and BMW that their methods can be improved, although these two graduates of London's AA have clearly reached a level of notoriety that permits them to take architecture itself in a new direction.

TEMPORARY CONTEMPORARY

The idea that architecture must be durable continues to hold sway for certain types of buildings. Museums, libraries, churches and banks usually have a bias toward permanence. And yet another side of contemporary design embraces the ephemeral, much as art has gone in the same direction. Then too, certain functions do not imply durability. One of the most inventive architects working today is Shigeru Ban. Ban is no stranger to temporary buildings as demonstrated by his Paper Refugee Shelter made with plastic sheets and paper tubes for the United Nations High Commission for Refugees (UNHCR). With the Bianimale Nomadic Museum, designed to show photographs by Gregory Colbert, Ban ventures into new territory. From March 5 to June 6, 2005, he created a 205-meter-long rectangular volume made essentially of shipping containers stacked on New York's Pier 54. It may be better to refrain from commentary on Colbert's pictures, but Ban's design does have something of "the atmosphere of a classical church," as the architect says. Though Japanese temples are rarely rectangular, there is also an Eastern feeling about the Nomadic Museum. Creating a feeling of spirituality out of steel containers and paper tubes is no small feat, but Shigeru Ban has shown repeatedly that unexpected materials can permit architectural innovation, even where permanence is not a goal. A more utilitarian demonstration of the Japanese architect's talents can be seen on the topmost level of the Pompidou Center in Paris, where he has installed his Paper Temporary Studio, a 115 m^2 arch made of paper tubes, timber, steel and PTFE membrane. While Ban works on the new facility of the Pompidou Center destined to the city of Metz, this office will remain on top of the Piano and Rogers building, almost like a reminder that the Pompidou Center was intended as a "flexible" structure.

Some young artists or architects turn their attentions to the ephemeral aspects of building for reasons of economy or because they are interested in somewhat neglected possibilities. This is definitely the case of two Germans with different approaches – the architect Andreas

Wenning and the artist Stephan Eberstadt. Wenning created baumraum in 2003 with an emphasis on tree-houses. Paying careful attention to the trees he builds in, Wenning demonstrates that the genre can be surprisingly rich in possibilities, most of which are not offered to more "down to earth" structures. Stefan Eberstadt has had an even more original idea with his Rucksack House, which is intended to simply hang from existing structures. As he says, "This reactivates the idea of the self-built anarchistic tree-house, this time, however, more prominently placed and structurally engineered." Eberstadt pleads for an increased awareness of the potential for interaction between contemporary art, architecture and other disciplines. His Rucksack House might be difficult to actually classify as art, except insofar as it offers a commentary on the hubris of architects, intent on setting the limits of their own structures as inviolable boundaries.

The Aga Khan Award for Architecture has long turned its attention to architectural forms that are rarely singled out in the professional press as examples of real, "useful" innovation. This must be the case of Nader Khalili's Sandbag Shelter Prototypes, recipient of a 2004 Aga Khan Award. Designed, like Ban's Paper Refugee Shelter, with the requirements of the UNHCR in mind, Khalili's system uses such readily available items as sand, earth or barbed wire to provide reliable and affordable housing. Such sandbag structures are inevitably ephemeral, but their simplicity and intelligence mean that they might well be more useful than any more "artistic" contribution to contemporary architecture. Neither complex computer programs nor technologically sophisticated materials are needed to bring architecture to people who could never afford even the basics of modern life. In this lies Nader Khalili's achievement.

Although statistics on church attendance in the West usually show a steady decline in religious fervor, architects are frequently called on to commemorate the rituals of life and death that the place of worship most often embodies. Architects have also tried, since the Second World War to come to grips with events whose horror goes beyond the restorative powers of any religion. The most visible and probably the most controversial of these efforts is Peter Eisenman's Monument to the Murdered Jews of Europe, located in the heart of Berlin, near both Pariser Platz and Potsdamer Platz. Eisenman's two-hectare field is occupied by 2751 blocks of grey concrete of heights varying between a few centimeters and four meters in height. The heaviness of this gesture is meant to mark the moral weight of the Shoah. In this respect the work serves a purpose even if it is not the type of function usually incarnated by architecture. Art then? And if neither art nor architecture could come to grips with such events, would Eisenman have invented a new approach, neither one nor the other and yet both at the same time?

Moshe Safdie has also dealt with the Shoah in his Holocaust History Museum at Yad Vashem. He has made a point of affirming "life after an experience of death," which may have been less the point of Eisenman's memorial. Yad Vashem is set in the Ein Kerem Valley, overlooking Jerusalem, and as such it can symbolize both the struggle and the triumphs of a people who have overcome so much adversity. Largely underground, Safdie's museum allows visitors to break into daylight only after they have experienced the exhibitions, while Eisenman's memorial lies open to the sky, bare and troubling in its graveyard grays. It seems certain that the Berlin memorial will continue to disturb visitors for some time to come, which is rarely the case of works of architecture. Here, meaning and form are intended to make certain that memory does not fade.

John Pawson is known for his minimalism. Indeed, his 1996 book *Minimum* was a bestseller. When he was asked by French Cistercian monks to work on a new monastery in the Czech Republic in 1999, he described it as the "project of a lifetime." Indeed, the monks had found that they had a great deal in common with the esthetics of Pawson, perhaps his handling of light in particular. The Monastery of Novy Dvûr is of course more than a place of worship, it is also the living space of the monks, and Pawson succeeded in combining the required practicality with an understated spirituality, basing the project partially in an abandoned 18th-century manor house located west of Prague. It has been said that the time of minimalism in contemporary architecture is past, and that today's designs are more likely to be complex or even decorative in their essence. Pawson proves that minimalism is more than a passing fashion. It is at the heart of Modernism, but it is also a recurrent theme of architecture and design over much longer periods, as the history of Japan might well prove.

While a monastery and memorials may garner an unusual amount of attention in today's architectural scene, a lighter, more cheerful expression of architectural invention deserves mention here if only because of its incongruity. Klein Dytham is a small Tokyo practice founded by Astrid Klein and Mark Dytham. Their Leaf Chapel, formed by two leaves made of glass and steel, is intended for weddings. Like an eyelid, the chapel opens at the appropriate moment (when the groom kisses the bride) to reveal a pond and garden. At only 168 m^2 this is a very small project, and yet it shows the adaptation of Western architects to a particularly Japanese view of weddings. Intended to inaugurate the "eternal" love of marriage, it is as airy and humorous as a passing cloud.

NATURE RULES
Though it may be that the fashion for virtual architecture is going the way of minimalism, some of the most interesting work being done currently involves sophisticated technology and the exploration of nature as a source for form and function. Whatever the future price of oil, ecologically oriented architecture has a bright future, if only for reasons of cost. The reduction of pollution is also a significant goal of what is commonly called "sustainability." The New York architect Michael McDonough, who worked for some time with SITE, has embarked on the construction of what might be called the ultimate sustainable house. His e-House "integrates over 100 new or advanced technologies (including high performance or historical or 'alternate' technologies) and proposes to develop a new lexicon for sustainable architecture theory." Energy efficiency is a goal, but even more the idea that the house can somehow form an "organic entity," respectful of its setting, or of local traditions. McDonough's effort to integrate the use of so many forms of technology is in itself interesting. He suggests that the very future of architecture may lie with such a holistic approach, one that makes use of as much knowledge as possible above and beyond the more basic structural language. Rather than creating a functioning shell, he proposes to make a building that will almost literally live and breathe with its occupants.

Dennis Dollens takes a different approach to nature, finding architectural inspiration in growth patterns. His recent work, such as the Digitally-Grown Tower published here, makes use of a program called Xfrog. As Dollens explains, "Xfrog is software made by a company called Greenworks in Germany. It employs botanic, L-system algorithms used in computational biological simulations to grow plants and landscapes for laboratory tests. Greenworks has taken L-systems and added proprietary programming that factors in things like gravity and phototropism and they have built an icon-based desktop. The software is basically used for futuristic landscapes or very realistic modeling for landscaping. I think I am the only person using it for such experimental architectural growth." In other words, what would happen if you could actually simulate botanic growth patterns in an architectural context? The result would most probably be efficient and would look quite different from existing architecture, while having a firm base in the reality of nature. Others like Frei Otto or Buckminster Fuller have experimented at the fringe between architecture and nature, but Dennis Dollens is using very recent computer technology to take this type of idea several steps further. Aside from his own designs, Dollens has worked to alert the academic community to the potential gains to be found in a cross-disciplinary approach that would enrich design through contact with science. As he writes, "…As designers, we should incorporate research methodologies and techniques rooted in science into the design process. For example, designers might look at the spatial, material, and structural qualities of shells, plants, or bones for attributes worth exploring. Such an engagement with process and research will eventually deepen our considerations of natural properties, subsequently manifested in environmentally responsible ways, while at the same time revealing forms extrapolated from nature—not merely designs emerging from *a priori* taste. There are potential collaborations in which scientists and designers could articulate and coordinate research goals, but for that to happen, a specific new type of design education must be evolved. One of the useful, if basic, guiding premises underlying such a development is the question: *How would nature solve this design problem?* The question could be incorporated easily into current design education as an evolutionary seed without overthrowing existing design pedagogy. Plant it and it will grow."

The Swiss architect Philippe Rahm has made quite a name for himself despite having actually built very little. With his former partner Gilles Décosterd (Décosterd & Rahm), he has actively explored underlying physiological factors that are frequently ignored or obviated in contemporary architecture. What happens, he asks, when factors like humidity, light, or oxygen content in the air are willfully manipulated? Taking virtual architecture a step further into the twilight zone of science, his *Ghost Flat* imagined a space whose furnishing and functions would be different according to the part of the light spectrum used. "The bedroom appears between 400 and 500 nanometers, the living room between 600 and 800 nanometers. The bathroom is localized in the ultraviolet, between 350 and 400." More worrisome is the work *ND Cult*. Imagine a roomy glass box with piped-in gas. Oxygen is reduced to six percent and the visitor enters "a space on the borderline of death, where perception and consciousness are modified in a way probably close to that of mystical states. Under these extreme physical conditions, the space is extremely dangerous, irreversible brain damage is possible and the risk of death is real." *ND* stands for Near Death. It might be interesting to recall Bill Viola's description of the third act of *Tristan* here: "We are plunged into the agony and delirium of death and suffering, replete with visions, dreams and hallucinatory revelations that play across the surface of a dying man's mind." Philippe Rahm's work has been shown extensively in art museums and Décosterd & Rahm were in charge of the Swiss Pavilion for the 2002 Venice Architecture Biennale. Their work there, called the Hormonorium, made use of 528 florescent tubes placed in the floor of the pavilion, with a resulting stimulation of the retina, which transmits information to the pineal gland causing a decrease in melatonin secretion. By so lowering the level of this hormone in the body, this environment allows us to experience a decrease in fatigue, a probable increase in sexual desire, and regulation of our moods. The architects also lowered the oxygen level in the pavilion from the normal 21 % to 14.5 %, or that found at an altitude of about 3000 meters in the Swiss mountains. As they explained, "This oxygen-rarified space causes slight hypoxia, which may initially be manifested by clinical states such as confusion, disorientation or bizarre behavior, but also a slight euphoria due to endorphin production. After about ten minutes, there is a measurable "natural" increase in erythropoietin (EPO) and hematocrit levels, as well as a strengthening of the cardiovascular and respiratory systems. The kidneys produce erythropoietin. This protein hormone reaches the bone marrow, where it stimulates the production of red blood cells, thus increasing the supply of oxygen to the muscles. Decreasing the oxygen level will therefore have a stimulating effect that may improve the body's physical capabilities by up to 10%."

MARCOS NOVAK is a professor at the University of California, Santa Barbara, where he is affiliated with the California NanoSystems Institute. As his UCSB biography has it, "Drawing upon architecture, music, and computation, and introducing numerous additional influences from art, science, and technology, his work intentionally defies categorization." Part of his new work published in this volume makes use of structural and functional magnetic resonance imaging scans of his own brain to create algorithmically generated spaces and forms. His concept of "transvergence" implies a meeting between science and art or architecture on a historic scale, a change of paradigm. The text reproduced below was written by Marcos Novak for *Architecture Now* to explain the state of his projects.

Recognizing the ongoing and ever-increasing importance of working with the granular, the elemental, the atomic, and also with the distributed, the parallel, and the emergent, at all levels from string theory to molecular biology, from material science to neurophysiology, from information technology to digital art, from granular navigable music to granular liquid architecture, this work examines how we might envision a mode of architecture that is not predicated on working with complete or preconceived forms, but one which assumes that forms develop as the outcome of processes that work at a granular and atomic level (in the original sense of "atomic" as being an element or monad that can no longer be subdivided).

Any informed reflection on the world as we know it recognizes that what we perceive as being substantial at our scale is not so: most of what appears to us as solid matter is predominantly void, so that the world is not composed of figure and ground in any absolute sense but is rather better thought of as a modulation of relations and densities.

Until recently, there was little one could do in terms of embracing this viewpoint as a design strategy. There were two main obstacles to this – number and control. Working with the very small implies working with huge numbers of tiny, hard to "grasp" elements. As is often the case with the initially unreachable, these two pragmatic obstacles hid a larger intellectual obstacle – that of actually conceiving what could be created not as preformed wholes but as aggregations of myriad parts ruled statistically and not individually.

Emerging technologies are enabling us to overcome the mechanical obstacles and challenging us to advance our theoretical reach and grasp – first in the realm of the virtual, and now increasingly in the realm of the material. Thus, we have an opportunity to reconsider our approach to making in a fundamental way. As nanotechnology and all the other technological and conceptual breakthroughs in our control of the very many and the very small are beginning to demonstrate, overcoming these obstacles offers a corresponding reward – the fine control over the gradation of and cross fading between attributes that would otherwise remain distinct, and therefore the possibility of inventing new types of inanimate and even animate matter with something approaching the generality, if not the ease, of inventing new timbres of sound.

The natural consequence of our pursuit of a "grand unified theory" reconciling the quantum mechanical with the relativistic descriptions on the universe is that the closer we get to understanding what the world is made of, the more empowered we become to alter everything above our most fundamental understanding. Why then not alter the elements themselves? The work shown here approaches these problems and possibilities from a variety of angles. The overriding notion is that of the "*alloatomic*," by which I mean a sense of the atomic that is not limited to the literal elements of which the world is made, but of "*allo*"-elements – other elements, of our own choice and invention. Just as fields such as *artificial life* and *artificial intelligence* do not limit themselves to the study of life or intelligence as they are, but extend themselves to consider life an intelligence *as they might be*, so too does the idea of the *alloatomic* extend itself to considerations of what the very small and elemental *might be*, and how we might learn to build with it. It should be clear that what I am describing is not limited to the physical and molecular, but applies also, and perhaps mostly, to the virtual, and therefore to the elemental as concept and abstraction.

Some of the work here is more purely "*alloatomic*" – trying to directly harness techniques for creating architectural form by commanding processes such as "*diffusion limited aggregation*" and other such techniques for modeling growth and pattern formation, allowing form to develop out of the manners in which large number or particles can adhere to or repel one another. Other work is far more abstract, drawing on neurophysiology and techniques such as fMRI – functional magnetic resonance imaging – of the brain (in this case, my own brain, in operation). Yet others draw upon CFP – computational fluid dynamics – imagine a "*liquid architecture*" consisting of the interplay of very dense liquid flows.

As with my previous work, this present work aims at continuing to articulate a continuum that ranges from the virtual to the actual, from the inanimate to the animate, from the musical to the material, to mention but a few of its axes. In the end, it is this continuum that is of interest, rather than any single experiment or project. Architecture begins as a modulation of space and form, presence and absence, solid and void; music modulates sound and silence, smoothness and harshness, stillness and turbulence, randomness and order, threaded with being, becoming, and nothingness. These lists are limited and partial, and could be endless, but what we can always factor out is the modulation of phenomena into patterns of variation that have both informational and human significance. Both the architecture and the music, and the *transarchitecture*, and any of the *transvergent* expressive forms we may encounter or invent, all are modulations. Understanding this, this work is an ongoing effort to learn how to modulate the new continua we are making.

Through all this runs an awareness of a perpetually changing mediated universe. Consciously exploring what I have named "*transvergence*," I am working on two parallel considerations of *(trans)architectural* research, practice, and pedagogy – first, the consideration of how new conditions lead to new species of architecture – and second, the consideration of how *(trans)architectural* research, practice, and pedagogy, if seen in a properly augmented and *speciated* manner, and if allowed their full imaginative and synthetic power, can provide singularly appropriate models for our creative engagement with the new worlds we are so rapidly creating, not only for architecture per se, but also for other expressive media formations, emerging or still to come.

© 2005 Marcos Novak for *Architecture Now*, volume 4

Novak might be considered a visionary who will have little practical impact on how things are built, or he may just be opening the door to new ways of seeing the world, not from a limited "professional" perspective, but from a broader viewpoint. Just as the "Renaissance Man" as exemplified by Da Vinci could be interested in biology, physics, art and architecture, so it may be that information technology can break the modern trend to blinkered specialization. Many significant figures of contemporary architecture, from Frank O. Gehry to Santiago Calatrava, have willfully broken the barriers between architecture, art or engineering. Understanding that science has made great progress, Novak and others like Dollens see no problem with making use of the imagery and process of other fields to innovate. Philippe Rahm takes the "obvious" facts of physiology and gives them a place in his architecture, virtual though it may be. Is it that surprising that in a building we live not only with space but also with conditions of humidity or oxygen content that have a strong impact on our comfort or discomfort? Purists will say that none of this has to do with architecture, but as advances in computer technology make the "non-standard" vision of building design a reality, the question of why barriers exist between disciplines at all is raised. Whether in a more modest and comprehensible way, as when the designer Patrick Jouin ventures deeper into the territory of architecture; when François Roche bases a project in the encounter of Charles Perrault and André Le Nôtre; or in the brave new world of Marcos Novak; there is one constant: architecture is out of the box.

EINLEITUNG

RAUS AUS DEM KASTEN

Die Architektur hat sich aus dem Kasten befreit, buchstäblich und symbolisch. Neue Bau- und Entwurfstechnologien tragen dazu bei, die gebaute Umwelt gänzlich umzuformen. Nicht zuletzt dank dieser Entwicklungen werden auch die Grenzen, die Architektur von Kunst und Design trennen, immer durchlässiger. Eine neue Vorstellung von Raum und wie mit ihm umzugehen ist bildete sich durch die Interpretation einer Reihe von Künstlern heraus, deren Ausdrucksformen zwingend die dritte Dimension einschließen. All dies bedeutet seltsamerweise nicht, dass die Moderne ausgedient hat. Es heißt nur, dass sich der Architektenschaft viele neue Möglichkeiten bieten, und dass selbst minimalistische Formen aus unterschiedlichen Überlegungen heraus zum Spektrum gehören. Das Ziel besteht gewiss nicht darin, einfach nur das Vorhergegangene zu wiederholen, sondern auch die Architektur neu zu überdenken. Dieses Buch umfasst keineswegs eine erschöpfende Auswahl der Architektur der letzten drei bis fünf Jahre, aber es gibt auf internationaler Ebene einen subjektiven Überblick über zahlreiche Bautypen und Trends. Es ist kein Zufall, dass ein Großteil der in diesem Buch behandelten Architekten in keinem der früheren Bände von *Architecture Now* enthalten ist. Zwar sind Gehry, Koolhaas oder Herzog & de Meuron vertreten, aber ebenso Patrick Jouin, Philippe Rahm sowie Klein Dytham. Bei Jouin handelt es sich um einen Designer, dessen Arbeiten, insbesondere in Verbindung mit seinem Auftraggeber, Starkoch Alain Ducasse, ihn auf das Gebiet der Architektur beförderten. Rahm (vormals Décosterd & Rahm) lotet die Grenzgebiete zwischen Physiologie und Architektur aus, während Klein Dytham die Szene in Tokio aufmischen mit Projekten wie der Green Green Screen, Omotesando, einem 274 m langen »Bauzaun«, oder ihrem SuperDeluxe Raum, den sie als »einen Ort für Spaß und Experimentieren« bezeichnen: Galerie, Bar, Küche, Jazzklub und Filmstudio, Kino, Bibliothek, Schule, Konzerthalle und Theater. Vergessen Sie ihre überkommenen Vorstellungen. Das hier ist »Architecture Now«!

GIMME SHELTER

Einstmals diente Architektur nur dazu, Schutz vor den Elementen und wilden Tieren zu bieten. Auch wenn Architekten sich bemühen, das Haus immer ungewöhnlicher zu gestalten, ist das »Dach überm Kopf« immer noch von vordringlicher Wichtigkeit. Die in Cañete, Peru, gelegene Casa Equis ist der geglückte Versuch der Architekten Jean-Pierre Crousse und Sandra Barclay, beide um die 40 Jahre alt, »die Intimität und Häuslichkeit zu schaffen, die man braucht, um in der Wüste zu leben, wo dieses Haus steht, ohne die Situation zu leugnen oder zu verfälschen«. Das Bild eines Kindes, das im weit über einen wilden Strand schwebenden, gläsernen Pool der Casa Equis schwimmt, ging durch die Architekturzeitschriften der Welt, so als habe man endlich ein Rezept für wahre Schwerelosigkeit entdeckt. Das Problem, dem sich David Chipperfield bei seinem Haus im spanischen Galicien gegenübersah, war etwas anderer Art. Das 210 m² große Wohnhaus musste nicht nur zum natürlichen Felsgestein passen, sondern auch zu einer vorhandenen Abfolge heterogener Häuser. Die Fähigkeit des Architekten, unter diesen Umständen eine zeitgemäße, vielfältige Modernität zu entwickeln, zeugt von einer Meisterschaft, die einen Wandel belegt: Die fortschreitende Verbesserung von Kommunikation, Information und Handel, bekannt unter dem Namen »Globalisierung«, führte zu einer neuen Spezies von Architekten, die ebenso im peruanischen Cañete wie im galicischen Corrubedo zu Hause ist. Sie wollen weder ein Pasticcio aus Versatzstücken lokaler Architektur, noch eine offenkundig fremde Sichtweise einführen, sondern in intelligenter und kohärenter Weise auf die vorhandenen Gegebenheiten reagieren. Die heutige Moderne hat nichts mehr mit der Geometrie Euklid'scher Lehrsätze zu tun, selbst wenn sich ein Architekt wie Chipperfield durch eine minimalistische Ästhetik auszeichnet. Es geht darum, Einfühlungsvermögen und Technik zu nutzen, um auf die Wünsche eines Auftraggebers eingehen zu können. Mit Sicherheit trifft das auf ein Projekt zu, bei dem der erfinderische, japanische Architekt Shuhei Endo mit einem steil ansteigenden Grundstück in Form eines 20 m langen Dreiecks konfrontiert war, dessen Breite zwischen 4 und 1,5 m beträgt. Sein Haus Rooftecture S zeigt, dass extreme Bedingungen zu ungewöhnlichen, ästhetisch faszinierenden Lösungen führen können. Angesichts der speziell entlang der Ostküste Japans hohen Siedlungsdichte, müssen Architekten häufig mit kleinen oder ungewöhnlich geformten Grundstücken zurechtkommen. Die jungen Architekten von Eastern Design errichteten ihr Slit House auf einer 50 m tiefen und 7,5 m breiten Fläche. Dieses Grundstück, dreimal so groß wie das von Rooftecture S, inspirierte zu einem bemerkenswerten Gebäude ohne wirkliche Fenster, aber mit 60 Schlitzen von 14 cm Breite. Bei den Japanern gilt das Spiel des Lichts in der Architektur an Orten mit wenigen Grünflächen als Ausdruck von Natur. Obgleich es sich beim Slit House um ein Rechteck aus Beton handelt, macht es sich die traditionelle Vorliebe für Licht zunutze, um mit der Eliminierung herkömmlicher Fenster zu experimentieren.

Überraschenderweise stößt man auch nahe des belgischen Hasselt auf fernöstliche Ästhetik. Bei der für Frédéric Chaillet, einen Seniorpartner des Architekturbüros Groep Delta entworfenen Villa C, kontrastieren eine massive, 26 m lange Mauer aus Waimes-Stein und eine vollverglaste Gartenfassade miteinander. Das nahe dem Speisezimmer gelegene Wasserbecken mit sieben Trittsteinen hat mit dem Faible des Besitzers für Asien zu tun und mit den schimmernden Lichtreflexen, die sich im Inneren des Hauses spiegeln. Die aus Stein, Stahl, Glas und Holz bestehende Villa C ist mit ihren starken Kontrasten ein hervorragendes Beispiel für die in der zeitgenössischen Architektur herrschende stilistische Freiheit. Die von den Pariser Architekten Jakob + MacFarlane entworfene Maison H auf Korsika ist zwar noch nicht gebaut, aber seine Gestaltung zeigt einen im Design der jüngeren Zeit ausgeprägten Trend, nämlich den Gebrauch von hoch entwickelter Computertechnik zur Erzeugung von Formen, die scheinbar der Erde selbst entsteigen. Wo die frühe Moderne in fast allen Fällen bestrebt war, der Erde nicht »zur Last zu fallen«, indem beispielsweise Bauten oft auf *pilotis* gestellt wurden, liegt es den Architekten heute weit näher zu »graben« oder sich unmittelbar von der Topografie eines Geländes inspirieren zu lassen.

UNTERKUNFT UND VERPFLEGUNG

Obschon Hotels strengen funktionalen Anforderungen entsprechen müssen, ist es ausgesprochen in Mode gekommen, sich bekannter Designer zu bedienen, um mehr Gäste anzuziehen. Ian Schragers Hotels mit Innenausstattungen von Designern wie Philippe Starck finden in vielen Städten Anklang. Die jungen Architekten von GRAFT bauten kürzlich mit einem relativ bescheidenen Budget Q!, ein Hotel in Berlin mit innovativem Ansatz. Die rot umhüllte Bar- und Restaurantlandschaft erinnert an die Projekte von Neil Denari, während in den Zimmern ein Kontinuum von Raum, Möblierung und Dekor dem Haus Atmosphäre verleiht. Für das vielleicht ultimative Designhotel forderte die spanische Kette Silken nicht weniger als 19 international renommierte Architekten und Designer auf, die 342 Zimmer des neuen Hotels Puerta América in Madrid auszustatten. Die Außenfassade wurde von Jean Nouvel entworfen, die Etagen unter anderem von Zaha Hadid, David Chipperfield, Mark Newson, Ron Arad, Arata Isozaki und John Pawson gestaltet. Diese Mixtur aus Architekten und Designern mag überraschen, aber die Grenzen zwischen den beiden Disziplinen sind fließend geworden, und Designer sind immer häufiger bestrebt zu bauen. Die Frage, wo »gutes« Design endet und Bigbusiness beginnt, stellt sich beim Hotel Puerta América, da die Gestaltung von Zimmern oder Fluren für das Hotel einer solchen Kette selbst für den begabtesten Kreativen eine einschüchternde Herausforderung darstellt.

Ein intelligenter, junger Designer, der gewiss den Ehrgeiz hat, auf das Gebiet der Architektur vorzudringen, ist der Franzose Patrick Jouin. Jouin machte sich einen Namen, indem er Restaurants für den Starkoch Alain Ducasse ausstattete. Für Ducasse gestaltete Jouin im noblen Schweizer Skiort Gstaad das Chlösterli. Der Gastronomiebetrieb ist in einem um 1700 von den Mönchen der Abtei Rougemont aus Holz erbauten, weitläufigen Chalet untergebracht und umfasst zwei Restaurants, eine Bar und eine Diskothek. Von Jouin entworfenes Mobiliar mit ironischen bäuerlichen Anklängen ziert die Restaurants. Ungeachtet der verschachtelten und eher dunklen Innenräume des alten Gebäudes verwendete Jouin in Gstaad einen neuen Stil, der kühlen Minimalismus zugunsten eines vielfältigeren, schmuckvolleren Dekors zurückstellt. Wenngleich Jouin nicht der einzige Designer ist, der sich in diese Richtung bewegt, ist er doch einer der bekanntesten. Sein Restaurant Mix im Mandalay Bay Hotel in Las Vegas soll dem extravaganten Ruf der Stadt gerecht werden. Da er sich einer an Vulkanen orientierten Bildsprache bediente, zögerte er nicht, einen Kronleuchter aus Muranoglas mit 15 000 mundgeblasenen Glaskugeln zu entwerfen.

Gut gestaltete Hotels stehen heutzutage keineswegs nur in Großstädten. Zwei in diesem Band publizierte Beispiele sind in den entlegensten Gegenden dieser Welt zu finden. Das ESO-Hotel in Cerro Paranal, Chile, wurde von den deutschen Architekten Auer+Weber in einer Höhe von 2400 m in den gebirgigen Zonen der Atacama-Wüste errichtet. Dort dient es den Wissenschaftlern und Besuchern des hier befindlichen Very Large Telescope (VLT). Das ESO-Hotel berücksichtigt seinen Standort in hervorragender Weise und bietet seinen Gästen überraschend viel Komfort. Das in erster Linie für weniger wissenschaftlich interessierte Touristen gedachte Longitude 131° ist Teil des von Philip Cox in Australien geplanten Yulara Tourist Resort. Der nahe gelegene Ayers Rock ist ein weithin bekanntes Wahrzeichen Australiens; die Temperaturen in dieser eher unwirtlichen Gegend liegen häufig über 40 Grad Celsius. Longitude 131° respektiert seine außergewöhnliche Umgebung, indem es auf Stahlstützen aufgeständert über dem Erdboden schwebt. Wie diese beiden Hotels belegen, ist die Vorstellung, »gute« Architektur sei nur für Connaisseurs von Interesse, nicht mehr gültig. Vielleicht aufgrund des öffentlichen Erfolges einer Reihe Aufsehen erregender »Architektenbauten« und auch weil Ketten wie Aman Resorts ein höheres Designniveau einführten, sind Projekte wie das Hotel Puerta América und diese beiden abgelegenen Häuser zunehmend häufiger anzutreffen.

Obwohl der praktische Aspekt von Hotelbauten häufig nicht zulässt, dass sie purer Ausdruck architektonischer Vorstellungen sind, werden computergestützte Herstellungsverfahren bald selbst auf diesem Gebiet Einzug halten. Das in Rotterdam ansässige Büro ONL [Oosterhuis_Lénárd] hat für Dubai ein höchst ungewöhnliches Hotel mit Namen Flyotel entworfen. Das mit fünf Sternen ausgezeichnete 600-Zimmer-Hotel lässt an einen zum Flug ansetzenden Vogel denken und wäre das erste Beispiel für »Non-Standard Design« bei einem Projekt dieser Größe. Die Anfang 2004 im Centre Pompidou veranstaltete Ausstellung »Non-Standard Architecture« stellte ONL neben elf weiteren Büros vor, darunter UN Studio, R&Sie (François Roche), Greg Lynn und Asymptote. Kurator Frédéric Migayrou zufolge war das Ziel der Ausstellung, »nicht nur Beispiele digitaler oder virtueller Architektur vorzustellen, die sich mit Fragen der Darstellung (wie Virtualität oder Hyperspace) beschäftigen, sondern auf gegenwärtige Modifikationen bei der Produktion von Architektur hinzuweisen. Die weit verbreitete Verwendung von auf algorithmischen Systemen basierenden Anwenderprogrammen setzt die Veränderung von Entwurfs- und Produktionsgeräten voraus. ›Non-Standard Architecture‹ ist eine auf der Nutzung digitaler Elemente basierende Überlegung zur Sprache der Architektur und ihrem Anwendungsbereich. Herkömmliche Bauverfahren können jetzt einer Produktion gegenübergestellt werden, die auf der Prototypisierung vorgefertigter Architekturelemente beruht.« Mit anderen Worten, Migayrou und einige der an der Ausstellung beteiligten Architekten sind davon überzeugt, dass ein System, mit dem sich besondere Formen zu den gleichen Kosten herstellen lassen wie standardisierte oder sich wiederholende, im Begriff ist, die Welt zu erobern. Kas Oosterhuis bestätigt, dass das Flyotel, an dessen internem Kai Wasserflugzeuge andocken können, »nur zehn Prozent mehr kosten wird, als ein Standardhochhaus«.

RAUM ERZEUGT KUNST

Schon seit längerem findet die Bauaufgabe Museum das besondere Interesse von Architekten. Frank Lloyd Wrights Guggenheim Museum in New York und zahlreiche weitere zeigten, dass ungewöhnliche oder interessante Architektur den Erfolg der jeweiligen Institution befördern, ja zuweilen das öffentliche Interesse wecken kann, selbst wenn die betreffende Kunstsammlung nicht gerade eindrucksvoll ist (Guggenheim Bilbao). Die Abenteuer von Thomas Krens, dem dynamischen Direktor der Guggenheim-Foundation, dauern an, während er in entfernten Weltgegenden ein Projekt nach dem anderen lanciert. Während es scheint, als solle Jean Nouvels Guggenheim Rio nicht realisiert werden, sorgte Krens für die Organisation eines Wettbewerbs für ein neues Museum in Guadalajara, Mexiko. Dieser zeitigte außer dem Entwurf des Siegers Enrique Norten weitere interessante Vorschläge wie den von Asymptote. Die New Yorker platzierten ihren Entwurf auf den Rand eines Canyons und ließen ihrer Fantasie und ihren Computern freien Lauf. So entstand eine plastische, nahezu fließende Form, für die die gleichen nicht-standardisierten Verfahren zum Einsatz kommen würden wie für das Flyotel von ONL. Ein weiteres Museum, das virtuell bleiben wird, ist François Roches Green Gorgon, ein Wettbewerbsbeitrag für Lausannes neues Museum für zeitgenössische Kunst. Das von der Natur inspirierte Green Gorgon mit seiner proteischen Form verkörpert die Überzeugung Roches, Architektur müsse eine Geschichte erzählen und solle mit »Fiktion« angereichert werden. In diesem Fall stellte die Zusammenarbeit von Charles Perrault (1628–1703), dem Autor des klassischen Märchenbuchs *Histoires ou contes du temps passé* (1697), und dem Gartenarchitekten André Le Nôtre (1613–1700) am Labyrinth von Versailles den Ausgangspunkt der Planung von R&Sie dar. Wie Roche erläutert, schufen Perrault und Le Nôtre weniger ein mathematisches Gebilde, als dass sie versuchten einen Ort zu gestalten, an dem sich die Besucher »verlieren« konnten. »Es ist genau diese heterotypische Dimension, die unseren Entwurf bedingt«, folgert Roche.

Man könnte sagen, dass Yoshio Taniguchi, der japanische Architekt, der für die kürzliche Umgestaltung des Museum of Modern Art in New York verantwortlich zeichnet, im Hinblick auf Museumsbauten das entgegengesetzte Ende des theoretischen Spektrums verkörpert. In Zusammenarbeit mit dem New Yorker Architekturbüro KPF und insbesondere mit Steven Rustow, gelang es Taniguchi, etwas von der wunderbaren Subtilität seiner japanischen Museen nach New York zu bringen. Es gibt jedoch eine Diskrepanz zwischen der schieren Größe von Räumen wie dem Atrium im zweiten Obergeschoss und der intimen Atmosphäre, von der die Rolle des MoMA als vorrangiger Ort zur Ausstellung der Kunst der Moderne abhing. Es mag sein, dass sich die Kuratoren mit dem neuen Raum einfach erst beschäftigen und Werke auswählen müssen, die ihn mit mehr Nachdruck und Berechtigung für sich beanspruchen. Gegenwärtig buhlt Barnett Newmans »Broken Obelisk«, von einem Kritiker als »mediokre Skulptur eines guten Malers« beschrieben, in dem übergroßen Raum erfolglos um Aufmerksamkeit. Das in seiner Maßstäblichkeit urbane und mit benachbarten Gebäuden in Einklang stehende MoMA Taniguchis stellt darüber hinaus auch das Ergebnis von Entscheidungen seitens des Kuratoriums dar, die dank einer höchst erfolgreichen Spendenkampagne möglich wurden. Große Ausstellungsflächen wurden eigens für Gewicht und Volumen einiger der schwergewichtigsten Skulpturen Richard Serras präpariert, aber die Frage mag gestattet sein, ob das MoMA wirklich der beste Ort für zeitgenössische Kunst ist. Es war und bleibt ein Tempel der Moderne des 20. Jahrhunderts. Dem MoMA ist zum guten Teil die geglückte Wandlung der modernen Kunst vom revolutionären Kampfstil zur anerkannten Norm zu verdanken. In der zeitgenössischen Kunst und erst recht in der Architektur jüngeren Datums werden neue Richtungen eingeschlagen, auf die Taniguchi und die Institution selbst möglicherweise nicht gut vorbereitet sind. Vielleicht entstehen neue Ausdrucksformen in einer groberen, feindseligeren Umgebung als die der spiegelnden Böden und weißen Flächen des MoMA.

Herzog & de Meuron wählten bei ihrer Erweiterung des Walker Art Center in Minneapolis einen anderen Weg. Die Schweizer Architekten schufen einen asymmetrischen mit geprägten Aluminiumpanelen verkleideten Block, aber die äußere Erscheinung der Architektur mag weniger entscheidend sein, als der Versuch, einen Ort zu schaffen, an dem sich Kunstformen auf »völlig überraschende und innovative Art und Weise« gegenseitig beeinflussen können. Ein Blick auf das Programm des Walker Art Museum zeigt, dass sein Motto »Wo Kunst und Leben sich treffen« sowohl zum Museum selbst als auch zu seiner neuen Architektur passt: Tanz, Performances, Film, Malerei, Musik und Theater sind sämtlich Teil der Mischung. Könnte es sein, dass der imposante weiße Kasten in der Tradition der Klassischen Moderne (MoMA) einfach nicht mehr zu der Fülle multidisziplinärer Formen passt, die auf die Künste einwirkt? Dies wäre in der Tat nicht so sehr ein Kommentar zum offenkundig großen Erfolg des MoMA, als zum Auftreten einer wirklich tief greifenden Veränderung in der Kunst. Während Taniguchi in der Schaffung eines Tempels für die Kunst des 20. Jahrhunderts schwelgte, stürzten sich Herzog & de Meuron beim Walker Art Center entschlossen ins 21. Jahrhundert.

Nicht alle neuen Museen sind bestrebt, Kunst und Architektur neu zu definieren. Das Naturwissenschaftliche Museum in Matsunoyama, Japan, von Tezuka Architects versucht gleichwohl, neue Wege zu erschließen. Die im Wesentlichen aus einer 111 m langen Röhre aus Corten-Stahl mit einem 34 m hohen Aussichtsturm bestehende Einrichtung soll dazu dienen, Leben unter der Oberfläche des hier reichlich vorhandenen Schnees zu beobachten. Obgleich Schneelasten von bis zu 2000 t jeglicher Bautätigkeit natürliche Grenzen setzen, begegneten Tezuka Architects einer scheinbaren Beschränkung mit Erfindungsreichtum. Das Museum, das einem riesigen Unterseeboot ähnelt, unterscheidet sich wesentlich von den meisten vorhandenen Museen. Der Form und Funktion nach ist ihre Stahlröhre einerseits Teil des Geländes, auf dem sie andererseits nur leicht aufliegen darf, da sie sich im Sommer um 20 cm ausdehnt. Es fiele schwer, diesen Bau als Teil eines spezifischen Trends einzustufen, selbst wenn er auf der letzten Architekturbiennale in Venedig als beispielhaft für die Tendenz gezeigt wurde, Architektur mit der Erde in Zusammenhang zu bringen. Er ist weder minimalistisch noch »non-standard«, und doch ist er ganz der Gegenwart zugehörig. Hier wie auch anderswo scheint Stil eher im Auge des Betrachters zu existieren als im Design selbst.

KUNST SCHAFFT RAUM

Die Beziehung zwischen Kunst und Architektur ist eine, die sich bis zu den frühesten überlieferten Bauten zurückverfolgen lässt, selbst wenn sich die Definition von Kunst seit der Zeit, als man sie als dekorativen Anteil von Kirchen oder Palästen betrachtete, wesentlich verändert hat. Man kann sagen, dass die Kunst etwas von ihrer Verbindung zur »realen« Welt aufgab, als Gemälde an Museumswände gehängt und Skulpturen auf Sockel gestellt wurden. Ein Teil des Siegeszugs der zeitgenössischen Kunst besteht darin, den Raum außerhalb der Museen zurückzuerobern, erneut ein »reales« Umfeld mitzugestalten. Das Interesse Anselm Kiefers am Raum ist bekannt, ob bei seinen Gemälden oder seinen häufig aus Blei bestehenden Metallskulpturen. Mehr als viele andere zeitgenössische Maler hat er in der Kunst seine eigene rätselhafte Welt geschaffen, eine, in der indirekte Verweise auf Mythen oder historische Tatsachen eine Art sedimentäre Geschichte erschaffen. Indem er seine Bilder mit Heu oder Sonnenblumensamen sowie mit einem oft auffällig dicken Impasto anreichert, hinterfragt er häufig die Vorstellung von Tiefe oder Perspektive mit Partikeln, die eine verlorene oder künftige Welt beschwören. So ist auch *La Ribaute*, Kiefers Besitz in den Cevennen und seine Wirkungsstätte während der letzten dreizehn Jahre, kein Atelier im herkömmlichen Sinn, sondern eher eine geschichtete Ansammlung von unter und über dem Erdboden gelegenen Räumen. Wie viele von Kiefers Bildern vermittelt *La Ribaute* das Gefühl, es stamme aus einer anderen Zeit oder es sei ein Überbleibsel irgendeiner unzureichend verstandenen Zivilisation. Es gibt keine Antwort auf die Frage, weshalb er helle Gewächshäuser errichtet hat und dunkle Welten aus Blei und Wasser, außer, dass diese Architektur der Ausdruck seiner Kunst, ja seiner selbst und seiner Zeit ist. Diese gebauten Formen könnten von einem esoterischen Wissen zeugen, dessen Bedeutung im Lauf der Zeit verloren ging, oder von dem schrecklichen Geheimnis einer unbehaglich nahen Zeit. Es heißt, der Unterschied zwischen Kunst und Architektur sei, dass letztere einem Zweck diene. Was aber wäre, wenn der Zweck darin bestünde, Kunst zu schaffen? Der ästhetische Impuls und die *raison d'être* hinter Kiefers Architektur ist seine Kunst, seine innere Welt. Visionäre Architekten wie Constant haben sich bisweilen neue Welten ausgedacht, und exzentrische Typen wie Simon Rodia, der Erbauer der Watts Towers, gaben ihren eigenen ästhetischen Empfindungen architektonische Form. Möglicherweise können konventionellere Architekten vom Beispiel Anselm Kiefers lernen.

Wahrscheinlich ist es genauso schwierig Architektur zu bestimmen wie Kunst. Viele Ausdrucksformen werden von diesen Oberbegriffen abgedeckt, selbst wenn das Kriterium der Funktionalität alles Gebaute gleichsam »verfolgt«. Einer der immer wiederkehrenden Gedanken in der zeitgenössischen Architektur mag am besten in den Worten Hamlets zum Ausdruck kommen: »O! That this too too solid flesh would melt, Thaw, and resolve itself into a dew.«[1] Das Blur Building, von Diller + Scofidio für die Schweizer Nationalausstellung Expo 02 in Yverdon entworfen, versuchte recht überzeugend, wie eine über dem See hängende Wolke auszusehen. Andere wollen Architektur schaffen, die fast wie ein lebendes Wesen auf ihre Besucher reagiert, während manche sich augenscheinlich mit dem rein Virtuellen zufrieden geben. Toyo Itos Tower of the Winds (Yokohama, Kanagawa, 1986) erinnert daran, dass eine auf der Grenze zur Kunst stehende, reaktive Architektur tatsächlich in der Lage ist, ihre Zeit zu prägen und die Frage aufzuwerfen, was eine Form letztlich bedeuten kann. Man stelle sich für einen Moment vor, auch Kunst könne raumbildend sein und ihm Bedeutung geben – oft in einer flüchtigeren Weise als Architektur. Aber das Blur Building und die temporären Pavillons der Serpentine Gallery in London zeigen, dass Dauerhaftigkeit von einigen nicht mehr für notwendig erachtet wird. Der amerikanische Videokünstler Bill Viola stellt sich seine Werke häufig in einem architektonischen Rahmen vor, und in der Tat erfordern deren Größe und Charakter meistens viel Raum und verändern ihn sogar. Bei Violas jüngster Zusammenarbeit mit dem Opern- und Theaterdirektor Peter Sellars und dem Dirigenten Esa-Pekka Salonen für einen vierstündigen Videofilm, der Richard Wagners Oper *Tristan und Isolde* begleiten soll, und eine Aufführung in Paris geht es um die Fragen von Bild, Raum und Darstellung, die am wirkungsvollsten an der Grenze zwischen Kunst und Architektur existieren. »Mir war von Anfang an klar, dass ich mit den Bildern nicht die Geschichte direkt illustrieren, sondern eine Bilderwelt schaffen wollte, die parallel zum Geschehen auf der Bühne existiert, so wie eine subtilere poetische Stimme die verbor-

---

[1] »O schmölze doch dies allzu feste Fleisch, Zerging und löst' in einen Tau sich auf!« (Hamlet, 1. Akt, 2. Szene, Zeile 129, in der Übers. v. A. W. von Schlegel)

genen Dimensionen unseres Innenlebens erzählt.«Die Bilder sollen als symbolische, innere Darstellungen fungieren, um, in den Worten von Seyyed Hossein Nasr, zu »Reflexionen der spirituellen Welt im Spiegel des Materiellen und Temporären« zu werden. Viola schreibt im Zusammenhang mit dem ersten Akt von Tristan vom »unendlichen Ozean einer unsichtbaren, immateriellen Welt« und fügt dem dritten Akt ein Bild von Feuer und Licht hinzu: »Akt III«, erläutert er, »beschreibt die Auflösung des Selbst in den Phasen des Sterbens, den heiklen und quälenden Prozess der Abtrennung und Auflösung der physischen, wahrnehmenden und begrifflichen Komponenten kognitiven Bewusstseins. Wir werden in Agonie und Delirium von Tod und Leiden gestürzt, voller Visionen, Träume und halluzinatorischer Offenbarungen, wie sie durch das Bewusstsein eines Sterbenden huschen. Wenn die Flammen von Leidenschaft und Fieber zuletzt das geistige Auge verschlingen und die Begierden des Körpers niemals befriedigt werden können, wird die Oberfläche zerschmettert und fällt zu Wellenmustern reinen Lichts zusammen.« Dies soll nicht heißen, dass Violas Bilder von Feuer, Wasser und Licht im gleichen Sinn Ausdruck von Architektur sind wie Kiefers Atelier. Viola benutzt Kunst, und in diesem Fall einen Bühnenraum, um Fragen von Leben und Tod zu evozieren. Ebenso wenig ist Architektur auf den geisttötenden Umgang mit beschränkten Budgets und die Platzierung von Notausgängen beschränkt. Zukunftsweisende Architektur löst den Kasten in Feuer und Licht auf und wird zum rein virtuellen Bild, aber durch sie werden Ideen geboren, nehmen die architektonischen Formen der Zukunft Gestalt an. Künstler wie Kiefer und Viola können in ästhetischer wie intellektueller Hinsicht dabei helfen, den Weg zu weisen.

GROß UND SEXY

Bekannte Architekten haben ihre Laufbahn häufig mit kleinen Projekten begonnen. Frank O. Gehry machte sich einen Namen mit Stücken von Maschendraht und Tarmac auf seinem Küchenboden. Wie Gehry herausfand, als er die Walt Disney Concert Hall in Los Angeles entwarf, sind große Projekte etwas ganz anderes. Andere Architekten verfassen Bücher und fertigen Zeichnungen an wie Rem Koolhaas und Zaha Hadid es taten, ehe sie erfolgreich wurden. Es dauert einfach seine Zeit, ehe ein Auftraggeber mit genügend Geld einem innovativen Architekten ein größeres Gebäude anvertraut. Das größte und politisch heikelste Projekt des brillanten Katalanen Enric Miralles wurde erst nach seinem frühen Tod fertig. Viele sind allerdings nach wie vor nicht von seinem Schottischen Parlament in Edinburgh überzeugt, das von seiner Partnerin und Ehefrau Benedetta Tagliabue von EMBT und der ortsansässigen Firma RMJM Scotland Ltd. fertig gestellt wurde. Die Komplexität des Gebäudes führte zu einer offiziellen Untersuchung des Projekts, die zu dem Schluss kam, die Kommunikation zwischen EMBT und RMJM sei unzureichend gewesen, desgleichen die Kontrolle der Ausgaben. Da überzogene Kosten für ein typisches Folgeproblem innovativer Architekten gehalten werden, trägt dieses Beispiel nicht gerade zur Verbesserung der Reputation dieses Berufsstandes bei. Das vielleicht übermäßig komplexe Parlamentsgebäude war nicht so sehr ein Opfer der Hybris des Architekten, als das bürokratischer Verzögerungen und Unentschlossenheit. In dem offiziellen Bericht zu dem Projekt, den Lord Fraser of Carmyllie dem schottischen Parlament am 24. Juni 2004 vorlegte, heißt es: »Wenn die Versuchung auch groß ist, die ganze Schuld auf ein verstorbenes, unberechenbares Architekturgenie aus Spanien, seine hypertrophe Arbeitsweise und die gespannte Beziehung zwischen seiner Witwe und RMJM in Edinburgh zu schieben, ist die Analyse des obersten Revisors doch unanfechtbar. Die Kosten stiegen, weil der Auftraggeber (zuerst der Außenminister und neuerdings das Parlament) Vergrößerungen und Änderungen wünschten oder sie zumindest in der einen oder anderen Form billigten.«[2]

[2] www.scottish.parliament.uk/vli/holyrood/inquiry/sp205–00.htm

Es mag sein, dass private Auftraggeber der Leistungsfähigkeit eines berühmten Architekten eher Impulse geben als öffentliche. Andererseits könnte es für begabte, an kleine Projekte gewöhnte Architekten in der Tat schwierig sein, plötzlich eine große Aufgabe zu übernehmen. Massimiliano Fuksas ist mit ziemlich großen Aufgaben vertraut, aber mit keinen vom Kaliber seiner Fiera Milano, dem neuen Messegelände der Stadt. Der in der Rekordzeit von 27 Monaten im Wesentlichen fertig gestellte Komplex umfasst nicht weniger als 1,4 Millionen m^2 Grundfläche und einen 1,5 km langen, zentralen Weg; das kunstvolle Auf und Ab der Wegüberdachung scheint das Produkt eines ausgeklügelten Computerprogramms zu sein. Der in Rom und Paris ansässige Fuksas verwendet jedoch für seine Entwurfszeichnungen keine Computer. Selbstverständlich machen seine Mitarbeiter regen Gebrauch von der neuesten Technik, aber der Architekt selbst zieht es vor, seine Gebäude zu zeichnen oder sogar zu malen, ehe sie in digitale Wunderwerke verwandelt werden. In diesem Fall regten ihn Stürme oder sogar Tornados zu der Überdachung des Gehwegs an. Es ist zwar viel von den Vorzügen des Computers die Rede, aber in Mailand ist zu sehen, dass Fuksas mit relativ traditionellen Mitteln in der Lage ist, in effizienter, termingerechter Weise eine sehr zeitgemäße Form zu erzeugen. Angesichts der oben beschriebenen, hinderlichen Begleitumstände blieb dieser Erfolg EMBT in Edinburgh versagt.

Rem Koolhaas könnte sehr wohl der zurzeit öffentlichkeitswirksamste Architekt sein, nicht zuletzt wegen seiner Bücher, von *Delirious New York* bis zu *S, M, L, XL*, und wegen seiner unverwechselbaren Persönlichkeit. Wenngleich von seinem Büro OMA viel die Rede ist, können die Bauten des Büros erst seit kurzem mit seiner Öffentlichkeitsarbeit Schritt halten. Koolhaas ist mit Recht stolz auf die neue Zentralbibliothek in Seattle. In für das Büro typischer Weise versuchte man nicht nur, der Bibliothek eine passende Hülle zu geben, sondern auch in konstruktiver und funktionaler Hinsicht innovativ vorzugehen. Der im Gegensatz zu den meisten Bibliotheken als »transparent und offen« gedachte Bau ist größtenteils verglast und erlaubt somit Blicke auf die Aktivitäten im Inneren. Die abgewinkelte Form ist nicht so sehr eine ästhetische Laune, als der gezielte Versuch, Art und Beschaffenheit des ins Innere einfallenden Lichts zu kontrollieren. Ein System »hängender Plattformen« sowie ein diagonales Raster, das bei Erdbeben und vor Windschäden schützen soll, gehören zu den konstruktiven Innovationen. Im Inneren der Bibliothek durchstößt eine Bücherspirale vier Ebenen des Magazins und fasst die komplette Sachbuchsammlung. Diese Spirale erleichtert die künftige Vergrößerung der Bücherbestände. Während man konstruktive Innovationen wohl von einem solch bekannten Architekten wie Koolhaas erwarten kann, ist es gewiss noch bedeutsamer, dass er es wagte, ein derart konservatives Milieu zu aktivieren wie das von Bibliothekaren, die nichts anderes gewöhnt sind als ordentlich sortierte, kilometerlange Magazine. Die Art und Weise, wie sich der Bau dem Publikum öffnet und dessen Nutzung des Gebäudes sind gleichfalls neuartig.

Zaha Hadid, ehemals Partnerin bei OMA, hat ebenfalls nach Jahren richtungweisender, grafischer Arbeit begonnen, vermehrt Bauten zu realisieren. Zwar galt sie 1988 bei der bahnbrechenden Ausstellung im MoMA neben Rem Koolhaas als eine der Begründerinnen des Dekonstruktivismus, aber ihre gegenwärtigen Arbeiten kennzeichnet eine viel fließendere Qualität, als die kantigen Kompositionen der russischen Konstruktivisten implizieren. Ihr als »Nervenzentrum der gesamten Fabrikanlage« bezeichnetes Zentralgebäude des BMW-Werks in Leipzig nimmt es mit einer Branche auf, deren Neigung zu architektonischer Innovation etwa so ausgeprägt ist wie die einer typischen Bibliothek. Wenn sie davon spricht, die Architektur zur Erzeugung einer »totalen Transparenz der internen Abläufe« zu nutzen, aber auch die Funktionen zu mischen, um »die traditionelle Abgrenzung von Statusgruppen zu vermeiden«, erklärt Hadid klipp und klar, dass sie wie Koolhaas nichts weniger als eine Revision eingefahrener Methoden anstrebt. Mit dem fließenden Charakter ihres Entwurfs stellt sie die festgelegte Routine in

Frage, die es Henry Ford erlaubte, seinen Kunden ein Model T in jeder Farbe zu versprechen, solange diese Schwarz war. Hadid hinterfragt darüber hinaus das modernistische Gebot streng geometrischer Grundrisse, indem sie organischeren, ununterbrochenen Bewegungen den Vorzug gibt. Faszinierend ist die Tatsache, dass sowohl in Seattle wie auch in Leipzig die Entwurfspräferenzen der Architekten tatsächlich mit der jeweils besten Lösung für die Auftraggeber übereinstimmten. Wo berühmte Architekten häufig bestrebt waren, ihre ästhetische Kennung an unpassender Stelle durchzusetzen, unternehmen Koolhaas und Hadid wirklich Schritte, um den Reiz so genannter intelligenter Architektur zu verstärken. Natürlich muss ein Architekt kämpfen, wenn er so fest etablierte Auftraggeber wie die Bibliothek von Seattle oder BMW davon überzeugen will, dass sich ihre jeweiligen Methoden verbessern lassen. Andererseits haben diese beiden Absolventen der Londoner Architectural Association eindeutig einen Bekanntheitsgrad erreicht, der es ihnen erlaubt, die Architektur selbst in eine neue Richtung zu lenken.

ZEITWEILIG ZEITGENÖSSISCH

Die Vorstellung, Architektur müsse dauerhaft sein, gilt nach wie vor für bestimmte Bauaufgaben. Museen, Bibliotheken, Kirchen und Banken favorisieren gewöhnlich Beständigkeit. Und doch begrüßt eine andere Seite zeitgenössischer Bauten das Flüchtige, wie sich auch die Kunst in die gleiche Richtung bewegt. Außerdem implizieren bestimmte Funktionen keine Dauerhaftigkeit. Unter den gegenwärtig aktiven Architekten ist Shigeru Ban einer der einfallsreichsten. Ban ist mit temporären Bauten wohlvertraut wie seine mit Plastikplanen und Pappröhren im Auftrag des Hohen Flüchtlingskommissars der UNO (UNHCR) hergestellten Paper Refugee Shelter (Flüchtlingsunterkünfte aus Karton) beweisen. Mit dem Bianimale Nomadic Museum, in dem Fotografien von Gregory Colbert gezeigt wurden, betrat Shigeru Ban Neuland. Für die Zeit vom 5. März bis zum 6. Juni 2005 schuf er am Pier 54 in New York einen 205 m langen, rechteckigen Baukörper, der im Wesentlichen aus gestapelten Schiffscontainern bestand. Bans Konstrukt hatte ihm selbst zufolge »etwas von der Atmosphäre einer klassischen Kirche«. Wenngleich japanische Tempel selten rechteckig sind, mutet das Nomadic Museum doch auch fernöstlich an. Mit Stahlcontainern und Papp-röhren eine spirituelle Atmosphäre zu erzeugen, ist ein wahres Meisterstück, aber Shigeru Ban hat wiederholt gezeigt, dass er mit ungewöhnlichen Materialien architektonisch innovativ arbeiten kann, gerade wenn es nicht um Dauerhaftigkeit geht. Eine mehr utilitaristische Demonstration der Talente des japanischen Architekten kann man auf der obersten Ebene des Centre Georges Pompidou in Paris sehen, wo er sein Paper Temporary Studio installiert hat; dabei handelt es sich um eine aus Papprollen, Bauholz, Stahl und PTFE-Folie bestehende, 115 m³ große Konstruktion mit einem Tonnendach. Solange Ban an der für die Stadt Metz vorgesehenen, neuen Zweigstelle des Centre Pompidou arbeitet, wird dieses Büro auf dem Bau von Piano und Rogers bleiben, beinahe als solle es daran erinnern, dass das Centre Pompidou als »flexibles« Gebäude gedacht war.

Einige junge Künstler und Architekten widmen sich den »flüchtigeren« Aspekten des Bauens aus ökonomischen Gründen oder weil sie sich für etwas aus dem Blick geratene Möglichkeiten interessieren. Dies trifft auf jeden Fall für die beiden mit unterschiedlichen Methoden arbeitenden Deutschen zu – den Architekt Andreas Wenning und den Künstler Stefan Eberstadt. Wenning gründete 2003 die Planungskooperative baumraum und widmet sich in erster Linie dem Bau von Baumhäusern. Wenning, der sehr schonend mit den Bäumen umgeht, in denen er baut, zeigt, dass die Möglichkeiten dieser Idee überraschend vielfältig und zumeist baumhausspezifisch sind. Stefan Eberstadt verfolgt mit seinem Rucksackhaus, das einfach an bestehende Gebäude angehängt werden soll, eine noch ausgefallenere Idee. Er erläutert: »Das Rucksackhaus reaktiviert die Idee des selbstgebauten, anarchistischen Baumhauses, hier allerdings an markanterem Ort und fachmännisch gebaut.« Eberstadt plädiert dafür, sich des Potenzials der Interaktion zwischen zeitgenössischer Kunst, Architektur und anderen Disziplinen stärker bewusst zu sein. Es mag schwer fallen, sein Rucksackhaus tatsächlich als Kunst einzustufen, höchstens insofern, als es einen Kommentar zur Hybris der Architekten liefert, die die Grenzen ihrer eigenen Bauten für unverletzlich halten.

Der Aga-Khan-Preis für Architektur hat seine Aufmerksamkeit schon seit längerem den Architekturformen zugewandt, die kaum je in der Fachpresse als Beispiele realer »nützlicher« Innovationen herausgestellt werden. Um ein solches Beispiel handelt es sich bei dem Prototyp für Schutzbauten aus Sandsäcken von Nader Khalili, dem Empfänger des Aga-Khan-Preises von 2004. Khalilis System, das ebenso wie Bans Paper Refugee Shelter den Bedingungen des UNHCR entsprechend konzipiert wurde, verwendet solche problemlos verfügbaren Materialien wie Sand, Erde und Stacheldraht, um daraus solide, kostengünstige Behausungen herzustellen. Derartige Sandsackkonstruktionen sind zwangsläufig vergänglich, aber ihre Einfachheit und Durchdachtheit bedeuten, dass sie möglicherweise nützlicher sind, als jeglicher Beitrag zur zeitgenössischen Architektur mit »künstlerischem« Anspruch. Es braucht weder komplexe Computerprogramme noch technisch anspruchsvolle Materialien, um Architektur zu Menschen zu bringen, die sich niemals auch nur die Grundlagen des modernen Lebens leisten könnten. Darin liegt Nader Khalilis Leistung.

Obgleich Statistiken über den Gottesdienstbesuch im Westen gewöhnlich einen stetigen Rückgang der religiösen Inbrunst ausweisen, werden Architekten häufig aufgefordert, für die Rituale von Leben und Tod einen angemessenen Ort zu schaffen. Seit dem Zweiten Weltkrieg haben Architekten darüber hinaus versucht, sich mit den Ereignissen auseinanderzusetzen, deren Schrecken die restituierenden Kräfte jeglicher Religion übersteigt. Der bekannteste und vermutlich umstrittenste dieser Versuche ist Peter Eisenmans Denkmal für die ermordeten Juden Europas, in der Nähe von Potsdamer und Pariser Platz im Herzen von Berlin gelegen. Auf Eisenmans 2 ha großem Areal stehen 2751 graue Betonblöcke, deren Höhe zwischen wenigen Zentimetern und 4 m variiert. Die Schwere der Blöcke soll die moralische Last der Shoah zum Ausdruck bringen. In dieser Hinsicht dient das Werk einem Zweck, selbst wenn es sich nicht um eine der architekturtypischen Funktionen handelt. Also Kunst? Und wenn weder Kunst noch Architektur mit solchen Ereignissen zu Rande kommen, könnte es sein, dass Eisenman einen neuen Ansatz gefunden hätte, der weder das eine, noch das andere und doch beides gleichzeitig ist?

Auch Moshe Safdie hat sich bei seinem Holocaust-Museum in Yad Vashed mit der Shoah auseinander gesetzt. Ihm ging es darum, »Leben nach der Erfahrung des Todes« zu bejahen, ein Gedanke, der bei Eisenmans Memorial vermutlich weniger eine Rolle spielte. Yad Vashem liegt im Ein-Kerem-Tal mit Blick auf Jerusalem und kann deshalb sowohl den Kampf als auch die Triumphe eines Volkes symbolisieren, das so überaus zahlreiche Widrigkeiten überwunden hat. Safdies Museum, das sich größtenteils unter der Erde befindet, entlässt seine Besucher erst ans Tageslicht, nachdem sie die Exponate erlebt haben, während Eisenmans Denkmal offen unter dem Himmel liegt, kahl und verstörend mit seinen morbiden Grautönen. Man kann davon ausgehen, dass es in Berlin seine Besucher noch längere Zeit aus der Ruhe bringen wird, ein seltener Fall bei Werken der Architektur. Hier sollen Bedeutung und Form die Gewähr dafür bieten, dass die Erinnerung nicht verblasst.

John Pawson ist bekannt für seinen Minimalismus, und sein 1996 erschienenes Buch *Minimum* erreichte unerwartet hohe Verkaufszahlen. Als er 1999 von französischen Zisterziensern den Auftrag erhielt, an einem neuen Kloster in der Tschechischen Republik zu arbeiten, bezeichnete er das als »einmalige Gelegenheit«. In der Tat hatten die Mönche festgestellt, dass sie vieles mit den ästhetischen Vorstellungen Pawsons gemein hatten, vielleicht insbesondere den Umgang mit Licht. Natürlich ist das Kloster Novy Dvûr ein Ort der Andacht, aber es ist zugleich der Lebensraum der Mönche, und es gelang Pawson, die nötigen praktischen Anforderungen mit einer maßvollen Spiritualität zu verbinden. Pawson brachte die Mönche in einem westlich von Prag gelegenen, verlassenen Herrenhaus des 18. Jahrhunderts unter, an das er drei Flügel anschloss. Es hieß, die Zeit des Minimalismus in der zeitgenössischen Architektur sei vorüber und die heutigen Entwürfe fielen im Wesentlichen eher komplex oder sogar dekorativ aus. Pawson beweist, dass der Minimalismus mehr als eine vorübergehende Modeerscheinung ist. Er gehört zum Wesen der Moderne und ist schon lange in Architektur und Design ein wiederkehrendes Thema, wie die Geschichte Japans sehr wohl belegen kann.

Während dem Kloster und der Gedenkstätte in der heutigen Architekturszene eine ungewöhnlich große Aufmerksamkeit zuteil wird, verdient hier auch ein leichterer, fröhlicherer Ausdruck architektonischen Erfindungsgeistes erwähnt zu werden, und sei es nur wegen seiner Andersartigkeit. Bei Klein Dytham handelt es sich um ein von Astrid Klein und Mark Dytham begründetes, kleines Architekturbüro in Tokio. Ihre Blatt-Kapelle, aus zwei Blattformen aus Glas und Stahl gebildet, ist für Hochzeiten gedacht. Wie ein Augenlid öffnet sich die Kapelle im passenden Moment – wenn der Bräutigam die Braut küsst – und gibt den Blick frei auf einen Garten mit kleinem Teich. Mit seinen 168 m^2 ist dies ein sehr kleines Projekt, das gleichwohl die Anpassung westlicher Architekten an spezifisch japanische Hochzeitsvorstellungen zeigt. Dafür gedacht, der Besiegelung der »ewig währenden« Liebe einen feierlichen Rahmen zu geben, geriet es so luftig und humorvoll wie ein vorüberziehendes Wölkchen.

DIE NATUR HERRSCHT

Wenngleich es sein kann, dass der Trend zur virtuellen Architektur den Weg des Minimalismus einschlägt, hat ein Teil der interessantesten, gegenwärtig in Arbeit befindlichen Projekte, mit komplexer Technik und dem Erforschen der Natur als Quelle für Form und Funktion zu tun. Ganz gleich wie der künftige Ölpreis aussehen wird, ökologisch ausgerichtete Architektur steht vor einer glänzenden Zukunft und sei es nur aus Kostengründen. Die Reduzierung der Umweltverschmutzung ist ein weiteres, wichtiges Ziel der so genannten Nachhaltigkeit. Der eine Zeit lang bei SITE tätige New Yorker Architekt Michael McDonough hat sich daran gemacht, das möglicherweise ultimative, nachhaltige Haus zu errichten. Sein e-House, so schreibt er, »integriert über 100 neue oder ausgereifte Technologien, darunter Hochleistungstechnologien, historische und alternative Technologien. Mit dem Haus schlagen wir die Entwicklung eines neuen Wortschatzes für nachhaltige Architekturtheorie vor.« Ein Ziel ist die sparsame Nutzung von Energie, aber noch wichtiger ist die Vorstellung, das Haus könne eine »organische Einheit« bilden, die ihre Umgebung und lokale Traditionen achtet. McDonoughs Bemühen, so viele technologische Möglichkeiten in kombinierter Form zu nutzen, ist schon an sich interessant. Er äußert die Ansicht, die wahre Zukunft der Architektur könne in einem solch holistischen Ansatz liegen, der sich über die grundlegendere, konstruktive Sprache weit hinaus so viel Wissen wie möglich zunutze macht. Anstatt eine funktionierende Hülle zu schaffen, spricht er sich dafür aus, ein Gebäude herzustellen, das beinahe buchstäblich mit seinen Bewohnern lebt und atmet.

Dennis Dollens nähert sich der Natur auf andere Weise und findet architektonische Anregungen in Wachstumsmodellen. Seine neuesten Arbeiten machen sich ein Programm namens Xfrog zunutze. Dollens erläutert: »Xfrog ist Software, die von der deutschen Firma Greenworks hergestellt wird. Sie nutzt botanische L-System-Algorithmen, die in computergestützten, biologischen Simulationen verwendet werden, um für Laborzwecke Pflanzen und Landschaften entstehen zu lassen. Greenworks nimmt die L-Systeme und ergänzt eigene Programmierungen, die Faktoren wie Schwerkraft und Fototropismus einberechnen und erstellt einen mithilfe von Icons operierenden Desktop. Die Software wird für futuristische Landschaften oder sehr realistische Landschaftsgestaltungen verwendet. Ich glaube, ich bin der einzige, der sie für derart experimentelles Architekturwachstum einsetzt.« Mit anderen Worten, was geschähe, wenn man tatsächlich botanische Wachstumsmodelle in einem Architekturkontext simulieren könnte? Das Ergebnis wäre höchstwahrscheinlich sehr effizient und sähe völlig anders aus als die vorhandene Architektur, wobei es eine solide Grundlage in der realen Natur hätte. Andere Architekten wie Frei Otto oder Buckminster Fuller experimentierten bereits an der Grenze zwischen Architektur und Natur. Dennis Dollens verwendet nun die neueste Computertechnik, um diese Ideen voranzutreiben. Abgesehen von seinen eigenen Entwürfen arbeitet Dollens daran, der akademischen Gemeinschaft den potenziellen Nutzen eines fachübergreifenden Vorgehens bewusst zu machen, das das Bauen durch Kontakt mit der Wissenschaft bereichern könnte. Er schreibt: »Als Designer sollten wir wissenschaftlich fundierte Methoden und Technologien in den Entwurfsprozess einbeziehen. Beispielsweise könnten Planer auf der Suche nach erforschenswerten Merkmalen die räumlichen, materiellen oder konstruktiven Eigenschaften von Muscheln, Pflanzen oder Knochen betrachten. Diese Beschäftigung mit Prozessen und Forschung wird schließlich unsere Rücksicht auf natürliche Eigenheiten verstärken. In der Folge wird sich dies wiederum in ökologisch vertretbaren Verfahren niederschlagen, während gleichzeitig von der Natur abgeleitete Formen zutage kommen – nicht nur Entwürfe, die vorrangig von den Vorlieben des Verfassers abhängen. Es ist eine Zusammenarbeit denkbar, bei der Wissenschaftler und Designer Forschungsziele formulieren und koordinieren; ehe das geschieht, müsste allerdings ein neuer Typ von Entwurfsausbildung entwickelt werden. Eine der nützlichen und elementaren Leitlinien, die einer solchen Entwicklung zugrunde lägen, wäre die Frage: Wie würde die Natur diese Entwurfsfrage lösen? Die Frage ließe sich leicht als evolutionärer Samen in die gegenwärtige Entwurfsausbildung einfügen, ohne die bestehende Pädagogik zu kippen. Einmal gepflanzt, wird er wachsen.«

Obwohl der Schweizer Architekt Philippe Rahm noch nicht viel gebaut hat, genießt er einen guten Ruf. Mit seinem früheren Partner Gilles Décosterd (Décosterd & Rahm) hat er grundlegende, physiologische Faktoren erforscht, die in der zeitgenössischen Architektur häufig außer Acht gelassen werden. Er fragt, was geschieht, wenn Faktoren wie Feuchtigkeit, Licht oder der Sauerstoffgehalt der Luft vorsätzlich manipuliert werden. Die virtuelle Architektur wird von ihm einen Schritt weiter in die Grauzone der Wissenschaft geführt, indem er mit *Ghost Flat* einen Raum vorstellt, dessen Möblierung und Funktionen sich in Abhängigkeit vom genutzten Teil des Lichtspektrums verändern. »Das Schlafzimmer erscheint zwischen 400 und 500, das Wohnzimmer zwischen 600 und 800 Nanometer Wellenlänge. Das Badezimmer ist auf den ultravioletten Bereich zwischen 350 und 400 Nanometer Wellenlänge beschränkt.« Beunruhigender ist das Projekt *ND Cult*. Man stelle sich einen geräumigen Glaskasten vor, in den Gas eingeleitet wird. Der Sauerstoff wird auf sechs Prozent reduziert, und der Besucher betritt »einen Raum an der Grenze zum Tod, in dem Wahrnehmung und Bewusstsein in einer Weise modifiziert werden, die vermutlich dem mystischer Zustände ähnlich ist. Unter diesen extremen physischen Bedingungen ist der Raum äußerst gefährlich, irreversible Hirnschädigung möglich und das Todesrisiko real.« *ND* bedeutet Near Death (dem Tod nahe). In diesem Zusammenhang ist es vielleicht interessant, an Bill Violas Beschreibung vom dritten Akt des »Tristan« zu erinnern: »Wir werden in Agonie und Delirium von Tod und Leiden gestürzt, voller Visionen,

Träume und halluzinatorischer Offenbarungen, wie sie durch das Bewusstsein eines Sterbenden huschen«. Philippe Rahms Schaffen wurde umfassend in Kunstmuseen ausgestellt, und Décosterd & Rahm zeichneten verantwortlich für den Schweizer Pavillon auf der Architekturbiennale 2002 in Venedig. Das *Hormonorium* verwendete 528 in den Boden des Pavillons eingelassene Leuchtröhren zur Stimulierung der Netzhaut, die Informationen an die Zirbeldrüse leitet und damit eine Abnahme der Melatoninproduktion bewirkt. Durch den so im Körper abgesenkten Hormonspiegel nimmt in diesem Raum die Müdigkeit ab, mit einiger Wahrscheinlichkeit steigt das sexuelle Lustempfinden und Stimmungsschwankungen werden reguliert. Darüber hinaus senkten die Architekten im Pavillon den Sauerstoffgehalt von den normalen 21 Prozent auf 14,5 Prozent ab, und damit auf den Wert, der auf einer Höhe von 3000 m in den Schweizer Alpen herrscht. Sie erläutern: »Die in diesem Raum vorhandene, dünne Luft verursacht einen leichten Sauerstoffmangel im Blut, der sich anfangs durch klinische Zustände wie Verwirrung, Desorientierung oder seltsames Verhalten äußern kann, aufgrund der Endorphinausschüttung aber auch durch leichte Euphorie. Nach etwa zehn Minuten tritt eine messbare, natürliche Erhöhung der Pegel von Erythroproietin (EPO) und Haematokrit auf, die eine Stärkung des Herz-Kreislauf-Systems und der Atmung zur Folge haben. Das Protein Erythroproietin wird in den Nieren gebildet, gelangt dann ins Knochenmark, wo es die Bildung von roten Blutkörperchen anregt und damit die Abgabe von Sauerstoff an die Muskeln erhöht. Das Senken des Sauerstoffgehalts hat demzufolge eine belebende Wirkung, die die physischen Fähigkeiten des Körpers um bis zu zehn Prozent steigern kann.«

MARCOS NOVAK lehrt an der University of California in Santa Barbara, wo er mit dem kalifornischen NanoSystems Institute zusammenarbeitet. In seiner von der Universität veröffentlichten Biografie heißt es: »Da Novak bei seiner Arbeit Architektur, Musik sowie elektronische Datenverarbeitung heranzieht und zahlreiche weitere Einflüsse aus Kunst, Wissenschaft und Technik verarbeitet, entzieht sie sich jeglicher Kategorisierung.« Bei einem Teil seiner in diesem Buch gezeigten Projekte nutzt er die konstruktive und funktionale magnetische Resonanztomografie seines eigenen Gehirns, um algorithmisch erzeugte Räume und Formen zu schaffen. Sein Begriff der »transvergence« impliziert einen Paradigmenwechsel bei der Begegnung von Wissenschaft und Kunst oder Architektur. Der folgende Text wurde von Marcos Novak für *Architecture Now* geschrieben, um den Stand seiner Projekte zu erläutern.

In Kenntnis der fortschreitenden, ständig zunehmenden Bedeutung der Arbeit mit dem Granulösen, Elementaren, Atomaren und Verteilten, dem Parallelen und Aufkommenden, auf sämtlichen Ebenen, von der Stringtheorie zur Molekularbiologie, von der Werkstoffkunde zur Neurophysiologie, von der Informationstechnik zur digitalen Kunst, von granulöser, lenkbarer Musik zu granulöser, fließender Architektur untersucht dieser Aufsatz, wie wir uns eine Architektur vorstellen könnten, die nicht auf der Arbeit mit fertigen oder vorgefassten Formen basiert, sondern davon ausgeht, dass sich Formen als Ergebnis von Prozessen entwickeln, die auf einer granulösen und atomaren Ebene funktionieren (im ursprünglichen Sinn von ›atomar‹ als einem nicht weiter teilbaren Element oder einer Monade.)

Jedes kenntnisreiche Nachdenken über die Welt, wie wir sie kennen, wird gewahr, dass das, was wir als substanziell wahrnehmen, in Wirklichkeit nicht so ist. Das Meiste, was uns als feste Materie erscheint, ist Leere, so dass die Welt nicht in irgendeinem absoluten Sinn aus Figur und Grund besteht, sondern dass man sie sich besser als Modulation von Verbindungen und Dichtigkeiten vorstellt.

Bis vor kurzem gab es nur wenig, was man im Hinblick auf die Übernahme dieses Standpunktes als Entwurfsstrategie tun konnte. Dem standen zwei Haupthindernisse im Weg – Anzahl und Kontrolle. Das Arbeiten mit sehr kleinen Teilchen impliziert die Arbeit mit einer riesigen Anzahl winziger, schwer ›fassbarer‹ Elemente. Wie es häufig mit dem ursprünglich Unerreichbaren geschieht, verbargen diese beiden pragmatischen Hindernisse eine höhere, intellektuelle Schranke – sich tatsächlich vorzustellen, was nicht als vorgeformte Einheiten geschaffen werden könnte, sondern als Zusammenballung von Myriaden statistisch und nicht einzeln beherrschbarer Teilchen.

Entstehende Technologien ermöglichen es uns, die mechanischen Hindernisse zu überwinden und fordern uns heraus, unsere theoretische Reichweite und unseren Zugriff voranzubringen – anfangs im virtuellen und jetzt zunehmend auch im materiellen Bereich. Auf diese Weise haben wir die Gelegenheit, unsere Herangehensweise an das »Machen« grundlegend neu zu überdenken. Wie Nanotechnologie und all die anderen technischen und kognitiven Triumphe bei unserer Beherrschung des sehr Zahlreichen und sehr Kleinen zu zeigen beginnen, geht mit der Überwindung dieser Hindernisse eine entsprechende Belohnung einher – die Feinkontrolle über Abstufung und Überblendung von Attributen, die ansonsten getrennt blieben und somit die Möglichkeit der Erfindung neuer Arten von unbelebter und sogar belebter Materie in einer Weise, die der Häufigkeit, wenn auch nicht der Mühelosigkeit nahe kommt, wie sie der Erfindung neuer Klangfarben zu eigen ist.

Die natürliche Folge unseres Strebens nach einer ›grandiosen, einheitlichen Theorie‹, die die quantenmechanischen mit den relativistischen Beschreibungen des Universums in Einklang bringt, ist: Je näher wir dem Verständnis kommen, woraus die Welt besteht, desto fähiger werden wir, alles über unser elementarstes Verständnis Hinausgehende zu verändern. Warum also nicht die Elemente selbst verändern? Die hier gezeigten Projekte nähern sich diesen Fragen und Möglichkeiten aus einer Vielzahl von Richtungen. Die beherrschende Vorstellung ist die des »*Alloatomischen*«, womit ich eine Ausprägung des Atomaren meine, die sich nicht auf die buchstäblichen Elemente beschränkt, aus denen die Welt besteht, sondern auf »allo«-*Elemente,* andere von uns selbst gewählte und erfundene Elemente. Ebenso wie sich Gebiete wie *künstliches Leben* und *künstliche Intelligenz* nicht auf die Untersuchung von Leben und Intelligenz in ihrem Ist-Zustand beschränken, sondern ihre Forschung auf Leben und Intelligenz *wie sie sein könnten* erweitern, so wird die Idee des *Alloatomischen* auf Überlegungen ausgedehnt, wie sehr Kleines und Elementares *sein könnte* und wie wir lernen könnten, damit zu bauen. Es sollte klar sein, dass das, wovon ich spreche, sich nicht auf das Physische und Molekulare beschränkt, sondern auch und vielleicht vorwiegend auf den virtuellen Bereich und es von daher auf das Elementare als Konzept und Abstraktion anwendbar ist.

Ein Teil der hier gezeigten Projekte ist ausschließlich »*alloatomisch*« – bei ihnen wird versucht, sich Techniken zur Schaffung architektonischer Formen direkt nutzbar zu machen, indem Prozesse wie »*diffusion limited aggregation*« sowie andere, ähnliche Techniken benutzt werden, die Wachstum und Musterbildung gestalten; so können sich Formen auf die Art und Weise entwickeln, in der sich große Mengen von Partikeln anziehen oder abstoßen. Andere Projekte sind weit abstrakter und nutzen Neurophysiologie oder Techniken wie fMRI (funktionale Magnetresonanzbildgebung) des Gehirns, in diesem Fall meines arbeitenden Gehirns. Andere wiederum verwenden CFP – computational fluid dynamics – man stelle sich eine ›flüssige Architektur‹ vor, bestehend aus dem Wechselspiel sehr dichter, flüssiger Strömungen.

Wie meine vorherige Arbeit zielt auch diese gegenwärtige Studie auf die weitergehende Artikulierung eines Kontinuums, das vom Virtu-ellen bis zum Tatsächlichen reicht, vom Unbelebten bis zum Belebten, vom Musikalischen zum Materiellen, um nur einige ihrer Leit-linien zu erwähnen. Im Endeffekt ist dieses Kontinuum von Interesse, nicht irgendein einzelnes Experiment oder Projekt. Architektur beginnt als Gestaltung von Raum und Form, Präsenz oder Absenz, Masse und Leere; Musik gestaltet Klang und Stille, Glätte und Rau-heit, Ruhe und Unruhe, Zufälligkeit und Ordnung, durchzogen von Sein, Werden und Nichts. Diese Aufzählungen sind begrenzt und sub-jektiv; sie könnten endlos sein, aber was wir immer ausschließen können, ist die Gestaltung von Phänomenen zu Variationsmustern, die sowohl informationelle wie menschliche Bedeutung haben. Architektur wie Musik und so genannte »Transarchitektur« sowie sämtliche »transvergenten« Ausdrucksformen, auf die wir stoßen oder die wir erfinden, sind alle Modulationen. Vor diesem Hintergrund ist diese Studie der laufende Versuch zu lernen, wie wir die von uns geschaffenen neuen Kontinua verändern können.

All diese Überlegungen sind durchzogen vom Wissen um ein sich ständig veränderndes, vermitteltes Universum. Da ich bewusst erfor-sche, was ich als »Transvergenz« bezeichne, arbeite ich an zwei parallelen Auffassungen von »(trans)architektonischer« Forschung, Praxis und Pädagogik: zuerst die Überlegung, wie neue Bedingungen zu neuen Arten von Architektur führen können und zweitens die Überlegung, wie »(trans)architektonische« Forschung, Praxis und Pädagogik – vorausgesetzt, sie wird in einer angemessen ergänzten und spezialisierten Weise gesehen und kann ihre ganze imaginative und synthetische Kraft entfalten – einzigartig passende Modelle für unsere kreative Beschäftigung mit den neuen Welten liefern können, die wir so eilig erzeugen, nicht nur für die Architektur per se, sondern auch für andere aufkommende oder künftige, aussagekräftige Medienstrukturen.

© 2005 Marcus Novak für *Architecture Now*, Band 4

Man könnte Novak für einen Visionär halten, der wenig praktischen Einfluss auf das tatsächliche Bauen haben wird; vielleicht öffnet er aber auch die Tür zu neuen Sichtweisen der Welt, nicht von einer begrenzten, »professionellen« Warte, sondern von einem globaleren Stand-punkt aus. Ebenso wie es dem von Leonardo da Vinci verkörperten Renaissancemenschen möglich war, sich für Biologie, Physik, Kunst und Architektur zu interessieren, könnte es sein, dass die Informationstechnik den modernen Trend zur Scheuklappenspezialisierung beenden kann. Zahlreiche bedeutende Vertreter der zeitgenössischen Architektur, von Frank O. Gehry bis Santiago Calatrava, haben absichtlich die Bar-rieren zwischen Architektur, Kunst oder Technik durchbrochen. In dem Wissen um die großen Fortschritte der Wissenschaft haben Novak und andere wie Dollens keine Schwierigkeiten damit, zum Zweck der Innovation von Bildsprache und Verfahren anderer Gebiete Gebrauch zu machen. Philippe Rahm nimmt die »offensichtlichen« Tatsachen der Physiologie und räumt ihnen Platz in seiner vorerst virtuellen Architektur ein. Ist es so überraschend, dass wir in einem Gebäude nicht nur mit dem Raum leben, sondern auch mit Feuchtigkeit oder Sauerstoffgehalt, die einen starken Einfluss auf unser Wohl- oder Unwohlsein haben? Puristen werden sagen, nichts davon habe etwas mit Architektur zu tun, aber in dem Maß wie Computertechnologie den »non-standard«-Entwurf zur Realität werden lässt, stellt sich die Frage, weshalb es überhaupt Barrieren zwischen Sachgebieten gibt. Sei es die maßvolle, nachvollziehbare Art, mit der der Designer Patrick Jouin sich weiter auf das Terrain der Architektur vorwagt, sei es François Roche, der ein Projekt auf die Begegnung von Charles Perrault und André Le Nôtre gründet, oder die schöne neue Welt von Marcos Novak: Es gibt eine Konstante – die Architektur ist aus dem Kasten heraus.

INTRODUCTION

HORS DE LA BOÎTE

Au propre comme au figuré, l'architecture a rompu avec la fameuse boîte. Les nouvelles technologies de conception et de construction commencent enfin à transformer notre façon d'aborder le bâti. Conséquence partielle de ces développements, les frontières qui séparent l'architecture de l'art et du design s'estompent. L'idée même d'espace et la façon dont il est manipulé évoluent grâce aux nouvelles perspectives ouvertes par un certain nombre d'artistes dont la pratique fait appel aux trois dimensions. Tout ceci ne signifie pas pour autant la mort du modernisme, mais simplement que les nouvelles possibilités offertes aux architectes sont si nombreuses que l'on peut même voir des solutions minimalistes naître de points de vue très différents. L'objectif n'est certainement pas de se contenter de reproduire ce qui a été fait auparavant, mais aussi de repenser l'architecture. Ce livre n'est en aucun cas une sélection exhaustive de l'architecture des trois ou quatre dernières années, mais un survol subjectif de multiples types de bâtiments et de tendances vus sous un angle international. Ce n'est pas un hasard si la plupart des architectes présentés dans cet ouvrage ne figuraient pas dans les précédents volumes d'*Architecture Now*. Gehry, Koolhaas ou Herzog & de Meuron sont là, mais aussi Patrick Jouin, Philippe Rahm et Klein Dytham. Jouin est un designer qui s'oriente vers le domaine de l'architecture, en particulier pour son client le célèbre chef Alain Ducasse. Rahm (récemment encore associé de l'agence Décosterd & Rahm) explore les frontières entre physiologie et architecture, tandis qu'Astrid Klein et Mark Dytham bousculent la scène tokyoïte avec des réalisations spectaculaires comme leur écran de verdure de 274 mètres de long (Green Green Screen, Omotesando) et leur superbe espace SuperDeluxe, qu'ils décrivent comme « un lieu de plaisir et d'expérimentation. Une galerie, un bar, une cuisine, un club de jazz et un studio de cinéma. Un cinéma. Une bibliothèque, une école, une salle de concert et un théâtre ». Laissez de côté vos idées préconçues. Voici ce qu'est l'architecture d'aujourd'hui…

ABRITE-MOI

Il y a fort longtemps, l'architecture servait essentiellement à se protéger des éléments, voire d'un loup éventuel. Avoir « un toit au-dessus de la tête » est aujourd'hui encore la préoccupation première, même si les architectes s'efforcent de rendre leurs maisons de plus en plus intéressantes. La Casa Equis, à Cañete (Pérou), est une surprenante tentative des architectes quarantenaires Jean-Pierre Crousse et Sandra Barclay pour « créer l'intimité ou les conditions de vie familiale requises pour vivre dans le désert où se trouve la maison, sans nier ni truquer la situation. » La photo d'un enfant nageant dans la piscine de verre de la Casa Equis suspendue très au-dessus d'une plage sauvage, a fait le tour des magazines d'architecture du monde entier, comme si l'on venait de découvrir la recette de l'apesanteur. Le problème auquel s'est trouvé confronté David Chipperfield dans sa maison de Galice était assez différent. Cette résidence de 210 m² devait s'adapter non seulement aux rochers présents sur le terrain mais aussi à une bande de maisons existantes de styles hétérogènes. Dans ces conditions difficiles, l'architecte a réussi magistralement à insuffler un esprit de modernité réel et diversifié qui montre que des changements sont décidément en cours. Le perfectionnement progressif des systèmes de communication, d'information et de commercialisation que recouvre le terme de « globalisation » a laissé le champ libre à une nouvelle génération d'architectes à l'aise aussi bien à Cañete, au Pérou, qu'à Corrubedo en Espagne. Leur but n'est pas de créer un pastiche d'architecture locale, ni d'imposer une vision par trop étrangère, mais de réagir au contexte de manière intelligente et cohérente. La modernité d'aujourd'hui ne s'appuie plus sur la géométrie de la boîte euclidienne, même si un architecte comme Chipperfield se fait toujours remarquer par son esthétique minimaliste. Il s'agit maintenant d'utiliser à la fois la sensibilité et les technologies pour répondre aux désirs des clients. Ce fut certainement le cas lorsque le très inventif architecte japonais Shuhei Endo se vit proposer un terrain triangulaire en pente abrupte de 20 m de long sur une profondeur allant de 4 à 1,5 m seulement… Sa Rooftecture S House démontre que des conditions extrêmes peuvent générer des solutions originales qui sont autant de défis esthétiques. La surpopulation urbaine du Japon, en particulier sur la côte est, confronte souvent les architectes à l'obligation de s'adapter à des terrains de configuration réduite ou bizarre. Les jeunes architectes de Easter Design ont édifié leur Slit House sur une parcelle de 50 m de long par 7,5 de large. Bien que presque trois fois plus grand que celui de la Rooftecture S, ce terrain étroit leur a inspiré une proposition remarquable, que caractérisent l'absence de vraies fenêtres et, surtout, la présence de pas moins de 60 fentes de 14 cm de large. Du fait que les espaces verts sont extrêmement rares dans leur pays, les Japonais considèrent que le jeu de la lumière dans une architecture est une manifestation de la nature. Bien qu'elle soit en fait un parallélogramme de béton, la Slit House fait appel à cette sensibilité traditionnelle à la lumière pour tenter d'éliminer la fenêtre classique.

L'esthétique orientale est également présente dans un lieu inattendu cette fois, à Hasselt en Belgique. La Villa C, conçue pour Frédéric Chaillet, associé senior de l'agence Groep Delta, joue du contraste entre une entrée signalée par un mur massif, quasi aveugle, de 26 m de long en pierre de Waimes et une façade sur jardin entièrement vitrée. L'utilisation d'un bassin réfléchissant à sept pas japonais près de la salle à manger rappelle l'intérêt du propriétaire pour l'Asie, ne serait-ce que par le miroitement de lumière qu'il crée à l'intérieur de la maison. Exploitant les puissants contrastes entre la pierre, l'acier, le verre et le bois, la Villa C est un excellent exemple du type de liberté stylistique qui règne dans l'architecture contemporaine. En Corse, la Maison H dessinée par les architectes parisiens Jakob + MacFarlane n'est pas encore sortie de terre, mais ses plans sont caractéristiques d'une des tendances fortes d'aujourd'hui : l'utilisation d'une technologie informatique sophistiquée pour créer des formes qui semblent jaillir du sol. Alors que les modernistes historiques cherchaient la plupart du temps à se poser légèrement sur le sol, juchant même parfois leurs constructions sur des pilotis, les architectes contemporains inclinent davantage à creuser ou à s'inspirer directement de la topographie du site.

TOUT CONFORT

Même si les hôtels doivent répondre à des contraintes fonctionnelles strictes, il est définitivement à la mode de faire appel à des designers réputés pour tenter d'attirer davantage de clients. Le style des hôtels de prestige de Ian Schrager, aux aménagements intérieurs signés par des célébrités comme Philippe Starck, a fait des émules dans de nombreuses villes. Les jeunes architectes de GRAFT ont récemment conçu l'hôtel Q ! à Berlin, d'une approche très inventive malgré la modestie de son budget. L'espace bar-restaurant, sorte de cocon rouge, fait penser au travail de Neil Denari mais le mobilier intégré et le décor des chambres réussissent à donner un style personnel à l'établissement. Pour ce que l'on pourrait qualifier de summum du « design hotel », la grande chaîne espagnole Silken a demandé à pas moins de dix-neuf architectes et designers de notoriété internationale de décorer les 342 chambres de son nouvel Hotel Puerta América à Madrid. Dans un immeuble signé Jean Nouvel, cet hôtel a ainsi vu ses étages aménagés par Zaha Hadid, David Chipperfield, Mark Newson, Ron Arad, Arata Isozaki et John Pawson. Ce mélange d'architectes et de designers peut surprendre, mais on constate aujourd'hui un effacement des frontières entre les deux disciplines, les designers cherchant de plus en plus à construire. Où le « Good Design » s'arrête-il et où débute le « big business »? C'est la question que soulève le Puerta América, car créer des chambres et des suites pour un établissement de chaîne est un défi périlleux, même pour le plus talentueux des créateurs.

Jeune et intelligent designer qui a certainement l'ambition de se frayer un chemin dans le domaine de l'architecture, le Français Patrick Jouin s'est déjà fait un nom en décorant des salles de restaurants pour le célèbre chef Alain Ducasse. C'est pour ce dernier qu'il a conçu le Chlösterli dans la station de ski de haut luxe de Gstaad. Aménagé dans un vaste chalet en bois construit vers 1700 par les moines de l'abbaye de Rougemont, le Chlösterli compte deux restaurants, un bar et une discothèque. Les meubles, également créés par Jouin non sans quelques clins d'œils aux thèmes alpins, animent avec grâce les salles de restaurant. En dépit de l'intérieur complexe et assez sombre du chalet, le designer a su apporter à Gstaad un style neuf, qui s'éloigne du minimalisme glacé au profit d'un décor plus varié, voire plus forte-ment orné. S'il n'est pas le seul designer à emprunter cette voie, Jouin est l'un des plus brillants. Son restaurant Mix pour l'hôtel à Mandalay Bay, Las Vegas, se propose de redonner tout son lustre à la réputation d'extravagance de la ville. Partant d'une iconographie volcanique, il n'a pas hésité à dessiner une gigantesque suspension composée de 15 000 sphères en verre de Murano…

Les hôtels bien conçus ne se cantonnent plus seulement aux grandes villes. Deux exemples publiés ici se trouvent en fait dans cer-taines des régions les plus reculées du monde. L'hôtel ESO à Cerro Paranal (Chili) a été édifié par les architectes allemands Auer + Weber à une altitude de 2400 m dans les montagnes du désert d'Atacama. Construit pour les utilisateurs du Très Grand Télescope (TGT) perché non loin de là, l'ESO prend remarquablement en compte ce site tout en offrant à ses hôtes un degré de confort inattendu. Principalement destiné à des touristes moins férus de sciences, Longitude 131° est une extension du complexe touristique de Yulara conçu par l'architecte Philip Cox. Bien que proche d'Ayers Rock, le fameux symbole de l'Australie, et situé dans une région assez inhospitalière où la température dépasse souvent 40°, cet hôtel respecte son impressionnant cadre naturel et se dresse sur des pilotis d'acier. Comme le montrent ces deux réalisa-tions, l'idée que la « bonne » architecture n'intéresse que les *cognoscenti* n'est plus valable. Peut-être du fait du succès public d'un certain nombre de constructions de « grands » architectes et aussi parce que des chaînes comme Aman Resorts ont imposé un standard de concep-tion élevé, des démarches comme celles du Puerta América ou de ces établissements perdus en pleine nature sont de plus en plus courantes.

Si l'aspect pratique de l'hôtellerie interdit parfois à ces réalisations d'exprimer un pur concept architectural, la conception et la réalisa-tion assistées par ordinateur vont bientôt ouvrir des voies nouvelles dans ce domaine. L'agence de Rotterdam ONL [Oosterhuis_Lénárd] a conçu un très étonnant hôtel pour Dubaï, le Flyotel. Évoquant un oiseau prêt à prendre son envol, cet établissement cinq étoiles de 600 chambres devrait être le premier exemple de conception architecturale « non-standard » appliquée à un aussi grand projet. Organisée par le Centre Pompidou à Paris fin 2003, l'exposition intitulée « Une architecture non-standard » présentait ONL et onze autres agences dont UN Stu-dio, R&Sie (François Roche), Greg Lynn et Asymptote. Son intention, selon son commissaire Frédéric Migayrou, n'était « pas tant de présenter des exemples d'architecture numérique ou virtuelle qui traitent des problèmes de la représentation (comme la virtualité et l'hyperespace) que de mettre en lumière les modifications apportées aujourd'hui à l'industrialisation de l'architecture. L'utilisation généralisée de logiciels appuyés sur des systèmes algorithmiques présuppose des changements dans les outils de conception et de production. L'architecture non-standard est une réflexion sur le langage de l'architecture et son champ d'application, à partir de l'exploitation d'éléments numériques. Les méthodes de construction traditionnelles peuvent maintenant être confrontées à une production reposant sur le prototypage ou la préfabrication d'éléments architecturaux ». Plus clairement encore, Migayrou et certains des architectes présents dans l'exposition sont convaincus qu'un système de lien direct de l'ordinateur à la fabrication permettant de créer des formes uniques pour le même prix que les formes standards, ou produites en série va bientôt bouleverser le monde. Kas Oosterhuis confirme que le Flyotel, prévu pour que des hydravions puissent s'amarrer à son quai intégré, coûtera « seulement 10% de plus qu'un immeuble de grande hauteur standard. »

L'ESPACE FAIT L'ART

Les musées ont longtemps été l'objet d'une attention particulière de la part des architectes. Le Guggenheim de Frank Lloyd Wright à New York et de nombreuses autres institutions ont montré qu'une architecture inhabituelle et même provocante pouvait exercer un impact notable sur le succès d'une institution, voire créer un afflux de public supplémentaire, même lorsque les collections présentées n'étaient pas d'une importance extrême (Guggenheim Bilbao). Les aventures de Thomas Krens, le dynamique directeur du Guggenheim, se poursuivent et il continue à lancer projet après projet sur différents points du globe. Si le Guggenheim de Jean Nouvel à Rio n'est pas près d'être construit, Krens a organisé un concours pour un nouveau musée à Guadalajara au Mexique. Remporté par Enrique Norten, il a suscité d'autres propositions intéressantes, par exemple celle d'Asymptote. En perchant leur projet au bord d'un canyon, les architectes new-yorkais ont lâché la bride à leur imagination et à leurs ordinateurs et créé une forme sculpturale, quasi liquide, qui aurait fait appel aux mêmes technologies non-standard que le Flyotel d'ONL. Un autre projet restera dans les cartons, celui de François Roche pour le nouveau musée d'art contemporain de Lausanne. Protéiforme et inspirée par la nature, sa « Green Gorgon » répond à la passion de l'architecte français pour une architecture qui raconte une histoire, qui soit enrichie par une fiction. Ici, c'est la collaboration entre Charles Perrault (1628–1703) auteur des *Histoires ou contes du temps passé* (appelés aussi *Contes de ma mère l'Oye*, 1697) et le jardinier André Le Nôtre (1613–1700) pour le labyrinthe de Versailles qui ont été le point de départ de la proposition de R&Sie. Pour Roche, Le Nôtre et Perrault n'ont pas tant créé un dessin mathématique qu'imaginé un lieu dans lequel les visiteurs accepteraient « de se perdre ». « C'est précisément cette dimension hétérotypique qui conditionne notre proposition », conclut François Roche.

On pourrait dire que Yoshio Taniguchi, l'architecte japonais auteur de la récente transformation du Museum of Modern Art de New York occupe l'extrémité opposée du spectre théorique, du moins pour ce qui concerne les musées. En collaboration avec les architectes new-yorkais KPF et en particulier Steven Rustow, Taniguchi a réussi à importer un peu de la merveilleuse subtilité japonaise à New York. Il subsiste néanmoins une fracture entre la dimension même des espaces, par exemple l'atrium du premier étage, et l'atmosphère d'intimité qui avait fait du MoMA le haut lieu de l'art moderne. Peut-être suffit-il désormais que les conservateurs du musée s'approprient ces nouveaux volumes et sélectionnent des œuvres qui l'habitent avec plus de force et de légitimité. Pour le moment, le *Broken Obelisk* de Barnett Newman, présenté par un critique comme « une médiocre sculpture d'un bon peintre », cherche en vain à attirer l'attention dans cet atrium surdimensionné. Urbain dans son échelle et ses rapports avec les immeubles avoisinants, ce MoMA tout neuf est aussi le fruit de décisions de conservateurs et d'administrateurs rendues possibles par des campagnes de financement fructueuses. De grandes galeries ont été spécifiquement conçues pour accueillir certaines des plus lourdes sculptures de Richard Serra, mais on peut se demander si ce musée est vraiment le lieu idéal pour présenter l'art contemporain. Il était et reste un temple de la modernité, telle qu'incarnée par le XXe siècle. Il est responsable pour une bonne part de la transition accomplie par l'art moderne entre les luttes révolutionnaires et la soumission aux normes. Mais ce qui se passe en art contemporain, et a fortiori dans l'architecture récente, dessine de nouvelles directions auxquelles et l'institution elle-même et Taniguchi n'apportent peut-être pas les solutions les plus adaptées. Les formes d'expression nouvelles seraient sans doute plus à leur place dans un environnement plus brut, voire hostile, que les sols polis et l'immense blancheur du MoMA.

Herzog & de Meuron ont choisi une approche différente pour l'extension du Walker Art Center à Minneapolis. Les architectes suisses ont imaginé une boîte tendue d'une résille d'aluminium, mais cet aspect extérieur est peut-être moins important que la volonté de créer un lieu dans lequel différentes formes d'art peuvent interagir de «façons entièrement inattendues et nouvelles». Un coup d'œil au programme du Walker montre que le slogan «Où l'art rencontre la vie» semble convenir à cette institution et à sa nouvelle architecture : danse, performances, cinéma, peinture, musique ou théâtre participent tous à cette fusion. Serait-ce que les versions plus traditionnelles de la grande boîte blanche (MoMA) ne sont plus adaptées à l'explosion de formes multidisciplinaires qui envahissent les arts ? Cette remarque porte d'ailleurs plus sur le changement majeur qu'ils connaissent que sur le succès du MoMA (à l'évidence très vif). Alors que Taniguchi s'est complu dans la création d'un temple pour l'art du XXe siècle, Herzog & de Meuron ont sauté avec ferveur dans le XXIe siècle.

Tous les nouveaux musées ne tentent pas de redéfinir l'art et l'architecture. Celui des sciences naturelles de Matsunoyama au Japon, par Tezuka Architects, cherche néanmoins à explorer de nouvelles pistes. Consistant essentiellement en un tube d'acier Corten de 111 mètres de long et une tour belvédère de 34 mètres de haut, ce nouvel équipement culturel est destiné à l'observation de la vie sous les abondantes chutes de neige locales. Bien que prendre en compte des charges de neige pouvant atteindre deux mille tonnes impose des contraintes techniques à n'importe quel bâtiment, Tezuka Architects ont fait de cette difficulté une source d'inventivité. Par sa forme et sa fonction, leur tube d'acier fait partie intégrante du terrain tout en reposant prudemment sur lui, puisqu'il subit une dilatation de 20 cm en été. Il serait difficile de classer ce travail dans une tendance actuelle spécifique, même s'il a été présenté à la dernière Biennale d'architecture de Venise comme représentatif des rapports entre le bâti et la terre. Cette approche n'est ni minimaliste ni non-standard et cependant très contemporaine. Ici comme ailleurs, le style semble davantage exister dans le regard du spectateur que dans le projet lui-même.

L'ART FAIT L'ESPACE

Les rapports entre l'art et l'architecture remontent aux premières constructions connues, même si la définition de l'art a substantiellement évolué depuis l'époque où elle ne concernait que le décor des églises ou des palais. On peut dire que l'art a abandonné certains de ses liens naturels avec le monde «réel» lorsque les peintures ont été accrochées aux murs des musées et les sculptures posées sur des socles. La conquête majeure de l'art contemporain a consisté à reprendre le contrôle de l'espace hors du musée, à réinvestir un environnement «réel». Le peintre Anselm Kiefer est connu depuis longtemps pour son intérêt pour l'espace, que ce soit dans ses peintures ou ses sculptures en métal (souvent en plomb). Plus que beaucoup d'autres peintres contemporains, il s'est créé son propre univers labyrinthique où les références indirectes aux mythes ou aux faits historiques constituent une sorte d'histoire sédimentaire. En incorporant du foin ou des graines de tournesol dans ses peintures et souvent d'épais empâtements, il remet en question la profondeur ou la perspective dans des œuvres qui évoquent un monde disparu, ou futur. Dans ce contexte, il peut sembler surprenant qu'au cours de ces treize dernières années il ait travaillé dans un atelier situé sur un terrain de 35 hectares à Barjac, dans les Cévennes. Ce n'est certainement pas un atelier au sens traditionnel, car *La Ribaute* est plus une superposition d'espaces au-dessus et en dessous du sol. Comme nombre des peintures de Kiefer, le lieu donne le sentiment de venir d'une autre époque, d'être le vestige de quelque civilisation encore mal connue. Il n'y a pas de réponse à la question du pourquoi de l'érection de ces serres étincelantes et de ces mondes obscurs d'eau et de plomb, si ce n'est que cette architecture est l'expression de son art, de l'artiste lui-même et de son époque. Ces formes construites seraient le témoignage d'une connaissance ésotérique dont le sens se serait perdu dans le temps, ou le terrible secret d'une époque trop proche pour ne pas mettre mal à l'aise. La différence entre l'art et l'architecture serait que cette dernière répond à un but, mais si ce but était justement de créer de l'art ? La pulsion esthétique, la raison d'être de « l'architecture » de Kiefer est son art, son monde intérieur. Des architectes authentiquement visionnaires comme Constant ont pu imaginer des mondes nouveaux et des figures excentriques comme Simon Rodia, qui a construit les Watts Towers à Los Angeles, ont donné une forme architecturale à leur sensibilité esthétique, mais il se pourrait que des architectes plus conventionnels aient aussi quelque chose à apprendre de l'exemple d'Anselm Kiefer.

Définir l'architecture est parfois aussi complexe que définir l'art. De nombreux types d'expression se cachent derrière ces mots attrape-tout, même si le critère de la fonction hante en permanence le bâti. L'une des idées récurrentes de l'architecture contemporaine est particulièrement bien exprimée par Hamlet dans la pièce de Shakespeare : « Ah ! Si cette chair trop solide pouvait se fondre, se dissoudre et se perdre en rosée ! ». Le Blur Building, conçu par Diller + Scofidio pour l'exposition nationale suisse Expo 02 à Yverdon-les-Bains, tentait de façon assez convaincante d'avoir l'air d'un nuage en suspension au-dessus du lac de Neuchâtel. D'autres parlent de créer une architecture qui réagirait à ses visiteurs, presque comme le ferait une créature vivante, tandis que certains semblent se contenter d'une approche purement virtuelle. La Tour des vents de Toyo Ito (Yokohama, Kanagawa, 1986) nous rappelle qu'une architecture réactive, à la frontière de l'art, peut marquer son temps et soulever la question simple du sens de la forme. On peut imaginer un instant que l'art peut, lui aussi, investir l'espace et lui donner sens, souvent de façon plus éphémère que l'architecture, mais le Blur Building ou les pavillons temporaires de la Serpentine Gallery à Londres montrent que la durabilité n'est plus une nécessité pour tous. Le vidéaste américain Bill Viola a souvent imaginé ses œuvres dans un cadre architectural, et leur échelle aussi bien que leur nature sont telles qu'elles requièrent généralement de l'espace et qu'elles le transforment. La récente collaboration de l'artiste avec le metteur en scène d'opéra et de théâtre Peter Sellars et le chef d'orchestre Esa-Pekka Salonen dans un film de quatre heures, qui accompagne l'opéra de Richard Wagner *Tristan et Isolde* à Paris, traite des enjeux d'image, d'espace et de représentation qui se bousculent aux frontières de l'art et de l'architecture. « Je voulais créer un monde d'images qui existe en parallèle à l'action se déroulant sur la scène », explique Viola, « … de la même façon qu'une voix poétique plus subtile nous ferait le récit des dimensions cachées de notre vie intérieure. Les images se veulent des représentations intérieures symboliques qui deviennent l'écho, pour reprendre les termes de Seyyed Hossein Nasr, des reflets du monde spirituel dans le miroir du matériel et du temporel ». Viola parle également de « l'océan infini d'un monde immatériel invisible » à propos du premier acte de *Tristan* et il nous propose une image de feu et de lumière pour le troisième acte. « L'acte III », explique-t-il, « décrit la dissolution du Soi dans les étapes de la mort, le processus délicat et cruel de la séparation et de la désintégration des composants physiques, de perception et de conceptualisation de la conscience. Nous sommes plongés dans l'agonie et le délire de la mort et de la souffrance, submergés par les visions, les rêves et les révélations hallucinées qui affleurent à l'esprit de l'homme en train de mourir. Lorsque les flammes de la passion et de la fièvre submergent la conscience et que le corps du désir s'enfuit à jamais, le miroir est voilé et s'évanouit dans des motifs de vagues et de pure lumière ». Ceci ne veut pas dire que les images de feu, d'eau et de lumière de Viola soient une expression d'architecture au même sens que l'atelier de Kiefer. Viola se sert de l'art, et ici de l'espace scénique, pour évoquer les enjeux de la vie et de la mort. L'architecture n'est pas pour autant condamnée à l'exercice lassant de la gestion des contraintes budgétaires et de l'implantation de sorties de secours. À la limite, elle dissout la boîte dans le feu et la lumière pour ne plus devenir qu'une image virtuelle, mais c'est précisément là que la pensée se produit, là où les bâtiments de demain prendront forme. Des artistes tels que Kiefer et Viola peuvent aider à montrer le chemin en termes esthétiques et intellectuels.

BIG AND SEXY

Les architectes devenus célèbres ont souvent commencé leur carrière par de petits projets. Frank O. Gehry s'est fait connaître par son utilisation de la résille métallique ou de l'asphalte sur le sol de sa cuisine, mais les grands projets sont une autre paire de manches, comme il a pu le découvrir en concevant le Walt Disney Concert Hall à Los Angeles. D'autres écrivent des livres ou dessinent avant de se retrouver en couverture des journaux, comme Rem Koolhaas ou Zaha Hadid. Il faut simplement du temps pour qu'un client assez fortuné fasse confiance à un architecte novateur et le charge d'un grand chantier. Le projet le plus important et le plus politiquement sensible du brillant architecte catalan Enric Miralles n'a été achevé qu'après sa mort prématurée. Beaucoup cependant ne sont toujours pas convaincus par cet immeuble du Parlement écossais (terminé par son associée et épouse Benedetta Tagliabue d'EMBT en collaboration avec l'agence locale RMJM Scotland Ltd.). Les complexités du projet ont conduit à la création d'une commission d'enquête qui a conclu à une insuffisance de communication entre EMBT et RMJM et à un contrôle des dépenses trop laxiste. Les dépassements budgétaires sont assez typiques des interventions des praticiens inventifs et cet exemple n'a pas contribué à relever la réputation de la profession. Peut-être parce qu'il était trop compliqué, le Parlement écossais a été la victime des retards et de l'indécision administratifs bien plus que de l'ego de l'architecte. Dans le rapport officiel remis par Lord Fraser of Carmyllie le 24 juin 2004, il est écrit : « Aussi tentant soit-il de reporter le blâme sur un génie architectural espagnol décédé, sur sa façon de travailler et sur les relations tendues entre sa veuve et RMJM à Édimbourg, l'analyse de l'auditeur général est incontestable. Les coûts se sont accrus parce que les clients (le secrétaire d'État en premier lieu, puis le Parlement) ont demandé des travaux supplémentaires et des modifications ou les ont, du moins, approuvés d'une façon ou d'une autre ».[1]

Il se peut que les clients privés stimulent davantage les grands architectes que la commande publique. Mais, là encore, il est parfois difficile pour des hommes de talent habitués à de petits projets de prendre brusquement en charge des chantiers importants. Massimiliano Fuksas est coutumier de chantiers d'assez grandes dimensions mais d'aucun à l'échelle de sa Fiera Milano, les nouvelles installations de la célèbre foire de la capitale lombarde. Achevé pour l'essentiel en un temps record de vingt-sept mois, ce complexe couvre pas moins de 1,4 millions de m² et se caractérise par une allée centrale de 1,5 km de long, dont le profil judicieux semble sorti d'un logiciel d'ordinateur

[1] www.scottish.parliament.uk/vli/holyrood/inquiry/sp205–00.htm

sophistiqué. En fait, Fuksas, basé à Rome et à Paris, ne se sert pas vraiment d'ordinateurs pour ses réalisations propres. Son agence utilise bien sûr abondamment les technologies les plus récentes, mais il préfère dessiner ou même peindre ses projets avant de les confier aux miracles de la numérisation. À Milan, il s'est inspiré des tempêtes ou même des tornades pour la couverture de l'allée. Bien que l'on fasse grand cas des prouesses de l'informatique, il est clair ici qu'en faisant appel à des moyens relativement traditionnels l'architecte a su créer une forme très contemporaine, de façon efficace et en respectant les délais. Son succès ôte à Édimbourg (EMBT) les circonstances atténuantes décrites plus haut.

Rem Koolhaas/OMA est sans doute l'architecte le plus en vue ces temps-ci, en grande partie grâce à ses livres, de *Delirious New York* à *S, M, L, XL* et à sa personnalité originale. Si l'on a beaucoup parlé de lui, ce n'est que récemment que ses réalisations ont commencé à s'élever au niveau de ses relations publiques. Il est fier, à juste titre, de la nouvelle Bibliothèque centrale de Seattle. Démarche typique de son agence, il s'est efforcé d'offrir à cet équipement public une enveloppe appropriée, bien sûr, mais aussi d'innover en termes de structure autant que de solutions fonctionnelles. Résolument «transparent et ouvert, contrairement à la plupart des bibliothèques, le bâtiment est en grande partie gainé de verre, ce qui permet de suivre ses activités aussi bien de l'intérieur que de l'extérieur. Sa forme inclinée est moins un caprice esthétique qu'un effort calculé pour contrôler le type et la qualité de la lumière qui pénètre dans les espaces intérieurs. Un système de «plates-formes flottantes» et une trame diagonale de protection contre tremblements de terre ou tornades représentent les innovations structurelles. Dans la bibliothèque même, une étonnante «Spirale de livres» traverse quatre niveaux de rayonnage, contient la collection complète des ouvrages documentaires et permet un accroissement de capacité dans le futur. Si l'innovation structurelle est ce que l'on peut attendre d'un architecte aussi connu, il est plus intéressant encore de voir que Koolhaas/OMA n'ont pas hésité à bousculer un milieu aussi conservateur que celui des bibliothécaires, plutôt habitués aux alignements soignés de kilomètres d'étagères. L'accueil du public et son utilisation des installations sont tout aussi inventifs.

Zaha Hadid, ancienne associée d'OMA, commence également à réaliser des projets sur un rythme soutenu, après des années de travail d'ordre plutôt conceptuel et graphique mais influent. Désignée lors de l'exposition fondatrice du MoMA de 1988 comme l'une des fondatrices de l'Architecture déconstructiviste aux côtés de Rem Koolhaas, elle fait preuve dans son travail actuel d'une souplesse assez éloignée des compositions anguleuses du mouvement russe. Son bâtiment central pour l'usine BMW de Leipzig, décrit comme le «centre nerveux de l'ensemble du complexe», a dû affronter un conservatisme ambiant aussi rétif à l'innovation architecturale que le monde des bibliothèques. Souhaitant utiliser l'architecture pour créer une «totale transparence de l'organisation interne», mais également pour mêler les fonctions «afin d'éviter la ségrégation habituelle de groupes enfermés dans leur statut», Hadid fait clairement comprendre que, comme Koolhaas, son but est bien de réviser des méthodes figées. Dans la fluidité de ses plans, elle remet en cause les alignements secs et desséchants du fordisme. Elle remet également en cause le dogme moderniste de plans strictement géométriques pour favoriser un flux de mouvements plus continu et plus organique. Ce qui surprend, à Seattle comme à Leipzig, c'est que les préférences naturelles des architectes semblent s'accorder avec les intérêts bien compris de leurs clients. Alors que de célèbres architectes ont souvent cherché à imposer leur esthétique personnelle dans des circonstances inappropriées, Koolhaas et Hadid ont accompli les efforts nécessaires pour rendre plus séduisante encore ce que l'on peut appeler une architecture «intelligente». Certes, convaincre des clients aussi établis que la Bibliothèque centrale de Seattle et BMW que leurs méthodes de travail pourraient être améliorées est toujours un combat, mais ces deux diplômés de l'Architectural Association de Londres ont atteint un niveau de notoriété internationale tel qu'il les autorise à infléchir le cours de l'histoire de l'architecture.

CONTEMPORAIN TEMPORAIRE

L'idée que l'architecture doive être durable tient bon pour certains types de bâtiments. Musées, bibliothèques, églises et banques apprécient généralement la notion de pérennité. Néanmoins, une autre face de la conception architecturale contemporaine s'intéresse, tout comme l'art, à l'éphémère. Certaines fonctions n'impliquent pas la durée. L'un des architectes les plus inventifs de notre époque est Shigeru Ban. Il est familier des constructions temporaires, comme le montrent ses abris en papier pour réfugiés réalisés en tubes de carton et films plastiques pour le Haut Commissariat aux Réfugiés (HCRNU). Avec son Musée nomade, conçu pour une exposition des photographies de Gregory Colbert à New York City du 5 mars au 6 juin 2005, il s'est aventuré sur un tout autre terrain. Il a imaginé un volume rectangulaire de 205 m de long essentiellement composé de conteneurs d'expédition, empilés sur le Pier 54. Même si l'on apprécie moyennement les images de Colbert, le projet de Ban possède indéniablement quelque chose de « l'atmosphère d'une église classique », selon ses propres termes. Et bien que les temples japonais soient rarement de forme rectangulaire, on trouve dans ce projet une touche orientale. Créer un sentiment de spiritualité à partir de conteneurs métalliques et de tubes en carton n'est pas une mince affaire, et Shigeru Ban a montré à de nombreuses reprises que des matériaux inattendus pouvaient ouvrir la voie à l'innovation architecturale, même lorsque la permanence n'est pas l'enjeu. Une démonstration plus utilitariste de ses talents peut se voir au sommet du Centre Pompidou à Paris où il a installé son Atelier éphémère sous une voûte de 115 m^2, faite de tubes de carton, de bois, d'acier et de membranes de PTFE. Pendant la durée des travaux du nouveau Centre Pompidou qu'il construit à Metz, cet atelier sera son bureau, tout en haut du bâtiment de Piano et Rogers. Il rappelle, à sa façon, que le Centre voulait être une structure « flexible. »

Certains jeunes artistes ou architectes s'intéressent aux aspects éphémères de la construction pour des raisons d'économie ou parce qu'ils explorent des domaines d'expérimentation un peu négligés. C'est sans aucun doute le cas de deux Allemands aux approches différentes, l'architecte Andreas Wenning et l'artiste Stefan Eberstadt. Wenning a créé baumraum en 2003, en s'appuyant sur l'engouement pour les maisons dans les arbres. Respectant au maximum les arbres dans lesquels il construit, il démontre que ce genre est étonnamment riche en possibilités dont la plupart sont refusées pour des structures qui auraient davantage « les pieds sur terre ». L'idée de Stefan Eberstadt, la Rucksack House, est encore plus originale, puisque cette « maison-sac à dos » entend tout simplement s'accrocher à des structures existantes. « Ceci réactive l'idée de la maison dans l'arbre artisanale, légèrement anarchique, mais, cette fois, implantée bien en évidence et passée au filtre de l'ingénierie. » Eberstadt plaide pour une conscience accrue du potentiel d'interactions entre l'art contemporain, l'architecture et d'autres disciplines. Peut-être est-il difficile de dire si sa Rucksack House appartient à la catégorie « art », mais elle nous offre en tout cas un commentaire sur la pseudo-élite des architectes qui font volontiers des limites de leurs constructions des frontières inviolables.

Le prix Aga Khan pour l'Architecture s'est longtemps intéressé à des formes architecturales rarement abordées par la presse professionnelle dans le cadre des innovations « utiles ». C'est le cas des prototypes d'abris en sacs de sable de Nader Khalili, lauréat du prix en

2004. Conçu selon les directives du HCR, comme l'abri en papier pour réfugiés de Shigeru Ban, son système fait appel à des matériaux aussi disponibles que le sable, la terre ou le fil de fer barbelé pour édifier un logement solide et très économique. Ces constructions en sacs de sable sont inévitablement éphémères, mais leur simplicité et leur intelligence signifient aussi qu'elle pourraient bien être plus utiles à l'architecture contemporaine que certaines contributions plus « artistiques. » Les logiciels complexes ou les matériaux d'une grande sophistication technique ne sont peut-être pas une condition *sine qua non* pour apporter l'architecture à des gens qui n'ont même pas accès au minimum nécessaire de la vie moderne. C'est la réussite de Nader Khalili.

Si les statistiques sur la fréquentation des églises en Occident révèlent un déclin régulier de la ferveur religieuse, les architectes n'en sont pas moins fréquemment appelés à commémorer les rites de la vie et de la mort autour desquels s'édifient généralement les lieux de culte. Ils ont également tenté, depuis la Seconde Guerre mondiale, de se colleter avec des événements historiques dont l'horreur va au-delà des consolations que peuvent apporter les religions. La plus visible et probablement la plus controversée de ces tentatives est le Mémorial aux Juifs assassinés d'Europe de Peter Eisenman, au cœur de Berlin, près de la Pariser Platz et de la Porte de Brandebourg. L'architecte a recouvert un terrain de deux hectares de 2751 stèles de béton gris de hauteurs variées, allant de quelques centimètres à quatre mètres de haut. Le poids de ce geste symbolise le poids moral de la Shoah. À cet égard, l'œuvre remplit un objectif, même si ce n'est pas le rôle le plus couramment imparti à l'architecture. Est-ce de l'art ? Et si ni l'art ni l'architecture ne pouvaient assumer de tels événements, Eisenman n'aurait-il pas inventé là une approche nouvelle qui n'est ni l'un ni l'autre, mais les deux à la fois ?

Moshe Safdie a lui aussi abordé le problème de la commémoration de la Shoah dans son musée de l'Histoire de l'Holocauste à Yad Vashem, où il a voulu affirmer une « vie après l'expérience de la mort », ce qui était sans doute moins le sens du travail berlinois d'Eisenman. Yad Vashem se trouve sur une coteau dominant la vallée d'Ein Kerem, à Jérusalem, et symbolise à la fois les combats et les triomphes d'un peuple qui a surmonté tant d'adversité. Souterrain dans sa majeure partie, le musée ne laisse les visiteurs retrouver la lumière naturelle qu'après qu'ils ont parcouru le contenu de l'exposition, alors que le mémorial d'Eisenman s'étend sous le ciel, nu et perturbant dans son gris sépulcral. Il semble certain que le mémorial berlinois continuera à longtemps déranger les visiteurs, ce qui est rarement le cas des œuvres architecturales. Le sens et la forme se conjuguent ici de telle sorte que le souvenir ne puisse s'effacer.

John Pawson est connu pour son minimalisme. En 1996, son livre *Minimum* a même été un best-seller. Lorsque des moines cisterciens français lui demandèrent en 1999 de réfléchir à un nouveau monastère en République tchèque, il y vit « le projet de sa vie ». Ces religieux avaient découvert qu'ils avaient de nombreux points en commun avec le minimalisme de l'architecte, en particulier son traitement de la lumière. Le monastère de Novy Dvûr est plus qu'un lieu de culte, il est aussi le lieu de vie des moines et Pawson a réussi à combiner ces aspects pratiques avec une spiritualité diffuse, tout en intégrant un manoir du XVIIIᵉ siècle longtemps abandonné, à l'ouest de Prague. On a pu dire que le temps du minimalisme en architecture était révolu et que les projets d'aujourd'hui sont d'une essence plus complexe, voire décorative. Pawson prouve que le minimalisme est plus qu'une vogue passagère. Il est au cœur du modernisme, mais constitue également un thème récurrent de l'histoire de l'architecture et du design sur de longues périodes, comme l'illustre l'histoire du Japon.

Si des monuments et un monastère peuvent attirer l'attention de la scène architecturale actuelle, une autre expression de l'invention architecturale, plus joyeuse, mérite d'être mentionnée ici, ne serait-ce que pour son décalage. Klein Dytham est une petite agence de Tokyo fondée par Astrid Klein et Mark Dytham. Leur « Leaf Chapel » (chapelle-feuille) formée de feuilles de verre et d'acier a été conçue pour des cérémonies de mariage. Telle une paupière, elle s'ouvre au moment approprié (lorsque le jeune marié embrasse la jeune épousée) pour dévoiler un jardin et un étang. Ce tout petit projet de 168 m² illustre néanmoins l'adaptation des architectes occidentaux à une vision assez particulière du mariage par les Japonais. Célébrant l'amour « éternel » sanctifié par le mariage, cette chapelle est aussi légère et amusante qu'un petit nuage passant dans le ciel.

LES LOIS DE LA NATURE

S'il se peut que la mode de l'architecture virtuelle suive les traces de celle du minimalisme, certaines des recherches les plus intéressantes menées actuellement concernent des technologies sophistiquées et l'exploration de nature en tant que source de formes et de fonctions. Quel que soit le prix futur du baril de pétrole, l'architecture de sensibilité écologique est assurée d'un brillant avenir, ne serait-ce que pour des raisons de coût. La réduction de la pollution est également un objectif important pour ce que l'on appelle aussi le « développement durable ». L'architecte new-yorkais Michael McDonough, qui a travaillé quelque temps avec SITE, s'est embarqué dans la construction de « la maison écologique absolue ». Sa e-House « intègre plus de cent technologies nouvelles ou d'avant-garde (dont des technologies hautes performances, historiques ou alternatives) et se propose de mettre au point un nouveau langage pour la théorie de l'architecture durable. » L'efficacité énergétique est un but, mais plus encore, l'idée que la maison puisse constituer d'une certaine façon une « entité organique », respectant son cadre ou les traditions locales. L'effort de l'architecte pour intégrer de si nombreuses formes de technologie est, en soi, intéressant. Il suggère que l'avenir même de l'architecture est lié à une approche aholistique ayant recours à des connaissances aussi nombreuses que possible au-delà du langage structurel de base. Plutôt que de créer une coquille qui « fonctionne », il propose une construction qui, littéralement, vivrait et respirerait à l'unisson avec ses occupants.

Dennis Dollens approche la nature de manière différente et trouve son inspiration architecturale dans les modèles de croissance. L'une de ses récentes recherches, la Digitally-Grown Tower publiée ici, utilise un logiciel appelé Xfrog. Dollens explique : « Xfrog est un logiciel allemand mis au point par la société Greenworks. Il utilise des algorithmes botaniques appelés L-systems qui sont utilisés en laboratoire pour les simulations numérisées de la pousse des plantes et de l'évolution des paysages. Greenworks a ajouté aux L-systems des capacités de programmation qui prennent en compte des éléments comme la gravité et le phototropisme et ont construit un »bureau« à base d'icônes. Ce logiciel sert essentiellement au dessin de paysages futuristes ou à la modélisation très réaliste de paysages. Je pense être le seul à l'utiliser pour l'étude expérimentale de la croissance architecturale. » En d'autres termes, qu'arriverait-il si vous pouviez réellement appliquer des modèles de croissance botanique simulée à un projet architectural ? Le résultat serait probablement riche en enseignements et prendrait des aspects assez différents de l'architecture existante, tout en reposant sur une base solide : la réalité de la nature. D'autres architectes, comme Frei Otto ou Buckminster Fuller, ont mené des expériences à la limite de l'architecture et de la nature, mais Dollens utilise les toutes dernières technologies informatiques pour pousser encore plus loin ce type de réflexion. Parallèlement à ses travaux personnels, il tente d'alerter la communauté universitaire sur les gains potentiels d'une approche transdisciplinaire susceptible d'enrichir la conception grâce aux contacts avec la science. Ainsi écrit-il : « …En tant que concepteurs, nous devrions intégrer les techniques et les méthodologies de la recherche scientifique dans notre processus de conception. Par exemple, des designers pourraient mettre à profit les qualités spatiales, matérielles et structurelles des coquillages, des plantes et des os. Un tel engagement dans la recherche et les processus pourra peut-être approfondir notre prise en compte des propriétés naturelles, qui seraient mises en œuvre, par la suite, de manière responsable à l'égard de l'environnement, tout en permettant l'émergence de formes extrapolées de celles de la nature et pas seulement de projets issus d'un goût a priori. Il existe des possibilités de collaborations entre scientifiques et créateurs. Ils pourraient articuler et coordonner leurs buts de recherche, mais pour que cela se produise, un nouveau type de formation spécifique à la conception doit apparaître. L'une des idées-forces, même si elle est très simple, qui sous-tendent un tel développement, est la question : *Comment la nature résoudrait-elle ce problème de conception ?* La question pourrait facilement être intégrée dans la formation actuelle au design et à l'architecture, comme une graine d'évolution qui ne renverserait pas forcément la pédagogie existante. Plantez-la et elle poussera. »

L'architecte suisse Philippe Rahm jouit déjà d'une certaine réputation, bien qu'il n'ait que peu construit. Avec son ancien associé, Gilles Décosterd (Décosterd & Rahm), il a très activement exploré des facteurs physiologiques que l'architecture contemporaine ignore ou repousse le plus souvent. Que se passe-t-il, demande-t-il, lorsque des facteurs comme l'humidité, la lumière ou la quantité d'oxygène dans l'air sont volontairement manipulés ? Emmenant l'architecture virtuelle un peu plus loin encore dans une zone sous-exploitée des sciences, son *Ghost Flat (Appartement fantôme)* imaginait un espace dont le mobilier et les fonctions se modifieraient selon la partie du spectre lumineux utilisé. « La chambre apparaît entre 400 et 500 nanomètres, le séjour entre 600 et 800. La salle de bains est localisée dans les ultraviolets, entre 350 et 400. » Plus inquiétante encore est l'œuvre intitulée *ND Cult*. Imaginez une spacieuse boîte de verre dans laquelle on injecterait du gaz à l'aide d'un tuyau. L'oxygène est réduit à 6% et le visiteur pénètre dans un « espace à la limite de la mort, où la perception et la conscience sont modifiés d'une façon probablement proche de celle d'états mystiques. Dans ces conditions physiques extrêmes, l'espace devient extrêmement dangereux, des atteintes irréversibles au cerveau peuvent se produire et le risque de mort est réel ». *ND* signifie *Near Death*, la « presque mort ». Il est intéressant ici de se rappeler la description du troisième acte de *Tristan et Isolde* par Bill Viola : « Nous sommes plongés dans l'agonie et le délire de la mort et de la souffrance, submergés par les visions, les rêves et les révélations hallucinées qui affleurent à l'esprit de l'homme en train de mourir. » L'œuvre de Philippe Rahm a été largement exposée dans des musées et Décosterd & Rahm ont été en charge du pavillon suisse de la Biennale d'architecture de Venise en 2002. Leur participation, appelée *Hormonorium*, fait appel à 528 tubes fluorescents répartis dans le sol du pavillon pour créer une stimulation de la rétine, laquelle transmet l'information à la glande pinéale, provoquant une diminution de la secrétion de mélatonine. « En réduisant le taux de cette hormone dans le corps, cet environnement nous permet d'expérimenter une diminution de la fatigue, un accroissement probable du désir sexuel et une régulation de l'humeur. » Les architectes avaient également abaissé le taux d'oxygène de 21 % à 14,5 %, c'est-à-dire celui existant à une altitude de 3000 m dans les Alpes suisses. « Ce volume d'air à oxygène raréfié provoque une légère hypoxie, qui peut dans un premier temps se manifester par des états cliniques comme la confusion, la désorientation ou un comportement bizarre, mais également une légère euphorie due à la production d'endomorphine. Au bout d'une dizaine de minutes, on constate une augmentation ‹ naturelle › du taux d'érythropoïétine (EPO), de l'hématocrite, ainsi qu'une accélération des systèmes respiratoires et cardio-vasculaires. Les reins produisent de l'EPO. Cette hormone protéique atteint la moelle épinière où elle stimule la production de globules rouges et donc accroît l'apport d'oxygène aux muscles. La diminution du taux d'oxygène exerce alors un effet stimulant qui peut améliorer les capacités physiques du corps jusqu'à 10%.

MARCOS NOVAK est professeur à l'Université de Californie à Santa Barbara, où il collabore avec le California NanoSystems Institute. Selon sa biographie universitaire, « … s'appuyant sur l'architecture, la musique et l'électronique en y mêlant de multiples influences supplémentaires venues des arts, des sciences et des technologies, son travail se refuse intentionnellement à toute catégorisation ». Une partie de ses récents travaux publiés ici utilise des images structurelles fonctionnelles de son propre cerveau, obtenues grâce aux techniques d'imagerie par résonance magnétique, pour créer des formes et des volumes par algorithmes. Son concept de « transvergence » implique une rencontre entre la science et l'art ou l'architecture à l'échelle historique, un changement de paradigme. Le texte ci-dessous a été rédigé par Marcos Novak pour *Architecture Now* pour expliquer l'état de ses recherches.

En prenant en compte l'importance toujours croissante du travail sur la matière granulaire, les éléments, les atomes mais aussi le distribué, le parallèle et l'émergeat, et ce, à tous les niveaux, de la théorie des cordes à la biologie moléculaire, de la science de la matière à la neurophysiologie, de la technologie de l'information à l'art numérique, de la musique navigable granulaire à l'architecture liquide granulaire, cette recherche étudie la façon dont nous pouvons envisager un mode d'architecture qui ne soit pas voué aux formes complètes et préconçues, mais assume que les formes se développent et sont l'aboutissement de processus qui œuvrent à un niveau granulaire et atomique (au sens originel d'« atomique », d'un élément ou d'une monade non subdivisible).

Toute réflexion informée sur le monde, tel que nous le connaissons, sait que ce que nous percevons comme substantiel à notre échelle ne l'est pas : la plus grande partie de ce qui nous semble être de la matière solide est surtout constituée de vide. Par conséquent, le monde ne se compose pas d'une figure et d'un fond au sens absolu, mais on doit plutôt l'envisager comme une modulation de relations et de densités.

Récemment encore, on ne pouvait pas faire grand-chose si l'on voulait s'approprier ce point de vue et en faire une stratégie de conception. Il y avait à cela deux obstacles principaux : le nombre et le contrôle. Travailler avec l'infiniment petit implique de se confronter à de gigantesques quantités d'éléments minuscules et difficiles à « saisir ». Comme c'est souvent le cas avec ce que l'on ne peut initialement atteindre, ces deux obstacles pragmatiques masquaient un obstacle intellectuel plus grand, celui de concevoir concrètement ce qui pouvait être créé, non comme des touts préformés, mais comme des agrégats de myriades de parties gérés statistiquement et non individuellement.

Les technologies émergentes nous permettent de dépasser les obstacles mécaniques et nous lancent le défi de faire avancer notre appréhension théorique, tout d'abord dans le domaine du virtuel, et maintenant de plus en plus dans celui du matériel. Ainsi avons-nous l'opportunité de reconsidérer notre approche du « faire » de façon fondamentale. Comme les nanotechnologies et toutes les autres percées technologiques et conceptuelles sur le contrôle des grands nombres et de l'infiniment petit commencent à le démontrer, surmonter ces obstacles offre une récompense : le contrôle précis de la gradation et des mélanges entre des attributs qui, sinon, resteraient distincts et donc la possibilité d'inventer de nouveaux types de matière inanimée et même animée, dans le cadre de quelque chose qui approche du caractère général, si ce n'est de la facilité, de l'invention de nouveaux timbres sonores.

La conséquence naturelle de notre recherche d'une « grande théorie unifiée » réconciliant le quantum mécanique et les descriptions relativistes de l'univers est que plus nous nous rapprochons de la compréhension de ce dont est fait le monde, plus nous acquérons le pouvoir de tout modifier au-delà de notre compréhension la plus fondamentale. Dès lors, pourquoi ne pas modifier les éléments eux-mêmes ? Le travail présenté ici est une approche de ces problèmes et ces hypothèses sous des angles variés. La notion principale est celle de l'*alloatomique,* autrement dit l'atomique qui ne se limite pas aux éléments littéraux dont le monde se compose, mais intègre des « allo- » éléments, d'autres éléments, issus de notre propre choix, inventés par nous. De même que des domaines comme *la vie artificielle* et *l'intelligence artificielle* ne se limitent pas à l'étude de la vie et de l'intelligence telles qu'elles sont mais s'étendent à la vie et à l'intelligence telles qu'elles *pourraient être*, l'idée de l'*alloatomique* s'étend à des considérations sur ce que l'infiniment petit et l'élémentaire *pourraient être* et comment nous pourions apprendre à construire avec eux. Il doit être clair que ce que je décris ne se cantonne pas au physique et au moléculaire, mais s'applique également, et peut-être principalement, au virtuel et donc à l'élémentaire en tant que concept et abstraction.

Certains travaux sont plus purement *alloatomiques* et essayent d'exploiter directement les techniques pour créer des formes architecturales en élaborant des processus comme la *diffusion à agrégation limitée* et d'autres techniques de ce type, permettant à la forme de se développer à partir des multiples façons dont de grandes quantités de particules peuvent s'agréger ou se repousser. Une autre partie du travail, beaucoup plus abstraite, s'appuie sur la neurophysiologie et des techniques comme la IRMF (imagerie par résonance magnétique fonctionnelle) du cerveau (en l'occurrence mon propre cerveau en action). D'autres s'appuient sur la DFC – dynamique des fluides computationnelle – pour imaginer une *architecture liquide* consistant en l'interaction de flux de liquides très denses.

Comme dans mes précédents travaux, cette phase a pour but de poursuivre l'articulation d'un continuum qui va du virtuel au réel, de l'inanimé à l'animé, du musical au matériel, pour ne mentionner que quelques-uns de ses axes. À la fin, c'est ce continuum qui est riche d'intérêt, plutôt qu'une expérimentation particulière ou un projet pris isolément. L'architecture commence comme une modulation d'espace et de forme, de présence et d'absence, de plein et de vide. La musique module le son et le silence, la douceur et la rudesse, le calme et la turbulence, le hasard et l'ordre, le tout tissé d'être, de devenir et de vide. Ces listes sont limitées et partielles et pourraient être sans fin, mais ce que nous pouvons toujours mettre en facteur est la modulation de phénomènes en modèles de variation qui ont un sens à la fois informel et humain. L'architecture comme la musique, la *transarchitecture* et n'importe quelle forme expressive *transvergente* que nous pouvons rencontrer ou inventer, toutes sont des modulations. Prenant ceci en compte, ce travail est un effort permanent pour apprendre comment moduler les nouveaux continuums que nous fabriquons.

De toutes ces considérations émerge la conscience d'un univers médiatisé en changement perpétuel. Explorant consciemment ce que j'ai nommé la *transvergence*, je travaille sur deux pistes parallèles de recherche (trans)architecturale, la pratique et la pédagogie. Il s'agit d'abord de voir comment ces conditions nouvelles génèrent une nouvelle espèce d'architecture, puis comment la recherche, la pratique et la pédagogie (trans)architecturales, considérées de manière enrichie et spécifique, et à condition que soit préservée leur puissance synthétique et d'imagination, peuvent offrir des modèles singuliers adaptés à notre engagement créatif en faveur des univers nouveaux que nous créons si rapidement, non seulement dans le domaine de l'architecture proprement dite, mais aussi dans celui d'autres formes d'expression, émergentes ou encore à venir.

© 2005 Marcos Novak pour *Architecture Now*, volume 4

Novak peut être considéré comme un visionnaire qui n'aura que peu d'impact pratique sur la manière dont les choses se construisent, mais peut-être ouvre-t-il la porte à de nouvelles façons de voir le monde, et pas uniquement dans une perspective « professionnelle » restreinte, mais d'un point de vue plus vaste. De même que l'homme de la Renaissance, dont Léonard de Vinci fut le parangon, pouvait s'intéresser à la biologie, à la physique, à l'art et à l'architecture, il est possible que les technologies de l'information arrivent à briser la tendance moderne des spécialisations à outrance. Nombre de représentants importants de l'architecture contemporaine, de Frank O. Gehry à Santiago Calatrava, ont volontairement rompu les barrières entre l'architecture, l'art et l'ingénierie. Comprenant que la science a accompli d'immenses progrès, Novak et d'autres, comme Dollens, ne voient aucun problème dans le fait d'utiliser l'imagerie et les processus mis au point dans d'autres domaines pour innover dans le leur. Philippe Rahm s'empare de faits « évidents » de la physiologie et leur accorde une place dans son architecture, aussi virtuelle soit-elle. Est-il si étonnant que dans un bâtiment, nous vivions non seulement à l'intérieur d'un volume mais aussi dans des conditions d'humidité et d'oxygène qui exercent un fort impact sur notre confort ? Les puristes diront que tout cela n'a rien à voir avec l'architecture. Pourtant, alors que les avancées de l'informatique font que la notion non-standard de la conception architecturale est devenue une réalité, la question du pourquoi des barrières entre les disciplines est soulevée. Que ce soit d'une façon plus modeste et compréhensible, comme lorsque le décorateur Patrick Jouin s'aventure sur le territoire de l'architecture, ou lorsque François Roche fait reposer un projet sur la rencontre entre Charles Perrault et André Le Nôtre, ou encore dans « le meilleur des mondes » de Marcos Novak, on ne peut que remarquer un point commun : l'architecture est sortie de la boîte.

DAVID ADJAYE

Adjaye/Associates, 23–28 Penn Street, London N1 5DL, UK
Tel: +44 20 77 39 49 69, Fax: +44 20 77 39 34 84, e-mail: info@adjaye.com
Web: www.adjaye.com

DAVID ADJAYE was born in 1966 in Dar-Es-Salaam, Tanzania. He studied at the Royal College of Art (Masters in Architecture, 1993), and worked in the offices of David Chipperfield and Eduardo Souto de Moura before creating his own firm in London in 2000 (Chassay Architects, 1988–90; David Chipperfield Architects, 1991; Eduardo Souto de Moura Architects, 1991; Adjaye & Russell, 1994–2000). He has been widely recognized as one of the leading architects of his generation in the UK, in part because of the talks he has given in various locations such as the Architectural Association, the Royal College of Art and Cambridge University, as well as Harvard, Cornell or the Universidad de Luisdad in Lisbon. He was also the co-presenter of the BBC's six-part series on modern architecture "Dreamspaces." Deyan Sudjic selected his Idea Store library in East London for the exhibition highlighting 100 projects that are changing the world at the 8th Venice Biennale of Architecture in 2002. His offices currently employs a staff of 35, and some of his key works are: Studio/home for Chris Ofili, London (1999); Extension to house, St. John's Wood (1998); Siefert Penthouse, London (2001); Elektra House, London (2001); Studio/gallery/home for Tim Noble and Sue Webster, London (2002); and the SHADA Pavilion, London (2000, with artist Henna Nadeem). Current work includes: The Nobel Peace Center, Oslo (published here, 2002–05); Bernie Grant Performing Arts Center, Tottenham London (2001–06); Stephen Lawrence Centre, Deptford, London (2004–06); a visual arts building for the London-based organizations inIVA/Autograph, and the Museum of Contemporary Art/Denver, Denver, Colorado (2004–06).

DAVID ADJAYE, 1966 in Daressalam, Tansania, geboren, studierte am Londoner Royal College of Art, wo er 1993 die Prüfung zum Master of Architecture ablegte. Ehe er im Jahr 2000 in London sein eigenes Büro eröffnete, arbeitete er von 1988 bis 1990 bei Chassay Architects, 1991 im Büro von David Chipperfield und bei Eduardo Souto de Moura und anschließend von 1994 bis 2000 im Büro Adjaye & Russell. Er gilt weithin als einer der führenden britischen Architekten seiner Generation. Diesen Ruf verdankt er z. T. den Vorträgen, die er in verschiedenen Institutionen wie der Architectural Association, dem Royal College of Art und den Universitäten Cambridge, Harvard, Cornell sowie der Universidad de Luisdad in Lissabon hielt. Darüber hinaus fungierte er als Co-Moderator von »Dreamspaces«, einer sechsteiligen Serie der BBC über moderne Architektur. Deyan Sudjic wählte seine »Idea-Store«-Bibliothek in East London für die Ausstellung der 100 Projekte, die die Welt verändert haben, aus; sie wurde im Rahmen der VIII. Architekturbiennale in Venedig gezeigt. Zu den bedeutendsten Arbeiten seines Büros, das gegenwärtig 35 Mitarbeiter beschäftigt, gehören: ein Studio mit Wohnung für Chris Ofili, London (1999), die Erweiterung eines Hauses in St. John's Wood (1998), das Siefert Penthouse, London (2001), das Elektra House, London (2001), ein Atelier mit Galerie und Wohnung für Tim Noble und Sue Webster, London (2002), sowie der SHADA Pavillon, London (2000), in Zusammenarbeit mit der Künstlerin Henna Nadeem. Zu seinen vor kurzem fertig gestellten bzw. im Bau befindlichen Projekten zählen: das hier publizierte Nobel-Friedenszentrum, Oslo (2002–05), das Bernie Grant Performing Arts Centre in Tottenham, London (2001–06), das Stephen Lawrence Centre in Deptford, London (2004–06), ein Kunstmuseum für die in London ansässigen Organisationen inIVA/Autograph sowie das Museum für zeitgenössische Kunst in Denver, Colorado (2004–06).

DAVID ADJAYE, né en 1966 à Dar-es-Salaam (Tanzanie), étudie au Royal College of Art (Master of Architecture, 1993), puis travaille dans les agences de David Chipperfield et d'Eduardo Souto de Moura avant de créer sa propre structure à Londres en 2000 (Chassay Architects, 1988–90 ; David Chipperfield Architects, 1991 ; Eduardo Souto de Moura Architects, 1991 ; Adjaye & Russell, 1994–2000). Il est généralement reconnu comme l'un des plus brillants architectes de sa génération au Royaume-Uni, entre autres, grâce aux conférences qu'il a données un peu partout, notamment à l'Architectural Association, au Royal College of Art, à Cambridge University, Harvard, Cornell ou l'Universidad de Luisdad à Lisbonne. Il a été coprésentateur, à la BBC, de deux épisodes de *Dreamspaces*, une série télévisée en six parties sur l'architecture. Sa bibliothèque Idea Store, dans l'East London, a été sélectionnée par Deyan Sudjic pour la grande exposition des « 100 projets qui ont changé le monde » présentée à la 8e Biennale d'architecture de Venise en 2002. Son agence emploie actuellement trente-cinq collaborateurs. Parmi ses principales réalisations : une maison-atelier pour Chris Ofili, Londres (1999) ; l'extension d'une maison, St. John's Wood (1998) ; la Siefert Penthouse, Londres (2001) ; la Maison Elektra, Londres (2001) ; l'atelier-galerie-maison de Tim Noble et Sue Webster, Londres (2002) et le Shada Pavilion, Londres (2000), en collaboration avec l'artiste Henna Nadeem. Ses chantiers actuels comprennent le Centre Nobel de la paix, Oslo (2002–05), publié ici ; le Bernie Grant Arts Centre, Tottenham, Londres (2001–06) ; le Stephen Lawrence Centre, Deptford, Londres (2004–06), et le Museum of Contemporary Art/Denver, Denver, Colorado (2004–06).

NOBEL PEACE CENTER

Oslo, Norway, 2002–05

Floor area: 1500 m². Client: Nobel Peace Institute. Cost: €14.1 million

The **NOBEL PEACE CENTER** was created by an act of the Norwegian Parliament in 2000. At first conceived as a museum for the Peace Prize, its function was subsequently enlarged to the explanation of conflicts and the role of the Prizewinners. As the Museum explains the selection of the architect after a competition, "The capacity for communication and dialogue through spatial manipulation was a decisive factor in commissioning architect David Adjaye and associates in London as the visual interpreter of the Center's concept. The global diversity of the Peace Prize, combined with a desire to create a Center that is dynamic and aesthetically cohesive – not merely visually pleasing, but engaging all the senses – also underpinned this decision. "Spatial manipulation" is what he calls his own work, and his projects are often the result of collaboration with artists, among them Chris Ofili, winner of the Turner Prize. Opened on June 11, 2005, the Center is located in the former Vestbanen Railway Station, an 1872 Italianate building set near the harbor and the City Hall of Oslo. A free-standing entrance portal that looks like a piece of contemporary sculpture greets visitors, its perforated skin forming a map of world-wide centers of conflict. Adjaye plays on color in the reception area (saturated red), in the Passage of Honor (gold) or in the Café de la Paix restaurant (green patterns designed by Chris Ofili). He has also collaborated for the exhibitions with the American David Small (Small Design Firm) who created video displays, working with material gathered by project historians, or an electronic "book" that recounts the life of Alfred Nobel. The cost of the building work was 14.1 million euros and the so-called Communications Project, of which the interior fittings are part, 7.4 million.

Das **NOBEL-FRIEDENSZENTRUM** wurde aufgrund eines Beschlusses des norwegischen Parlaments von 2000 gebaut. Ursprünglich sollte ein Museum für den Friedenspreis errichtet werden, dessen Funktion wurde aber erweitert und umfasst jetzt auch die Erläuterung von Konflikten und Informationen zur Rolle der Preisträger. Die Auswahl des Architekten wurde folgendermaßen begründet: »Die Förderung von Kommunikation und Dialog durch die Gestaltung des Raums war ein wichtiger Grund, Adjaye/Associates als visuelle Interpreten des Konzeptes des Friedenszentrums zu beauftragen. Die globale Vielseitigkeit des Friedenspreises in Verbindung mit dem Wunsch, ein dynamisches und ästhetisch einheitliches Zentrum zu schaffen, das nicht nur optisch gefällt, sondern alle Sinne in Anspruch nimmt, unterstützte die Entscheidung. ›Raummanipulation‹ nennt Adjaye seine Architektur, und bei seinen Projekten arbeitet er oft mit Künstlern zusammen, unter ihnen Chris Ofili.« Das Zentrum wurde am 11. Juni 2005 eröffnet und befindet sich im ehemaligen Vestbanen-Bahnhof, einem Gebäude von 1872 im italienischen Stil in der Nähe des Hafens und des Rathauses von Oslo. Ein freistehender, einer zeitgenössischen Skulptur ähnelnder Portalbogen begrüßt den Besucher. Seine perforierte Oberfläche zeigt eine Landkarte der weltweiten Konfliktgebiete. Im Gebäude spielt Adjaye mit Farben: Der Eingangsbereich ist in sattem Rot gehalten, »Der Weg der Ehre« in Gold und das Restaurant Café de la Paix in grünen Mustern, die Ofili gestaltete. Die Ausstellungen wurden zusammen mit dem Amerikaner David Small, der die Videofilme schuf, konzipiert. Small arbeitete dabei u. a. mit Material, das Historiker sammelten, und mit einem elektronischen »Buch«, das das Leben von Alfred Nobel ausführlich darstellt. Die Kosten für das Gebäude lagen bei umgerechnet 14,1 Millionen Euro, das »Kommunikationsprojekt«, zu dem die Innenraumgestaltung gehört, belief sich auf 7,4 Millionen Euro.

Le **CENTRE NOBEL DE LA PAIX** a été créé par un acte du Parlement norvégien en 2000. Conçu pour être le musée du prix Nobel de la paix, sa fonction a été élargie à l'explication des conflits et du rôle des titulaires du prix. L'institution a justifié son choix de l'architecte : « L'aptitude à la communication et au dialogue par la manipulation spatiale a été un facteur clé dans notre décision de confier aux Londoniens Adjaye/Associates l'interprétation visuelle du concept du Centre. La diversité internationale du prix Nobel de la paix, combinée au désir de créer un Centre dynamique et esthétiquement cohérent – visuellement agréable et engageant dans tous les sens du terme – explique également cette décision ». La « manipulation spatiale » est l'une des expressions d'Adjaye pour décrire son travail, et ses projets résultent souvent d'une collaboration avec des artistes, parmi lesquels Chris Ofili, prix Turner 1998. Ouvert le 11 juin 2005, le Centre est installé dans l'ancienne gare de chemin de fer de Vestbanen, bâtiment italianisant de 1872, à proximité du port et de l'hôtel de ville d'Oslo. Un portail d'entrée indépendant, semblable à une sculpture contemporaine, accueille les visiteurs, sa peau perforée dessinant une carte des conflits dans le monde. Adjaye joue sur la couleur dans la zone d'accueil (rouge saturé), dans le passage d'honneur (or) ou dans le restaurant du Café de la Paix (motifs verts de Chris Ofili). Pour les expositions, il a collaboré avec l'Américain David Small qui a créé des installations vidéo à partir de matériaux réunis par des historiens et un « livre » électronique sur la vie d'Alfred Nobel. Le coût du bâtiment s'est élevé à 14,1 millions d'euros et le projet dit « de communication », dont faisait partie l'aménagement intérieur, à 7,4 millions d'euros.

The former Vestbanen Railway Station (1872) was refurbished and a powerful rectangular entrance canopy added opposite the main entrance of the building.

Der ehemalige Vestbanen-Bahnhof von 1872 wurde umgebaut; vor dem Haupteingang wurde ein schwerer rechteckiger Portalbogen platziert.

L'ancienne gare de Vestbanen (1872) a été restaurée et un portique rectangulaire aux formes puissantes implanté devant l'entrée du bâtiment.

The red entrance area and the spectacular Passage of Honor, with its portraits of Nobel Peace Prize laureates, set the tone of the project, using the generous spaces of the building to their maximum effect.

Der rote Eingangsbereich und der spektakuläre »Weg der Ehre« mit Porträts der Nobelpreisträger bestimmen die Atmosphäre im Gebäude und nutzen dessen großzügige Räumlichkeiten mit maximaler Wirkung.

L'entrée de couleur rouge et le spectaculaire « passage d'honneur » orné des portraits des lauréats du prix Nobel de la paix donnent le ton à ce projet qui tire le maximum d'effets des généreux volumes du bâtiment.

ASYMPTOTE

Asymptote Architecture, 561 Broadway, Suite 5A, New York, New York 10012, USA
Tel: +1 212 343 7333, Fax: +1 212 343 7099, e-mail: info@asymptote.net
Web: www.asymptote.net

Lise Anne Couture was born in Montreal in 1959. She received her Bachelor of Architecture degree from Carlton University, Canada, and her Master of Architecture degree from Yale. She has been a Design Critic in the Master of Architecture program at Parsons School of Design, New York. Couture currently holds the Davenport chair at Yale University School of Architecture. Hani Rashid received his degree as Master of Architecture from the Cranbrook Academy of Art, Bloomfield Hills, Michigan. He is presently a professor of Architecture at Columbia University in New York and at the Swiss Federal Institute of Technology (ETH) in Zurich. They created **ASYMPTOTE** in 1987. Projects include their 1988 prize-winning commission for the Los Angeles West Coast Gateway 1989; a commissioned housing project for Brig, Switzerland; and their participation in the 1993 competition for an Art Center in Tours, France (1993). Other work by Asymptote includes a theater festival structure built in Denmark in 1997, a virtual trading floor for the New York Stock Exchange, and the Guggenheim Virtual Museum, a multimedia project aimed at creating an on-line museum. In 2001, Asymptote participated in competitions for the Daimler-Chrysler and Mercedes-Benz Museums in Stuttgart, an expansion of the Queens Museum, and the Eyebeam Center in New York. Most recently Asymptote completed the construction of HydraPier in Harlemmermeer, the Netherlands, a public building housing technology and art located near Schipol Airport. They also finished the Carlos Miele Flagship Store on West 14th Street in Manhattan in 2003. Asymptote was involved in the design of the 2004 Venice Biennale of Architecture, *Metamorph* and a new theater for the Hans Christian Andersen festival in Odense, Denmark. Asymptote is also completing a Crematorium and Memorial Chapel in Rotterdam.

Lise Anne Couture, geboren 1959 in Montreal, erwarb ihren Bachelor of Architecture an der Carlton University in Kanada und ihren Master of Architecture an der Yale University. Anschließend war sie im Rahmen des Master-of-Architecture-Programms als Designkritikerin an der Parsons School of Design in New York tätig. Couture hat derzeit den Davenport Lehrstuhl an der Yale University School of Architecture an der Cranbrook Academy of Art in Bloomfield Hills, Michigan. Gegenwärtig ist er als Professor für Architektur an der Columbia University in New York und der Eidgenössischen Technischen Hochschule (ETH) in Zürich tätig. Zusammen gründeten sie 1987 das Architekturbüro **ASYMPTOTE**. Zu ihren Projekten gehören der preisgekrönte Entwurf für den Los Angeles West Coast Gateway (1988–89), ein Wohnhausprojekt in Brig in der Schweiz und ihr Wettbewerbsbeitrag für ein Kunstzentrum im französischen Tours (1993), außerdem ein Bau für ein Theaterfestival in Dänemark (1997), ein virtuelles Börsenparkett für die New Yorker Börse sowie das Guggenheim Virtual Museum, ein Multimediaprojekt, das ein Online-Museum präsentiert. 2001 beteiligte sich Asymptote an den Wettbewerben für das Mercedes-Benz-Museum in Stuttgart, den Erweiterungsbau des Queens Museum of Art und das Eyebeam Center, beide in New York. In jüngster Zeit realisierte Asymptote in den Niederlanden, nahe dem Flughafen Schiphol in Harlemmermeer das Projekt HydraPier, ein Ausstellungsgebäude für die Präsentation von Technologie und Kunst. Außerdem wurde 2003 der Carlos Miele Flagship Store in der West 14th Street in Manhattan fertig gestellt. Asymptote war am Ausstellungsdesign »Metamorph« der Architekturbiennale von 2004 in Venedig und am Entwurf eines neuen Theaters für das Hans Christian Andersen Festival im dänischen Odense beteiligt und plant derzeit ein Krematorium mit Friedhofskapelle in Rotterdam.

Lise Anne Couture, née à Montréal en 1959, est Bachelor of Architecture de la Carlton University, Canada, et Master of Architecture de Yale. Elle a été « Design Critic » du cursus de maîtrise d'architecture de la Parsons School of Design (New York) et est actuellement titulaire de la chaire Davenport de la Yale University School of Architecture. Hani Rashid est Master of Architecture de la Cranbrook Academy of Art à Bloomfield Hills, Michigan. Il est professeur d'architecture à Columbia University (New York) et à l'Institut fédéral suisse de technologie (ETH, Zurich). Ensemble, ils ont créé **ASYMPTOTE** en 1987. Parmi leurs réalisations et projets : celui, primé, de la compétition pour la West Coast Gateway, Los Angeles (1988) ; un immeuble de logements, Brig, Suisse (1991) ; leur participation au concours de 1993 pour un Centre d'art à Tours, France (1993) ; une structure pour un festival de théâtre, Århus, Danemark (1997) ; une salle des marchés virtuelle pour le New York Stock Exchange et le Guggenheim Virtual Museum, projet multimédia de musée en ligne. En 2001, Asymptote a participé aux concours pour les musées Daimler-Chrysler et Mercedes Benz à Stuttgart, l'extension du Queens Museum et le Eyebeam Center à New York. Plus récemment, l'agence a achevé la construction de l'HydraPier à Harlemmermeer (Pays-Bas), bâtiment consacré aux arts et à la technologie près de l'aéroport de Schipol et le magasin-pilote Carlos Miele, West 14th Street à Manhattan (2003). Ils ont participé à la conception de *Metamorph*, la 9e Biennale d'architecture de Venise (2004) et d'un nouveau théâtre pour le Hans Christian Andersen Festival à Odense (Danemark). Asymptote achève actuellement un crématorium et une chapelle du souvenir à Rotterdam.

GUGGENHEIM GUADALAJARA

Guadalajara, Mexico, 2004–05

Floor area: 26 248 m². Client: Solomon R. Guggenheim/Guggenheim Museum. Cost: $210 million

Although Asymptote lost this limited competition to Enrique Norten, their surprising proposal for the new **GUGGENHEIM GUADALAJARA** deserves to be seen. Sitting on the precipitous edge of a cliff overlooking a vast natural area outside the city, the project proposed, as the architects said, to create a new kind of public space. In their words, "This extension of the city that projects out towards the limitless horizon of the natural landscape is a spectacular urban balcony that functions simultaneously as a dramatic viewing platform, a gateway, a gathering place, an urban theater and an outdoor exhibition space. Defined by the four sculptural corner building volumes that rise up from the ground plane and the sweeping undulating surfaces of the museum suspended above, this remarkable space that transitions between the city and the extraordinary expanse of the canyon beyond is the threshold to the Museum itself. In this dynamic public space visitors can access the diverse public amenities housed in the corner buildings, wander among large-scale sculptures on exhibit or enter the Museum interior via its dramatically ascending escalators set against an extraordinary panorama." The flowing computer-generated forms of the Museum are recognizable as the work of Asymptote, but here on a larger scale than any of their built work. Exhibition galleries were to be located "on two upper levels connected by bridges and balconies that overlook the atrium space while a special Multimedia Gallery located on a lower level in the southwest corner is directly accessible from the atrium." The architects were careful to create relatively "neutral" exhibition spaces so that the architecture would not overwhelm the art.

Auch wenn nicht Asymptote, sondern Enrique Norten den Wettbewerb für sich entschied, verdient der überraschende Entwurf für das neue **GUGGENHEIM MUSEUM** in Guadalajara Beachtung. Das Projekt befindet sich an der Kante eines jäh abfallenden Felsens. Außerhalb der Stadt gelegen, bietet sich hier ein Blick über die weite, unberührte Umgebung. Die Architekten schlugen mit ihrem Entwurf vor, eine neue Art von öffentlichem Raum zu schaffen. Mit ihren Worten »ist diese Erweiterung der Stadt in Richtung des endlosen Horizontes der natürlichen Landschaft ein spektakulärer urbaner Balkon, der gleichzeitig als Aussichtspunkt, als Tor, als Versammlungsort, als urbanes Theater und als Ausstellungsraum im Freien dient. Dieser bemerkenswerte Außenraum, der den Übergang zwischen der Stadt und der Weite des Canyons bildet, ist die Schwelle zum eigentlichen Museum. Er wird durch die vier skulpturalen Eckgebäude, die sich von der Grundebene erheben, und durch die welligen Oberflächen des Museums darüber definiert. Von diesem dynamischen, öffentlichen Raum werden die verschiedenen Einrichtungen in den vier Eckgebäuden erschlossen. Die Besucher können zwischen den großformatigen Skulpturen umherwandern oder sich in das Museum begeben, indem sie die Rolltreppen benutzen, die dem außergewöhnlichen Panorama gegenüberstehen.« Die fließenden, computergenerierten Formen sind typisch für die Projekte von Asymptote; hier treten sie jedoch in einem größeren Maßstab als bei ihren bisher gebauten Projekten auf. Die Ausstellungsgalerien sollten »auf zwei oberen Ebenen angeordnet werden, die durch Brücken und Balkone miteinander verbunden sind; von dort aus überblickt man das Atrium, während eine spezielle Multimediagalerie auf der unteren Ebene in der südwestlichen Ecke direkt vom Atrium aus zugänglich ist.« Mit Bedacht haben die Architekten einen relativ »neutralen« Ausstellungsraum geschaffen, damit die Architektur nicht die Kunst überwältigt.

Bien qu'Asymptote ait perdu ce concours sur invitation pour un nouveau **MUSÉE GUGGENHEIM** à Guadalajara au bénéfice d'Enrique Norten, leur étonnante proposition mérite d'être connue. Posé en bordure d'une falaise donnant sur une immense zone naturelle en dehors de la ville, le projet se proposait, comme l'expliquent les architectes, de créer un nouveau type d'espace public : « Cette extension de la ville qui se projette vers l'horizon infini du paysage naturel est un spectaculaire balcon urbain qui fonctionne à la fois comme une plate-forme d'observation, une porte d'entrée, un lieu de réunion, un théâtre urbain et un espace d'exposition en plein air. Délimité par les quatre bâtiments d'angles sculpturaux qui jaillissent du sol et par la silhouette sinueuse du musée suspendu au-dessus d'eux, ce remarquable espace qui fait la transition entre la ville et l'extraordinaire domaine naturel du canyon est le seuil d'entrée au musée lui-même. À partir de ce volume dynamique, les visiteurs accèdent aux différentes installations situées dans les bâtiments d'angle, déambulent au milieu des sculptures monumentales ou pénètrent à l'intérieur du musée par des escaliers mécaniques spectaculaires avec, en toile de fond, un fabuleux panorama. » Ces formes fluides générées par ordinateur sont caractéristiques du travail d'Asymptote, mais n'avaient jamais été exploitées à aussi grande échelle. Les galeries d'exposition devaient être installées « aux deux niveaux supérieurs connectés par des passerelles et des balcons surplombant l'atrium, tandis qu'une galerie spécifiquement dédiée au multimédia serait, au niveau inférieur sud-ouest, directement accessible depuis l'atrium ». Les architectes avaient prévu des espaces d'exposition relativement « neutres » afin que l'architecture ne domine pas les œuvres d'art.

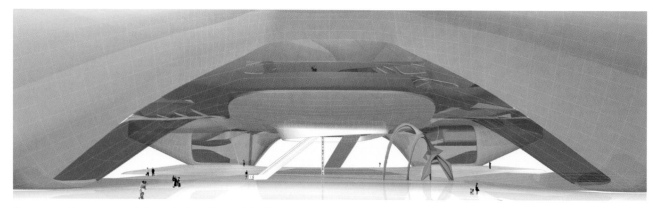

The open, arching spaces created below the museum permit the exhibition of large-scale sculptures like the Calder stabile seen here.

In dem offenen, sich wölbenden Raum unter dem Museum können großformatige Skulpturen ausgestellt werden, z. B. diese Calder-Skulptur.

Les volumes ouverts et voûtés sous le musée permettent d'exposer des sculptures de grandes dimensions, comme ce stabile de Calder.

Asymptote's computer drawings for the Guggenheim Guadalajara emphasize a dream-like atmosphere and a spatial continuity into which works of art can be inserted, or even projected.

Asymptotes Computerdarstellungen des Guggenheim Guadalajara transportieren eine traumähnliche Stimmung und den Eindruck eines fließenden Raums, in den Kunstwerke eingefügt oder projiziert werden können.

Les images de synthèse d'Asymptote pour le Guggenheim de Guadalajara illustrent une atmosphère irréelle et une continuité spatiale dans laquelle des œuvres d'art pourraient être insérées ou même projetées.

Sitting on a cliff looking out on a vast natural panorama, Asymptote's design has a spacecraft feeling with escalators rising like gangways from the covered plaza visible in this image. Works by Richard Serra (left) and Richard Long (center) take on a special resonance in this unexpected setting.

Das Museum, hoch oben auf einem Felsen gelegen, bietet einen weiten Blick ins Umland. Asymptotes Entwurf weckt Assoziationen an ein Raumschiff; hier zu sehen sind die Rolltreppen, die wie Gangways von der überdeckten Plaza auf die höhere Ebene führen. Arbeiten von Richard Serra (links) und Richard Long (Mitte) bekommen in dieser ungewöhnlichen Umgebung eine besondere Wirkung.

Implanté au sommet d'une falaise face à un immense panorama naturel, le projet d'Asymptote dégage une atmosphère de vaisseau spatial. Caractéristiques : ces escaliers-passerelles mécaniques spectaculaires s'élevant depuis la place couverte. Les œuvres de Richard Serra (à gauche) et de Richard Long (au centre) prennent une résonance particulière dans ce cadre étonnant.

AUER+WEBER

Auer+Weber+Architekten
Haussmannstrasse 103a
70188 Stuttgart
Germany

Tel: +49 711 26 84 04 0
Fax: +49 711 26 84 04 88
e-mail: pr@auer-weber.de
Web: www.auer-weber.de

ESO Hotel ▶

Fritz Auer, born in Tübingen in 1933, studied at the Technische Hochschule in Stuttgart beginning in 1953. He obtained a scholarship from the Cranbrook Academy of Arts and received his Master of Architecture degree there in 1959. He became a partner in the firm of Behnisch & Partner in 1966 and created the office **AUER+WEBER** in 1980. Carlo Weber was born in Saarbrücken in 1934 and also attended the Technische Hochschule in Stuttgart before going to the Beaux Arts in Paris. Like Auer, he became a partner at Behnisch & Partner in 1966. They have worked extensively on urban renewal, in Bonn, Stuttgart and other cities. They completed the University Library of Magdeburg in 2003; the Welle department store in Bielefeld in 2003; and are working on the Science Park of Ulm; the Alter Hof urban renewal project in Munich; retirement centers in Landau, Pforzheim-Huchenfeld and Keltern-Ellmendingen; the General Archives of Karlsruhe and the District Administration Center in Tübingen.

Fritz Auer, 1933 in Tübingen geboren, begann sein Studium 1953 an der Technischen Hochschule in Stuttgart. Er erhielt ein Stipendium von der Cranbrook Academy of Arts und schloss dort 1959 mit einem Master of Architecture ab. 1966 wurde er Partner im Büro Behnisch & Partner und gründete 1980 das Architekturbüro **AUER+WEBER**. Carlo Weber, geboren 1934 in Saarbrücken, studierte ebenfalls an der Technischen Hochschule Stuttgart, bevor er nach Paris ging, um dort die Ecole des Beaux-Arts zu besuchen. Wie Auer wurde er 1966 Partner im Büro Behnisch & Partner. Auer+Weber haben sich ausgiebig mit Stadterneuerung in Bonn, Stuttgart und anderen Städten beschäftigt. 2003 wurde die Universitätsbibliothek in Magdeburg fertig gestellt, ebenfalls 2003 das Welle-Kaufhaus in Bielefeld. Derzeit in der Planung sind der Wissenschaftspark in Ulm, das Sanierungsprojekt Alter Hof in München, Altenzentren bzw. Pflegestifte in Landau, Pforzheim-Huchenfeld und Keltern-Ellmendingen, das Generallandesarchiv in Karlsruhe und das Landratsamt in Tübingen.

Fritz Auer, né à Tübingen en 1933, a commencé ses études à la Technische Hochschule de Stuttgart en 1953. Il a été boursier de la Cranbrook Academy of Arts où il a obtenu son Master of Architecture en 1959. Devenu partenaire de l'agence Behnisch & Partner en 1966, il a créé sa propre structure, **AUER+WEBER**, en 1980. Carlo Weber, né à Sarrebruck en 1934, a également commencé ses études à la Technische Hochschule de Stuttgart, puis les a poursuivies à l'École nationale supérieure des beaux-arts de Paris. Comme Auer, il a été partenaire de Behnisch & Partner. Ils ont eu en charge de nombreux projets de rénovation urbaine, notamment à Bonn et à Stuttgart. Parmi leurs réalisations : la Bibliothèque universitaire de Magdebourg (2003) et le grand magasin Welle à Bielefeld (2003). Ils travaillent actuellement au projet de Parc des sciences d'Ulm, à celui de la rénovation urbaine de l'Alter Hof à Munich, à des maisons de retraite à Landau, Pforzheim-Huchenfeld et Keletern-Ellmendingen, des Archives générales de Karlsruhe et du Centre administratif du district de Tübingen.

ESO HOTEL

Cerro Paranal, Chile, 1998–2002

Floor area: 12 000 m². Cubic volume: 40 000 m³. Client: ESO European Southern Observatory, Munich.
Cost: €11 million

This 12 000 m², 11 million euro hotel is located at an altitude of 2400 m in the mountainous northern area of the Atacama desert in Chile. The reason for this unusual location is the proximity of the Very Large Telescope (VLT) on the Cerro Paranal. Operated by the European Southern Observatory (ESO), an organization based in Munich, the VLT is "the most powerful telescope based on earth." The **ESO HOTEL** serves the scientists and engineers who work in the facility. As the architects describe it, "For the relatively short time of their stays under extreme climatic conditions – intense sunlight, extreme dryness, high wind speeds, great fluctuations in temperature and the danger of earthquakes – a place has been created far away from civilization where they can relax and rest between the strenuous phases of their work. Reminiscent of an oasis, it provides 120 hotel rooms, a canteen and lounge areas, as well as a swimming pool, fitness center and library." Auer+Weber have set the hotel into a natural depression in the ground, allowing only a 35-meter-wide dome over the central lounge to rise above the horizon line. This obviously unusual setting seems to have inspired the architects to create a structure which is at once in harmony with the surroundings and yet provides refuge and a point from which to observe nature.

Das 12 000 m² große, 11 Millionen Euro teure Hotel befindet sich auf einer Höhe von 2400 m in der bergigen Atacamawüste im Norden Chiles. Grund für diesen ungewöhnlichen Standort ist die Nähe zum Riesenteleskop auf dem Cerro Paranal, das vom European Southern Observatory (ESO), einer Organisation mit Sitz in München, betrieben wird. Das Very Large Telescope (VLT) ist »das stärkste Teleskop der Erde«. Das **ESO HOTEL** steht den Wissenschaftlern und Ingenieuren, die in der Einrichtung arbeiten, zur Verfügung. Die Architekten beschreiben es so: »Für die relativ kurze Zeit, die die Mitarbeiter unter extremen klimatischen Bedingungen – intensive Sonneneinstrahlung, extreme Trockenheit, starke Windgeschwindigkeiten, große Temperaturunterschiede und die Gefahr von Erdbeben – hier verbringen, wurde weit weg von der Zivilisation ein Ort geschaffen, an dem man sich entspannen und zwischen den anstrengenden Phasen der Arbeit ausruhen kann. Das Hotel ähnelt einer Oase; es bietet 120 Hotelzimmer, eine Kantine, Loungebereiche, einen Swimmingpool, ein Fitnesszentrum und eine Bibliothek.« Auer+Weber haben das Hotel in einer natürlichen Senke angeordnet, so dass nur die flache Kuppel über der zentralen Lounge mit einem Durchmesser von 35 m über die Horizontlinie hinausragt. Die außergewöhnliche Lage hat die Architekten dazu inspiriert, ein Gebäude zu schaffen, das einerseits mit der Umgebung harmoniert, gleichzeitig aber ein Refugium und ein Ort für Naturbeobachtungen ist.

Cet hôtel de 12 000 m² réalisé pour un budget de 11 millions d'euros est situé à 2400 m d'altitude dans le nord du désert montagneux d'Atacama au Chili. La raison du choix de ce site étrange est la proximité du Très Grand Télescope du Cerro Paranal. Géré par l'European Southern Observatory basé à Munich, le TGT est le plus puissant télescope jamais construit. L'**HÔTEL ESO** est destiné aux scientifiques et ingénieurs qui y travaillent. Les architectes présentent ainsi l'esprit de leur projet : « Pour la durée relativement brève de leurs séjours dans des conditions climatiques particulièrement rudes – soleil intense, sècheresse extrême, vents très forts, grandes fluctuations de la température et risques sismiques – il fallait créer un lieu où l'on puisse se détendre et se reposer entre des tours de service épuisants. Rappelant une oasis, [l'hôtel] offre 120 chambres, un restaurant, des salles de repos, une piscine, un centre de remise en forme et une bibliothèque. » Auer+Weber ont implanté le bâtiment au cœur d'une dépression naturelle. Seule la coupole de 35 mètres de diamètre coiffant le salon central s'élève au-dessus de la ligne d'horizon. Ce site étonnant leur a inspiré une structure qui s'harmonise à son cadre naturel, tout en offrant un refuge et un endroit d'où l'on peut observer la nature.

In this lunar landscape, the architecture takes on an ethereal presence, its repetitive façade emitting light from cutouts that alternate with more open glazed areas.

Die Architektur hat in dieser Mondlandschaft eine unwirkliche Präsenz. Die ausgestanzten Fensteröffnungen in der gleichmäßigen Fassade reflektieren das Licht; dazwischen sind verglaste Flächen angeordnet.

Dans ce paysage lunaire, l'architecture revêt une présence éthérée. La lumière émane de la façade au rythme répétitif, à travers des découpes alternant avec des plans vitrés.

Though it appears to be no more than a bar from certain angles, the hotel is carefully inserted into the dry, undulating landscape whose only other remarkable feature is the ESO telescope.

Aus bestimmten Blickwinkeln betrachtet scheint das Hotel die Form eines einfachen Riegels zu haben. Tatsächlich ist es jedoch behutsam in die trockene, bergige Umgebung eingefügt, in der ansonsten nur das ESO-Teleskop auffällt.

Bien que, sous certains angles, il fasse penser à une barre, l'hôtel est judicieusement inséré dans son paysage lunaire et désertique, à proximité de l'autre intervention humaine remarquable dans la région, le Très Grand Télescope ESO.

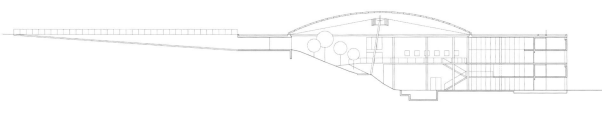

Where the earth offers a spectacle of desolation, the architects have correctly chosen to make use of light. The earth and the sky are the spectacle here and the hotel opens toward both, while protecting its residents from the surrounding harshness.

Wo die Erde nur ein »Schauspiel der Verlassenheit« bietet, haben sich die Architekten richtigerweise dafür entschieden, das Licht zu nutzen. Erde und Himmel sind hier die wesentlichen Elemente, und beiden öffnet sich das Hotel. Gleichzeitig schützt es seine Bewohner vor der unwirtlichen Umgebung.

Parce que le sol lui-même n'offre qu'un spectacle de désolation, les architectes ont décidé d'utiliser la lumière au maximum. La terre et le ciel sont le spectacle sur lequel s'ouvre cet hôtel chargé de protéger ses hôtes d'un environnement hostile.

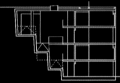

SHIGERU BAN

Shigeru Ban Architects
5–2–4 Matsubara
Setagaya-ku, Tokyo 156-0043
Japan

Tel: +81 333 24 67 60
Fax: +81 333 24 67 89
e-mail: tokyo@shigerubanarchitects.com
Web: www.shigerubanarchitects.com

Bianimale Nomadic Museum ▶

Born in 1957 in Tokyo, **SHIGERU BAN** studied at the Southern California Institute of Architecture (SciArc) from 1977 to 1980. He attended the Cooper Union School of Architecture, where he studied under John Hejduk (1980–82). He worked in the office of Arata Isozaki (1982–83) before founding his own firm in Tokyo in 1985. His work includes numerous exhibition designs like the Alvar Aalto show at the Axis Gallery, Tokyo (1986). His buildings include the Odawara Pavilion, Kanagawa (1990); the Paper Gallery, Tokyo (1994); the Paper House, Lake Yamanaka (1995); and the Paper Church, Takatori, Hyogo (1995). He has also designed ephemeral structures such as his Paper Refugee Shelter made with plastic sheets and paper tubes for the United Nations High Commission for Refugees (UNHCR). He designed the Japanese Pavilion at Expo 2000 in Hanover. Current work includes a small museum of Canal History in Pouilly-en-Auxois, France; the Schwartz Residence, Sharon, Connecticut; Forest Park Pavilion – Bamboo Gridshell-02, St. Louis, Missouri; Mul(ti)houses, Mulhouse, France; Sagaponac House/Furniture House-05, Long Island, New York; Hanegi Forest Annex, Setagaya, Tokyo; and the new Pompidou Center in Metz, France.

SHIGERU BAN, 1957 in Tokio geboren, studierte von 1977 bis 1980 am Southern California Institute of Architecture (SCI-Arc) und von 1980 bis 1982 bei John Hejduk an der Cooper Union School of Architecture in New York. Von 1982 bis 1983 arbeitete er im Büro von Arata Isozaki und gründete 1985 seine eigene Firma in Tokio. Shigeru Ban gestaltete zahlreiche Ausstellungen, so die 1986 in der Galerie Axis in Tokio gezeigte Alvar-Aalto-Schau. Zu seinen Bauten gehören u. a. der Odawara Pavillon in Kanagawa (1990), die Paper Gallery in Tokio (1994), das Paper House am Yamanaka-See (1995) und die Paper Church in Takatori, Hyogo (1995). Ban hat auch Behelfsbauten entworfen wie sein für den Hohen Flüchtlingskommissar der Vereinten Nationen (UNHCR) aus Plastikfolie und Pappröhren gebauter Paper Refugee Shelter. Für die Expo 2000 in Hannover plante er den japanischen Pavillon. Zu seinen jüngsten Projekten zählen ein kleines Museum für die Geschichte des Kanalbaus im französischen Pouilly-en-Auxois, das Haus Schwartz in Sharon, Connecticut, der Forest Park Pavilion – Bamboo Gridshell-02 in St. Louis, Missouri, die Mul(ti)houses im französischen Mulhouse, das Haus Sagaponac/Furniture House-05 in Long Island, New York, sowie ein Gebäude in Hanegi Forest, Setagaya, Tokio, und das Centre Pompidou in Metz.

Né en 1957 à Tokyo, **SHIGERU BAN** étudie au Southern California Institute of Architecture (SCI-Arc) de 1977 à 1980, puis à la Cooper Union School of Architecture, où il suit l'enseignement de John Hejduk (1980–82). Il travaille pour Arata Isozaki (1982–83), avant de fonder son agence à Tokyo en 1985. Il a conçu de nombreuses expositions (notamment celle sur Alvar Aalto, Axis Gallery, Tokyo, 1986). Parmi ses réalisations architecturales : le Pavillon Odawara, Kanagava (1990) ; la Paper Gallery, Tokyo (1997) ; la Maison de papier, Lac Yamanaka (1995) et l'Église de papier, Takatori, Hyogo (1995). Il conçoit également des structures éphémères, comme son abri pour réfugiés en feuilles de plastique et tubes de carton, pour le Haut Commissariat aux Réfugiés (HCR) des Nations Unies. Il a signé le pavillon japonais à l'Expo 2000 de Hanovre. Parmi ses réalisations figurent le Centre d'interprétation du canal de Bourgogne (Pouilly-en-Auxois, France) et, en cours, la Schwartz Residence (Sharon, Connecticut) ; le Forest Park Pavilion – Bamboo Gridshell-02 (Saint Louis, Missouri) ; Mul(ti)houses (Mulhouse, France) ; Sagaponac House/Furniture House-05 (Long Island, New York) ; un bâtiment dans la forêt de Hanegi (Setagaya, Tokyo) et le nouveau Centre Pompidou à Metz (France).

BIANIMALE NOMADIC MUSEUM

New York, New York, USA, 2005

Floor area: 4180 m². Client: Ashes and Snow, LLC.
Cost: not disclosed

The **BIANIMALE NOMADIC MUSEUM** was a 4180 m² structure intended to house *Ashes and Snow*, an exhibition of large-scale photographs by Gregory Colbert, on view in New York from March 5 to June 6, 2005. No less than 205 meters long, the 16-meter-high rectangular building was made up essentially of steel shipping containers and paper tubes made from recycled paper, with inner and outer waterproof membranes and coated with a waterproof sealant. Located on Pier 54 on Manhattan's Lower West side, the building had a central 3.6-meter-wide wooden walkway composed of recycled scaffolding planks lined on either side with river stones. The overall impression of this structure was not unlike that of a temple, or as the architect wrote, "The simple triangular gable design of the roof structure and ceremonial, columnar interior walkway of the museum echo the atmosphere of a classical church." The first building to be made from shipping containers in New York, the Nomadic Museum is an intriguing effort to employ recyclable materials to create a large-scale structure. Despite the rather difficult access to the site and high entrance fee, many New Yorkers went to visit Ban's museum, perhaps more intrigued by its spectacular outer and interior forms than by the theatrical photographs of Colbert.

Das 4180 m² große **NOMADISCHE MUSEUM** wurde eigens für die Ausstellung »Ashes and Snow« errichtet. Die Show, vom 5. März bis zum 6. Juni 2005 in New York zu sehen, zeigte die großformatigen Fotografien von Gregory Colbert. Nicht weniger als 205 m lang, bestand die 16 m hohe rechteckige Konstruktion im Wesentlichen aus Frachtcontainern und Pappröhren aus recyceltem Papier, die innen und außen mit einer wasserdichten Folie versehen und wasserundurchlässig imprägniert waren. Standort der Konstruktion war der Pier 54 auf der Lower West Side im Süden Manhattans. Ein 3,6 m breiter Weg aus recycelten Gerüstbrettern, auf beiden Seiten mit Flussbettsteinen gefasst, führte durch die Mitte des Gebäudes. Der Gesamteindruck ähnelte dem eines Tempels oder mit den Worten des Architekten: »Das dreieckige, einfache Satteldach und der zeremonielle, von Stützen gesäumte innere Weg des Museums erinnern an die Atmosphäre in einer alten Kirche.« Das Nomadische Museum war das erste Gebäude in New York, das aus Frachtcontainern gebaut wurde – ein verblüffender Versuch, recycelbares Material für eine Konstruktion in großem Maßstab zu verwenden. Trotz des hohen Eintrittgeldes und des eher schwierigen Zugangs zum Standort besuchten viele New Yorker Shigeru Bans Museum. Möglicherweise waren sie mehr an dessen spektakulären inneren und äußeren Formen als an den theatralischen Fotografien von Colbert interessiert.

Ce **MUSÉE NOMADE** était une structure éphémère de 4180 m² conçue pour l'exposition de photographies de très grand format de Gregory Colbert, « Ashes and Snow », organisée par la Bianimale Foundation que dirige l'artiste, qui s'est déroulée à New York (Hudson River at 13th Street) du 5 mars au 6 juin 2005. Cette construction rectangulaire de 205 m de long sur 16 m de haut était essentiellement composée de conteneurs d'expédition en acier et de tubes de carton recyclé, totalement imperméabilisés et gainés d'un isolant étanche. Installé sur le Pier 54 dans le quartier du Lower West Side à Manhattan, le bâtiment était traversé par une allée centrale de 3,6 m de large en planches d'échafaudage recyclées, bordées de galets des deux côtés. L'impression donnée était celle d'un temple où, comme l'a écrit l'architecte, « le dessin très simple du pignon triangulaire de la toiture et l'allée principale bordée de colonnes évoquaient l'atmosphère d'une église classique ». Premier bâtiment réalisé à New York à partir de conteneurs, le Nomadic Museum est une intéressante tentative d'utilisation à grande échelle de matériaux recyclables. Malgré l'accès assez difficile au site et le prix élevé de l'entrée, de nombreux New-Yorkais ont visité cette exposition, peut-être plus par curiosité pour cette construction spectaculaire que pour les photographies théâtrales de Colbert.

Built out of paper tubes and shipping containers, Ban's Nomadic Museum actually seemed very much at home in its dockside setting.

Bans Nomadic Museum aus Pappröhren und Frachtcontainern passte in die Umgebung der Docks sehr gut hinein.

L'environnement portuaire convenait parfaitement au Nomadic Museum de Ban, construit à partir de conteneurs d'expédition en acier et de tubes en carton.

By alternating the alignments of the containers, Ban made the long building much more visually interesting than it might have been had he simply stacked the elements in solid rows.

Ban ordnete die Container auf Lücke an. Dadurch wurde das lange Gebäude optisch viel interessanter, als wenn er die Container einfach nur aufeinander gestapelt hätte.

En alternant ses alignements de conteneurs, Ban a rendu cette longue construction plus intéressante visuellement qu'avec un empilement uniforme.

Although the Nomadic Museum was extremely simple, and repetitive in its structural principles, the vast interior space with its controlled natural lighting and central wooden walkway immediately took on the appearance of a temple-like space.

Obwohl das Nomadic Museum ein extrem einfaches Gebäude mit einer repetitiven Struktur war, strahlte der riesige Innenraum mit seiner kontrolliert eingesetzten Tageslichtbelichtung und dem hölzernen Mittelgang eine sakrale Atmosphäre aus.

De principe structurel extrêmement simple et répétitif, le Nomadic Museum n'en offre pas moins un vaste volume intérieur doté d'un éclairage naturel contrôlé et d'une allée centrale en bois qui évoque l'image d'un temple.

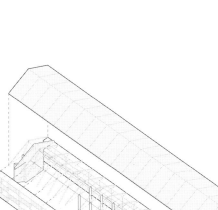

PAPER TEMPORARY STUDIO

6th floor terrace, Centre Georges Pompidou, Paris, France, 2004

Floor area: 115 m². Client: Shigeru Ban Architects. Cost: not disclosed

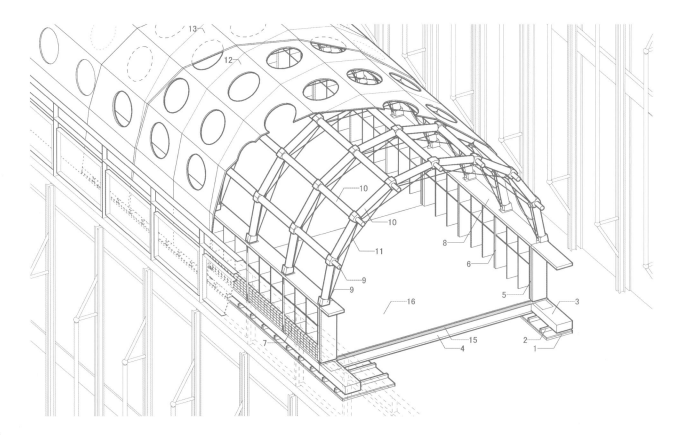

As Shigeru Ban describes this project, "After winning the competition for Centre Pompidou Metz, Centre Pompidou's new facility in the city of Metz, I suggested half jokingly to Mr Bruno Racine, the director of the Centre Pompidou that 'The agreed design fee is not sufficient for an architectural office from a foreign country like us to rent an office in Paris. So if you could lend us space on the terrace, we can build our temporary office.' Unexpectedly, Racine agreed and Ban created a 115 m² temporary arched office on top of the Piano & Rogers landmark. With the approval of Renzo Piano, Ban designed a paper tube structure with some use of timber and steel. The roof is made of titanium dioxide PTFE membrane, regular PTFE membrane, and PVC membrane. The interior is finished with tile carpet, wood deck and Vitra furniture. Since one of Racine's original requirements was that the office be fully visible to Centre Pompidou visitors, Shigeru Ban concludes, 'Please come visit us when you have chance to come to Paris. Though as we are part of the exhibit, it would require that you buy an admission ticket at the entrance.'"

Shigeru Ban beschreibt dieses Projekt so: »Nachdem ich den Wettbewerb für das Centre Pompidou Metz (eine neue Dependance des Centre Pompidou) gewonnen hatte, schlug ich dem Direktor, Bruno Racine, halb im Scherz vor: ›Das Entwurfshonorar reicht für ein Architekturbüro aus dem Ausland wie wir es sind nicht aus, Büroräume in Paris zu mieten. Wenn Sie uns Platz auf Ihrer Terrasse überlassen, können wir dort ein temporäres Büro bauen.‹ Wider Erwarten stimmte Racine zu, und Ban entwarf ein 115 m² großes, halbtonnenförmiges Büro auf dem Dach des Wahrzeichens von Piano und Rogers. Mit Renzo Pianos Zustimmung entwickelte Ban eine Konstruktion aus Pappröhren, die durch wenig Holz und Stahl ergänzt wird. Das Dach besteht aus einer PTFE-Folie aus Titandioxid, einer normalen PTFE-Folie und einer PVC-Folie. Der Innenraum ist mit Teppichfliesen, einem Holzdeck und Möbeln von Vitra gestaltet. Da eine der ursprünglichen Forderungen von Racine war, dass das Büro jederzeit für Besucher des Centre Pompidou zu besichtigen sei, sagt Shigeru Ban: »Bitte besuchen Sie uns, wenn Sie die Möglichkeit haben, nach Paris zu kommen. Da wir Teil der Ausstellung sind, müssen Sie dafür aber eine Eintrittskarte für das Museum kaufen.«

Shigeru Ban présente ainsi ce projet : « Après avoir remporté le concours du Centre Pompidou à Metz, j'ai expliqué en plaisantant à demi à Bruno Racine, directeur du Centre, que les honoraires d'une agence étrangère comme la nôtre ne nous permettaient pas de louer des bureaux à Paris et donc, que s'il nous prêtait un peu d'espace sur sa terrasse, nous pourrions y construire des bureaux temporaires. » Surprise : Bruno Racine donna son accord et Ban créa ces bureaux en forme d'arche de 115 m² tout en haut du monument signé par Piano et Rogers. Avec l'approbation de Renzo Piano, Ban conçut une structure faite de tubes de carton et de diverses pièces de bois et d'acier. Le toit se compose de trois membranes en PTFE au dioxyde de titane, PTFE classique et PVC. Le sol est en bois recouvert de dalles de moquettes et les meubles viennent de chez Vitra. Comme l'une des demandes de Bruno Racine était que les visiteurs du Centre puissent voir ces bureaux, Ban les y invite : « Venez donc nous voir si vous avez la chance de passer par Paris, mais comme nous faisons partie des pièces exposées, vous devrez acheter un billet d'entrée... »

Sitting on top of the Pompidou Center, just opposite the Georges Restaurant and the entrance to the temporary exhibition areas, Ban's studio is alien to the Piano and Rogers architecture, and yet somehow fits in comfortably.

Bans Büro auf dem Dach des Centre Georges Pompidou liegt direkt gegenüber dem Restaurant »Georges« und dem Eingang zu den Sonderausstellungen. Mit der Architektur von Piano und Rogers hat es wenig gemein, fügt sich aber trotzdem gut ein.

Tout en haut du Centre Pompidou, face au restaurant Georges et à l'entrée des expositions temporaires, l'atelier de Ban, s'il reste étranger à l'architecture de Piano et Rogers, ne s'en est pas moins confortablement installé.

A flexible, bright and open workspace allows Ban and his team to be permanently in proximity to their client for the Pompidou Center Metz project on which he is working.

Der flexibel nutzbare, helle und offene Arbeitsraum von Ban und seinem Team liegt in der Nähe des Büros seines Auftraggebers – derzeit plant Ban das Centre Pompidou Metz.

Cet espace de travail flexible, ouvert et lumineux, permet à Shigeru Ban et à son équipe de travailler à proximité de leur commanditaire pour le Centre Pompidou de Metz.

Visitors to the Pompidou Center's exhibitions can get a glimpse inside the Paper Temporary Studio after they pass through the ticketing area near the building's famous moving walkway.

Nachdem die Besucher des Centre Georges Pompidou in der Nähe der berühmten Rolltreppen ihre Eintrittskarte gekauft haben, können sie einen Blick in das Paper Temporary Studio werfen.

Les visiteurs des expositions du Centre peuvent apercevoir le Paper Temporary Studio après la billetterie, à quelques mètres seulement du fameux escalier mécanique.

BARCLAY & CROUSSE

Barclay & Crousse Architecture
7, Passage Saint Bernard
75011 Paris
France

Tel: +33 149 23 51 36
Fax: +33 148 07 88 32
e-mail: atelier@barclaycrousse.com
Web: www.barclaycrousse.com

Casa Equis ►

JEAN-PIERRE CROUSSE was born in 1963. He was educated at the Universidad Ricardo Palma in Lima, Peru and at Milan Polytechnic, Milan, Italy were he received a European architecture degree. **SANDRA BARCLAY** was born in 1967 and also studied at the Universidad Ricardo Palma, before getting a French architecture degree (D. P. L. G.) at the Ecole d'architecture de Paris-Belleville (1993). Their built work includes the reconstruction of the Musée Malraux, Le Havre, France (1999); an office building in Malakoff, Paris, France (2003); the M House, Cañete, Peru (2001); B House, Cañete, Peru (1999); and a renovation of the City Hall of Epinay-sur-Seine, France (2004). Projects include the H House in the Gers region of France (2005); the B&F House in the Haute Savoie region of France and welfare housing in Malakoff, Paris (2005).

JEAN-PIERRE CROUSSE, geboren 1963, studierte an der Universidad Ricardo Palma in Lima, Peru, und am Politecnico in Mailand, wo er einen europäischen Architekturabschluss erwarb. **SANDRA BARCLAY** wurde 1967 geboren und studierte ebenfalls an der Universidad Ricardo Palma, bevor sie 1993 ihren französischen Architekturabschluss (D. P. L. G.) an der Ecole d'Architecture de Paris-Belleville machte. Zu ihren realisierten Projekten gehören die Sanierung des Musée Malraux in Le Havre (1999), ein Bürogebäude in Malakoff, Paris (2003), das Haus B und das Haus M in Cañete, Peru (1999 und 2001), und die Instandsetzung des Rathauses von Epinay-sur-Seine (2004). Projektiert sind u. a. das Haus H im Departement Gers (2005), das Haus B&F in der Haute Savoie und ein sozialer Wohnungsbau in Malakoff, Paris (2005).

JEAN-PIERRE CROUSSE, né en 1963, a étudié à l'Universidad Ricardo Palma à Lima (Pérou) et à l'École Polytechnique de Milan où il a obtenu son diplôme européen d'architecte. **SANDRA BARCLAY**, née en 1967, a également fait ses études à l'Universidad Ricardo Palma, puis à l'École d'architecture de Paris-Belleville (1993). Elle est architecte D. P. L. G. Parmi leurs réalisations : la rénovation du musée Malraux, Le Havre, France (1999) ; un immeuble de bureaux, Malakoff, France (2003) ; la maison B et la maison M (1999 et 2001, Cañete, Pérou) et la rénovation de l'hôtel de ville d'Épinay-sur-Seine, France (2004). Ils ont actuellement en projet la Maison H dans le Gers (2005), la Maison B&F en Haute-Savoie et des logements sociaux à Malakoff.

CASA EQUIS

Cañete, Peru_2003

Floor area: 174 m². Client: Juan Carlos Verme. Cost: $75 000

CASA M

CASA EQUIS

This 174 m² residence was built in the same area as the architects' B House and their earlier M House (located directly next to the Casa Equis). As the architects say, the project "attempts to create the intimacy or domesticity necessary in order to live in the desert where the house is located, without denying or falsifying the situation." They chose to fully occupy the site and to create "a pure prism, that landed in the dunes, but gives the impression that it was always there." Their concept was to dig the living spaces out of the "pre-existing" prism, "a little like archeologists clearing away the sand and revealing Pre-Columbian ruins." Creating a maximum amount of ambiguity between exterior and interior spaces, they attempted to relate each area of the house to the sky or the neighboring ocean. Cut into the hillside, the house has an upper level entry from the road with and social spaces (living/dining, kitchen and suspended swimming pool), and a lower level with master bedroom, children's room and guest room, terraces and a beach entrance. The Casa Equis won the prize for the best work of architecture at the Fourth Ibero-American Architecture Biennale in Lima, Peru (2004).

Das 174 m² große Einfamilienhaus befindet sich in derselben Gegend wie das Haus B und das frühere Haus M der Architekten, das direkt neben der Casa Equis steht. Wie Barclay & Crousse sagen, versuchen sie mit dem Projekt »die Intimität und Häuslichkeit zu schaffen, die man braucht, um in der Wüste zu leben, wo dieses Haus steht, ohne die Situation zu leugnen oder zu verfälschen«. Sie entschieden sich dafür, das Grundstück komplett zu bebauen und »ein reines Prisma« zu schaffen, »das in den Dünen gelandet ist, aber den Eindruck vermittelt, als ob es schon immer hier gewesen sei«. Die konzeptionelle Idee war, die Wohnräume aus einem gedanklich schon vorhandenen Prisma »auszugraben«, »ungefähr so, wie Archäologen Sand abtragen, um präkolumbianische Ruinen freizulegen.« Jeder Bereich des Hauses sollte in einen Bezug zum Himmel und zum nahe gelegenen Ozean gesetzt werden, wodurch ein Maximum an Doppeldeutigkeit zwischen Außen- und Innenraum erreicht wurde. Das Haus ist in das hügelige Terrain eingeschnitten; auf der oberen Ebene liegen der straßenseitige Eingang und die gemeinschaftlich genutzten Räume (Wohn- und Essraum, Küche) sowie ein aufgeständerter Swimmingpool. Auf der unteren Ebene sind das Elternschlafzimmer, ein Kinder- und Gästezimmer, Terrassen sowie ein Strandeingang angeordnet. Die Casa Equis gewann den ersten Preis in der Kategorie Architektur bei der IV. Iberoamerikanischen Architekturbiennale in Lima (2004).

Cette résidence de 174 m² a été construite non loin de la Maison B et de la Maison M réalisées par les mêmes architectes. Pour ses auteurs, ce projet tente de « créer l'intimité ou les conditions de vie familiale requises pour vivre dans le désert où se trouve la maison, sans nier ni truquer la situation ». Ils ont choisi d'occuper la totalité du terrain et de créer « un prisme pur, qui aurait atterri dans les dunes, tout en donnant l'impression d'avoir toujours été là ». Leur concept était de creuser la zone de vie dans le prisme « préexistant », « un peu comme des archéologues dégagent le sable pour mettre au jour des ruines précolombiennes ». En créant le maximum d'ambiguïté entre les espaces intérieurs et extérieurs, ils ont voulu créer un lien entre chaque zone de la maison et le ciel ou l'océan tout proche. Découpée dans le flanc de la dune, l'entrée de la maison donnant sur la route est au niveau supérieur, qui regroupe les parties communes (séjour, salle à manger, cuisine, piscine suspendue), tandis qu'au niveau inférieur se trouvent la chambre principale, celle des enfants, une chambre d'amis, des terrasses et l'accès à la plage. Cette maison a remporté le prix de la meilleure œuvre à la 4e Biennale ibéro-américaine d'architecture de Lima en 2004.

The earlier Casa M by the same architects and the Casa Equis sit side-by-side on a cliff above the ocean. Variations on a theme, they both offer luxury and sophistication in a very rough natural setting.

Die Casa M und die Casa Equis – beide von Barclay & Crousse – liegen nebeneinander auf einem Felsen über dem Ozean. Als Variationen eines Themas bieten sie den Bewohnern Luxus und Kultiviertheit in einer kargen Natur.

Conçues par les mêmes architectes, la Casa M (plus ancienne) et la Casa Equis ont été édifiées côte à côte sur une falaise dominant l'océan. Variations sur un même thème, elles offrent à la fois luxe et sophistication dans un cadre naturel sauvage.

Alternating opaque and transparent surfaces, the architects use a strict, geometric vocabulary that opens toward the powerful natural setting while setting clear defensive boundaries.

Die Architekten benutzen ein streng geometrisches Vokabular aus geschlossenen und transparenten Flächen. Sie öffnen das Haus zur dominanten Umgebung, schaffen gleichzeitig aber auch klare und schützende Grenzen.

Alternant surfaces opaques et transparentes, les architectes ont utilisé un vocabulaire géométrique strict qui permet une ouverture sur un cadre naturel très présent tout en fixant clairement des limites quasi défensives.

The suspended pool, where a child seems to hover far above the crashing waves, is one of the more unusual features of the Casa Equis.

Der brückenartige Pool, in dem ein Kind hoch über der Brandung zu schweben scheint, ist eine Besonderheit der Casa Equis.

La piscine suspendue dans laquelle une enfant semble flotter au-dessus de vagues déferlantes de l'océan, est l'un des éléments les plus surprenants de la Casa Equis.

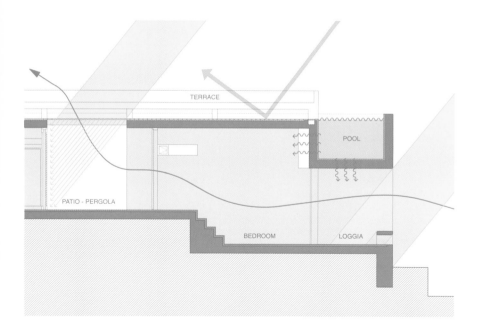

TERRACE

POOL

PATIO - PERGOLA

BEDROOM

LOGGIA

*By closing the horizontal surfaces
and opening the vertical ones to the
light and air of the ocean, the
architects create a sheltered and yet
remarkably open space.*

*Mit geschlossenen horizontalen
Flächen und vertikalen, zum Licht
und der Luft des Ozeans geöffneten
Flächen schaffen die Architekten
einen geschützten, aber bemerkenswert offenen Außenraum.*

*En jouant sur la fermeture des plans
horizontaux et l'ouverture des plans
verticaux vers la lumière et l'air de
l'océan, les architectes ont créé un
volume ouvert mais protégé.*

Large flat surfaces of color with ample use of light wood intentionally give a warmer aspect to the interior than to the exterior of the house. Sparsely furnished, the house is fully turned toward the spectacle of nature, while offering its residents a high level of civilized amenity.

Großzügige Farbflächen und viel helles Holz geben den Innenräumen bewusst einen wärmeren Ton als der äußeren Hülle. Das sparsam möblierte Haus ist vollständig auf das Naturschauspiel ausgerichtet und bietet seinen Bewohnern gleichzeitig ein hohes Maß an Komfort.

Ses vastes plans colorés et l'utilisation généreuse du bois clair donnent à l'intérieur un aspect plus chaleureux que celui de l'extérieur. Meublée avec parcimonie, la maison est tournée vers le spectacle de la nature, tout en offrant à ses résidents un excellent niveau de confort raffiné.

BAUMRAUM

baumraum
Andreas Wenning
Roonstrasse 49
28203 Bremen
Germany

Tel: +49 421 70 51 22
Fax: +49 421 794 63 51
e-mail: a.wenning@baumraum.de
Web: www.baumraum.de

Plendelhof Tree House ▶

Andreas Wenning was born in 1965. He studied as a cabinet maker in Weinheim, Germany (1982–85), and as an architect at the Technical University of Bremen where he obtained his degree in 1995. He worked in the office of Jose Garcia Negette in Sydney, Australia (2000–01) and he created his own office, **BAUMRAUM**, in Bremen in 2003. Aside from the tree house published here, he has worked on web-like "grabnet" rope structures for trees (Lower Saxony Horticultural Show, Wolfsburg, 2004) or organized seminars on "The Body Language of Trees," or "Building a Tree House without Impairing the Tree." His firm offers to build unique tree houses for clients. He has just finished a pavilion made of Corten steel for the Science Center of the University of Bremen.

Andreas Wenning wurde 1965 geboren. Von 1982 bis 1985 machte er eine Lehre als Möbeltischler in Weinheim. 1995 erwarb er an der Hochschule Bremen sein Architekturdiplom. Er arbeitete im Büro von Jose Garcia Negette in Sydney (2000–01) und gründete 2003 in Bremen sein eigenes Büro **BAUMRAUM**. Neben dem hier gezeigten Baumhaus entwarf Wenning netzartige, in Bäumen aufgehängte Seilkonstruktionen (»Fangnetze«) für die Niedersächsische Gartenschau 2004 in Wolfsburg und hielt Seminare, z. B. »Die Körpersprache von Bäumen« oder »Baumhäuser bauen ohne Beschädigung des Baumes«. Das Büro bietet den Bau von einzigartigen Baumhäusern an. Erst kürzlich wurde ein Pavillon für das Wissenschaftszentrum der Universität Bremen aus Corten-Stahl fertig gestellt.

Andreas Wenning, né en 1965, a étudié l'ébénisterie à Weinheim, Allemagne (1982–85) et l'architecture à l'Université technique de Brême, dont il est sorti diplômé en 1995. Il a travaillé dans l'agence Jose Garcia Negette à Sydney, Australie (2000–01) et créé la sienne, **BAUMRAUM**, à Brême en 2003. En dehors de la « maison dans l'arbre » publiée ici, il a élaboré des structures en cordage « grabnet » pour arbres, Exposition horticole de Basse-Saxe, Wolfsburg (2004) et organisé des séminaires sur « Le langage corporel des arbres » ou « Construire une maison dans les arbres sans abîmer les arbres ». Son agence propose de construire des maisons dans les arbres originales. Il vient d'achever un pavillon en acier Corten pour le Centre des sciences de l'Université de Brême.

PLENDELHOF TREE HOUSE

Gross-Henstedt, Germany, 2002–03

Floor area: 6 m² plus 4 m² terrace. Client: Andreas Wenning. Cost: €14 500

Andreas Wenning designed this tree house for two beech trees located at the Plendelhof Stables, about 30 kilometers south of Bremen, Germany. Set 8.6 meters off the ground the 950-kilo structure measures 7.5 x 2.6 meters and is two meters high. The triangular main frame is made of 100mm x 200mm larch beams. It is covered with larch boards, with 80mm of insulation between the inner and outer panels. The insulation allows the tree house to be used even in winter with a small heater inside. The total cost of the project was 14 500 euros. The house was designed to be small and yet to provide enough comfort for sleeping. Views in all directions and a sun terrace were also part of the original goals of the design. The architect opted for a "suspended structure anchored to the beeches with steel ropes." Assembled to the greatest extent possible on the ground, the house had to be easy to install without damage to the trees. Wenning also insists that the tree house does not "restrict the movement of the trees in terms of wind and growth." Although children can use this tree house, given its height off the ground it seems almost better suited to adults. Entered through a hatch, the tree house has a boat-like atmosphere inside.

Auf dem Plendelhof etwa 30 km südlich von Bremen befindet sich das von Andreas Wenning entworfene Baumhaus. Die in zwei Buchen gebaute, 950 kg schwere Konstruktion schwebt 8,6 m über dem Boden, misst 7,5 x 2,6 m und ist 2 m hoch. Der tragende, dreieckige Rahmen besteht aus Lärchenhölzern mit Querschnitten von 100 x 200 mm. Er ist mit zwei Schichten aus Lärchenholzbrettern verkleidet, zwischen denen eine 80 mm starke Dämmung angeordnet ist. Aufgrund der Dämmung und eines kleinen Heizgerätes kann das Baumhaus sogar im Winter benutzt werden. Die Gesamtkosten lagen bei 14 500 Euro. Das Haus sollte eher klein sein, aber ausreichenden Komfort bieten, um darin zu schlafen. Ziel des Entwurfs war auch, Ausblicke in alle Richtungen zu bieten und eine Sonnenterrasse vorzusehen. Der Architekt entschied sich für eine »Konstruktion, die mit Stahlseilen in den Buchen verankert ist«. Das Baumhaus wurde zum größten Teil auf der Erde zusammengefügt und sollte mit einfachen Mitteln an den Bäumen befestigt werden können, ohne diese zu beschädigen. Wenning besteht darauf, dass es »die Bewegung der Bäume, die durch Wind oder Wachstum verursacht werden, nicht behindert«. Auch wenn Kinder das Baumhaus benutzen können, ist es aufgrund seiner Höhe besser für Erwachsene geeignet. Eine Luke bildet den Eingang; in seinem Inneren herrscht eine bootsartige Atmosphäre.

Andreas Wenning a conçu cette maison à proximité des écuries de Plendelhof, à 30 km environ au sud de Brême. Calée entre deux hêtres à 8,6 m du sol, cette construction de 950 kg mesure 7,5 x 2,6 m pour 2 m de haut. L'ossature principale, triangulaire, est en poutres de mélèze de 10 x 20 cm de section. L'ensemble est habillé à l'intérieur comme à l'extérieur de planches de mélèze séparées par 80 mm de matériau isolant, ce qui permet d'utiliser la maison même en hiver, avec un petit radiateur. Le budget total du projet s'est élevé à 14 500 euros. La maison est petite, mais suffisante pour y dormir, et offre un petit solarium et des perspectives dans toutes les directions. L'architecte a opté pour une « structure suspendue accrochée aux arbres par des câbles d'acier ». Assemblée pour sa plus grande partie au sol, elle a pu être hissée sans dommage pour les arbres. Wenning insiste sur le fait que cette maison « n'entrave pas le mouvement des arbres, qu'il soit dû au vent ou à leur croissance ». Si les enfants peuvent l'utiliser, elle semble mieux adaptée à des adultes tant elle est loin du sol. À l'intérieur, où l'on pénètre par une trappe, on se sent comme dans un bateau.

The tree house obviously obeys different rules than its earthbound cousins, but Andreas Wenning has done everything necessary to protect the trees while creating a spectacular modern getaway almost nine meters off the ground.

Ein Baumhaus gehorcht zweifellos anderen Regeln als seine bodenständigen Verwandten. Andreas Wenning hat alles dafür getan, die Bäume zu schützen und einen spektakulären, modernen Rückzugsort fast 9 m über dem Erdboden zu schaffen.

La maison dans l'arbre obéit à des règles différentes de celles qui sont appliquées à ses cousines terrestres. Andreas Wenning a tout fait pour respecter les arbres, tout en créant ce spectaculaire abri moderne à près de neuf mètres du sol.

The triangular plan of the tree house is visible in these images, as is the careful placement of windows that allow visitors to take full advantage of the unexpected view.

Hier zu sehen sind der dreieckige Grundriss des Baumhauses und die überlegte Anordnung der Fenster, die dem Besucher optimale und überraschende Ausblicke bieten.

Ces images mettent en évidence le plan triangulaire de la maison et la disposition étudiée des fenêtres qui permettent de profiter pleinement de vues surprenantes.

BEKKERING ADAMS

Bekkering Adams architecten
Sint Jobsweg 30
3024 EJ Rotterdam
The Netherlands

Tel: +31 104 25 81 66
Fax: +31 104 25 89 46
e-mail: info@bekkeringadams.nl
Web: www.bekkeringadams.nl

Juliette Bekkering was born in Sorengo, Switzerland in 1963. She received her degree in architecture from the Technical University in Delft in 1989. She went on to do post-graduate work in urban design at the Polytechnic University of Barcelona (1993). From 1989 to 1994 she worked with Michiel Riedijk and OMA in Rotterdam. Beginning in 1995, she was an associated project architect with Neutlings Riedjik for their fire stations in Maastricht and Breda. She created her own office, Juliette Bekkering Architecten, in Rotterdam in 1997. Monica Adams was born in Meppel, the Netherlands in 1964. She also graduated from the Technical University in Delft in 1989. She worked with Sutcliffe and Copeland in London before becoming a project architect with Mecanoo in Rotterdam in 1991. She joined Erick van Egeraat when he set up EEA in 1995, and set up the firm's London office in 1998. In March 2005, Juliette Bekkering and Monica Adams created **BEKKERING ADAMS** architecten. Work includes the Maashaven OZ de Zuidpunt Offices, apartments and municipal office, Feijenoord, Rotterdam (2004), and the Vlissingen Middleburg fire station, Middleburg (2004).

Juliette Bekkering, 1963 in Sorengo in der Schweiz geboren, machte ihr Architekturdiplom 1989 an der Technischen Universität Delft. Als Graduierte arbeitete sie 1993 an der Universitat Politècnica de Catalunya in Barcelona im Bereich Städtebaulicher Entwurf. Von 1989 bis 1994 war sie in Rotterdam bei Michiel Riedijk und im OMA tätig; von 1995 an war sie, in Projektpartnerschaft mit Neutlings Riedijk, Projektleiterin für die Feuerwehrwachen in Maastricht und Breda. 1997 gründete sie in Rotterdam ihr eigenes Büro Juliette Bekkering. Auch Monica Adams, geboren 1964 in Meppels, Niederlande, machte ihr Diplom 1989 an der Technischen Universität Delft. Bevor sie 1991 Projektleiterin bei Mecanoo in Rotterdam wurde, arbeitete sie bei Sutcliffe and Copeland in London. Als Erick van Egeraat 1995 EEA gründete, wurde sie dort Mitarbeiterin und ging 1998 nach London, um das dortige Büro von EEA zu leiten. Im März 2005 gründeten Juliette Bekkering und Monica Adams Bekkering **BEKKERING ADAMS** architecten. Projekte der Architektinnen sind u. a. die Büros Maashaven O. Z. de Zuidpunt (Wohnungen, Büros und Gemeindebüro) in Feijennoord, Rotterdam (2004), und die Feuerwache Vlissingen-Middelburg in Middelburg (2004).

Juliette Bekkering, née à Sorengo en Suisse, est diplômée d'architecture de l'Université technique de Delft (1989), puis a poursuivi ses études d'urbanisme à l'Université polytechnique de Barcelone (1993). De 1989 à 1994, elle a travaillé avec Michiel Riedijk et OMA à Rotterdam. Début 1995, elle est architecte de projet associée à Neutlings Riedijk pour leurs casernes de pompiers de Maastricht et de Breda. Elle a créé son agence, Juliette Bekkering Architecten, à Rotterdam en 1997. Monica Adams, née à Meppel (Pays-Bas) est également diplômée de l'Université technique de Delft (1989). Elle a travaillé pour Sitcliffe et Copeland à Londres avant de devenir architecte de projet pour Mecanoo à Rotterdam en 1991. Elle a rejoint Erik van Egeraat lorsqu'il a constitué EEA en 1995 et ouvert une agence à Londres en 1998. En mars 2005, elle a rejoint Juliette Bekkering dans son agence devenue **BEKKERING ADAMS** architecten. Elles ont réalisé les appartements et bureaux municipaux de Maashaven OZ de Zuidpunt Offices, Feijenoord, Rotterdam (2004) et le poste d'incendie de Vlissingen, Middleburg (2004).

BOOSTER PUMP STATION EAST

Amsterdam East, The Netherlands, 2003–05

Floor area: 650 m². Client: DWR, Dienst Waterbeheer en Riolering.
Cost: €1.2 million

This facility houses three pumps intended to collect the sewage of Amsterdam East and to send it to a new central sewage purification plant in Amsterdam West. The site is relatively natural and near to a future harbor for yachts. The architects explain that "Since the main function of the building is to shelter and stop the sound of the pumps, the building could be treated as a sculpture. The program and the directions found in the site dictate the shape. A concrete skin is molded around the functional elements of the program. The volume cantilevers to accommodate the mezzanine for operating the pumps, it dents where the entry doors are located, and wraps around the heavy in- and outgoing pipes. The roof is treated like the fifth elevation, in order to make a truly all-round object. The distinct crystal-like shape of the building gives it an ever-changing appearance." Built in blue-green and marble pigmented concrete, the structure has a web-like bas-relief pattern wrapped around it and is sandblasted in the upper areas to create a "refined and filigree look." The 650 m² facility was completed in April 2005 and features external graphics (molded at the base of the structure) playing on the word "Booster" and night lighting fixtures placed in the cantilevers and "cannelures" in the concrete.

In der Anlage sind drei Pumpen untergebracht, die das Abwasser von Amsterdam-Ost sammeln und zu einem neuen, zentralen Klärwerk im Westen Amsterdams leiten sollen. Das Grundstück ist relativ ursprünglich; in seiner Nähe wird ein Jachthafen entstehen. Die Architektinnen erklären: »Da die wesentliche Funktion des Gebäudes darin besteht, die Pumpen vor der Witterung zu schützen und Geräuschemissionen zu verhindern, konnten wir es wie eine Skulptur behandeln. Das Programm und die Richtungen, die wir auf dem Grundstück vorfanden, diktierten seine Form. Eine Betonhülle wurde um die funktionalen Elemente herumgeformt: Um das Zwischengeschoss, von dem aus die Pumpen betrieben werden, aufzunehmen, kragt der Baukörper aus; wo die Eingangstüren liegen, ist er eingezogen, und die großen Zu- und Abwasserrohre werden von ihm umhüllt. Damit das Gebäude tatsächlich von allen Seiten einen objekthaften Charakter bekam, wurde das Dach als fünfte Ansicht behandelt. Durch die eigenständige, kristalline Form wirkt der Bau immer wieder anders.« Das Gebäude aus blaugrün marmoriertem Beton weist allseitig ein netzartiges, flaches Reliefmuster auf; in den oberen Bereichen wurde es sandgestrahlt, um eine »differenzierte und filigrane« Wirkung zu erzielen. 2005 wurde die 650 m² große Anlage fertig gestellt. Zusätzlich ist die Außenwand mit grafischen Elementen versehen die mit dem Wort »Booster« spielen. Im unteren Bereich erscheinen sie in der kannelurenartig gerillten Oberfläche als Reliefs. Nachts werden die Auskragungen durch die Beleuchtung in Szene gesetzt.

Cette installation abrite trois pompes de collecte des eaux usées d'Amsterdam-Est qui les expédie vers une nouvelle station de traitement à Amsterdam-Ouest. Le site relativement naturel se trouve à proximité d'un futur port de plaisance. Selon les architectes, « comme la principale fonction de ce bâtiment est d'abriter des pompes et de masquer leur nuisance sonore, il pouvait être traité comme une sculpture. Le programme et les orientations fournies par le terrain dictaient sa forme. Une peau de béton a été coulée autour des éléments fonctionnels. Le volume est en porte-à-faux pour recevoir une mezzanine destinée au poste de commande. Il s'incurve au niveau des portes d'entrée et se déploie autour des énormes tuyaux d'entrée et de sortie. Le toit est traité comme une cinquième façade afin de créer un objet visible sous toutes ses faces. La forme clairement cristalline du bâtiment lui confère un aspect perpétuellement changeant. » Construite en béton marbré bleu-vert teinté dans la masse, la structure est totalement recouverte d'un motif de lignes entrecroisées traité en bas-relief et sablée dans sa partie supérieure pour créer un « aspect raffiné et filigrané. » Cet édifice de 650 m² a été achevé en avril 2005. Il se signale par une ornementation typographique jouant sur le mot « Booster » et des éclairages nocturnes placés dans les porte-à-faux et les « cannelures » du béton.

Bekkering and Adams have used surface and form to maximum effect in designing this pumping station, showing that industrial facilities are not condemned to their usual drab or ugly appearance.

Beim Entwurf der Pumpstation gestalteten Bekkering und Adams die Oberfläche und Form des Gebäudes höchst effektvoll und zeigten so, dass industrielle Anlagen nicht unbedingt hässlich und düster sein müssen.

Bekkering et Adams ont exploité au maximum les possibilités de formes et de surfaces pour concevoir cette station de pompage prouvant que les installations industrielles ne sont pas toujours sinistres et laides.

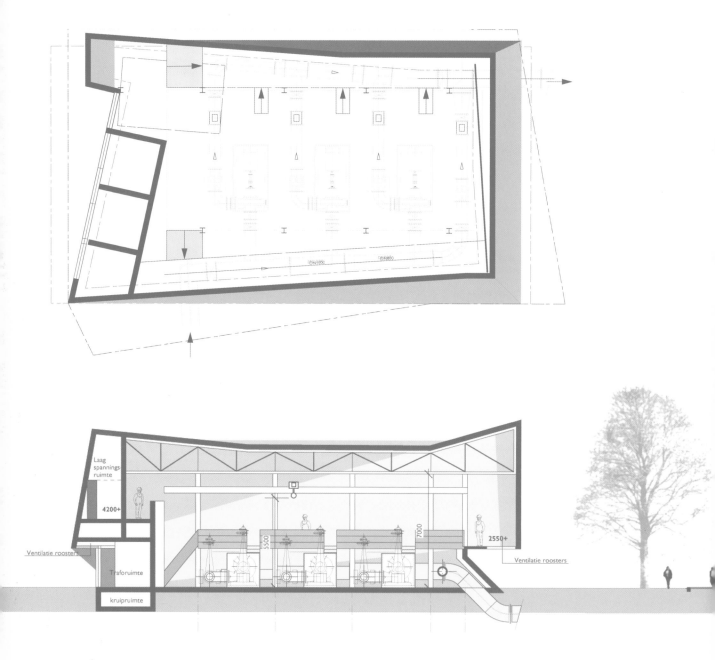

Laag
spannings
ruimte

4200+

Ventilatie roosters

Traforuimte

kruipruimte

5500

7000

2550+

Ventilatie roosters

Despite the unexpected appearance
of the pumping station, a plan and
section show that the structure easily
contains its functional elements without undue loss of space.

Grundriss und Schnitt machen deutlich: Trotz seines überraschenden
Äußeren nimmt das Gebäude die
funktionalen Elemente ohne Raum-
verlust problemlos auf.

Malgré son aspect inattendu, cette
structure accueille facilement ses
composantes fonctionnelles sans
perte de place, comme le montrent
le plan et la coupe.

CARAMEL

Caramel Architekten ZT GmbH
Katherl.Haller.Aspetsberger
Schottenfeldgasse 72/2/3
1070 Vienna
Austria

Tel: +43 15 96 34 90
Fax: +43 15 96 34 90 20
e-mail: kha@caramel.at
Web: www.caramel.at

House H ▶

CARAMEL was created in 2000 by Günter Katherl, born in 1965 in Vöcklabruck, Austria, Martin Haller, born in 1966 in Mittelberg, Vorarlberg, and Ulrich Aspetsberger, born in 1967 in Linz. Their most recent commissions have resulted from their successful participation in international competitions. In addition to the realization of three large-scale projects – Wifi in Dornbirn (an advanced training center); Transfusionsmedizin LKH-Salzburg hospital institute, and the Betriebsgebäude, Ansfelden (plant facility) – the trio also devotes themselves to design studies and unconventional single-family dwelling projects. Other areas of activity include lectures, teaching, and art projects, such as a remote-controlled "rain cloud" with which Caramel provided a "cool" surprise to visitors on the grounds of the Venice Architecture Biennale in 2004.

CARAMEL wurde 2000 von Günter Katherl, geboren 1965 in Vöcklabrück, Österreich, Martin Haller, geboren 1966 in Mittelberg, Vorarlberg, und Ulrich Aspetsberger, geboren 1967 in Linz, gegründet. Ihre neuesten Aufträge entwickelten sich aus ihrer erfolgreichen Teilnahme an internationalen Wettbewerben. Zusätzlich zu der Realisierung von drei großen Projekten – Wifi in Dornbirn (ein modernes Trainingszentrum), ein Krankenhausinstitut für Transfusionsmedizin für das LKH Salzburg und die Betriebswerkstätte in Ansfelden – arbeitet das Trio an Entwurfsstudien und unkonventionellen Einfamilienhausprojekten. Die Architekten halten außerdem Vorträge, unterrichten und beschäftigen sich mit Kunstprojekten, beispielsweise der ferngesteuerten »Regenwolke«, mit der Caramel 2004 den Besuchern der Architekturbiennale in Venedig eine »kühle« Überraschung bereitete.

L'agence **CARAMEL** a été fondée en 2000 par trois architectes autrichiens : Günter Katherl (né en 1965 à Vöcklabruck), Martin Haller (né en 1966 à Mittelberg) et Ulrich Aspetsberger (né en 1967 à Linz). Leurs succès à divers concours internationaux leur ont valu récemment un certain nombre de commandes. En dehors de trois projets à grande échelle – Wifi à Dornbin (un centre de formation avancée), l'Institut médical de transfusion de l'hôpital LKH-Salzbourg et une usine à Ansfelden – le trio se consacre à des recherches de design et des projets de maisons individuelles hors des sentiers battus. Leurs activités comprennent également des conférences, l'enseignement et des projets artistiques comme le *Nuage de pluie* télécommandé avec lequel ils ont surpris les visiteurs de la 9e Biennale d'architecture de Venise en 2004.

HOUSE H
Linz, Austria, 2002–04

Floor area: 249 m². Volume: 790 m³. Client: not disclosed.
Cost: €350 000

This 245 m² residence is located on an 820 m² site overlooking the city of Linz and the Alps in the distance. Built with reinforced concrete and a fine steel structure, the house is clad in "polyurethane foil which was sprayed on a layer of oriented strand board (OSB), creating a homogenous surface that extends to the roof, walls and the bottom of the 13.5-meter cantilevered living room. This cantilever protects the children's play area from the rain and sun. The house is entered on the west side of the middle floor that contains a foyer, the kitchen, and a children's playroom. A half story up, the floating, glazed living room offers a panoramic view to the south. The angled overhang of the living room is clearly the defining architectural gesture of the house. Above the kitchen, the architects created a small TV lounge and an office. The ground floor is set into a slope that opens to the garden. A master bedroom, three children's rooms and two bathrooms, a fitness area and a wine cellar make up this lower level. Caramel collaborated with interior designer Friedrich Stiper for this house, as they had on another project for the same client, a conversion for the Linz-based advertising company "Reklamebüro" completed in 2000. The garden design was the work of Doris Pühringer.

Das 245 m² große Einfamilienhaus mit Blick auf die Stadt Linz (und Fernblick auf die Alpen) steht auf einem 820 m² großen Grundstück. Es besteht aus Stahlbeton sowie einer filigranen Stahlkonstruktion und ist mit einer Schicht aus Polyurethan umhüllt, die auf OSB-Platten (Oriented Strand Board) gesprüht wurde. Diese homogene Oberfläche findet sich auch auf dem Dach, den Wänden und der Unterseite des 13,5 m weit auskragenden Wohnraums. Die Auskragung schützt den Spielbereich der Kinder vor Regen und Sonne. Man betritt das Haus auf der Westseite der mittleren Ebene, wo sich der Eingangsbereich, die Küche und ein Spielraum für die Kinder befinden. Ein halbes Geschoss darüber bietet der fließende, verglaste Wohnraum einen Panoramablick Richtung Süden. Ganz offensichtlich definiert die architektonische Geste des winkelförmig auskragenden Wohnraums das Haus. Über der Küche ordneten die Architekten eine kleine TV-Lounge und ein Büro an. Das Erdgeschoss ist in einen Hang hinein geschoben, der sich zum Garten hin öffnet. Auf dieser unteren Ebene liegen das Elternschlafzimmer, drei Kinderzimmer, zwei Badezimmer, ein Fitnessbereich und ein Weinkeller. Wie bei einem anderen Projekt für denselben Bauherrn (einem Umbau für die in Linz ansässige Werbeagentur »Reklamebüro«, der 2000 fertig gestellt wurde) arbeitete Caramel bei diesem Projekt mit dem Innenarchitekten Friedrich Stiper zusammen. Der Entwurf für den Garten stammt von Doris Pühringer.

Cette résidence de 245 m² est située sur un terrain de 820 m² dominant la ville de Linz et donnant, au loin, sur les Alpes. Elle est bâtie en béton armé sur une ossature en acier et habillée d'un film de polyuréthane projeté sur des panneaux d'OSB pour créer une surface homogène qui recouvre la toiture, les murs et la base d'un séjour de 13,5 m de long en porte-à-faux. Ce dernier protège la zone de jeux des enfants du soleil et de la pluie. On entre par le côté ouest de l'étage intermédiaire qui comprend le vestibule, la cuisine et la salle de jeux. Un demi-étage plus haut, le séjour vitré, comme suspendu, offre une vue panoramique plein sud. Son porte-à-faux incliné constitue le geste architectural majeur de la maison. Au-dessus de la cuisine ont été créés un petit salon de télévision et un bureau. Le rez-de-chaussée, découpé dans la pente et ouvrant sur le jardin, est réservé à la chambre de maîtres et à trois chambres d'enfants, deux salles de bains, une salle de gymnastique et un cellier. Caramel a collaboré avec l'architecte d'intérieur Friedrich Stiper avec lequel l'agence avait déjà travaillé sur un autre projet pour le même client, le réaménagement de l'agence de publicité Reklamebüro de Linz, achevé en 2000. Le jardin a été dessiné par Doris Pühringer.

With its spectacular cantilevered volume, House H has an unexpected sequence of strong cutaway shapes inside as well (below). Ample glazing around the cantilevered living space emphasizes an impression of lightness given by the house as seen from certain angles.

Der spektakulär auskragende Baukörper des Hauses H weist auch in seinem Inneren einige kräftige subtraktive Schnitte auf (unten). Die großzügige Verglasung des Wohnraums verstärkt den Eindruck der Leichtigkeit, den das Haus aus verschiedenen Blickwinkeln bietet.

Dans son porte-à-faux spectaculaire, la maison H présente une séquence inattendue de formes découpées aussi bien à l'intérieur qu'au-dessous. Sous certains angles, les vastes ouvertures vitrées autour du séjour renforcent l'impression de légèreté.

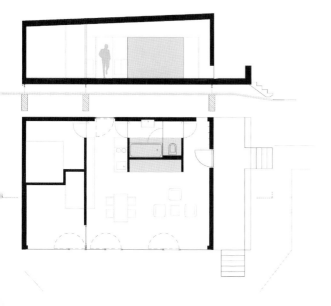

CASEY BROWN

Casey Brown Architecture
Level 1/ 63 William Street
NSW 2010 East Sydney
Australia

Tel: +61 293 60 79 77
Fax: +61 293 60 21 23
e-mail: cba@caseybrown.com.au
Web: www.caseybrown.com.au

James-Robertson House ▶

Robert Brown received his degrees in architecture from the University of New South Wales (1976 and 1979) and from Columbia University Graduate School of Architecture in New York (1992–93). He worked with Fisher Lucas Architects in Sydney (1976), Julian Harap Architects in London (1983) and with the Heritage Council NSW (1984–86) before creating Dawson Brown Partnership (1986–89), Dawson Brown + Ackert Architecture (1989–92) and Dawson Brown Architecture (1993–2004). In 2004, he created the firm **CASEY BROWN** with partner Caroline Casey. The James-Robertson House published here won a 2004 Residential Architecture Award from the Royal Australian Institute of Architects (NSW Chapter). Recent projects include the Sastrugi Ski Lodge, Thredbo (2000); Graigee Lee House, Palm Beach, Sydney (2001); Bungan Beach House, Bungan Beach, Sydney (2003). Current projects include: Djikul 5 Star boutique Hotel, Palm Cove, Queensland; Cliff House, Coogee, Sydney; Whale Beach House, Whale Beach, Sydney.

Robert Brown studierte an der University of New South Wales Architektur (Abschlüsse 1976 und 1979) und später an der Columbia University Graduate School of Architecture in New York (1992–93). 1976 arbeitete er in Sydney bei Lucas Architects, 1983 bei Julian Harap Architects in London und 1984 bis 1986 beim Heritage Council von New South Wales. Anschließend gründete er Dawson Brown Partnership (1986–89), später Dawson Brown + Ackert Architecture (1989–92) und Dawson Brown Architecture (1993–2004). Zusammen mit Caroline Casey eröffnete Brown 2004 **CASEY BROWN**. Das hier gezeigte James-Robertson House gewann 2004 einen Preis des Royal Australian Institute of Architects (Verband New South Wales) in der Kategorie Wohnbauten. Zu seinen neueren Projekten gehören die Sastrugi Ski Lodge in Thredbo (2003), das Graigee Lee House in Palm Beach, Sydney (2001), und das Bungan Beach House in Bungan Beach, Sydney (2003). Neueste Projekte sind u. a. das kleine und exklusive Djikul 5 Star Hotel in Palm Cove, Queensland, das Cliff House in Coogee, Sydney, und das Whale Beach House in Whale Beach, Sydney.

Robert Brown est diplômé en architecture de l'Université de Nouvelle-Galles du Sud (1976 et 1979) et de la Graduate School of Architecture de Columbia University à New York (1992–93). Il a travaillé pour Fisher Lucas Architects à Sydney (1976), Julian Harap Architects à Londres (1983) et le Heritage Council NSW (1984–86) avant de fonder Dawson Brown Partnership (1986–89), Dawson Brown + Ackert Architecture (1989–92) et Dawson Brown Architecture (1993–2004). En 2004, il a créé l'agence **CASEY BROWN** avec sa partenaire Caroline Casey. La James-Robertson House présentée ici a remporté le prix de l'Architecture résidentielle 2004 du Royal Australian Institute of Architects (pour la Nouvelle-Galles du Sud). Parmi ses récents projets : la Sastrugi Ski Lodge, Thredbo (2000) ; la maison Graigee Lee, Palm Beach, Sydney (2001) ; la maison de plage de Bungan, Bungan, Sydney (2003). Il travaille actuellement au « boutique-hôtel » 5 étoiles Djikul (Palm Cove, Queensland), et sur deux maisons à Sydney, Cliff House et Whale Beach House.

JAMES-ROBERTSON HOUSE

Great Mackerel Beach, New South Wales, Australia, 2001–03

Floor area: 183 m². Client: Marcia and Dougal James-Robertson.
Cost: €1.26 million

Although Great Mackerel Beach is located relatively close to the city of Sydney, it can only be acceded to by ferry, which means that its fifty houses are very secluded. The architect Robert Brown and his family spend time there, as do Marcia and Dougal James-Robertson, his clients for this residence. The black-painted exposed steel frame pavilions are anchored in the rock and set on a massive sandstone retaining wall. Largely glazed, the sidewalls and roofs are covered in corrugated copper. They are set on a massive, irregular wall of sandstone blocks, carved by hand from the cliff-side site. The lower double pavilion contains guest bedrooms with a kitchen and dining and living area on the top floor. The upper pavilion contains the owner's private area. The interior design work was done by Robert Brown's partner Caroline Casey, and includes a silver ash dining table four meters long and 60 mm thick. The site area is 720 m² and the house has a floor area of 183 m².

Great Mackerel Beach befindet sich relativ nah bei Sydney, ist aber nur mit der Fähre zu erreichen. Die 50 Häuser, die es dort gibt, liegen daher sehr für sich. Wie die Bauherren Marcia und Dougal James-Robertson verbringen der Architekt Robert Brown und seine Familie hier oft ihre Zeit. Die Pavillons mit einer schwarz gestrichenen, sichtbaren Stahlkonstruktion sind im Felsboden verankert und stehen auf einer massiven Stützmauer aus Sandstein. Die Dächer und die seitlichen, großflächig verglasten Wände sind mit gewelltem Kupferblech verkleidet. Den Sockel der Pavillonbauten bildet eine schwere, unregelmäßige Wand aus Sandsteinblöcken; diese wurden aus der Felsküste auf dem Grundstück in Handarbeit herausgeschnitten. Im tiefer gelegenen zweigeschossigen Pavillon befinden sich auf der unteren Ebene Schlafräume für Gäste, darüber eine Küche, Ess- und Wohnraum. Der obere Pavillon ist dem Besitzer vorbehalten. Die Innenräume wurden von Robert Browns Partnerin Caroline Casey gestaltet: Dazu gehört ein 4 m langer Esstisch aus Silberesche mit einer 60 mm dicken Tischplatte. Das Grundstück ist 720 m² groß, die Gesamtfläche des Hauses beträgt 183 m².

Bien que Great Mackerel Beach soit relativement proche de Sydney, on ne peut y accéder que par un ferry, ce qui explique le calme dont jouissent ses cinquante maisons. L'architecte Robert Brown et sa famille y séjournent, ainsi que Marcia et Dougal James-Robertson, ses clients. Les pavillons à ossature en acier peint en noir, ancrés dans la roche, semblent posés sur un mur de soutènement en grès massif. Ils sont largement vitrés et leurs murs latéraux, ainsi que leurs toits, sont habillés de cuivre ondulé. Le double pavillon inférieur regroupe les chambres d'invités, une cuisine ainsi qu'une zone de repas et de séjour à l'étage. Le pavillon supérieur contient la suite du propriétaire. L'aménagement intérieur a été exécuté par l'associée de Robert Brown, Caroline Casey, et comprend une table de repas en hêtre cendré de 4 m de long et 6 cm d'épaisseur. La surface du terrain est de 720 m², celle de la maison de 183 m².

The James-Robertson House is dug into a steep site whose vegetation has been protected, accentuating the contrast between nature and the light and airy openness of the architecture.

Das James-Robertson House steht auf einem steil abfallenden Grundstück. Die Vegetation konnte erhalten werden, wodurch der Kontrast zwischen der Natur und der leichten, luftigen Offenheit der Architektur betont wird.

La maison James-Robertson est nichée dans une pente abrupte dont la végétation a été préservée, ce qui accentue le contraste entre la nature luxuriante et la légèreté aérienne de l'architecture.

The upper volume containing the owner's space is visible in the image to the far right, with the guest pavilions below. Floor-to-ceiling glazing allows unobstructed views of the remarkable natural setting.

Ganz rechts: Der obere Baukörper enthält die Räume des Bauherrn; darunter liegen die Pavillons für die Gäste. Geschosshohe Fenster gewähren unverstellte Ausblicke auf die einzigartige Umgebung.

Le volume du haut contient l'appartement du propriétaire, visible à l'extrême droite. Les pavillons des invités sont situés en dessous. Le vitrage intégral offre une vue totalement dégagée sur le remarquable cadre naturel.

The lower, double volume, with the dining area, also seen on the right hand page and on the previous page. Although its lines are clean and direct, the architecture offers an unexpected flow of spaces from one area to the next, and out toward the water.

Der untere Zwillingsbaukörper mit dem Essbereich (zu sehen ebenfalls auf der rechten und auf der vorher-gehenden Seite): Die Linienführung der Architektur ist sauber und direkt und bietet überraschend fließende Räume zwischen den verschiedenen Bereichen und zum Ozean.

Le double volume inférieur comprend la zone des repas (page de droite et page précédente). Grâce à ses lignes nettes et directes, l'architecture crée un étonnant flux spatial d'une zone à l'autre, ainsi que vers l'extérieur et l'océan.

The black, exposed steel frame of the house contrasts with the corrugated copper used for the roofs in these images. Above, a rear entrance path made of wood with natural rocks accentuates the Japanese feeling evident in some aspects of the house.

Die sichtbare schwarze Stahlkonstruktion kontrastiert mit den Dächern aus gewelltem Kupferblech. Oben: Ein hölzerner Weg führt zu einem hangseits liegenden Eingang. Das Holz in Verbindung mit dem natürlichen Felsgestein unterstreicht die japanisch anmutende Atmosphäre, die in einigen Bereichen des Hauses zu spüren ist.

L'ossature apparente en acier peint en noir contraste avec le cuivre ondulé utilisé en toiture. Ci-dessus, le cheminement en bois flanqué de rochers naturels qui conduit à l'entrée arrière accentue l'esprit japonisant évident de certains aspects de la maison.

DAVID CHIPPERFIELD

David Chipperfield Architects
1A Cobham Mews, Agar Grove
London NW1 9SB
UK

Tel: +44 20 72 67 94 22
Fax: +44 20 72 67 93 47
e-mail: info@davidchipperfield.co.uk
Web: www.davidchipperfield.co.uk

Teruel Urban Development ▶

Born in London in 1953, **DAVID CHIPPERFIELD** obtained his Diploma in Architecture from the Architectural Association (AA, London, 1978). He worked in the offices of Norman Foster and Richard Rogers, before establishing David Chipperfield Architects (London, 1984). Built work includes: Arnolfini Arts Center (Bristol, 1987); Design Store (Kyoto, 1989); Matsumoto Headquarters Building (Okayama, Japan, 1990); Plant Gallery and Central Hall of the Natural History Museum (London, 1993); Wagamama Restaurant (London, 1996); River & Rowing Museum (Henley-on-Thames, 1996). His recent and current work includes: Landeszentralbank (Gera, Germany); Housing (Berlin Spandau); Office building (Dusseldorf); reconstruction of the Neues Museum (Berlin, 2000–09); the Ansaldo City of Cultures (Milan, 2000–07); Figge Art Museum (Davenport, Iowa, 2000–05); the San Michele Cemetery (Venice, Italy, 1998–2013); and the design of numerous Dolce & Gabbana shops beginning in 1999.

Der 1953 in London geborene **DAVID CHIPPERFIELD** erhielt 1978 sein Architekturdiplom von der Architectural Asociation (AA) in London. Ehe er 1984 David Chipperfield Architects in London eröffnete, arbeitete er in den Büros von Norman Foster und Richard Rogers. Realisierte Projekte von Chipperfield sind u. a.: Arnolfini Arts Center, Bristol (1987), Design Store, Kioto (1989), Matsumoto Headquarters Building, Okayama (1990), Plant Gallery und Central Hall des Natural History Museum, London (1993), Wagamama Restaurant, London (1996), und das River & Rowing Museum in Henley-on-Thames (1996). Zu seinen jüngsten oder noch im Bau befindlichen Projekten zählen: die Landeszentralbank in Gera (1994–2001), Wohnungsbau in Berlin-Spandau, ein Bürogebäude in Düsseldorf, die Rekonstruktion des Neuen Museums auf der Museumsinsel in Berlin (2000–09), Ansaldo City of Cultures, Mailand (2000–07), Figge Art Museum in Davenport, Iowa (2000–05), die Erweiterung des Friedhofs San Michele in Venedig (1998–2013) sowie seit 1999 die Gestaltung zahlreicher Läden für Dolce & Gabbana.

Né à Londres en 1953, **DAVID CHIPPERFIELD** est diplômé de l'Architectural Association (1978). Il a travaillé dans les agences de Norman Foster et Richard Rogers avant de créer David Chipperfield Architects à Londres en 1984. Parmi ses réalisations : Arnolfini Arts Center, Bristol (1987) ; Design Store, Kyoto (1989) ; immeuble du siège de Matsumoto, Okayama, Japon (1990) ; la galerie des Plantes et le hall central du Natural History Museum, Londres (1993) ; Wagamama Restaurant, Londres (1996) ; River and Rowing Museum, Henley-on-Thames (1996). Ses travaux récents et en cours de chantier comprennent : la Landeszentralbank (Gera, Allemagne) ; un immeuble de logements (Berlin Spandau) ; un immeuble de bureaux (Düsseldorf) ; la reconstruction du Neues Museum, Berlin (2000–09) ; la Cité des cultures Ansaldo, Milan (2000–07) ; le Figge Art Museum, Davenport, Iowa, États-Unis (2000–05) ; le cimetière de San Michele, Venise (1998–2013) et la conception de nombreuses boutiques Dolce & Gabbana depuis 1999.

TERUEL URBAN DEVELOPMENT

Teruel, Spain, 2001–2003

Floor area: 7215 m². Client: Diputación General de Aragon.
Cost: €5.8 million

The Mudejar architecture of Teruel, built by Moorish craftsmen under Christian rule, was inscribed on the UNESCO World Heritage list in 1986. This is an indication of how delicate any contemporary intervention in such a location must be. The city, located about an hour and half from Valencia, has a population of 32 000 persons. As the architects explain it, "The project consists of reforming the access from the railway station to the Paseo del Ovalo, an historic promenade built on the site of the city walls. This promenade is one of the many sensitive monuments in this world heritage city. The immediate environment leading to the promenade has been improved with the addition of planting, street furniture and upgrading the quality of finishes and providing additional lighting." Carried out in association with the firm b720 Arquitectura, the project covers a total area of 7215 m². The contract value given by the architects is 5.8 million euros. A tall cavity inserted by the architects into the city wall leads to a lobby with a top-lit glazed elevator shaft. The elevator goes up 25 meters to the old town and a new square. The project was awarded the 2004 European Prize for Urban Public Space given jointly by the Centre de Culture Contemporània de Barcelona (CCCB), the Architekturzentrum Wien (AzW), the Institut Français d'Architecture (IFA), the Netherlands Architecture Institute (NAI) and The Architecture Foundation.

Die von maurischen Handwerkern unter christlicher Herrschaft geschaffene Mudéjar-Architektur im spanischen Teruel wurde 1986 von der UNESCO zum Weltkulturerbe erklärt. Jeder Eingriff an diesem Ort muss also mit der entsprechenden Sensibilität vorgenommen werden. In Teruel, das von Valencia in etwa 1,5 Stunden mit dem Auto zu erreichen ist, leben etwa 32 000 Menschen. Die Architekten erklären: »Das Projekt wird von der Neuformulierung des Zugangs vom Bahnhof zum Paseo del Ovalo bestimmt, einer historischen Promenade an der einstigen Stadtmauer. Diese Promenade ist eins von vielen Denkmälern in der Weltkulturerbestadt. Die direkte Umgebung, die zur Promenade hinleitet, wurde durch Anpflanzungen, Straßenmöbel, verbesserte Oberflächen und eine zusätzliche Beleuchtung aufgewertet.« Das Projekt, das in Partnerschaft mit dem Büro b720 Arquitectura ausgeführt wurde, hat eine Gesamtfläche von 7215 m²; die Baukosten werden von den Architekten mit umgerechnet 5,8 Millionen Euro angegeben. In einem hohen Hohlraum, der in die Stadtmauer eingelassen wurde, führt ein von oben belichteter, verglaster Aufzug zu einem »Stadtfoyer«. Dieser Aufzug, der einen Höhenunterschied von 25 m überwindet, verbindet die Altstadt mit einem neuen Platz. 2004 erhielt das Projekt den Europäischen Preis für öffentlichen Raum, der zusammen vom Centre de Culture Contemporània de Barcelona (CCCB), dem Architekturzentrum Wien (AzW), dem Institut Français d'Architecture (IFA), dem Niederländischen Architekturzentrum (NAI) und The Architecture Foundation vergeben wurde.

Les constructions de style mudejar de Teruel, édifiées par des artisans maures pour des catholiques, sont inscrites au Patrimoine mondial de l'Humanité par l'Unesco depuis 1986, ce qui laisse imaginer la difficulté de toute intervention contemporaine dans un site aussi protégé. La ville, située à une heure et demie de Valence, compte 32 000 habitants. Comme l'explique l'architecte, « il s'agissait de transformer l'accès, depuis la gare, au Paseo del Ovalo, promenade historique aménagée sur les anciens murs d'enceinte de la ville. Elle figure parmi les monuments particulièrement sensibles de cette cité du Patrimoine mondial. Ses abords immédiats ont été améliorés par des plantations, un nouveau mobilier urbain, des finitions de qualité et un meilleur éclairage public ». Réalisé en association avec l'agence b720 Arquitectura, le projet couvre une aire totale de 7215 m² pour un budget de 5,8 millions d'euros. Une étroite cavité aménagée par les architectes dans les remparts ouvre sur un hall abritant un ascenseur au toit vitré. La cabine mène, vingt-cinq mètres plus haut, à la vieille ville et à une nouvelle place. Le projet a reçu en 2004 le Prix européen pour les espaces publics urbains, attribué conjointement par le Centre de culture contemporaine de Barcelone (CCCB), l'Architekturzentrum de Vienne (AzW) l'Institut français d'architecture (IFA) l'Institut d'architecture néerlandais (NAI) et The Architecture Foundation.

Chipperfield masters a minimalist series of pathways and openings that succeed in bringing modernity to an ancient setting without interfering with the very spirit of the place.

Chipperfield schafft eine minimalistische Abfolge von Wegen und Öffnungen, mit der er Modernität an diesen historischen Ort bringt, ohne dessen Aura zu zerstören.

Chipperfield a parfaitement maîtrisé la succession d'ouvertures et de passages qui réussit à moderniser le cadre ancien sans interférer avec l'esprit du lieu.

With its strong angled surfaces, Chipperfield's entrance volumes might bring to mind the sculptures of a Richard Serra.

Die mächtigen, gefalteten Flächen des Eingangsbaukörpers erinnern an Skulpturen von Richard Serra.

Les volumes de l'entrée aux plans fortement inclinés font penser aux sculptures de Richard Serra.

HOUSE IN GALICIA

Corrubedo, Galicia, Spain, 1996–2002

Floor area: 210 m². Client: Dr. Evelyn Stern.
Cost: not disclosed

This 210 m² private house was designed by David Chipperfield for a site on the main street of a small fishing village, located on Spain's northwestern Atlantic coast. Contrary to other houses built along the harbor, this residence seeks to make the most of the views available here. As the architect describes the project, "From the sea, the collection of individual and apparently random buildings in Corrubedo form a kind of village elevation – a thin ribbon of buildings that although made up of houses of varying heights and geometries, still presents itself as a unified and solid arrangement. The introduction of a new house with different priorities had to take into consideration its place within this wall. Looking to provide a sense of continuity, the house sits on a solid stone and concrete base, and its upper mass, like the neighboring houses, is punctured by small windows. Placed like a shelf between these two conditions, a large panoramic window, extending the full width of the house, provides all-encompassing views across the beach and harbor." With a stone base reflecting the rocks on the beach, the house assumes a whiter appearance and a more angled geometry as it rises. The architect succeeds both in integrating the house into what appears to be a hodgepodge of different structures along the harbor and at the same time in creating an obviously new and exciting form.

An der Atlantikküste im Nordwesten Spaniens befindet sich an der Hauptstraße des kleinen Fischerdorfes Corrubedo das Grundstück, für das David Chipperfield dieses 210 m² große Einfamilienhaus entwarf. Im Gegensatz zu anderen Häusern am Hafen versucht dieses Haus, aus der Aussicht, die sich hier bietet, das Beste zu machen. Der Architekt: »Vom Meer aus bildet die Ansammlung von unterschiedlichen und offenkundig zufälligen Gebäuden eine Art Dorfansicht – ein dünnes Häuserband, das sich, obwohl es aus Häusern verschiedener Höhe und Geometrien besteht, trotzdem als einheitliches und solides Arrangement darstellt. Bei der Einfügung eines neuen Hauses mit anderen Vorgaben musste der Platz, den es in dieser ›Wand‹ einnimmt, berücksichtigt werden. Um das Gefühl der Kontinuität aufrecht zu erhalten, hat das Haus eine feste Basis aus Stein und Beton; der obere Bereich ist, wie bei den Nachbarhäusern, durch kleine Fenster durchbrochen. Zwischen diesen beiden unterschiedlichen Bereichen ist – wie ein Regalfach – ein großes Panoramafenster eingeschoben, das die volle Breite des Hauses einnimmt und Weitwinkelausblicke über den Strand und den Hafen bietet.« Der Steinsockel nimmt Bezug auf die Felsen am Strand; weiter oben wird das Haus weiß und bekommt eine komplexere Geometrie. Dem Architekten ist es gelungen, das Haus sowohl in seinen Kontext zu integrieren, der als ein Durcheinander von verschiedenen Baukörpern am Hafen erscheint, als auch eine eindeutig neue und inspirierte Form zu schaffen.

Cette résidence privée de 210 m² a été conçue par David Chipperfield pour une parcelle située dans la rue principale d'un petit village de pêcheurs sur la côte atlantique, au nord-ouest de l'Espagne. L'architecte décrit ainsi son projet : « Vu de la mer, cet agglomérat de bâtiments disposés apparemment au hasard forme une sorte de rempart du village, un mince ruban de constructions qui, bien que constitué de maisons de hauteurs et de formes diverses, se présente comme un tout solidaire et massif. Y introduire une nouvelle maison aux priorités différentes impliquait de lui attribuer sa place dans ce ‹mur›. Afin de participer à cette continuité, la maison repose sur une base pleine en pierre et béton et sa partie supérieure, comme celle des maisons voisines, est percée de petites fenêtres. Insérée comme une étagère entre ces deux parties, une vaste fenêtre panoramique se déploie sur toute la largeur de la maison, offrant une vue panoramique sur la plage et le port. » Sur sa base de pierre qui rappelle les rochers du littoral, la maison développe un aspect plus léger et lumineux et une géométrie plus anguleuse en s'élevant. L'architecte a réussi à intégrer sa réalisation dans ce méli-mélo de constructions bordant le port tout en créant une forme stimulante, résolument moderne.

While fitting into the wall-like sequence of existing houses, the architect nonetheless fundamentally challenges the established order, with his large openings contrasting with the more closed façades of neighboring buildings.

Chipperfield passt das Haus in die wandartige Sequenz der bestehenden Häuser ein; gleichzeitig stellt er die vorhandene Ordnung in Frage, indem er große Öffnungen vorsieht, die mit den geschlosseneren Fassaden der Nachbargebäude kontrastieren.

Même s'il respecte le rythme de l'alignement de maisons existantes, l'architecte défie cet ordre établi par de grandes ouvertures qui contrastent avec les façades fermées des constructions anciennes.

White simplicity is the ruling esthetic idea here, with ample views toward the ocean. Equally austere furniture emphasizes the view as opposed to drawing attention to the architecture.

Weiße Einfachheit und weite Ausblicke auf den Atlantik bestimmen die Ästhetik. Auch die zurückhaltende Möblierung betont den Ausblick, nicht die Architektur.

Ici, le parti pris esthétique est celui de la simplicité et de la blancheur immaculée. Le mobilier, tout aussi austère, met en valeur la vue sur l'océan au lieu d'attirer l'attention sur l'architecture.

Panoramic openings almost give the impression that the architect has framed the view in a cinematographic mode, and yet this is not video art, it is the juxtaposition of smooth whiteness and nature's variety.

Panoramafenster vermitteln fast den Eindruck, als hätte der Architekt den Ausblick in filmischer Weise gerahmt. Allerdings geht es hier nicht um Videokunst, sondern um die Gegenüberstellung eines eleganten weißen Baukörpers mit der sich ständig verändernden Natur.

Les ouvertures panoramiques donneraient presque l'impression que l'architecte a voulu cadrer le paysage de façon cinématographique. Ce n'est pas pour autant de l'art vidéo, mais la simple juxtaposition de la variété de la nature et de la délicate blancheur de l'architecture.

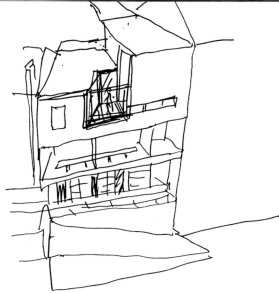

A night view shows the contrast between the ample openings in Chipperfield's house and the more closed facades nearby. To the left, a sketch by Chipperfield shows the form of the house.

Die Nachtansicht verdeutlicht den Kontrast zwischen den großen Öffnungen des Chipperfield-Hauses und den geschlosseneren Fassaden der Nachbargebäude. Links: Eine Skizze von Chipperfield zeigt die Form des Hauses.

Vue de nuit montrant le contraste entre les amples ouvertures de la maison de Chipperfield et celles, beaucoup plus réduites, de ses voisines. À gauche, un croquis de l'architecte.

COX RICHARDSON

Cox Richardson Architects & Planners
Level 2, 204 Clarence Street
Sydney NSW 2000
PO Box Q193 NSW 1230
Australia

Tel: +61 292 67 95 99
Fax: +61 292 64 58 44
e-mail: sydney@cox.com.au
Web: www.cox.com.au

PHILIP COX graduated from Sydney University in architecture in 1962. He was a Royal Australian Institute of Architects (RAIA) silver medalist and was awarded the NSW Board of Architects Traveling Scholarship. He graduated from Sydney University with a diploma in Town & Country Planning in 1972. From 1963 to 1967, Philip Cox worked with Ian McKay. The Cox Group was created in Sydney in 1967 as Philip Cox & Partners. The firm now has offices in Sydney, Perth, Brisbane, Melbourne and Canberra as well as in Beijing and Dubai, and they currently employ 250 persons in Australia. Philip Cox has received numerous awards in recognition of his contribution to architecture, including the RAIA Gold Medal in 1984. He is a Professor of Architecture at the University of NSW, a member of International Advisory Committee for the National University of Singapore and member of the International Advisory to the Urban Redevelopment Authority of Singapore. Major projects include: Yulara Tourist Resort, Central Australia (1984); Sydney Football Stadium, Moore Park, NSW (1988); National Tennis Center, Melbourne, VIC (1988); Sydney Exhibition Center, Darling Harbor, NSW (1988); Sydney International Aquatic Centre, Homebush Bay, NSW (1994); Star City, Pyrmont, Sydney, NSW (1997); Singapore Expo, Singapore (1999); and the Sydney SuperDome and Car Park, Homebush Bay, NSW (1999). Current work includes the Qingdao Beijing Olympics Sailing Facility.

PHILIP COX machte 1962 an der Sydney University seinen Architekturabschluss. Vom Royal Australian Institute of Architects (RAIA) wurde er mit einer Silbermedaille ausgezeichnet, und die Architektenkammer von New South Wales verlieh ihm ein Reisestipendium. 1972 erwarb er, ebenfalls an der Sydney University, einen Abschluss in Stadt- und Regionalplanung. Von 1963 bis 1967 arbeitete Philip Cox bei Ian McKay. The Cox Group wurde 1967 unter dem Namen Philip Cox & Partners in Sydney gegründet. Das Büro unterhält Zweigstellen in Sydney, Perth, Brisbane, Melbourne und Canberra, außerdem in Peking und Dubai. In Australien beschäftigt es zurzeit 250 Mitarbeiter. Philip Cox' Beitrag zur Architektur wurde durch eine Vielzahl von Auszeichnungen gewürdigt, z. B. 1984 mit der RAIA Goldmedaille. Er ist Professor für Architektur an der University of New South Wales, Mitglied des Internationalen Beratergremiums der National University of Singapore und Mitglied des Internationalen Beratungsgremiums des Amts für Stadterneuerung in Singapur. Zu seinen Großbauten gehören das Yulara Tourist Resort in Zentralaustralien (1984), das Sydney Football Stadion in Moore Park (1988), das National Tennis Center in Melbourne (1988), das Sydney Exhibition Center in Darling Harbor (1988), das Sydney International Aquatic Center in Homebush Bay (1994), Star City in Pyrmont, Sydney (1997), ferner die Singapore Expo in Singapur (1999) und der Sydney SuperDome und Car Park in Homebush Bay (1999). Die Olympischen Sportstätten der Segler in Qingdao, Peking, sind derzeit im Bau.

PHILIP COX est diplômé en architecture (1962) urbanisme et aménagement rural (1972) de l'Université de Sydney. Il a reçu une bourse de voyage du New South Wales Board of Architects et la médaille d'argent du Royal Australian Institute of Architects (RAIA). De 1963 à 1967, il a travaillé avec Ian McKay, puis a créé à Sydney, en 1967, Philip Cox & Partners, qui s'est développé à l'échelle nationale et internationale pour devenir ensuite le Cox Group : l'agence, qui emploie 250 personnes en Australie, possède aujourd'hui des bureaux à Sydney, Perth, Brisbane, Melbourne, Canberra, comme à Pékin et Dubaï. Philip Cox a reçu de nombreuses récompenses pour ses contributions à l'architecture dont la Médaille d'or du RAIA en 1984. Il est professeur d'architecture de l'Université de Nouvelle-Galles du Sud et membre du Comité consultatif international pour l'Urban Redevelopment Authority de Singapour. Parmi ses réalisations majeures : Yulara Tourist Resort, Territoire-du-Nord (1984) ; le stade de football de Sydney, Moore Park (1988) ; le Centre national du tennis, Melbourne (1988) ; le Centre d'expositions de Sydney, Darling Harbor (1988) ; le Centre aquatique international de Sydney, Homebush Bay (1994) ; Star City, Pyrmont, Sydney (1997) ; Singapore Expo, Singapour (1999), le Superdome de Sydney, Homebush Bay (1999). Il réalise actuellement les équipements pour les compétitions de voile des Jeux olympiques de Pékin.

LONGITUDE 131°

Yulara, Northern Territory, Australia, 2002

Area: 15 tents, each 40 m²; central facility: 500 m² on two floors. Client: Voyages Resorts & Hotels.
Cost: €3.15 million

The fifteen tents of the facility are stretched in a wide arc in the vast emptiness surrounding Ayers Rock, visible above right.

Die 15 »Hotelzelte« sind in der riesigen Leere, die Ayers Rock umgibt, entlang einer geschwungenen Linie angeordnet (oben rechts).

Les quinze « tentes » de l'hôtel dessinent un arc dans le désert d'Ayers Rock (en haut à droite).

This "self-contained boutique hotel" with fifteen rooms is located just two kilometers from the Kata Tjuta National Park and within view of Ayers Rock. It is an extension to the 200-hectare Yulara Tourist Resort, completed by Philip Cox in 1984. Located south-west of the city of Alice Springs, the Park is the heart of the Aboriginal land of Australia, and contains two world-renowned natural monuments – Ayers Rock, also known as *Uluru*, a mass of arkosic sandstone that rises 348 meters out of the desert floor, considered to be sacred ground by the Aborigines, and *Kata Tjuta*, also known as *The Olgas*, a group of thirty rounded red domes as high as 546 meters. With summer temperatures rising above 40° and dune flora and fauna to protect, the hotel is raised up on steel piles, and roofed in three layers of fabric. The architects explain, "The rooms are a simple box plan, with sliding panels that open half the façade and fully glazed south-facing walls making the most of the expansive view. The walls diverge slightly to open the view still further."

Das »selbstständig funktionierende Boutique-Hotel« mit 15 Räumen ist nur 2 km vom Kata Tjuta National Park entfernt und liegt in Sichtweite von Ayers Rock. Es bildet die Erweiterung des 200 ha großen, ebenfalls von Philip Cox geplanten Yulara Tourist Resort, das 1984 fertig gestellt wurde. Der südwestlich von Alice Springs gelegene Park ist das Herz des von den Aborigines bewohnten Gebietes und bietet zwei weltweit bekannte Naturdenkmäler – Ayers Rock, auch *Uluru* genannt, ein massiver Felsen aus Sandstein, der 348 m aus der ebenen Wüste emporragt und von den Ureinwohnern als heiliger Ort angesehen wird, und *Kata Tjuta*, auch bezeichnet als *The Olgas*, eine Gruppe von 30 gerundeten, roten, bis zu 546 m hohen Felsen. Wegen der Temperaturen, die im Sommer auf über 40° Celsius steigen, und um die Dünenfauna und -flora zu schützen, steht das Hotel auf Stahlstützen und hat ein dreilagiges Dach aus Stoff. Die Architekten erläutern: »Die Räume haben einen einfachen Rechteckgrundriss. Mit Schiebeelementen kann die Hälfte der Fassade geöffnet werden; die vollständig verglaste Fassade nach Süden nutzt den weiten Ausblick optimal aus. Um den Ausblick noch weiter zu vergrößern, sind die Wände leicht gegeneinander verschoben.«

Ce «boutique hotel autarcique» de quinze chambres se trouve à deux kilomètres à peine du parc national d'Uluru-Kata Tjuta, en vue d'Ayers Rock. C'est une extension du Yulara Tourist Resort de 200 hectares achevé par Cox en 1984. Au sud-ouest d'Alice Springs, le parc se trouve au cœur du pays aborigène et contient deux monuments naturels célèbres dans le monde entier, Ayers Rock, également appelé Uluru, monolithe de grès rouge dominant le désert de ses 348 m et considéré comme un territoire sacré par les Aborigènes, et Kata Tjuta (ou les monts Olgas), groupe de trente rochers arrondis rouges dont l'altitude s'élève jusqu'à 546 m. Parce que les températures grimpent à plus de 40° en été et que la flore et la faune spécifiques des dunes doivent être protégées, l'hôtel est posé sur des pilotis d'acier et sa toiture est constituée de trois couches de toile. L'architecte explique que «les chambres sont dessinées sur le plan d'une simple boîte, avec des panneaux coulissants qui ouvrent la moitié de la façade, entièrement vitrée vers le sud pour bénéficier au maximum de la vue. Les murs s'écartent légèrement pour amplifier encore la vision panoramique».

The central facility of Longtitude 131 is more than ten times larger than the guest tents, and yet it assumes a similar architectural vocabulary. The whole sits lightly on the land.

Das Hauptgebäude von Longtitude 131° ist mehr als zehnmal so groß wie ein Hotelzelt, zeigt jedoch ein ähnliches architektonisches Vokabular. Die gesamte Anlage wird durch Leichtigkeit gekennzeichnet.

Le bâtiment central de Longitude 131 (ci-dessous) est plus de dix fois plus grand que les pavillons des hôtes, tout en reprenant le même vocabulaire architectural. L'ensemble est délicatement posé sur le sol du désert.

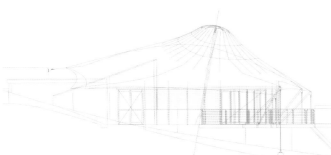

With their stretched canopies offering some protection from the difficult climate, the tents are glazed and lifted above the earth. To the left, a section of the central building.

Die aufgespannten Vordächer bieten etwas Schutz vor dem Wüstenklima. Die »Zelte« sind aufgeständert und an einer Seite verglast; links ein Schnitt durch das Hauptgebäude.

Les tentes, munies d'auvents de toile tendue pour protéger de la redoutable chaleur, sont vitrées et sur pilotis. À gauche, un partie du bâtiment central.

ODILE DECQ

Odile Decq Benoît Cornette
Architectes Urbanistes
11, rue des Arquebusiers
75003 Paris
France

Tel: +33 142 71 27 41
Fax: +33 142 71 27 42
Web: www.odbc-paris.com

ODILE DECQ was born in 1955 and obtained her degree in architecture (DPLG) at UP6 in Paris in 1978. She studied urbanism at the Institut d'Etudes Politiques in Paris (1979). Her partner Benoît Cornette passed away in 1998. She has designed a number of apartment buildings in Paris (1988, 1995, 1997 and currently); three buildings for Nantes University (1993–98); the presentation of the French Pavilion at the 1996 Architecture Biennale in Venice; and the Shiatzy Chen fashion boutique on the rue Saint-Honoré in Paris. She has worked recently on a refurbishment of the Conference Hall of Unesco in Paris, a renovation of the Cureghem Veterinary School in Brussels, and extension of the Belloy Clinique in Paris. Winner of the Golden Lion at the Venice Architecture Biennale, 1996; the 1999 Benedictus Award for the Faculty of Economics and the Law Library at the University of Nantes; she has taught at the Ecole Spéciale d'Architecture in Paris since 1992, and has been a guest professor at the Technische Hochschule,Vienna (1998), and the Bartlett School of Architecture, London (1998/1999/2000).

ODILE DECQ, geboren 1955, machte 1978 ihr Architekturdiplom (D. P. L. G.) an der UP6 in Paris. 1979 studierte sie am Institut d'Etudes Politiques, ebenfalls in Paris, Urbanismus. Ihr Partner, Benoît Cornette, starb 1998. Decq hat in Paris eine Reihe von Apartmenthäusern entworfen (1988, 1995, 1997 und zurzeit), drei Gebäude für die Universität in Nantes (1993–98), den Französischen Pavillon für die Architekturbiennale 1996 in Venedig und die Verkaufsräume für Shiatzy Chen an der Rue Saint-Honoré in Paris. In jüngerer Zeit war sie für die Instandsetzung des Konferenzsaales der UNESCO in Paris verantwortlich, außerdem für die Sanierung der Cureghem Veterinärschule in Brüssel sowie für die Erweiterung des Belloy Krankenhauses in Paris. Sie ist Gewinnerin des Goldenen Löwen der Architekturbiennale 1996 in Venedig und des Benedictus-Preises für die Wirtschaftsfakultät und die Rechtsbibliothek der Universität Nantes. Seit 1992 unterrichtet sie an der Ecole Spéciale d'Architecture in Paris; sie war Gastprofessorin an der Technischen Hochschule Wien (1998) und an der Bartlett School of Architecture in London (1998/1999/2000).

ODILE DECQ, née en 1955, a obtenu son diplôme d'architecte DPLG de l'UP6 (École d'architecture de Paris-La Villette) en 1978 et a étudié l'urbanisme à l'Institut d'Études Politiques de Paris (1979). Son associé, Benoît Cornette, est décédé en 1998. Elle a conçu un certain nombre d'immeubles de logements à Paris (1988, 1995, 1997 et actuellement), trois immeubles pour l'Université de Nantes (1993–98), la présentation du pavillon français à la 6e Biennale d'architecture de Venise (1996) et la boutique de mode Shiatzy Chen, rue Saint-Honoré à Paris. Elle a travaillé récemment au réaménagement de la salle de conférence de l'Unesco à Paris, à la rénovation de l'École vétérinaire Cureghem à Bruxelles et à l'extension de la clinique Belloy à Paris. Elle a remporté le Lion d'or de la Biennale d'architecture de Venise en 1996, le Benedictus Award 1999 pour la Faculté d'économie et la bibliothèque de la Faculté de droit de l'Université de Nantes. Elle enseigne à l'École spéciale d'architecture de Paris depuis 1992 et a été professeur invité à la Technische Hochschule de Vienne, Autriche (1998) et à la Bartlett School of Architecture, Londres (1998–2000).

LIAUNIG MUSEUM

Neuhaus, Austria, 2005–07

*Floor area: 4500 m². Client: Herbert Liaunig Museumsverwaltung.
Cost: €8 million*

*The Liaunig Museum is one of a
number of exercises by contemporary
architects in the area of topographic
insertion. Here, the architecture
appears to emerge from the landscape. Seen from above, it becomes
almost invisible.*

*Das Liaunig-Museum ist in der zeit-
genössischen Architektur ein Beispiel
für die Einfügung eines Gebäudes in
die Topografie. In diesem Fall scheint
die Architektur aus der Landschaft
»aufzutauchen«. Von oben gesehen ist
sie fast unsichtbar.*

*Le Liaunig Museum est une illus-
tration de ces exercices sur l'insertion topographique que mènent
certains architectes contemporains.
Ici, l'architecture semble émerger
du paysage. Vue du ciel, elle est
presque invisible.*

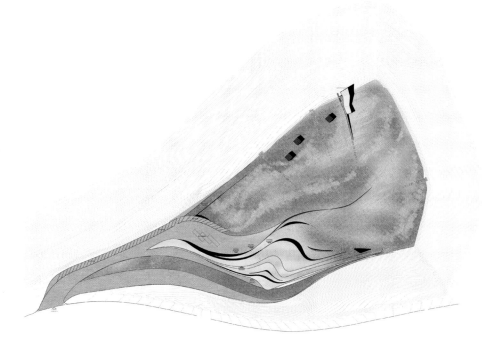

In February 2004, Odile Decq won the international competition to design this 4500 m² museum intended to house the substantial collection of Austrian art formed by Herbert Böckl and Fritz Wotruba, and she describes her scheme as "a concept that plays with the landscape." The undulating roof is to be made of prefabricated concrete. Decq's description of the project as a "landscape museum" is accentuated by the interaction of interior and exterior spaces. As she writes, "On the façade lines become waves, then the envelope becomes an in-between space: outside and inside, enclosed and open, a building and a landscape, Art and Nature. A walk through the building becomes a sequential discovery, becomes an event. The walk to reach the entrance, the foyer itself, the ramps, the exhibition rooms … every space is conceived to lead the visitor to move, to travel through the building, to experience the art exhibitions. Spaces are never centered. The perspectives are tangential and allow for a series of sequential points of view." Featured at the 2004 Venice Architecture Biennale in the section devoted to landscape and architecture, the Liaunig Museum is a particularly important demonstration of the vitality of contemporary French architecture.

Im Februar 2004 gewann Odile Decq den internationalen Wettbewerb für das 4500 m² große Museum, in dem die umfangreiche Sammlung österreichischer Kunst von Herbert Böckl und Fritz Wotruba ihren ständigen Platz finden soll. Sie beschreibt ihren Entwurf »als ein Konzept, das mit der Landschaft spielt«. Das wellenförmige Dach soll aus vorgefertigten Betonelementen bestehen. Decqs Bezeichnung des Projektes als »Landschaftsmuseum« wird durch das Zusammenspiel von Innen- und Außenräumen verdeutlicht. Sie sagt: »Auf der Fassade werden aus Linien Wellen, dann wird aus der Hülle ein Zwischenraum: außen und innen, umschlossen und offen, ein Gebäude und eine Landschaft, Kunst und Natur. Der Gang durch das Gebäude wird zu einer sequenziellen Entdeckungsreise, zu einem Ereignis. Das Erreichen des Eingangs, das Foyer selbst, die Rampen, die Ausstellungsräume …. jeder Raum ist so entworfen, dass er den Besucher einlädt, sich zu bewegen, durch das Gebäude zu reisen, die Kunst zu erleben. Die Räume sind nie zentriert. Perspektiven sind tangential und gestatten eine Abfolge von Sichtweisen.« Bei der Architekturbiennale in Venedig wurde das Liaunig-Museum in der Kategorie »Landschaft und Architektur« präsentiert und demonstriert besonders nachdrücklich die Vitalität der zeitgenössischen französischen Architektur.

C'est en février 2004 qu'Odile Decq a remporté le concours international pour la conception de ce musée de 4500 m² destiné à l'importante collection d'art autrichien constituée par Herbert Böckl et Fritz Wotruba. La description du projet par l'architecte insiste sur l'interaction entre l'intérieur et l'extérieur, sous le vaste toit ondulé en béton préfabriqué. Pour elle, il s'agit « d'un concept de jeu avec le paysage… Sur la façade, les lignes deviennent des vagues, puis l'enveloppe se transforme en un espace entre-deux: dedans et dehors, fermé et ouvert, bâtiment et paysage, art et nature. Se promener dans le musée devient une découverte séquentielle, un événement. La distance pour atteindre l'entrée, le hall d'accueil lui-même, les rampes, les galeries d'exposition… tout est conçu pour pousser le visiteur à se déplacer, à voyager à travers le bâtiment, à aller à la rencontre des œuvres d'art. Les espaces ne sont jamais centrés. Les perspectives sont tangentielles et autorisent une série de points de vue séquentiels ». Présenté à la Biennale d'architecture de Venise 2004 dans la section « Paysage et architecture », le Liaunig Museum est une démonstration particulièrement significative de la vitalité de l'architecture française contemporaine.

Computer views of the museum as
it will be seen from the exterior and
two interior images emphasize the
degree to which the structure will
be integrated into the site, echoing
the mountains in the background.

Die Computergrafiken zeigen die
Außenansicht des Museums sowie
zwei Innenansichten und verdeutlichen die starke Integration des
Gebäudes in die Topografie; dabei
nimmt die Architektur das Thema der
Berge der Umgebung auf.

Les images de synthèse du musée
vu de l'extérieur et deux vues d'intérieurs mettent en évidence le degré
d'intégration au site qui fait écho aux
montagnes dans le lointain.

DILLER + SCOFIDIO + RENFRO

Diller + Scofidio + Renfro, 36 Cooper Sq 5F, New York, New York 10003, USA
Tel: +1 212 260 7971, Fax: +1 212 260 7924
e-mail: disco@dillerscofidio.com, Web: www.dillerscofidio.com

Elizabeth Diller is Professor of Architecture at Princeton University and Ricardo Scofidio is Professor of Architecture at The Cooper Union in New York. According to their own description, "**DILLER + SCOFIDIO + RENFRO** is a collaborative, interdisciplinary studio involved in architecture, the visual arts and the performing arts. The team is primarily involved in thematically-driven experimental works that take the form of architectural commissions, temporary installations and permanent site-specific installations, multimedia theater, electronic media, and print." Charles Renfro was born in Houston, Texas in 1964. Prior to joining Diller + Scofidio in 1997, Renfro worked with several offices in New York including Smith-Milller+Hawkinson and Ralph Appelbaum Associates. He was promoted to partner in 2004. Their work includes "Slither," 100 units of social housing in Gifu, Japan, and *Moving Target*, a collaborative dance work with Charleroi/Danse Belgium. Installations by Diller + Scofidio have been seen at the Cartier Foundation in Paris (*Master/Slave*, 1999); the Museum of Modern Art in New York and the Musée de la Mode in Paris. Recently, they completed The Brasserie Restaurant, Seagram Building, New York (1998-99); the Blur Building, Expo 02, Yverdon-les-Bains, Switzerland (2000-02) and were selected as architects for the Institute of Contemporary Art in Boston, the Eyebeam Institute in the Chelsea area of Manhattan, and Lincoln Center, New York. They recently completed *Facsimile*, a permanent media installation for the San Francisco Arts Commission at the new Moscone Convention Center West, as well as a master plan for Brooklyn Academy of Music Cultural District in collaboration with Rem Koolhaas. They designed the Viewing Platforms at Ground Zero in Manhattan, and they are also working on a major project to redesign the area surrounding the Tivoli Park in Copenhagen.

Elizabeth Diller ist als Professorin für Architektur an der Princeton University, Ricardo Scofidio als Professor für Architektur an der Cooper Union School of Architecture in New York tätig. Ihrer eigenen Beschreibung zufolge ist »**DILLER + SCOFIDIO + RENFRO** ein interdisziplinäres Gemeinschaftsprojekt, das sich mit Architektur, bildender und darstellender Kunst beschäftigt. Das Team führt hauptsächlich experimentelle Arbeiten durch, die sich auf der Grundlage von Architektur, Installation, Multimediapräsentation, elektronischen Medien und Druckgrafik mit bestimmten Themen auseinandersetzen.« Charles Renfro, geboren 1964 in Houston, Texas, arbeitete für verschiedene New Yorker Architekturbüros – darunter Smith-Miller+Hawkinson und Ralph Appelbaum Associates – bevor er seine Tätigkeit bei Diller + Scofido aufnahm. 2004 wurde er Partner. Zu ihren Projekten zählen u. a.: »Slither«, 100 Sozialwohnungen in Gifu, Japan, und *Moving Target*, eine Tanztheaterproduktion in Zusammenarbeit mit der Tanzformation Charleroi/Danse Belgium. Installationen von Diller + Scofidio wurden in der Fondation Cartier in Paris (*Master/Slave*, 1999), im Museum of Modern Art in New York und im Musée de la Mode in Paris gezeigt. Zu ihren neueren Architekturarbeiten gehören das Restaurant The Brasserie im Seagram Building in New York (1998–99) und das Blur Building für die Expo 2002 im schweizerischen Yverdon-les-Bains (2000–02). Außerdem erhielten sie die Aufträge für das Institute of Contemporary Art in Boston, das Eyebeam Institute im Stadtteil Chelsea in Manhattan sowie das Lincoln Center in New York. Kürzlich wurde *Facsimile*, eine ständige Medieninstallation für die San Francisco Arts Commission am neuen Moscone Convention Center West fertig gestellt; ebenso – in Zusammenarbeit mit Rem Koolhaas – ein Master Plan für die Brooklyn Academy of Music Cultural District. Sie haben die Aussichtsplattform für Ground Zero in Manhattan entworfen und arbeiten an einem Großprojekt zur Umgestaltung der Umgebung des Tivoli in Kopenhagen.

Elizabeth Diller est professeur associé à Princeton et Ricardo Scofidio professeur d'architecture à The Cooper Union, New York. Selon eux, « **DILLER + SCOFIDIO + RENFRO** est une agence interdisciplinaire coopérative qui se consacre à l'architecture, aux arts plastiques et à ceux du spectacle. L'équipe travaille essentiellement sur des recherches thématiques expérimentales qui peuvent prendre la forme de commandes architecturales, d'installations temporaires, d'installations permanentes adaptées au site, de théâtres multimédia, de médias électroniques et d'édition ». Charles Renfro est né à Houston, Texas, en 1964. Avant de rejoindre Diller + Scofidio en 1997, il a travaillé pour plusieurs agences new-yorkaises dont Smith-Miller+Hawkinson et Ralph Appelbaum Associates. Il est devenu partenaire en 2004. Parmi leurs projets récents : Slither, 100 logements sociaux (Gifu, Japon), *Moving Target*, œuvre chorégraphique en collaboration avec Charleroi/Danse (Belgique). Des installations de Diller + Scofidio ont été présentées à la Fondation Cartier à Paris, *Master/Slave* (1999) au Museum of Modern Art de New York et au musée de la Mode à Paris. Plus récemment, ils ont achevé le restaurant Brasserie, Seagram Building, New York (1998–99); le pavillon d'exposition Blur Building, Expo 02, Yverdon-les-Bains, Suisse (2002) et ont été sélectionnés pour l'Institute of Contemporary Art de Boston, l'Eyebeam Institute à Manhattan (Chelsea) et le Lincoln Center (New York). Ils ont dernièrement livré *Facsimile*, une installation média permanente pour la San Francisco Arts Commission, au nouveau Moscone Convention Center West, ainsi que le plan directeur de la Brooklyn Academy of Music Cultural District en collaboration avec Rem Koolhaas. Ils ont conçu les plates-formes d'observation de Ground Zero à Manhattan et travaillent également sur un important projet de restructuration des abords immédiats du parc de Tivoli à Copenhague.

THE HIGH LINE

New York, New York, USA, 2004

Length: 2.5 km. Client: Friends of the High Line. Cost: not disclosed

The **HIGH LINE** is an unused elevated railway spur running about 2.5 kilometers from the Jacob Javits Convention Center in New York to Gansevoort Street in the meatpacking district on Manhattan's Lower West Side. The so-called West Side Improvement Project, including the High Line, built because of the number of accidents involving trains serving Manhattan's docks, was put into effect in 1929. Intended to avoid the negative effects of subway lines over crowded streets, the High Line cuts through the center of city blocks. Increasing truck traffic led to the demolition of parts of the High Line in the 1960s and a halt to train operations in 1980. Despite efforts to demolish the remaining structure to allow new construction, a good part of the High Line survived and a group called Friends of the High Line, created in 1999, eventually convinced authorities to renovate it rather than to allow its destruction. Diller + Scofidio + Renfro have participated in a collective proposal for the High Line including the landcape architects Field Operations, the artist Olafur Eliasson, the Tanya Bonakdar Gallery, the engineers Buro Happold and a number of other parties to renovate and bring new life to a disused part of the city. As they say, "Inspired by the melancholic, unruly beauty of the High Line, where nature has reclaimed a once vital piece of urban infrastructure, the team retools this industrial conveyance into a postindustrial instrument of leisure reflection about the very categories of 'nature' and 'culture' in our time. By changing the rules of engagement between plant life and pedestrians, our strategy of agri-tecture combines organic and building materials into a blend of changing proportions that accommodate the wild, the cultivated, the intimate, and the hyper-social." The United States Senate voted a credit of 18 million dollars for the project in July 2005, and the Museum of Modern Art in New York presented an exhibition of the Diller + Scofidio + Renfro scheme until October 30, 2005.

Die **HIGH LINE** ist eine 2,5 km lange, nicht mehr benutzte Hochbahntrasse, die von der Gansevoort Street im Meatpacking District auf der Lower West Side von Manhattan bis zum Jacob Javits Convention Center führt. Der Bau der High Line war Teil des so genannten West Side Improvement Project, das 1929 eingerichtet wurde, da es zu zahlreichen Unfällen mit den die Docks andienenden Zügen gekommen war. Um die negativen Auswirkungen von Stadtbahnen, die direkt über vielbefahrenen Straßen verlaufen, zu vermeiden, wurde die High Line so gelegt, dass sie die Blöcke mittig durchschneidet. Aufgrund des erhöhten LKW-Verkehrs wurden in den 1960er Jahren Teile der High Line abgebrochen; 1980 wurde der Zugverkehr ganz eingestellt. Obwohl es Versuche gab, die noch vorhandenen Abschnitte abzureißen und eine neue Konstruktion zu errichten, blieb ein größerer Teil der High Line erhalten. Die Friends of the High Line setzten sich seit 1999 gegen den Abriss und für die Sanierung ein und konnten die zuständigen Behörden überzeugen. Diller + Scofidio + Renfro haben – zusammen mit den Landschaftsarchitekturbüro Field Operations, dem Künstler Olafur Eliasson, der Tanya Bonakdar Gallery, dem Ingenieurbüro Happold und vielen anderen Beteiligten – einen Vorschlag erarbeitet, wie die Konstruktion saniert und dieser ausrangierte Teil der Stadt wiederbelebt werden kann. Sie sagen: »Die melancholische, ungestüme Schönheit der High Line und die Tatsache, dass sich die Natur hier ein früher wichtiges Element der städtischen Infrastruktur zurückerobert hat, inspirierte uns. Das Team deutet die industrielle Transporttrasse in ein postindustrielles Instrument der Reflexion über Freizeit um. Dabei geht es genau um die Kategorien ›Natur‹ und ›Kultur‹ in der heutigen Zeit. Indem wir die Regeln der gegenseitigen Verpflichtungen zwischen der Pflanzenwelt und den Fußgängern ändern, verbindet unsere Strategie der ›Agritektur‹ organische Materialien und Baumaterialien zu einer Mischung mit veränderlichen Anteilen, die das Wilde, das Kultivierte, das Persönliche und das Hypersoziale umfasst.« Im Juli 2005 stimmte der amerikanische Senat einem Kredit von umgerechnet 15 Millionen Euro zu; in einer Ausstellung bis zum 30. Oktober 2005 zeigte das Museum of Modern Art in New York das Konzept von Diller + Scofidio + Renfro.

La **HIGH LINE** est une ancienne voie ferrée aérienne serpentant sur 2,5 km, du Jacob Javits Convention Center jusqu'à Gansevoort Street, à Meatpacking District (quartier des bouchers) dans le Lower West Side à Manhattan. Le West Side Improvement Project, qui comprenait la High Line construite en surélévation en réaction aux nombreux accidents provoqués par les trains qui desservaient les docks de Manhattan, datait de 1929. Pour pallier les inconvénients de lignes de métro passant au-dessus des rues bondées, la High Line passe carrément au milieu des blocs d'immeubles. L'accroissement de la circulation des camions a conduit à la démolition partielle de cette ligne dans les années 1960 et le trafic ferroviaire y a définitivement cessé en 1980. Malgré plusieurs tentatives de démolition de l'ensemble pour permettre de nouvelles constructions, une bonne partie de la ligne subsiste et une association, les Amis de la High Line, créée en 1999, a fini par convaincre les autorités de la rénover plutôt que de la supprimer. Diller + Scofidio + Renfro ont participé à un collectif regroupant, entre autres, les architectes paysagistes Field Operations, l'artiste Olafur Eliasson, la Tanya Bonakdar Gallery, les ingénieurs Buro Happold, collectif qui se proposait de redonner vie à ce quartier abandonné. « Inspirés par la beauté anarchique et mélancolique de la High Line, où la nature a reconquis un élément d'infrastructure urbaine jadis vital, nous avons transformé cet outil industriel en un instrument postindustriel de loisirs, en une réflexion sur la signification réelle des classifications entre « nature » et « culture » de notre époque. En changeant les règles des rapports entre la vie végétale et les piétons, notre stratégie d'*agri-tecture* mélange matériaux organiques et matériaux de construction selon des proportions variables pour accueillir le sauvage et le cultivé, l'intime et l'hypersocial. » Le Sénat américain a voté, en juillet 2005, un crédit de 15 millions d'euros pour le projet de Diller + Scofidio + Renfro, qui a été exposé au Museum of Modern Art de New York.

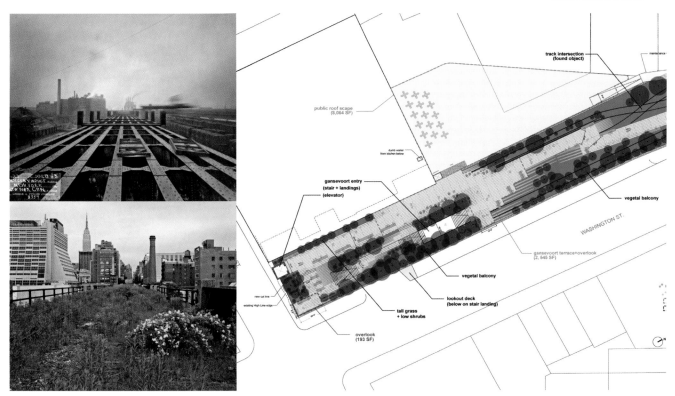

The High Line squeezes between buildings on Manhattan's Lower West Side. Drawings above give an idea of the variety of architectural and botanical solutions chosen by the architects involved.

Die High Line schlängelt sich durch die Häuser auf Manhattans Lower West Side. Die Zeichnungen zeigen die vielfältigen architektonischen und landschaftsplanerischen Lösungen der verschiedenen Architekten.

La High Line se faufile entre les bâtiments du Lower West Side de Manhattan. Les dessins ci-dessus donnent une idée de la variété des solutions architecturales et végétales retenues par les architectes.

DENNIS DOLLENS

Dennis Dollens
40 Camino Cielo
Santa Fe, New Mexico 87 506
USA

Tel: +1 505 988 9236
Fax: +1 505 988 5820
e-mail: exodesic@mac.com
Web: www.tumbletruss.com

Digitally-Grown Tower ▶

Born in Los Angeles in 1950, **DENNIS DOLLENS** has taught Design Biomimetics in the Genetic Architectures Program and in the Department of Ecology and Architecture at the Universitat Internacional de Catalunya's School of Architecture (Barcelona) for four years. He lectures internationally on Digital-Biomimetic Architecture and on his work in schools of industrial design and architecture. He is currently working on a PhD at the University of Strathclyde, Glasgow. His studios are in Santa Fe, New Mexico and Barcelona, Spain and his most recent books are *D2A: Digital to Analog* (translated into Spanish and published as *De lo digital a lo analógico*) and *DBA: Digital-Botanic Architecture*. His current architectural work includes the Spiral Bridge, Pyrenées, France (with Ignasi Pérez Arnal, 2004); Digital-Computing Center, Marfa, Texas (2005–); and a residence in Santa Fe, New Mexico (2004–).

DENNIS DOLLENS, 1950 in Los Angeles geboren, lehrte an der Architekturfakultät der Universitat Internacional de Catalunya in Barcelona im Programm Genetische Architektur biomimetisches Entwerfen, außerdem unterrichtete er vier Jahre lang am Fachbereich Ökologie und Architektur. An Architektur- und Designfakultäten in zahlreichen Ländern hält er Vorträge über seine Projekte und zum Thema »Digital-biomimetische Architektur«. Derzeit promoviert er an der University of Strathclyde, Glasgow. Er hat Ateliers in Santa Fe, New Mexico, und in Barcelona. In jüngster Zeit veröffentlichte er zwei Bücher, *D2A: Digital to Analog*, das auch auf Spanisch erschien (*De lo digital a lo analógico*), und *DBA: Digital-Botanic Architecture*. Zu seinen neuesten Projekten gehören die Spiralbrücke in den französischen Pyrenäen (mit Ignasi Pérez Arnal, 2004), das Digital-Computing Center in Marfa, Texas (2005–), und ein Wohnhaus in Santa Fe, New Mexico (2004–).

Né à Los Angeles en 1950, **DENNIS DOLLENS** a enseigné la biomimétique du design dans le cadre du programme d'architectures génétiques et au département d'écologie et d'architecture de l'École d'architecture de l'Universitat Internacional de Catalunya (Barcelone) pendant quatre ans. Il donne des conférences dans de nombreux pays sur l'architecture numérique-biomimétique et sur son œuvre dans des écoles de design industriel et d'architecture. Il prépare actuellement un PhD à l'Université de Strathclyde à Glasgow. Il a des agences à Santa Fe (Nouveau-Mexique) et Barcelone (Espagne) et a récemment publié *D2A ; Digital to Analog* et *D-B-A : Digital-Botanic Architecture*. Ses dernières réalisations architecturales comprennent le Pont en spirale, Pyrénées, France (avec Ignasi Pérez Arnal, 2004), le Digital-Computing Center, Marfa, Texas (2005–) et une maison à Santa Fe, Nouveau-Mexique (2004–).

DIGITALLY-GROWN TOWER

New York, New York, USA, 2005

Floor area: 22 500 m². Height: 42.5 m. Client: Lumen, Inc.
Cost: $27 million

Imagined for a site on Manhattan's Lower East Side, this tower was designed with software called Xfrog. Made by the German firm Greenworks, Xfrog consists of "botanic, L-system algorithms used in computational biological simulations to grow plants and landscapes for laboratory tests and simulations." The work done by Dollens consists in "changing the software's growth parameters in order to direct digital growth from reproducing botanic organisms like trees or shrubs into producing architectural elements like an experimental frame for a new building." Beginning with the seed pods of penstemon (*Penstemon palmeri*), Dollens proposes a design that has a radically different appearance from almost any existing tower, and yet has a solid basis in the forms of nature. Further, digitally-driven manufacturing can be adapted to this type of concept. Dollens writes, "The unifying concept behind this project is that computational growth of architectural structures and systems can be influenced by biomimetic observations without falling into traditional categories of 'organic architecture.' In addition, the potential of biological science, biotechnology, and digital manufacturing, arriving at a union where architectural production and new possibilities for non-toxic architecture come together, begins to make sense."

Der Turm, geplant für die Lower East Side in Manhattan, wurde mit der Software Xfrog entworfen. Das von der deutschen Firma Greenworks entwickelte Programm besteht aus »botanischen, L-System-Algorithmen, die in ›computerbiologischen‹ Simulationen verwendet werden, um Pflanzen und Landschaften für Labortests und -simulationen zu generieren«. Dollens »verändert die Wachstumsparameter des Programms, so dass die Reproduktion botanischer Organismen wie Bäume oder Sträucher in eine Produktion architektonischer Elemente – z. B. ein experimentelles Tragwerk für ein neues Gebäude – umgewandelt wird.« Ausgehend von den Schoten der Pflanze Penstemon palmeri schlägt Dollens einen Turm vor, der sich radikal von fast allen gebauten Türmen unterscheidet. Seine solide Basis sind jedoch Formen aus der Natur. Darüber hinaus kann eine digital gestützte Produktion aus diesem Entwurfskonzept abgeleitet werden. Dollens schreibt: »Grundgedanke des Projektes ist, dass computergeneriertes Wachstum von architektonischen Strukturen und Systemen durch biomimetische Beobachtungen beeinflusst werden kann, ohne in die bekannten Kategorien einer organischen Architektur zu verfallen. Dass die Potenziale der Biologie, Biotechnologie und der digitalen Produktion gebündelt werden, ist sinnvoll. Daraus ergeben sich neue Möglichkeiten einer schadstofffreien Architektur.«

Cette tour a été conçue à l'aide du logiciel Xfrog, pour un terrain du Lower East Side à Manhattan. Mis au point par la société allemande Greenworks, Xfrog consiste en « algorithmes botaniques dits L-systems, utilisés pour les simulations biologiques virtuelles étudiant en laboratoire la croissance des végétaux et l'évolution des paysages ». Le travail de Dennis Dollens a consisté à « modifier les paramètres de croissance du logiciel pour réorienter la croissance numérique des organismes botaniques de reproduction – arbres et buissons –, vers la production d'éléments architecturaux comme, par exemple, une ossature expérimentale pour une nouvelle construction ». Partant de graines de penstemon (*Penstemon palmeri*), il propose ainsi un plan dont l'aspect diffère de presque toutes les tours existantes à ce jour, tout en s'appuyant sur une base formelle naturelle solide. Des processus de fabrication pilotée par ordinateur peuvent être adaptés à ce type de concept. Dollens écrit : « Le concept qui sous-tend ce projet est que la croissance virtuelle des structures et systèmes architecturaux peut être influencée par des observations biomimétiques sans tomber dans les catégories traditionnelles de l'architecture dite ‹ organique ›. De plus, la possibilité d'une collaboration de la biologie, de la biotechnologie et de la fabrication numérisée au bénéfice d'une production architecturale et de nouvelles possibilités d'architecture non toxique commence à faire sens. »

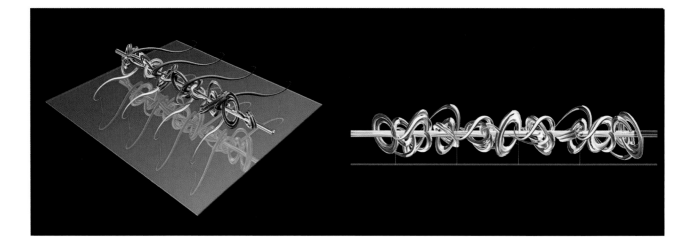

Using a program intended to mimic plant growth, Dennis Dollens has created the basis for a different type of architecture, whose esthetics owe more to biology than to Euclidean geometry.

Dennis Dollens verwendet ein Programm, das den Wuchs von Pflanzen simuliert und schafft so die Basis für einen neuartigen Architekturtypus, dessen Ästhetik mehr mit Biologie als mit euklidischer Geometrie zu tun hat.

Grâce à un programme qui reproduit les schémas de croissance des plantes, Dennis Dollens a jeté les bases d'une architecture d'un type nouveau dont l'esthétique doit plus à la biologie qu'à la géométrie euclidienne.

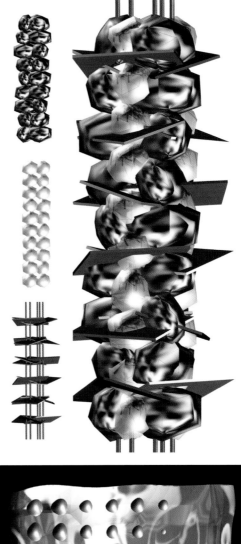

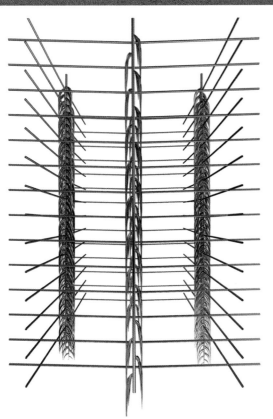

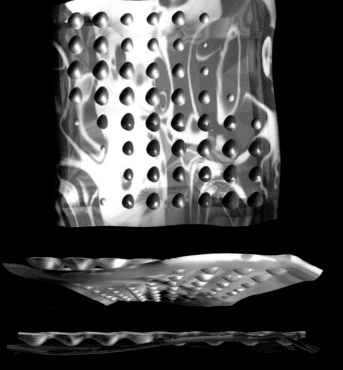

EASTERN DESIGN

Eastern Design Office, Inc.
Chezmoi Espoir 202 12 Sumizome-cho
Fukakusa Fushimi-ku, Kyoto
Japan

Tel/Fax: +81 756 42 96 44
e-mail: eastern@sweet.ocn.ne.jp
Web: www.eastern.e-arc.jp

Slit House ▶

The principals of **EASTERN DESIGN OFFICE** are Anna Nakamura, born in 1974, and educated at the Faculty of Engineering, Hokkaido University, and Taiyo Jinno, born in Aichi in 1968. He obtained a Master of Architecture degree from the Graduate School of Science and Technology, Nihon University. They created their firm in Kyoto in 2003. Thus far, they have won first prize in an international invited competition for Water Sports World in the Haihe District of Tianjin, China (2003); second prize in an international invited competition for the Urban Planning of the Tianjin Development Zone, China (2004); and second prize in an international invited competition for the Wrestling Arena for the 2008 Summer Olympic Games in Beijing (China Agricultural University Gymnasium). Their built works are the Slit House, Shiga, Japan (2005), published here, and the Horizontal Slit House, Shiga, Japan (2005). As Nakamura and Jinno say, "Eastern Design Office has its base in Kyoto and acts in Japan and China. The name 'Eastern' implies 'architecture from the East.' We are seeking a design possibility with "Slit.' It relies on an architectural technique that has existed since ancient times. But 'Slit' is now our design method, one we have adapted to change an aspect of contemporary architecture."

Anna Nakamura, geboren 1974, und Taiyo Jinno, geboren 1968 in Aichi, sind die Partner von **EASTERN DESIGN OFFICE**. Anna Nakamura studierte an der Fakultät Bauingenieurwesen der Hokkaido Universität, Taiyo Jinno erwarb seinen Master of Architecture an der Graduate School of Science and Technology der Nihon Universität. 2003 gründeten sie in Kioto ihr eigenes Büro. Bislang gewannen sie den ersten Preis im international eingeladenen Wettbewerb für die Water Sports World im Haihe-Bezirk in Tianjin, China (2003), sowie den zweiten Preis in einem ebenfalls international eingeladenen Wettbewerb für eine Ringer-Arena für die Olympischen Sommerspiele 2008 in Peking (China Agricultural University Gymnasium). Realisierte Projekte des Büros sind das hier publizierte Slit House und das Horizontal Slit House, beide im japanischen Shiga (2005). Nakamura und Jinno sagen: »Eastern Design Office hat seine Basis in Kioto und ist in Japan und China tätig. Der Name ›Eastern‹ impliziert ›Architektur aus dem Osten‹. Mit ›Slit‹ (Schlitz) suchen wir nach einer Möglichkeit zu entwerfen. Sie beruht auf einer architektonischen Technik, die es von alters her gibt. Aber der Schlitz ist jetzt unsere Entwurfsmethode, eine die wir angepasst haben, um eine Seite der zeitgenössischen Architektur zu verändern.«

Les associés de **EASTERN DESIGN OFFICE** sont Anna Nakamura, née en 1974 et formée à la Faculté d'ingénierie de l'Université d'Hokkaido, et Taiyo Jinno, né en 1968, Master of Architecture de l'École supérieure de science et de technologie de la Nihon University. Ils ont fondé leur agence à Kyoto en 2003 et, depuis, remporté le premier prix d'un concours international sur invitation pour l'urbanisme de la zone de développement de Tianjin, Chine (2004) et le second prix d'un concours international sur invitation pour le stade de lutte des Jeux olympiques d'été 2008 à Pékin. Ils ont réalisé la Slit House, Shiga, Japon (2005), publiée ici, et l'Horizontal Slit House, Shiga, Japon (2005). Selon leurs propres termes, « Eastern Design Office est basé à Kyoto et travaille en Chine et au Japon. Le nom ‹ Eastern › (Oriental) implique ‹ une architecture orientale ›. Nous recherchons des possibilités de conception autour de ‹ Slit › (la fente). Nous nous appuyons sur une technique architecturale qui existe depuis très longtemps. Mais ‹ Slit › est une méthode de conception que nous avons adaptée pour influer sur un aspect de l'architecture contemporaine ».

SLIT HOUSE

Shiga Prefecture, Japan, 2004–05

Floor area: 210 m². Client: Niwaka, Inc.
Cost: € 405 000

Creating an ambiguity between interior and exterior, the thick concrete walls of the Slit House also redefine the window in architectural terms.

Die dicken Betonwände des Slit House führen zu einer Ambivalenz von innen und außen und definieren das architektonische Element »Fenster« neu.

Par l'ambiguïté qu'ils entretiennent entre l'intérieur et l'extérieur, les épais murs de béton de la Slit House redéfinissent la notion même de fenêtre en termes architecturaux.

Set on a long, narrow site, 50m deep and just 7.5 m wide, this unusual house features no less than 105 m of wall length with 60 slits and no actual windows. One of its narrow sides faces the street, and the other a river. As the architects say, "This method of slits is our challenge to the window." The slits involved are 14 cm wide, and the structural nature of the house depends directly on the proliferation of these openings. The architects write, "The slits screen inner privacy from view from the outside. But the slits bring light into the house." They emphasize that the residence is occupied by an old woman and say, "The slits remind us of our memory of poetic scenery. It is like a stream of light through the *fusuma* or *shoji* of Japanese traditional architecture or a stream of light from a skylight in ancient stone architecture." This architecture has a silent ambiance as though it were in the middle of a solitary jar, and a poetic clearness that evokes endless space. Built with reinforced concrete, the one-story house occupies a site that measures 318 m² and has a total floor area of 210 m².

Das ungewöhnliche Haus auf einem langen, schmalen Grundstück (50 m lang, aber nur 7,5 m breit) hat eine Wandlänge von nicht weniger als 105 m; die Wände sind an 60 Stellen geschlitzt, haben aber keine herkömmlichen Fenster. Die eine Schmalseite des Hauses liegt zur Straße, die andere zu einem Fluss. Dazu sagen die Architekten: »Mit der Methode des Schlitzens fordern wir das Fenster heraus.« Die Schlitze sind 14 cm breit; das statische System des Hauses hängt direkt mit der großen Anzahl dieser Öffnungen zusammen. Die Architekten schreiben: »Die Schlitze schirmen die Privatsphäre im Inneren des Hauses vor Blicken von außen ab. Aber sie bringen Licht in das Haus hinein.« Sie weisen darauf hin, dass das Haus von einer alten Dame bewohnt wird und sagen: »Die Schlitze erinnern uns an eine poetische Szenerie: wie das Licht, das durch eine *fusuma* oder *shoji*, also die traditionelle japanische Schiebetür fällt, oder wie ein Lichtstrahl durch das Oberlicht in einem alten Gebäude aus Stein.« Diese Architektur hat eine stille Atmosphäre, als ob sie sich im Zentrum eines für sich stehenden Behältnisses befände, und eine poetische Klarheit, die endlosen Raum evoziert. Das eingeschossige Haus aus Stahlbeton bedeckt eine 318 m² große Fläche und hat eine Bruttogeschossfläche von 210 m².

Implantée sur un terrain de 50 m de long sur à peine 7,5 m de large, cette curieuse maison de 210 m² en béton armé ne possède pas moins de 105 m de murs percés de 60 fentes, et pas une seule vraie fenêtre. L'une de ses étroites façades donne sur une rue, l'autre sur un fleuve. Pour les architectes, « cette méthode de fente est notre défi par rapport à la fenêtre ». Les fentes sont larges de 14 cm et la structure de la maison dépend directement de la prolifération de ces ouvertures. « Les fentes protègent l'intimité de l'extérieur. Mais elles apportent aussi la lumière dans la maison. » Ils mettent en valeur l'idée que la maison est occupée par une vieille dame… « Elles réveillent en nous des souvenirs de paysages poétiques. Ces fentes font penser à un flot de lumière qui passerait à travers le *fusuma* ou le *shoji* de l'architecture japonaise traditionnelle ou à la lumière tombant d'une verrière dans l'architecture ancienne en pierre. » Cette architecture dégage une atmosphère de silence et une clarté poétique qui évoque un espace infini.

Although its slits occasionally give it a fortress-like appearance, the house has a rich and varied relationship with the sky and with daylight.

Die Schlitze geben dem Haus einen fast festungsähnlichen Charakter. Trotzdem werden vielfältige Bezüge zum Himmel und zum Tageslicht geschaffen.

Même si les fentes donnent parfois à cette maison l'aspect d'une forteresse, elle entretient une relation riche et variée avec le ciel et la lumière naturelle.

Traditional Japanese objects and furniture seem to fit well into what is otherwise an extremely contemporary space.

Die traditionellen japanischen Objekte und Möbelstücke fügen sich gut in die ultramodernen Räume ein.

Les meubles et objets japonais traditionnels semblent parfaitement à leur place dans ce volume d'esprit extrêmement contemporain.

STEFAN EBERSTADT

Stefan Eberstadt
Westendstrasse 30
80339 Munich
Germany

Tel: +49 89 16 70 98
Fax: +49 89 50 09 67 56
e-mail: stefan.eberstadt@adbk.mhn.de
Web: www.fiedler.url.de/303.0.html

Rucksack House ▶

Born in 1961, the artist **STEFAN EBERSTADT** lives and works in Munich. He worked as an apprentice carpenter and studied sculpture at the Academy of Fine Arts in Munich from 1982 to 1988 under Eduardo Paolozzi. He also studied in London and Bath during the same period. He received a Fellowship from the Bavarian Academy of Beaux Arts in 1993, the Travel Grant to New York City from the Bavarian State in 1994 and the Project Scholarship for Fine Art from the City of Munich in 2004. From 1995 to 2001 he taught at the Academy of Fine Arts in Munich. His work has been shown internationally, in particular at the Gallery Ulrich Fiedler in Cologne and the Rocket Gallery in London. He is currently preparing a solo show in Cologne and was included in *Come-in. Interior as Medium of Contemporary Art in Germany*, a touring exhibition hosted by the Museum of Contemporary Art in Saõ Paulo.

Der 1961 geborene Künstler **STEFAN EBERSTADT** lebt und arbeitet in München. Er war Auszubildender in einer Tischlerei und studierte u. a. unter Eduardo Paolozzi von 1982 bis 1988 Bildhauerei an der Akademie der Bildenden Künste in München. In diesem Zeitraum studierte er auch in London und Bath. 1993 erhielt er von der Bayerischen Akademie der Schönen Künste ein Stipendium, 1994 vom Freistaat Bayern ein Reisestipendium nach New York und 2004 von der Stadt München ein Projektstipendium. Von 1995 bis 2001 unterrichtete er an der Akademie der Bildenden Künste in München. Seine Arbeit wird international gezeigt, speziell in der Galerie Ulrich Fiedler in Köln und der Rocket Gallery in London. Derzeit bereitet er eine Einzelausstellung in Köln vor; er hat außerdem an der Tourneeausstellung *Come-in. Interieur als Medium der zeitgenössischen Kunst in Deutschland*, kuratiert vom Museum of Contemporary Art, São Paulo, teilgenommen.

Né en 1961, l'artiste **STEFAN EBERSTADT** vit et travaille à Munich. Il a été apprenti charpentier et a étudié la sculpture auprès d'Eduardo Paolozzi à l'Académie des beaux-arts de Munich de 1982 à 1988. Il a également suivi des cours à Londres et Bath au cours de la même période. Il a reçu une bourse de l'Académie bavaroise des beaux-arts et la Bourse de voyage à New York du Land de Bavière en 1994 ainsi que la Bourse de projet pour les beaux-arts de la Ville de Munich en 2004. De 1995 à 2001, il a enseigné à l'Académie des beaux-arts de Munich. Son œuvre a été présentée dans de nombreux pays, en particulier à la galerie Ulrich Fiedler à Cologne et à la Rocket Gallery à Londres. Il prépare actuellement une exposition personnelle à Cologne et figure dans *Come-in, Interior as Medium of Contemporary Art in Germany*, exposition itinérante organisée par le musée d'Art contemporain de São Paulo.

RUCKSACK HOUSE

Leipzig/Cologne, Germany, 2004–05

Floor area: 9 m². Client: Prototype by Stefan Eberstadt, Munich and courtesy Fiedler Contemporary, Cologne.
Cost: €25 000 (production cost); €50 000 (prototype)

Stefan Eberstadt had the unusual idea of simply adding space to an existing building. As he says, "New space gets slung onto an existing space by a simple, clear and understandable method. This reactivates the idea of the self-built anarchistic tree house, this time however, more prominently placed and structurally engineered. Our common perception needs to be challenged since it gets irritated when the plain façade of a building is suddenly interrupted by a box-shaped volume edging out into the realm of the street." Working with Thomas Beck, a structural engineer from Munich, he devised a welded steel structure with plywood cladding that was hung by steel cables from the Federkiel Stiftung/Halle 14 in Leipzig from September to November 2004 in the context of the exhibition *Xtreme Houses*. It was presented again in Cologne in September 2005 during the international architectural symposium *Plan05 – Forum of Contemporary Architecture*. Measuring 250 x 360 x 250 cm, the **RUCKSACK HOUSE** is "an attempt to explore the boundary between architecture and art." It has been described as a "walk-in sculpture" but it clearly has an architectural presence. Eberstadt concludes: "Today the task for art is to influence the design and the aesthetic structures of our environment. Art cannot be seen as an isolated factor, rather it should challenge and interact with other fields like architecture and design. In order to exist, art has to get involved in fields operating outside of its own."

Stefan Eberstadt hatte die ungewöhnliche Idee, Raum einfach an ein bestehendes Gebäude anzufügen. Er sagt: »Neuer Raum wird auf einfache, klare und verständliche Weise an vorhandenen Raum ›drangeworfen‹. Damit wird die Idee des selbstgebauten, anarchistischen Baumhauses reaktiviert; hier jedoch tritt es deutlicher in Erscheinung und ist baukonstruktiv durchgearbeitet. Unsere alltägliche Wahrnehmung wird dabei herausgefordert: Eine glatte Fassade, die plötzlich durch einen kistenartigen, in den Straßenraum hineinragenden Baukörper unterbrochen wird, erzeugt Irritationen.« In Zusammenarbeit mit Thomas Beck, einem Statiker aus München, entwickelte Eberstadt eine geschweißte Stahlkonstruktion mit einer Sperrholzverkleidung, die mithilfe von Stahlseilen von der Halle 14 der Leipziger Baumwollspinnerei (Stiftung Federkiel) abgehängt wurde. Diese Aktion fand von September bis November 2004 im Zusammenhang mit der Ausstellung *Xtreme Houses* statt. Auf dem internationalen Architektursymposion *Plan05 – Forum für Zeitgenössische Architektur* wurde die Konstruktion im September 2005 in Köln noch einmal gezeigt. Das **RUCKSACKHAUS** mit den Maßen 250 x 360 x 250 cm ist »der Versuch, die Grenzen zwischen Architektur und Kunst zu erforschen«. Es wurde als begehbare Skulptur bezeichnet, hat aber eine deutliche architektonische Präsenz. Abschließend sagt Eberstadt: »Heute besteht die Aufgabe der Kunst darin, das Design und die ästhetischen Strukturen unserer Umwelt zu beeinflussen. Kunst kann nicht als ein isolierter Faktor gesehen werden, vielmehr sollte sie andere Bereiche – z. B. Architektur und Design – herausfordern und mit ihnen interagieren. Um zu existieren, muss Kunst Bereiche mit einbeziehen, die sich außerhalb ihrer eigenen Sphäre befinden.«

Stefan Eberstadt a eu l'idée simple de donner du volume à un bâtiment existant. Il explique : « Le nouveau volume est greffé sur celui existant au moyen d'une méthode simple, claire et compréhensible. Ceci réactive l'idée de la maison dans l'arbre à caractère anarchique, ‹ à construire soi-même ›, mais implantée de façon plus visible et structurellement mieux étudiée. Notre perception a besoin d'être mise au défi car elle s'irrite de voir la façade neutre d'un immeuble brutalement interrompue par un volume en forme de boîte se projetant vers la rue. » En collaboration avec Thomas Beck, ingénieur structurel munichois, il a conçu une structure en acier soudé habillée de contreplaqué, accrochée par des câbles en acier en haut de la Halle 14 de la Federkiel Stiftung à Leipzig où se tenait, de septembre à novembre, l'exposition *Xtreme Houses*. Le projet fut exposé à nouveau à Cologne en septembre 2005 lors du symposium international d'architecture *Plan05 – Forum of Contemporary Architecture*. Cette **MAISON SAC À DOS** de 2,50 x 3,60 x 2,50 m, est « une tentative d'exploration des frontières entre l'art et l'architecture ». Elle a été décrite comme une « sculpture pénétrable » mais possède à l'évidence une présence architecturale. Eberstadt conclut : « Aujourd'hui, l'art a pour rôle d'influencer le design et les structures esthétiques de notre environnement. Il ne peut être considéré comme un facteur isolé, mais doit se confronter et interagir avec d'autres secteurs comme l'architecture et le design. Pour exister, l'art doit s'impliquer dans des champs autres que le sien ».

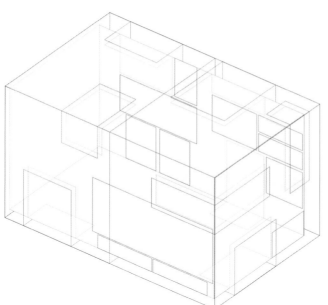

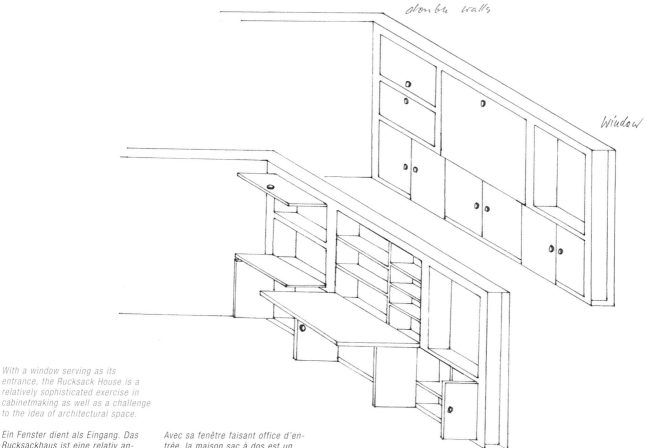

double walls

Window

With a window serving as its entrance, the Rucksack House is a relatively sophisticated exercise in cabinetmaking as well as a challenge to the idea of architectural space.

Ein Fenster dient als Eingang. Das Rucksackhaus ist eine relativ anspruchsvolle »Tischlerarbeit« und stellt die Vorstellung von architektonischem Raum auf die Probe.

Avec sa fenêtre faisant office d'entrée, la maison sac à dos est un exercice de menuiserie assez sophistiqué et un défi à l'idée même d'espace architectural.

PETER EISENMAN

Eisenman Architects P.C.
41 West 25th Street
New York, New York 10011
USA

Tel: + 1 212 645 1400
Fax: + 1 212 645 0726
e-mail: info@eisenmanarchitects.com
Web: www.eisenmanarchitects.com

Having established his reputation as a theorist, **PETER EISENMAN** came into view first as a member of the "New York Five" with Meier, Hejduk, Gwathmey and Graves. He set up his practice in 1980, and came to the attention of a wider public with the very visible Wexner Center for the Visual Arts at Ohio State University, Columbus, Ohio (1982-89). Born in Newark, New Jersey in 1932, he received architecture degrees from Columbia, and a PhD at the University of Cambridge, England. Peter Eisenman has taught at Cambridge, Princeton, Yale and Harvard as well as the University of Illinois, Ohio State University and the Cooper Union School of Architecture in New York. His major projects include the Koizumi Sangyo Building, Tokyo, Japan (1987-89); Greater Columbus Convention Center, Columbus, Ohio (1989-93); Aronoff Center for Design and Art, University of Cincinnati, Cincinnati, Ohio (1988-96); and the unbuilt Max Reinhardt Haus, Berlin, Germany (1992-93). He also designed the Staten Island Institute of Arts and Sciences (1997). He participated in the competition for the new World Trade Center in 2002 with Richard Meier, Charles Gwathmey and Steven Holl. Recent projects include a 48-story office tower on the Friedrichstrasse in Berlin, a museum for digital art in Hsinchu, Taiwan, the City of Culture of Galicia in Santiago de Compostela, Spain and a 68,000-seat stadium for the Arizona Cardinals in Phoenix, Arizona.

PETER EISENMAN begründete seinen Ruf durch seine theoretischen Arbeiten. Als Mitglied der New York Five, der auch Richard Meier, John Hejduk, Charles Gwathmey und Michael Graves angehörten, trat er erstmals in Erscheinung. 1980 gründete er sein Büro. Einer breiteren Öffentlichkeit wurde er durch das eigenwillige Wexner Center for the Visual Arts der Ohio State University in Columbus, Ohio (1982–89), bekannt. Der 1932 in Newark, New Jersey, geborene Eisenman studierte an der Columbia University Architektur und promovierte an der Universität Cambridge in England. Peter Eisenman hat in Cambridge, Princeton, Yale und Harvard gelehrt, außerdem an der University of Illinois, der Ohio State University und an der Cooper Union School of Architecture in New York. Zu seinen wichtigsten Projekten gehören das Koizumi Sangyo Gebäude in Tokio (1987–89), das Greater Columbus Convention Center in Columbus, Ohio (1989–93), das Aronoff Center for Design and Art der University of Cincinnati, Ohio (1988–96), und das nicht realisierte Max-Reinhardt-Haus in Berlin (Planung 1992–93). Auch der Entwurf für das Staten Island Institute of Arts and Sciences stammt von ihm (1997). Gemeinsam mit Richard Meier, Charles Gwathmey und Steven Holl nahm er 2002 am Wettbewerb für das neue World Trade Center teil. Neuere Projekte sind u. a. ein 48-geschossiges Bürohaus in der Friedrichstraße in Berlin, das Museum of Digital Arts in Hsinchu, Taiwan, das Kulturzentrum für die Kulturhauptstadt Santiago de Compostela in Galicien und ein Stadion für die Arizona Cardinals in Phoenix, Arizona, mit 68 000 Sitzplätzen.

À l'origine théoricien réputé, **PETER EISENMAN** s'est fait connaître comme membre des « New York Five » avec Meier, Hejduk, Gwathmey et Graves. Il a créé son agence en 1980 et s'est fait remarquer d'un public plus large avec son très spectaculaire Wexner Center for the Visual Arts, Ohio State University, Columbus, Ohio (1982–89). Né à Newark (New Jersey) en 1932, il est diplômé en architecture de Columbia University et Ph. D. de l'Université de Cambridge (U. K.). Il a enseigné à Cambridge, Princeton, Yale et Harvard, University of Illinois, Ohio State University et Cooper Union School of Architecture à New York. Parmi ses projets majeurs : l'immeuble Koisumi Sangyo, Tokyo (1987–89) ; le Greater Columbus Convention Center, Columbus, Ohio (1989–93) ; le Aronoff Center for Design and Art, University of Cincinnati, Ohio (1988–96) et la Max Reinhardt Haus, non encore construite, Berlin (1992–93). Il a également conçu le Staten Island Institute of Arts and Sciences (1997) et a participé au concours pour le nouveau World Trade Center de New York en 2002, avec Richard Meier, Charles Gwathmey et Steven Holl. Ses projets récents comprennent une tour de bureaux de 48 étages sur la Friedrichstrasse à Berlin, un musée d'art numérique à Hsinchu (Taiwan), la Cité de la culture de Galice à Saint-Jacques-de-Compostelle (Espagne) et un stade de 68 000 places pour les Arizona Cardinals à Phœnix (Arizona).

MEMORIAL TO THE MURDERED JEWS OF EUROPE

Berlin, Germany, 2004

Floor area: 19 000 m². Client: Stiftung Denkmal für die emordeten Juden Europas. Cost: €25 million

Originally submitted in 1997 as a collaborative effort with the sculptor Richard Serra, Peter Eisenman's project for a **MEMORIAL TO THE MURDERED JEWS OF EUROPE** was ratified in June 1999 in a 314-209 vote by the German Parliament. Located in the heart of Berlin close to the Brandenburg Gate and Pariser Platz, the memorial covers two hectares with 2751 blocks of gray concrete of heights varying between a few centimeters and four meters. The last of these was put into place in mid-December 2004. A number of controversies dogged the project, and Eisenman was forced to scale down the original design by politicians who felt it was too imposing for a site in the midst of Berlin's redevelopment area. Close to the location of Hitler's chancellery and the bunker where he died, as it is to the new Potsdamer Platz, the monument is an impressive array that might recall either a graveyard or a cityscape depending on the viewer's personal reactions. The fact that Eisenman is, in his own words, a "non-practicing Jew," here gives a legitimacy that others might not have had to a project that does not serve a purpose in the traditional architectural sense. A memorial, it is also in many ways like a sculpture, or a work of art, albeit one charged with historical meaning. It is massive and undeniable in its physical presence. It will surely long remain as a reminder of events that should not be forgotten.

Der Bildhauer Richard Serra und Peter Eisenman reichten 1997 zusammen einen Entwurf für das **MAHNMAL FÜR DIE ERMORDETEN JUDEN EUROPAS** ein. Im Juni 1999 wurde der Entwurf, nunmehr nur noch von Peter Eisenman bearbeitet, mit einem Abstimmungsergebnis von 314 zu 209 vom Deutschen Bundestag genehmigt. Das Mahnmal liegt mitten in Berlin, unweit des Brandenburger Tors und des Pariser Platzes, und nimmt eine Fläche von 2 ha in Anspruch. 2751 Blöcke aus grauem Beton, in unterschiedlichen Höhen zwischen wenigen Zentimetern und 4 m, bedecken das Feld. Der letzte Block wurde Mitte Dezember 2004 aufgestellt. Eine Reihe von Kontroversen begleitete das Projekt, und Eisenman musste den ursprünglichen Entwurf verkleinern, da verschiedene Politiker meinten, das Projekt sei zu beherrschend für das Bebauungsgebiet im Herzen der Stadt. Es befindet sich in der Nähe der Reichskanzlei Hitlers und des Bunkers, in dem er Selbstmord beging, sowie auch des neuen Potsdamer Platzes. Je nach persönlicher Reaktion des Betrachters ruft die imposante Anordnung Erinnerungen an einen Friedhof oder an eine Stadtlandschaft hervor. Die Tatsache, dass Eisenman — mit eigenen Worten — ein »nicht-praktizierender« Jude ist, verschaffte ihm möglicherweise eine besondere Legitimation. Im traditionellen architektonischen Sinn hat das Projekt keine Funktion. Es ist ein Mahnmal, aber in vielerlei Hinsicht auch eine Skulptur, ein Kunstwerk — wenn auch eines mit einer durch die Geschichte begründeten Bedeutung. Es ist massiv und in seiner physischen Präsenz nicht zu übersehen. Sicherlich wird es für lange Zeit an Ereignisse erinnern, die nicht vergessen werden sollten.

Proposé à l'origine en 1997 en collaboration avec le sculpteur Richard Serra, ce projet de **MÉMORIAL POUR LES JUIFS ASSASSINÉS D'EUROPE** a été approuvé en juin 1999 par un vote du Parlement allemand. Situé au cœur de Berlin, près de la porte de Brandebourg et de la Pariser Platz, le Mémorial couvre deux hectares avec ses 2751 blocs de béton gris de hauteur variable (de quelques centimètres à quatre mètres). La dernière stèle a été mise en place en décembre 2004. Un certain nombre de controverses ont été soulevées par ce projet et Eisenman fut forcé d'en réduire les dimensions originales, car des politiciens pensaient qu'il était trop important pour le centre de la capitale. Proche de la chancellerie du Reich, du Bunker de Hitler et la Potsdamer Platz, ce monument est un impressionnant déploiement de formes qui peuvent rappeler un cimetière ou un paysage urbain, selon les réactions personnelles qu'il suscite en chaque spectateur. Le fait qu'Eisenman soit, selon ses propres termes, un « Juif non-pratiquant » lui donne une légitimité que d'autres n'auraient peut-être pas eue sur un projet qui ne répond pas à une fonction architecturale traditionnelle. C'est un mémorial, mais aussi, à de très nombreux égards, une sculpture ou une œuvre d'art chargée d'histoire. Ce monument massif s'impose par sa présence physique indéniable. Il restera certainement longtemps un rappel d'événements qui ne doivent pas être oubliés.

In its irregular repetitions, the Memorial sometimes creates an abstract pattern (right, lower) but more often brings to mind a vast expanse of unmarked tombs.

In seiner unregelmäßigen Wiederholung schafft das Mahnmal ein abstraktes Muster (rechts unten), noch eher erinnert es aber an ein Feld unzähliger unbenannter Gräber.

Avec son système de répétition/variation, le Mémorial en arrive parfois à créer un motif abstrait (en bas à droite) mais il évoque surtout un vaste champ de tombes anonymes.

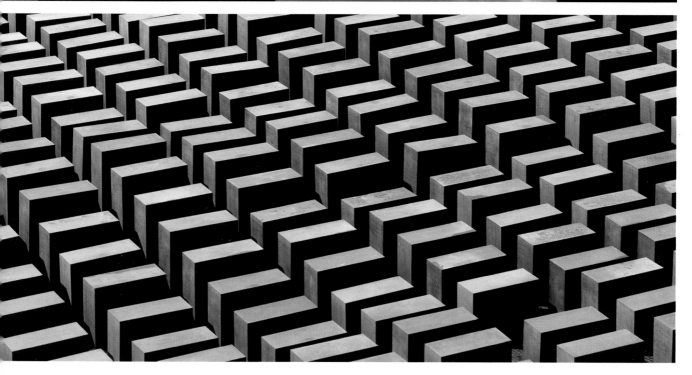

Seen from various angles, Eisenman's Memorial takes on the appearance of a cityscape, or more frequently, of a graveyard. Tombs, or tombstones, echo the modern buildings in the background, but also forcefully recall the events that they commemorate. Their weight is undeniable.

Aus bestimmten Perspektiven gesehen erinnert Eisenmans Mahnmal an eine Stadtlandschaft – noch häufiger jedoch an einen Friedhof. Die »Grabsteine« verweisen auf die modernen Gebäude im Hintergrund, rufen aber auch die Geschehnisse der Vergangenheit eindringlich in Erinnerung. Ihr Gewicht ist unbestreitbar.

Sous divers angles, le Mémorial d'Eisenman peut prendre l'aspect d'un paysage urbain ou plus probablement d'un cimetière. Les tombes ou stèles font écho aux immeubles récents qui les entourent, mais rappellent aussi avec force les événements qu'elles commémorent. Leur présence et leur poids sont incontestables.

EMBT

EMBT – Miralles Tagliabue Arquitectes Associats SL
Passatge de la Pau, 10 Bis. Pral.
08002 Barcelona
Spain

Tel: +34 934 12 53 42
Fax: +34 934 12 37 18
e-mail: publicacio@mirallestagliabue.com
Web: www.mirallestagliabue.com

Born in Barcelona in 1955, **ENRIC MIRALLES** received his degree from the Escuela Técnica Superior de Arquitectura in that city in 1978. He died in 2000. He lectured there, at Columbia University in New York, at Harvard, and at the Architectural Association in London. He formed a partnership with Carme Pinós in 1983, and won a competition for the Igualada Cemetery Park on the outskirts of Barcelona in 1985 (completed in 1992). Contrary to the minimalism of other local architects like Albert Viaplana and Helio Piñón, with whom he worked from 1974 to 1984, or Estève Bonnel, Miralles was known for the exuberance of his style. While interested in deconstruction as it is applied to literature, Miralles is skeptical about its application to architecture. His work includes the Olympic Archery Ranges, Barcelona (1989–91), the La Mina civic center, Barcelona (1987–92), the Morella Boarding School, Castelló (1986–94), and the Huesca Sports Hall (1988–94). **BENEDETTA TAGLIABUE** was born in Milan and graduated from the Instituto Universitario di Architettura di Venezia in 1989. She studied and worked in New York (with Agrest & Gandelsonas) from 1987 to 1989. She worked for Enric Miralles beginning in 1992, first becoming a partner, then leading the studio after the death of Miralles.

ENRIC MIRALLES (1955–2000) wurde in Barcelona geboren und studierte dort an der Escuela Técnica Superior de Arquitectura, an der er später auch lehrte. Außerdem unterrichtete er an der Columbia University in New York, in Harvard und an der Architectural Association in London. Mit Carme Pinós gründete Enric Miralles 1983 ein Büro. 1985 gewann er den Wettbewerb für die Friedhofsanlage Igualada am Stadtrand von Barcelona (Fertigstellung 1992). Im Gegensatz zu anderen katalanischen Architekten wie Albert Viaplana und Helio Piñón, für die er von 1974 bis 1984 arbeitete, oder auch Estève Bonnel, ist Miralles' Architektur nicht dem Minimalismus verpflichtet, sondern zeichnet sich durch eine überschwängliche Sprache aus. Er war am Dekonstruktivismus in der Literatur interessiert, stand seiner Anwendung in der Architektur jedoch skeptisch gegenüber. Zu seinen Projekten gehören die olympischen Anlagen für das Bogenschießen in Barcelona (1989–91), das La-Mina-Gemeindezentrum in Barcelona (1987–92), das Morella-Internat in Castelló (1986–94) und das Sportzentrum in Huesca (1988–94). **BENEDETTA TAGLIABUE**, geboren in Mailand, machte 1989 am Instituto Universitario di Architettura di Venezia ihren Abschluss. Von 1987 bis 1989 studierte und arbeitete sie in New York (bei Agrest & Gandelsonas). Seit 1992 war sie für Enric Miralles tätig, wurde seine Partnerin und übernahm nach dessen Tod die Leitung des Büros.

Né à Barcelone en 1955 et mort en 2000, **ENRIC MIRALLES** était diplômé de la Escuela Tecnica Superior de Arquitectura de cette ville (1978). Il y a enseigné ainsi qu'à Columbia University à New York, à Harvard et à l'Architectural Association de Londres. Il s'est associé à Carme Pinós en 1973 et a remporté le concours pour le parc du cimetière d'Igualada, dans la banlieue de Barcelone, en 1985 (achevé en 1992). À l'opposé du minimalisme d'autres praticiens catalans, comme Albert Viaplana et Helio Pinón avec lesquels il a travaillé de 1974 à 1984, ou encore Esteve Bonell, Miralles était connu pour l'exubérance de son style. Intéressé par le déconstructivisme en littérature, il s'est toujours montré sceptique sur ses applications à l'architecture. Son œuvre comprend le stade de tir à l'arc des Jeux olympiques de Barcelone (1989–91); le centre municipal de La Mina, Barcelone (1987–92); le pensionnat de Morella, Castello (1986–94) et la salle de sport de Huesca (1988–94). **BENEDETTA TAGLIABUE**, née à Milan, est diplômée de l'Istituto universitario di architettura de Venise (1989). Elle a étudié et travaillé à New York (chez Agrest et Gandelsonas) de 1987 à 1989 puis, à partir de 1992, avec Enric Miralles, dont elle fut la compagne. Elle a pris la direction de l'agence à sa mort.

SCOTTISH PARLIAMENT

Edinburgh, UK, 1998–2004

Floor area: 31 894 m². Client: Scottish Parliament.
Cost: €370 million

Inaugurated by Queen Elizabeth II on October 9, 2004, four years after the death of Enric Miralles, the **SCOTTISH PARLIAMENT** was from the outset a contro-versial project, in part because of its sensitive site at the end of the Royal Mile in Edinburgh. The project was carried out in a joint venture by Enric Miralles, Benedetta Tagliabue EMBT Arquitectes Associats and RMJM Scotland, M. A. H. Duncan, T. B. Stewart. With a site area of 18 289 m² plus 17 329 m² that was landscaped and a total floor area of 31 894 m², the building was created essentially with precast concrete, metal frames and laminated wood. As the architects wrote, "The land itself will be a material, a physical building material… the Scottish Parliament will be slotted into the land… to carve in the land the form of gathering people together." 14 000 tons of granite from Kemnay Quarry in Aberdeenshire were used as were 2000 tons of Black Belfast granite imported from South Africa for the overlaid mosaic panels. The profile of these panels is intended to evoke the outline of the *Reverend Robert Walker skating in Duddingston Loch,* a painting by Henry Raeburn conserved at the Scot-tish National Gallery. Winner of a 2005 RIBA Architecture Award, the Parliament building elicited this commentary: "The building is a statement of sparkling excellence. On the Memory Wall, one of the statements reads, 'Say little and say it well.' This building is definitely saying a lot rather than little, but it definitely says it well." The most distinctive exterior feature of the building, aside from its obvious complexity, is the roof inspired by upturned boats. Press sources indicate that the final cost of the project was some 635 million euros (the architects list 370 million euros as the cost), whereas the July 1998 budget had been fixed at 80 million euros. A public inquiry held at the Land Court in Edinburgh, headed by Lord Fraser of Carmyllie, concluded that the two architectural firms involved had had great difficulty communicating, and that costs had not been sufficiently controlled by all concerned. Lord Fraser issued a series of ten recommendations to avoid such difficulties for future Scottish public projects.

Vier Jahre nach Enric Miralles' Tod eröffnete Königin Elisabeth II. am 9. Oktober 2004 das neue **SCHOTTISCHE PARLAMENTSGEBÄUDE**. Von Beginn an war das Projekt umstritten, was zT. an seinem sensiblen Standort am Ende der Royal Mile in Edinburgh liegt. Das Parlamentsgebäude ist ein Gemeinschaftsprojekt von Enric Miral-les, Benedetta Tagliabue EMBT Arquitectes Associats und RMJM Scotland, M. A. H. Duncan, T. B. Stewart. Das Grundstück ist 31 894 m² groß, 17 329 m² davon wurden landschaftsplanerisch gestaltet. Betonfertigteile und ein Tragwerk aus Stahl und Brettschichtholz sind für das Gebäude charakteristisch. Die Architekten schreiben: »Das Terrain selbst wird ein Material sein, ein physisches Baumaterial … das Parlamentsgebäude wird in das Terrain ›eingenutet‹ sein … um in den Boden die Form, die sich bildet, wenn Menschen zusammenkommen, einzumeißeln.« 14 000 t Granit aus den Steinbrüchen von Kemnay in Aberdeenshire wurden verbaut, außerdem 2000 t Black-Belfast-Granit aus Südafrika, die für die äußere, mosaikartige Verkleidung verwendet wurden. Das Muster soll an den Umriss eines Gemäldes von Henry Raeburn erin-nern, das in der Scottish National Gallery hängt: *Reverend Robert Walker skating in Duddingston Loch.* Das Gebäude wurde mit dem 2005 RIBA Architecture Award aus-gezeichnet und gab Anlass zu folgendem Kommentar: »Das Gebäude ist ein brillantes Statement. Eine Aussage auf der ›Wand der Erinnerung‹ lautet: ‚Sag wenig, aber das Wenige gut‹. Dieses Gebäude sagt definitiv viel, nicht wenig, aber ganz sicher sagt es das gut.« Neben seiner offensichtlichen Komplexität sind das prägnanteste äußere Merkmal des Gebäudes die Dachkonstruktionen, die an umgedrehte Boote erinnern. Presseberichten zufolge beliefen sich die Kosten des Gebäudes auf umge-rechnet 635 Millionen Euro (die Architekten geben die Kosten mit 370 Millionen Euro an). Im Juli 1998 waren die Kosten auf 80 Millionen Euro festgelegt worden. Eine öffentliche Untersuchung durch das Landgericht Edinburgh unter Vorsitz von Lord Fraser of Carmyllie kam zu dem Ergebnis, dass die beiden beteiligten Architekturbüros sehr schlecht miteinander kommunizierten und dass die Kosten von allen Beteiligten nicht ausreichend kontrolliert worden waren. Eine Liste mit zehn Empfehlungen wurde herausgegeben, um bei zukünftigen öffentlichen Bauten in Schottland ähnliche Probleme zu vermeiden.

Inauguré par la reine Elizabeth II le 9 octobre 2004, quatre ans après la disparition d'Enric Miralles, le **PARLEMENT ÉCOSSAIS** aura été dès le départ un pro-jet controversé, en partie parce qu'il était situé dans une zone sensible à l'extrémité du Royal Mile à Édimbourg. Il a été réalisé collectivement, par Enric Miralles, Bene-detta Tagliabue EMBT Arquitectes Associats et RMJM Scotland, M. A. H. Duncan, T. B. Stewart. Sur un terrain de 31 894 m² dont 17 329 m² ont été paysagés, le bâtiment à ossature de métal est essentiellement construit en béton préfabriqué et bois lamellé-collé. Comme l'écrit l'architecte, « le sol lui-même sera un matériau, un matériau physique de construction… le Parlement écossais sera inséré dans le sol… de façon à graver dans la terre l'empreinte d'un lieu fait pour réunir les gens. » 14 000 tonnes de granit de la carrière de Kemnay dans l'Aberdeenshire ont été utilisées ainsi que 2000 tonnes de granit Black Belfast importé d'Afrique du Sud pour former une mosaïque de panneaux. Le profil de ces panneaux est censé évoquer les contours d'une œuvre du peintre Henry Raeburn, *Le Révérend Robert Walker patinant sur le Loch de Duddington,* conservée à la National Gallery écossaise. Le bâtiment a remporté le prix d'architecture 2005 du RIBA, accompagné du commentaire suivant : « Cette réalisation est une brillante affirmation d'excellence. Sur le ‹ Mur de la mémoire ›, une des citations dit ‹ Parlez peu et parlez bien ›. Non seulement ce bâtiment dit beaucoup plus que ‹ peu ›, mais il le dit particulièrement bien. » L'élément extérieur le plus caractéristique, en dehors d'une évidente complexité, est le toit inspiré de coques de bateaux inversées. Des sources journalistiques ont parlé d'un coût final de quelque 635 millions d'euros (contre les 370 millions indiqués par les architectes) alors que le budget avait été fixé, en 1998, à 80 millions d'euros. Une enquête publique, menée par Lord Fraser of Carmyllie, a conclu que les deux agences d'archi-tecture mises en cause avaient eu la plus grande difficulté à communiquer et que les coûts n'avaient pas été suffisamment contrôlés par les services concernés. Lord Fraser a publié une série de dix recommandations pour éviter que les mêmes problèmes se reproduisent pour de futurs projets publics en Écosse.

In the context of Edinburgh's very traditional "Royal Mile" the new Scottish Parliament stands out as being quite different, which has of course led to a good deal of criticism.

Im Kontext von Edinburghs altehrwürdiger Royal Mile fällt das neue Schottische Parlament besonders auf, was natürlich schon zu Kritik von vielen Seiten geführt hat.

Dans le contexte du très traditionaliste Royal Mile d'Édimbourg, le nouveau Parlement écossais affirme sa différence et cela a entraîné, comme l'on pouvait s'y attendre, de multiples controverses.

This image shows the rather abrupt transition from Edinburgh's stone architecture to that of the new Parliament building. Although there are other modern buildings nearby, the EMBT design brings a surprisingly complex vision of contemporary architecture to the area.

Edinburghs steinerne Architektur und das neue Parlamentsgebäude stehen recht übergangslos nebeneinander. In der näheren Umgebung gibt es auch andere moderne Gebäude, im Bau von EMBT manifestiert sich jedoch eine überraschend komplexe Vorstellung von aktueller Architektur.

On voit bien ici la transition assez brutale entre l'architecture de pierre de la capitale écossaise et celle du Parlement. Même si d'autres bâtiments modernes se trouvent à proximité, le projet d'EMBT impose sa vision très complexe de l'architecture contemporaine dans un quartier protégé.

Large glazed areas bring a good deal of the Scottish capital's limited supply of daylight into the building. This is no minimalist design, in fact it might be considered something of the opposite, a dense, almost willfully "difficult" vision.

Große Glasflächen bringen einen hohen Anteil des in der schottischen Hauptstadt nicht im Übermaß vorhandenen Lichts in das Gebäude. Das Parlament ist kein minimalistischer Bau – ganz im Gegenteil stellt es eine dichte, fast absichtlich »schwierige« Vision vor.

De vastes pans vitrés compensent la faiblesse de la lumière naturelle qui, en Écosse, dure de longs mois. Le projet du Parlement, qui est tout sauf minimaliste – et peut-être même à l'exact opposé – exprime une vision dense qui recherche presque volontairement la difficulté.

The visitor or user of the building is bombarded with a cacophony of forms that does not appear to resolve itself into an "organic" type of architecture. Highly original, the building is the result of a complex and criticized selection and control process.

Der Besucher bzw. Benutzer wird mit einer Kakofonie von Formen bombardiert, die aber nicht in eine organische Architektur münden. Das einzigartige Gebäude ist das Resultat eines komplexen und kontroversen Auswahl- und Kontrollprozesses.

Le visiteur ou l'usager de ce bâtiment est bombardé d'une cacophonie de formes ne pouvant se réduire à un vocabulaire de type organique. Très original, le Parlement est l'aboutissement d'un processus de sélection et de contrôle complexe, et critiqué.

SHUHEI ENDO

Shuhei Endo Architecture Institute
Domus AOI 5F, 5–15–11, Nishitenma, Kita-ku
Osaka 530–0047
Japan

Tel: +81 663 12 74 55
Fax: +81 663 12 74 56
e-mail: endo@paramodern.com
Web: www.paramodern.com

Rooftecture S ▶

Born in Shiga Prefecture in 1960, **SHUHEI ENDO** obtained his masters degree from the Kyoto City University of Art in 1986. He worked after that with the architect Osamu Ishii and established his own firm, the Shuhei Endo Architecture Institute, in 1988. His work has been widely published and he has received numerous prizes including the Andrea Palladio International Prize in Italy (1993). His recent work includes his Slowtecture S, Maihara, Shiga (2002); Growtecture S, Osaka (2002); Springtecture B, Biwa-cho, Shiga (2002); Bubbletecture M, Maihara, Shiga (2003); Rooftecture C, Taishi, Hyogo (2003); Rooftecture H, Kamigori, Hyogo (2004); and Bubbletecture O, Maruoka, Fukui (2004).

SHUHEI ENDO, 1960 in der Präfektur Shiga geboren, erwarb 1986 seinen Masterabschluss an der Kyoto City University of Art in Kioto. Danach arbeitete er bei Osamu Ishii und gründete 1988 sein eigenes Büro, das Shuhei Endo Architecture Institute. Für seine Bauten, die umfassend publiziert wurden, hat er zahlreiche Preise erhalten, darunter den italienischen Andrea Palladio International Award (1993). Zu seinen jüngsten Bauten gehören Slowtecture S in Maihara, Shiga (2002), Growtecture S in Osaka (2002), Springtecture B in Biwa-cho, Shiga (2002), Bubbletecture M in Maihara, Shiga (2003), Rooftecture C in Taishi, Hyogo (2003), Rooftecture H in Kamigori, Hyogo (2004) und Bubbletecture O in Maruoka, Fukui (2004).

Né dans la préfecture de Shiga en 1960, **SHUHEI ENDO** est Master of Architecture de l'Université d'art de Kyoto (1986). Il a ensuite travaillé auprès de l'architecte Osamu Ishii et créé son agence, Shuhei Endo Architecture Institute, en 1988. Son œuvre a été largement publiée et il a reçu de nombreux prix, dont le Prix international Andrea Palladio en Italie (1993). Parmi ses travaux récents : la Slowtecture S, Maihara, Shiga (2002) ; la Growtecture S, Osaka (2002) ; la Rooftecture C, Taishi, Hyogo (2003) ; la Rooftecture H, Kamigori, Hyogo (2003) et lka Bubbletecture O, Maruoka, Fukui (2004).

ROOFTECTURE S

Kobe, Hyogo, 2005

Floor area: 66 m². Client: Ryosuke and Yasuko Uenishi.
Cost: €120 000

This 66 m² steel frame house occupies just 50.3 m² of the total 130 m² triangular lot. Twenty meters long, the site varies in depth between 1.5 and 4 meters. This is in part due to the steep inclination of the location, facing the Inland Sea. It is covered in galvanized steel sheet. Interior materials include galvanized steel, plywood and wood flooring. As Endo says, "The main theme of this house has been the archaic problem involving slopes and architecture… States of liberation and closure created though the interaction with the slope define this house's spatial quality." Perched on a retaining wall, the house has a wrap-around roof that undoubtedly dictated the choice of its name **ROOFTECTURE S**. Japanese houses are often quite small, given the high population density, particularly along the country's east coast. Like much of Endo's other work, this house challenges the assumptions of architecture and finds an appropriate solution for a particularly difficult and tight location.

Das 66 m² große Haus mit einer Stahlskelettkonstruktion nimmt nur 50,3 m² des dreieckigen, 130 m² großen Grundstücks ein. Dieses hat eine Länge von 20 m, seine Breite beträgt 1,5 bis 4 m. Das liegt z. T. an der steil ansteigenden Topografie des Standortes am japanischen Binnenmeer. Das Haus ist mit verzinktem Stahlblech eingedeckt. Zu den Materialien im Inneren gehören verzinkter Stahl, Sperrholz und Fußböden aus Holz. Endo erläutert: »Das Hauptthema dieses Hauses ist das grundlegende Problem, das sich aus einer Hanglage in Verbindung mit Architektur ergibt… Stadien zwischen Befreiung und Umschließung, die durch die Wechselwirkungen zwischen Hang und Haus entstehen, bestimmen die räumlichen Qualitäten des Hauses.« Das Dach, das dem auf eine Stützmauer aufgesetzten Haus seinen Namen **ROOFTECTURE S** gab, wickelt sich um den Baukörper. Wohnhäuser in Japan sind oft recht klein, was an der hohen Bevölkerungsdichte speziell an der Ostküste des Landes liegt. Wie viele andere Gebäude Endos fordert Rooftecture S die gängigen Vorstellungen von Architektur heraus und findet für ein besonders schwieriges und enges Grundstück eine angemessene Lösung.

Cette maison à ossature de bois de 66 m² de surface n'occupe que 50,3 m² d'une parcelle triangulaire de 130 m². En effet, le terrain de vingt mètres de long donnant sur la mer Intérieure du Japon est très fortement incliné et ne mesure que 1,5 à 4 m de profondeur. La maison est recouverte de tôle d'acier galvanisé et utilise à l'intérieur le même acier, le contreplaqué et des planchers en bois. Pour Endo, « le thème principal de cette maison était l'éternel problème posé par les rapports entre une pente et l'architecture… Des situations de libération et de fermeture se créent par interaction avec la pente et définissent le caractère spatial de cette maison ». Juchée sur un mur de soutènement, elle a un toit enveloppant, comme drapé autour d'elle, qui lui vaut son nom de **ROOFTECTURE S**. Les maisons japonaises sont souvent assez petites du fait de la densité démographique du pays, en particulier sur la côte est. Comme beaucoup d'autres réalisations d'Endo, celle-ci remet en cause les certitudes de l'architecture et apporte une solution appropriée à un terrain particulièrement étroit et difficile.

An exercise in extremes, the Rooftecture S design is an ingenious solution to the problems posed by a lot that many would consider unusable. Endo has fashioned an intelligent response to the narrow and abrupt site.

Rooftexture S könnte man als »Extremarchitektur« bezeichnen. Der Entwurf löst die Probleme des Grundstücks, das viele für unbebaubar halten, auf geniale Weise. Endo hat das Haus intelligent an das enge und steile Grundstück angepasst.

Exercice extrême, le projet de la Rooftecture S est la solution aux problèmes posés par un terrain que beaucoup auraient jugé inutilisable. Endo a imaginé une réponse intelligente à ce site étroit et escarpé.

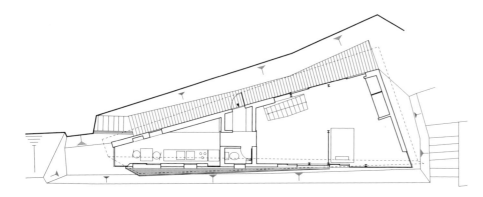

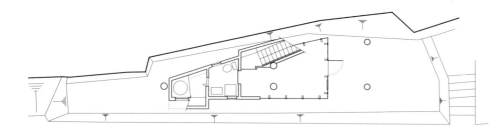

Inside, the house brings to mind ship design to some extent, one of few comparable types of equally constrained space.

Die Innenarchitektur des Hauses erinnert teilweise an Bootsbau: Nur dort gibt es ein vergleichbar knappes Raumangebot.

L'intérieur de la maison rappelle dans une certaine mesure celui d'un bateau, l'un des rares types de volume aussi contraignant.

FLANK

FLAnk, Inc., 548 West 28th Street, Suite 234, New York
New York 10011, USA

Tel: +1 212 352 8224, Fax: +1 212 675 8126
e-mail: info@flankonline.com
Web: www.flankonline.com/

FLANK is an architecture and real-estate development firm created in January 2002 in New York. Its principals are Jonathan Kully and Michael Walsdorf. Kully and Walsdorf both graduated from Columbia University's Graduate School of Architecture in May 2002. FLAnk is currently a nine-person firm that seeks to "blur the delineation between architecture and development, appropriating characteristics from each." Prior to attending Columbia, Jonathan Kully acted as a strategic planner at the corporate offices for The Gap, while Michael Walsdorf proceeded directly from undergraduate studies. FLAnk is currently involved in several development projects in Manhattan, acting as design coordinator and in certain cases project management including the following recent projects: 454 West 20th Street, New York – renovation of a landmark brownstone in Chelsea. Flank designed and developed the property; 145 6th Avenue, coordinated renovation of the base building and assisted in the preparation for a future tower addition;157 Hudson Street – coordinated the retrofit and renovation of a landmark building as well as several interior modifications; 520 West 27th Street, coordinated design and pre-construction of a new commercial condominium, and managed development team throughout the project; 135 West 4th Street, design and development of a residential conversion of an existing church. FLAnk's aim, as they say, is that "by controlling the entire process from capital structures, to design, to pre-construction, through construction management, we are able to construct innovative buildings at a fraction of the market's cost."

FLANK, im Januar 2002 in New York gegründet, ist gleichzeitig Architekturbüro und Projektentwickler. Geschäftsführende Partner sind Jonathan Kully und Michael Walsdorf. Beide studierten an der Columbia University's Graduate School of Architecture und machten dort im Mai 2002 ihren Master of Architecture. FLAnk hat derzeit neun Mitarbeiter. Ziel des Büros ist es, »die Grenzen zwischen Architektur und der Entwicklung von Grundstücken zu überwinden und sich die charakteristischen Merkmale beider Tätigkeitsbereiche zunutze zu machen«. Jonathan Kully war als Strategieplaner für das Bekleidungsunternehmen The Gap tätig, bevor er an der Columbia University studierte; Michael Walsdorf begann direkt nach der Schulausbildung zu studieren. FLAnk ist zurzeit mit der möglichen Bebauung von verschiedenen Grundstücken in Manhattan beschäftigt. Dabei fungiert das Büro als Entwurfsberater und übernimmt in einigen Fällen auch das Projektmanagement. Projekte sind u. a.: 454 West 20th Street, New York – Sanierung eines denkmalgeschützten Brownstones in Chelsea (Entwurf und Entwicklung), 145 6th Avenue – Koordination der Sanierung des unteren Gebäudeteils und Entwurf einer Hochhausaufstockung, 157 Hudson Street – Koordination der Nachrüstung und Sanierung sowie verschiedener Umbauten im Inneren eines denkmalgeschützten Gebäudes, 520 West 27th Street – Koordination des Entwurfs und der vorbereitenden Planung eines Neubaus mit Eigentumswohnungen sowie Management des Entwicklungsteams, 135 West 4th Street – Entwicklung und Entwurf des Umbaus einer Kirche in Wohnungen. FLAnk formuliert seine Strategie so: »Indem wir den ganzen Prozess, von der Frage der Finanzierung über den Entwurf und die vorbereitende Planung bis zur Bauleitung kontrollieren, können wir innovative Gebäude zu einem Bruchteil des Marktpreises anbieten.«

FLANK est une agence d'architecture et de promotion immobilière créée en janvier 2002 à New York. Ses associés sont Jonathan Kully et Michael Walsdorf, tous deux diplômés de la Columbia University's Graduate School of Architecture en mai 2002. FLAnk emploie neuf personnes qui cherchent à « réduire les frontières entre l'architecture et la promotion, en s'appropriant les caractéristiques de chacun de ces domaines ». Avant d'étudier à Columbia, Kully était planner stratégique pour Gap, tandis que Michael Walsdorf était encore au collège. L'agence travaille actuellement à plusieurs projets de promotion à Manhattan, comme coordinatrice et dans certains cas gestionnaire de projet, en particulier sur les chantiers new-yorkais de : 454 West 20th Street, rénovation d'un immeuble « brownstone » typique de Chelsea ; 145 6th Avenue, coordination de la rénovation d'un immeuble et assistance à la préparation d'une future extension en tour ; 157 Hudson Street, coordination de la réhabilitation d'un immeuble classé et de plusieurs modifications intérieures ; 520 West 27th Street, coordination de la conception et travaux préparatoires pour un nouvel immeuble en copropriété et gestion du projet ; 135 West 4th Street, conception et promotion de la conversion d'une église en appartements. L'objectif de FLAnk est le suivant : « En contrôlant la totalité du processus, de la structuration du capital à la conception, des travaux préparatoires à la gestion de la construction, nous sommes en mesure de construire des bâtiments novateurs pour une part infime des coûts du marché ».

GATEWAY BRIDGE

New York, New York, USA, 2002-04

Floor area: 75 000 m² (15 000 m² per level). Client: Port Authority of New York and New Jersey.
Cost: $450 million

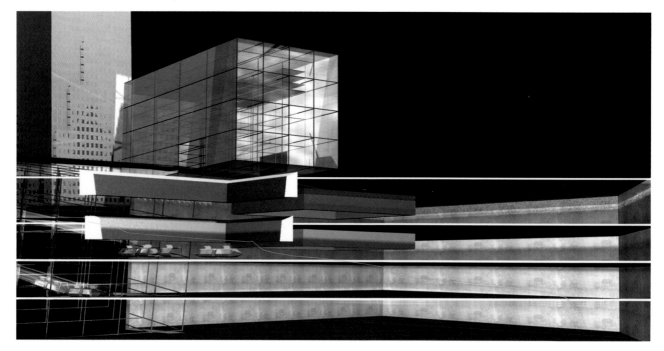

A subterranean section showing vehicular paths and the memorial assembly space.

Der unterirdische Schnitt zeigt die Verkehrswege und den Gedenkraum.

La coupe souterraine montre les accès en voiture et le hall d'accueil du Mémorial.

This project was first conceived as an unsolicited proposal following the events of September 11, 2001. As the architects explain, "this Node relocates the concentration of capital, ideas, and transportation to a suspended location above the Hudson River... Our bridge is programmed with office space, mixed income housing, entertainment venues, cultural institutions, and passage for pedestrians, trains, and vehicles." And they conclude that "the bridge seeks to be more than just a passage between New Jersey and the city by becoming part of the cityscape itself." Although it was not retained amongst the projects that are advancing in and around the former World Trade Center site, Flank entered the project in the "**GATEWAY BRIDGE**" competition organized by *New York Magazine*. The judge for the competition won by FLAnk was Richard Meier. Meier declared: "This proposal separates vehicular and pedestrian traffic and is visually innovative. The result has potential to be a lively addition to the Manhattan skyline and is a design with high artistic and symbolic values. It is original and memorable."

Das Projekt war zuerst nur ein Vorschlag, der nach dem 11. September 2001 ohne Auftrag erarbeitet wurde. »Kapital, Ideen und Transportwege werden auf einen über dem Hudson River gelegenen Ort als neuen Knotenpunkt der Stadt verlegt... Auf der Brücke gibt es Büros, Wohnungen für Menschen mit unterschiedlichem Einkommen, Unterhaltungsangebote und kulturelle Einrichtungen; außerdem können Fußgänger, Fahrzeuge und Züge die Brücke passieren«, erläutern die Architekten und schließen: »Die Brücke will mehr als nur eine Verbindung zwischen New Jersey und der Stadt sein, indem sie zu einem Teil der Stadtlandschaft selbst wird.« Die Brücke gehört nicht zu den Projekten auf dem Grundstück des ehemaligen World Trade Centers oder in dessen Umgebung, die weiterentwickelt werden. Trotzdem reichte FLAnk das Projekt beim vom *New York Magazine* durchgeführten **GATEWAY-BRIDGE**-Wettbewerb ein und gewann. Richard Meier, Juror des Wettbewerbs beurteilte das Projekt folgendermaßen: »Der motorisierte Verkehr wird bei diesem Vorschlag vom Fußgängerverkehr getrennt. Das Projekt ist visuell innovativ und hat das Potenzial, der Skyline von Manhattan ein starkes Element hinzuzufügen. Es ist ein Entwurf von hohem künstlerischem und symbolischem Wert. Er ist originell und denkwürdig.«

Ce projet était à l'origine une proposition libre conçue à la suite des événements du 11 septembre 2001. Pour FLAnk, « ce point nodal restitue la concentration de capital, d'idées et de transports dans un lieu en suspension au-dessus de l'Hudson... Notre pont répond à un programme de bureaux, de logements de divers types, de lieux de spectacles, d'institutions culturelles et de voies de circulation pour les piétons, les trains et les voitures... Il ne cherche pas à être plus qu'un passage entre le New Jersey et la ville, bien intégré dans le paysage urbain ». Bien que le projet n'ait pas été retenu pour le site du World Trade Center, FLAnk l'a présenté au concours du « **GATEWAY BRIDGE** » organisé par le *New York Magazine*. Le juge du concours remporté par l'agence était Richard Meier, qui a déclaré : « Cette proposition qui sépare la circulation des piétons de celle des véhicules est visuellement novatrice. Elle possède l'atout d'être un ajout dynamique à la silhouette urbaine de Manhattan et d'incarner des valeurs artistiques et symboliques élevées. C'est un projet original et qui marque les esprits. »

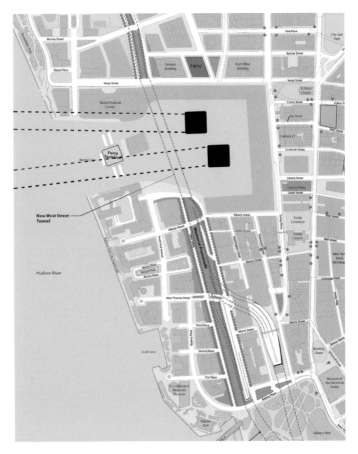

Right, a map illustrating the trajectory bridge in relation to the context. Below, the bridge looking south.

Rechts: Lageplan mit Brücke im Kontext. Unten: Blick Richtung Süden mit Brücke.

À droite, carte situant le pont dans son contexte. Ci-dessous, le pont vers le sud.

MASSIMILIANO FUKSAS

M Fuksas Arch
Piazza del Monte di Pietà, 30
00186 Rome
Italy

Tel: +39 06 68 80 78 71
Fax: +39 06 68 80 78 72
e-mail: m.fuksas@fuksas.it
Web: www.fuksas.it

MASSIMILIANO FUKSAS was born in 1944 in Rome. He received his degree in architecture at the University of La Sapienza in 1969. He created the agency Granma (1969–88) with Anna Maria Sacconi, and opened an office in Paris in 1989. He won the 1999 Grand Prix d'Architecture in France, and has written the architecture column of the Italian weekly *L'Espresso* beginning in 2000. He was the Director of the 7th Architecture Biennale in Venice (1998–2000). His presence in France was notably marked by the Médiathèque in Rézé (1987–91); the National Engineering School in Brest (ENIB ISAMOR, 1990–92); the Maison des Arts at the Michel de Montaigne University in Bordeaux (1992–95); Maximilien Perret High School, Alfortville, near Paris (1995–97). His Corten steel entrance for the caves at Niaux (1988–93) shows, as did the Maison des Arts in Bordeaux, that Fuksas has a sustained interest in contemporary sculpture and art. In 1995–2001 he built the Twin Tower, a 150-meter-high headquarters for Wienerberger in Vienna, Austria; and the Piazza Mall, an entertainment center, commercial and office complex in Eindhoven, The Netherlands (1999–2004). More recently, Fuksas has completed the Ferrari Research Center, Maranello, Italy (2001–04) and is presently working on three large-scale projects: European Convention Center (EUR) in Rome and two rock-and-roll concert halls (Zénith) in Strasbourg and Amiens.

Der 1944 in Rom geborene **MASSIMILIANO FUKSAS** studierte an der Università di Roma »La Sapienza« Architektur und machte 1969 sein Diplom. Zusammen mit Anna Maria Sacconi gründete er das Büro Granma, das von 1969 bis 1988 bestand. 1989 eröffnete er in Paris ein neues Büro. 1999 gewann er den französischen Grand Prix d'Architecture. Seit 2000 schreibt er die Architekturkolumne für das Wochenmagazin *L'Espresso*. Fuksas war Direktor der VII. Architekturbiennale in Venedig (1998–2000). Bekannt wurde er in Frankreich durch folgende Gebäude: die Médiathèque in Rézé (1987–91), die Ecole Nationale d'Ingénieurs et Institut Scientifique in Brest (ENIB ISAMOR, 1990–92), die Maison des Arts der Université Michel de Montaigne in Bordeaux (1992–95) und das Lycée Maximilien Perret in Alfortville nahe Paris (1995–97). Der Eingang aus Corten-Stahl für die Höhlen von Niaux (1988–93) zeigt ebenso wie die Maison des Arts in Bordeaux Fuksas' beständiges Interesse an zeitgenössischer Bildhauerei bzw. Kunst. 1995 bis 2001 wurden die Twin Towers, die 150 m hohe Zentrale von Wienerberger in Wien realisiert, 1999 bis 2004 die Piazza Mall, ein Komplex mit Büro-, Laden- und Unterhaltungsnutzung in Eindhoven, Niederlande. Vor kurzem wurde das Forschungszentrum von Ferrari in Maranello, Italien (2001–04), fertig gestellt. Zurzeit plant Fuksas drei große Projekte: das European Convention Center (EUR) in Rom und zwei Rock-and-Roll-Konzerthallen (Zénith) in Straßburg und Amiens.

Né en 1944 à Rome, **MASSIMILANO FUKSAS** est diplômé d'architecture de l'Université La Sapienza (1969). Il a créé l'agence Gramma (1969–88) avec Anna Maria Sacconi et ouvert une agence à Paris en 1989. Grand prix d'architecture 1999 en France, il a par ailleurs tenu une rubrique d'architecture dans l'hebdomadaire italien *L'Espresso* à partir de 2000. Il a été le directeur de la 7e Biennale d'architecture de Venise (1998–2000). Sa présence en France a été marquée par la construction de la Médiathèque de Rézé (1987–91); l'École nationale d'ingénierie de Brest, Enib Isamor (1990–92); la Maison des arts de l'Université Michel de Montaigne à Bordeaux (1992–95); le collège Maximilien Perret à Alfortville près de Paris (1995–97). De même que la Maison des arts de Bordeaux, l'entrée en acier Corten qu'il a créée pour les grottes préhistoriques de Niaux (1988–93) montre son indéfectible intérêt pour la sculpture et l'art contemporains. En 1999–2001, il a construit les Twin Towers, un immeuble de bureaux de 150 m de haut pour Wienerberger (Vienne, Autriche), et le Piazza Mall, centre de loisirs, centre commercial et complexe de bureaux à Eindhoven, Pays-Bas (1999–2004). Plus récemment, il a achevé le Centre de recherche Ferrari, Maranello, Italie (2001–04) et travaille actuellement à trois importants projets: le Centre européen de congrès à Rome et deux Zénith, salles de concert rock, à Strasbourg et Amiens.

NEW MILAN TRADE FAIR

Pero-Rho, Milan, Italy, 2002–05

Total floor area: 2 000 000 m², building floor area: 1 000 000 m²; exhibition floor area: more than 400 000 m².
Client: Fondazione Fiera Milano. Cost: €750 million

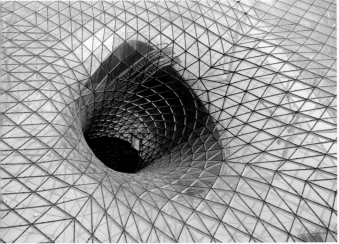

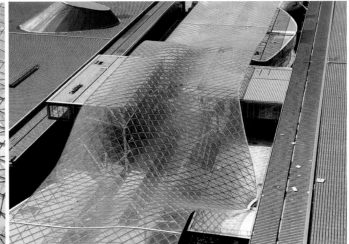

Massimilliano Fuksas's vision of the central glass-covered walkway of the Fiera Milano is related to drawings he made of vortices or storm formations.

Die Idee eines zentralen, glasüberdachten Weges für die Fiera Milano hat Massimiliano Fuksas aus Zeichnungen entwickelt, die er von Strudel- und Wirbelformationen machte.

La vision de l'allée couverte de la Fiera Milano par Massimiliano Fuksas se rapproche des dessins de vortex ou de formations d'orages.

An aerial view gives a clear idea of the size and volume of the complex, with the main walkway slicing through the middle of the more ordinary exhibition areas to the right and left.

Das Luftbild vermittelt einen Eindruck von der Größe des Projektes. Der Hauptweg verläuft mitten durch das ansonsten weniger spektakuläre Ausstellungsgelände.

Vue aérienne montrant les dimensions impressionnantes du complexe. L'allée principale se fraye un chemin au milieu de pavillons d'exposition plus traditionnels.

Easily the largest project that Massimiliano Fuksas has ever been involved in, the new **FAIR OF MILAN** measure no less than 1.4 million square meters. Fuksas won a 2001 competition against the likes of Santiago Calatrava, the German firm von Gerkan Marg und Partner and the Italian Mario Bellini, and completed his enormous task in just over 27 months. At its height, the Fiera Milano was the largest civilian construction project underway in the world. The most architecturally interesting feature of the complex is its central "urban promenade," a 1.5 km covered walkway with a dynamic glass canopy design that flows over the crowded people movers in patterns that bring to mind clouds or even tornados. Given the rather extreme conditions imposed by the large scale of the Fiera Milano and the very short construction schedule, it might have been expected that Fuksas would do no more than a competent job, but he has gone much further, almost reinventing the idea of fair grounds and above all adding his own personal, artistic touch. Although his walkway may bring to mind certain computer-generated forms, the source of his ideas is in drawings and models which often approach the quality of artworks in and of themselves.

Bei weitem das größte Projekt von Massimiliano Fuksas ist die neue **MAILÄNDER MESSE** mit nicht weniger als 1,4 Millionen m². Fuksas gewann 2001 den Wettbewerb, an dem u. a. Santiago Calatrava, Von Gerkan, Marg und Partner sowie Mario Bellini teilgenommen hatten; in nur 27 Monaten wurde das enorme Bauvorhaben durchgeführt. Auf dem Höhepunkt der Bautätigkeit war die Fiera Milano die größte zivile Baustelle der Welt. Das interessanteste Merkmal der Anlage ist die zentrale »urbane Promenade«, ein 1,5 km langer überdeckter Weg mit einem dynamisch »fließenden« Vordach, unter dem die Messefahrzeuge, die für den Transport der Besucher eingesetzt werden, hin- und herfahren. Dabei evozieren die Formen des Daches Bilder von Wolken, sogar von Tornados. In Anbetracht der Bedingungen, die die enorme Größe der Fiera Milano und die extrem kurze Bauzeit darstellten, hätte man erwarten können, dass Fuksas die ihm gestellte Aufgabe kompetent lösen würde – und nicht mehr. Tatsächlich ist er aber viel weiter gegangen: Fast könnte man sagen, er habe die Idee aller Messegelände neu erfunden und vor allem seine persönliche, künstlerische Sichtweise eingebracht. Der Messeweg mag an bestimmte computergenerierte Formen erinnern, die Ideen basieren jedoch auf Fuksas' Zeichnungen und Modellen, die oft selbst die Qualität von Kunstwerken annehmen.

Le nouveau complexe de la **FOIRE DE MILAN**, certainement le plus important projet, et de loin, dans lequel ait jamais été impliqué Massimilano Fuksas, couvre pas moins de 1,4 million de m². Il en a remporté le concours en 2001 face à Santiago Calatrava, à l'agence allemande Von Gerkan, Marg und Partner et à l'Italien Mario Bellini, et a achevé cette tâche immense en un peu plus de 27 mois seulement. À un certain moment, ce chantier était le plus important projet civil en construction dans le monde. Sa caractéristique la plus intéressante est une « promenade urbaine », allée de 1,5 km de long couverte par un long ruban de verre suspendu, se déployant au-dessus des trottoirs roulants en adoptant des formes qui rappellent des nuages, voire des tornades. Compte tenu des contraintes extrêmes de cette énorme entreprise et de ses délais très courts, on aurait pu s'attendre à ce que Fuksas se contente de faire un travail pertinent, mais il est allé beaucoup plus loin en réinventant pratiquement l'idée de foire et surtout en y ajoutant sa propre touche artistique. Bien que cette allée évoque certaines formes générées par ordinateur, ses plans sont, en fait, issus de dessins et de maquettes dont la qualité approche souvent celle d'œuvres d'art.

Despite an extremely tight design to completion schedule, Fuksas has given the Fiera Milano an unexpectedly light and airy feeling.

Trotz des extrem engen Terminrahmens hat Fuksas für die Fiera Milano eine überraschend leichte und luftige Atmosphäre geschaffen.

Malgré des délais de concours extrêmement serrés, Fuksas a réussi à donner à la Foire de Milan un caractère étonnamment léger et aérien.

Along the spine of the central axis, a certain number of pod-like volumes house functions ranging from press areas to cafés.

Entlang des Rückgrates findet sich eine Reihe kokonartiger Volumina, in denen z. B. Räume für die Presse und Cafés untergebracht sind.

Le long de l'axe central, divers volumes en formes de cosses abritent des activités variées, de la salle de presse aux cafés.

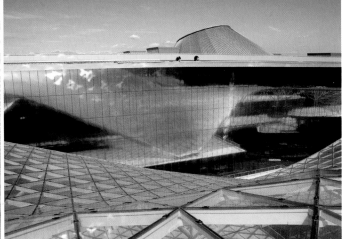

Fuksas adopts an essentially industrial vocabulary to the needs of large-scale exhibitions, using volcano-like protrusions from the main buildings to bring ample light into the actual show spaces.

Im Prinzip passt Fuksas ein dem Industriebau entliehenes Vokabular den Anforderungen einer Großmesse an. Die vulkanähnlich geformten Ausstülpungen aus den Dächern bringen viel Licht in die Ausstellungshallen.

Fuksas a adopté un vocabulaire essentiellement industriel pour répondre aux besoins des expositions à grande échelle. Dans le bâtiment principal, des saillies aux allures de volcans permettent un meilleur éclairage des espaces d'exposition.

GA.A ARCHITECTS

Ga.A Architects, 891–15 Bang-bae-dong, Secho-gu, Seoul 137–814, Korea
Tel: +82 25 23 34 43, Fax: +82 25 23 51 21
e-mail: moonchoi21@hotmail.com, Web: www.gaa-arch.com

Mass Studies, 683–140 Hannam 2-Dong, Fuji Bldg. 4F, Yongsan-Gu, Seoul 140–892, Korea
Tel: +82 79 06 52 8/9, Fax: +82 27 90 64 38
e-mail: office@massstudies.com, Web: www.massstudies.com

Slade Architecture, 150 Broadway, 807, New York, New York 10038, USA
Tel: +1 212 677 6380, Fax: +1 212 677 6330
e-mail: info@sladearch.com, Web: www.sladearch.com

Moongyu Choi, principal of **GA.A ARCHITECTS**, was born in Cheongju, Korea, in 1961. He received his B. A. and M. E. in Architectural Engineering from Yonsei University (Seoul, Korea) and Master of Architecture from Columbia University Graduate School of Architecture. After graduating he worked with Toyo Ito Architects in Tokyo. In 1999 he founded his practice Ga.A Architects in Seoul. Minsuk Cho was born and raised in Seoul, Korea. He received a Bachelor of Science in Architectural Engineering from Yonsei University (Seoul, Korea) and a Masters of Architecture from the Graduate School of Architecture at Columbia. He began his career working for Kolatan/MacDonald Studio, and Polshek & Partners in New York, and later moved to OMA in Rotterdam. With his business partner James Slade he established Cho Slade Architecture in 1998 in New York City. Their work received a number of awards including two Progressive Architecture Awards (Citations) and the Architectural League of New York's Young Architects Award in 2000. Since 2003, Minsuk Cho has been very actively engaged in his own firm in Korea, Mass Studies. James Slade studied at Cornell and Columbia, receiving his architecture degree in 1993. He worked in the offices of Rick Mather, Polshek & Partners, and Richard Gluckman, before creating Cho Slade in 1997 and Slade Architecture in 2002.

Moongyu Choi, Geschäftsführer von **GA.A ARCHITECTS**, wurde 1961 in Cheongju (Korea) geboren. Er studierte an der Yonsei University in Seoul Bauwesen; seinen Master of Architecture machte er an der Graduate School of Architecture der Columbia University in New York. Anschließend arbeitete er für Toyo Ito Architects in Tokio. 1999 gründete er sein Büro Ga.A Architects in Seoul. Minsuk Cho stammt aus Seoul. Er erwarb seinen Bachelor of Science im Fach Bauwesen an der Yonsei University und, wie Choi, seinen Master of Architecture an der Graduate School of Architecture der Columbia University. Zunächst arbeitete er für Kolatan/MacDonald Studio und Polshek & Partners in New York, später bei OMA in Rotterdam. Zusammen mit James Slade gründete er 1998 in New York Cho Slade Architecture. Das Büro wurde schon mehrfach ausgezeichnet, u. a. mit zwei Progressive Architecture Awards (Lobende Erwähnungen) und 2000 mit dem Young Architects Award der Architectural League of New York. Seit 2003 engagiert sich Minsuk Cho sehr aktiv in seinem eigenen Büro Mass Studies in Korea. James Slade studierte in Cornell und an der Columbia University und machte dort 1993 seinen Abschluss als Architekt. Er arbeitete für Rick Mather, Polshek & Partners und Richard Gluckman, bevor er 1997 Cho Slade Architecture und 2002 Slade Architecture gründete.

Moongyu Choi, qui dirige **GA.A ARCHITECTS**, est né en 1961 à Cheongju (Corée du Sud). Il est Bachelor of Arts et Master of Engineering en ingénierie architecturale de l'Université Yonsei (Séoul) et Master of Architecture de la Graduate School of Architecture de Columbia University (New York). Il a travaillé pour Toyo Ito Architects à Tokyo (1991–92) avant de créer son agence, Ga.A Architects, à Séoul en 1999. Minsuk Cho est né et a étudié à Séoul. Il est Bachelor of Science en ingénierie architecturale de l'Université Yonsei (Séoul) et Master of Architecture de la Graduate School of Architecture de Columbia University. Il a débuté sa carrière au Kolatan/MacDonald Studio, avant de travailler pour Polshek & Partners à New York et OMA à Rotterdam. Avec son associé, James Slade, il a fondé Cho Slade Architecture en 1998 à New York. Leurs réalisations ont reçu plusieurs récompenses, dont deux Progressive Architecture Awards (citations, 1999 et 2003) et le prix de l'Architectural League of New York's Young Architects en 2000. Depuis 2003, Minsuk Cho s'est beaucoup impliqué dans son agence coréenne, Mass Studies. James Slade a étudié à Cornell University et Columbia University dont il a été diplômé en 1993. Il a travaillé dans les agences de Rick Mather, Polshek & Partners, et Richard Gluckman, avant de fonder Cho Slade en 1997 et Slade Architecture en 2002.

DALKI THEME PARK

Heyri Art Valley, Paju, Korea

Floor area: 1115 m². Client: Ssamzie Corporation/Hokyun Chun, President.
Cost: $2.2 million

Described by James Slade as an "equal partnership" between his firm, Ga.A Architects and Mass Studies from Seoul, the **DALKI THEME PARK** is unusual in that it is inspired by a fictional girl. As the architects explain it, "Dalki is a cartoon character invented to market clothes and other products for children and teenagers. She is an imaginary girl who lives in a garden with her friends. Dalki Theme Park is a building where these imaginary characters interact with human visitors in a real, physical setting. The space accommodates shopping, playing, eating and lounging as well as exhibits dealing with scale, nature and the Dalki characters." With an area of approximately 1200 m², the pavilion designed by the three firms is in Heyri Art Valley, a planned 55-hectare residential community, located one hour north of Seoul and very close to the Unification Observation Tower, built in the Demilitarized Zone (DMZ) between the two Koreas. Slade explains that the "building was about negotiating the boundary between the imagined (cartoon characters) and the real (visitors), and that led the architects to propose a "forest" as the theme, with spaces, above the forest, inside the trees and under the forest, with the structure rising up on pilotis as it emerges from the ground. For the shady lower level, lights, fog machines, fans and heaters "generate artificial climatic conditions."

James Slade beschreibt die Zusammenarbeit am **DALKI-THEMENPARK** als »gleichwertige Partnerschaft« seines Büros, von Ga.A Architects und Mass Studies. Der Dalki-Themenpark ist insofern ungewöhnlich, als er von einem fiktiven Mädchen inspiriert wurde. Die Architekten erläutern: »Dalki ist eine Comicfigur, die erfunden wurde, um Kleidung und andere Produkte für Kinder und Teenager zu vermarkten. Sie ist ein virtuelles Mädchen, das zusammen mit seinen Freunden in einem Garten lebt. Der Dalki-Themenpark ist ein Gebäude, in dem diese virtuellen Charaktere mit realen Besuchern in einer realen, physischen Umgebung interagieren. Das Gebäude umfasst Shopping-, Spiel-, Gastronomie- und Loungebereiche, außerdem Ausstellungen zu den Themen Maßstab, Natur und Dalki-Charaktere.« Das von den drei Büros geplante Gebäude mit einer Fläche von 1200 m² befindet sich im Heyri Art Valley, einer am Reißbrett entworfenen 55 ha großen Wohngegend, die in etwa einer Stunde von Seoul aus zu erreichen ist. Sie liegt nördlich der Stadt, unweit des so genannten Unification Observation Towers, der in der entmilitarisierten Zone (DMZ) zwischen den beiden Koreas steht. James Slade erklärt: »Thema des Projektes ist es, die Grenzen zwischen dem Virtuellen (den Comicfiguren) und dem Realen (den Besuchern) auszuloten. Das führte uns dazu, einen ›Wald‹ als Motiv vorzuschlagen, mit Räumen über dem Wald, in den Bäumen und unter dem Wald. Dazu wird der aus dem Boden auftauchende Baukörper auf Stützen gestellt. Auf der eher dunklen Ebene im Untergeschoss werden durch Beleuchtung, Nebelmaschinen, Ventilatoren und Heizgeräte künstliche klimatische Bedingungen geschaffen.«

Présenté par James Slade comme un « partenariat à égalité » entre son agence, Ga.A Architects et Mass Studies, le **PARC À THÈME DE DALKI** est inspiré par un personnage de fiction. Comme l'expliquent les architectes, « Dalki est un personnage de bande dessinée imaginé pour promouvoir des vêtements et des produits pour enfants et adolescents. C'est une petite fille qui vit avec ses amis dans un jardin. Le parc à thème est un bâtiment dans lequel ces personnages imaginaires interagissent avec les visiteurs dans un cadre réaliste, physique. Les espaces sont conçus pour le commerce, le jeu, la restauration et la détente, aussi bien que pour des expositions qui jouent sur l'idée de nature et ses rapports d'échelle avec les personnages de Dalki ». Le pavillon de 1200 m² environ se trouve sur le site de Heyri Art Valley, un domaine résidentiel de 55 hectares à une heure de Séoul et à proximité de la Tour d'observation de l'Unification construite dans la zone démilitarisée entre les deux Corées. Slade explique que « le bâtiment traite des frontières entre l'imaginaire (les personnages de bande dessinée) et le réel (les visiteurs), ce qui a conduit à la proposition du thème de la ‹ forêt › qui comporte des espaces au-dessus de la forêt, dans les arbres et en sous-bois, la construction sur pilotis paraissant jaillir du sol. Aux niveaux inférieurs ombragés, des lumières, des machines à brouillard, des ventilateurs et des bouches d'air chaud recréent des conditions climatiques artificielles ».

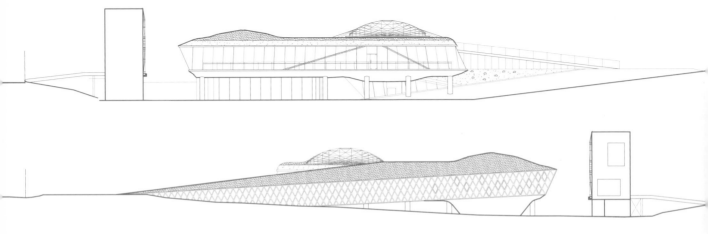

Rising up out of the earth like an intrusion of fantasy into the real world, the fully glazed main building sits above the ground on skewed columns.

Wie ein Eindringling aus einer Fantasiewelt schwebt das vollständig verglaste Hauptgebäude auf geneigten Stützen über dem Erdboden.

S'élevant du sol comme une intrusion du monde imaginaire dans le monde réel, le bâtiment principal, entièrement habillé de verre, repose au sol sur des colonnes obliques.

Humorous and unusual in its appearance, the Dalki Theme Park is an effort to give form to the kind of fantasy world that usually does not influence architecture so directly.

Der Dalki-Themenpark – humorvoll und ungewöhnlich gestaltet – ist der Versuch, der Fantasiewelt, die normalerweise keinen so direkten Einfluss auf Architektur hat, eine Form zu geben.

D'un aspect curieux et traité avec beaucoup d'humour, le parc à thème de Dalki est une tentative pour faire vivre un univers de fantaisie dont on n'imaginait pas qu'il puisse influencer à ce point l'architecture.

Large open spaces with a themed interior design blend seamlessly with the architecture itself. A site plan to the right shows the form of the building.

Weite, offene Räume mit einer thematischen Innenraumgestaltung verbinden sich mit der Architektur zu einer Einheit. Der Lageplan rechts zeigt die Form des Gebäudes.

À l'intérieur, autour de différents thèmes, de vastes espaces ouverts se fondent sans heurts à l'architecture. Le plan du site, à droite, montre la forme du bâtiment.

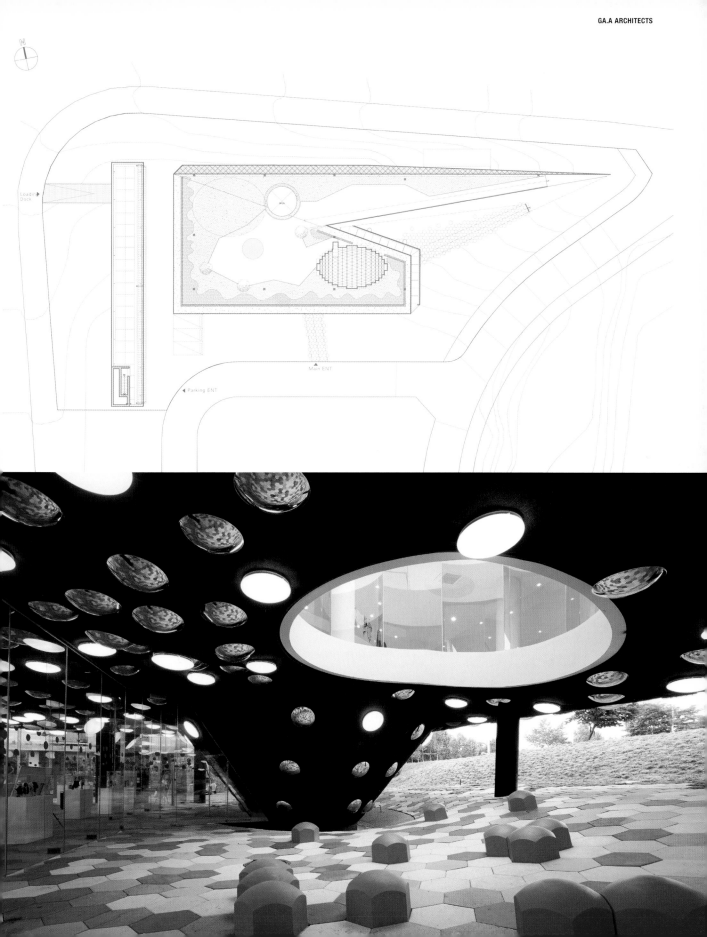

FRANK O. GEHRY

Gehry Partners, LLP
12541 Beatrice Street
Los Angeles, California 90066
USA

Tel: +1 310 482 3000
Fax: +1 310 482 3006

Born in Toronto, Canada in 1929, **FRANK O. GEHRY** studied at the University of Southern California, Los Angeles (1949–51), and at Harvard (1956–57). Principal of Gehry Partners, LLP, Los Angeles, since 1962, he received the 1989 Pritzker Prize. Some of his notable projects are the Loyola Law School, Los Angeles (1981–84); the Norton Residence, Venice, California (1983); California Aerospace Museum, Los Angeles (1982–84); Schnabel Residence, Brentwood (1989); Festival Disney, Marne-la-Vallée, France (1989–92); Guggenheim Museum, Bilbao, Spain (1991–97); Experience Music Project, Seattle, Washington (1995–2000); and the unbuilt Guggenheim Museum (New York, 1998–). Recent work includes: DG Bank Headquarters, Berlin, Germany (2000); Fisher Center for the Performing Arts at Bard College, Annandale-on-Hudson, New York (2002); Walt Disney Concert Hall, Los Angeles (2003); the Massachusetts Institute of Technology Stata Complex, Cambridge, Massachusetts (2003); and the MARTa Herford, Herford, Germany (2001–05), published here.

FRANK O. GEHRY, 1929 in Toronto geboren, studierte von 1949 bis 1951 an der University of Southern California (USC) in Los Angeles und von 1956 bis 1957 in Harvard. Seit 1962 ist er Leiter der Firma Gehry Partners, LLP, in Los Angeles. 1989 erhielt er den Pritzker-Preis. Zu seinen bekanntesten Bauten gehören die Loyola Law School in Los Angeles (1981–84), das California Aerospace Museum in Los Angeles (1982–84), die Villa Norton im kalifornischen Venice (1983), die Villa Schnabel in Brentwood (1989), das Festival Disney im französischen Marne-la-Vallée (1989–92), das Guggenheim Museum in Bilbao (1991–97) und das Experience Music Project in Seattle, Washington (1995–2000). Sein 1998 entworfener Bau für das Guggenheim Museum in New York blieb bislang unrealisiert. Zu seinen jüngsten Projekten zählen: die Zentrale der DG Bank in Berlin (2001), das Fisher Center for the Performing Arts am Bard College in Annandale-on-Hudson, New York (2002), die Walt Disney Concert Hall in Los Angeles (2003), der Stata Complex für das Massachusetts Institute of Technology in Cambridge (2003) sowie das hier gezeigte MARTa Herford (2001–05).

Né à Toronto au Canada en 1929, **FRANK O. GEHRY** étudie à l'University of Southern California, Los Angeles (1949–51), puis à Harvard (1956–57). Directeur de l'agence Gehry Partners, LLP, Los Angeles, depuis 1962, il reçoit en 1989 le prix Pritzker. Parmi ses projets les plus remarqués : la Loyola Law School, Los Angeles (1981–84); la Norton Residence, Venice, Californie (1983); le California Aerospace Museum, Los Angeles (1982–84); la Schnabel Residence, Brentwood (1989); Festival Disney, Marne-la-Vallée, France (1989–92); le Guggenheim Museum, Bilbao, Espagne (1991–97); Experience Music Project, Seattle, Washington (1995–2000) et le Guggenheim Museum de New York (1998–) non encore construite. Parmi ses chantiers récents : le siège de la DG Bank, Berlin, Allemagne (2000); le Fisher Center for the Performing Arts at Bard College, Annandale-on-Hudson, New York (2000–03); le Walt Disney Concert Hall, Los Angeles (2003); le Massachusetts Institute of Technology Stata Complex, Cambridge, Massachusetts (2003) et le MARTa Herford, Herford, Allemagne (2001–05), publié ici.

MARTA HERFORD
Herford, Germany, 2001–05

Floor area: 7000 m² (3200 m² new construction). Client: City of Herford.
Cost: €28.8 million

The exterior of the museum retains all of the humorous, almost anthropomorphic wit of Gehry, despite its extensive use of brick, an unfamiliar material for the California architect.

Trotz des reichlich verwendeten Backsteins (ungewöhnlich für den Architekten) bewahrt das Äußere des Museums Gehrys typischen humorvollen, fast anthropomorphen Esprit.

L'extérieur du musée conserve l'esprit d'humour, presque anthropomorphique de Gehry, malgré l'utilisation extensive de la brique, matériau peu courant pour l'architecte.

A small town of 65 000 people, Herford is located between Dortmund and Hanover. According to the museum's artistic director, Jan Hoet, former director of the SMAK museum in Ghent, Belgium, Herford had "two options – either to sleep or to turn toward the future." Hoet's vision of the future is the 29 million euro, 7000 m² design concocted by Frank Gehry. Intended to incorporate a part of an "existing industrial building with new buildings located to the south and to the north." The southern extension includes 730 m² of multipurpose exhibition space surrounding a 445 m², 22-meter-high main gallery. To the north a 345 m² space is devoted to furniture design. A restaurant in the southeast corner overlooks the adjacent river. The new structures are clad in brick and stainless steel and bring to mind the forms of the Guggenheim Bilbao, also designed by Gehry. Jan Hoet is a well-known personality in the European contemporary arts scene and he certainly doesn't mind stirring up reactions, for and against such an ambitious project. Gehry too is no stranger to controversy. With annual operating costs of about three million euros and a large budget overrun, the **MARTA HERFORD** has indeed been the object of much criticism.

Die Kleinstadt Herford mit 65 000 Einwohnern liegt zwischen Dortmund und Hannover. Jan Hoet, künstlerischer Leiter des Museums und ehemaliger Direktor des SMAK Museums in Gent ist der Meinung, dass Herford »zwei Optionen hatte – entweder zu schlafen oder sich der Zukunft zuzuwenden«. Hoets Vision der Zukunft ist der 29 Millionen Euro teure, 7000 m² große, von Frank Gehry erdachte Bau. Der Entwurf soll »ein vorhandenes Industriegebäude mit neuen Gebäuden im Süden und Norden« verbinden. Die südliche Erweiterung umfasst u. a. eine multifunktionale Ausstellungsfläche von 730 m², die um eine 445 m² große, 22 m hohe Hauptgalerie herum organisiert ist. Im Norden ist eine Ausstellungsfläche von 345 m² für Möbeldesign vorgesehen. Ein Restaurant in der südöstlichen Ecke überblickt den nahe gelegenen Fluss. Die Formen der mit Backstein und Edelstahl verkleideten Neubauten erinnern an Gehrys Museum in Bilbao. Jan Hoet ist in der zeitgenössischen europäischen Kunstszene eine bekannte Persönlichkeit und es macht ihm sicherlich nichts aus, mit so einem ehrgeizigen Projekt Reaktionen – pro oder kontra – hervorzurufen. Gehry sind Kontroversen ebenfalls nicht fremd. Mit jährlichen Betriebskosten von 3 Millionen Euro und einer beträchtlichen Überschreitung der Baukosten stand das **MARTA HERFORD** auch tatsächlich schon oft in der Kritik.

Herford est une ville de 65 000 habitants située entre Dortmund et Hanovre. Selon Jan Hoet, directeur artistique du musée et ancien directeur du SMAK de Gand en Belgique, Herford avait deux options : « Soit s'endormir, soit se tourner vers le futur. » La vision du futur de Hoet est ce musée de 29 millions d'euros et 7000 m² créé par Frank Gehry. Le projet était d'harmoniser « un bâtiment industriel existant avec de nouvelles constructions implantées au nord et au sud du premier ». L'extension sud comprend 730 m² d'espaces d'exposition polyvalents, entourant la galerie principale de 445 m² et 22 m de haut. À l'angle sud-est a été aménagé un restaurant donnant sur le fleuve. Les nouvelles constructions sont habillées de brique et d'acier inoxydable et font penser au Guggenheim Bilbao, dont Gehry est également l'auteur. Jan Hoet est une personnalité de la scène de l'art européenne et n'a certainement pas peur de susciter des réactions – pour ou contre cet ambitieux projet – tandis qu'une bonne controverse ne saurait déranger l'architecte. Avec son coût de fonctionnement de 3 millions d'euros environ et un important dépassement de budget, le **MARTA HERFORD** a déjà été l'objet de nombreuses critiques.

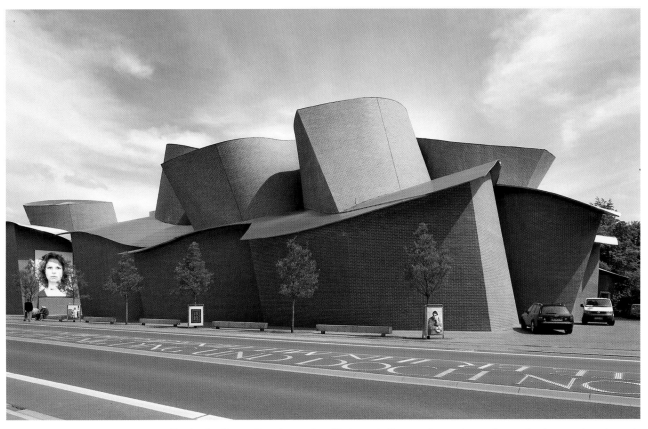

Like dancing figures, the volumes of the museum dip and twist in ways that make obvious that this is not just another ordinary building in Herford.

Wie tanzende Figuren neigen und drehen sich die Volumina und machen klar: Dies ist mehr als ein weiteres gewöhnliches Gebäude in Herford.

Comme des danseurs, les volumes du musée plongent et se tordent d'une façon qui les distingue radicalement des autres constructions à Herford.

The museum cafeteria retains much of the architectural excitement that Gehry knows so well how to generate, despite a budget which obviously did not permit much extravagance.

Ganz offensichtlich erlaubte das Budget keine Extravaganzen, dennoch ist im Museumscafé die architektonische Spannung zu spüren, die Gehry immer wieder herzustellen weiß.

La cafeteria du musée témoigne de cette effusion architecturale que Gehry sait si bien orchestrer malgré un budget qui ne prêtait apparemment pas à de telles extravagances.

This is clearly not the Guggenheim Bilbao. Despite the curving exterior forms, the interior often assumes a more measured rectilinearity (below) than Gehry's Spanish masterpiece.

Eindeutig nicht das Guggenheim Bilbao: Trotz der kurvigen Formen außen zeigt sich innen oft eine maßvollere Rechtwinkligkeit (unten) als in Gehrys spanischem Meisterwerk.

Ce n'est certainement pas le Guggenheim de Bilbao. Malgré ses formes extérieures incurvées, l'intérieur se plie souvent à une rectilinéarité plus mesurée (ci-dessous) que le chef d'œuvre de Gehry en Espagne.

GRAFT

GRAFT Gesellschaft von Architekten mbH
Borsigstrasse 33
10115 Berlin
Germany

Tel: +49 30 24 04 79 85
Fax: +49 30 24 04 79 87
e-mail: berlin@graftlab.com
Web: www.graftlab.com

GRAFT was created in Los Angeles in 1998 "as a label for architecture, art, music and the pursuit of happiness". Lars Krückeberg, Wolfram Putz and Thomas Willemeit are the partners of GRAFT, which today employs about 20 architects and artists in the US, Europe and in Asia. GRAFT has offices in Los Angeles and Berlin and Beijing. Lars Krückeberg was educated at the Technische Universität Braunschweig, Braunschweig as an engineer (1989–96) and at SciArc in Los Angeles (1997–98). Wolfram Putz attended the Technische Universität Braunschweig (1988–95), the University of Utah, Salt Lake City (1992–93) and SciArc in Los Angeles (1996–98). Thomas Willemeit also was educated in Braunschweig and at the Bauhaus Dessau (1991–92) before working in the office of Daniel Libeskind (1998–2001). Taking advantage of their German background combined with U.S. training, GRAFT declares "We can see an architecture of new combinations, the grafting of different cultures and styles. The English word graft includes a variety of meanings and multiple readings. It has a particular meaning in the terminology of botany, the grafting of one shoot onto a genetically different host. The positive properties of two genetically different cultures are combined in the new biological hybrid." They have built a studio and house for the actor Brad Pitt in Los Angeles (2000–03); designed a private dental clinic in Berlin and a nightclub at the Treasure Island Casino in Las Vegas; and are working on the Dominion, another design hotel located in Vancouver, Canada (2004–05).

GRAFT wurde 1998 in Los Angeles »als Label für Architektur, Kunst, Musik und das Streben nach Glück« gegründet. Lars Krückeberg, Wolfram Putz und Thomas Willemeit sind die Partner von GRAFT; derzeit beschäftigen sie ungefähr 20 Architekten und Künstler in den USA, Europa und Asien. GRAFT unterhält Büros in Los Angeles, Berlin und Peking. Lars Krückeberg studierte Ingenieurwesen an der Technischen Universität Braunschweig (1989–96), außerdem an der SCI-Arc in Los Angeles (1997–98). Auch Wolfram Putz studierte an der Technischen Universität Braunschweig (1988–95), dann an der University of Utah in Salt Lake City (1992–93) und an der SCI-Arc in Los Angeles (1996–98). Thomas Willemeit studierte ebenfalls in Braunschweig, außerdem am Bauhaus in Dessau (1991–92), bevor er im Büro von Daniel Libeskind arbeitete (1998–2001). Den deutschen Hintergrund und die Ausbildung in den USA nutzend, formuliert GRAFT sein Programm: »Wir stellen uns eine Architektur vor, die von neuen Kombinationen lebt, die verschiedene Kulturen und Stile ›veredelt‹. Das englische Wort ›graft‹ hat mehrere Bedeutungen, kann unterschiedlich verstanden werden. Im Bereich der Botanik bedeutet ›to graft‹, dass ein Schössling auf eine fremde Gastpflanze aufgepropft wird. Die positiven Eigenschaften der beiden genetisch voneinander verschiedenen Kulturen werden in einem neuen biologischen Hybrid miteinander verbunden.« GRAFT hat u. a. ein Studio und ein Wohnhaus für den Schauspieler Brad Pitt entworfen (2000–03) sowie eine private Dentalklinik in Berlin und einen Nachtklub für das Treasure Island Casino in Las Vegas; derzeit in Planung ist das Dominion, ein Design Hotel in Vancouver (2004–05).

GRAFT, « label pour l'architecture, l'art, la musique et la poursuite du bonheur », a été créé à Los Angeles en 1998. Lars Krückeberg, Wolfram Putz et Thomas Willemeit sont les associés de GRAFT qui emploie aujourd'hui une vingtaine d'architectes et d'artistes aux États-Unis, en Europe et en Asie. L'agence possède des bureaux à Los Angeles, Berlin et Pékin. Lars Krückeberg a été formé à l'ingénierie à la Technische Universität de Braunschweig (1989–96) et à SciArc à Los Angeles (1997–98). Wolfram Putz a étudié à la même université (1988–95), à celle de l'Utah à Salt Lake City (1992–93) et à SciArc à Los Angeles (1996–98). Thomas Willemeit a également étudié à Braunschweig et au Bauhaus Dessau (1991–92) avant de travailler auprès de Daniel Libeskind (1998–2001). En s'appuyant sur leurs formations allemande et américaine, GRAFT déclare : « Nous pouvons entrevoir une architecture de combinaisons nouvelles, la greffe de différents styles et cultures. Le terme anglais ‹ to graft › possède toute une variété de sens et de lectures. Il a une signification particulière en botanique : le greffage sur un hôte génétiquement différent. Les caractères propres à deux cultures génétiquement différentes se combinent alors en un nouvel hybride biologique. » Ils ont construit un atelier et une maison pour l'acteur Brad Pitt à Los Angeles (2000–03), conçu une clinique dentaire privée à Berlin, un nightclub pour le Treasure Island Casino à Las Vegas, et travaillent actuellement sur le projet Dominion, un « design hotel » à Vancouver, Canada (2004–05).

HOTEL Q!
Berlin, Germany, 2002–04

Floor area: 2973 m². Client: Wolfgang Loock.
Cost: €1 million (interior design)

Located on the Knesebeckstrasse, just around the corner from the busy Kurfürstendamm, Q! is a design hotel that takes many leads from predecessors such as the Schrager hotels in London (St Martins Lane) or the United States (Morgans, Delano, Mondrian etc.). Hotel operator Wolfgang Loock called them in 2002 after seeing the Hollywood Hills studio they designed for Brad Pitt in *Architectural Digest*. Though they did not design the seven-story building that houses the hotel, GRAFT managed to give a distinctive look to the interior, beginning with the 260 m² ground floor with its reception desk, lounge-bar and restaurant. White translucent curtains shield the hotel desk from the street but once inside the visitor is immediately confronted by wrap-around red surfaces that look more Californian than New Berlin. Six floors with twelve rooms per floor and a penthouse on the seventh floor make up the rest of the 2973 m² structure. Working with an interior design budget of approximately one million euros, Wolfgang Putz succeeded in imposing a unified esthetic sense, admittedly influenced in part by the work of Neil Denari. Guest rooms also feature wrapped surfaces where walls become desks or ceilings. Smoked oak floors and subtle ceiling designs based on the photographs of Christian Thomas aim to give a "cocoon-like feeling" to the rooms. The architects do succeed in breaking down the strict barriers between floor and ceiling, desk and bed, and in this they have given a unique ambiance to Q!

In der Knesebeckstraße, nicht weit vom belebten Kurfürstendamm, liegt das Hotel Q!, dessen Design sich in vielen Bereichen an Vorgängern wie den Schrager Hotels in London (St. Martin's Lane) oder in den USA (Morgans, Delano, Mondrian etc.) orientiert. Nachdem er in »Architectural Digest« einen Bericht über das von GRAFT entworfene Hollywood Hills Studio für Brad Pitt gesehen hatte, rief Wolfgang Loock, der Betreiber des Hotels 2002 bei GRAFT an. Obwohl der Entwurf für das siebengeschossige Gebäude, in dem sich das Hotel befindet, nicht von GRAFT stammt, gelang es den Architekten, im Inneren des Hotels ein eigenständiges Design durchzusetzen – beginnend mit dem 260 m² großen Erdgeschoss mit der Rezeption, einer Lounge/Bar und einem Restaurant. Weiße, durchscheinende Vorhänge schirmen die Rezeption von der Straße ab; erst einmal drinnen, wird der Besucher sogleich mit umlaufenden roten Oberflächen konfrontiert, die mehr an Kalifornien als an das neue Berlin denken lassen. Der Rest des 2973 m² großen Hotels umfasst sechs Geschosse mit jeweils zwölf Hotelzimmern sowie ein Penthouse. Mit einem Budget von etwa 1 Million Euro für die Innenausstattung gelang es Wolfgang Putz, eine einheitliche Ästhetik zu schaffen, die, wie er selbst sagt, teilweise von Neil Denaris Projekten beeinflusst ist. Auch in den Hotelzimmern gibt es sich abwickelnde Oberflächen, Wände werden so zu Tischen oder Unterdecken. Fußböden aus geräucherter Eiche und subtile Deckengrafiken, deren Grundlage Fotografien von Christian Thomas bilden, sollen in den Räumen eine »kokonartige Atmosphäre« erzeugen. Und tatsächlich gelingt es den Architekten, die strengen Grenzen zwischen Boden und Decke, Tisch und Bett aufzuheben und dadurch im Q! ein einzigartiges Ambiente zu schaffen.

Situé sur la Knesebeckstrasse, presque à l'angle du Kurfürstendamm, Q! est un « design hotel » qui s'inspire beaucoup de précurseurs comme les hôtels Schrager à Londres (St. Martins Lane) ou aux États-Unis (Morgan, Delano, Mondrian, etc.). Gérant d'hôtels, Wolfgang Loock a fait appel à GRAFT en 2002 après avoir vu le studio d'Hollywood Hills réalisé pour Brad Pitt dans *Architectural Digest*. Bien qu'elle n'ait pas conçu l'immeuble de sept étages qui accueille l'hôtel, l'agence a réussi à donner un style très personnel aux aménagements intérieurs, à commencer par les 260 m² de la réception, du bar et du restaurant. Des rideaux translucides blancs isolent la réception de la rue, mais une fois entré, le visiteur est confronté à des plans enveloppants rouges de style plus californien que néo-berlinois. Six niveaux de douze chambres et une penthouse au septième constituent le reste de cet ensemble de 2973 m². Pour un budget d'aménagement intérieur d'environ 1 million d'euros, Wolfram Putz a réussi à imposer une esthétique harmonieuse, influencée en partie, admet-il, par le travail de Neil Denari. Les chambres présentent le même type de surfaces enveloppantes qu'au rez-de-chaussée, qui font que les murs deviennent bureaux ou plafonds. Les sols en chêne fumé et le décor subtil des plafonds, inspirés des photos de Christian Thomas, accentuent cette impression de cocon. Les architectes ont, en effaçant les strictes barrières entre sol et plafond, bureau et lit, su créer cette atmosphère si personnelle à l'hôtel Q!.

The smooth red wrap-around design of the lobby and bar area of the hotel sets the tone for the entire project. Walls become furniture and there is almost no differentiation between the walls and ceilings.

Die glatte rote Umhüllung ist das wesentliche Gestaltungsmerkmal der Lobby und der Bar und bestimmt den Ton im Gebäude. Die Wände werden zu Möbelstücken, Wand und Decke verschmolzen.

Le principe d'enveloppe rouge utilisé pour le hall d'accueil et le bar donne le ton au projet. Les murs deviennent meubles et la distinction entre murs et plafonds s'efface.

The architects have created a varied sequence of spaces throughout the hotel, using mostly cooler colors in the rooms, but have maintained the idea that furniture emerges from architectural surfaces as though the entire design were part of a continuous entity.

Die Architekten haben eine differenzierte Abfolge von Räumen geschaffen. Die Hotelzimmer sind überwiegend in kälteren Farben gehalten, aber auch hier werden die Möbel aus den raumbegrenzenden Flächen geformt, als ob die gesamte Gestaltung Teil eines zusammenhängenden Ganzen wäre.

Les architectes ont créé une séquence variée de volumes dans tout l'hôtel, faisant appel à des couleurs plus apaisantes dans les chambres. Ils y ont cependant poursuivi l'idée de meubles émergeant du bâti considéré comme une entité continue.

Using a flooring product called Marmoleum Real 3127, the architects have extended their idea of an internal "landscape" throughout the hotel. The upper level penthouse offers more generous spaces than the "normal" rooms.

Die Böden bestehen aus Marmoleum Real 3127. Die Architekten weiteten die Idee einer innenräumlichen Landschaft auf das ganze Hotel aus. Das Penthouse bietet mehr Platz als die Standardzimmer.

À l'aide d'un revêtement de sol, le Marmoleum Real 3127, les architectes ont développé leur idée de « paysage » interne sur l'ensemble de l'hôtel. La penthouse du niveau supérieur offre des espaces plus généreux que les chambres types.

A spa is a part of any self-respecting "design" hotel and Q! is no exception. Angled surfaces that offer unexpected uses are present throughout, thanks to the clever work of GRAFT.

Ein Spa gehört zu jedem Designhotel, das etwas auf sich hält; Q! bildet da keine Ausnahme. Geneigte Flächen können ungewöhnlich genutzt werden und dank GRAFTs Kreativität kommen sie überall zum Einsatz.

Tout design hotel qui se respecte doit posséder un spa et le Q ! ne fait pas exception. Des plans inclinés se prêtent à des usages originaux, grâce à l'intelligent travail de GRAFT.

The continuity between floor, bathtub and bed is to say the least unusual, but it works well in the rooms of the hotel.

Die Einheit von Boden, Badewanne und Bett ist, vorsichtig ausgedrückt, ungewöhnlich, funktioniert in den Hotelzimmern aber gut.

La continuité entre le sol, la baignoire et le lit est pour le moins inhabituelle, mais fonctionne très bien dans le cadre de cet hôtel.

GROEP DELTA

Groep Delta Architectuur
Ilgatlaan 9
3500 Hasselt
Belgium

Tel: +32 11 28 49 69
Fax: +32 11 28 11 85
e-mail: info@groepdelta.com
Web: www.groepdelta.com

Villa C

GROEP DELTA is split into three organizations. One is for urbanization and is called Groep Delta Stedenbouw. The other two are Groep Delta Architectuur and Groep Delta Renovatie & Interieur. Their focus is on inner city projects and they design few houses. The director of the three groups is Juul Vanleysen. Vanleysen, the architect of the Villa C, was born in 1965. He graduated from the Sint-Lucas Higher Institute for Architecture in Ghent in 1988. The son of one of the founders of the firm, Vanleysen became a partner in 2000. Groep Delta employs 26 persons. The firm's recent work includes a showroom/flagship store for Vitra in Brussels; two showrooms for Mini Cooper cars in Antwerp and three "boutique-style" offices for Assubel Insurance in Brussels.

GROEP DELTA aus dem belgischen Hasselt besteht aus drei Büros: Das eine beschäftigt sich mit Städtebau und nennt sich Groep Delta Stedenbouw, die anderen beiden sind Groep Delta Architectur und Groep Delta Renovatie & Interieur. Ihr Schwerpunkt sind innerstädtische Projekte, aber auch einige Häuser wurden bislang geplant. Chef der drei Büros ist Juul Vanleysen. Vanleysen, Architekt der Villa C, wurde 1965 geboren und studierte am Institut Supérieur d'Architecture Saint-Luc de Wallonie in Gent, wo er 1988 seinen Abschluss machte. Er ist der Sohn eines der Gründer von Groep Delta und wurde 2000 Partner des Büros. Insgesamt hat das Büro 26 Mitarbeiter. Zu den jüngeren Projekten gehören ein Showroom/Flagship Store für Vitra in Brüssel, zwei Showrooms für den Mini Cooper in Antwerpen und drei shopartige Büros für die Assubel Versicherung in Brüssel.

GROEP DELTA est divisé en trois unités. La première, Groep Delta Stedenbouw, se consacre à l'urbanisme, les deux autres sont Groep Delta Architectuur et Groep Delta Renovatie & Interieur. L'agence s'intéresse aux projets d'urbanisme et conçoit également quelques maisons individuelles. Le directeur de ces trois départements, Juul Vanleysen, architecte de la Villa C, est né en 1965. Fils du fondateur de l'agence, il en est devenu associé en 2000 après avoir étudié à l'Institut supérieur d'architecture Sint-Lucas à Gand, dont il est sorti diplômé en 1988. Groep Delta emploie 26 collaborateurs. Parmi ses récentes réalisations : un showroom-magasin Vitra à Bruxelles ; deux showrooms pour les voitures Mini Cooper à Anvers et trois bureaux « boutique-style » pour les Assurances Assubel à Bruxelles (2001–03).

VILLA C

Zonhoven, Belgium, 1999–2001

Floor area: 320 m². Client: Frédéric Chaillet.
Cost: not disclosed

Frédéric Chaillet, a senior partner of Groep Delta, decided to entrust his partners, Juul Vanleysen and Luc Buelens, managing partner of Groep Delta Renovatie & Interieur, with the design and construction of his new 360 m² square house on an 8663 m² piece of farmland just outside of Hasselt. Vanleysen created a two-level design with an extremely slim roof, allowing for glass walls with practically no frames on the garden side. The entrance side is a massive 26-meter-long wall made of Waimes stone, punctuated only by a steel door and a cantilevered carport. The roof is supported by six thin but massive steel columns. The only real departure from a purely modernist plan was the unusual truncated red cedar shingle-clad cone that houses the fireplace and projects above the thin roof of the dining space. "I told Juul Vanleysen that I wanted a square house, because that is the way I think," says Chaillet. "I was against this intrusion but now it has become one of my favorite spaces." The garden was created by the landscape architect Michel Pauwels, but Chaillet's interest in Asia certainly had an influence on its spare forms, particularly in the pond with seven stepping stones and a concrete platform, located near the dining room space. A constant theme on the garden side is the close connection of the interior to the exterior. There are no curtains and even the master bathroom has a large door opening directly from the shower into the garden. Bedrooms for the owners and their two small children are located on the upper level and also look out into the spacious garden. Custom-designed furniture for the children's area is echoed in the dressing rooms by a wenge-clad block containing drawers and cupboards for the adults. A Paolo Piva bed facing a double-height window dominates the master bedroom. A discreet steel spiral stairway allows access to the ground level television room. The large plasma screen here is one of the few visible indications of the presence of modern technology in the house, though the residence is fully wired and computer-controlled.

Frédéric Chaillet, Seniorpartner von Groep Delta, entschied sich dafür, seinen Partnern Juul Vanleysen und Luc Buelens, geschäftsführender Partner von Groep Delta Renovatie & Interieur, den Entwurf seines neuen Hauses anzuvertrauen. Das 8663 m² große Stück Land, auf dem das 360 m² große Haus steht, liegt etwas außerhalb von Hasselt. Vanleysen entwarf ein zweigeschossiges Haus mit einem extrem dünnen und leichten Dach, das auf der Gartenseite praktisch rahmenlose Glaswände ermöglicht. Die Eingangsseite besteht aus einer massiven, 26 m langen Wand aus Steinen aus dem Ort Waimes, die nur durch eine Stahltür und ein auskragendem Carport unterbrochen wird. Das Dach wird von sechs dünnen Stahlstützen mit massiven Querschnitten getragen. Der einzige echte Unterschied zu einem rein klassisch-modernen Grundriss ist der ungewöhnliche, mit roten Zedernholzschindeln verkleidete Kegelstumpf; er ragt über das dünne Dach des Esszimmers hinaus und beherbergt den Kamin. »Ich habe Juul Vanleysen gesagt, dass ich ein rechteckiges Haus haben möchte, weil ich auch so denke.«, sagt Chaillet. »Ich war gegen diese ›Einmischung‹, aber nun ist es einer meiner liebsten Orte.« Der Landschaftsarchitekt Michel Pauwels hat den Garten entworfen, aber sicherlich beeinflusste Chaillets Interesse an Asien dessen sparsame Formen. Besonders bei dem an der Esszimmerfassade gelegenen Teich mit seinen sieben Stufen und einer Plattform aus Beton wird dies deutlich. Ein durchgängiges Thema auf der Gartenseite ist die enge Verbindung von Außen- und Innenraum. Es gibt keine Vorhänge, und selbst die Dusche des Hauptbadezimmers hat eine große Tür, die direkt in den Garten führt. Das Schlafzimmer der Eltern und die Zimmer der beiden kleinen Kinder liegen im Obergeschoss und blicken ebenfalls in den großzügigen Garten. Speziell angefertigte Möbel für den Kinderbereich finden in den Ankleidezimmern der Erwachsenen in Form eines mit Wengeholz verkleideten Blocks mit Schubladen und Schränken ihre Entsprechung. Ein von Paolo Piva entworfenes Bett gegenüber einem zweigeschossigen Fenster dominiert das Elternschlafzimmer, das durch eine diskrete Wendeltreppe mit dem TV-Raum im Erdgeschoss verbunden ist. Der große Plasmabildschirm ist eines der wenigen sichtbaren Zeichen moderner Technologie im Haus; tatsächlich ist es jedoch komplett verkabelt und computergesteuert.

Frédéric Chaillet, associé senior de Groep Delta Architectuur, a décidé de confier à ses associés Juul Vanleysen et Luc Buelens (associé gérant de Renovatie & Interieur), la conception et la construction de sa nouvelle maison de 360 m² sur un terrain agricole de 8663 m² à la sortie d'Hasselt. Vanleysen a conçu une maison sur deux niveaux, à la toiture extrêmement fine et aux murs de verre pratiquement sans cadre côté jardin. La façade de l'entrée est un mur massif de 26 m de long en pierre de Waimes, simplement ponctué d'une porte en acier et d'un abri pour voitures en porte-à-faux. Le toit est soutenu par six fines colonnes d'acier massif. Le seul écart par rapport à une approche purement moderniste est le curieux cône tronqué, recouvert de bardeaux de cèdre, qui protège la cheminée et s'élance au-dessus du mince toit de la zone des repas. « J'avais dit à Juul Vanleysen que je voulais une maison carrée, car c'est ma façon de penser, » précise Chaillet, « j'étais contre cette digression, mais c'est maintenant l'un de mes endroits favoris. » Le jardin a été dessiné par l'architecte paysagiste Michel Pauwels, mais l'intérêt de Chaillet pour l'Asie a sans aucun doute influencé ses formes épurées, en particulier celles de la pièce d'eau à sept pas japonais en pierre et de la plate-forme de béton accolée à la façade de la salle à manger. La connexion étroite entre intérieur et extérieur est un thème récurrent dans le traitement du jardin. Il n'y a aucun rideau dans la maison, et même la salle de bains principale ouvre directement sur le jardin par une grande porte. Les chambres du propriétaire et de ses deux jeunes enfants se trouvent à l'étage et donnent également sur la verdure. Le style du mobilier, spécifiquement créé pour les enfants, se retrouve en écho dans les dressing-rooms ou le massif bloc plaqué de wengé contenant tiroirs et rangements. Un lit de Paolo Piva fait face à une baie double hauteur qui domine la chambre de maîtres, et un discret escalier en spirale dessert la salle de télévision au rez-de-chaussée. Le grand écran plasma est l'un des rares signes de présence de la technologie moderne. Pourtant, la maison est entièrement câblée et gérée par ordinateur.

The rough stone outer wall offers few clues of the essential open and fully-glazed garden façade of the Villa C. A pond with stepping stones runs along the back side of the house.

Die Außenwand aus rauem Bruchstein zur Straße gibt keinen Hinweis auf die geöffnete, vollständig verglaste Gartenseite. Dort ist ein Wasserbecken mit Trittstufen angeordnet.

Les murs en pierre brute ne donnent guère d'indices sur la façade arrière entièrement vitrée donnant sur le jardin. Un bassin à pas japonais court le long de cette partie de la maison.

The architects have contrasted an unusual shingle-covered cone with an extremely refined floor-to-ceiling glazing for the dining area that faces the pond at the rear of the house.

Der ungewöhnliche, mit Schindeln verkleidete Kegelstumpf bildet einen Kontrast zur geschosshohen High-techverglasung des Essbereichs. Dieser ist zum Wasserbecken auf der Gartenseite orientiert.

Pour l'aire des repas qui fait face au bassin situé à l'arrière de la maison, les architectes ont joué du contraste entre un curieux cône à couverture en bardeaux de cèdre et le raffine-ment des murs de verre sans cadre.

A shower opens directly toward the garden, and heightens the impression that the entire house has been carefully designed, right down to the bathroom fixtures.

Die Dusche hat einen direkten Zugang zum Garten; dies verstärkt den Eindruck, dass das ganze Haus – bis hin zu den Armaturen der Badezimmer – sorgfältig entworfen wurde.

La salle de douche, qui ouvre sur le jardin, confirme le sentiment que la totalité de la maison a été conçue avec le plus grand soin, jusqu'à sa robinetterie.

The rough stone of the outer façade appears inside the house, but cedes immediately to a much more refined and smooth dark wall where ceramics are displayed. The main living area is situated to the right of the image above, through the openings in the black wall.

Der raue Bruchstein der äußeren Fassade findet sich auch im Inneren des Hauses. Er korrespondiert hier jedoch mit einer viel edleren, glatten und dunkel gehaltenen Wand, die der Ausstellung von Keramiken dient. Den Wohnraum betritt man durch die Öffnungen in der dunklen Wand, rechts auf dem Foto.

La pierre brute de la façade sur rue contraste, à l'intérieur, avec un mur sombre au traitement satiné et subtil, sur lequel sont présentées des œuvres en céramique. On accède au séjour principal par l'ouverture pratiquée dans le mur noir, à droite sur la photo.

ZAHA HADID

Zaha Hadid
Studio 9
10 Bowling Green Lane
London EC1R OBQ
UK

Tel: +44 20 72 53 51 47
Fax: +44 20 72 51 83 22
e-mail: mail@zaha-hadid.com
Web: www.zaha-hadid.com

BMW Central Building

ZAHA HADID studied architecture at the Architectural Association in London (AA) beginning in 1972 and was awarded the Diploma Prize in 1977. She then became a partner of Rem Koolhaas in the Office for Metropolitan Architecture (OMA) and taught at the AA. She has also taught at Harvard, the University of Chicago, in Hamburg and at Columbia University in New York. Well known for her paintings and drawings, she has had a substantial influence despite having built relatively buildings. She has completed the Vitra Fire Station, Weil-am-Rhein, Germany (1990–94) and exhibition designs such as that for *The Great Utopia*, Solomon R. Guggenheim Museum, New York (1992). Significant competition entries include her design for the Cardiff Bay Opera House (1994–96); and the Habitable Bridge, London (1996); or the Luxembourg Philharmonic Hall, Luxembourg (1997). More recently, Zaha Hadid has entered a phase of active construction with such projects as the Bergisel Ski Jump, Innsbruck (2001–02); Lois & Richard Rosenthal Center for Contemporary Art, Cincinnati, Ohio (1999–2003); and Central Building of the new BMW Assembly Plant in Leipzig (2005). She is working on the Price Tower Arts Center, Bartlesville, Oklahoma; Doha Tower, Doha, Qatar; and made a proposal for the 2012 Olympic Village, New York. In 2004, Zaha Hadid became the first woman to win the coveted Pritzker Prize.

ZAHA HADID studierte ab 1972 an der Architectural Association (AA) in London und erhielt 1977 den Diploma Prize. Danach wurde sie Partnerin von Rem Koolhaas im Office for Metropolitan Architecture (OMA). Sie lehrte an der Architectural Association (AA), in Harvard, an der University of Chicago, in Hamburg und an der Columbia University in New York. Hadid ist besonders durch ihre Gemälde und Zeichnungen bekannt geworden. Obwohl nur wenige ihrer Entwürfe realisiert wurden, so das Feuerwehrhaus der Firma Vitra in Weil am Rhein (1990–94), gehört sie zu den einflussreichsten Vertreterinnen ihrer Zunft. 1992 entwarf sie das Ausstellungsdesign für *The Great Utopia* im New Yorker Solomon R. Guggenheim Museum. Zu ihren bedeutendsten Wettbewerbsbeiträgen gehören Entwürfe für das Cardiff Bay Opera House (1994–96), für die Habitable Bridge in London (1996) und die Philharmonie in Luxemburg (1997). In jüngster Zeit begann für Zaha Hadid eine Phase des aktiven Bauens mit Projekten wie der Bergisel-Sprungschanze in Innsbruck (2001–02), dem Lois & Richard Rosenthal Center for Contemporary Art, Cincinnati, Ohio (1999–2003), und dem Zentralgebäude des neuen BMW-Werkes in Leipzig. Derzeit in Planung sind das Price Tower Arts Center in Bartlesville in Oklahoma und der Doha Tower in Doha im Emirat Katar. Außerdem hat sie einen Entwurf für das Olympische Dorf 2012 in New York erarbeitet. Anfang 2004 wurde Zaha Hadid als erste Frau mit dem begehrten Pritzker-Preis ausgezeichnet.

Née en 1950 à Bagdad, **ZAHA HADID** a étudié l'architecture à l'Architectural Association (AA) de Londres de 1972 à 1977, date à laquelle elle reçoit le prix Diploma. Elle est ensuite associée de l'agence de Rem Koolhaas, Office for Metropolitan Architecture (OMA), et enseigne à l'AA, à Harvard, à l'Université de Chicago, à Columbia University (New York) et à l'Université de Hambourg. Très connue pour ses peintures et dessins, elle exerce une réelle influence, même si elle construit assez peu pendant longtemps. Parmi ses réalisations : le poste d'incendie de Vitra, Weil-am-Rhein, Allemagne (1990–94) et des projets pour des expositions comme *La Grande Utopie* au Solomon R. Guggenheim Museum, New York (1992). Elle a participé à des concours dont les plus importants sont le projet de la Cardiff Bay Opera House, Pays-de-Galles (1994–96), un pont habitable, Londres (1996) et la salle de concerts philharmoniques de Luxembourg (1997). Plus récemment, elle est entrée dans une phase d'importants chantiers avec des projets comme le tremplin de saut à ski de Bergisel (2001–02, Innsbruck, Autriche) ; le Lois and Richard Rosenthal Center for Contemporary Art, Cincinnati, Ohio (1999–2003) et le bâtiment central de l'usine BMW de Leipzig (2003–04) publié ici. Elle travaille actuellement aux projets du Price Tower Arts Center (Bartlesville, Oklahoma) et de la Doha Tower (Doha, Quatar) et a présenté une proposition pour le village des Jeux olympiques de New York en 2012. En 2004, elle a été la première femme à remporter le très convoité prix Pritzker.

BMW PLANT LEIPZIG – CENTRAL BUILDING

Leipzig, Germany, 2003–04

Floor area: 25 000 m². Client: BMW AG, Munich. Cost: €54 million

Simply put, in the words of the architects, "It was the client's objective to translate industrial architecture into an aesthetic concept that complies equally with representational and functional requirements. In the transition zones between manufacturing halls and public space, the **CENTRAL BUILDING** acts as a 'mediator,' impressing a positive permanent impact upon the eye of the beholder in a restrained semiotic way." Zaha Hadid was asked to design this building, described as the "nerve center of the whole factory complex," subsequent to an April 2002 competition she won when the layout of adjacent manufacturing buildings had already been decided. Suppliers chosen for the rest of the factory provided many pre-fabricated elements, in harmony with the "industrial approach to office spaces" decided by BMW. Used as the entrance to the entire plant, the Central Building connects the three main manufacturing departments. The nerve-center concept is rendered all the more clear in that "the central area as a 'market place' is intended to enhance communication by providing staff with an area with which to avail themselves of personal and administrative services." A system of cascading floors allows views of different parts of the manufacturing process, ranging from assembly to the auditing area described as "a central focus of everybody's attention." The building itself is made with "self-compacting concrete and a roof structure assembled with a series of H-steel beams." The architect intends to use the architecture to create an "overall transparency of the internal organization," but also to mix functions "to avoid the traditional segregation of status groups." Particular attention was also paid to the inevitable car parking area in front of the building by "turning it into a dynamic spectacle in its own right."

Bei dem neuen **ZENTRALGEBÄUDE** für BMW ging es, so die Architekten, um Folgendes: »Das Ziel des Bauherrn war es, Industriearchitektur in ein ästhetisches Konzept zu übersetzen, das sowohl Repräsentations- als auch funktionale Anforderungen erfüllt. Im Übergang zwischen Produktionshallen und öffentlichem Bereich fungiert das Zentralgebäude als ein Vermittler, der auf zurückhaltende Weise einen dauerhaften, positiven Eindruck auf dem Auge des Betrachters hinterlässt.« Zaha Hadid wurde mit dem Entwurf des Gebäudes, das als »Nervenzentrum der gesamten Fabrikanlage« bezeichnet wird, beauftragt, nachdem sie im April 2002 den Wettbewerb hierfür gewonnen hatte. Zu diesem Zeitpunkt war das Konzept der angrenzenden Produktionshallen schon festgelegt. Firmen, die Teile für diese Bereiche der Anlage lieferten, wurden beim Zentralgebäude mit der Produktion vieler vorgefertigter Elemente beauftragt. Auf diese Weise wurde »der industrielle Charakter der Büroräume«, für den man sich bei BMW entschieden hatte, umgesetzt. Als Zugang zu allen Bereichen der Anlage verbindet das Zentralgebäude die drei Produktionsabteilungen. Das Konzept des Nervenzentrums wird mit dem »zentralen Bereich, der als ›Marktplatz‹ fungieren soll« besonders deutlich. »Er soll die Kommunikation zwischen den Mitarbeitern fördern und persönliche und verwaltungstechnische Dienstleistungen anbieten.« Ein System von kaskadenartigen Ebenen erlaubt Blicke in verschiedene Bereiche, von der Montage bis zum Testbereich, der als »ein Schwerpunkt des allgemeinen Interesses« beschrieben wird. Das Gebäude wurde aus »selbstverdichtendem Beton hergestellt und hat eine Dachkonstruktion aus Doppel-T-Trägern«. Die Absicht der Architektin war es, eine »umfassende Transparenz der internen Organisation« zu schaffen und Funktionsbereiche zu mischen, »um die traditionelle Trennung verschiedener ›Statusgruppen‹ der Mitarbeiter zu vermeiden«. Besondere Aufmerksamkeit wurde auch den unvermeidlichen Stellplatzflächen vor dem Gebäude geschenkt, indem »diese selbst in ein dynamisches Spektakel verwandelt« wurden.

Selon les termes de l'architecte, « l'objectif du client était de traduire l'architecture industrielle en un concept esthétique qui s'accorde aussi bien avec des exigences fonctionnelles que de représentation. Dans les zones de transition entre les ateliers de fabrication et les espaces publics, le **BÂTIMENT CENTRAL** joue le rôle d'un ‹ médiateur ›, exerçant un impact positif sur le regard du spectateur de façon sémiotique et contrôlée. » Zaha Hadid s'est vue confier la conception de ce bâtiment, décrit comme « le centre névralgique de l'ensemble du complexe de l'usine » après avoir remporté un concours, organisé en avril 2002, alors que les plans d'un bâtiment de fabrication adjacent avaient déjà été décidés. Les fournisseurs choisis pour le reste de l'usine ont fourni des éléments préfabriqués correspondant à « l'approche industrielle des espaces de bureaux » décidée par BMW. Situé à l'entrée du complexe, le Bâtiment central connecte les trois grands départements de fabrication. Le concept de centre névralgique se traduit par « une zone centrale qui est une ‹ agora › dont le rôle est d'améliorer la communication en offrant un espace où on trouve tous les services personnels et administratifs ». La disposition en cascade des différents niveaux montre tous les stades de la chaîne de production, de l'assemblage au contrôle, décrit comme « le centre de l'attention de tous ». Le bâtiment est en « béton auto-compactant et possède une toiture faite d'une série de poutres en acier profilé en H ». Pour Zaha Hadid, l'architecture sert à créer une « transparence d'ensemble de l'organisation interne », mais aussi à mêler les fonctions « pour éviter la traditionnelle ségrégation hiérarchique ». Une attention particulière a été portée aux parkings face à l'entrée du bâtiment pour « en faire un spectacle dynamique en soi ».

The wrapping, forward leaning forms of the building give it a dynamic aspect, as though it were ready to speed away just like the cars it is intended to produce.

Die fließenden, sich nach vorne neigenden Formen verleihen dem Gebäude seine dynamische Wirkung – als ob es jederzeit davonschießen könnte, wie die Fahrzeuge, die hier produziert werden sollen.

Les formes enveloppantes inclinées vers l'avant donnent au bâtiment un aspect dynamique, « prêt à démarrer » comme les voitures qui y sont produites.

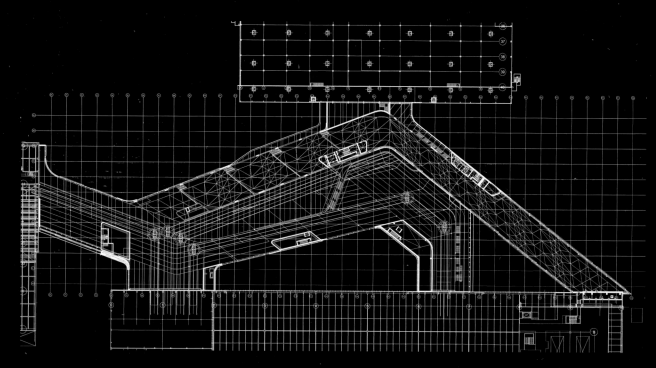

These images show clearly that this is more than just a pretty façade covering a conventional building.

Hier wird deutlich, dass es sich um mehr als ein konventionelles Gebäude mit einer interessanten Hülle handelt.

Ces images montrent qu'il ne s'agit pas d'une jolie façade recouvrant un bâtiment conventionnel.

HERRMANN + BOSCH /
ARCHITEKTENGRUPPE STUTTGART

Herrmann + Bosch, Freie Architekten BDA, Teckstrasse 56, 70190 Stuttgart, Germany
Tel: +49 711 26 84 11 10, Fax: +49 711 2 68 41 11 29, e-mail: info@herrmann-bosch.de
Web: www.herrmann-bosch.de

Dieter Herrmann was born in 1938 and studied at the Technical University of Stuttgart (1958–65), before working in the office of Behnisch & Partner, Stuttgart (1966–78). In partnership with Gerhard Bosch, he created the office of **HERRMANN + BOSCH** in 1992. Gerhard Bosch was born in 1955, and studied at the University of Stuttgart (1977–85). He is a professor of wood construction at the University of Applied Sciences in Biberach. Knut Lohrer, born in 1937, studied architecture at the Technical University of Stuttgart (1958–65). He created his own office, Atelier Lohrer, in Stuttgart in 1973 and worked on several museum and exhibition design projects with Dieter Herrmann. Since 2002, he has been an architectural advisor for the Sultanate of Oman. Uli Pfeil was born in 1956 and studied architecture at the University of Stuttgart (1977–84). He worked in the offices of Dieter Herrmann and Atelier Lohrer (1984–91) before creating his own office in Stuttgart in 1991. Dieter Keck was born in 1946 and studied at the University of Applied Sciences in Karlsruhe (1969–73). They recently completed a 13-story administrative building for the Landwirtschaftliche Sozialversicherung insurance company in Stuttgart-Kaltental and are currently working on a number of retirement homes in Germany. Important buildings planned by Herrmann + Bosch include the Daimler-Benz-Museum (in collaboration with Knut Lohrer and H. G. Merz, Stuttgart, 1984–86); the Limes-Museum (in collaboration with Knut Lohrer, Aalen, 1985–87); the Fachhochschule für Technik, Esslingen (University of Applied Science, 1992–96); and the Haus Rohrer Höhe home for the elderly (Stuttgart, 1996–98).

Dieter Herrmann, geboren 1938, studierte in Stuttgart (1958–65). Von 1966 bis 1978 arbeitete er im Büro Behnisch & Partner, Stuttgart. Zusammen mit Gerhard Bosch gründete er 1992 das Büro **HERRMANN + BOSCH**. Gerhard Bosch, geboren 1955, studierte in Stuttgart (1977–85). Er ist Professor für Holzkonstruktionen an der Hochschule Biberach. Knut Lohrer, geboren 1937, studierte Architektur an der Technischen Universität Stuttgart (1958–65). 1973 gründete er sein eigenes Büro Atelier Lohrer in Stuttgart und arbeitete zusammen mit Dieter Herrmann an verschiedenen Museums- und Ausstellungsprojekten. Seit 2002 ist er architektonischer Berater des Sultanats Oman. Uli Pfeifer, geboren 1956, studierte ebenfalls Architektur an der Technischen Universität Stuttgart (1977–84). Er arbeitete im Büro von Dieter Herrmann und im Atelier Lohrer (1984–91), bevor er 1991 sein eigenes Büro in Stuttgart gründete. Dieter Keck, geboren 1946, studierte an der Fachhochschule Karlsruhe (1969–73). Kürzlich wurde ein von Herrmann + Bosch zusammen mit Keck geplantes 13-geschossiges Verwaltungshochhaus für die Landwirtschaftliche Sozialversicherung in Stuttgart-Kaltental fertig gestellt. Außerdem sind bei Herrmann + Bosch derzeit eine Reihe von Seniorenheimen in Deutschland in Planung. Zu den wichtigen Gebäuden des Büros gehören das Daimler-Benz-Museum (in Zusammenarbeit mit Lohrer und H. G. Merz) Stuttgart (1984–86), das Limes-Museum (in Zusammenarbeit mit Lohrer) in Aalen (1985–87), die Fachhochschule für Technik, Esslingen (1992–96), und das Seniorenwohnheim Haus Rohrer Höhe, Stuttgart (1996–98).

Dieter Herrmann, né en 1938, a étudié dans la même université (1958–65) avant de travailler pour Behnisch & Partner à Stuttgart (1966–78). En partenariat avec Gerhard Bosch, il a créé l'agence **HERRMANN + BOSCH** en 1992. Gerhard Bosch, né en 1955, a étudié à l'Université de Stuttgart (1977–85). Il enseigne la construction en bois à l'Université des sciences appliquées de Biberach. Knut Lohrer, né en 1937, est diplômé en architecture de l'Université technique de Stuttgart (1958–65). Il a créé son agence, Atelier Lohrer, à Stuttgart en 1973 et travaillé sur plusieurs projets de musées et d'expositions avec Dieter Herrmann. Depuis 2002, il est conseiller en architecture pour le sultanat d'Oman. Uli Pfeil, né en 1956, a étudié l'architecture à l'Université de Stuttgart (1977–84) et a travaillé pour Herrmann et l'Atelier Lohrer (1984–91) avant de créer sa propre agence à Stuttgart en 1991. Dieter Keck, né en 1946, a étudié à l'Université des sciences appliquées de Karlsruhe (1969–73). Ensemble, ils ont récemment achevé un immeuble de bureaux de 13 étages pour la compagnie d'assurances Landwirtschaftliche Sozialversicherung à Stuttgart-Kaltental et travaillent sur un certain nombre de projets de maisons de retraite en Allemagne. Parmi leurs réalisations les plus importantes : le musée Daimler-Benz, en collaboration avec Knut Lohrer et H. G. Merz, Stuttgart (1984–86) ; le Limes-Museum, en collaboration avec Knut Lohrer, Aalen (1985–87) ; la Fachhochschule für Technik, Esslingen (1992–96) et la maison de retraite Haus Rohrer Höhe, Stuttgart (1996–98).

INDOOR BATH FARMHOUSE

Klein Pöchlarn, Austria, 2000–02

Floor area: 107 m². Client: Mr. Weissensteiner.
Cost: €310 000

This 107 m² addition to a farmhouse was designed between June 2000 and October 2001. Hertl says that "The bath is designed to simulate a contemporary grotto, a hollow space in a green solid, that aims to reach the mystique and sensuousness of an antique bath." In this description, and perhaps in an unassuming way in the actual structure, there is an echo of Peter Zumthor's Thermal Baths in Vals. Employing "simple and modest elements" such as a "hollow solid with a corner in glass, cubicle, bench and wine-cellar," the architect used green glazed concrete so that "even the pool glimmers green." A glazed façade with red louvers on the interior gives some sense of the outside environment, but there is an uncompromising geometric strength in the basic rectangular volume imagined by Gernot Hertl. Despite the rather hard lines of the design, the combination of the green surfaces, water and the imagined bath do evoke the sensuality alluded to in the architect's description.

Das 107 m² große Nebengebäude eines Bauernhofs wurde zwischen Juni 2000 und Oktober 2001 entworfen. Hertl sagt dazu: »Das Bad soll eine moderne ›Grotte‹ sein, ein hohler Raum in einem massiven Grün, der an die mystischen und sinnlichen Qualitäten eines Bades der Antike anknüpft.« In dieser Beschreibung und vielleicht in der Bescheidenheit des realen Baukörpers sind Anklänge an das Thermalbad in Vals von Peter Zumthor zu spüren. Die »einfachen und bescheidenen Elemente« – z. B. ein »ausgehöhlter massiver Körper mit einer Ecke aus Glas, ein kleiner, abgetrennter Ruheraum, eine Bank und ein Weinkeller« sind aus grün lasiertem Beton, so dass »sogar der Pool grün schimmert«. Eine Glasfassade mit roten Lamellen auf der Innenseite stellt eine gewisse Verbindung zur Umgebung her; die kompromisslose geometrische Strenge des einfachen rechtwinkligen Baukörpers dominiert jedoch. Trotz der eher strengen Linien des Entwurfs rufen die grünen Oberflächen und das Wasser in Kombination mit der Vorstellung, hier ein Bad zu nehmen, die Sinnlichkeit hervor, auf die der Architekt in seiner Beschreibung verweist.

Cette extension de 107 m² d'un bâtiment de ferme a été conçue de juin 2000 à octobre 2001. Hertl explique que « le pavillon de bains est conçu pour simuler une grotte contemporaine, un volume creux dans un solide vert qui veut atteindre au caractère mystique et sensuel des bains antiques ». Dans cette description et peut-être aussi dans la réalisation de ce petit projet, on trouve comme un écho des Bains de Vals par Peter Zumthor. Utilisant des « éléments simples et modestes » comme « un solide creux doté d'un angle en verre, une cabine, un banc et une cave à vin », l'architecte a utilisé un béton verni en vert pour que « même le bassin ait des reflets verts ». La façade en verre à persiennes intérieures rouges crée une perception particulière de l'environnement extérieur, mais la puissance géométrique du volume rectangulaire imaginé par Hertl s'impose néanmoins. Malgré des lignes assez dures, l'association des surfaces vertes et de l'eau évoque la sensualité à laquelle l'architecte fait allusion dans sa description.

A hint of color is all that relieves the apparent austerity of the bathhouse. There is a solidity and integrity in the design that gives it a presence beyond its small size.

Nur die Farbe schwächt die Strenge des Badehauses ein wenig ab. Das kleine Gebäude strahlt Solidität und Integrität aus und hat eine Präsenz, die über seine tatsächliche Größe hinausgeht.

Seule la couleur anime l'austérité apparente de cette maison de bains. Son aspect massif et sa cohérence confèrent au projet une présence très forte pour ses dimensions.

HERZOG & DE MEURON

Herzog & de Meuron
Rheinschanze 6
4056 Basel
Switzerland

Tel: +41 613 85 57 40
Fax: +41 613 85 57 58
e-mail: info@herzogdemeuron.com

Allianz Arena ▸

Jacques Herzog and Pierre de Meuron were both born in Basel in 1950. They received degrees in architecture at the ETH in Zurich in 1975 after studying with Aldo Rossi, and founded their firm **HERZOG & DE MEURON** Architecture Studio in Basel in 1978. Harry Gugger and Christine Binswanger joined the firm in 1991, while Robert Hösl and Ascan Mergenthaler became partners in 2004. Their built work includes the Antipodes I Student Housing at the Université de Bourgogne, Dijon (1991–92), the Ricola Europe Factory and Storage Building in Mulhouse (1993) and a gallery for a private collection of contemporary art in Munich (1991–92). Most notably they were chosen early in 1995 to design the new Tate Gallery extension for contemporary art, situated in the Bankside Power Station on the Thames opposite Saint Paul's Cathedral, which opened in May 2000. They were also short listed in the competition for the new design of the Museum of Modern Art in New York (1997). More recently, they have built the Forum 2004 Building and Plaza, Barcelona (2002–04), the Prada Aoyama Epicenter in Tokyo (2003), and plan to build the CaixaForum-Madrid and the National Stadium, Main Stadium for the 2008 Olympic Games in Beijing.

Jacques Herzog und Pierre de Meuron wurden beide 1950 in Basel geboren. Sie studierten bei Aldo Rossi an der ETH in Zürich, wo sie 1975 ihr Diplom machten. 1978 gründeten sie in Basel das Büro **HERZOG & DE MEURON**. Harry Gugger und Christine Binswanger arbeiten seit 1991 dort, 2004 wurden Robert Hösl und Ascan Mergenthaler Partner. Zu den Bauten von Herzog & de Meuron gehören das Studentenwohnheim Antipodes I der Université de Bourgogne in Dijon (1991–92), das Ausstellungsgebäude für eine Privatsammlung moderner Kunst in München (1991–92) und das Fabrik- und Lagergebäude der Firma Ricola Europe in Mulhouse (1993). 1995 erhielten sie ihren bedeutendsten Auftrag: die Planung der »Tate Modern«, des in der Bankside Power Station untergebrachten Museums für zeitgenössische Kunst als Erweiterung der Tate Gallery in London. Das gegenüber der St. Paul's Cathedral an der Themse gelegene Gebäude wurde im Mai 2000 eröffnet. Beim Wettbewerb für die Umgestaltung des Museum of Modern Art in New York (1997) kamen Herzog & de Meuron in die engere Wahl. In jüngster Zeit haben sie u. a. das Gebäude und den Platz »Forum 2004« in Barcelona (2002–04) sowie das Prada Aoyama Epicenter in Tokyo (2003) realisiert; in Planung sind u. a.: das CaixaForum-Madrid und das Hauptstadion für die Olympischen Spiele 2008 in Peking.

Jacques Herzog et Pierre de Meuron sont tous deux nés à Bâle en 1950. Diplômés en architecture de l'Institut fédéral suisse de technologie (ETH) de Zurich (1975) où ils étudient auprès d'Aldo Rossi, ils fondent **HERZOG & DE MEURON** Architecture Studio, à Bâle, en 1978. Harry Gugger et Christine Binswanger les rejoignent en 1991, suivis de Robert Hösl et Ascan Mergenthaler en 2004. Parmi leurs premières réalisations remarquées : le foyer d'étudiants Antipodes I pour l'Université de Bourgogne, Dijon (1991–92), l'usine-entrepôt Ricola Europe, Mulhouse (1993) et une galerie pour une collection privée d'art contemporain, Munich (1989–92). Ils ont été sélectionnés en 1995 pour l'installation de la Tate Modern de Londres dans une ancienne centrale électrique, Bankside Power Station, au bord de la Tamise, face à la cathédrale Saint-Paul, réalisation qui fut inaugurée en mai 2000. Ils ont fait partie des architectes retenus pour le concours de la transformation du Museum of Modern Art de New York (1997). Plus récemment, ils ont construit le bâtiment et la place du Forum 2004 à Barcelone (2002–04), le Prada Aoyama Epicenter à Tokyo (2003) et travaillent aux projets du Caixa Forum-Madrid et du Stade national, principal stade des Jeux olympiques qui se tiendront à Pékin en 2008.

ALLIANZ ARENA

Munich, Germany, 2002–05

Floor area: 171 000 m². Built-up floor area stadium: 37 600 m².
Client: Allianz Arena – München Stadion GmbH. Cost: € 280 million (estimate)

Intended for use during the 2006 FIFA World Cup, the **ALLIANZ ARENA** offers a total of 66 000 covered seats. Its 37 600 m² footprint corresponds to 171 000 m² of gross floor area. Its circumference is 840 m. As the architects explain, "Three themes define our architectural and urban concept for the world championship football stadium in Munich: 1) the presence of the stadium as an illuminated body that can change its appearance and is situated in an open landscape; 2) the procession-like arrival of fans in a landscaped area; and 3) the crater-like interior of the stadium itself." Located between the airport and downtown Munich in an open area, the Allianz Arena is covered with large EFTE cushions that can each be lit separately in white, red or light blue. A digital control system permits changes in the color scheme, in particular in order to identify the home team playing (FC Bayern Munich or TSV 1860). The idea of a stadium that is entirely colored in this way is quite new. Vogt Landschaftsarchitekten from Zurich designed the landscaping, formed by swathes of green together with meandering asphalt paths. Given that the Arena is intended only for football games, the seating arrangement does not have to be changed and great attention has been taken to bringing the spectators as close as possible to the playing field.

Die **ALLIANZ ARENA**, einer der Austragungsorte der Fußballweltmeisterschaft 2006, hat 66 000 überdachte Plätze. Die 37 600 m² große Grundfläche bietet eine Bruttogeschossfläche von 171 000 m², der Umfang des Stadions misst 840 m. Die Architekten erläutern: »Drei Themen definieren unseren architektonischen und städtebaulichen Ansatz für das Weltmeisterschaftsstadion in München: 1) die Präsenz des Stadions als illuminierter Baukörper, der sein Äußeres verändern kann und in eine offene Landschaft eingebettet ist, 2) die prozessionsartige Annäherung der Fans in einer landschaftsplanerisch gestalteten Umgebung und 3) der kraterähnliche Innenraum des Stadions.« Die Allianz Arena, ungefähr in der Mitte zwischen dem Flughafen und der Innenstadt Münchens in freier Landschaft gelegen, wird von großen Kissen aus EFTE-Folie überdeckt; jedes dieser Kissen kann weiß, rot oder blau leuchten. Ein digitales Kontrollsystem erlaubt Veränderungen des farbigen Gesamtbildes, insbesondere um kenntlich zu machen, welche Mannschaft gerade ein Heimspiel hat (FC Bayern München oder TSV 1860). Die Idee eines Stadions, das auf diese Weise farbig gestaltet wird, ist recht neu. Vogt Landschaftsarchitekten aus Zürich haben die Außenanlagen – gemähte Rasenstreifen und mäandrierende Asphaltwege – gestaltet. Da die Arena nur für Fußballspiele genutzt werden soll, gibt es eine feste Bestuhlung; außerdem wurde sehr viel Wert darauf gelegt, die Zuschauer so nah wie möglich an das Spielfeld zu bringen.

Édifié en prévision de la Coupe du monde de football 2006, l'**ALLIANZ ARENA** offre 66 000 places et 171 000 m² de surface utile pour une emprise au sol de 37 600 m². « Trois thèmes définissent notre concept architectural et urbain pour le stade de football du championnat du monde à Munich », expliquent les architectes : « 1) la présence du stade, en tant que corps illuminé qui peut changer d'aspect et se trouve au milieu d'un espace ouvert ; 2) l'arrivée processionnelle des supporters dans une zone paysagée et 3) l'intérieur du stade même, en forme de cratère. » Situé entre l'aéroport et le centre ville dans une zone dégagée, le stade est couvert d'énormes coussins en EFTE dont chacun peut s'éclairer séparément en blanc, rouge ou bleu clair. Un système de commande par ordinateur modifie les couleurs, par exemple pour identifier l'équipe locale qui joue (FC Bayern Munich ou TSV 1860). Cette idée de stade « colorisable » est nouvelle. Vogt Landschaftsarchitekten, de Zurich, a créé les aménagements paysagers alternant les bandes de gazon et de sinueuses allées goudronnées. Le stade étant exclusivement conçu pour le football, l'implantation des sièges n'a pas à être modulable et l'on a pu faire en sorte que les spectateurs soient aussi près que possible du terrain.

Giving a new appearance to as "ordinary" a structure as a football stadium is no small task. Herzog & de Meuron have also given variety to the exterior of the building through the use of light and color.

Einem Funktionsgebäude wie einem Fußballstadion ein modernes Aussehen zu geben, ist nicht ganz leicht. Durch den Einsatz von Licht und Farbe kann die Außenfassade verändert werden.

Donner un aspect moderne à une structure aussi « ordinaire » qu'un stade de football n'est pas une mince affaire. Herzog & de Meuron ont rendu modulable l'aspect extérieur du bâtiment en jouant avec lumière et couleur.

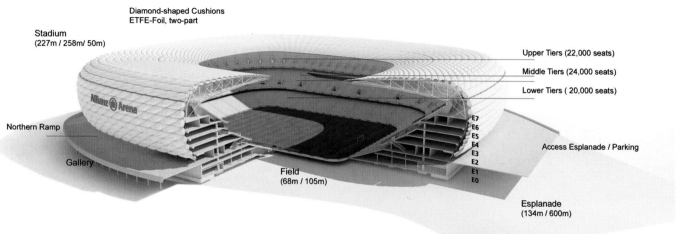

Diamond-shaped Cushions
ETFE-Foil, two-part

Stadium
(227m / 258m/ 50m)

Upper Tiers (22,000 seats)

Middle Tiers (24,000 seats)

Lower Tiers (20,000 seats)

Northern Ramp

E7
E6
E5
E4
E3
E2
E1
E0

Access Esplanade / Parking

Gallery

Field
(68m / 105m)

Esplanade
(134m / 600m)

Unlike some well-known architects who have difficulty working on a large scale, Herzog & de Meuron have succeeded in creating an elegant design intended for the use of very large numbers of people.

Im Gegensatz zu anderen berühmten Architekten, denen es schwer fällt, Großbauten zu planen, ist Herzog & de Meuron ein elegantes Bauwerk gelungen, das von sehr vielen Menschen genutzt wird.

Contrairement à certains grands architectes qui ont des difficultés à travailler sur des projets de grandes dimensions, Herzog & de Meuron ont réussi à créer un style élégant destiné au public le plus vaste.

The round shape of the Arena itself is echoed in the landscaping and approach roads leading to the parking areas.

Die runde Form der Allianz Arena findet sich in der landschaftsplanerischen Gestaltung und in der Anlage der Zufahrtsstraßen wieder.

La forme ronde de l'Allianz Arena se retrouve dans les aménagements paysagers et les voies d'accès aux parkings.

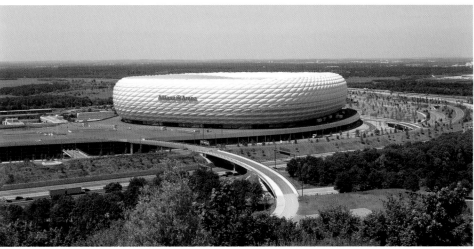

WALKER ART CENTER

Minneapolis, Minnesota, USA, 2003–05

Floor area: 11 800 m² (expansion). Client: Walker Art Center.
Cost: $38.2 million

This project includes an 11 800 m² expansion (about the equivalent of the existing space). The architects emphasize that the **WALKER ART CENTER** is more than a museum, since its directors insist on its role as a hub for local cultural life, and wish to place more emphasis on electronic media and performing arts. The new space includes a theater, compared by the architects to "a down-sized version of the Scala in Milan or the open-air Globe theater of Shakespeare's day." In fact the new spaces can be used to interweave different art forms in "entirely unexpected and innovative ways." Though their own addition, with its folded forms and large, irregular windows seems quite different from the original Edward Larabee Barnes (1915–2004) building, it intentionally plays on the stricter existing structure and enlivens it. As the architects say about the windows, "They look accidental but are homologous forms, showing a kinship in value and structure, somewhat like the shapes of a silhouette cutting." Doubling the available amount of gallery space, the renovated Walker includes a 1.5 hectare garden extending the Minneapolis Sculpture garden to the south; a 280 m² "event space" with views of the city, which can be rented out for community use; a "destination restaurant;" and a new 350-seat "multidisciplinary performing arts studio." The new 21-meter-high tower is distinctively clad in custom stamped aluminum mesh.

Das Projekt umfasst eine 11 800 m² große Erweiterung, die damit ungefähr die Größe des bestehenden Museums hat. Die Architekten betonen, dass das **WALKER ART CENTER** mehr ist als ein Museum, da es eine zentrale Rolle im örtlichen kulturellen Leben spielt und seine Direktoren eine stärkere Gewichtung der elektronischen Medien und der darstellenden Künste anstreben. Die Erweiterung beinhaltet ein Theater, das von den Architekten mit »einer verkleinerten Version der Mailänder Scala oder Shakespeares nach oben offenem Globe Theatre« verglichen wird. Tatsächlich können die neuen Räume dazu benutzt werden, verschiedene Kunstformen »auf gänzlich unerwartete und innovative Art« zu verbinden. Obwohl die Erweiterung mit ihren gefalteten Formen und den großen, unregelmäßigen Fenstern mit dem bestehenden Gebäude von Edward Larabee Barnes (1915–2004) nicht viel gemeinsam zu haben scheint, ist das Spiel mit dem vorhandenen strengeren Baukörper und dessen Belebung beabsichtigt. Die Architekten äußern sich zu den Fenstern folgendermaßen: »Sie sehen aus wie zufällig entworfen, aber sie haben homologe Formen, die eine Verwandtschaft in Wertigkeit und Konstruktion zeigen.« Die Galeriefläche wurde verdoppelt: Dazu gehört ein 1,5 ha großer Garten, der den Minneapolis Sculpture Garden nach Süden hin ergänzt, ein 280 m² großer Raum für Events, der von der Gemeinde gemietet werden kann, ein Toprestaurant sowie ein neues »multidisziplinäres Studio für darstellende Künste« mit 350 Plätzen. Der neue 21 m hohe Turm wird durch sein speziell angefertigtes Aluminiumnetz gekennzeichnet.

Ce projet de réaménagement du **WALKER ART CENTER** comprend aussi une extension de 11 800 m² (l'équivalent des espaces existants). Les architectes expliquent que ce Centre est le noyau de la vie culturelle locale et que ses administrateurs souhaitaient mettre l'accent sur les médias électroniques et les arts du spectacle. Le nouvel espace contient un théâtre qu'Herzog & de Meuron comparent à « une version réduite de la Scala de Milan ou du théâtre du Globe de Shakespeare ». En fait, ces installations peuvent générer des rencontres entre différentes formes artistiques de « façons entièrement nouvelles et inattendues ». Bien que la nouvelle extension, avec ses formes repliées et ses vastes ouvertures, semble trancher avec les lignes strictes du bâtiment d'origine signé Edward Larabee Barnes (1915–2004), elle joue de ce contraste tout en l'animant. Au sujet des fenêtres, les architectes précisent que « si elles ont l'air d'être disposées au hasard, ce sont des formes homologues qui mettent en évidence une parenté de valeur et de structure ». Outre le doublement des galeries d'exposition, le Walker rénové possède un jardin de 1,5 hectare qui prolonge vers le sud le Jardin de sculptures de Minneapolis, un « espace pour événements » de 280 m² loué pour manifestations locales, un restaurant de qualité et un nouveau « studio multidisciplinaire d'arts du spectacle » de 350 places. La nouvelle tour de 21 mètres se fait remarquer par son habillage en panneaux d'aluminium.

Though certainly not anthropomorphic in its apparent design, the Walker Art Center extension has an unusual almost "living" presence.

Obwohl sicherlich kein anthropomorphes Gebäude, hat die Erweiterung des Walker Art Center eine ungewöhnliche, fast »lebendige« Präsenz.

Très loin d'être anthropomorphique, le Walker Art Center n'en dégage pas moins une présence « vivante ».

The architects master the use of
powerful interior forms that have a
clear continuity with the outside of
the building. Nor are these forms created at the expense of the functionality of the building.

Den Umgang mit expressiven Innen-
raumformen, die in einem klaren
Zusammenhang mit dem Äußeren
des Gebäudes stehen, beherrschen
die Architekten meisterhaft. Diese
Formen beeinträchtigen die Funktionalität nicht.

Les architectes maîtrisent l'utilisation
de puissantes formes intérieures
dans une continuité évidente avec
celles de l'extérieur. Elles n'ont pas
pour autant été créées aux dépens
du fonctionnalisme du bâtiment.

DE YOUNG MUSEUM

San Francisco, California, USA, 2002-05

*Area: 27 220 m². Client: Fine Arts Museums of San Francisco (FAMSF).
Cost: $135 million*

The Swiss architects Herzog & de Meuron have had something of a double-feature, opening a new building for the Walker Art Center in Minneapolis and for the **DE YOUNG MUSEUM** in San Francisco in the space of less than a year. Founded in 1895 in San Francisco's Golden Gate Park, the de Young museum can be considered an integral part of the cultural fabric of the city. With a construction cost of 135 million dollars and a total project cost of 202 million dollars, this is no MoMA, but it is the Swiss pair's biggest new museum structure, since Tate Modern in London was actually a rehabilitation. It replaces the former facility on the same site that was damaged by the 1989 Loma Prieta earthquake. An interesting feature of the project is that it reduces the de Young's footprint by 37 % and returns nearly one hectare of open space to Golden Gate Park. The building's dramatic copper façade is perforated and textured to replicate the impression made by light filtering through a tree canopy, creating an artistic abstraction on the exterior of the museum that is linked to the de Young's park setting. The copper skin, chosen for its changeable quality through oxidation, will assume a green patina over time that will blend with the surrounding environment. The northeast corner of the building features a 44-meter spiral tower.

Mit dem neuen Walker Art Center in Minneapolis und dem **DE YOUNG MUSEUM** in San Francisco – beide Museen wurden innerhalb eines Jahres eröffnet – hatten die Schweizer Architekten Herzog & de Meuron einen Doppelerfolg. 1895 gegründet, gilt das De Young Museum in San Franciscos Golden Gate Park als wesentlicher Bestandteil des kulturellen Lebens der Stadt. Mit Baukosten von umgerechnet etwa 110 Millionen Euro und Gesamtkosten von 170 Millionen Euro reicht es zwar nicht an die Dimensionen des neuen MoMA heran, ist aber der bislang größte Museumsneubau der Schweizer Architekten, da es sich bei der Tate Modern in London ja um den Umbau eines bestehenden Gebäudes handelt. Der Neubau ersetzt das alte Museum am selben Ort; dieses wurde 1989 während des Loma-Prieta-Erdbebens beschädigt. Interessant ist, dass das neue De Young Museum gegenüber dem Altbau eine um 37 Prozent reduzierte Grundfläche aufweist und dem Golden Gate Park fast einen Hektar unbebauter Fläche »zurückgibt«. Die Textur der dramatischen, gelochten Kupferfassade erinnert an Licht, das durch das Blattwerk eines Baums sickert. Diese künstlerische Abstraktion verbindet das Museum mit seiner Parkumgebung. Die Kupferhaut, gewählt aufgrund ihrer sich durch Oxidation verändernden Oberflächenqualität, wird im Lauf der Zeit eine grüne Patina bekommen und sich so der Umgebung weiter anpassen. An der Nordostecke des Gebäudes befindet sich ein 44 m hoher, spiralförmig gedrehter Turm.

Herzog & de Meuron ont connu une sorte de double triomphe en ouvrant en moins d'un an le nouveau bâtiment du Walker Center à Minneapolis et celui du **DE YOUNG MUSEUM** à San Francisco. Fondé en 1895 et implanté dans le Golden Gate Park à San Francisco, le De Young Museum fait partie intégrante du tissu culturel de la ville. Construit pour un budget global de 170 millions d'euros (dont 110 millions pour la seule construction), ce n'est pas un projet de l'envergure de celui du MoMA, mais néanmoins la plus grande réalisation muséale du duo suisse, puisque la Tate Modern de Londres était en fait une réhabilitation. Ce nouveau bâtiment de 27 220 m² commandé par le Fine Arts Museum de San Francisco (FAMSF) remplace l'ancien, endommagé par le tremblement de terre de Loma Prieta en 1989. Une des caractéristiques intéressantes de ce projet est de réduire de 37% l'emprise au sol initiale et de restituer près d'un hectare de terrain au Golden Gate Park. La spectaculaire façade de cuivre perforé et texturé imite la lumière filtrant à travers le faîte des arbres, créant une image abstraite et artistique qui intègre encore davantage le musée à son cadre de verdure. La peau de cuivre, choisie pour sa capacité à évoluer avec le temps en s'oxydant, prendra une patine verte qui se fondra dans l'environnement. L'angle nord-est du bâtiment est signalé par une tour en spirale de 44 m de haut.

Standing out against the landscape the forms of the de Young Museum do not immediately bring to mind any architectural precedent. Herzog & de Meuron have again expressed their frequent interest in surface and form in a highly original manner.

Die mit der Landschaft kontrastieren-den Formen des De Young Museums lassen zunächst keine architektoni-schen Vorbilder erkennen. Herzog & de Meuron bringen hier erneut ihr Interesse an Oberfläche und Form auf einzigartige Weise zum Ausdruck.

Se détachant sur le paysage, la silhouette du De Young Museum n'évoque aucun précédent architec-tural. Herzog & de Meuron expriment, ici encore, leur intérêt pour la forme et la surface, d'une façon extrême-ment originale.

Interior views of the museum make it clear that its rather unusual exterior does not keep it from having functional, indeed inspiring spaces within.

Innenansichten des Museums verdeutlichen, dass es trotz der eher ungewöhnlichen äußeren Form von innen funktional und inspirierend ist.

Les vues intérieures du musée montrent que l'extérieur inhabituel ne l'empêche pas d'offrir des volumes intérieurs fonctionnels et motivants.

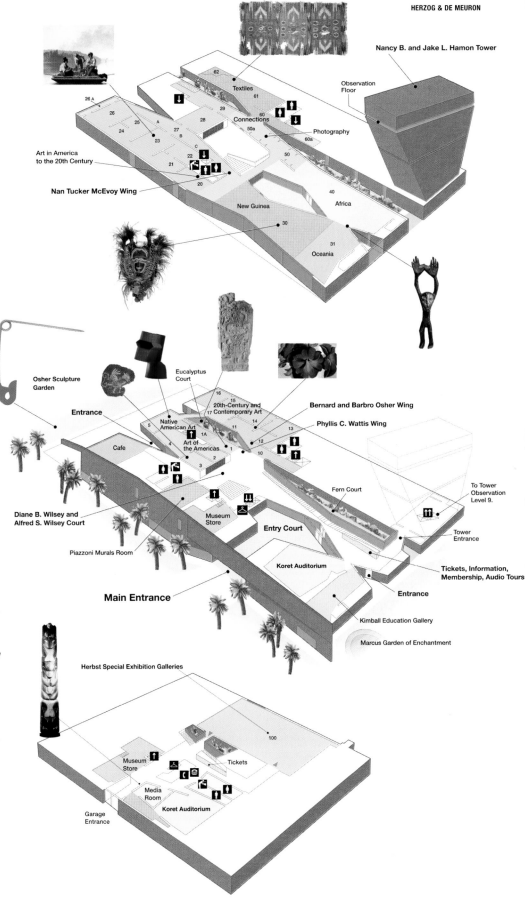

Nancy B. and Jake L. Hamon Tower

Observation Floor

Textiles

Connections

Photography

Art in America to the 20th Century

Nan Tucker McEvoy Wing

New Guinea

Africa

Oceania

Osher Sculpture Garden

Eucalyptus Court

20th-Century and Contemporary Art

Bernard and Barbro Osher Wing

Entrance

Native American Art

Phyllis C. Wattis Wing

Cafe

Art of the Americas

Diane B. Wilsey and Alfred S. Wilsey Court

Museum Store

Fern Court

To Tower Observation Level 9.

Entry Court

Tower Entrance

Piazzoni Murals Room

Koret Auditorium

Tickets, Information, Membership, Audio Tours

Main Entrance

Entrance

Kimball Education Gallery

Marcus Garden of Enchantment

Herbst Special Exhibition Galleries

Museum Store

Tickets

Media Room

Koret Auditorium

Garage Entrance

Many recently designed museum facilities by other architects either present a banal plan that is opposed to clever exterior effects, or impose unusable space on institutions. Herzog & de Meuron succeed in innovating in both exterior and interior design, on the surface, and in depth.

Viele Museen der jüngeren Zeit haben entweder einen banalen Grundriss, der raffiniert eingesetzten Fassadeneffekten gegenübersteht, oder den Museen werden unbrauchbare Räumlichkeiten aufgezwungen. Herzog & de Meuron dagegen gelingt es, sowohl innen als auch außen – also die Oberfläche und die Tiefe betreffend – neue Wege zu gehen.

Dans de nombreux équipements muséaux récents, les architectes ont soit conjugué un plan intérieur banal avec d'intelligents effets extérieurs, soit imposé des espaces pratiquement inutilisables. Herzog & de Meuron ont, quant à eux, su innover dans la conception de l'extérieur comme de l'intérieur, en surface comme en profondeur.

STEVEN HOLL

Steven Holl Architects, P. C.
450 West 31ˢᵗ Street, 11ᵗʰ floor
New York, New York 10001, USA

Tel: +1 212 629 7262, Fax: +1 212 629 7312
e-mail: mail@stevenholl.com, Web: www.stevenholl.com

Born in 1947 in Bremerton, Washington, **STEVEN HOLL** obtained his Bachelor of Architecture degree from the University of Washington (1970). He studied in Rome and at the Architectural Association in London (1976). He began his career in California and opened his own office in New York in 1976. Holl has taught at the University of Washington, Syracuse University, and since 1981 at Columbia University. His notable buildings include: Hybrid Building, Seaside, Florida (1984–88); Berlin AGB Library, Berlin, Germany, competition entry (1988); Void Space/Hinged Space, Housing, Nexus World, Fukuoka, Japan (1989–91); Stretto House, Dallas, Texas (1989–92); Makuhari Housing, Chiba, Japan (1992–97); Chapel of St. Ignatius, Seattle University, Seattle, Washington (1994–97); Kiasma Museum of Contemporary Art, Helsinki, Finland (1993–98). His work includes an extension to the Cranbrook Institute of Science, Bloomfield Hills, Michigan (1996–99). Winner of the 1998 Alvar Aalto Medal, Steven Holl recently completed the Bellevue Art Museum, Bellevue, Washington, and an expansion and renovation of the Nelson Atkins Museum of Art (Kansas City, Missouri). Other recent work includes the Knut Hamsun Museum, Hamarøy, Norway; an Art and Art History Building for the University of Iowa, Iowa City, Iowa; and the College of Architecture at Cornell University, Ithaca, New York (2004). He completed the Turbulence House in New Mexico for the artist Richard Tuttle in 2005, and he recently won the competition for the Knokke-Heist Casino in Belgium and completed the Pratt Institute Higgen Hall Center Wing, in Brooklyn. Steven Holl is also working on a new residence at the Swiss Embassy in Washington, D. C. He was one of the six finalists for the Louvre's new building in Lens, France.

STEVEN HOLL, 1947 in Bremerton, Washington, geboren, machte 1970 seinen Bachelor of Architecture an der University of Washington. Er studierte in Rom und an der Architectural Association in London (1976). Für kurze Zeit war er in Kalifornien tätig, bevor er 1976 in New York sein eigenes Büro eröffnete. Steven Holl hat an der University of Washington und an der Syracuse University unterrichtet; seit 1981 lehrt er an der Columbia University. Zu seinen wichtigsten Projekten gehören: das Hybrid Building, Seaside, Florida (1984–88), die Erweiterung der Amerika-Gedenkbibliothek in Berlin (Wettbewerbsbeitrag 1988), Void Space/Hinged Space, Wohnblock, Nexus World, Fukuoka, Japan (1989–91), das Stretto House, Dallas (1989–92), Makuhari Wohnhäuser, Chiba, Japan (1992–97), die St. Ignatius Kapelle, Seattle University, Seattle (1994–97), und das Kiasma Museum of Contemporary Art, Helsinki (1993–98). Holl plante außerdem die Erweiterung des Cranbrook Institute of Science, Bloomfield Hills, Michigan (1996–99). 1998 gewann er die Alvar-Aalto-Medaille. Vor kurzem wurden das Bellevue Art Museum in Bellevue, Washington, und die Erweiterung und Sanierung des Nelson Atkins Museum of Art in Kansas City, Missouri, fertig gestellt. Andere Projekte der jüngsten Zeit sind u. a. das Knut-Hamsun-Museum in Hamarøy, Norwegen, ein Gebäude für Kunst und Kunstgeschichte für die University of Iowa in Iowa City und das College of Architecture der Cornell University in Ithaca, New York (2004). 2005 wurde das Turbulence House in New Mexico für den Künstler Richard Tuttle fertig gestellt. Kürzlich hat Holl den Wettbewerb für das Knokke-Heist Kasino in Belgien gewonnen und stellte den Flügel des Pratt Institute Higgen Hall Center in Brooklyn fertig. Steven Holl plant außerdem ein neues Wohnhaus für die Botschaft der Schweiz in Washington, D. C. Er war einer der sechs Endrundenteilnehmer für das neue Louvre-Gebäude in Lens, Frankreich.

Né en 1947 à Bremerton (Washington), **STEVEN HOLL** est Bachelor of Architecture de l'Université de Washington (1970), puis a étudié à Rome et à l'Architectural Association, Londres (1976). Il débute sa carrière en Californie et ouvre sa propre agence à New York, en 1976. Il enseigne à l'Université de Washington, à Syracuse University et, depuis 1981, à Columbia University. Principales réalisations : Hybrid Building, Seaside, Floride (1984–88) ; participation au concours de la Bibliothèque AGB, Berlin (1988) ; immeuble d'appartements Void Space/Hinged Space, Nexus World, Fukuoka, Japon (1989–91) ; Stretto House, Dallas, Texas (1989–92) ; immeuble d'appartements Makuhari, Chiba, Japon (1992–97) ; musée d'Art contemporain Kiasma, Helsinki, Finlande (1993–98) ; rénovation et extension du Cranbrook Institute of Science, Bloomfield Hills, Michigan (1996–99). Distingué par la Médaille Alvar Aalto en 1998, il a récemment terminé le Bellevue Art Museum (Bellevue, Washington), l'extension et rénovation du Nelson Atkins Museum of Art, Kansas City, Missouri, et le Knut Hamsun Museum (Hamarøy, Norvège) ; le bâtiment pour l'art et l'histoire de l'art de l'Université de l'Iowa (Iowa City, Iowa) et le College of Architecture de Cornell University, Ithaca, New York (2004). Il a achevé la Turbulence House au Nouveau-Mexique pour l'artiste Richard Tuttle en 2005 et le Pratt Institute Higgen Hall Center Wing à Brooklyn et a remporté le concours pour le Casino de Knokke-Heist (Belgique). Il travaille actuellement à une nouvelle résidence pour l'ambassade suisse à Washington et fait partie des six finalistes du concours pour la nouvelle implantation du Louvre à Lens (France).

LOISIUM VISITOR CENTER AND HOTEL

Langenlois, Vienna, 2001–05

Floor area: Visitor Center 1200 m²; Hotel 7000 m². Client: Kellerwelt Betriebs GmbH & Co KG.
Cost: Visitor Center €2.2 million; Hotel €8.6 million

This complex includes a café, wine shop, souvenir shop, seminar rooms, event spaces, offices, restaurant, spa, and an 82-room hotel. The Visitor Center measures 1200 m² in floor area and cost 2.2 million euros, while the 7000 m² hotel cost 8.6 million. Situated sixty minutes west of Vienna in Langenlois, the largest wine-growing town in Austria, **LOISIUM** became a complete, wine-themed tourist destination with the opening of the luxury hotel there in October 2005. Basing his design on the location and the proximity of historic wine cellars, Holl first created the cube-shaped Visitors' Center that leans five degree toward a ramp leading to the wine cellar network. Built mostly with reinforced concrete, one-third of the Center is sunken below grade. The visible sections are clad in 4 mm-thick "Marine" aluminum, a special alloy with extremely good resistance properties. Connected to existing cellar passageways by a ninety-meter-long tunnel, the architecture creates a link between basement, ground and upper levels that reinforces the subterranean aspect of the wine cellar network. Holl's well-known mastery of light and form takes on a particularly interesting resonance in the context of Europe's old traditions, giving them life, and adding a historic depth to the architect's work that lacks in a U. S. context.

Der Komplex umfasst ein Café, eine Weinhandlung, einen Souvenirladen, Seminarräume, Räume für Sonderveranstaltungen, Büros, ein Restaurant, ein Spa, und ein 82-Zimmer-Hotel. Die Kosten des 1200 m² großen Besuchszentrums betrugen 2,2 Millionen Euro, die des Hotels (mit einer Gesamtfläche von 7000 m²) 8,6 Millionen Euro. Langenlois, die größte Weinbaustadt in Österreich, liegt westlich von Wien und ist mit dem Auto in einer Stunde von dort aus zu erreichen. Hier befindet sich **LOISIUM**, das durch die Eröffnung eines Luxushotels im Oktober 2005 zu einem ganz dem Wein gewidmeten Ziel für Touristen wurde. Der Ort und die Nähe zu den historischen Weinkellern bildeten die Grundlage für Holls Entwurf. Er entwickelte zuerst das Besuchszentrum in Form eines mächtigen Kubus, der sich mit einem Winkel von fünf Grad aus der Senkrechten zu einer Rampe neigt, die zu dem System von Weinkellern führt. Das Besuchszentrum, das weitgehend in Stahlbeton ausgeführt wurde, liegt zu einem Drittel in der Erde. Die von außen sichtbaren Teile des Gebäudes wurden mit 4 mm dickem, seewasserbeständigem Aluminium verkleidet, das extrem widerstandsfähig ist. Die zwischen den Weinkellern vorhandenen Gänge wurden an das neue Gebäude durch einen 90 m langen Tunnel angeschlossen. So wurde eine Verbindung zwischen dem Untergeschoss, dem Erdgeschoss und den Obergeschossen geschaffen, wodurch die Tatsache, dass sich das System der Weinkeller unter der Erde befindet, betont wird. Holls bekannte Meisterschaft, mit Licht und Form umzugehen, erweist sich im Kontext europäischer Traditionen als besonders interessant. Er erfüllt sie mit Leben; sie wiederum geben seinem Gebäude eine historische Tiefe, die in einer US-amerikanischen Umgebung nicht vorhanden wäre.

Ce complexe comprend un hôtel de 82 chambres, des bureaux, des salles de séminaires, des salles pour événements, un restaurant, un café, une boutique de vins, une de souvenirs et un spa. Le Centre de 1200 m² a coûté 2,2 millions d'euros et l'hôtel de 7000 m², 8,6 millions. Situé à une heure de Vienne, à Langenlois, capitale autrichienne du vin, **LOISIUM** est devenue une destination touristique pour les œnophiles, qui s'est vue couronnée par l'ouverture de cet hôtel de luxe en octobre 2005. S'inspirant du site et de la proximité de caves historiques, Holl a d'abord créé le Centre de visites, de forme cubique, incliné à 5° vers une rampe qui conduit au réseau de caves. Bâti essentiellement en béton armé, le Centre est au tiers enterré. Les parties visibles sont habillées d'un alliage d'aluminium « marine » de 4 mm d'épaisseur et d'une remarquable résistance. Relié aux caves par un tunnel de 90 m de long, le bâtiment fait corps avec le sol et le sous-sol, ce qui renforce l'aspect souterrain du réseau de caves. La maîtrise de la lumière et des formes qui sont la marque de l'architecte trouve une résonance particulière dans ce contexte de vieilles traditions européennes, les revitalise et confère à cette œuvre une dimension historique qu'elle n'aurait su trouver en Amérique.

The Loisium Hotel (left page) stands out from the vineyards, an enigmatic sculp-tural presence. In the Visitor Center (above), traditional window sequences are abandoned in favor of an irregular pattern of slits and openings that bring light into the building in unexpected ways.

Das Hotel Loisium (linke Seite) in den Weinbergen hat eine rätselhafte, skulpturale Präsenz. Statt herkömmlicher Fenster gibt es im Besucherzentrum (oben) unregelmäßig angeordnete Schlitze und Öffnungen, die das Innere auf ungewöhnliche Weise belichten.

Sculptural et énigmatique, l'hôtel de Loisium (page gauche) se détache sur son environnement de vignobles. Les séquences traditionnelles de fenêtres du centre d'accueil des visiteurs (ci-dessus) ont été abandonnées au profit d'un motif irrégulier de fentes et d'ouvertures qui canalisent la lumière de façon inattendue.

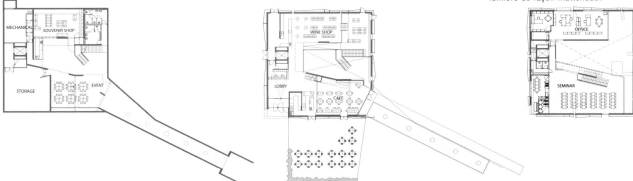

Steven Holl continues the logic
of the façade of his building inside,
with openings and color effects
that enliven the space.

Steven Holl führt die Logik der
Fassade im Inneren weiter. Öffnungen
und Farbeffekte werden gezielt eingesetzt, um den Raum zu beleben.

Steven Holl poursuit la logique de sa
façade à l'intérieur, avec des ouvertures et des effets de couleurs qui
animent l'espace.

Light, space and even water are part
of the architect's intentional exploration of sensations, in the phenom-
nology of architecture.

Licht, Raum und sogar Wasser sind
Teil von Holls Erforschung der Wahrnehmung von Architektur.

La lumière, l'espace et même l'eau
participent à l'exploration intention-
nelle des sensations dans une phéno-
ménologie de l'architecture.

WHITNEY WATER PURIFICATION FACILITY AND PARK

New Haven, Connecticut, USA, 1998–2005

*Floor area: 13 006 m². Client: South Central Connecticut Regional Water Authority.
Cost: $46 million*

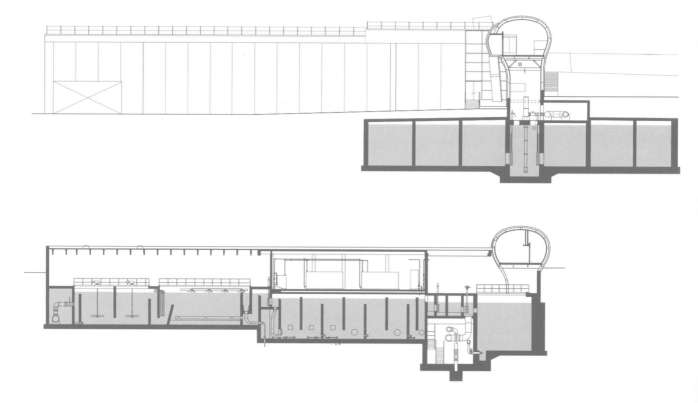

Taking on the mechanical requirements of a water purification facility, Steven Holl succeeds in giving an original form to his design, at once linked to the earth and distinct from it.

Indem er sich mit den funktionalen Anforderungen einer Wasseraufbereitungsanlage auseinandersetzt, findet Holl eine signifikante Form für das Gebäude, das einerseits mit dem Erdboden verbunden ist, sich andererseits aber klar von ihm abhebt.

Tout en prenant en compte les contraintes techniques de cette installation de traitement des eaux, Steven Holl est parvenu à lui donner une forme originale à la fois liée au terrain et distincte de lui.

Steven Holl explains that "The design fuses the architecture of the water purification plant with the landscape to form a public park. Water treatment facilities are located beneath the park, while the public and operational programs rise up in a 110 m long stainless steel sliver expressing the workings of the plant below and forming a reflective horizon line in the landscape. Like an inverted drop of water, the sliver shape creates a curvilinear interior space which opens to a large window view of surrounding landscape." The architect invested himself fully in the technical aspects of the project, seeing to it that the project was as fully "green" and sustainable as possible. A heat pump system with 88 wells saves 850 000 kilowatts in energy costs annually, while the fact that the plant itself is set into the ground, below lake level, allows it to use the pressure of gravity to feed in the water as opposed to energy-consuming pumps. The excavated debris from the site was reused and recyclable materials were used wherever possible. Existing wetland and natural vegetation were preserved, while a green roof system requiring very little maintenance was designed for the facility. Capable of treating 60 million liters of water per day, the plant measures 13 000 m² and cost 46 million dollars to build.

Steven Holl erläutert: »Der Entwurf verbindet die Architektur der Wasseraufbereitungsanlage mit der Landschaft, um so einen öffentlichen Park zu schaffen. Die Anlagen zur Behandlung des Wassers liegen unter der Erdoberfläche und sind in einem 110 m langen ›Span‹ aus Edelstahl angeordnet. Er bringt die Funktionen der Anlage im Untergrund zum Ausdruck und bildet eine reflektierende Horizontlinie in der Landschaft. An einen umgedrehten Wassertropfen erinnernd, formt der Span einen geschwungenen Innenraum, der sich mit einem großzügigen Ausblick zur Landschaft der Umgebung öffnet.« Der Architekt machte sich sehr umfassend mit der technischen Seite des Projekts vertraut und setzte sich dafür ein, dass die Anlage so ökologisch wie möglich gebaut wurde. Durch das Wärmepumpensystem mit 88 Behältern werden jährlich 850 000 Kilowattstunden Energie gespart, und durch die Verlegung der eigentlichen Anlage ins Erdreich, unterhalb der Seeoberfläche, wird das Wasser durch die Erdanziehungskraft in die Anlage eingeleitet, ohne dass dafür energieaufwendige Pumpen notwendig wären. Der Erdaushub für das Gebäude konnte wiederverwendet werden; wo immer möglich kamen recycelbare Materialien zum Einsatz. Feuchtgebiete und die natürliche Vegetation wurden erhalten, ferner wurde ein Gründach mit sehr geringem Wartungsaufwand entwickelt. Die Anlage mit einer Fläche von 13 000 m² reinigt täglich 60 Millionen l Wasser; die Gesamtkosten beliefen sich auf umgerechnet 38,5 Millionen Euro.

Steven Holl explique que « ce projet opère la fusion entre l'architecture de cette installation de purification de l'eau et son paysage pour donner naissance à un parc public. Le traitement de l'eau est effectué en sous-sol, tandis que les salles de contrôle et les espaces ouverts au public sont abrités dans un ‹ tuyau › d'acier inoxydable de 110 m de long qui exprime la nature de l'installation souterraine et dessine une ligne d'horizon qui réfléchit le paysage. Comme une goutte d'eau inversée, cette forme délimite un volume intérieur curviligne qui s'ouvre par une vaste baie sur l'environnement ». Steven Holl s'est personnellement investi dans les aspects techniques du projet, de sorte que le résultat est aussi écologique que possible. Un système de pompe à chaleur de 88 puits permet une économie d'énergie de 850 000 Kw annuels. La position enterrée de l'unité de traitement, en dessous du niveau du lac, permet par ailleurs d'utiliser la pression de la gravité pour l'alimentation en eau et de se passer de pompes grandes consommatrices d'énergie. Les déblais de l'excavation ont été réutilisés et des matériaux recyclables choisis à chaque fois que cela était possible. Les zones marécageuses et la végétation existantes ont été préservées et une toiture végétalisée à maintenance réduite mise en place. Cette installation susceptible de traiter 60 millions de litres d'eau par jour, d'une superficie de 13 000 m², a coûté 38,5 millions d'euros.

Water treatment facilities are certainly not known for their design qualities, but here, as in any other work of his architecture, Steven Holl also pays careful intention to the creation of unusual interiors, where light and space interact in unexpected ways.

Wasseraufbereitungsanlagen zeichnen sich gewöhnlich sicher nicht durch ihre gestalterischen Qualitäten aus. Bei dieser Anlage schafft Holl – wie bei allen seinen Gebäuden – Innenräume, in denen Licht und Raum auf unerwartete Weise miteinander in Beziehung treten.

Les installations de traitement des eaux ne sont certainement pas réputées pour leur qualité esthétique mais ici, comme dans n'importe quelle autre de ses réalisations, l'architecte porte une attention soignée à la création de volumes intérieurs inhabituels dans lesquels la lumière et l'espace interagissent de façon inattendue.

There is something of a spaceship about the Whitney building, an alien craft that does not just sit on the earth but also rises from it.

Das Whitney-Gebäude hat etwas von einem Raumschiff – ein fremdes Fahrzeug, das nicht nur auf der Erde steht, sondern auch in die Höhe strebt.

Il y a, dans ce bâtiment de Whitney, quelque chose d'un vaisseau extraterrestre qui se serait posé sur terre ou qui jaillirait des profondeurs.

JAKOB + MACFARLANE

Jakob + MacFarlane SARL d'Architecture
13–15, rue des Petites Écuries
75010 Paris
France

Tel: +33 144 79 05 72
Fax: +33 148 00 97 93
e-mail: info@jakobmacfarlane.com
Web: www.jakobmacfarlane.com

Renault Square Com

DOMINIQUE JAKOB, born in 1966, received her degree in art history at the Université de Paris 1 (1990) before obtaining her degree in architecture at the École d'Architecture Paris-Villemin (1991). She has taught at the École Spéciale d'Architecture (1998–99) and the École d'Architecture Paris-Villemin (1994–2000). Born in New Zealand in 1961, **BRENDAN MACFARLANE** received his Bachelor of Architecture at SCI-Arc (1984); and his Master of Architecture degree at Harvard Graduate School of Design (1990). He has taught at the Berlage Institute, Amsterdam (1996); the Bartlett School of Architecture in London (1996–98) and the École Spéciale d'Architecture in Paris (1998–99). Both Jakob and MacFarlane have worked in the office of Morphosis in Santa Monica. Their main projects include the T House, La-Garenne-Colombes, France (1994, 1998), the Georges Restaurant in the Pompidou Center, Paris, France (1999–2000); and the restructuring of the Maxime Gorki Theater, Petit-Quevilly, France (1999–2000). Recent work includes: La Fanal Theater, Saint-Nazaire, France (2004); an office building for a reinsurance company in Paris (2004); and plans for new facilities on the Paris docks (2004).

DOMINIQUE JAKOB, geboren 1966, machte 1990 an der Université Paris 1 ihren Abschluss in Kunstgeschichte. Ihr Architekturstudium an der Ecole d'Architecture Paris-Villemin schloss sie1991 ab. Sie unterrichtete von 1998 bis 1999 an der Ecole Spéciale d'Architecture und von 1994 bis 2000 an der Ecole d'Architecture Paris-Villemin. Der 1961 in Neuseeland geborene **BRENDAN MACFARLANE** erlangte 1984 seinen Bachelor of Architecture an der SCI-Arc und 1990 seinen Master of Architecture an der Graduate School of Design in Harvard. Er hat am Berlage-Institut in Amsterdam gelehrt (1996), an der Bartlett School of Architecture in London (1996–98) und an der Ecole Spéciale d'Architecture in Paris (1998–99). Sowohl Jakob als auch MacFarlane haben bei Morphosis in Santa Monica gearbeitet. Zu ihren wichtigsten Projekten gehören die Maison T in La-Garenne-Colombes, Frankreich (1994, 1998), das Restaurant Georges im Centre Georges Pompidou in Paris (1999–2000) und der Umbau des Maxim-Gorki-Theaters in Petit-Quevilly, Frankreich (1999–2000). Neuere Projekte des Büros sind u. a. das Theater La Fanal in Saint-Nazaire, Frankreich (2004), ein Bürogebäude für eine Versicherungsgesellschaft in Paris (2004) und Planungen für neue Nutzungen der Docks in Paris (2004).

DOMINIQUE JAKOB, née en 1966, est titulaire d'une licence en histoire de l'art de l'Université de Paris I (1990) et diplômée de l'École d'architecture de Paris-Villemin (1991). Elle a enseigné à l'École spéciale d'architecture (1998–99) et à l'École de Paris-Villemin (1994–2000). Né en Nouvelle-Zélande en 1961, **BRENDAN MACFARLANE** est Bachelor of Architecture du Southern California Institute of Architecture, SCI-Arc (1984) et Master of Architecture de la Graduate School of Design de Harvard (1990). Il a enseigné au Berlage Institute à Amsterdam (1996), à la Bartlett School of Architecture de Londres (1996–98) et à l'École spéciale d'architecture à Paris (1998–99). Tous deux ont travaillé à l'agence Morphosis à Santa Monica. Parmi leurs principaux projets : la Maison T, La Garenne-Colombes, France (1994 et 1998) ; le restaurant Georges, Centre Georges Pompidou, Paris (1999–2000), la restructuration du théâtre Maxime Gorki, Petit-Quevilly, France (1999–2000) ; le théâtre Le Fanal, Saint-Nazaire, France (2004) ; un immeuble de bureaux pour une compagnie de réassurance, Paris (2004) et les Docks de Paris, un projet pour de nouveaux équipements culturels et sportifs sur les quais de Seine, Paris (2004).

RENAULT SQUARE COM

Boulogne-Billancourt, France, 2002–05

Floor area: 14 500 m². Client: Régie Renault.
Cost: €23 million

The distinctive skylights of Vasconi's factory remain, but Jakob + MacFarlane have given a new luminosity and transparency to the Renault factory building.

Die charakteristischen Oberlichter von Vasconis Gebäude blieben. Jakob + MacFarlane haben dem ehemaligen Renaultwerk jedoch zu neuer Leuchtkraft und Transparenz verholfen.

Les verrières originales de l'usine créée par Vasconi subsistent, mais Jakob + MacFarlane ont donné à ces installations une luminosité et une transparence nouvelles.

In the early 1980s, the French automobile company Renault asked the architect Claude Vasconi to design about twenty new buildings to replace ageing factory facilities located on the Séguin Island in the Seine at the western extremity of Paris, and on the right bank of the river. As it happens, he built only one structure, called 57 Métal. Never used as a factory, Métal 57 has been converted by Jakob + MacFarlane into a communications center for Renault. With ceiling heights ranging between six and twelve meters, Métal 57 posed a challenge to the architects, intent on keeping something of the original spirit of the 15 000 m^2 building while turning it into a viable facility. Meant to be a place to base Renault's public relations staff of 250–300 people, and to present new cars to the press and leaders in the automobile industry, the company envisioned a venue where its marketing groups from around the world could come for meetings, entertainment, dining, and other events showcasing its cars. Three auditoriums seating 100, 300 and 500 persons respectively were added to one side of the shed-like structure. Completed in 2005 for 23 million euros, the conversion successfully creates open, airy spaces ideally suited to showing cars. The architects partially lined the vast exhibition area with large, 7-centimeter-thick structural honeycomb panels faced in resin-coated aluminum. With exposed steel frames backing "pleated" white walls, the architects created display backdrops against which they can hang automobiles like works of art. As MacFarlane points out, "the wall material, made for aeronautics industry fuselages, is interesting because of its flatness and lightness."

In den frühen 1980er Jahren beauftragte der französische Autohersteller Renault den Architekten Claude Vasconi mit dem Entwurf von etwa 20 neuen Gebäuden als Ersatz für die in die Jahre gekommenen Fabrikanlagen auf der Seine-Insel Séguin im äußersten Westen von Paris und auf dem rechten Seineufer. Tatsächlich wurde aber nur einer dieser Entwürfe realisiert, das so genannte Métal-57-Gebäude. Métal 57 wurde jedoch nie als Werk benutzt und von Jakob + MacFarlane in ein Kommunikationszentrum für Renault umgebaut. Mit Deckenhöhen zwischen 6 und 12 m stellte Métal 57 eine Herausforderung für die Architekten dar: Einerseits wollten sie etwas von der ursprünglichen Atmosphäre des 15 000 m^2 großen Gebäudes erhalten, es aber andererseits in ein gut nutzbares Kommunikationszentrum verwandeln. 250 bis 300 Mitarbeiter der PR-Abteilung sollen hier arbeiten; außerdem dient es dazu, der Presse und wichtigen Personen der Automobilindustrie die neusten Modelle zu präsentieren. Renault stellte sich einen Ort vor, an dem seine Marketingteams aus der ganzen Welt für Meetings, Unterhaltungsveranstaltungen, Diners und andere Events, bei denen Autos vorgestellt werden, zusammenkommen. Drei Auditorien mit 100, 300 und 500 Plätzen wurden an der einen Seite des hallenartigen Baukörpers angefügt. 2005 wurde das 23 Millionen Euro teure Gebäude fertig gestellt. Mit dem Umbau ist es gelungen, offene, großzügige Räume zu schaffen, die sich ideal für die Präsentation von Autos eignen. Die riesigen Ausstellungsräume wurden z. T. mit großen, 7 cm dicken Paneelen mit einem Wabenkern und einer Oberfläche aus kunstharzbeschichtetem Aluminium ausgekleidet. Die Architekten entwarfen sichtbare Stahlkonstruktionen, die »gefältete« weiße Wände halten; an diesen Wänden können Automobile wie Kunstwerke aufgehängt werden. MacFarlane dazu: »Das Interessante am Material der Wand, das eigentlich zur Herstellung von Flugzeugrümpfen verwendet wird, ist seine glatte Oberfläche und sein geringes Gewicht.«

Au début des années 1980, le constructeur automobile Renault avait demandé à l'architecte Claude Vasconi de concevoir une vingtaine de bâtiments pour remplacer ses usines vieillissantes de l'île Seguin et de la rive droite de la Seine à Boulogne-Billancourt. Finalement, il ne réalisa qu'un seul bâtiment, appelé 57 Métal. Jamais utilisé en tant qu'usine, le lieu a été converti par Jakob + MacFarlane en Centre de communication Renault. L'ensemble, doté de plafonds de six à douze mètres de haut, représentait un défi pour les architectes, qui voulaient conserver en partie l'esprit d'origine de cette construction de 15 000 m^2 tout en la transformant en un équipement efficace. Ce lieu était destiné à accueillir les 250 à 300 personnes du département des relations presse de la firme et à présenter les nouveaux modèles aux journalistes et aux décideurs du secteur automobile. Renault prévoyait aussi d'y recevoir ses équipes de marketing du monde entier, qui pourraient s'y réunir, y travailler, se restaurer et assister à des événements organisés autour des voitures. Trois auditoriums de 100, 300 et 500 places sont venus se greffer au flanc de l'ancien bâtiment-hangar. Achevée en 2005 pour un budget de 23 millions d'euros, cette conversion a réussi à créer des espaces aérés et ouverts, parfaitement adaptés à leur fonction. Les architectes ont en partie habillé la vaste surface d'exposition de panneaux structurels en nid d'abeille d'aluminium de 7 cm d'épaisseur doublés de résine en façade. À partir d'une ossature apparente en acier qui soutient des murs blanc «plissés», ils ont créé des cimaises sur lesquelles sont accrochées les voitures, comme des œuvres d'art. Comme MacFarlane le fait remarquer, «ce matériau mural, fabriqué pour les fuselages d'avion, est intéressant pour sa légèreté et sa minceur».

The main floor of the factory has been converted to a bright exhibition space. The angled surfaces are a product of the aeronautics industry.

Die Hauptebene der ehemaligen Fabrik wurde in einen hellen Ausstellungsraum umgewandelt. Die geneigten Flächen sind aus dem Flugzeugbau.

L'étage de l'usine a été transformé en un lumineux espace d'exposition. La technologie des plans inclinés est issue de l'industrie aéronautique.

Conference rooms and office spaces are inserted into the former factory space along either side of the main axis. Working with a limited budget, the architects have succeeded in giving the entire space a contemporary and efficient feeling.

Entlang der Hauptachse wurden auf beiden Seiten Konferenz- und Büroräume eingefügt. Trotz begrenzter finanzieller Mittel ist es den Architekten gelungen, dem ganzen Komplex ein modernes und ökonomisches Flair zu geben.

Des salles de réunion et des bureaux viennent s'insérer dans le volume de l'ancienne usine, de chaque côté de l'axe principal. Avec un budget limité, les architectes ont su donner à la totalité de cet espace industriel une allure moderne et efficace.

H HOUSE

Propriano, Corsica, France, 2003

Floor area: 900 m². Client: Mr H.
Cost: €650 000

The architects explain that in the **H HOUSE**, presented in the 9th Architecture Biennale in Venice, they used the natural topography of the site in order to generate the forms of the structure. "We made a digital model of the site topography," says MacFarlane, "we then superimposed over this matrix a surface cloned from the first model. Next, the programmatic elements were introduced between these two virtual surfaces. We then let them seep and deform like living shapes, appropriating their environment. The result is a series of cellular spaces appearing on a surface guided by a three-dimensional matrix of the topography." Certainly part of a trend to make use of the land in contemporary architecture, this particular project was actually chosen by the Biennale's director, Kurt Forster, in a section he called "Transformation," where the ability of contemporary architecture to adapt to circumstances was the theme. In their earlier Georges restaurant in the Pompidou Center, Jakob + MacFarlane used the original orthogonal grid set down by Piano and Rogers and morphed it on a computer to create the bulbous forms of the restaurant facilities. In a sense, the H House applies this method to natural topography.

MAISON H wurde auf der IX. Architekturbiennale in Venedig gezeigt. Die Architekten erläutern, dass sie die natürliche Topografie des Grundstücks benutzten, um die Formen der Konstruktion zu bestimmen. »Wir haben ein digitales Modell der Topografie angefertigt«, sagt MacFarlane, »anschließend haben wir diese Matrix mit der Oberfläche, die wir vom ersten Modell klonten, überlagert. Dann wurde das Raumprogramm zwischen diese beiden virtuellen Oberflächen gelegt. Wir ließen es ›einsickern‹, wodurch es sich veränderte (ähnlich wie sich in der Natur Formen verändern) und sich der Umgebung anpasste. Das Ergebnis ist eine Serie von zellenartigen Räumen, die auf der Oberfläche auftauchen, die von der dreidimensionalen Matrix der Topografie bestimmt ist.« Sicherlich folgt das Gebäude dem aktuellen Trend in der Architektur, das Gelände für den Entwurf zu benutzen. Dieses spezielle Projekt wurde vom Direktor der Biennale, Kurt Forster, für die Kategorie »Transformation« ausgewählt; Thema dieser Sektion war die Fähigkeit heutiger Architektur, sich den Gegebenheiten anzupassen. In ihrem Restaurant Georges im Centre Georges Pompidou benutzten Jakob + MacFarlane das ursprüngliche, von Piano und Rogers festgelegte Raster und wandelten es am Computer in eine blasenartige Form um. In gewisser Weise wird bei der Maison H dieselbe Methode auf die natürliche Topografie angewendet.

Les architectes expliquent que pour la **MAISON H**, présentée à la 9e Biennale d'architecture de Venise, ils se sont servi de la topographie du site pour générer une forme. « Nous avons réalisé un modèle numérique de la topographie et surimposé à cette matrice une surface clonée à partir de la première. Puis, les éléments programmatiques ont été insérés entre ces deux surfaces virtuelles. Nous les avons ensuite laissé s'infiltrer et se déformer comme des éléments vivants pour qu'ils s'approprient leur environnement. Le résultat est une série d'espaces cellulaires apparaissant en surface mais guidés par la matrice tridimensionnelle de la topographie. » Dans le cadre d'une tendance à utiliser davantage la topographie dans l'architecture contemporaine, ce projet a été choisi par le directeur de la Biennale vénitienne, Kurt Forster, pour la section intitulée « Transformation » dont le thème était la capacité de l'architecture contemporaine à exploiter le contexte du site. Dans leur restaurant Georges (antérieur), Jakob + MacFarlane se sont servi de la trame définie à l'origine par Piano et Rogers et traitée par ordinateur pour obtenir les formes bulbeuses de plusieurs salles du restaurant. D'une certaine façon, la Maison H applique cette méthode à la topographie naturelle.

The H House, something like the Liaunig Museum by Odile Decq, also reproduced in this volume, is one of a number of contemporary efforts to generate architectural form from topopgraphy. It seems to emerge from the ground of the site.

La Maison H, un peu comme le Liaunig Museum d'Odile Decq également reproduit dans ces pages, est l'une des récentes tentatives de création d'une forme architecturale à partir de la topographie. La maison semble surgir du sol.

Wie das Liaunig-Museum von Odile Decq gehört die Maison H zu den aktuellen Projekten, die versuchen, aus der Topografie eine architektonische Formensprache zu entwickeln. Das Haus scheint aus dem Erdboden emporzuwachsen.

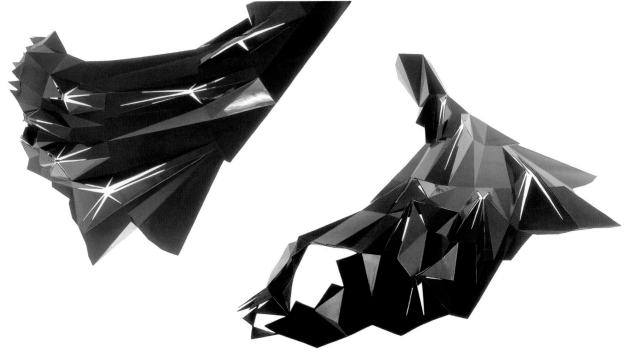

PATRICK JOUIN

Agence Patrick Jouin
8, Passage de la Bonne Graine
75011 Paris
France

Tel: +33 155 28 89 20
Fax: +33 158 30 60 70
e-mail: agence@patrickjouin.com
Web: www.patrickjouin.com

Chlösterli ►

Born in Nantes in 1967, **PATRICK JOUIN** studied at the Ecole Nationale Supérieure de Création Industrielle (ENSCI) in Paris and received his diploma in 1992. He worked in 1992 as a designer at the Compagnie des Wagons-Lits, and for the two following years at Tim Thom, Thomson multimedia under Philippe Starck, who was then artistic director of the brand. From 1995 to 1999, Patrick Jouin was a designer in Philippe Starck's Paris studio. He has designed numerous objects and pieces of furniture, but his architectural work includes: the Alain Ducasse au Plaza Athénée Restaurant, Paris (2000); 59 Poincaré Restaurant, Paris (2000); Plastic Products Factory, Nantes (2001); Plaza Athénée Bar (2001); Spoon Byblos Restaurant, Saint Tropez (2002); Mix New York Restaurant for Alain Ducasse (2003); the Chlösterli with two restaurants, Gstaad, Switzerland (2003); the Mix Restaurant in Las Vegas (2004); and the Terrasse Montaigne, Plaza Athénée (2005). His recent *Solid* collection of furniture for the Belgian firm MGX uses the sophisticated technique of stereolithography to create remarkable, unique polymer objects.

Der 1967 in Nantes geborene **PATRICK JOUIN** studierte an der Ecole Nationale Supérieure de Création Industrielle (ENSCI) in Paris und machte dort 1992 seinen Abschluss. Im selben Jahr arbeitete er als Designer für die Compagnie des Wagons-Lits, in den beiden darauf folgenden Jahren bei Tim Thom, Thomson Multimedia, für Philippe Starck, der damals Art Director für die Marke war. Von 1995 bis 1999 war Patrick Jouin Designer bei Philippe Starck in Paris. Er hat zahlreiche Objekte und Möbelstücke entworfen, aber auch u. a. folgende Gebäude und Einrichtungen: das Restaurant Alain Ducasse im Plaza Athénée in Paris (2000), das Restaurant 59 Poincaré in Paris (2000), eine Fabrik für Produkte aus Kunststoff in Nantes (2001), die Plaza Athénée Bar (2001), das Restaurant Spoon Byblos in Saint-Tropez (2002) und das Mix New York Restaurant für Alain Ducasse (2003), außerdem das Chlösterli mit zwei Restaurants in Gstaad, Schweiz (2003), das Mix Restaurant in Las Vegas (2004) und die Terrasse Montaigne im Plaza Athénée (2005). Bei seiner neuen Möbelkollektion *Solid* für die belgische Firma MGX setzt er eine anspruchsvolle Technik, die Stereolithografie, ein, um bemerkenswerte, einzigartige polymere Objekte herzustellen.

Né à Nantes en 1967, **PATRICK JOUIN** a étudié à l'École nationale supérieure de création industrielle (Ensci) à Paris dont il est sorti diplômé en 1992. Il a ensuite travaillé pour la Compagnie des Wagons-Lits, puis les deux années suivantes au sein de Tim Thom, le département de design de Thomson Multimédia animé par Philippe Starck. De 1995 à 1999, il a été designer chez celui-ci. Il a conçu de nombreux objets et éléments de mobilier. Ses interventions architecturales comprennent : le restaurant du Plaza Athénée pour Alain Ducasse, Paris (2000), le Restaurant 59 Poincaré, Paris (2000) ; une usine de produits en plastique, Nantes (2001) le bar du Plaza Athénée (2003) ; le restaurant Spoon Byblos, Saint-Tropez (2000) ; le restaurant Mix pour Alain Ducasse, New York (2003) ; le Chlösterli avec deux restaurants, Gstaad, Suisse (2003) ; le restaurant Mix, Las Vegas (2004) et la Terrasse Montaigne, Plaza Athénée (2005). *Solid*, sa récente collection de meubles pour le fabricant belge MGX, fait appel à des techniques sophistiquées de stéréolithographie pour de remarquables objets uniques en polymères.

CHLÖSTERLI
Gstaad, Switzerland, 2003

Floor area: 700 m² (bar, lounge, discotheque, 2 restaurants, 2 kitchens). Client: Michel Pastor.
Cost: not disclosed

Located outside the town, on the main road leading into Gstaad, **CHLÖSTERLI** was created by Patrick Jouin inside a traditional Swiss chalet, built around 1700 by the monks of the Rougemont Abbey. Although the designer did add a comfortable outside terrace, he essentially left the exterior of the wooden building as it was. Inside, a 6-meter-long wall of glass containing an exceptional wine collection cuts the space in two. The kitchen is on one side of this wall, and two restaurants, a bar and a discotheque on the other. A slate floor with some luminous colored glass inserts marks the disco area, while the architect plays in a clever way on the traditional chalet interiors of the country, using milking pots as champagne chillers for example. In the bar, video screens evoke the chimney and fireplaces that modern regulations and an old wooden building don't allow. Much of the interior furnishing is Jouin's own creation, including the tables, lighting, and dining room seating with the *Mabelle* chair from his 2003 furniture collection of Cassina.

Das traditionelle, außerhalb von Gstaad an der Hauptstraße in die Stadt gelegene Schweizer Chalet wurde um 1700 von Mönchen der Rougemont-Abtei errichtet und beherbergt das von Patrick Jouin umgestaltete Restaurant **CHLÖSTERLI**. Eine komfortable Außenterrasse kam hinzu, ansonsten blieb die Hülle des Holzbaus intakt. Das Innere des Gebäudes wird durch eine 6 m lange Glaswand, die eine außergewöhnliche Weinsammlung aufnimmt, in zwei Teile geteilt. Auf der einen Seite befindet sich die Küche, auf der anderen Seite liegen zwei Restaurants, eine Bar und eine Diskothek. Der Bereich der Diskothek wird durch einen Schieferboden mit einigen farbig leuchtenden Glaseinsätzen gekennzeichnet. Der Architekt spielt geschickt mit der traditionellen Einrichtung eines Chalets und verwendet beispielsweise Milchkannen als Sektkühler. In der Bar werden auf Videobildschirmen Schornstein und Kamin simuliert; aufgrund der heutigen Bauvorschriften war ein echter Kamin in dem alten Gebäude nicht zulässig. Ein großer Teil der Inneneinrichtung stammt von Jouin: Tische, Beleuchtungskörper und die Restaurantbestuhlung mit dem *Mabelle*-Stuhl sind aus seiner Kollektion 2003 für Cassina.

C'est en dehors de la ville, sur la route principale conduisant à Gstaad, que Patrick Jouin a aménagé le **CHLÖSTERLI** à l'intérieur d'un chalet traditionnel construit vers 1700 par les moines de l'abbaye de Rougemont. Bien qu'il ait ajouté une confortable terrasse, il a laissé quasiment intact l'extérieur du bâtiment en bois. À l'intérieur, un mur de verre de 6 m de long, contenant une exceptionnelle collection grands crus, coupe le volume en deux avec, d'un côté, la cuisine et de l'autre, deux restaurants, un bar et une discothèque. Le sol en ardoise ponctué d'inserts de verre de couleur rétro-éclairés marque la zone de la discothèque. Ailleurs, l'architecte joue intelligemment sur les aspects traditionnels de la décoration de chalet, utilisant par exemple des pots à lait comme seaux à champagne. Dans le bar, un écran vidéo évoque le feu de bois que les règlements modernes et les constructions anciennes en bois interdisent de nos jours. La plus grande partie du mobilier est signée de Jouin, en particulier les tables, les luminaires et les sièges de la salle à manger qui ne sont autres que les fauteuils *Mabelle* de sa collection 2003 éditée par Cassina.

Aside from an outside terrace, Jouin did not really modify the exterior of the old chalet, which is located on the main entrance road to Gstaad.

Abgesehen von der Außenterrasse hat Jouin das Äußere des Chalets kaum verändert. Das Chalet liegt an der Hauptstraße nach Gstaad.

En dehors de la terrasse (page précédente), Jouin n'a pas vraiment modifié le vieux chalet situé en bordure de la principale route d'accès à Gstaad.

The outside terrace of the restaurant offers an excellent view of the surrounding countryside and mountains without altering the very old feeling of the main building.

Die Außenterrasse bietet einen schönen Blick auf die bergige Landschaft der Umgebung; die Stimmung in dem uralten Chalet verändert sich durch diese Terrasse aber nicht.

La terrasse du restaurant offre une vue remarquable sur la campagne et les montagnes environnantes, sans trahir l'impression de construction très ancienne que donne le chalet.

A discothèque and bare space on the ground floor making use of floor blocks lit from below, and a spectacular wine cellar inserted into a glass wall. A private dining room on the upper floor is visible at the top of the image on this page.

Die Diskothek und die Bar im Erdgeschoss werden durch einzelne Fußbodenfelder von unten beleuchtet. Die spektakuläre Weinsammlung ist in eine Glaswand integriert. Diese Seite: Oben im Bild ein Essraum für geschlossene Gesellschaften.

La discothèque, le bar du rez-de-chaussée au sol éclairé et une spectaculaire cave à vin enchâssée dans un mur de verre. À l'étage, une salle à manger privée, visible en haut de la photo de cette page.

Throughout the different areas on the ground and upper floors, Jouin makes clever use of traditional elements in a modern context. For a bar area (left page, bottom, middle) he uses video screens with pictures of cozy fires, in particular because current fire regulations did not allow for a real fireplace. He mixes his own existing furniture designs with newly created chairs, tables and accessories.

In allen Bereichen des Erd- und Obergeschosses mischt Jouin geschickt traditionelle Elemente in den modernen Umbau. Im Barbereich (linke Seite, unten Mitte) lodern auf Bildschirmen Kaminfeuer. Dies ist vor allem den heutigen Brandschutzvorschriften geschuldet, die einen echten Kamin nicht zuließen. Jouin verwendet seine früheren Möbelentwürfe ebenso wie neu entworfene Stühle, Tische und Accessoires.

Au rez-de-chaussée comme à l'étage, Jouin a habilement réutilisé des éléments traditionnels dans un contexte moderne. Ainsi dans le bar (page de gauche, en bas et au centre), des écrans vidéo diffusent des images de feu de bois, la réglementation ne permettant pas d'installer une vraie cheminée. Il a mélangé ses meubles déjà édités à de nouveaux modèles de fauteuils, tables et accessoires.

MIX VEGAS

Las Vegas, Nevada, USA, 2005

Floor Area: 1485 m². Client: Mandalay Bay Hotel.
Cost: $15 million

Patrick Jouin took some pleasure in the apparent contradiction of creating a large restaurant for the world-renowned chef Alain Ducasse in a Las Vegas Strip hotel, the Mandalay Bay. As he says, the design "lives up to Las Vegas's reputation for extravagance." Perched on top of the hotel, the restaurant offers desert and city panoramas for clients. As the firm's description has it, "Mix combines two very different atmospheres: the deep, sexy, entrancing red in the bowels of the bar; and the purity of whiteness, translucent, in suspension, as airy as the skies, in the restaurant." The 300-seat elliptical lounge is "built around a structure that rises up like a bouquet of coral, a vision of magma, fire, or volcanic energy." The main dining room has a 10-meter ceiling and features a Murano chandelier made of 15 000 hand-blown glass bubbles. Here, as in the restaurant at Chlösterli, Jouin used his *Mabelle* chairs manufactured by Cassina. The restaurant seats 240 including 40 terrace seats. A part of the restaurant floor is covered with polycarbonate tiles that contain a molded-in layer of lace that Jouin calls "a modern version of interior carpeting." The budget for the project was 15 million dollars.

Patrick Jouin erhielt den Auftrag, im Mandalay Bay, einem Hotel am Strip von Las Vegas, ein Restaurant für den weltweit bekannten Restaurantbesitzer und Chefkoch Alain Ducasse einzurichten. Der offenkundige Gegensatz reizte ihn. Wie er sagt, »entspricht der Entwurf dem Ruf von Las Vegas, Extravagantes zu bieten«. Das im obersten Geschoss des Hotels gelegene Restaurant bietet dem Besucher einen weiten Blick über die Wüste und die Stadt. Laut Selbstbeschreibung des Hotels ist das Restaurant eine Mischung aus »zwei ganz verschiedenen Atmosphären: Das tiefe Rot der Schalen an der Bar ist sexy und hinreißend, das reine Weiß im Restaurant ist dagegen transluzent, in der Schwebe und luftig wie der Himmel.« Die elliptische Lounge mit 300 Plätzen wurde »um eine Konstruktion herumgebaut, die wie ein Korallenzweig in die Höhe wächst und an Magma, Feuer und vulkanische Energie erinnert.« Der Kronleuchter aus Muranoglas im 10 m hohen Hauptspeisesaal des Restaurants besteht aus 15 000 mundgeblasenen Glaskugeln. Wie bei den Restaurants im Chlösterli kommt der von Jouin entworfene *Mabelle*-Stuhl von Cassina zum Einsatz. Das Restaurant hat 240 Plätze, 40 davon auf der Terrasse. Ein Teil des Restaurantbodens besteht aus Polykarbonatfliesen, in die ein Spitzengewebe eingegossen wurde – Jouin nennt dies eine »moderne Teppichvariante«. Die Kosten für das Projekt betrugen umgerechnet etwa 12,5 Millionen Euro.

Patrick Jouin a certainement pris plaisir à cette contradiction apparente : créer un vaste restaurant dans un hôtel sur le Strip de Las Vegas pour le célèbre et très raffiné chef Alain Ducasse. Comme il l'explique, « il s'agissait de se mettre au niveau de la réputation d'extravagance de Las Vegas ». Perché au sommet de l'hôtel, le restaurant offre un panorama sur la ville et le désert. Selon le descriptif officiel : « Mix combine deux atmosphères très différentes : le rouge profond, sexy, ensorcelant des boyaux du bar et la pureté du restaurant tout de blancheur, de transparences, aussi aérien que le ciel. » La salle en ellipse de 300 couverts est « construite autour d'une structure qui se dresse comme un bouquet de corail, une vision de magma, de feu, d'énergie volcanique ». Le plafond de la salle à manger principale s'élève à 10 m de haut et s'orne d'un lustre en Murano composé de 15 000 bulles de verre soufflé. Comme dans le restaurant Chlösterli, Jouin a utilisé le siège *Mabelle* édité par Cassina. Le restaurant propose 240 places, dont 40 en terrasse. Une partie du sol est en dalles de polycarbonate à inclusions de dentelle, « une version moderne de la moquette », selon Patrick Jouin. Le budget de cette réalisation s'est élevé à 12,5 millions d'euros.

The fact that contemporary design is tending to become more flamboyant and less minimalist certainly fits the mood of this project. Jouin takes on the capital of kitsch with good design that will still please the crowds.

Dass aktuelles Design eher zum Pompösen als zum Minimalistischen tendiert, zeigt sicherlich dieses Projekt. Jouin nimmt sich der »Hauptstadt des Kitsch« an und überzeugt mit gutem Design auch die Massen.

Le fait que le design contemporain tende à devenir moins minimaliste et beaucoup plus flamboyant a certainement servi l'atmosphère de ce projet. Jouin a insufflé dans la capitale du kitsch un peu de ce « good design » qui devrait plaire aux foules.

For all its bright colors and curvy furniture, Mix also capitalizes on its location in the heart of architectural extravagance that some call bad taste – large windows open out onto the Las Vegas skyline.

Über die starken Farben und geschwungenen Möbel hinaus schlägt Mix auch Vorteil aus dem Standort im Herzen der architektonischen Extravaganz, die manche „schlechten Geschmack" nennen – große Fenster öffnen sich zur Skyline von Las Vegas.

Par ses couleurs éclatantes et son mobilier en courbes, Mix capitalise également sur sa situation au cœur de cette extravagance architecturale que certains qualifieront de mauvais goût, aperçue à travers ses immenses baies ouvertes sur le panorama de Las Vegas.

The vast space and location of the Mix project make it about as different as it could be from the old wood of Gstaad, but Patrick Jouin employs his own Mabelle armchair (Cassina) in both locations. There is a kind of old fashioned glamor in his use of thousands of hand-blown glass bubbles.

Das Mix und das Chlösterli in Gstaad könnten unterschiedlicher nicht sein – aufgrund der Dimension des Raumes und des Genius Loci. In beiden Projekten verwendet Jouin jedoch den von ihm entworfenen Mabelle-Stuhl von Cassina. Tausende von mundgeblasenen Glaskugeln verbreiten so etwas wie altmodischen Glamour.

Rien n'est plus différent du Chlösterli de Gstaad que les généreux espaces du Mix ce qui n'a pas empêché Patrick Jouin d'utiliser son fauteuil Mabelle (Cassina). Les milliers de sphères de verre soufflé apportent une touche glamour désuète.

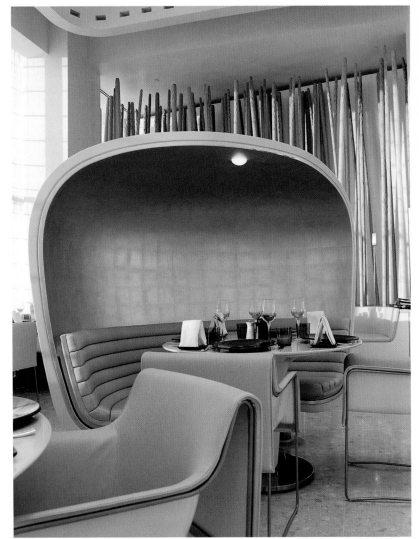

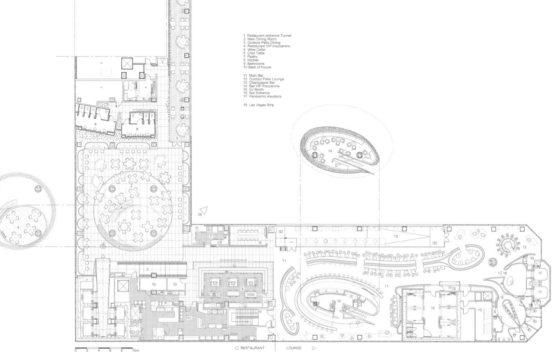

1 Restaurant entrance Tunnel
2 Main Dining Room
3 Outdoor Patio Dining
4 Restaurant VIP mezzanine
5 Wine Cellar
6 Chef Table
7 Pastry
8 Kitchen
9 Bathrooms
10 Back of House

11 Main Bar
12 Outdoor Patio Lounge
13 Champagne Bar
14 Bar VIP mezzanine
15 DJ Booth
16 Bar Entrance
17 Panoramic elevators

18 Las Vegas Strip

◁ RESTAURANT   LOUNGE ▷

With a deft sense of color and movement, Patrick Jouin animates the
large dining space of Mix, giving it
an elegance that seems quite fresh
and new, especially in Las Vegas.

Mit Geschick und Sinn für Farbe und
Bewegung belebt Jouin den großen
Essbereich des Mix und verleiht ihm
eine Eleganz, die – besonders in Las
Vegas – neu und frisch wirkt.

Avec un sens très vif de la couleur et
du mouvement, Patrick Jouin a animé
la vaste salle à manger du Mix pour
lui donner une élégance nouvelle et
pleine de fraîcheur, surtout pour Las
Vegas.

Lightness and a certain visual complexity combine to give an atmosphere to the space that is carried
through in the furniture, and even
in the table settings.

Leichtigkeit und eine besondere
visuelle Komplexität verbinden sich
zu einer räumlichen Atmosphäre,
die sich bis in die Möblierung und
Tischware hinein fortsetzt.

La légèreté et une certaine complexité visuelle se combinent et créent
une atmosphère qui se retrouve
jusque dans le mobilier et même la
vaisselle de table.

NADER KHALILI

Nader Khalili
Cal-Earth Institute
10376 Shangri La Avenue
Hesperia, California 92345
USA

Tel: +1 760 244 0614
Fax: +1 760 244 2201
e-Mail: calearth@aol.com
Web: www.calearth.org

NADAR KHALILI was born in 1937 in Iran and trained there as an architect as well as in Turkey and the United States. From 1970 to1975, he practiced architecture in Iran, and has since dedicated himself to research into building with earth. He has been a licensed architect in the State of California since 1970. He has served as a consultant to the United Nations (UNIDO) and a contributor to NASA. Khalili founded the California Institute of Earth Art and Architecture (Cal-Earth) in Hesperia, California in 1986, and has been directing the Architectural Research Program at Sci-Arc in Los Angeles since 1982. He has received awards from organizations such as the California chapter of the American Institute of Architects, for Excellence in Technology; the United Nations and HUD (U. S. Department of Housing and Urban Development), for "Shelter for the Homeless"; and the American Society of Civil Engineers (Aerospace Division), for his work in lunar-base-building technology. He is the author of five published books, including two translations of the work of the thirteenth-century Sufi poet, Jalal-e-Din Mohammad Rumi. Khalili's architectural works include the design of a future-oriented community of 5000 inhabitants (1988); Malekshahr of Isfahan, a community for 20 000 that was partially built before 1979; and more than 100 projects for conventional buildings.

NADER KHALILI, geboren 1937 im Iran, studierte in seinem Heimatland, in der Türkei und in den USA Architektur. Von 1970 bis 1975 arbeitete er im Iran als Architekt; seitdem widmet er sich der Erforschung des Bauens mit Erde. Seit 1970 ist er in Kalifornien zeichnungsberechtigter Architekt. Khalili war als Berater für die Vereinten Nationen (UNIDO) tätig und hat bei Projekten der NASA mitgewirkt. 1986 gründete er das Californian Institute of Earth Art and Architecture (Cal-Earth) in Hesperia, Kalifornien; seit 1982 ist er Leiter des Forschungsprogramms Architektur an der SCI-Arc in Los Angeles. Khalili wurde von verschiedenen Institutionen ausgezeichnet, so z. B. vom kalifornischen Verband des American Institute of Architects für herausragende Leistungen im Bereich Technologie, von den Vereinten Nationen und von HUD (Amerikanische Behörde für Wohnen und Stadtentwicklung) für »Obdach für Obdachlose« sowie von der Amerikanischen Gesellschaft für Bauingenieure (Abteilung Luftfahrt) für seine Arbeit über Bautechnologien auf dem Mond. Nader Khalili hat fünf Bücher geschrieben, darunter zwei Übersetzungen des Sufi-Dichters Jalal-e-Din Mohammad Rumi aus dem 13. Jahrhundert. Zu den architektonischen Arbeiten Khalilis gehören der Entwurf für eine zukunftsorientierte Gemeinde mit 5000 Einwohnern (1988), die Gemeinde Malekshahr in Isfahan für 20 000 Einwohner, die vor 1979 in Teilen realisiert wurde, und mehr als 100 in bautechnischer Hinsicht konventionelle Gebäude.

Né en 1937 en Iran, **NADER KHALILI** y a étudié l'architecture, ainsi qu'en Turquie et aux États-Unis. De 1970 à 1975, il a pratiqué en Iran et s'est, depuis, consacré à la recherche sur la construction en terre. Il est architecte licencié de l'État de Californie depuis 1970. Consultant auprès des Nations Unies (United Nations Industrial Development Organization) et collaborateur de la Nasa, il a fondé le California Institute of Earth Art and Architecture (Cal-Earth) à Hesperia (Californie) en 1986 et dirige l'Architectural Research Program de SCI-Arc à Los Angeles depuis 1982. Il a reçu des prix d'organismes tels que l'antenne californienne de l'American Institute of Architects pour l'excellence en technologie, les Nations Unies et le Département américain du logement et de l'urbanisme (HUD) pour son « Abri pour les sans-abri » et de l'American Society of Civil Engineers (division aérospatiale) pour ses travaux sur les technologies de construction de bases lunaires. Il est l'auteur de cinq ouvrages, dont deux traductions de l'œuvre du poète soufi du XIIIe siècle Jalal-e-Din Mohammad Rumi. Parmi ses réalisations architecturales, on note : la conception d'une ville futuriste de 5 000 habitants (Californie, 1988, restée à l'état de prototype) ; Malekshahr d'Isphahan, ville de 20 000 habitants partiellement édifiée vers 1979, et plus de 100 projets de réalisations conventionnelles.

SANDBAG SHELTER PROTOTYPES

Various locations, 1992–

Floor area: single unit 400 m² or double unit 800 m². Client: Iran office of UNDP/UNHCR and others.
Cost: $2300 for a single unit or $2800 for a double unit, 25% extra for each additional unit

A winner of the 2004 Aga Khan Award for Architecture, the **SANDBAG SHELTER PROTOTYPES** designed by Nader Khalili were described in the jury citation as follows: "These shelters serve as a prototype for temporary housing using extremely inexpensive means to provide safe homes that can be built quickly and have the high insulation values necessary in arid climates. Their curved form was devised in response to seismic conditions, ingeniously using sand or earth as raw materials, since their flexibility allows the construction of single- and double-curvature compression shells that can withstand lateral seismic forces. The prototype is a symbiosis of tradition and technology. It employs vernacular forms, integrating load-bearing and tensile structures, but provides a remarkable degree of strength and durability for this type of construction, that is traditionally weak and fragile, through a composite system of sandbags and barbed wire." Khalili basically found that stacking sandbags in circular plans to form domed structures, with barbed wire laid between each row to prevent the bags from shifting, was a way of providing readily available and stable housing. Nor is this concept merely theoretical since prototype sandbag shelters have been built in Iran, Mexico, India, Thailand, Siberia, and Chile. The prototypes received California building permits and have also met the requirements of the United Nations High Commission for Refugees (UNHCR) for emergency housing. Both the UNHCR and the United Nations Development Program (UNDP) used the system in 1995 to provide temporary shelters for a flood of refugees coming into Iran from Iraq.

Die **PROTOTYPEN VON SCHUTZBAUTEN AUS SANDSÄCKEN** wurden 2004 mit dem Aga-Khan-Preis für Architektur ausgezeichnet. Die Jury beschreibt sie folgendermaßen: »Diese Schutzbauten sind Prototypen von temporären Häusern, die mit extrem preiswerten Mitteln errichtet werden können. Sie stellen sichere Unterkünfte bereit, können schnell gebaut werden und haben einen hohen Wärmedämmwert, der im Wüstenklima notwendig ist. Ihre gekrümmte Form wurde als Antwort auf seismische Bedingungen entwickelt. Auf geniale Weise wird Sand oder Erde als Rohmaterial verwendet, da die Flexibilität dieser Materialien die Konstruktion von einfach und zweifach gekrümmten, auf Druck belasteten Hüllen erlaubt, die seismischen Horizontallasten standhalten können. Der Prototyp ist eine Symbiose von Tradition und Technologie. Er verwendet Formen, die auf dem Land gebräuchlich sind, integriert druck- und zugbelastete Strukturen, bietet aber einen bemerkenswerten Grad an Festigkeit und Haltbarkeit für eine Konstruktion dieser Art, die sonst eher schwach und instabil ist. Dies wird durch eine Kompositsystem aus Sandsäcken und Stacheldraht erreicht.« Sandsäcke werden kreisförmig ausgelegt und dann so aufgeschichtet, dass sie eine Kuppel formen. Um ein Verrutschen der Säcke zu verhindern, wird zwischen jede Reihe Stacheldraht gelegt. Auf diese Weise, so fand Khalili heraus, können schnell herzustellende und stabile Unterkünfte gebaut werden. Das Konzept ist nicht theoretischer Natur: Solche Schutzbauten wurden schon im Iran, in Mexiko, Indien, Thailand, Sibirien und Chile errichtet. Die kalifornische Baubehörde genehmigte die Prototypen; sie entsprechen auch den Standards des Hochkommissars für Flüchtlinge der Vereinten Nationen (UNHCR) für Notunterkünfte. Sowohl der UNHCR als auch das Entwicklungsprogramm der Vereinten Nationen (UNDP) benutzte das System 1995, um temporäre Unterkünfte für die Flüchtlinge aus dem Irak in den Iran zu bauen.

Les **PROTOTYPES D'ABRIS EN SACS DE SABLE** conçus par Nader Khalili, lauréat du Prix d'architecture Aga Khan 2004, étaient présentés de la façon suivante par le jury : « Ces abris sont des prototypes de logements temporaires créés à l'aide de moyens extrêmement bon marché, afin d'offrir un foyer solide rapidement constructibles et présentent le haut degré d'isolation thermique indispensable dans les climats arides. Leurs formes courbes ont été conçues pour supporter des secousses sismiques, et utilisent ingénieusement comme matières premières le sable et la terre, dont la souplesse permet la construction de coques à simple ou double courbe en compression qui peuvent résister aux forces sismiques latérales. Ces prototypes sont une symbiose de tradition et de technologie. Ils font appel à des formes vernaculaires, intégrant des structures porteuses et en traction, tout en offrant un remarquable niveau de résistance et de durabilité pour ce type de construction, traditionnellement léger et fragile, grâce à un système composite de sacs de sable et fil de fer barbelé. » À l'origine, Khalili a découvert que le fait d'empiler des sacs de sable en cercle pour former des structures en coupole et de les stabiliser par du fil de fer barbelé intercalé entre chaque strate était un moyen d'obtenir des logements stables et faciles à construire. Son concept n'est pas resté purement théorique, puisque des prototypes ont déjà été construits en Iran, au Mexique, en Inde, en Thaïlande, en Sibérie et au Chili. Ils ont reçu un permis de construire en Californie et sont conformes à la réglementation du Haut Commissariat des Nations Unies aux Réfugiés pour les logements d'urgence. Le HCR et le Programme de développement des Nations Unies (PDNU) ont utilisé ce système dès 1995 pour répondre aux afflux de réfugiés arrivant d'Irak en Iran.

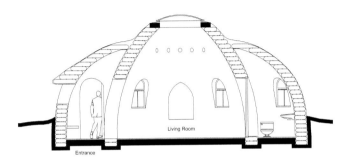

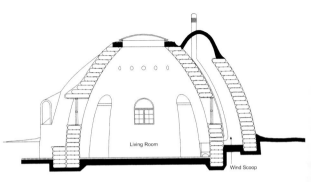

The sandbag shelters can be arranged in various configurations, with a simplicity of construction that can be mastered even by persons who have no knowledge of building.

Aus den Sandsäcken können verschiedene Haustypen gebaut werden. Alle Behausungen sind auch von Menschen, die über keine Baukenntnisse verfügen, einfach herzustellen.

Les abris en sacs de sable peuvent adopter différentes configurations, tout en gardant une simplicité de construction maîtrisable même par des gens qui n'ont aucune connaissance dans ce domaine.

Using sandbags and barbed wire, normally associated more with disaster and conflict than with hope to build, Nader Khalili has devised an inversion of the downward spiral that affects so many across the world.

Nader Khalili benutzt Sandsäcke und Stacheldraht – Materialien, die man normalerweise eher mit Katastrophen und Konflikten als mit Hoffnung verbindet –, um die Negativspirale, die so viele Menschen weltweit betrifft, in eine positive umzudrehen.

À partir de sacs de sable et de fil de fer barbelé – matériaux que l'on associe plus aux désastres et conflits qu'aux espoirs –, Nader Khalili propose une solution pour inverser la spirale vers le bas qui affecte tant d'individus dans le monde.

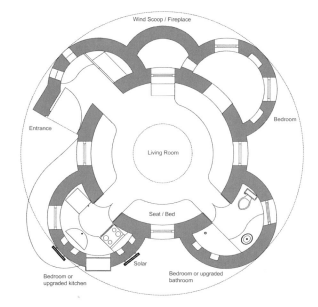

A plan to the right shows how the lobed and domed structures can be adapted to various degrees of sophistication, to include a kitchen or bathroom as well as the central living space. The plentiful raw materials used ensure that this type of shelter could be erected almost anywhere in the world.

Der Grundriss rechts zeigt, dass die kuppelförmigen Konstruktionen aus Sand und Stoff auch höheren Ansprüchen gerecht werden und eine Küche und/oder ein Badezimmer sowie den zentralen Wohnraum aufnehmen können. Aufgrund der reichlich vorhandenen Rohmaterialien kann diese Art der Unterkunft fast überall auf der Welt gebaut werden.

Le plan à droite montre comment ces petites constructions à coupole peuvent acquérir divers degrés de sophistication et comprendre une cuisine, une pièce d'eau ou un séjour central. Le choix de matériaux économiques et abondants fait que ce type d'abri peut être édifié presque n'importe où dans le monde.

Wind Scoop / Fireplace

Bedroom

Entrance

Living Room

Seat / Bed

Bedroom or
upgraded kitchen

Solar

Bedroom or upgraded
bathroom

ANSELM KIEFER

White Cube Gallery
48 Hoxton Square
London N1 6PB
UK

Tel: +44 20 79 30 53 73
Fax: +44 20 77 49 74 80
email: enquiries@whitecube.com
Web: www.whitecube.com

La Ribaute

ANSELM KIEFER was born in 1945 in Donaueschingen (Baden-Württemberg). In 1965, he started studying law and Romance languages at the Albert Ludwigs University, Freiburg in Breisgau and he spent time in Paris. Between 1966 and 1970 he studied art with Peter Dreher and Horst Antes at the Staatliche Hochschule der Bildenden Künste, in Freiburg and Karlsruhe. He had his first one-man show at the Galerie am Kaiserplatz in Karlsruhe in 1969. He studied at the Düsseldorf Kunstakademie under Joseph Beuys (1970–72). After a 1978 solo exhibition at the Kunsthalle Bern, he had a traveling show that went to the Städtische Kunsthalle, Düsseldorf, the Musée d'Art Moderne de la Ville de Paris and the Israel Museum in Jerusalem. A traveling show that went to the United States in 1987–89 confirmed his substantial international reputation. His interest in architectural environments was shown when he acquired a former brick factory in Höpfingen (near Heidelberg), planning to install his major project *Zweistromland* there (1988). It was in 1992 that he settled in Barjac (Cévennes), France, and started to transform his 35-hectare studio compound *La Ribaute* into an environment that might well be called a work of architecture.

ANSELM KIEFER wurde 1945 in Donaueschingen (Baden-Württemberg) geboren. 1965 begann er ein Jura- und Romanistikstudium an der Albert-Ludwig-Universität in Freiburg im Breisgau und hielt sich in Paris auf. Von 1966 bis 1970 studierte er bei Peter Dreher und Horst Antes an den Staatlichen Hochschulen der Bildenden Künste in Freiburg und Karlsruhe. Seine erste Einzelausstellung hatte er 1969 in der Galerie am Kaiserplatz in Karlsruhe. Von 1970 bis 1972 studierte er an der Düsseldorfer Kunstakademie bei Joseph Beuys. Nach einer Einzelausstellung 1978 in der Kunsthalle Bern ging eine Wanderausstellung von ihm an die Städtische Kunsthalle Düsseldorf, zum Musée d'Art Moderne de la Ville de Paris und zum Israelischen Museum in Jerusalem. 1987 bis 1989 stellte Kiefer in verschiedenen Orten in den USA aus und festigte sein internationales Renommee. Kiefers Interesse an seiner architektonischen Umgebung zeigte sich, als er 1988 eine ehemalige Ziegelei in Höpfingen im Odenwald kaufte, um dort sein Großprojekt *Zweistromland* zu installieren. 1992 ließ er sich in Barjac in den französischen Cevennen nieder. Er begann, das 35 ha große Gelände *La Ribaute*, auf dem sein Atelier steht, in ein Environment zu verwandeln, das man ohne Probleme als architektonisches Projekt bezeichnen kann.

ANSELM KIEFER est né en 1945 à Donaueschingen (Bade-Wurtemberg). En 1965, il débute des études de droit et de langues romanes à l'Université Albert Ludwig de Fribourg-en-Brisgau puis séjourne à Paris. De 1966 à 1970, il étudie l'art auprès de Peter Dreher et Horst Antes à la Staatliche Hochschule der Bildenden Künste à Fribourg et Karlsruhe. Sa première exposition personnelle a lieu à la galerie « am Kaiserplatz » à Karlsruhe en 1969. Il étudie ensuite auprès de Joseph Beuys à la Kunstakademie de Düsseldorf (1970–72). Après une exposition personnelle à la Kunsthalle de Berne, une exposition itinérante sur son travail est accueillie par la Städtische Kunsthalle de Düsseldorf, le musée d'Art moderne de la Ville de Paris et le Musée d'Israël à Jérusalem. Une autre exposition parcourt les États-Unis en 1987–89 et confirme sa réputation internationale, déjà substantielle. Son intérêt pour l'environnement architectural se révèle lorsqu'il acquiert une ancienne briqueterie à Höpfingen (près d'Heidelberg) où il projette d'installer son projet majeur, *Zweistromland* (1986–89). C'est en 1992 qu'il s'installe en France, à Barjac, dans les Cévennes et se lance dans l'aménagement des 35 hectares de sa propriété de *La Ribaute* en un environnement que l'on peut qualifier d'œuvre architecturale.

LA RIBAUTE

Barjac, France, 1992–

Floor area: 35 ha (total studio area). Client: Anselm Kiefer. Cost: not disclosed

Although Kiefer's studio is very much the expression of his own creative world, its unexpected or even upsetting esthetics challenge preconceived ideas of architecture.

Das Atelier bringt sehr deutlich Kiefers persönliche kreative Welt zum Ausdruck. Die unerwartete und sogar bedrückende Ästhetik fordert gängige Vorstellungen von Architektur heraus.

Si l'atelier de Kiefer est l'expression de son univers créatif personnel, son esthétique surprenante, voire dérangeante, remet en question beaucoup d'idées préconçues sur l'architecture.

Located near Nîmes in southern France, Barjac is where the German painter Anselm Kiefer has chosen to build his very unusual studio. Rather than one space, the painter has chosen to create an interlocking web of buildings, curious concrete towers, a greenhouse, and underground depositories for his work. A central dimly-lit space, lined with lead-and partly filled with water, is at the heart of the complex, or perhaps it is the artist's stage set designed for the opera *Electra* (Teatro San Carlos, Naples, 2003). In both cases, there is a sense of vertiginous digging or of rising up from the ashes of the modern world to look at the stars. Kiefer rarely renders his references explicit, preferring a certain ambiguity, combined with an obvious repulsion for the horrors brought about by his own country during the War. Architecture is frequently present in Kiefer's paintings, and its role too is bathed in ambiguity. One of his works, *The Unknown Painter* (Dem unbekannten Maler, 1982. Boymans van Beuningen Museum, Rotterdam) shows part of one of Munich's "Honor Temples" (*Ehrentempeln*, 1935). The author Daniel Arasse has proven that Anselm Kiefer's "unknown painter" is none other than Hitler himself, who was often called an "artist" or a "painter" by such figures as Goebbels. Arasse has also compared Kiefer's work itself to a labyrinth, an image particularly well suited to **LA RIBAUTE**. In the sense that painters or architects often share the dream of creating their own worlds, Kiefer's studio in Barjac is a logical extension of his work from two dimensions into three. Kiefer has frequently created sculptures, but in this instance, the third dimension takes on a more complete expression, and inevitably becomes a work of architecture, and of art.

Der deutsche Maler Anselm Kiefer hat sich Barjac in der Nähe von Nîmes in Südfrankreich ausgesucht, um hier sein sehr ungewöhnliches Atelier zu bauen. Der Maler entschied sich dafür, nicht einen einzigen Raum zu schaffen, sondern ein ineinander greifendes System aus Gebäuden, kuriosen Betontürmen, einem Gewächshaus und unterirdischen Lagern. Ein zentraler, wenig beleuchteter Raum, der mit Blei ausgekleidet und teilweise mit Wasser gefüllt ist, bildet den Mittelpunkt der Anlage – vielleicht handelt es sich hierbei um den Bühnenentwurf für die Oper *Elektra*, den der Künstler 2003 für das Teatro San Carlos in Neapel schuf. In jedem Fall wird das Gefühl vermittelt, dass hier ein wirbelndes Graben bzw. ein Auferstehen aus der Asche der modernen Welt – um die Sterne zu betrachten – stattfindet. Kiefer äußert sich nur selten ausdrücklich zu den Bezügen seiner Arbeit, zieht eine gewisse Doppeldeutigkeit vor. Gekoppelt ist diese mit einem ganz offensichtlichen Abscheu vor dem Leid, das sein Land während des Zweiten Weltkrieges über andere brachte. In seinen Bildern ist Architektur oft präsent, und ihre Rolle ist oft sehr widersprüchlich. Eine seiner Arbeiten, *Dem unbekannten Maler* (1982, Boymans-van-Beuningen-Museum in Rotterdam), zeigt einen Teil eines der Ehrentempel in München von 1935. Der Autor Daniel Arasse hat nachgewiesen, dass Anselm Kiefers »unbekannter Maler« niemand anderes als Hitler selbst ist, der von Leuten wie Goebbels oft als »Künstler« oder »Maler« bezeichnet wurde. Außerdem verglich Arasse Kiefers Œuvre insgesamt mit einem Labyrinth, ein Bild, das besonders gut auf **LA RIBAUTE** zutrifft. In dem Sinn, dass Maler und Architekten oft den Traum haben, ihre eigene Welt zu erschaffen, ist Kiefers Atelier in Barjac eine logische Erweiterung seiner Arbeit von der Zwei- in die Dreidimensionalität. Kiefer hat schon viele bildhauerische Werke geschaffen, aber in diesem Fall nimmt die dritte Dimension eine umfassendere Form an und wird unweigerlich zu Architektur – und zu Kunst.

C'est à Barjac, non loin de Nîmes dans le sud de la France, qu'Anselm Kiefer a choisi d'installer son très étrange atelier. Plutôt qu'un espace unique, il a opté pour un réseau imbriqué de constructions, de tours de béton, d'une serre et de réserves souterraines pour ses œuvres. Un espace central faiblement éclairé, doublé de plomb et partiellement rempli d'eau, occupe le cœur de ce complexe (peut-être est-ce le décor par Kiefer conçu pour l'opéra *Elektra* au Teatro San Carlo de Naples en 2003). Le lieu dégage un sentiment de profondeur vertigineuse et, en même temps, d'ascension vers les étoiles à partir d'un monde réduit en cendres. Kiefer donne rarement la clé de ses références, préférant cultiver une certaine ambiguïté, associée à la répulsion pour les horreurs causées par son pays au cours de la dernière guerre. L'une de ses œuvres de 1983, *Dem unbekannten Maler* (Au peintre inconnu, musée Boymans van Beuningen, Rotterdam) montre une partie d'un des « Temples d'honneur » munichois (*Ehrentempeln*) de 1935. L'historien d'art Daniel Arasse a montré que ce « peintre inconnu » n'était autre que Hitler, que d'aucuns qualifiaient « d'artiste » ou de « peintre ». Arasse a également comparé l'œuvre même de Kiefer à un labyrinthe, image qui convient particulièrement à l'impression laissée par **LA RIBAUTE**. Dans la mesure où nombre de peintres et d'architectes partagent un même rêve – créer leur propre univers –, l'atelier de Kiefer à Barjac est l'extension tridimensionnelle logique de son œuvre. Kiefer a fréquemment créé des sculptures, mais, ici, la troisième dimension acquiert un sens encore plus fort pour devenir vraiment une œuvre d'architecture. Et d'art.

A military or prison-like atmosphere
sometimes inhabits these images,
as though the artist were exhuming
the ghosts of the century gone by.

Eine militärische oder gefängnisartige
Atmosphäre ist diesen Bildern inne –
als ob der Künstler die Geister des
vergangenen Jahrhunderts beschwören würde.

Une atmosphère militaire ou carcé-
rale émane parfois de ces images,
comme si l'artiste avait exhumé
quelque fantôme du XXᵉ siècle.

Greenhouses, tunnels and shards of pottery are all part of the universe to which Kiefer has given form at La Ribaute. For those who know his paintings, much of this imagery will seem familiar.

Gewächshäuser, Tunnel und zerbrochene Pflanztöpfe sind Teile des Universums, dem Kiefer in La Ribaute Form gegeben hat. Wer seine Bilder kennt, ist mit dieser Bilderwelt zum großen Teil vertraut.

Serres, tunnels et tessons de poteries font partie de l'univers auquel Kiefer a donné forme à La Ribaute. Une iconographie que connaissent bien les amateurs de ses peintures.

KLEIN DYTHAM

Klein Dytham architecture
AD Bldg 2nd Floor
1–15–7 Hiro
Shibuya-ku
Tokyo 150–0012
Japan

Tel: +81 357 95 22 77
Fax: +81 357 95 22 76
e-mail: kda@klein-dytham.com
Web: www.klein-dytham.com

Undercover Lab ▶

KLEIN DYTHAM Architecture was created in Tokyo by Astrid Klein and Mark Dytham in 1991. Winners of the 1993 Kajima Space Design Award for the best young practice in Japan. Astrid Klein was born in Varese, Italy in 1962. She studied at the Ecole des Arts Décoratifs in Strasbourg, France (1986), and received a degree in architecture from the Royal College of Art, London in 1988. In 1988, she also worked in the office of Toyo Ito in Tokyo. Mark Dytham was born in Northamptonshire, England, in 1964 and attended the Newcastle University School of Architecture, graduating in 1985. He then also attended the Royal College of Art, London (1988). He worked in both the office of Skidmore Owings and Merrill in Chicago and with Toyo Ito in Tokyo before creating KDa. He has been an assistant professor at Tokyo Science University. Their recent projects include the Leaf Chapel and Undercover Lab published here as well as the Idée Workstation (Shimouma, Tokyo), and Cats Eyes, a fashion store in Harajuku, Tokyo.

KLEIN DYTHAM Architecture wurde 1991 von Astrid Klein und Mark Dytham in Tokio gegründet. 1993 waren sie die Gewinner des Kajima Space Design Award für das beste junge Büro in Japan. Astrid Klein, geboren 1962 in Varese, Italien, studierte an der Ecole des Arts Décoratifs in Straßburg (1986) und schloss 1988 ihr Architekturstudium am Royal College of Art in London ab. 1988 war sie auch im Büro von Toyo Ito in Tokio tätig. Mark Dytham wurde 1964 in Northamptonshire, England, geboren, studierte an der Newcastle University School of Architecture und machte dort 1985 seinen Abschluss. Er studierte ebenfalls am Royal College of Art in London (1988). Dytham arbeitete bei Skidmore, Owings and Merrill in Chicago und bei Toyo Ito in Tokio, bevor er sich mit Klein zusammentat. Außerdem war er Wissenschaftlicher Mitarbeiter an der Tokyo Science University. Zu den neueren Projekten des Büros gehören die hier gezeigte Blatt-Kapelle und das Undercover Lab, ferner die Idée Workstation in Shimouma, Tokio, und Cats Eyes, ein Modegeschäft in Harajuku, Tokio.

KLEIN DYTHAM Architecture a été créée à Tokyo par Astrid Klein et Mark Dytham en 1991, et a remporté en 1993 le prix de conception d'espace Kajima pour la meilleure jeune agence au Japon en 1993. Astrid Klein est née à Varese (Italie) en 1962. Elle a étudié à l'École des arts décoratifs de Strasbourg en 1986 et est diplômée en architecture du Royal College of Art de Londres (1988). La même année, elle a travaillé à Tokyo chez Toyo Ito. Mark Dytham, né en 1964 dans le Northamptonshire (Angleterre), est diplômé de la Newcastle University School of Architecture (1985). Il a ensuite étudié au Royal College of Art de Londres (1988), puis a travaillé dans les agences de Skidmore Owings and Merrill à Chicago et avec Toyo Ito à Tokyo, avant de créer KDa. Il a été assistant-professeur à l'Université des sciences de Tokyo. Parmi leurs récents projets : la Leaf Chapel et l'Undercover Lab publiés ici, le poste de travail Idée (Shimouma, Tokyo) et la boutique de mode Cats Eyes (Harajuku, Tokyo).

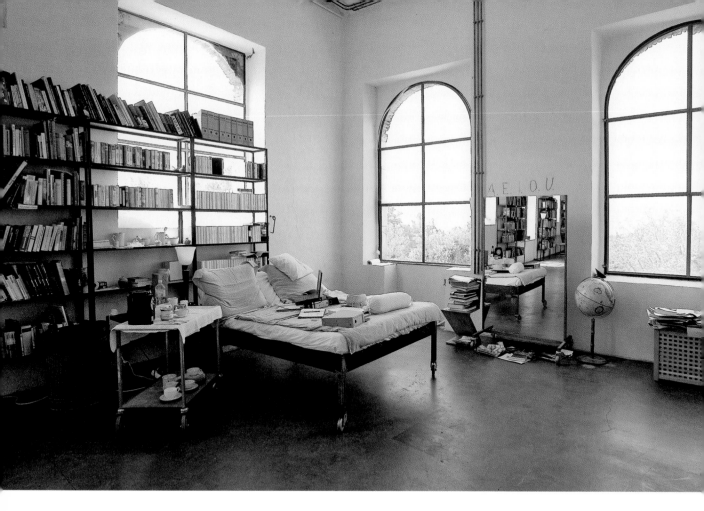

The artist in his working space, where classification plays as much of a role as a kind of imaginary archaeology which obviously evokes the "real" world.

Der Künstler in seinem Arbeitsraum. Klassifizierung spielt hier genauso eine Rolle wie eine Form von »imaginärer Archäologie«, die ganz offensichtlich die »reale« Welt evoziert.

L'artiste sur son lieu de travail, où la classification a son rôle à jouer, comme une sorte d'archéologie imaginaire évoquant le monde « réel ».

UNDERCOVER LAB

Harajuku, Tokyo, Japan, 2000–01

Floor area: 639 m². Client: Undercover Co. Ltd.
Cost: not disclosed

"**UNDERCOVER LAB** is a building, which is undercover. Not only is it tucked away in the back streets of Harajuku, but the site is also very deceiving," say the architects. The steel frame and reinforced concrete atelier and showroom for a fashionable designer occupies 206 m² of a 345 m² site and develops a total floor area of 639 m². Including a studio, press showroom and office, the design is based on a dramatically cantilevered black tube that allows for a twenty-meter-long hangar intended to display a "one season fashion collection." Five cars can be parked below the overhang, further optimizing the use of precious Tokyo land. Since the main part of the site is actually located behind a 10-meter driveway, the architects asked themselves "How could we make the building impressive and commanding when the main bulk of the building was set back 10 meters. The tube seemed a natural way to bring the building to the street…" They further explain that the tube was made to look "as anonymous as possible, almost like a shipping container where you have no idea of its contents."

»**UNDERCOVER LAB** ist ein geheimes Gebäude. Es liegt nicht nur in einer Seitenstraße von Harajuku, auch das Grundstück täuscht den Besucher«, sagen die Architekten. Das Atelier und der Showroom eines gefragten Designers bestehen aus einer Stahlkonstruktion und Stahlbeton. Das Gebäude nimmt 206 m² des 345 m² großen Grundstücks ein. Seine Gesamtfläche beträgt 639 m². Der Entwurf wird von einem dramatisch auskragenden schwarzen Quader bestimmt. In ihm befindet sich eine 20 m lange Halle, in der die aktuelle Kollektion gezeigt wird. Ferner gibt es das Atelier, einen Showroom für die Presse und ein Büro. Unter dem auskragenden Quader können fünf Autos parken, wodurch die Nutzung des so wertvollen Tokioer Bodens noch weiter optimiert wird. Da sich der wesentliche Teil des Grundstücks hinter einer 10 m langen Zufahrt befindet, fragten sich die Architekten: »Wie können wir ein eindrucksvolles Gebäude bauen, wenn das Hauptvolumen des Gebäudes 10 m von der Straße entfernt liegt? Der Quader schien ein natürliches Mittel zu sein, um das Gebäude an die Straße anzubinden …« Weiter erklären sie, dass der Quader »so anonym wie möglich« aussehen soll, »fast wie ein Frachtcontainer, bei dem man keine Ahnung hat, was er enthält«.

« **UNDERCERCOVER LAB** est un bâtiment… clandestin. Non seulement il est en retrait au fond d'une des ruelles secondaires de Harajuku, mais son terrain est également très trompeur », expliquent les architectes. La structure en acier et en béton armé de cet atelier/showroom pour un styliste de mode occupe 206 m² d'un terrain de 345 m² pour une surface utile totale de 639 m². Le projet comprend un atelier, un showroom de presse et un bureau. Il met en scène une sorte de tube noir en porte-à-faux spectaculaire, qui abrite un hall de vingt mètres de long dans lequel toute la collection entière d'une saison peut être présentée. Cinq voitures peuvent stationner sous ce porte-à-faux, ce qui est une façon d'optimiser l'utilisation du précieux sol tokyoïte. La plus grande partie du terrain se trouvant au fond d'une allée de 10 m de long, les architectes se sont demandé : « Comment rendre le bâtiment impressionnant et dominant lorsque sa masse principale doit être en retrait de dix mètres ? Le tube nous a paru une manière naturelle de ramener le tout vers la rue… [nous l'avons rendu] aussi anonyme que possible, presque comme un conteneur d'expédition dont on ne sait pas ce qu'il contient. »

An ample interior working space mixes brick and wood, with a ceiling made from wooden concrete forms. The architects combine roughness, surprise and a sure sense of volume to make the Undercover Lab a kind of hidden world for the fashion designers in the midst of Tokyo's bustle.

Der Arbeitsraum wird durch Ziegelstein und Holz gekennzeichnet (die Decke besteht aus hölzernen Schalelementen für Beton). Die Architekten vermischen raue und überraschende Elemente; mit sicherem Gefühl für Raum machen sie das Undercover Lab für die Modedesigner zu einem versteckten Ort inmitten von Tokios Hektik.

Le vaste atelier de travail associe la brique, le bois et un plafond en bois. Les architectes ont combiné brutalité, effets de surprise et un sens très sûr des volumes pour faire de l'Undercover Lab l'univers secret d'un styliste de mode en plein cœur de l'animation de Tokyo.

The spectacular cantilever of the Undercover Lab is its identifying feature, seen in the image above, and in section below right.

Die spektakuläre Auskragung ist das identifikationsstiftende Merkmal des Undercover Lab, zu sehen oben und in der Ansicht unten rechts.

Le porte-à-faux spectaculaire de l'Undercover Lab (photo ci-dessus et coupe ci-dessous, à droite) fait aussi office de signal d'identification.

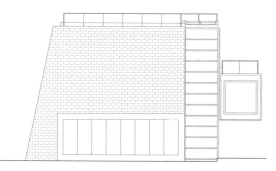

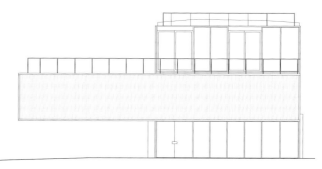

LEAF CHAPEL

Kobuchizawa, Yamanashi, Japan, 2003–04

Floor area: 168 m². Client: Risonare (Hoshino Resort).
Cost: not disclosed

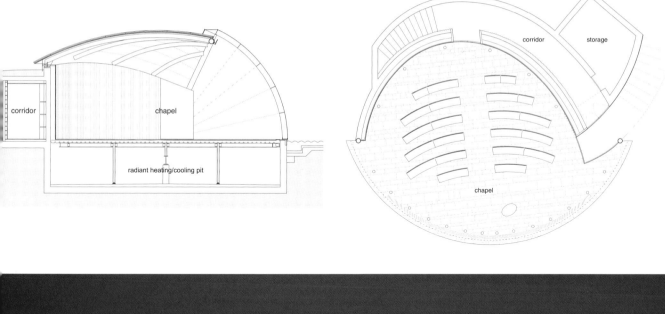

corridor

chapel

radiant heating/cooling pit

corridor

storage

chapel

Seen against the background of the rather unattractive complex into which it is inserted, the Leaf Chapel is seen here with its dome of veil partially lifted. From within the chapel (right) newlyweds are granted a vision of paradise.

Vor dem Hintergrund des eher unattraktiven Komplexes, in den die Blatt-Kapelle hineingesetzt wurde, ist sie hier mit angehobener Kuppel zu sehen. Rechts: Innen bietet sich den frisch Vermählten eine »Vision des Paradieses«.

Se détachant sur le fond du complexe assez peu séduisant dans lequel elle s'insère, la Leaf Chapel, sa coupole en partie relevée. De l'intérieur de la chapelle (à droite) les nouveaux mariés sont censés avoir une vision du paradis.

Located on the grounds of the Risonare Hotel, this wedding chapel is "formed by two leaves – one glass, one steel – which have seemingly fluttered to the ground." The white steel leaf is perforated with 4700 holes, each of which has an acrylic lens, "similar to a bride's veil made of delicate lace." The eleven-ton steel shell silently lifts in 38 seconds at the end of the ceremony, much as the groom lifts the bride's veil to kiss her. A pond with stepping stones and a green natural setting await the newlyweds. Black timber walls and benches for 80 guests, and a black granite floor intentionally create a contrast within the 168 m^2 chapel to the "bright white purity of the occasion." Though the architects insist on the leaf metaphor, the shape of the chapel and its opening lid also invite comparisons to an eye. Given the Japanese passion for wedding chapels which do not necessarily carry with them a religious connotation, Klein Dytham have shown their capacity to respond to the tastes and needs of their clients.

Die Hochzeitskapelle liegt auf dem Grundstück des Risonare Hotels und wird »durch zwei scheinbar auf den Boden gefallene Blätter, eines aus Glas, das andere aus Stahl, gebildet«. Das weiße »Blatt« aus Stahl ist mit 4700 Löchern perforiert. In jedem Loch befindet sich eine Linse aus Acryl, so dass ein Bild entsteht, das »dem feinen Spitzenschleier einer Braut ähnelt«. Am Ende jeder Zeremonie hebt sich – in 38 Sekunden – leise die 11 t schwere Stahlschale so, wie der Bräutigam den Schleier der Braut hebt, wenn er sie küsst. Ein Teich mit Trittsteinen und eine natürliche grüne Umgebung erwarten die frisch Verheirateten. Die schwarzen Holzwände und Bänke für 80 Gäste sowie der schwarze Granitfußboden der 168 m^2 großen Kapelle bilden einen bewussten Kontrast zur »schneeweißen Reinheit des Anlasses«. Obwohl die Architekten auf der Blattmetaper bestehen, ruft die Form der Kapelle mit dem sich öffnenden »Lid« Assoziationen an ein Auge hervor. In Anbetracht der besonderen Vorliebe der Japaner für Hochzeitskapellen – nicht unbedingt haben diese auch eine religiöse Konnotation – beweisen Klein Dytham ihre Fähigkeit, auf den Geschmack und die Bedürfnisse ihrer Bauherren zu reagieren.

Située sur le domaine du Risonare Hotel, cette chapelle de mariage est «formée de deux feuilles – une de verre et une d'acier – qui semblent être tombées au sol en virevoltant». «La feuille blanche en acier, perforée de 47 000 trous, dont chacun est doté d'une petite lentille en acrylique, est ‹semblable à un voile de mariée en dentelle délicate›.» La coquille d'acier de 11 onze tonnes se relève en 38 secondes à la fin de la cérémonie, un peu comme lorsque le jeune marié soulève le voile de l'épousée pour l'embrasser. Un bassin à pas japonais et un cadre de verdure naturel accueillent les jeunes mariés. À l'intérieur des 168 m^2 de la chapelle, des murs et des bancs pour 80 invités en bois noirci et un sol en granit noir créent volontairement un contraste avec «la pureté immaculée de l'occasion». Bien que les architectes insistent sur la métaphore de la feuille, la forme et l'ouverture de la chapelle font également penser à un œil. Quand on connaît la passion des Japonais pour les chapelles, qui ne comporte pas forcément de connotation religieuse, Klein Dytham ont montré ici leur capacité à répondre aux goûts et aux attentes de leurs clients.

MATHIAS KLOTZ

Mathias Klotz
Los Colonos 0411
Providencia
Santiago
Chile

Tel: +56 22 33 66 13
Fax: +56 22 32 24 79
e-mail: mathiasklotz@mi.cl
Web: www.mathiasklotz.com

MATHIAS KLOTZ was born in 1965 in Viña del Mar, Chile. He received his architecture degree from the Pontificia Universidad Católica de Chile in 1991. He created his own office in Santiago the same year. He has taught at several Chilean universities and was Director of the School of Architecture of the Universidad Diego Portales in Santiago (2001–03). Recent work includes: the Casa Viejo, Santiago (2001); the Smol Building, Concepción (2001); the Faculty of Health, Universidad Diego Portales, Santiago (2004); and the remodeling of the Cerro San Luis House, Santiago (2004). Current projects include: the Techos House, Villa La Angostura, Argentina; Kegevic House, Cachagua; and the Ochoalcubo House, Marbella; 20 one-family houses in La Dehesa, Santiago; and the Buildings Department San Isidro, Buenos Aires, Argentina. His work has been exhibited at the GA Gallery in Tokyo, at Archilab, Orléans, France (2000), and at MoMA in New York where he was a finalist for the 1998 Mies van der Rohe Prize. He participated in the Chinese International Practical Exhibition of Architecture in Nanjing in 2004, together with such architects as David Adjaye, Odile Decq, Arata Isozaki and Kazuyo Sejima.

MATHIAS KLOTZ, 1965 in Viña del Mar in Chile geboren, schloss sein Architekturstudium an der Pontificia Universidad Católica de Chile 1991 ab. Im selben Jahr gründete er in Santiago sein eigenes Büro. Er hat an verschiedenen Universitäten in Chile unterrichtet und war von 2001 bis 2003 Direktor der Architekturfakultät der Universidad Diego Portales in Santiago. Neuere Projekte von ihm sind u. a. die Casa Viejo in Santiago (2001), das Smol-Gebäude in Concepción (2001), die Fakultät für Gesundheitswesen der Universidad Diego Portales (2004) und der Umbau des Hauses Cerro San Luis in Santiago (2004). Zu den in der Planung bzw. im Bau befindlichen Projekten gehören das Techos-Haus in Villa La Angostura in Argentinien, das Kegevic-Haus in Cachagua und das Ochoalcubo-Haus in Marbella, ferner 20 Einfamilienhäuser in La Dehesa, Santiago, und die Bauabteilung San Isidro in Buenos Aires. Seine Projekte wurden in der GA Gallery in Tokio, auf der Archilab in Orléans (2000) und im MoMA in New York ausgestellt. 1998 war er in New York Finalist für den Mies-van-der-Rohe-Preis. 2004 hat Klotz – zusammen mit Architekten wie David Adjaye, Odile Decq, Arata Isozaki und Kazuyo Sejima – an der Chinese International Practical Exhibition of Architecture in Nanjing teilgenommen.

MATHIAS KLOTZ est né en 1965 à Viña del Mar au Chili. Il est sorti diplômé en architecture de la Pontificia Universidad Católica de Chile en 1991 et a créé sa propre agence à Santiago la même année. Il a enseigné dans plusieurs universités chiliennes et a dirigé l'École d'architecture de l'Universidad Diego Portales à Santiago (2001–03). Parmi ses œuvres récentes : la Casa Viejo, Santiago (2001) ; centre commercial Smol, Concepción (2002) ; la faculté de médecine de l'Universidad Diego Portales, Santiago (2004) ; la rénovation de la Casa Cerro San Luis, Santiago (2004) ; Casa Techitos (Villa La Angostura, Argentine) ; la Casa Kegevic (Cachagua) ; la Casa Orchoalcubo (Marbella) ; vingt maisons individuelles (La Dehesa, Santiago) et le Département de la construction (San Isidro, Buenos Aires, Argentine). Ses travaux ont été exposés à la GA Gallery à Tokyo, à Archilab, Orléans, France (2000) et au MoMA à New York. En 1998, il a été finaliste du prix Mies van der Rohe. Il a participé à l'Exposition internationale d'architecture pratique de Nanjing, Chine (2004) aux côtés de confrères comme David Adjaye, Odile Decq, Arata Isozaki et Kazuyo Sejima.

VIEJO HOUSE
Santiago de Chile, Chile, 2001–02

Floor area: 750 m². Client: Veronica Viejo.
Cost: €1 million

The strict lines of the house and its thick concrete shell do not exclude the luxurious openness seen in this image.

Die strengen Linien des Hauses und seine massive Betonhülle schließen eine luxuriöse Offenheit im Inneren nicht aus.

Les lignes strictes de la maison et son épaisse coque de béton n'excluent pas un luxueux sentiment d'ouverture, comme le montre cette photo.

The circular pattern of openings in the concrete is echoed by larger circular openings in the roof of the house.

Das Motiv der kreisförmigen Öffnungen im Beton findet sich in den großen runden Öffnungen im Dach des Hauses wieder.

Les oculus pratiqués dans le béton trouvent un écho dans les vastes ouvertures circulaires ménagées dans la toiture.

This family house located in a residential area of Santiago is set on a 3700 m² site and has a built area of 700 m². A 12 x 40 m rectangle, the house was built entirely out of reinforced concrete. Circular windows mark one long closed façade, while the opposite face of the house opens entirely toward a swimming pool with a wooden terrace. Another terrace, on the roof, offers a 360° view of the hills surrounding Santiago, while round skylights bring daylight into the interior. Since another house had been built on the site in the 1950s, the architect was able to take advantage of large, existing trees. The architect explains that "the program, classic for a family with two children, was organized around two corridors, one interior and other exterior running from the entrance, through the public and service areas to the more private areas. This is a quiet work that resolves constructive and programmatic problems with simplicity, working different textures for the concrete on site as well as the different heights on the interior areas, depending on their use and proportions." Powerful and yet practical, the **VIEJO HOUSE** demonstrates the ability of the architect to use concrete as the main building material of a comfortable, even luxurious house.

Das Einfamilienhaus in einer Wohngegend von Santiago steht auf einem 3700 m² großen Grundstück und hat eine Gesamtfläche von 700 m². Das rechteckige Haus mit den Außenmaßen 12 x 40 m wurde komplett aus Stahlbeton errichtet. Kreisrunde Fenster kennzeichnen die lange, ansonsten geschlossene Fassade; dagegen ist die gegenüberliegende Seite vollständig zu einem Swimmingpool und einer holzgedeckten Terrasse geöffnet. Eine weitere Terrasse auf dem Dach des Hauses bietet einen Panoramablick auf die Santiago umgebenden Berge. Das Haus wird über runde Oberlichter zusätzlich belichtet. Auf dem Grundstück stand ein Haus aus den 1950er Jahren, das abgerissen wurde; den Bestand an alten großen Bäumen bezog der Architekt aber in die Planung mit ein. Klotz erläutert: »Das für eine Familie mit zwei Kindern typische Raumprogramm wurde mithilfe von zwei Fluren organisiert: einem inneren und einem äußeren Flur, der vom Eingang durch die ›öffentlicheren‹ Bereiche und die Servicezone zu den privateren Räumen führt. Dies ist ein ›stilles‹ Haus. Konstruktive und durch das Raumprogramm auftretende Fragen wurden auf einfache Weise beantwortet. Vor Ort stellte man verschiedene Betonoberflächen her, die Innenräume erhielten, je nach Nutzung und gewünschter Proportion, unterschiedliche Höhen.« Kraftvoll und praktisch – die **CASA VIEJO** zeigt die Fähigkeit des Architekten, Beton als Hauptbaumaterial einzusetzen, und er schafft mit ihm ein komfortables, sogar luxuriöses Haus.

Cette maison de famille située dans un quartier résidentiel de Santiago est implantée sur un terrain de 3700 m² et offre une surface utile de 700 m². Ce rectangle de 12 x 40 m a été entièrement construit en béton armé. Des ouvertures circulaires ponctuent une longue façade fermée, tandis que la façade opposée s'ouvre entièrement sur une terrasse en bois et une piscine. Une autre terrasse sur le toit offre une vue à 360° sur les collines entourant Santiago, tandis que les verrières rondes ménagées dans son sol éclairent l'intérieur. Comme une autre maison avait été édifiée sur ce terrain dans les années 1950, l'architecte a pu profiter de la présence de grands arbres. Il explique que « le programme classique pour une famille avec deux enfants s'organise autour de deux corridors, l'un intérieur, l'autre extérieur, partant de l'entrée et desservant les zones de réception et de service jusqu'aux parties plus privées. Il s'agit d'un travail serein qui résout les problèmes de construction et de programme avec simplicité, propose des textures de béton variées et différentes hauteurs de pièces selon leur usage et leurs proportions ». De formes puissantes tout en restant fonctionnelle, la **MAISON VIEJO** illustre la capacité de l'architecte à utiliser le béton comme matériau principal pour une maison confortable, voire luxueuse.

A canopied car park and a sunscreen demonstrate the architect's deft alternation of dense opacity with airy lightness. Heavy materials seem to hover in space, offering protection and a promise of solidity to the residents.

Die überdeckten Stellplätze und der Sonnenschutz machen den geschickten Wechsel von dichter Opazität und luftiger Leichtigkeit deutlich. Schwere Materialien scheinen zu schweben, bieten Schutz und versprechen Solidität.

Un parking sous auvent et un écran solaire illustrent l'habileté de l'architecte à alterner opacité et légèreté aérienne. Les matériaux lourds semblent flotter dans l'espace tout en offrant leur protection et leur garantie de solidité aux occupants.

MARCIO KOGAN

Marcio Kogan
Alameida Tiete, 505
04616–001 São Paulo SP
Brazil

Tel: +55 11 30 81 35 22
Fax: +55 11 30 63 34 24
e-mail: mk-mk@uol.com.br
Web: www.marciokogan.com.br

BR Hous

Born in 1952, **MARCIO KOGAN** graduated in 1976 from the School of Architecture at Mackenzie University in São Paulo. In 1983, he received an IAB (Instituto de Arquitetos do Brazil) Award for the Rubens Sverner Day-Care Center. He received other such awards for his Goldfarb Residence (1991); the Larmond Store (1995); UMA Store (1999); or for the BR House (published here, 2004). In 2003, he made a submission for the World Trade Center Site Memorial, and in 2002, he completed a Museum of Microbiology in São Paulo. He worked with Isay Weinfeld on the Fasano Hotel in São Paulo. He also participated with Weinfeld in the 25th São Paulo Biennale (2002) and worked with him on the Escola Cidade Jardim/ Play Pen, also in São Paulo. Kogan is known for his use of box-like forms, together with wooden shutters, trellises and exposed stone.

Der 1952 geborene **MARCIO KOGAN** machte 1976 seinen Abschluss an der Escuela de Arquitectura der Universidad Mackenzie in São Paulo. Das von ihm geplante Rubens-Sverner-Tagespflegezentrum wurde 1983 mit einem Preis des IAB (Instituto de Arquitetos do Brazil) ausgezeichnet. Weitere Preise des IAB erhielt er für die Goldfarb Residence (1991), den Larmond Store (1995), für den UMA Store (1999) und für das hier gezeigte BR Haus (2004). 2003 reichte er einen Entwurf für das Mahnmal auf dem Grundstück des World Trade Center ein, 2002 wurde das Museum für Mikrobiologie in São Paulo fertig gestellt. Das Fasano Hotel in São Paulo plante er in Partnerschaft mit Isay Weinfeld. Ebenfalls mit Weinfeld nahm er 2002 auch an der 25. São Paulo Biennale und an der Escola Cidade Jardim/Play Pen in São Paulo teil. Typisch für Kogans Architektur sind kistenartigen Formen, Fensterläden und Spaliere aus Holz sowie die Verwendung von Naturstein.

Né en 1952, **MARCIO KOGAN** est diplômé de l'École d'architecture de l'Université Mackenzie à São Paulo (1976) et a été primé par l'IAB (Institut des architectes du Brésil) pour le dispensaire Rubens Sverner, la résidence Goldfarb (1991), le magasin Larmond (1995), le magasin UMA (1999) et la Mmaison BR (2004) publiée ici. En 2002, il a achevé un musée de microbiologie à São Paulo et, en 2003, a proposé un projet au concours pour le mémorial du World Trade Center à New York. Il a conçu, avec Isay Weinfeld, l'hôtel Fasano à São Paulo et a également participé, avec Weinfeld, à la 25e Biennale de São Paulo (2002) et collaboré avec lui au projet de la Escola Cidade Jardim/Play Pen, toujours à São Paulo. Il est connu pour son utilisation de la forme de la boîte, de volets et treillis en bois et de la pierre apparente.

BR HOUSE

Araras, Rio de Janeiro, Brazil, 2002–04

Floor area: 739 m². Client: not disclosed.
Cost: $1 million

Located on a 6820 m² site, this rectangular house has a floor area of 739 m². The architect describes the residence himself in clear terms: "The two-story house is made of concrete, metal, wood, aluminum and glass and is totally integrated with the forest landscape of this mountainous region of Rio de Janeiro (Petrópolis). The first floor has four suites, guest bathroom, kitchen and living/dining rooms. The ground floor has a heated pool, dry sauna with a large fixed glass wall so that one can contemplate the landscape. The house represents the idea of two monolithic concrete blades containing the boxes of the first floor, raised on stilts and stone box. The wood-covered façade consists of a light filter (vertical wooden strips) which, on the terraces of the suites, open completely. At nightfall, this "skin" looks as though it is totally lit, surrounded by the beautiful mountainous forest." The idea of lifting structures up on pilotis is fairly common in Brazil. What is not at all obvious in this house, is that Marcio Kogan was called into the project after another architect had been dismissed by the clients and Kogan had to deal with an existing steel frame. Seemingly making this apparent handicap into an advantage, the essentially geometric rigor of the architectural solutions blends seamlessly with a sensual and very Brazilian presence of nature.

Das rechteckige, 739 m² große Haus befindet sich auf einem Grundstück mit einer Fläche von 6820 m². Der Architekt beschreibt das Wohnhaus so: »Das zweigeschossige Haus besteht aus Beton, Metall, Holz, Aluminium und Glas und ist vollständig in die Waldlandschaft der bergigen Region Petrópolis von Rio de Janeiro integriert. Im ersten Obergeschoss gibt es vier Suiten, ein Gästebadezimmer, eine Küche sowie Ess- und Wohnräume. Auf der Erdgeschossebene liegen ein beheiztes Schwimmbad und eine Trockensauna mit einer großen festverglasten Glaswand, so dass die Landschaft gegenwärtig ist. Bestimmt wird das Haus von der Idee zweier monolithischer ›Klingen‹ aus Beton (die Decken), die die ›Kisten‹ des ersten Obergeschosses aufnehmen. Sie wurden mithilfe der Stützen und einer ›Steinkiste‹ angehoben. Die holzverkleidete Fassade wirkt als Lichtfilter und besteht aus vertikalen Holzlamellen. Sie lässt sich im Bereich der Terrassen der Schlafräume komplett öffnen. Nachts scheint diese Hülle — umgeben von dem wunderbaren Bergwald — komplett zu leuchten.« Die Idee, Gebäude auf Stützen zu stellen, ist in Brasilien nicht ungewöhnlich. Man bemerkt es gar nicht, aber Marcio Kogan wurde beauftragt, nachdem sich die Bauherren von einem anderen Architekten getrennt hatten. Kogan musste daher die schon fertige Stahlkonstruktion in seinen Entwurf integrieren. Dieses scheinbare Handicap wendete er zum Guten: Die im Grundsatz geometrische Strenge der Lösung fügt sich ohne Schwierigkeiten in die sinnliche und sehr brasilianische Präsenz der Natur ein.

Située sur un terrain de 6820 m², cette maison rectangulaire mesure dispose de 739 m² de surface utile. L'architecte la décrit ainsi lui-même : « Cette maison sur deux niveaux est en béton, métal, bois, aluminium et verre, et totalement intégrée au paysage forestier de cette région montagneuse de l'État de Rio de Janeiro (Petrópolis). L'étage réunit quatre suites, des salles de bains pour invités, une cuisine et le séjour/salle-à-manger. Le rez-de-chaussée est occupé par une piscine chauffée, un sauna sec à grande paroi fixe en verre d'où l'on peut contempler le paysage. La maison est construite sur l'idée de deux lames de béton monolithes contenant les boîtes de l'étage soutenues par des pilotis et une boîte en pierre. La façade en bois se présente sous forme d'un écran léger (baguettes de bois verticales) qui s'ouvre entièrement sur les terrasses des suites. La nuit, cette ‹ peau › semble totalement lumineuse, entourée par la magnifique forêt de cette zone montagneuse. » L'idée d'élever les maisons sur pilotis est assez courante au Brésil, ce qui ne l'est pas, en revanche, c'est que Kogan a été appelé sur ce projet après qu'un de ses confrères ait été écarté, et qu'il a dû composer avec une structure en acier existante. Transformant ce handicap en avantage, la rigueur essentiellement géométrique des solutions architecturales retenues les fait se fondre dans une nature très présente, sensuelle, très typiquement brésilienne.

Lifting his house up on pilotis like many modern Brazilian buildings, Kogan also contrasts a rough stone base with smoother or more sophisticated surfaces in wood, glass, steel or concrete.

Wie viele andere moderne Häuser in Brasilien steht das BR Haus auf Pilotis. Der grobe Steinsockel kontrastiert mit glatteren und edleren Oberflächen aus Holz, Glas, Stahl und Beton.

En élevant la maison sur des pilotis, Kogan a également fait contraster la base en pierre brute avec des surfaces plus douces et plus sophistiquées en verre, bois, acier ou béton.

An elevation shows the strictly rectangular shape of the house, with its essential living space lifted up off the ground.

Die Ansicht zeigt die streng rechtwinklige Form des Hauses. Der Wohnraum liegt im ersten Obergeschoss.

Élévation montrant la forme strictement rectangulaire de la maison, dont la partie séjour est surélevée par rapport au sol.

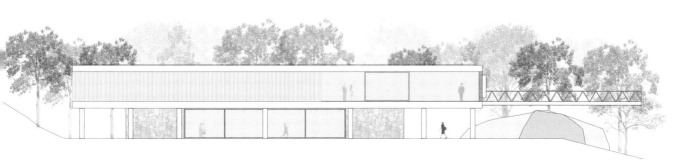

Trees come up through the wooden surface of a terrace, emphasizing the proximity of nature, which is in any case visible through the large glazed surfaces of the house.

Bäume wachsen durch den Holzfußboden der Terrasse und betonen die Nähe zur Natur. Diese ist ohnehin aufgrund der großen Verglasungen des Hauses sehr präsent.

Des arbres poussent à travers la terrasse en bois. Ils renforcent la proximité de la nature, visible à travers les vastes pans de verre de la maison.

Floor-to-ceiling windows bring the surrounding natural setting almost into the living room, while ample but strictly aligned furniture also contrasts with the profusion of greenery seen outside.

Geschosshohe Fenster bringen die natürliche Umgebung fast in den Wohnraum hinein. Großzügige, streng ausgerichtete Möbel bilden dabei einen Gegensatz zum verschwenderischen Grün der Natur.

Des ouvertures sol-plafond font quasiment entrer l'environnement naturel dans la maison, tandis que le mobilier, de proportions généreuses mais strictement aligné, contraste avec la profusion végétale que l'on aperçoit à l'extérieur.

A site plan shows the car park and approach bridge, leading to the outdoor terrace and into the rectangular volume of the house. Rough stones and water define lower level spaces, while the living room (right) remains smoothly horizontal.

Der Lageplan zeigt die überdeckten Stellplätze und die Zugangsbrücke, die auf die Außenterrasse führt, von wo aus das Haus betreten wird. Grobes Felsgestein und Wasser definieren die Räume der unteren Ebene. Rechts: Der Wohnraum ist elegant horizontal gegliedert.

Le plan du site montre le parking et le passerelle qui mène à la terrasse et à l'intérieur du rectangle de la maison. Un mur de pierres brutes et un bassin délimitent les espaces du niveau inférieur, tandis que le séjour (à droite) affiche une horizontalité douce et reposante.

REM KOOLHAAS/OMA

Office for Metropolitan Architecture
Heer Bokelweg 149
3032 AD Rotterdam
The Netherlands

Tel: +31 102 43 82 00
Fax: +31 102 43 82 02
e-mail: office@oma.nl
Web: www.oma.nl

REM KOOLHAAS created the Office for Metropolitan Architecture (**OMA**) in 1975 together with Elia and Zoe Zenghelis and Madelon Vriesendorp. Born in Rotterdam in 1944, Koolhaas tried his hand as a journalist for the *Haagse Post* and as a screenwriter before studying at the Architectural Association in London. He became well known after the 1978 publication of his book *Delirious New York*. OMA is led today by four partners, Rem Koolhaas, Ole Scheeren, Ellen van Loon, and Joshua Prince-Ramus. Their built work includes a group of apartments at Nexus World, Fukuoka (1991), and the Villa dall'Ava, Saint-Cloud (1985–91). Koolhaas was named head architect of the Euralille project in Lille in 1988, and has worked on a design for the new Jussieu University Library in Paris. His 1400 page book *S,M,L,XL* (Monacelli Press, 1995) has more than fulfilled his promise as an influential writer. He won the 2000 Pritzker Prize and the 2003 Praemium Imperiale Award for architecture. More recent work of OMA includes a House, Bordeaux, France (1998), the campus center at the Illinois Institute of Technology (1998), the new Dutch Embassy in Berlin (2000–04), as well as the Guggenheim Las Vegas (2000–01), Prada boutiques in New York and Los Angeles, and the 1850-seat Porto Concert Hall (2005). OMA participated in the Samsung Museum of Art (Leeum) in Seoul with Mario Botta and Jean Nouvel. Current work has included the design of OMA's largest project ever: the 575 000 m² Headquarters and Cultural Center for China Central Television (CCTV) in Beijing; and the New City Center for Almere for which the firm has drawn up the master plan.

Zusammen mit Elia und Zoe Zenghelis sowie Madelon Vriesendorp gründete **REM KOOLHAAS** 1975 das Office for Metropolitan Architecture (**OMA**). Der 1944 in Den Haag geborene Koolhaas arbeitete als Journalist für die *Haagse Post* und als Drehbuchautor, bevor er an der Architectural Association in London studierte. Er wurde mit seinem 1978 erschienenen Buch *Delirious New York* weithin bekannt. OMA wird heute von vier Partnern geführt: Rem Koolhaas, Ole Scheeren, Ellen van Loon und Joshua Prince-Ramus. Zu ihren Bauten gehören u. a. die Villa dall'Ava im französischen Saint-Cloud (1985–91) und Wohnungen in Nexus World im japanischen Fukuoka (1991). 1988 wurde Koolhaas die Leitung des Euralille-Projekts in Lille übertragen; außerdem erarbeitete er einen Entwurf für die neue Bibliothek der Universität Jussieu in Paris. Mit seinem 1400 Seiten starken Buch *S,M,L,XL* (Monacelli Press, 1995) hat er seinen Status als einflussreicher Theoretiker und Autor bestätigt. Im Jahr 2000 erhielt Koolhaas den Pritzker-Preis und 2003 den Architekturpreis Praemium Imperiale. Gebäude von OMA sind u. a. ein Wohnhaus in Bordeaux (1998), das Campus-Zentrum des Illinois Institute of Technology (1998), die Niederländische Botschaft in Berlin (2000–04), das Guggenheim Museum in Las Vegas (2000–01), Boutiquen für Prada in New York und Los Angeles und ein Konzertsaal in Porto mit 1850 Plätzen (2005). Mit Mario Botta und Jean Nouvel hat Koolhaas das Samsung Museum für Kunst (Leeum) in Seoul geplant. Zu den derzeitigen Projekten gehört der bislang größte Auftrag für OMA: das rund 600 000 m² umfassende Verwaltungs- und Kulturgebäude für China Central Television (CCTV) in Peking sowie das neue Stadtzentrum von Almere in den Niederlanden, für das OMA den Masterplan entworfen hat.

REM KOOLHAAS est né à Rotterdam en 1944. Avant d'étudier à l'Architectural Association de Londres, il s'essaye au journalisme pour le *Haagse Post* et à l'écriture de scénarii. Il fonde l'Office for Metropolitan Architecture (**OMA**) à Londres en 1975 et devient célèbre grâce à la publication, en 1978, de son ouvrage *Delirious New York*. OMA est dirigé par quatre partenaires, Rem Koolhaas, Ole Scheeren, Ellen van Loon et Joshua Prince-Ramus. Parmi leurs réalisations : un ensemble d'appartements à Nexus World, Fukuoka, Japon (1991) ; la villa dall'Ava, Saint-Cloud, France (1985–91). Koolhaas est nommé architecte en chef du projet Euralille à Lille en 1988 et propose un projet de bibliothèque pour la Faculté de Jussieu à Paris. Son livre de 1400 pages, *S,M,L,XL* (Monacelli Press, 1995), confirme son influence et son impact de théoricien. Il a remporté le prix Pritzker en 2000 et le Praemium Imperiale en 2003. Parmi ses réalisations récentes : une maison à Bordeaux (1998), le campus de l'Illinois Institute of Technology (1998), la nouvelle ambassade des Pays-Bas à Berlin (2000–04), le Guggenheim Las Vegas (2000–01), des boutiques Prada à New York et Los Angeles et tout récemment, la Casa da Musica, salle de concert de 1850 places, à Porto, Portugal (2005). Son agence a conçu le Samsung Museum of Art (Leeum) à Seoul en coopération avec Mario Botta et Jean Nouvel, et travaille actuellement sur son plus important projet à ce jour, le siège et le centre culturel de la Télévision nationale chinoise (CCTV) à Pékin (575 000 m²), et le nouveau centre-ville d'Almere (Pays-Bas).

SEATTLE CENTRAL LIBRARY

Seattle, Washington, USA, 2004

Floor area: 30 000 m². Client: Seattle Central Library. Cost: $165.5 million (including Temporary Central Library)

The new **CENTRAL LIBRARY**, located on Fourth Avenue in Seattle, is drawing more than 8000 visitors a day, or twice as many as the old building. OMA worked with the Seattle firm LMN Architects on this project, which was the third Central Library built on the same site. The total cost of the 30 000 m² structure, including 10 million dollars for the Temporary Central Library, was 165.5 million dollars. It has a capacity for 1.45 million books. The structure is covered with nearly 10 000 pieces of glass, of which half are triple-layered with an expanded metal mesh sandwiched between the two outer layers in order to protect the interior against heat and glare. A reason for the use of this much glass was the architects' desire to make the building "transparent and open," qualities not always associated with libraries. Passers-by can see activity on every floor of the building. The unusual shape of the building is partially related to efforts to control the type and quantity of light reaching interior spaces. A particularly striking overhang covers the entry on the Fourth Avenue side of the library. A system of "floating platforms" and a diagonal grid designed to protect against earthquakes or wind damage are amongst other structural innovations in the design. Within the library, a unique "Books Spiral" penetrates four levels of the stacks and contains the nonfiction collection, allowing for increased capacity and easier expansion of the number of books in the future. The 275-seat Microsoft Auditorium, located on Level 1, is considered by the Library to be its "centerpiece." Level 2 is a staff floor, and Level 3 includes the base of the building's atrium, book return and check out facilities, or the "Norcliffe Foundation Living Room," a reading area with a ceiling height of fifteen meters. Four meeting rooms are located on Level 4, and a large space called the "Mixing Chamber" compared by the architects to a "trading floor for information" is used to "go for help with general questions or in-depth research." The "Books Spiral" reaches from Level 6 to Level 9, while a reading room with a capacity for 400 persons is located on Level 10. The top floor is occupied by administrative offices and a staff lunch room.

8000 Besucher kommen täglich in die neue **ZENTRALBIBLIOTHEK** an der Fourth Avenue in Seattle, doppelt so viele wie in die alte. An dem Projekt – es ist bereits die dritte Zentralbibliothek auf dem Grundstück – waren neben OMA auch LMN Architects aus Seattle beteiligt. Die Gesamtkosten des 30 000 m² großen Gebäudes belaufen sich auf umgerechnet 139 Millionen Euro. Darin enthalten sind etwa 8,5 Millionen Euro für eine temporäre Bibliothek. 1,45 Millionen Bücher haben hier ihren Platz. Der Bau ist mit fast 10 000 Glaspaneelen eingedeckt. Die Hälfte dieser Paneele hat einen dreilagigen Aufbau: Zwischen zwei Glasscheiben ist ein Metallnetz angeordnet, um den Innenraum vor zuviel Hitze und vor Spiegelungen zu schützen. Ein Grund für die Verwendung von so viel Glas ist der Wunsch des Architekten, das Gebäude »transparent und offen« zu gestalten – Qualitäten, die man nicht unbedingt mit einer Bibliothek in Verbindung bringt. Passanten können sehen, dass auf jeder Ebene des Hauses Aktivitäten stattfinden. Die ungewöhnliche Form des Gebäudes hängt z. T. mit Überlegungen zusammen, wie die Tageslichtart und -menge in den Räumen kontrolliert werden können. Der Eingang an der Fourth Avenue wird von einer besonders eindrucksvollen Auskragung überdeckt. Ein System von »schwebenden Ebenen« und ein diagonaler Gitterrost, der die seismischen Kräfte sowie die Windlasten aufnimmt, gehören zu den konstruktiven Neuerungen des Gebäudes. Im Inneren der Bibliothek durchdringt eine »Bücherspirale«, die alle Sachbücher enthält, die vier aufeinander gestapelten Büchergeschosse. Die Spiralform erlaubt es, die Nutzerkapazitäten und die Zahl der Bücher in Zukunft zu erhöhen. Das »Microsoft-Auditorium« mit 275 Plätzen auf der Ebene eins wird von den Bibliotheksmitarbeitern als Herz des Baus betrachtet. Auf der Ebene zwei liegen die Räume für die Angestellten. Das Atrium des Gebäudes beginnt auf Ebene drei, außerdem befinden sich hier u. a. die Buchrückgabe und der »Norcliffe Foundation Living Room«, eine Lesezone mit einer Deckenhöhe von 15 m. Ebene vier nimmt vier Konferenzräume und einen großen Raum, das so genannte »Mixing Chamber«, auf. Dieser Raum wird von den Architekten mit einem Börsenparkett für Informationen verglichen. Er wird benutzt, wenn man »in grundsätzlichen Fragen Hilfe sucht oder Grundsatzforschung betreibt«. Die Bücherspirale reicht von Ebene sechs bis Ebene neun, auf der Ebene zehn befindet sich ein Lesesaal für 400 Personen. Die Büros der Verwaltung und eine Kantine für die Mitarbeiter sind auf der obersten Ebene angeordnet.

Située sur Fourth Avenue, la nouvelle **BIBLIOTHÈQUE CENTRALE** de Seattle, dont la capacité est de 1,45 million d'ouvrages, attire déjà plus de 8000 visiteurs par jour, soit deux fois la fréquentation de la précédente. OMA a collaboré sur ce projet – la troisième bibliothèque édifiée sur le même site – avec l'agence de Seattle LMN Architects. Le budget total de ce bâtiment de 30 000 m² s'est élevé à 139 millions d'euros dont 8,5 millions pour la Bibliothèque centrale temporaire, le temps du chantier. L'ensemble est habillé de près de 10 000 panneaux de verre dont la moitié de triple épaisseur : entre les deux vitrages externes est inséré un tissu de métal étiré qui protège l'intérieur de la lumière excessive et de la chaleur. La raison de cette utilisation massive du verre était le souhait de l'architecte de rendre le bâtiment « transparent et ouvert », qualités qui ne vont pas forcément de pair avec les bibliothèques. Les passants peuvent ainsi voir toutes les activités qui s'y déroulent, à chaque niveau. La forme originale du bâtiment est due en partie à la volonté de contrôler le type et la quantité de lumière susceptible d'atteindre l'intérieur. Un porte-à-faux spectaculaire protège l'entrée sur Fourth Avenue. Un système de « plates-formes flottantes » et une structure en diagonale, conçus pour résister aux tremblements de terre ou aux tornades, font partie des autres innovations structurelles du projet. Une « Spirale des livres » accueillant les ouvrages documentaires court sur quatre niveaux de rayonnages, permettant aussi d'augmenter la capacité de stockage dans le futur. Au niveau 1, l'auditorium Microsoft de 250 places est considéré comme le point central de la bibliothèque. Au niveau 2 se trouvent les bureaux du personnel et au niveau 3 la base de l'atrium, le bureau de prêt des ouvrages et la Norcliffe Foundation Living Room, une zone de lecture bénéficiant d'une hauteur sous plafond de 15 mètres. Quatre salles de réunion sont situées au niveau 4, ainsi qu'un vaste espace appelé « Chambre de mixage » comparé par les architectes à « une salle de marché de l'information, pour aider à répondre aux questions d'ordre général et aux recherches approfondies ». La « Spirale des livres » s'élève du niveau 6 au niveau 9 tandis qu'une salle de lecture de 400 places occupe le niveau 10. Le dernier niveau est occupé par des bureaux et par le restaurant du personnel.

The dynamic angles of the Library set it aside from its urban neighbors. It looks almost as though it might be capable of moving away from the site under its own power.

Durch ihre dynamischen Winkel unterscheidet sich die Zentralbibliothek von ihren innerstädtischen Nachbarn. Fast meint man, sie könne sich aus eigener Kraft von dem Grundstück entfernen.

Les pans inclinés dynamiques de la Bibliothèque la détachent visuellement de son voisinage urbain. On pourrait presque la croire capable de se déplacer d'elle-même.

Despite the unexpected angles of the building, each facet is calculated on the basis of function and sunlight considerations.

Die Winkel im Gebäude mögen zufällig erscheinen, tatsächlich wurde aber jede Facette auf der Basis von Funktion und Belichtung berechnet.

Les étonnantes facettes des façades ont été calculées en fonction de critères fonctionnels pour un éclairage naturel.

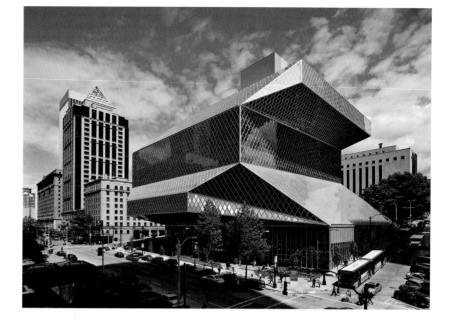

The angled glass façades of the Library allow for generous and active interior spaces, where one level proceeds to the next without the usual strict division of floors.

Die geneigten Glasfassaden ermöglichen großzügige und aktiv zu nutzende Innenräume. Ohne die übliche Trennung der Geschosse geht eine Ebene in die nächste über.

Les parois de verre inclinées de la Bibliothèque laissent place à des salles spacieuses et fonctionnelles, où l'on passe d'un niveau à l'autre sans séparation traditionnelle.

Interior features and the vast over-head array of metal and light create an impression of a city within the city, where certain spaces are defined by their function but also, clearly, by their architecture.

Besondere räumliche Elemente und die riesigen Überkopfverglasungen aus Metall und Licht vermitteln den Eindruck einer Stadt in der Stadt. Spezielle Zonen werden durch ihre Funktion definiert – natürlich aber auch durch die Architektur.

L'aménagement intérieur, les immenses volumes de métal et la lumière créent une impression de ville dans la ville. Certains espaces sont définis par leur fonc-tion autant que par leur architecture.

Although many more traditional libraries have had vast reading rooms, the Seattle Library has a profusion of unexpected spaces, where floors levels shift and develop before the visitor's eyes.

Große Lesesäle gab und gibt es auch in vielen älteren Bibliotheken. Die Zentralbibliothek in Seattle wartet jedoch mit einer Fülle von überraschenden Räumen auf, in denen sich die Ebenen neigen und sich dem Besucher sukzessiv erschließen.

Si beaucoup de bibliothèques plus traditionnelles possèdent de vastes salles de lecture, celle de Seattle offre une profusion d'espaces inattendus dans lesquels les niveaux s'entrecroisent et se déploient devant le visiteur.

In contrast with the many vast open spaces, the Library also offers more intimate areas near the book shelves (right). Stairways are not hidden like fire escapes, but participate in the invitation to explore the building (below).

Im Gegensatz zu den vielen riesigen offenen Räumen gibt es in der Zentralbibliothek im Bereich der Buchregale auch intimere Bereiche (rechts). Die Treppen werden nicht wie Sicherheitstreppenhäuser versteckt, sondern sind Teil der Einladung, das Gebäude zu erkunden (unten).

Outre ses vastes espaces ouverts, la bibliothèque met à disposition des aires plus intimes à proximité des rayonnages de livres (à droite). Les escaliers ne sont pas dissimulés comme des issues de secours, mais sont au contraire une invitation à visiter le bâtiment (en bas).

Rem Koolhaas has been quoted as saying that the Seattle Library is his "masterpiece." Though it can be expected that the Dutchman and his firm (OMA) will build many more significant buildings, the library is a symphonic orchestration that allays function and form in new ways, no small accomplishment where the handling of books is concerned.

Rem Koolhaas hat die Bibliothek in Seattle als sein Meisterstück bezeichnet. Man kann von dem Niederländer erwarten, dass er noch viele weitere bedeutende Gebäude realisiert – die Bibliothek wird als »sinfonische Orchestrierung«, die Form und Funktion auf neue Weise miteinander in Einklang bringt, Bestand haben. Keine geringe Leistung, wenn es um den Umgang mit Büchern geht.

Rem Koolhaas aurait dit que cette bibliothèque était son « chef-d'œuvre ». On peut espérer que le Néerlandais et son équipe d'OMA réaliseront d'autres projets encore plus significatifs, mais cette bibliothèque est une orchestration symphonique qui réunit de manière novatrice la forme et la fonction, ce qui n'est pas une mince réussite dans le domaine de la conservation des livres.

KENGO KUMA

Kengo Kuma & Associates
2–24–8 BY-CUBE 2–4F
Minami Aoyama
Minato-ku
Tokyo 107–0062
Japan

Tel: +81 334 01 77 21
Fax: +81 334 01 77 78
e-mail: kuma@ba2.so-net.ne.jp
Web: www.kkaa.co.jp

Born in 1954 in Kanagawa, Japan, **KENGO KUMA** graduated in 1979 from the University of Tokyo with a Masters in Architecture. In 1985–86 he received an Asian Cultural Council fellowship Grant and was a Visiting Scholar at Columbia University. In 1987 he established the Spatial Design Studio, and in 1991 he created Kengo Kuma & Associates. His work includes: the Gunma Toyota Car Show Room, Maebashi (1989); Maiton Resort Complex, Phuket, Thailand; Rustic, Office Building, Tokyo; Doric, Office Building, Tokyo; M2, Headquarters for Mazda New Design Team, Tokyo (all in 1991); Kinjo Golf Club, Club House, Okayama (1992); Kiro-san Observatory, Ehime (1994); Atami Guest House, Guest House for Bandai Corp, Atami (1992–95); Karuizawa Resort Hotel, Karuizawa (1993); Tomioka Lakewood Golf Club House, Tomioka (1993–96); Toyoma Noh-Theater, Miyagi (1995–96); and the Japanese Pavilion for the Venice Biennale, Venice, Italy (1995). He has recently completed the Stone Museum (Nasu, Tochigi) and a Museum for the work of Ando Hiroshige (Batou, Nasu-gun, Tochigi). He completed the Nagasaki Prefecture Art Museum in March 2005; the Fukusaki Hanging Garden in January 2005; LVMH Osaka in 2004; One Omotesando, Tokyo (2003); and the Great (Bamboo) Wall guest house, Beijing (2002).

KENGO KUMA, geboren 1954 in Kanagawa, Japan, schloss 1979 sein Studium an der Universität Tokio mit dem Master of Architecture ab. Von 1985 bis 1986 arbeitete er mit einem Stipendium des Asian Cultural Council als Gastwissenschaftler an der Columbia University in New York. 1987 gründete Kuma das Spatial Design Studio und 1991 das Büro Kengo Kuma & Associates in Tokio. Zu seinen Bauten gehören: der Gunma Toyota Car Showroom in Maebashi, Japan (1989), die Ferienanlage Maiton in Phuket, Thailand, die Bürogebäude Rustic und Doric sowie M2, der Hauptsitz für die Designabteilung von Mazda, alle 1991 in Tokio ausgeführt, ferner das Klubhaus des Kinjo Golf Club in Okayama (1992), das Gästehaus für die Firma Bandai Corporation in Atami (1992–95), ein Hotel in Karuizawa (1993), das Klubhaus des Lakewood Golf Club in Tomioka (1993–96), das Observatorium Kiro-san in Ehime (1994), der Japanische Pavillon auf der Biennale in Venedig (1995) und das No-Theater in Toyama, Miyagi (1995–96). Seine neuesten Projekte sind das Steinmuseum in Nasu, Tochigi, sowie ein Museum für die Werke von Ando Hiroshige in Batou, Nasu-gun, Tochigi. Das Kunstmuseum der Präfektur Nagasaki wurde im März 2005 fertig gestellt, die Hängenden Gärten von Fukusaki im Januar 2005, das LVMH Osaka 2004, One Omotesando in Tokio 2003 und das Gästehaus Great (Bamboo) Wall in Peking 2002.

Né en 1954 à Kanagawa, au Japon, **KENGO KUMA** est Master of Architecture de l'Université de Tokyo (1979). En 1984–86, il bénéficie d'une bourse de l'Asian Cultural Council et est chercheur invité à la Columbia University (New York). En 1987, il crée le Spatial Design Studio et, en 1991, Kengo Kuma & Associates. Parmi ses réalisations : le Car Show Room Toyota de Gunma, Maebashi (1989) ; le Maiton Resort Complex, Phuket, Thaïlande (1991) ; le Rustic Office Building, Tokyo (1991) ; l'immeuble de bureaux Doric, Tokyo (1991) ; le siège du département de design de Mazda, Tokyo (1991) ; le Club House du Kinjo Golf Club, Okayama (1992) ; l'Observatoire Kiro-San, Yoshiumi, Ochi-gun, Ehime (1994) ; la Guest House d'Atami pour Bandaï Corp, Atami (1992–95) ; le Karuizawa Resort Hotel, Karuizawa (1993) ; le Club House du Tomioka Lakewood Golf, Tomioka (1993–96) et le théâtre Nô Toyoma, Miyagi (1995–96) et le pavillon japonais de la Biennale de Venise en 1995. Il a récemment construit le musée de la Pierre, Nasu, Tochigi, le musée Ando Hiroshige, Batou, Nasu-gun, Tochigi, la « Grande muraille de bambou », maison d'hôtes, Pékin (2002), One Omotesando, Tokyo (2003), le siège de LVMH à Osaka (2004), et vient d'achever les jardins suspendus de Fukusaki (janvier 2005) ainsi que le musée d'Art de la Préfecture de Nagasaki (mars 2005) présenté ici.

NAGASAKI PREFECTURAL MUSEUM
Nagasaki, Nagasaki, 2003–05

*Floor area: 9898 m². Client: Nagasaki Prefecture.
Cost: € 36 million*

*Kengo Kuma uses a succession of
vertical elements, not unlike a screen,
or perhaps a bamboo forest to define
the major elements of the museum,
creating an impression of lightness.*

*Mit einer Vielzahl von vertikalen Ele-
menten, die wie ein Screen oder ein
Bambuswald wirken, definiert Kengo
Kuma die wichtigen Bereiche des
Museums und erzielt den Eindruck
von Leichtigkeit.*

*Kengo Kuma utilise une succession
d'éléments verticaux – une sorte
d'écran ou peut-être de forêt de
bambous – pour délimiter les principaux éléments du musée et créer
une impression de légèreté.*

As Kengo Kuma explains, the fact that Nagasaki was the only port permitted to remain open while Japan was closed to the rest of the world, it boasts a substantial collection of Spanish and Portuguese works of art. The 12 679 m² site had the particularity of having a canal run through it. Kuma explains that "To make the canal one with the art museum, I created an intermediate space along the canal, and made it a promenade for city residents and a place for appreciating works of art. This space was protected from the strong sun by stone louvers that created a breezy, pleasant shade." A "box-shaped" glass bridge crosses the canal, making it visible to all the visitors of the museum. The roof of the structure is also used as a gallery space with a view of the city's port. With a footprint of 6248 m² and a floor area of 9898 m², this is a large structure, handled with the typical subtlety and intelligence that the architect always demonstrates. Kengo Kuma is also quite outspoken about certain aspects of the design. As he says, "In Nagasaki, I developed a new supporting detail for stone louvers using solid steel columns. Nagasaki, located in southern Japan, is known for its Colonial-style veranda architecture using wooden latticework. The detail I used here is a contemporary version of this traditional architecture; it also is a criticism of contemporary Japanese architecture that ignores both indigenous climate and landscape."

Die Tatsache, dass Nagasaki der einzige offene Hafen war, als sich Japan gegenüber dem Rest der Welt verschloss, führte zum Entstehen einer grundlegenden Sammlung spanischer und portugiesischer Kunstwerke, erläutert Kengo Kuma. Das 12 679 m² große Grundstück weist als Besonderheit einen Kanal auf. Dazu Kuma: »Um aus dem Kanal und dem Museum eine Einheit zu machen, habe ich einen Zwischenraum entlang des Kanals geschaffen und hier eine Promenade für die Bewohner der Stadt angeordnet. Dies ist ein Ort, um die Kunstwerke zu würdigen. Steinlamellen schützen vor der starken Sonneneinstrahlung und sorgen für eine luftige, angenehme Verschattung.« Eine kistenartige Brücke aus Glas stellt eine Verbindung über dem Kanal her und macht ihn so für alle Besucher des Museums erlebbar. Das Dach des Gebäudes, das auch als Galerie benutzt wird, bietet einen Blick auf den Hafen von Nagasaki. Mit einer Grundfläche von 6248 m² und einer Gesamtfläche von 9898 m² ist das Museum ein großes Gebäude, das mit der für den Architekten typischen Sensibilität und Intelligenz entwickelt wurde. Kengo Kuma äußert sich recht offen über bestimmte Aspekte des Entwurfs. So sagt er: »In Nagasaki habe ich ein neues Auflagerdetail für die Steinlamellen entwickelt, indem ich massive Stahlstützen benutzte. Nagasaki im Süden Japans ist bekannt für seine Verandenarchitektur im Kolonialstil mit Spalieren aus Holz. Das Detail, das ich hier verwendete, ist eine moderne Version dieser traditionellen Architektur. Es ist auch eine Kritik an der modernen japanischen Architektur, die sowohl das Klima vor Ort als auch die Landschaft ignoriert.«

Comme l'explique Kengo Kuma, le fait que Nagasaki ait été le seul port ouvert, lorsque le Japon était isolé du reste du monde, explique qu'il possède une substantielle collection d'art espagnol et portugais. L'une des caractéristiques du terrain de 12 679 m² était la présence d'un canal. «Pour que le canal ne fasse qu'un avec le musée, j'ai créé un volume intermédiaire le long de celui-ci. J'en ai fait une promenade pour les citadins qui est, en même temps, un nouveau lieu pour la découverte d'œuvres d'art. Cet espace est protégé du soleil par des brise-soleil de pierre qui créent une ombre agréable et aérée. Une passerelle de verre ‹en forme de boîte› traverse le canal, désormais visible par tous les visiteurs du musée. Le toit sert également d'espace d'exposition et offre une vue sur le port.» Avec une emprise au sol de 6248 m² et une surface utile de 9898 m², il s'agit d'un grand bâtiment, traité avec la subtilité et l'intelligence dont l'architecte a toujours fait preuve. Kengo Kuma s'exprime très volontiers sur certains aspects de son projet : «À Nagasaki, j'ai mis au point de nouveaux supports pour les brise-soleil de pierre, à base de colonnes en acier massif. Nagasaki, dans le Japon du Sud, est connue pour son architecture à vérandas de style colonial et leurs claustras en lattis de bois. Le système que j'utilise est une version contemporaine de cette architecture traditionnelle, c'est aussi une critique d'une architecture japonaise contemporaine qui ignore à la fois le climat et le paysage.»

The museum straddles a canal in an almost effortless way, obviating the programmatic difficulty imposed on the architect.

Die Museumsbrücke überspannt scheinbar mühelos einen Kanal. Die Probleme, die das Raumprogramm mit sich brachte, werden so gelöst.

Le musée franchit un canal, gommant sans effort cette difficulté du programme imposé.

Floor to ceiling glazing and extremely thin support columns give an impression of extremely light architecture in these views.

Eine geschosshohe Verglasung und sehr schlanke Stützen vermitteln den Eindruck extremer Leichtigkeit.

Des murs de verre sur toute la hauteur et des colonnes de soutien extrêmement fines créent une impression d'extrême légèreté.

The high ceilings and verticality of spaces give a slightly technological aspect to the museum, but unite its design and allow the works to speak for themselves.

Die hohen Räume und ihre Vertikalität geben dem Museum eine leicht technische Prägung, vereinheitlichen aber den Entwurf und lassen die Kunstwerke für sich selbst sprechen.

Les hauts plafonds et la verticalité des espaces confèrent au musée un aspect un peu technologique, tout en renforçant l'unité du plan et en laissant aux œuvres exposées la liberté de s'exprimer.

HENNING LARSEN

Henning Larsens Tegnestue
Vesterbrogade 76
1620 Copenhagen V
Denmark

Tel: +45 82 33 30 00
Fax: +45 82 33 30 99
e-mail: hlt@hlt.dk
Web: www.hlt.dk

Copenhagen Opera House

HENNING LARSEN was born in 1925. He attended the Royal Academy of Fine Arts in Copenhagen where he received a degree in architecture in 1950. He then studied at the AA in London (1951–52) and at MIT (1952). He created his firm HLT in 1959 in Copenhagen. HLT had a staff of 90 persons in early 2005, and was run and owned by Larsen and six partners: Peer Teglgaard Jeppesen, Lars Steffensen, Troels Troelsen, Mette Kynne Fransen, Louis Becker and Michael Christensen. His work includes the Ministry of Foreign Affairs in Riyadh, Saudi Arabia, winner of a 1989 Aga Khan Award for Architecture (1982–84); the expansion of the Freie Universität, Berlin (1973–82); the Nation Center in Nairobi Kenya, built for the Aga Khan (1987–92); University of Physics and Astronomy, Stockholm (1998–2000); and the IT University of Copenhagen (2002–04). Work in progress includes the Eyes of Tirana, a three-building mixed-use complex of 48 000 m² with a 26-story tower in Tirana, Albania; the Copenhagen Business School. A considerable part of HLT's work has been won through competitions. Approximately 50 percent of their projects have been built in Denmark. As the firm explains, "The architectural aim of HLT is to design the physical surroundings – from urban area development plans, urban spatiality and buildings, to components and furniture design – in a way that ensures the user a perceptual design and a solid functionality."

HENNING LARSEN, geboren 1925, studierte an der Königlichen Akademie der Künste in Kopenhagen und schloss sein Architekturstudium 1950 ab. Anschließend studierte er an der Architectural Association in London (1951–52) und am Massachusetts Institute of Technology (1952). 1959 gründete er sein Büro HLT in Kopenhagen. Anfang 2005 hatte das Büro 90 Mitarbeiter. Es gehört Larsen und seinen sechs Partnern – Peer Teglgaard Jeppesen, Lars Steffensen, Troels Troelsen, Mette Kynne Fransen, Louis Becker und Michael Christensen – und wird von ihnen gemeinsam geführt. Folgende Projekte wurden u. a. realisiert: das Außenministerium in Riad, Saudi Arabien (Gewinner des Aga-Khan-Preises für Architektur, 1982–84), ein Erweiterungsbau für das Physik-Institut der Freien Universität Berlin (1973–82), das Nation Center in Nairobi, Kenia (für den Aga Khan, 1987–92), die Universität für Physik und Astronomie in Stockholm (1998–2000) und die IT Universität in Kopenhagen (2002–04). Zu den zurzeit in Planung bzw. im Bau befindlichen Projekten gehören »Die Augen von Tirana«, ein multifunktionaler Komplex aus drei Gebäuden mit insgesamt 48 000 m² mit einem 26-geschossigen Turm in Tirana, Albanien, ferner die Copenhagen Business School. Ein beträchtlicher Anteil der Bauten des Büros resultieren aus gewonnenen Wettbewerben. Ungefähr die Hälfte aller Projekte wurde in Dänemark realisiert. Das Büro formuliert seine architektonische Zielsetzung so: »HTL ist bestrebt, die physische Umgebung zu entwerfen – angefangen mit städtebaulichen Entwicklungsplanungen, über urbane Räume und Gebäude bis hin zu Konstruktionselementen und Möbeln – auf eine Weise, die dem Benutzer ein erkennbares Entwurfskonzept und eine solide Funktionalität bietet.«

Né en 1925, **HENNING LARSEN** est diplômé en architecture de l'Académie royale des bBeaux-aArts de Copenhague (1950) et a ensuite étudié à l'AA de Londres, (1951–52) et au MIT, Boston (1952), avant d'ouvrir son agence, HLT, en 1959 à Copenhague. Elle compte aujourd'hui six dirigeants associés – Larsen, Peer Teglgaard Jeppesen, Lars Steffensen, Troels Troelsen, Mette Kynne Fransen, Louis Becker et Michael Christensen – et 90 quatre-vingt-dix collaborateurs. Parmi ses réalisations : le ministère des affaires étrangères de Riyadh, Arabie saoudite (1982–1984), récompensé par le prix Aga Khan pour l'architecture en 1989 ; l'extension de la Freie Universität de Berlin (1973–82) ; le Nation Center, construit pour l'Aga Khan, Nairobi, Kenya (1987–92) ; l'Université de physique et d'astronomie de Stockholm (1998–2000) ; l'Université d'IT, Copenhague (2002–04). Actuellement en chantier : les « Les Yeux de Tirana », complexe un ensemble de trois immeubles d'habitations, de bureaux et de commerces de 418 000 m² en trois immeubles, dont une tour de 26 niveaux étages (Tirana, Albanie) ; la Business School de Copenhague (2005–07). Une proportion considérable de ces projets a été remportée à l'occasion de concours et environ 50% d'entre eux ont été réalisés au Danemark. Comme l'explique l'agence : « L'objectif architectural de HLT est de concevoir un environnement physique – des plans d'urbanisme, des espaces urbains et des immeubles jusqu'aux composants divers et mobilier – de sorte que l'utilisateur perçoit la qualité de conception et bénéficie d'un fonctionnalisme évident. »

COPENHAGEN OPERA HOUSE

Copenhagen, Denmark, 2001–04

*Floor area: 41 000 m². Client: The A. P. Møller and Chastine Mc-Kinney Møller Foundation.
Cost: $442 million (estimate)*

It was in the year 2000 that the City of Copenhagen asked three architects, West 8, Sjoerd Soeters and Henning Larsens Tegnestue, to prepare a study of the future urban development of the city's harbor. Larsen was given responsibility for the inner harbor, while the other two firms worked on the northern and southern areas. As they explain, "We suggested three large building volumes situated at Dokøen, Christiansholm and Kvæsthusbroen in order to create a new strong cultural center with the water and the harbor as the unifying elements." The completion of this study in 2000 coincided with the offer of the A. P. Møller Foundation to donate an opera and ballet house to the city. Larsen was selected to design the structure, located in the central harbor facing Amalienborg, the Royal residence. As the firm describes their building, "An opera house comprises a variety of functions and rooms divided into two main areas: the front of the house and the backstage. The front of the house consists of the foyer and the auditorium, whereas the backstage contains the stage area including workshop facilities, dressing rooms, costume shops, administration offices and rehearsal facilities for singers, choir, soloists, orchestra and ballet. The spectacular floating cantilevered roof is the unifying element of the Opera, and its architectural function is to bring together and control the various spaces. The interaction of the auditorium shell and the public harbor space is the key element of the design." The large, 1400-seat auditorium is at the center of this 41 000 m², but it includes a total of six performance stages and a smaller studio stage. Unseen, as much as 13 meters below sea level, rehearsal rooms and other facilities occupy 12 000 m². The striking roof with its 32-meter overhang covers a four-story arched foyer. A paved area in front of the structure leads directly to the harbor.

2000 erhielten drei Architekturbüros – West 8, Sjoerd Soeters und Henning Larsens Tegnestue – von der Stadt Kopenhagen den Auftrag, Studien für die zukünftige städtebauliche Entwicklung des Kopenhagener Hafens anzufertigen. Larsen wurde die Planung des inneren Hafens übertragen, die beiden anderen Büros befassten sich mit dem nördlichen bzw. südlichen Bereich. HLT erläutern: »Wir schlugen drei große Baukörper am Dokøen, Christiansholm und Kvæsthusbroen vor, um ein neues und kraftvolles kulturelles Zentrum zu schaffen. Das Wasser und der Hafen bilden dabei den übergeordneten Hintergrund.« Die Fertigstellung der Studie im Jahr 2000 fiel mit dem Angebot der Stiftung A. P. Møller zusammen, der Stadt ein Opern- und Balletthaus zu stiften. Larsen wurde für den Entwurf des Gebäudes ausgewählt. Es befindet sich im Zentralhafen gegenüber Amalienborg, dem königlichen Schloss. Das Büro beschreibt das Gebäude so: »Ein Opernhaus beinhaltet eine Vielzahl von Funktionen und Räumen, die in zwei Hauptbereiche aufgeteilt sind – einen vorderen und einen hinteren Teil. Im vorderen Teil befinden sich das Foyer und der Zuschauerraum, der hintere Teil umfasst den Bühnenbereich, zu dem die Werkstätten, die Künstlergarderoben, die Gewandmeisterei, die Büros der Verwaltung sowie Probebühnen und -räume für die Sänger, den Chor, die Solisten, das Orchester und das Ballett gehören. Das spektakulär vorkragende, schwebende Dach ist das bauliche Element der Oper, das alle Bereiche vereint. Seine architektonische Funktion besteht darin, die verschiedenen Räume zusammenzufassen und zu ›kontrollieren‹. Die Wechselwirkung zwischen der ›Schale‹ des Auditoriums und dem öffentlichen Hafenraum bestimmt den Entwurf.« Der große Zuschauerraum mit 1400 Plätzen ist das Herzstück des 41 000 m² großen Baus; außerdem gibt es sechs weitere Bühnen und eine kleinere Studiobühne. Unsichtbar, bis zu 13 m unterhalb des Meeresspiegels, liegen – auf einer Fläche von 12 000 m² – die Proberäume und andere Nutzungsbereiche. Unter dem beeindruckenden, 32 m vorkragenden Dach befindet sich das viergeschossige geschwungene Foyer. Ein gepflasterter Bereich vor dem Gebäude führt direkt zum Hafen.

C'est en 2000 que la ville de Copenhague a demandé à trois architectes, West 8, Sjoerd Soeters et Henning Larsens Tegnestue, d'étudier le développement de la zone portuaire de la capitale. Larsen a pris en charge le port intérieur tandis que les deux autres agences se chargeaient des zones nord et sud. Comme ils l'expliquent : « Nous avons suggéré la construction de trois grands volumes à Dokøen, Christiansholm et Kvæsthusbroen, afin de créer un centre culturel consistant fort, unifié par la présence de l'eau et du port. » L'achèvement de cette étude en 2000 coïncida avec l'offre de la Fondation A. P. Møller d'offrir le financement d'un lieu pour l'opéra et la danse à Copenhague. Larsen a été sélectionné pour en concevoir le bâtiment situé dans le port central, face à Amalienborg, la résidence royale. L'agence présente ainsi son projet : « Un opéra remplit comporte une certaine variété de fonctions et de salles que l'on peut répartir en deux zones principales : le ‹devant et l'arrière de la scène› et les coulisses. La première zone consiste en un foyer et une grande salle, la seconde comprend la scène, les ateliers, les loges des artistes, les ateliers de costumes, les bureaux de l'administration et les studios de répétition pour les chanteurs, les chœurs, les solistes, l'orchestre et le ballet. Le spectaculaire toit en suspension porte-à-faux, dont la fonction architecturale consiste à réunir et contrôler les différents volumes, est l'élément unificateur majeur. L'interaction entre la coque de la salle et le lieu d'accueil du public donnant sur le port est un autre élément clé du projet. »La grande salle de 1400 places occupe est le cœur de ce monument de 41 000 m² qui comprend par ailleurs six salles de spectacles et une scène plus petite. Les salles de répétition et autres équipements, invisibles car implantés jusqu'à 13 m sous le niveau de la mer, occupent 12 000 m². Les spectaculaires 32 m de porte-à-faux du toit recouvrent surplombent le foyer incurvé en arc de cercle sur quatre niveaux. Devant le bâtiment, une aire pavée descend jusqu'à l'eau.

The extremely thin canopy above the entrance plaza might bring to mind certain designs of Jean Nouvel (Tours or Lucerne) but Larsen's Royal Danish Opera remains a truly unique piece of architecture, a cultural symbol for the Danish capital.

Das extrem flache Vordach über der Eingangsplaza erinnert ein wenig an Jean Nouvels Entwürfe für Tours und Luzern. Gleichwohl ist Larsens Opernhaus ein einzigartiges Bauwerk und kulturelles Symbol der dänischen Hauptstadt.

L'auvent d'une grande finesse qui surplombe le parvis de l'entrée peut rappeler certains projets de Jean Nouvel (Tours ou Lucerne), mais l'Opéra royal du Danemark de Larsen reste une œuvre originale qui est devenue le nouveau symbole culturel de la capitale danoise.

Sitting near the water, the Opera appears, in the views above, to resemble a great ocean liner that has pulled up in the port. A section (below) confirms the nautical appearance and design of the structure.

Oben: Das am Wasser gelegene Opernhaus wirkt wie ein im Hafen vor Anker liegender Ozeandampfer. Der Schnitt (unten) verdeutlicht das nautische Erscheinungsbild und Design des Gebäudes.

Implanté en bordure de mer, l'Opéra fait penser, dans les images ci-dessus, à un grand paquebot venu s'ancrer dans le port. La coupe ci-dessous confirme l'aspect et la conception "nautique" de la structure

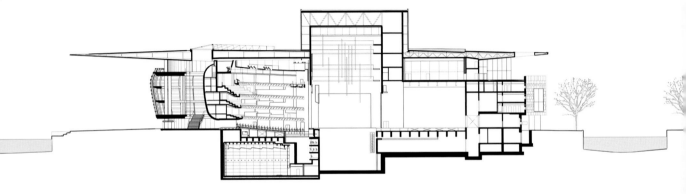

The full auditorium takes on the warmth that may seem to be missing from much of the rest of the architecture of the Opera. This might not, however, be construed as a fault of the architecture, since the living heart of the project is the concert hall.

Der Hauptsaal beansprucht die Wärme für sich, die vielen anderen Räumen des Opernhauses zu fehlen scheint. Dies sollte aber nicht als ein Mangel der Architektur gewertet werden, da das Herzstück des Gebäudes ja der Hauptsaal ist.

La grande salle exprime une chaleur qui peut sembler faire défaut à une grande partie du reste du bâtiment. Elle représente le cœur du projet.

MAYA LIN

Maya Lin Studio
112 Prince Street
New York, New York 10012
USA

Tel: +1 212 941 6463
Fax: +1 212 941 6464
e-mail: mlinstudio@earthlink.net

Riggio-Lynch Chapel

MAYA LIN, born in 1959, attended Yale College and the Yale School of Architecture, receiving her Masters in Architecture in 1986. She created her office, Maya Lin Studio, in New York the same year. By that time she had already created what remains her most famous work, the Vietnam Veterans' Memorial on the Mall in Washington D.C. (1981). Other sculptural work includes her Civil Rights Memorial in Montgomery, Alabama (1989); and *Groundswell*, at the Wexner Center of the Arts, Columbus, Ohio (1993). She completed the design for the Museum of African Art in New York (with David Hotson, 1993); the Weber Residence, Williamstown, Massachusetts (1994); and the Asia/Pacific/American Studies Department, New York University, New York (1997). Recent work includes the Greyston Bakery, Greyston Foundation, Yonkers, New York (2003); the Langston Hughes Library, Childrens' Defense Fund, Clinton, Tennessee (1999, with Martella Associates, Architects); and the Riggio-Lynch Chapel, Children's Defense Fund (2004), published here.

MAYA LIN, geboren 1959, studierte am Yale College und an der Yale School of Architecture, wo sie 1986 ihren Master of Architecture erwarb. Im selben Jahr gründete sie ihr eigenes Büro Maya Lin Studio. Zu diesem Zeitpunkt hatte sie schon ihr bis heute bekanntestes Werk, das Vietnam Veterans' Memorial an der Mall in Washington D.C., geschaffen (1981). Andere bildhauerische Arbeiten sind u.a. das Civil Rights Memorial in Montgomery, Alabama (1989), und *Groundswell* für das Wexner Center of Arts in Columbus, Ohio (1993). Realisierte Bauten sind das Museum of African Art in New York (mit David Hotson, 1993), die Weber Residence in Williamstown, Massachusetts (1994), und das Asia/Pacific/American Studies Department der New York University in New York (1997). Zu ihren jüngsten Projekten gehören die Greyston Bäckerei der Greyston Foundation in Yonkers, New York (2003) sowie die Langston-Hughes-Bibliothek (mit Martella Associates, Architects, 1999) und die Riggio-Lynch-Kapelle, beide für den Childrens' Defense Fund in Clinton, Tennessee (2004).

MAYA LIN, née en 1959, a fait ses études au Yale College et à la Yale School of Architecture, Master of Architecture (1986). Elle ouvre son agence, Maya Lin Studio, à New York la même année, mais a déjà créé ce qui reste à ce jour son œuvre la plus célèbre, le Mémorial des vétérans de la guerre du Vietnam sur le National Mall de Washington (1981). Elle a réalisé d'autres œuvres de nature sculpturale, comme le Mémorial des droits civiques à Montgomery, Alabama (1989) et *Groundswell* pour le Wexner Center for the Arts, Columbus, Ohio (1993). Par ailleurs, elle a réalisé le Museum for African Art, New York (avec David Hotson, 1993); la Weber Residence, Williamstown, Massachusetts (1994) et le département des études Asie/Pacifique/Amérique de la New York University, New York (1997). Parmi ses récents travaux : la Greyston Bakery, Greyston Foundation, Yonkers, New York (2003); la Langston Hughes Library (avec Martella Associates, Architects) et la Riggio-Lynch Chapel publiée ici, pour le Children's Defense Fund, Clinton, Tennessee (1999 et 2004).

RIGGIO-LYNCH CHAPEL

Clinton, Tennessee, USA, 2004

Floor area: 887 m². Client: The Children's Defense Fund.
Cost: $2.2 million

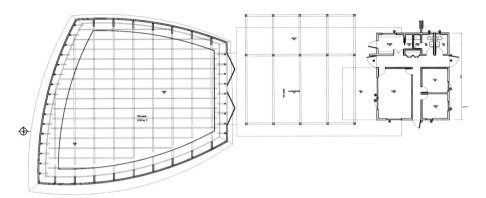

Lin's asymmetrical plan and the ship-like nature of the design are obvious in the drawings to the left and the image above.

Links: Der Grundriss zeigt die Asymmetrie der Kapelle. Oben: Der an ein Schiff erinnernde Gebäudekörper.

Le plan asymétrique de Maya Lin et la nature nautique du projet sont évidents dans les dessins (à gauche) et l'image ci-dessus.

Working with Bialosky + Partners, Architects & Planners, Maya Lin created this 887 m² chapel with architectural grade glu-lam beams, concrete floors and a cypress wood exterior. As she explains, "The concept for the design of the Chapel comes from The Children's Defense Fund's Motto: 'Dear Lord be good to me. The Sea is so wide and my boat is so small.' The abstracted image of a boat or ark that is constructed out of wood and forms the main body of the Chapel is at the heart of the design." The simple yet sculptural presence of the main building is unusual and succeeds in sublimating the boat image while making the reference clear and present. Maya Lin also conceived the structure, with its open passageway to a small concrete administrative building and meeting room, so that it could on some occasions receive large numbers of people, without overwhelming the other structures on Haley Farm. Once the retreat of the author Alex Haley, the Farm is the Children's Defense Fund's center for leadership training and the development of new ideas to help America's children. Lin's Langston Hughes Library is located on the same Farm. The new chapel is named after the main donor for the project, Leonard Riggio, chairman of the booksellers Barnes & Noble, and William Lynch, a political activist and former New York City Deputy Mayor.

In Zusammenarbeit mit den Architekten Bialosky + Partners entwarf Maya Lin die 887 m² große Kapelle, die mit hochwertigen Leimholzbindern, Betonböden und einer Außenverkleidung aus Zypressenholz ausgestattet ist. Lin erläutert das Projekt: »Das Konzept für den Bau der Kapelle basiert auf dem Leitspruch des Childrens' Defense Fund: ›Lieber Gott, sei gut zu mir. Das Meer ist so groß und mein Boot ist so klein.‹ Herzstück des Entwurfs ist das abstrahierte Bild eines Bootes oder einer Arche aus Holz, das den Hauptraum der Kapelle bildet.« Die einfache, sculpturale Präsenz des Hauptgebäudes ist ungewöhnlich und überhöht auf überzeugende Weise das Bild des Bootes; gleichzeitig ist die Referenz klar und präsent. Maya Lin entwarf auch das Gesamtkonzept der Anlage: Dazu gehört ein offener Gang zu einem kleinen Verwaltungsgebäude (mit angeschlossenem Versammlungsraum) aus Beton. So können bei besonderen Anlässen viele Besucher empfangen werden, ohne die Kapazitäten der anderen Gebäude auf dem Gelände zu überfordern. Einst ein Rückzugsort des Schriftstellers Alex Haley, ist die Farm das Zentrum des Childrens' Defense Fund, in dem das Führungspersonal der Organisation ausgebildet wird und neue Ideen entwickelt werden, um den Kindern in Amerika zu helfen. Auch die von Lin entworfene Langston-Hughes-Bibliothek befindet sich auf dem Gelände. Die neue Kapelle wurde nach den Hauptsponsoren Leonard Riggio, Vorsitzender des Buchverlags Barnes & Noble, und William Lynch, politischer Aktivist und früherer Zweiter Bürgermeister von New York City, benannt.

En collaboration avec Bialosky + Partners, Architects & Planners, Maya Lin a conçu cette chapelle de 887 m² dont la construction fait appel à des poutres en bois lamellé-collé, des sols en béton et des façades en cyprès. Pour elle, « le concept de cette chapelle vient de la devise du Children's Defense Fund – *Seigneur, sois bon avec moi, la mer est si vaste et mon bateau si petit.* L'image abstraite d'un bateau ou d'une ‹ arche de Noé › en bois est au cœur de la conception ». La forte présence du bâtiment principal, à la fois simple et sculptural, parvient à sublimer l'image d'un bateau tout en conservant la clarté de la référence. Maya Lin a également conçu la structure, avec son passage ouvert vers un petit bâtiment administratif en béton et une salle de réunion qui peut recevoir à certaines occasions un grand nombre de fidèles, sans envahir les autres installations du domaine de Haley Farm. Jadis retraite de l'auteur Alex Haley, la ferme est le centre du Children's Defense Fund pour la formation au leadership et la recherche d'idées nouvelles pour l'aide aux enfants américains. La bibliothèque Langston Hughes, également de Lin, est située à proximité. La nouvelle chapelle porte les noms de son principal donateur, Leonard Riggio, président de la chaîne de librairies Barnes & Noble, et de William Lynch, politicien et ancien maire adjoint de New York.

Eschewing Modernist symmetry, Maya Lin achieves a sense of motion and a connection to the origins of the church with her design.

Maya Lin vermeidet die Symmetrie der Moderne; sie erzeugt ein Gefühl von Bewegung und stellt einen Bezug zu den kirchlichen Ursprüngen her.

Loin de la symétrie moderniste, Maya Lin insuffle la notion de mouvement à ce projet et recrée le lien avec les origines historiques de l'église.

LLPS ARQUITECTOS

llps arquitectos
Estébanez Calderón 5, 6° F
28 020 Madrid
Spain

Tel: +34 915 71 15 54
Fax: +34 915 71 15 54
e-mail: info@llps-arquitectos.com
web. www.llps-arquitectos.com

Juan Llorente Orejas, Eduardo Pérez Gomez and Miguel Ángel Sánchez García were all born in 1972 in Madrid, and studied at the Escuela Técnica Superior de Arquitectura de Madrid (1997 and 1998). Juan Llorente Orejas worked in the offices of Javier Bellosillo and Estanislao Pérez-Pita; Eduardo Pérez Gómez with Andrés Perea Ortega, Javier Bellosillo, Alberto Campo Baeza, and Estanislao Pérez-Pita, while Miguel Ángel Sánchez García worked for Andrés Perea Ortega, Alberto Campo Baeza, Estanislao Pérez-Pita before the three partners founded **LLPS ARQUITECTOS** in 1997. Their projects include a fast food restaurant in Madrid (1996); the House in Humanes published here (2001); the Municipal Sports Hall, Las Palmas de Gran Canaria (2002); Social Housing, Madrid (2003); Apartment Building; Guadalajara, Spain (2004); a Social Center, Almoguera, Spain (2004); and an office for architects in Guadalajara (2004).

Juan Llorente Orejas, Eduardo Pérez Gómez und Miguel Ángel Sánchez García, alle 1972 in Madrid geboren, studierten an der Escuela Técnica Superior de Arquitectura in Madrid (Abschluss 1997 und 1998). Juan Llorente Orejas war bei Javier Bellosillo und Estanislao Pérez-Pita beschäftigt. Eduardo Pérez Gómez arbeitete bei Andrés Perea Ortega, Javier Bellosillo, Alberto Campo Baeza und bei Estanislao Pérez-Pita. Miguel Ángel Sánchez García war bei Andrés Perea Ortega, Alberto Campo Baeza und ebenfalls bei Estanislao Pérez-Pita tätig. 1997 gründeten die drei Partner **LLPS ARQUITECTOS**. Sie haben u. a. folgende Projekte realisiert: ein Fast-Food-Restaurant in Madrid (1996), das hier gezeigte Haus in Humanes (2001), eine Gemeindesporthalle in Las Palmas, Gran Canaria (2002), sozialen Wohnungsbau in Madrid (2003) und ein Apartmenthaus in Guadalajara (2004) sowie ein Sozialzentrum in Almoguera (2004) und Büroräume für Architekten in Guadalajara (2004).

Juan Llorente Orejas, Eduardo Pérez Gómez et Miguel Ángel Sánchez Garcia sont tous trois nés à Madrid en 1972 et ont étudié à l'Escuela Técnica Superior de Arquitectura de Madrid, ETSAM (1997 et 1998). Juan Llorente Orejas a travaillé dans les agences de Javier Bellposillo, Alberto Campo Baeza et Estanslao Pérez-Pita, Miguel Ángel Sánchez Garcia pour Andrés Perea Ortega, Alberto Campo Baeza, Estanislao Pérez-Pita avant que les trois associés ne fondent **LLPS ARQUITECTOS** en 1997. Parmi leurs projets : un établissement de restauration rapide, Madrid (1996) ; la maison à Humanes publiée ici (2001) ; une salle municipale des sports, Las Palmas de Gran Canaria (2002) ; des logements sociaux, Madrid (2003) ; un immeuble d'appartements, Guadalajara (2004) ; un centre social, Almoguera (2004) et une agence d'architecture, Guadalajara (2004).

HOUSE IN HUMANES

Humanes, Guadalajara, Spain, 2001

Floor area: 209 m². Client: Pedro Ramón López Vázquez.
Cost: €150 000

Designed in 1999, this 209 m² house occupies a 2000 m² site and is made of concrete, stone, wood and steel. Set in the village of Humanes in the province of Guadalajara, the site offers views of fields and mountains. The client requested a fireplace and a large covered terrace that can be used for summer dining. Placing the residence at the southeast of the lot, the architects sought to create a protected outdoor space with a visual relation to the landscape. As they explain, "The key element of the project is a triple vertical space that is generated by the living-room around the chimney... The formal language of the project is created by the superposition of two blocks resulting in an L-shaped building, articulated by the vertical space of the chimney. The first block is a one-story volume that includes the dining room, kitchen, a bathroom and the master bedroom, located as required by the client on the ground floor. The other block is a two-story volume. In the lower area a longitudinal space contains the living room, which continues outwards towards a porch, doubling its dimensions. The other bedrooms and a bathroom are located on the upper floor of this volume."

Das Haus mit einer Grundfläche von 209 m² wurde 1999 entworfen. Es steht auf einem 2000 m² großen Grundstück; hauptsächlich verwendete Materialien sind Beton, Stein, Holz und Stahl. Vom Grundstück, das im Dorf Humanes in der Region Guadalajara liegt, bietet sich ein Blick über Felder und Berge. Der Bauherr wünschte einen offenen Kamin und eine große überdachte Terrasse, auf der man im Sommer das Abendessen einnehmen kann. Die Architekten platzierten das Haus in der süd-östlichen Ecke des Grundstücks, um so einen geschützten Außenraum zu schaffen, der einen Sichtbezug zur Landschaft hat. Sie erläutern: »Das wesentliche Element des Entwurfs ist ein dreigeschossiger vertikaler Raum, der sich aus der Anordnung des Wohnraumes um den Kamin ergibt... Die formale Sprache des Hauses wird durch die Überlagerung von zwei Volumen bestimmt. Dadurch ergibt sich ein L-förmiges Gebäude, das durch den vertikalen Raum des Kamins gegliedert wird. Das eine Volumen ist der eingeschossige Baukörper mit Essraum, Küche, Badezimmer und Schlafzimmer der Bauherren. Auf ihren Wunsch liegt der letztgenannte Raum im Erdgeschoss. Der andere Gebäudeteil ist zweigeschossig: Auf der unteren Ebene liegt der längliche Wohnraum, der sich nach außen auf die überdachte Terrasse ausdehnt und so seine Größe verdoppelt. Im Obergeschoss liegen weitere Schlafzimmer und ein Badezimmer.«

Située dans le village d'Humanes, dans la province de Guadalajara, cette maison de 209 m² en béton, pierre, bois et verre, a été conçue en 1999 pour un terrain de 2000 m² qui donne sur des champs et des montagnes. Le client souhaitait une cheminée et une grande terrasse couverte pour ses dîners d'été. En implantant la maison au sud-est de la parcelle, les architectes ont cherché à créer un espace extérieur protégé en relation visuelle avec le paysage : « L'élément clé du projet est le triple volume vertical du séjour autour de la cheminée... Le langage formel est ici créé par la superposition de deux blocs, ce qui donne une construction en L, articulée par la verticale de la cheminée. Le premier bloc est un volume d'un seul niveau qui reçoit la salle à manger, la cuisine, une salle de bains et la chambre principale en rez-de-chaussée, comme le voulait le client. L'autre bloc est un volume de deux niveaux avec, en bas, le séjour, en longueur, qui se poursuit vers l'extérieur par un porche et double ainsi sa dimension et, au-dessus, les autres chambres et une salle de bains. »

The powerful interpenetrating volumes of the house are designed in a mode of minimalist austerity, which certainly does not diminish their power, quite the contrary.

Die kraftvollen, sich durchdringenden Volumina des Hauses sind durch minimalistische Strenge gekennzeichnet. Dies mindert ihre Kraft nicht, sondern verstärkt sie noch.

Les puissants volumes imbriqués de la maison de Humanes sont dessinés dans un esprit minimaliste qui renforce leur pouvoir.

Using sunlight and the effects created by successive volumes and alternation of transparent and opaque surfaces, the architects come close to a sense of perfect design, where light and shadow change space with each passing hour.

Die Architekten arbeiten mit dem Sonnenlicht und den Effekten, die sich aus der Abfolge der Volumina ergeben; auch durch den Wechsel von transparenten und opaken Flächen kommen sie einem »perfekten« Entwurf nahe. Licht und Schatten verändern die Räume ständig.

En utilisant la lumière naturelle et les effets générés par la succession des volumes et l'alternance de surfaces transparentes et opaques, les architectes se rapprochent d'une architecture parfaite dans laquelle l'ombre et la lumière modifient la perception de l'espace au fil des heures.

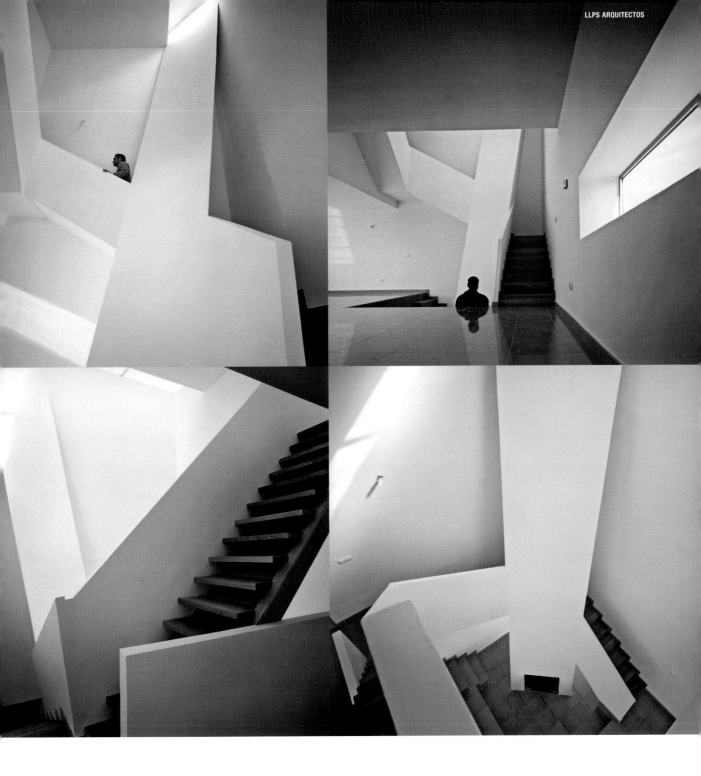

Stairways and interpenetrating volumes create a sense of labyrinthine complexity despite the overall simplicity of the design.

Treppen und die sich durchdringenden Baukörper schaffen trotz der insgesamt einfachen Gebäudestruktur eine labyrinthartige Komplexität.

Les escaliers et les volumes imbriqués créent une complexité de labyrinthe malgré la simplicité d'ensemble de la conception.

LTL LEWIS.TSURUMAKI.LEWIS

LTL Architects, PLLC
147 Essex Street, New York, New York 10002
USA

Tel: +1 212 505 5955, Fax: +1 212 505 1648
e-mail: office@LTLwork.net, Web: www.LTLarchitects.com

Paul Lewis received his Master of Architecture from Princeton University in 1992, and studied previously at Wesleyan University (B. A. 1988). He is a principal and founding partner of **LEWIS TSURUMAKI LEWIS**, created in 1993. He was an associate at Diller + Scofidio, New York (1993–97). Marc Tsurumaki received his Master of Architecture degree from Princeton in 1991, after attending college at the University of Virginia. He worked as a project architect in the office of Joel Sanders in New York (1991–97) prior to creating Lewis Tsurumaki Lewis. David J. Lewis completed his architectural studies at Princeton in 1995 after attending Cornell and Carlton College. He was the Publications Director, Cornell University, College of Architecture, Art, and Planning (1997–98). He worked at Peter Guggenheimer, Architects, PPC, New York as an assistant (1995–96) and in the office of Daniel Libeskind in Berlin (1993) before creating LTL. The firm's recent built projects include: Bornhuetter Hall, Wooster, Ohio (2004); Tides Restaurant, New York (2005); Figge Residence, Wooster, Ohio (2004); Xing Restaurant, New York (2005): and the Ini Ani Coffee Shop, New York (2004). Current projects are: Arthouse Renovation and Expansion, Austin, Texas (2005, contemporary art museum); Residential Tower, Las Vegas, Nevada (2005); Dash Dogs Restaurant, New York (2005); Alexakos Gymnasium, Southhampton, New York (2006); Brown University Bio-Medical Center Renovation; Providence, Rhode Island (2005); HPD Housing, East New York, New York (2006); Allentown House Allentown, Pennsylvania (2006); and the Burns Townhouse, Philadelphia, Pennsylvania (2006).

Paul Lewis studierte erst an der Wesleyan University (B. A. 1988), dann machte er 1992 an der Princeton University seinen Master of Architecture. Er ist Gründungspartner und Geschäftsführer des 1993 eröffneten Büros **LEWIS TSURUMAKI LEWIS**. Bei Diller + Scofidio in New York war er von 1993 bis 1997 assoziierter Partner. Marc Tsurumaki studierte an der University of Virginia und an der Princeton University (Master of Architecture 1991). Bevor er Lewis Tsurumaki Lewis gründete, war er von 1991 bis 1997 Projektarchitekt bei Joel Sanders in New York. David J. Lewis schloss sein Architekturstudium 1995 in Princeton ab, davor studierte er in Cornell und am Carlton College. Von 1997 bis 1998 war er Publications Director am College of Architecture, Art and Planning der Cornell University. Vor der Gründung von LTL arbeitete David Lewis als Assistent bei Peter Guggenheimer, Architects, PPC, in New York und 1993 bei Daniel Libeskind in Berlin. Neuere Projekte des Büros sind u. a. die hier gezeigte Bornhuetter Hall in Wooster, Ohio (2004), das Tides Restaurant in New York (2005), die Figge Residence in Wooster, Ohio (2004), das Xing Restaurant in New York (2005) und der Ini Ani Coffee Shop in New York (2004). Zurzeit in Planung bzw. im Bau sind die Sanierung und Erweiterung des Arthouse (ein Museum für zeitgenössische Kunst) in Austin, Texas (2005), ein Wohnhochhaus in Las Vegas (2005), das Dash Dogs Restaurant in New York (2005), die Alexakos Sporthalle in Southhampton, New York (2006), ferner die Sanierung des Biomedizinischen Zentrums der Brown University in Providence, Rhode Island (2005), HPD Housing in East New York, New York (2006), das Allentown House in Allentown, Pennsylvania (2006), und das Burns Townhouse in Philadelphia, Pennsylvania (2006).

Après avoir étudié à la Wesleyan University (Bachelor of Arts, 1988), Paul Lewis a reçu son Master of Architecture de Princeton University en 1992. Il est le cofondateur et dirigeant directeur de **LEWIS TSURUMAKI LEWIS** (LTL), agence créée en 1993. Il a été associé de Diller + Scofidio, New York (1993–97). Marc Tsurumaki est Master of Architecture M. Arch. de Princeton (1991) après des études à l'Université de Virginie. Il a travaillé comme architecte de projet chez Joel Sander à New York (1991–97) avant de créer LTL. David J. Lewis, après Cornell et Carlton College a achevé ses études d'architecture à Princeton en 1995. Il a été directeur des publications au College of Architecture, Art and Planning de Cornell University (1997–98), a travaillé comme assistant chez Peter Guggenheimer, Architects, PPC, New York (1995–96) et dans l'agence de Daniel Libeskind à Berlin (1993), avant de créer LTL. Parmi les récentes réalisations de l'agence : Bornhuetter Hall, Wooster, Ohio (2004) ; Tides Restaurant Restaurant à New York (2005) ; Ini Ani Coffee Shop à New York (2004). En projet actuellement : rénovation et extension de l'Arthouse, Austin, Texas (2005) ; une tour d'appartements, Las Vegas (2005) ; le Dash Dogs Restaurant à New York (2005) ; l'Alexakos Gymnasium à Southampton, New York (2006) ; la rénovation du Centre biomédical de Brown University, Providence, Rhode Island (2005) ; les logements HPD, East New York (2006) ; Allentown House, Allentown, Pennsylvanie (2006) et l'hôtel de ville Burns, Philadelphie, Pennsylvanie (2006).

FLUFF BAKERY

New York, New York, USA, 2004

Floor area: 72 m². Client: Chow Down Mgt. Inc. Cost: $250 000

Created at 751 Ninth Avenue in New York for a cost of $250 000, this 72 m² space has unusual walls and ceilings, created with strips of felt and stained plywood each individually put in place. A ceiling light was "designed as a custom horizontal chandelier, composed of 42 dimmable incandescent lights connected to a series of branching stainless steel metal armatures." As the architects explain, "This design/build project explores a new architectural surface made from an excessive repetition and assembly of common, banal and cheap materials. More akin to a gallery installation, the interior surface and the chandelier were built and installed by the architects." The strip cladding also creates a dynamic effect that sweeps visitors into the space beginning with a floor-to-ceiling glass façade. Despite their rather sophisticated background, the architects demonstrate with the **FLUFF BAKERY** that they are willing to get directly involved in an original, small-scale project.

751 Ninth Avenue lautet die Adresse der Bäckerei Fluff in New York. Die Baukosten für den 72 m² großen Raum betrugen umgerechnet 210 500 Euro. Die ungewöhnliche Wand- und Deckenverkleidung besteht aus dünnen Filzstreifen und gebeiztem Sperrholz, jeder Streifen wurde einzeln montiert. Die Deckenbeleuchtung bildet ein »speziell angefertigter ›horizontaler Kronleuchter‹. Er besteht aus 42 dimmbaren Leuchtstoffröhren, die an sich verzweigenden Stahlarmen befestigt sind.« Die Architekten erläutern: »Mit dem Entwurf bzw. dem realisierten Raum erforschen wir eine neue architektonische Oberfläche, die aus der exzessiven Wiederholung und der Verwendung von gewöhnlichen, einfachen und billigen Materialien entsteht. Die Oberflächen und der ›Kronleuchter‹ – Elemente, die eher Installationen in einer Galerie ähneln – wurden von den Architekten selbst hergestellt und montiert.« Die streifenartige Wandverkleidung hat auch einen dynamischen Effekt, der den Besucher in den Raum hineinzieht. Eingeleitet wird dieser Effekt durch die raumhoch verglaste Fassade. Ihren eher intellektuellen Anspruch hinter sich lassend beweisen die Architekten mit der **BÄCKEREI FLUFF**, dass sie bereit sind, sich auf ein originelles, kleines Projekt einzulassen.

Aménagé 751 Ninth Avenue à New York pour un budget de 210 000 d'euros, ce local de 72 m² présente de curieux murs et plafonds revêtus de minces bandes de feutre et de contreplaqué teinté, mises en place une par à une. Au plafond est suspendu un luminaire « conçu comme un lustre horizontal sur mesure composé de 42 tubes fluorescents rhéostatés montés sur une série de branches en acier inoxydable ». Comme l'explique l'architecte : « De sa conception à sa réalisation, ce projet explore une nouvelle surface architecturale composée d'une répétition et d'un assemblage pléthoriques de matériaux communs et bon marché dans un esprit d'excès. Tenant plus de l'installation d'une galerie d'art, ces surfaces et ce lustre ont été fabriqués et installés par nous. » Le « bardage » de fins bandeaux crée un effet dynamique qui happe les clients dans le volume ouvert sur la rue par une façade en verre du sol au plafond. Malgré leur formation assez sophistiquée, les architectes démontrent avec la **BOULANGERIE FLUFF** qu'ils n'hésitent pas à s'impliquer directement à fond dans un projet original, même de petite échelle.

The architects are given to complex effects created with "ordinary" materials. Here, reflections and lighting combine to make it difficult to determine where inside begins and outside ends.

Mit »gewöhnlichen« Materialien erzielen die Architekten komplexe Effekte. Reflexionen und die Belichtung führen hier dazu, dass nicht ohne Weiteres erkennbar ist, wo innen anfängt und außen aufhört.

Les architectes ont privilégié les effets complexes créés par des matériaux « ordinaires ». Ici, reflets et éclairage naturel se combinent pour rendre indiscernable la limite entre l'intérieur et l'extérieur.

BORNHUETTER HALL

The College of Wooster, Wooster, Ohio, USA, 2003–04

Floor area: 4413 m². Client: The College of Wooster.
Cost: $6.9 million

Though campus buildings obey an
implacable economic logic and are
rarely permitted to show much architectural originality, LTL has managed
here to give variety to the entrance
sequence, which confirms the
impression that minimalism is no
longer quite in fashion.

Campusgebäude gehorchen einer
unerbittlichen ökonomischen Logik
und zeichnen sich nur selten durch
architektonische Originalität aus.
LTL gelingt es jedoch, die Eingangs-
sequenz sehr abwechslungsreich
zu gestalten. Der Eindruck, dass
der Minimalismus ein wenig aus
der Mode gekommen ist, wird hier
bestätigt.

Sur les campus, les bâtiments
obéissent à une logique économique
implacable et ne s'autorisent que
rarement à faire preuve d'originalité
architecturale. LTL a pourtant réussi
à apporter de la variété dans la
séquence de l'entrée, confirmant
l'impression que le minimalisme est
un peu passé de mode.

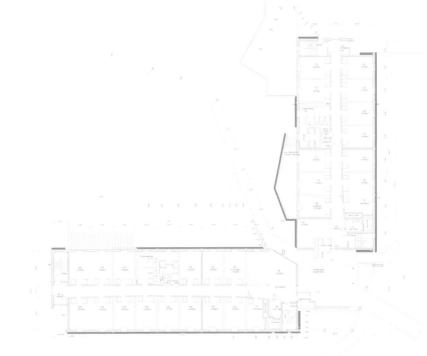

This new residence hall for Wooster College includes housing for 185 students, "a director's apartment, seven lounges, six study nooks and a large multipurpose room." Extensive interviews with students, staff, administrators, donors and trustees were carried out before the completion of the design. Formed out of two separate wings joined together by an outdoor courtyard, **BORNHUETTER HALL** is intended to maximize spaces for gathering and social interaction. The architects proudly underline that "The building was built in fourteen months, on time and under budget." Built for a total budget of 8.7 million dollars, of which 6.9 million was devoted to the construction, the building includes a screen of structural glass at the entrance, and pre-patinated copper cladding in the interior of the courtyard. Working with the clients and users of the building, LTL succeeded in creating a convivial atmosphere with relatively limited means, and above all respected the creative aspect of their work in spite of the complex requirements of such a facility.

Das neue Wohngebäude des Wooster College umfasst Wohnungen für 185 Studenten, »eine Wohnung für den Direktor, sieben Lounges, sechs ›Studierecken‹ und einen großen multifunktionalen Raum«. In der Entwurfsphase wurden mit den Studenten, den Angestellten, der Verwaltung, den Spendern und den Treuhändern ausführliche Gespräche geführt. Das Gebäude besteht aus zwei voneinander getrennten Flügeln, die um einen Innenhof angeordnet sind. Mit der **BORNHUETTER HALL** soll das Angebot für Aufenthaltsräume und soziale Kontakte vergrößert werden. Die Architekten betonen nicht ohne Stolz, dass »das Gebäude in 14 Monaten gebaut wurde, innerhalb des Zeitplans blieb und weniger kostete als veranschlagt«. Die Gesamtkosten des Gebäudes betrugen umgerechnet 7,3 Millionen Euro, 5,8 Millionen davon waren reine Baukosten. Der Hofbereich ist nach außen durch eine Wand mit Glasstreifen abgeschlossen, die Fassaden im Hofbereich sind mit vorpatinierten Kupferblechen bekleidet. Indem die Architekten mit den Bauherren und Nutzern zusammenarbeiteten, ist es ihnen gelungen, mit relativ begrenzten Mitteln eine kommunikative Atmosphäre zu schaffen; vor allem aber ließen sie, trotz der komplexen Anforderungen einer solchen Einrichtung, den kreativen Aspekt ihrer Arbeit nicht zu kurz kommen.

Ce nouveau pavillon pour le Wooster College comprend des logements pour 185 étudiants, un appartement pour le directeur, sept salons, six petits bureaux d'étude et une grande salle polyvalente. De multiples entretiens avec les étudiants, le personnel, les administrateurs, les donateurs et les membres du conseil d'administration ont été menés pour nourrir ce projet. Constitué de deux ailes séparéesreliées connectées par une cour, **BORNHUETTER HALL** a voulumet l'accent maximiser sur les relations sociales et les espaces prévus pour les rencontres. Les architectes soulignent avec fierté que « le bâtiment a été édifié en quatorze mois, dans les délais et dans le cadre du budget prévu ».« Réalisé pour un montant total de 7,3 millions d'euros (dont 5,8 pour la construction seule), il se présente sous la forme d'un écran de verre structurel à l'entrée et d'un habillage de cuivre pré-patiné sur la cour intérieure. En travaillant en étroite relation avec le client et les utilisateurs, LTL a réussi à créer une atmosphère conviviale malgré des moyens relativement limités et, surtout, à maintenir sa créativité malgré les multiples contraintes qu'impose ce type d'équipement.

The entrance screen of Bornhuetter Hall divides the exterior world from the inner area of the facility, and yet it does not separate inside and outside.

Die offene Wand im Eingangsbereich schirmt den Innenbereich von der Außenwelt ab, trennt die beiden Bereiche aber nicht vollständig voneinander.

La paroi ouverte dans l'entrée protège l'espace intérieur du monde extérieur, sans séparer tout à fait les deux domaines.

The challenge for the architects was to create agreeable space in the context of limited budgets and strict programmatic requirements, and they seem to have succeeded quite well.

Die Herausforderung bestand darin, mit einem begrenzten Budget angenehme Räume zu schaffen. Dies ist den Architekten offenbar recht gut gelungen.

Le défi que les architectes ont parfaitement relevé consistait à créer un espace agréable dans le cadre d'un budget limité et d'une programmation rigoureuse.

MICHAEL MALTZAN

Michael Maltzan Architecture, Inc.
2801 Hyperion Avenue, Suite 107
Los Angeles, California 90027
USA

Tel: +1 323 913 3098
Fax: +1 323 913 5932
e-mail: info@mmaltzan.com
Web: www.mmaltzan.com

MICHAEL MALTZAN was born in 1959 in Levittown, New York. He holds both a Bachelor of Fine Arts and a Bachelor of Architecture from Rhode Island School of Design (1984, 1985) and a Master of Architecture degree from Harvard (1987). Since establishing his own firm in 1995, Michael Maltzan has been responsible for the design of a wide range of arts, educational, commercial, institutional and residential projects including the Mark Taper Center/Inner-City Arts campus, Harvard/Westlake School's Feldman/Horn Center for the Arts, the Getty Information Institute Digital Laboratory, and MoMA QNS in Long Island City which opened in June 2002. Recent work includes the design of the Kidspace Children's Museum in Pasadena, California, and the UCLA Hammer Museum in Los Angeles. More recently he has worked on the new Sonoma County Museum in Santa Rosa; the Fresno Metropolitan Museum; Pavilion n° 16 for the Architecture Park in Jinhua, China; and the Biblioteca degli Alberti at the Giardini di Porta Nuova in Milan. Maltzan has served as design instructor, lecturer, and visiting critic at The Architectural League of New York, Rhode Island School of Design, UCLA, USC, Harvard University, University of Waterloo, and SCI-Arc.

MICHAEL MALTZAN, geboren 1959 in Levittown im Bundesstaat New York, machte seinen Bachelor of Fine Arts und den Bachelor of Architecture an der Rhode Island School of Design (1984, 1985) und seinen Master of Architecture in Harvard (1987). Seit der Gründung seines eigenen Büros 1995 hat Michael Maltzan Gebäude mit einer großen Bandbreite an Nutzungen entworfen: Kunst- und Bildungsstätten, kommerzielle und institutionelle Einrichtungen sowie Wohnhäuser. Dazu gehören das Mark Taper Center, der Inner City Arts Campus in Harvard, das Feldman/Horn Center for the Arts der Harvard/Westlake School in North Hollywood, ferner das Getty Information Institute Digital Laboratory und MoMA QNS in Long Island City, das im Juni 2002 eröffnet wurde. Zu den neueren Projekten des Büros gehören das Kidspace Children's Museum in Pasadena, Kalifornien, und das UCLA Hammer Museum in Los Angeles. Derzeit in Planung sind das neue Sonoma County Museum in Santa Rosa, das Fresno Metropolitan Museum, der Pavillon Nr. 16 für den Architekturpark in Jinhua, China, sowie die Biblioteca degli Alberti an den Giardini di Porta Nuova in Mailand. Maltzan hält Vorträge und war als Dozent für Entwurf und als Gastkritiker für die Architectural League of New York, die Rhode Island School of Design, die UCLA, USC (University of Southern California), Harvard University, University of Waterloo und das SCI-Arc tätig.

MICHAEL MALTZAN est né en 1959 à Levittown, New York. Il est Bachelor of Arts et Bachelor of Architecture de la Rhode Island School of Design (1984–85) et Master of Architecture de Harvard (1987). Depuis la création de son agence en 1995, il a réalisé un grand nombre de projets dans le domaine des arts, de l'éducation, du commerce, des institutions publiques et du logement, dont le Mark Taper Center/Inner-City Arts campus, le Feldman/Horn Center for the Arts de la Westlake School à Harvard, le Getty Information Institute Digital Laboratory et le MoMA QNS à Long Island City qui a ouvert ses portes en juin 2002. Il travaille actuellement à la conception du Kidspace Children's Museum à Pasadena, Californie, et au UCLA Hammer Museum à Los Angeles. Il a récemment reçu commande du nouveau Musée du comté de Sonoma à Santa Rosa, du Metropolitan Museum de Fresno, du Pavillon 16 du Parc d'architecture de Jinhua (Chine) et de la Biblioteca degli Alberti aux Giardini di Puorta Nuova à Milan. Maltzan a été enseignant en conception, conférencier et critique invité à l'Architectural League de New York, à la Rhode Island School of Design, à UCLA, et USSC, à Harvard University, University of Waterloo et SCI-Arc.

FRESNO METROPOLITAN MUSEUM

Fresno, California, USA, 2005–07

Floor area: 7044 m² (new construction) + 1880 m² (renovation). Client: Fresno Metropolitan Museum.
Cost: $43 million

Located in the agricultural region of California's Central Valley, Fresno is one of the fastest-growing cities in the state. The **METROPOLITAN MUSEUM** wished to give more coherence to a diverse collection and they called on Michael Maltzan not only to create space for them, but also to help in finding a "cohesive vision" for the institution. This private art and science museum occupied the former building of the *Fresno Bee* newspaper in the so-called uptown Cultural Arts District, across the street from the future site of the Central California History Museum, and near the proposed site for the Fresno Central Library. As Michael Maltzan says, "One of the main challenges in the development of a new home for the Museum is the relationship the new building would have to its existing home, the extent to which one acknowledges the institution's origins with the desire to forge new identities." Renovation of the existing building for administrative use amounts to about 2000 m², while the new construction covers roughly 7000 m². The project includes exhibition galleries and a café, store, media center and the museum's "support wing." The architect explains that "the building's structure lifts a rational, regular grid of two-way steel trusses nine meters above the museum's open public plaza. This floating field of structure encloses the museum's primary galleries, and is tethered to the ground through a faceted, twisted web of structural scaffolds." The cantilevered building offers none of the rectangular predictability of the older wing, and indeed does not appear to have façades in the traditional sense.

Fresno ist eine der am schnellsten wachsenden Städte Kaliforniens. Sie liegt im landwirtschaftlich geprägten Central Valley. Das **METROPOLITAN MUSEUM**, das sich für seine heterogene Sammlung einen stärkeren Zusammenhalt wünschte, wendete sich an Michael Maltzan. Es sollten nicht nur neue Räume geschaffen werden, Maltzan sollte auch dabei helfen, eine »verbindende Vision« für die Institution zu finden. Die private Kunst- und Techniksammlung ist im ehemaligen Gebäude der Tageszeitung *Fresno Bee* im so genannten Uptown Cultural Arts District untergebracht. Auf der gegenüberliegenden Straßenseite befindet sich der zukünftige Standort des Zentralkalifornischen Historischen Museums und in der Nähe die geplante Zentralbibliothek von Fresno. Michael Maltzan erläutert: »Eine der wesentlichen Herausforderungen im Prozess, neue Räume für die Sammlung zu schaffen, besteht in der Beziehung, in der das neue Gebäude zu seinem Standort stehen wird und in der Frage, inwieweit man die Ursprünge des Museums respektiert und gleichzeitig neue Identitäten schafft.« Rund 2000 m² des bestehenden Gebäudes wurden für administrative Zwecke instand gesetzt. Der neue Bau hat eine Fläche von etwa 7000 m². Das Raumprogramm beinhaltet Ausstellungsräume und ein Café, einen Museumsshop, ein Medienzentrum und Sekundärräume. Der Architekt erklärt, dass »die konstruktiven Elemente des Gebäudes ein rationales, regelmäßiges Gitter aus doppelten Stahlträgern tragen, das die offene Museumsplaza in 9 m Höhe überspannt. Dieses schwebende Konstruktionselement schließt die Hauptausstellungsräume gegen den Außenraum ab und ist mit dem Boden durch ein facettiertes, gedrehtes Netz aus konstruktiven Gerüsten verbunden«. Das auskragende Gebäude bietet nicht die rechtwinklige Vorhersehbarkeit des alten Gebäudes – tatsächlich scheint es gar keine Fassaden im traditionellen Sinn zu haben.

Situé en pleine zone agricole de la vallée centrale de Californie, Fresno est l'une des villes de cet État qui connaît le plus fort taux de croissance. Le **METROPOLITAN MUSEUM** souhaitait donner une plus grande cohérence à ses diverses collections et a fait appel à Michael Maltzan pour créer un nouvel espace et l'aider à définir une « vision cohérente » de l'institution. Ce musée privé d'art et des sciences occupait l'ancien immeuble du journal *Fresno Bee* dans le quartier culturel, face au futur site du Central California History Museum et près du terrain envisagé pour la Fresno Central Library. Comme l'explique Michael Maltzan : « L'un des enjeux principaux de la création d'un nouveau lieu pour le musée est la relation du nouveau bâtiment avec l'ancien, ou la mesure dans laquelle on reconnaît les origines de l'institution et le désir de se forger une identité nouvelle. » La rénovation de l'immeuble existant pour les bureaux administratifs représente environ 2000 m², la construction neuve environ 7000 m². Le projet comprend des galeries d'exposition, un café, une boutique, un centre médias et « l'aile technique » du musée. Les architectes expliquent que « la structure du bâtiment s'appuie sur une grille régulière et rationnelle de poutres en acier bidirectionnelles à neuf mètres au-dessus de la place du musée. Cette structure suspendue regroupe les principales galeries et se rattache au sol par un réseau d'échafaudages structurels en torsion et à facettes ». Le bâtiment en porte-à-faux est bien différent du style de l'aile ancienne et ne semble même pas posséder de façade au sens traditionnel du terme.

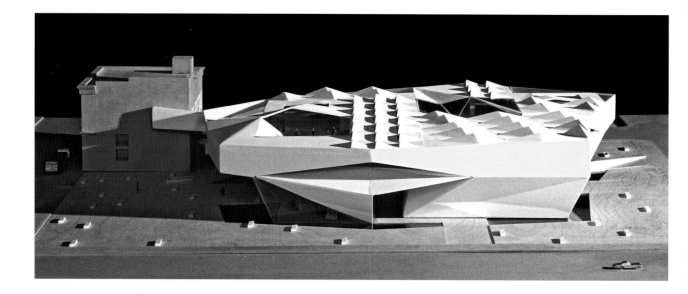

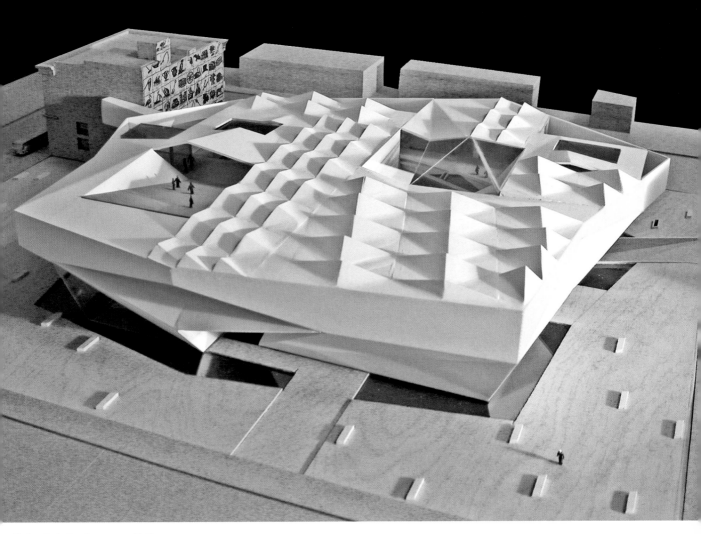

Maltzan's design does away with the traditional juxtaposition of façades to a roof. Here the façades are dissolved into rising planes and interpenetrating spaces, while the roof takes on an unusual degree of variation and opening.

Maltzan überwindet den traditionellen Gegensatz zwischen Fassade und Dach. Die Fassaden werden hier in geneigte Ebenen und sich durchdringende Räume aufgelöst. Das Dach ist variantenreich gestaltet und mit Oberlichtern ausgestattet.

Le projet de Maltzan élimine la traditionnelle juxtaposition des façades et du toit. Ici, les façades se dissolvent dans des plans et des volumes qui s'interpénétrent tandis que la toiture se permet un degré inhabituel de variations et d'ouvertures.

MANSILLA+TUÑÓN

Mansilla+Tuñón arquitectos
Rios Rosas 11, 6º
28003 Madrid
Spain

Tel/Fax: +34 913 99 30 67
e-mail: circo@circo.e.telefonica.net
Web: www.mansilla-tunon.com

MUSAC Art Center

EMILIO TUÑÓN and **LUIS MANSILLA** were both born in Madrid, respectively in 1958 and 1959, and received their doctorates from the ETSAM in 1998. They created their firm in Madrid in 1992. They are both full professors in the Architectural Design Department of the Architecture School of Madrid. In 1993, they created a "thinking exchange cooperative" called Circo with Luis Rojo and they publish a bulletin of the same name. Their built projects include the Archeological and Fine Arts Museum of Zamora (1996); Indoor Swimming Pool in San Fernando de Henares (1998); Fine Arts Museum of Castellón (2001); Auditorium of León (2002); Regional Library and Archive of Madrid (2003); and the MUSAC Art Center in León (2004). They won competitions for the urban planning of Valbuena in Logroño and a Public Library in Calle de los Artistas in Madrid in 2003; and for the Town Council of Lalin (2004), and the Helga Alvear Foundation in Cáceres (2005). They have been finalists for the last four Mies van der Rohe Awards (1997, 1999, 2001 and 2003).

EMILIO TUÑÓN, 1958 in Madrid geboren, und **LUIS MANSILLA**, 1959 ebenfalls in Madrid geboren, promovierten 1998 an der ETSAM (Escuela Técnica Superior de Arquitectura) in Madrid. 1992 gründeten sie dort ihr Büro. Beide haben eine Vollprofessur im Fachgebiet Architektonischer Entwurf an der ETSAM inne. 1993 gründeten sie zusammen mit Luis Rojo eine »Gedankenaustausch-Kooperative«, Circo genannt, und geben seitdem ein Themenheft mit demselben Namen heraus. Zu den realisierten Gebäuden des Büros gehören das Archäologische Museum und Museum für Kunst in Zamora (1996), ein Hallenbad in San Fernando de Henares (1998), das Museum für Bildende Kunst in Castellón (2001) und ein Auditorium in León (2002), ferner die Regionalbibliothek und das Regionalarchiv von Madrid (2003) und das Kunstzentrum MUSAC in León (2004). 2003 haben sie einen städtebaulichen Wettbewerb für Valbuena in Logroño und einen Wettbewerb für eine öffentliche Bücherei in der Calle de los Artistas in Madrid gewonnen, außerdem Wettbewerbe für das Gebäude des Stadtrats von Lalin (2004) und die Helga-Alvear-Stiftung in Cáceres (2005). Sie waren bereits viermal Finalisten für den Mies-van-der-Rohe-Preis (1997, 1999, 2001 und 2003).

EMILIO TUÑÓN et **LUIS MANSILLA** sont nés à Madrid, respectivement en 1958 et 1959 et sont tous deux docteurs de l'Etsam (1998). Ils ont créé leur agence madrilène en 1992 et sont professeurs au département de Conception architecturale de leur ancienne école. En 1993, ils ont créé une «coopérative d'échanges d'idées» appelée «Circo» avec Luis Rojo et publient un bulletin du même nom. Parmi leurs réalisations : le Musée d'archéologie et des beaux-arts de Zamora (1996); une piscine couverte à San Fernando de Henares (1998); le Musée des beaux-arts de Castellon (2001); l'Auditorium de León (2002); la Bibliothèque régionale et les Archives de Madrid (2003) et le Musac, Musée d'art contemporain de Castille et León (2004). Ils ont remporté des concours pour l'urbanisme de Valbuena à Logroño, pour une bibliothèque publique, calle de los Artistas à Madrid, en 2003, pour le Conseil municipal de Lalin (2004) et pour la Fondation Helga Alvear à Cáceres (2005). Ils ont été finalistes des quatre derniers prix Mies van der Rohe (1997, 1999, 2001 et 2003).

MUSAC

Museo de Arte Contemporáneo de Castilla y León, León, Spain, 2002–04

Floor area: 10 000 m². Client: Gesturcal S. A., Junta de Castilla y León.
Cost: €24 million

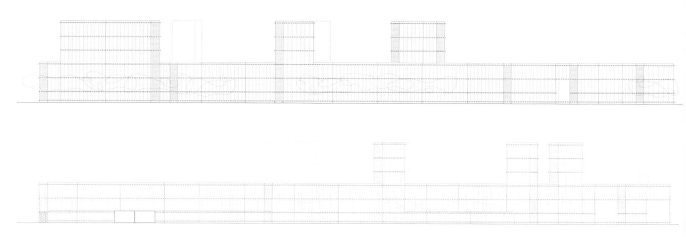

The architects use color like an abstract pattern akin to a work of art executed at architectural scale. With minimal exterior detailing, they allow color to take on a central role in the design.

Die Architekten setzen Farbe als abstraktes Muster ein; dieses wirkt als ein Kunstwerk in einem architektonischen Maßstab. Die äußere Fassade zeigt nur wenige Details und überlässt der Farbe die Hauptrolle.

Les architectes utilisent la couleur comme un motif abstrait, un peu comme dans une œuvre d'art, mais à l'échelle de l'architecture. Avec très peu d'effets extérieurs, ils laissent la couleur prendre la vedette.

Located on the Avenida de los Reyes Leoneses is a 10 000 m² building with white concrete walls and large areas of colored glazing. The architects explain that "**MUSAC** is a new space for culture, regarded as something that visualizes the connections between man and nature. A cluster of chained but independent rooms permit exhibitions of differing sizes and types. Each of the jaggedly shaped rooms constructs a continuous yet spatially differentiated area that opens onto the other rooms and courtyards, providing longitudinal, transversal and diagonal views. Five hundred prefab beams enclose a series of spaces that feature systematic repetition and formal expressiveness. Outside, the public space takes on a concave shape to hold the activities and encounters, embraced by large colored glass in homage to the city as the place for interpersonal relationships." Cheerful and varied in its appearance, MUSAC certainly takes a different esthetic approach than many contemporary art museums, where there is an emphasis on a more discreet Modernism. But the architects have a ready explanation for this difference. "In contrast to other types of museum spaces that focus on the exhibition of frozen historic collections, MUSAC is a living space that opens its doors to the wide-ranging manifestations of contemporary art," they declare.

Das Kunstzentrum **MUSAC** an der Avenida de los Reyes Leoneses in Léon ist ein 10 000 m² großes Gebäude mit weißen Wänden aus Sichtbeton und großen, farbig verglasten Flächen. Die Architekten erläutern: »MUSAC ist ein neuer Ort für Kultur. Kultur wird hier als etwas betrachtet, das die Beziehungen zwischen Mensch und Natur vergegenwärtigt. Eine Gruppe von ineinander greifenden, aber voneinander unabhängigen Räumen ermöglicht Ausstellungen verschiedener Größe und Art. Jeder der winkligen Räume ist Teil eines Raumkontinuums, gleichzeitig aber räumlich differenziert und öffnet sich zu anderen Räumen und Innenhöfen, wodurch sich Sichtachsen in Längs-, Quer- und Diagonalrichtung ergeben. 500 vorgefertigte Träger begrenzen das Raumsystem, das von der systematischen Wiederholung und formalen Expressivität bestimmt wird. Der Außenbereich hat eine konkave Form, um den öffentliche Raum für Aktivitäten und Begegnungen zu fassen. Er wird durch große farbige Glasscheiben, eine Hommage an die Stadt als Ort zwischenmenschlicher Beziehungen, gerahmt.« Fröhlich und differenziert gestaltet, folgt MUSAC sicherlich einem anderen ästhetischen Ansatz als viele moderne Kunstmuseen, die einem diskreteren Modernismus verpflichtet sind. Für diesen Unterschied haben die Architekten eine Erklärung parat: »Im Gegensatz zu anderen Museumsräumen, die der Ausstellung von ›gefrorenen‹ historischen Sammlungen dienen, ist MUSAC ein lebendiger Ort, der seine Türen den sehr unterschiedlichen Äußerungen der neuen Kunst öffnet.«

Situé Avenida de los Reyes Leoneses, le bâtiment de ce musée, qui conjugue murs de béton blanc et vastes pans de verre de couleur, totalise 10 000 m². Les architectes expliquent que « le **MUSAC** est un nouvel espace pour la culture, un lieu qui doit mettre en lumière les connexions entre l'homme et la nature. L'assemblage de salles reliées entre elles mais indépendantes permet des expositions de toute nature. Chaque élément découpé de ce ‹ puzzle › détermine un espace continu mais spatialement différencié, qui ouvre sur d'autres salles et des cours tout en ménageant des perspectives longitudinales, transversales et diagonales. Cinq cents poutres préfabriquées enferment une série d'espaces qui jouent de la répétition systématique et de l'expressivité formelle. À l'extérieur, l'espace public s'incurve pour accueillir les activités et les rencontres. Il est couvert de verre de couleurs en hommage à la ville, lieu par excellence des relations humaines ». D'aspect joyeux et très diversifié, le MUSAC a adopté une approche esthétique différente de celle de beaucoup de musées d'art contemporain, où l'on préfère un modernisme plus discret. Mais les architectes ont une explication toute prête à cette différence : « Par contraste avec d'autres types de musées qui se consacrent à l'exposition de collections historiques figées, le MUSAC est un espace vivant qui ouvre ses portes aux multiples manifestations de l'art contemporain. »

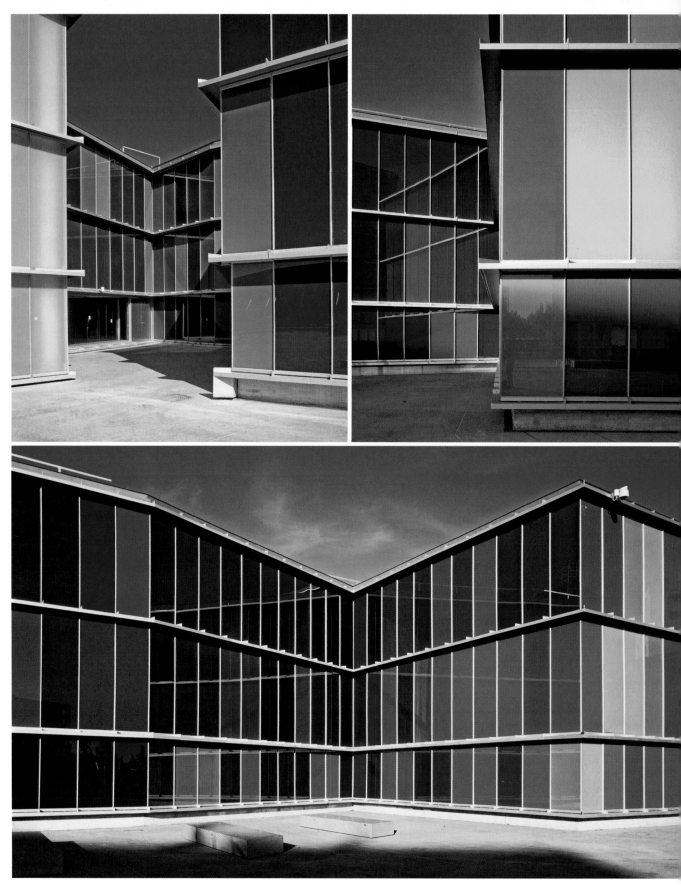

As the drawing below and the images on this double page demonstrate, colors are applied like a continuous canvas, made up of a chromatic orchestration that may or may not follow the sequence of the electromagnetic spectrum.

Wie diese Bilder und die Zeichnung zeigen, wurden die Farben gewissermaßen auf eine umlaufende Leinwand »aufgetragen«. Ihre chromatische Ausformulierung folgt teilweise der Abfolge im elektromagnetischen Spektrum.

Comme le montrent le dessin ci-dessous et les images de cette double page, les couleurs sont appliquées selon un canevas continu à partir d'une orchestration chromatique qui suit, ou non, le spectre lumineux.

Interior spaces are generous and
sometimes darker than might be
expected given the explosion of
colors seen on the exterior.

Les généreux volumes intérieurs sont
parfois plus sombres que l'on pourrait s'y attendre après l'explosion de
couleurs de l'extérieur.

Die Innenräume sind weiträumig
und mitunter dunkler als man
in Anbetracht der Farbexplosion
außen erwarten könnte.

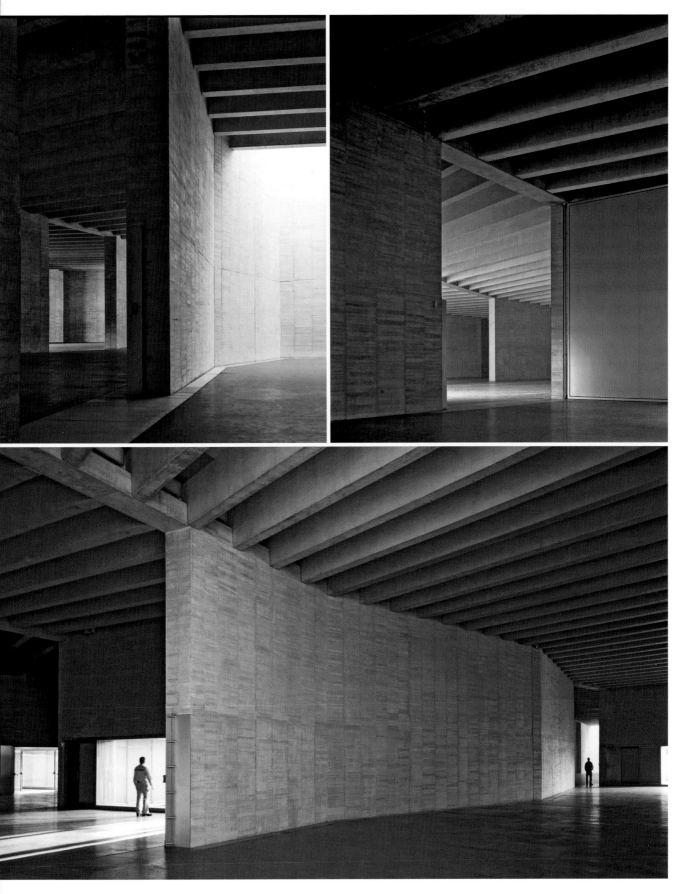

While color is the defining element of the exterior, it gives way inside to a limited palette which permits the exhibition areas to offer a neutral backdrop to the works to be shown.

Während nach außen die Farbe das definierende Element ist, wird im Inneren eine eingeschränkte Farbpalette verwendet, um einen neutralen Hintergrund für die Kunst zu schaffen.

Si la couleur est l'élément clé pour l'extérieur, elle laisse place, à l'intérieur, à une palette limitée qui permet aux aires d'exposition d'offrir un environnement neutre aux œuvres d'art.

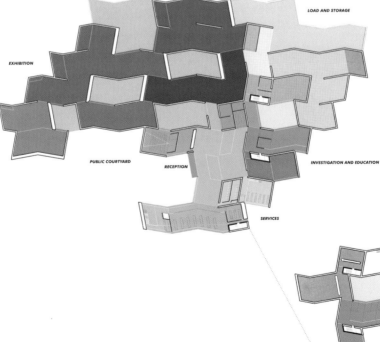

EXHIBITION

LOAD AND STORAGE

PUBLIC COURTYARD

RECEPTION

INVESTIGATION AND EDUCATION

SERVICES

The plan above shows overlapping zones that house the various museum functions. Within, the symphony of outside colors is left aside, and more solid, concrete surfaces make their appearance.

Der Grundriss zeigt ineinander über-gehende Zonen, in denen die ver-schiedenen Funktionen des Museums angeordnet sind. Innen wird die Farbigkeit zugunsten massiver Beton-oberflächen aufgegeben.

Le plan ci-dessus montre la super-position des zones qui accueillent les différentes fonctions du musée. À l'intérieur, la symphonie de cou-leurs est écartée au profit de plans de béton brut.

● ENTRANCE	● MULTI-USE ROOM	● PATIO
● MAIN LOBBY	● RESTAURANT	● RESTORATION WORKSHOP
● EXHIBITION ROOM 1	● SHOP	● STORAGE
● EXHIBITION ROOM 2	● TOILETS	● LOADING AREA
● EXHIBITION ROOM 3	● LIBRARY	● CONTROL AREA
● EXHIBITION ROOM 4	● EDUCATIONAL WORKSHOP	● TECHNICAL AREA
● EXHIBITION ROOM 5	● OFFICE	● VEHICLE ENTRANCE
● EXHIBITION PATIO	● STAFF	

MICHAEL MCDONOUGH

Michael McDonough Architect, 131 Spring Street
New York, New York 10012, USA

Tel: +1 212 431 3723, Fax: + 1 212 431 7465
e-mail: here@michaelmcdonough.com, Web: www.michaelmcdonough.com

Since the founding of his architecture and design firm in 1984, **MICHAEL MCDONOUGH** has completed commercial spaces such as galleries, showrooms, public buildings, shops, and exhibits, as well as residential projects, including homes and lofts throughout the United States and Europe, consults world-wide on corporate futurism, personal environments, and product development. His design philosophy is "rooted in systems convergence theory, synthesizing traditional and modern design, emphasizing new materials and sustainable technologies." As an architect, McDonough has designed facilities and consulted for such companies as Lufthansa German Airlines, Frogdesign, Frankfurt Airport Authority, Aveda Corporation, Stephen Sprouse Fashion, and Seaside Community Development Corporation; as well as designing over 50 private residences, exhibitions, and conceptual projects. As an industrial designer, his collections include tabletop objects, jewelry, and furniture. He designed the McEasy Collection of lounge furniture for ICF Unika Vaev Nienkämper, and Eco-sTuff!, a line of ecological furniture made of 100% post-consumer recycled newspaper. McDonough holds a B.A. in English from the University of Massachusetts, and Master of Architecture from the University of Pennsylvania, where he was an Editor of *VIA*. He also completed additional studies in architecture and art at the Massachusetts Institute of Technology. Presently, he is a contributing editor and writer at *Metropolitan Home*. He has also written on design for *The New York Times*, *Wired*, and other publications. Novelist Tom Wolfe dedicated his controversial book on architecture, *From Bauhaus to Our House*, to McDonough. McDonough's first book, *Malaparte: A House Like Me* was published by Clarkson Potter/Publishers in 1999.

Seit der Gründung seines Architektur- und Designbüros 1984 hat **MICHAEL MCDONOUGH** zahlreiche kommerzielle und private Bauten realisiert. Zu den kommerziellen Projekten gehören Galerien, Showrooms, öffentliche Gebäude, Läden und Ausstellungen, zu den privaten Wohnhäuser und Lofts in den USA und Europa. Er ist weltweit als Berater für »Corporate Futurism«, private Environments und Produktentwicklung tätig. Seine Entwurfsphilosophie hat »ihre Wurzeln in der Systemkonvergenztheorie, die traditionelles und modernes Design miteinander verbindet und neue Materialien und nachhaltige Technologien verwendet«. Als Architekt hat McDonough die Einrichtungen diverser Unternehmen – z. B. für die Lufthansa, Frogdesign, den Frankfurter Flughafen, Aveda Kosmetik, Stephen Sprouse Mode und die Seaside Community Development Corporation – entworfen und diese Unternehmen beraten. Mehr als 50 Privathäuser, Ausstellungen und konzeptionelle Projekte stammen von ihm. Als Industriedesigner entwarf er Tischwaren, Schmuck und Möbel. Er hat die Loungemöbel der McEasy Kollektion für ICF Unika Vaev Nienkämper und Eco-sTuff!, eine Kollektion von ökologischen Möbeln, die zu 100 Prozent aus recyceltem Zeitungspapier bestehen, entworfen. McDonough hat einen B. A. in Englisch von der University of Massachusetts und einen Master of Architecture von der University of Pennsylvania, wo er Herausgeber von *VIA* war. Ferner schloss er zusätzliche Architektur- und Kunststudien am Massachusetts Institute of Technology ab. Derzeit ist er Mitherausgeber und Autor von »Metropolitan Home«. Zum Thema Design hat er Beiträge für die *New York Times*, *Wired* und andere Publikationen geschrieben. Der Romanautor Tom Wolfe widmete ihm sein umstrittenes Buch *From Bauhaus to Our House*. McDonoughs erstes Buch *Malaparte: A House Like Me* erschien 1999 bei Clarkson Potter/Publishers.

Depuis la fondation de son agence d'architecture et de design, **MICHAEL MCDONOUGH** a réalisé des points de vente, des boutiques, des showrooms, des bâtiments publics et des expositions aussi bien que des projets résidentiels dont des maisons et des lofts, aux États-Unis et en Europe. Il a donné des consultations dans le monde entier sur le futur consultant international pour les questions de développement des entreprises, d'environnements personnels et de développement de produits. Sa philosophie du design est « enracinée dans la théorie de convergence des systèmes, elle fait la synthèse entre les conceptions moderne et traditionnelle et met l'accent sur les nouveaux matériaux innovants et les technologies durables ». En tant qu'architecte, il a conçu des équipements et a été consultant pour des entreprises comme Lufthansa, Frogdesign, l'aéroport de Francfort, Aveda Corporation, Stephen Sprouse Fashion, Seaside Community Development Corporation et il est l'auteur de plus de 50 cinquante résidences privées, expositions et projets conceptuels. Designer industriel, il a réalisé des objets d'art de la table, des bijoux et des meubles. Il a conçu la collection de mobilier de salon McEasy pour ICF Unika Vaev Nienkämper ainsi qu'Eco-sTuff!, une ligne de mobilier écologique en papier journal 100% recyclé. McDonough est Bachelor of Art en anglais de l'Université du Massachusetts et Master of Architecture de l'Université de Pennsylvanie où il était le rédacteur en chef de *VIA*. Il a également suivi des études complémentaires en art et architecture au Massachusetts Institute of Technology. Actuellement, il est éditorialiste et rédacteur pour *Metropolitan Home*. Il a également écrit sur le design dans *The New York Times*, dans *Wired* et d'autres publications. Il est le dédicataire du célèbre et controversé ouvrage de Tom Wolfe sur l'architecture, *From Bauhaus to Our House*. Son premier livre, *Malaparte : A House Like Me*, a été publié par Clarkson Potter/Publishers en 1999.

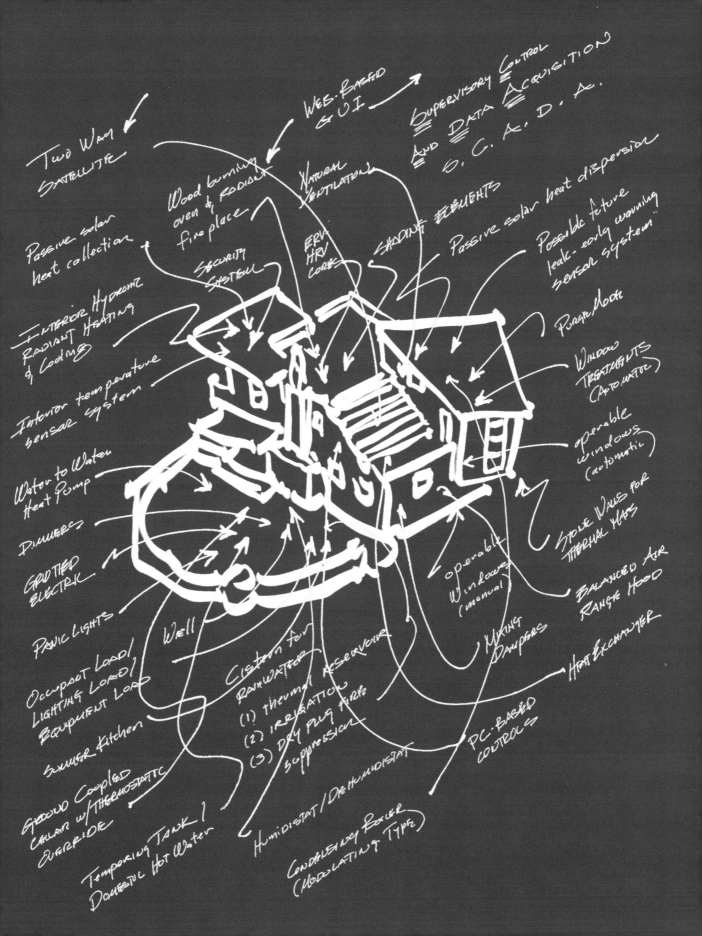

E-HOUSE

Hudson Valley, New York, USA, 2002–05

Floor area: 235 m². Client: Michael McDonough Architect.
Cost: not disclosed

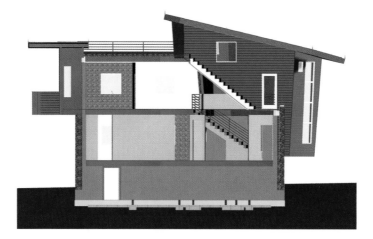

Michael McDonough calls the **E-HOUSE** "a laboratory for new technologies in the guise of a contemporary home." Much more than a "green" house, McDonough's creation involved careful analysis of the site, use of local materials and artisans, and careful research of all possible ways of making it both reactive and sensitive to its users and its environment. McDonough explains that "Importantly, the project aspires to set new standards for building design, integrates over 100 new or advanced technologies (including high performance or historical or 'alternate' technologies) and proposes to develop a new lexicon for sustainable architecture theory." He makes references not only to the 18th-century Dutch Colonial homestead ruins found on the site, but also to the Casa Malaparte and its south-facing monumental stairway. Two trapezoidal extensions are designed to capture a view and to catch the first light of day all year long. An "experimental radiant heating, cooling, and snowmelt system with rainwater thermal storage cisterns and heat exchangers" is one feature of the residence, which can be controlled and monitored from a distance with a dedicated web site. McDonough explains that "The e-House will have a SCADA – Supervisory Control and Data Acquisition – system in conjunction with an Internet portal and management software. This means the house acts as an organic entity, enabled through currently available networking, hardware and software technologies. It ... will be capable of making low-level decisions related to systems management."

Michael McDonough nennt das **E-HOUSE** »ein Laboratorium für neue Technologien, verkleidet als modernes Haus«. Viel mehr als ein »grünes« Haus beinhaltete seine Planung eine sorgfältige Untersuchung des Grundstücks, die Einbeziehung von Materialien und Handwerkern der Region sowie eine aufwendige Erforschung aller Möglichkeiten, das Haus so zu gestalten, dass es sensibel auf seine Nutzer und seine Umgebung reagieren kann. McDonough meint: »Es ist wichtig, dass wir mit dem Projekt anstreben, neue Standards für den Entwurf von Gebäuden zu setzen. Es integriert über 100 neue oder ausgereifte Technologien, darunter Hochleistungstechnologien, historische und alternative Technologien. Mit dem Haus schlagen wir die Entwicklung eines neuen Wortschatzes für nachhaltige Architekturtheorie vor.« McDonough bezieht sich nicht nur auf die Ruinen eines niederländischen Kolonialhauses aus dem 18. Jahrhundert, die auf dem Grundstück gefunden wurden, sondern auch auf die Casa Malaparte und ihre nach Süden orientierte monumentale Treppe. Zwei trapezförmige Anbauten sollen einen Ausblick bieten und das ganze Jahr über das erste Tageslicht einfangen. Ein wichtiges Element des Hauses ist das »experimentelle Strahlwärme-, Kühl- und Schneeschmelzsystem mit Auffangwärmetanks für Regenwasser sowie Wärmetauschern«. Es kann aus der Distanz über eine spezielle Website überwacht und kontrolliert werden. McDonough erläutert: »Das e-House wird über ein SCADA-System (Überwachende Kontrolle und Datenaufnahme) verfügen, in Verbindung mit einem Internetportal und einer Managementsoftware. Das bedeutet, dass sich das Haus als organisches Ganzes verhält. Die derzeit zur Verfügung stehende Vernetzung, die Hardware- und Softwaretechnologien ermöglichen dies. Es ... wird dazu in der Lage sein, untergeordnete, das Systemmanagement betreffende Entscheidungen selbst zu treffen.«

Michael McDonough dit que sa **E-HOUSE** est «un laboratoire de nouvelles technologies déguisé en maison contemporaine». Ce travail, qui est beaucoup plus qu'une maison «verte», a entraîné une analyse approfondie du site, le recours à des artisans et des matériaux locaux et une recherche sur toutes les manières possibles de rendre cette maison aussi réactive et sensible que possible, tant à ses usagers qu'à son environnement. McDonough explique : «Il est important de noter que le projet aspire à fixer de nouveaux standards de conception de l'habitat, d'intégrer plus de 100 technologies nouvelles ou d'avant-garde (dont des technologies haute performance, historiques ou ‹alternatives›) et se propose de mettre au point un nouveau lexique de la théorie de l'architecture durable. » L'architecte ne fait pas seulement référence aux ruines de la maison du XVIIIe siècle de style colonial hollandais existant sur le terrain mais aussi à la Casa Malaparte et à son escalier monumental. Deux extensions trapézoïdales ont été aménagées pour capter la vue et les premiers rayons du soleil tout au long de l'année. Un «système expérimental de chauffage radiant, de rafraîchissement et de fonte de la neige radiant avec des citernes de stockage de l'eau de pluie et des échangeurs de chaleur» est l'un des équipements contrôlables et pilotables à distance *via* un site internet. L'architecte explique également que «la e-House sera équipée de SCADA – système de contrôle, de supervision et d'acquisition de données – qui œuvrera en conjonction avec un portail internet et un logiciel de gestion. Ceci signifie que la maison agit comme une entité organique, ce que permettent les technologies informatiques actuellement disponibles. Elle ... sera en mesure de prendre certaines décisions à partir des systèmes de gestion ».

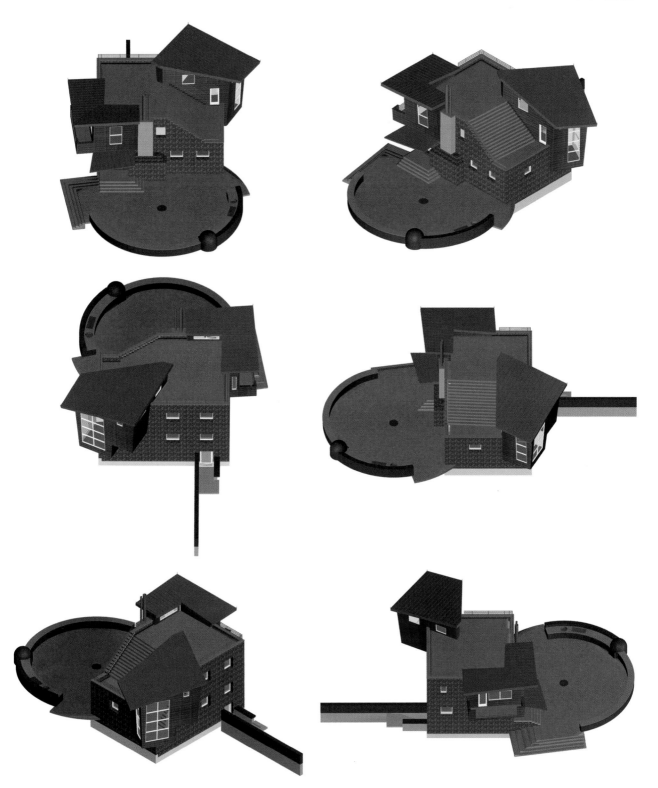

The e-House gives the impression of being a collage of disparate elements, whose shape and positioning is more related to environmental forces than esthetic ones.

Das e-House wirkt wie eine Collage aus verschiedenen Elementen, deren Form und Position eher durch ökologische Kriterien als durch ästhetische Überlegungen bestimmt werden.

La e-House donne l'impression d'un collage d'éléments disparates dont la forme et le positionnement dépendent plus de l'environnement que de critères esthétiques.

RICHARD MEIER

Richard Meier & Partners
475 Tenth Avenue
New York, New York 10018
USA

Tel: +1 212 967 6060
Fax: +1 212 967 3207
e-mail: mail@richardmeier.com
Web: www.richardmeier.com

RICHARD MEIER was born in Newark, New Jersey in 1934. He received his architectural training at Cornell University, and worked in the office of Marcel Breuer (1960–63) before establishing his own practice in 1963. In 1984, he became the youngest winner of the Pritzker Prize, and he received the 1988 RIBA Gold Medal. His notable buildings include The Atheneum, New Harmony, Indiana (1975–79); Museum of Decorative Arts, Frankfurt, Germany (1979–84); High Museum of Art, Atlanta, Georgia (1980–83); Canal Plus Headquarters, Paris, France (1988–91); City Hall and Library, The Hague, The Netherlands (1990–95); Barcelona Museum of Contemporary Art, Barcelona, Spain (1988–95); and the Getty Center, Los Angeles, California (1984–97). Recent work includes the U. S. Courthouse and Federal Building, Phoenix, Arizona (1995–2000); Jubilee Church, Rome (2003); Crystal Cathedral International Center for Possibility Thinking, Garden Grove, California (2003); Arp Museum, Rolandseck, Germany; and the Yale University History of Art and Arts Library, New Haven (2001), and the 66 restaurant in New York (2001–02). Present work includes the Beach House, a 12-story glass enclosed condominium located on Collins Avenue in Miami (2004–07); the ECM City Tower, Pankrac City, Prague, Czech Republic (2004–07); 165 Charles Street (2003–05), a 16-story residential building located in Manhattan near the architect's Perry Street apartments (1999–2002); and the Ara Pacis Museum, Rome, Italy (1995–2006).

RICHARD MEIER, geboren 1934 in Newark, New Jersey, studierte an der Cornell University und arbeitete von 1960 bis 1963 im Büro von Marcel Breuer, bevor er 1963 sein eigenes Büro gründete. 1984 wurde er – als jüngster Gewinner – mit dem Pritzker-Preis ausgezeichnet, 1988 erhielt er die RIBA Gold Medal. Zu seinen wichtigsten Gebäuden gehören: The Atheneum, New Harmony, Indiana (1975–79), das Museum für Kunsthandwerk in Frankfurt am Main (1979–84), das High Museum of Art in Atlanta, Georgia (1980–83), die Zentrale von Canal Plus in Paris (1988–91), das Rathaus mit Bibliothek in Den Haag (1990–95), das Museum für zeitgenössische Kunst in Barcelona (1988–95) und das Getty Center in Los Angeles (1984–97). Zu seinen jüngsten Projekten zählen das US Courthouse and Federal Building in Phoenix, Arizona (1995–2000), die Kirche des Heiligen Jahres in Rom (2003), das Chrystal Cathedral International Center for Possibility Thinking in Garden Grove, Kalifornien (2003), das Arp-Museum in Rolandseck (1995–2005), die Yale University History of Art and Arts Library in New Haven (2001) und das Restaurant 66 in New York (2001–02). Derzeit in der Planung bzw. im Bau befindliche Projekte sind u. a.: das Beach House, ein vollständig verglastes zwölfgeschossiges Gebäude mit Eigentumswohnungen auf der Collins Avenue in Miami (2004–07), der ECM City Tower in Pankrac, Prag (2004–07), 165 Charles Street (2003–05), ein 16-geschossiges Wohngebäude in der Nähe der Perry Street Apartments (1999–2002, ebenfalls von Richard Meier) in Manhattan, und das Ara-Pacis-Museum in Rom (1995–2006).

Né à Newark (New Jersey), en 1934, **RICHARD MEIER** a étudie à Cornell University, et travaille dans l'agence de Marcel Breuer (1960–63) avant de s'installer à son compte en 1963. Prix Pritzker 1984, Royal Gold Medal, 1988. Principales réalisations : The Athenaeum, New Harmony, Indiana, États-Unis (1975–79) ; Musée des Arts décoratifs de Francfort-sur-le-Main (1979–84) ; High Museum of Art, Atlanta, Géorgie (1980–83) ; siège de Canal +, Paris (1988–91) ; hôtel de ville et bibliothèque, La Haye (1990–95) ; Musée d'Art contemporain de Barcelone (1988–95) ; Getty Center, Los Angeles, Californie (1984–96). Travaux récents : Tribunal fédéral et immeuble de l'administration fédérale à Phoenix, Arizona (1995–2000) ; l'Église du Jubilée, Rome (2003) ; le Crystal Cathedral International Center for Possibility Thinking, Garden Grove, Californie (2003) ; le Arp Museum, Rolandseck, Allemagne (1995–2005) ; la Yale University History of Art and Arts Library, New Haven (2001), et le restaurant 66 à New York (2001–02) ; Beach House, un immeuble en copropriété sur Collins Avenue à Miami (2004–07) ; la tour ECM, Pankrak City, Prague (2004–07) ; un immeuble d'habitation de 16 étages au 165 Charles Street, Manhattan (2003–05), non loin de ses appartements du 173/176 Perry Streets (1999–2002), et le musée de l'Ara Pacis, Rome, Italie (1995–2006).

MUSEUM FRIEDER BURDA

Baden-Baden, Germany, 2001–04

Floor area: 2000 m². Client: Stiftung Frieder. Burda Cost: €20 million

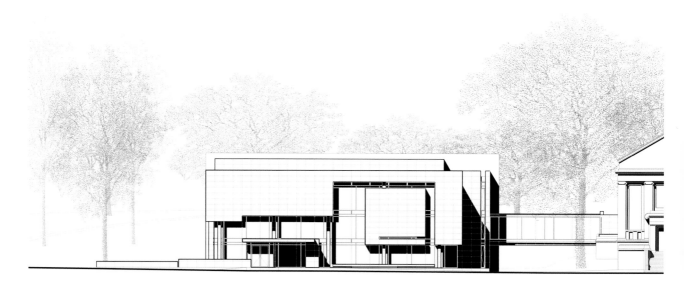

The 15-meter-high structure has an approximate overall size of 2000 m² with an exhibition space of 1000 m². With four stories, including the entry level, the structure is clad in white enameled metal panels. As the architect says, "The new museum for the Frieder Burda Collection in Baden-Baden is designed to be in harmony with the surrounding Lichtentaler Allee Park and to compliment the adjacent Kunsthalle. The overall size and proportions of the new building are in scale with the Kunsthalle creating a sense of unity, while each institution maintains its own unique identity." A glazed bridge links the museum to the plinth of the Kunsthalle in a manner that does not disturb the architecture of the existing structure. Although he does employ a selected palette of materials and a specified architectural vocabulary, Richard Meier shows, with a building like the **MUSEUM FRIEDER BURDA**, that these self-imposed limitations can indeed lead to a great variety of buildings and indeed to a more and more masterful treatment of spaces and light. As described by the museum, "The Frieder Burda collection, rooted in German Expressionism, is comprised of more than 500 paintings, sculptures and works on paper. The collection focuses on classical, modern and contemporary art and includes works by Gerhard Richter, Sigmar Polke and Arnulf Rainer, as well as eight works by Pablo Picasso. In addition to paintings from Adolph Gottlieb, De Kooning, Pollock and Rothko, the collection includes an important work by Clyfford Still. The collection's German post-war selections feature work by George Baselitz, along with two well-known works by his early companion in Berlin, Eugen Schönebeck. Also noteworthy is Anselm Kiefer's nearly six-meter-long painting, *Böhmen liegt am Meer*."

Das 15 m hohe Gebäude mit einer Gesamtfläche von insgesamt ca. 2000 m² umfasst 1000 m² Ausstellungsfläche. Die vier Geschosse (inkl. Eingangsgeschoss) sind komplett mit weiß emaillierten Metallpaneelen verkleidet. Der Architekt erläutert: »Das neue Museum für die Sammlung Frieder Burda in Baden-Baden soll sich harmonisch in den Park an der Lichtentaler Allee einfügen und die nahe gelegene Staatliche Kunsthalle ergänzen. Die Gesamtgröße des neuen Gebäudes und seine Proportionen orientieren sich an denen der Kunsthalle, wodurch ein einheitliches Ensemble geschaffen wird, die spezielle Identität beider Institutionen aber bestehen bleibt.« Eine verglaste Brücke verbindet das neue Museum mit dem Sockel der Kunsthalle, ohne deren Architektur zu stören. Obwohl er nur wenige Materialien und ein spezielles architektonisches Vokabular verwendet, zeigt Richard Meier mit einem Gebäude wie dem **MUSEUM FRIEDER BURDA**, dass diese selbstauferlegte Beschränkung zu sehr verschiedenen Gebäuden und zu einem immer anspruchsvolleren Umgang mit Raum und Licht führen kann. Die Sammlung des Museums wird folgendermaßen beschrieben: »Die im deutschen Expressionismus verwurzelte Sammlung Frieder Burda umfasst mehr als 500 Gemälde, Skulpturen und Arbeiten auf Papier. Sammlungsschwerpunkte sind die Kunst der Klassischen Moderne und moderne und zeitgenössische Kunst. Vertreten sind u. a. Gerhard Richter, Sigmar Polke und Arnulf Rainer sowie acht Arbeiten von Pablo Picasso. Außer Werken von Adolph Gottlieb, De Kooning, Pollock und Rothko ist auch eine bedeutende Arbeit von Clyfford Still Teil der Sammlung. Die deutsche Kunst nach dem Zweiten Weltkrieg wird u. a. durch Georg Baselitz und zwei bekannte Werke von Eugen Schönebeck, einem Kollegen von Baselitz aus seinen frühen Berliner Jahren, repräsentiert. Ebenfalls erwähnenswert ist das fast 6 m lange Bild *Böhmen liegt am Meer* von Anselm Kiefer.«

Ce bâtiment de 15 mètres de haut, habillé de panneaux de métal émaillé blanc, offre une surface totale d'environ 2000 m² sur quatre niveaux, dont la moitié est réservée aux galeries d'exposition. Selon la description de l'architecte, « le nouveau musée de la collection Frieder Burda à Baden-Baden est conçu pour être en harmonie avec son environnement, celui du Lichtentaler Allee Park et de la Kunsthalle adjacente, qu'il vient compléter. Les dimensions et les proportions de la nouvelle construction sont à l'échelle de la Kunsthalle pour créer un sentiment d'unité tout en conservant l'identité de chaque institution ». Une passerelle de verre relie le musée à la base de la Kunsthalle sans nuire à l'architecture de celle-ci. Même s'il reste fidèle à sa palette de matériaux et son vocabulaire architectural personnels, Richard Meier montre avec le **MUSÉE FRIEDER BURDA** que des contraintes bien comprises peuvent générer une grande variété de propositions et un traitement de plus en plus magistral de l'espace et de la lumière. Quant au musée même, « la collection Frieder Burda, qui prend ses racines dans l'expressionnisme allemand, compte plus de cinq cents peintures, sculptures et travaux sur papier. Elle est centrée sur l'art classique, moderne et contemporain, avec des œuvres de Gerhard Richter, Sigmar Polke et Arnulf Rainer, ainsi que huit Pablo Picasso. Hormis des tableaux de Adolph Gottlieb, De Kooning, Pollock et Rothko, elle comprend également une œuvre importante de Clyfford Still. La sélection d'art allemand de l'après-guerre présente des travaux de Georg Baselitz et deux œuvres célèbres du compagnon berlinois de ses débuts, Eugen Schönebeck. On note également la peinture de près de six mètres de long d'Anselm Kiefer, *Böhmen liegt am Meer* ».

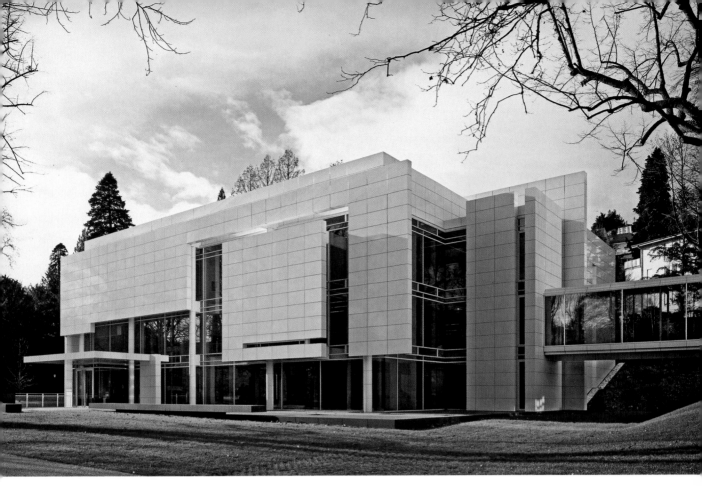

Richard Meier remains faithful to his white, geometric rigor, and yet in the case of the Burda Collection, he attains new degrees of aesthetic complexity or perfection. Opaque white screens alternate with the setback glazing in a pattern that might be compared to a musical partition.

Richard Meier bleibt seiner geometrisch weißen Strenge treu. Mit der Sammlung Burda erreicht er jedoch einen neuen Grad an ästhetischer Komplexität und Perfektion. Weißopake Flächen wechseln mit der zurückgesetzten Verglasung zu einem Muster, das mit einer musikalischen Komposition verglichen werden kann.

Richard Meier reste fidèle au blanc et à la rigueur géométrique. Ici, il atteint une fois de plus de nouveaux degrés de complexité dans sa perfection esthétique. Les écrans blancs opaques alternent avec les plans vitrés en retrait selon un motif comparable à une partition musicale.

As always, Meier masters the use of light and interpenetrating interior spaces. His trademark walkways or gangways permit varying views of the architecture and of the outside gardens.

Wie immer beherrscht Richard Meier den Umgang mit Licht und sich durchdringenden Innenräumen meisterhaft. Rampen und Brücken – seine Markenzeichen – ermöglichen unterschiedliche Blicke auf die Architektur und den Garten.

Comme toujours, Meier maîtrise l'utilisation de la lumière et de l'interpénétration des volumes intérieurs. Les passages ou coursives qui sont sa marque offrent des points de vues variés sur l'architecture ou les jardins.

MORPHOSIS

Morphosis
2041 Colorado Avenue
Santa Monica, California 90404
USA

Tel: +1 310 453 2247
Fax: +1 310 829 3270
e-mail: studio@morphosis.net
Web: www.morphosis.net

Caltrans District 7 Headquarters

MORPHOSIS principal Thom Mayne, born in Connecticut in 1944, received his Bachelor of Architecture in 1968 at USC, and his Masters of Architecture degree at Harvard in 1978. He created Morphosis in 1979 with Michael Rotondi, who left to create his own firm, Roto. He has taught at UCLA, Harvard, and Yale and SCI-Arc, of which he was a founding Board Member. Some of the main buildings of Morphosis are the Lawrence House (1981); Kate Mantilini Restaurant, Beverly Hills (1986); Cedar's Sinai Comprehensive Cancer Care Center, Beverly Hills (1987); Crawford Residence, Montecito (1987–92); Yuzen Vintage Car Museum, West Hollywood (project, 1992), as well as the Blades Residence, Santa Barbara, California (1992–97) and the International Elementary School, Long Beach, California (1997–99). More recent work includes the San Francisco Federal Building; University of Cincinnati Student Recreation Center; the NOAA Satellite Operation Facility in Suitland, Maryland; and a proposal for the 2012 Olympics in New York City made prior to the selection of London. Thom Mayne was the winner of the 2005 Pritzker Prize.

Geschäftsführer Thom Mayne, geboren 1944 in Connecticut, machte seinen Bachelor of Architecture 1968 an der University of Southern California (USC) und seinen Master of Architecture 1978 in Harvard. Zusammen mit Michael Rotondi gründete er 1979 **MORPHOSIS**. Michael Rotondi führt inzwischen sein eigenes Büro Roto. Thom Mayne hat an der UCLA, in Harvard, Yale und an der SCI-Arc – deren Gründungsmitglied er war – unterrichtet. Einige von Morphosis' wichtigsten Gebäuden sind das Lawrence House (1981), das Kate Mantilini Restaurant in Beverly Hills (1986), das Cedar's Sinai Comprehensive Cancer Care Center, ebenfalls in Beverly Hills (1987), die Crawford Residence in Montecito (1987–92) und das Yuzen Vintage Car Museum in West-Hollywood (Projekt, 1992), ferner die Blades Residence in Santa Barbara, Kalifornien (1992–97), und die Internationale Grundschule in Long Beach, Kalifornien (1997–99). Zu den neueren Projekten des Büros gehören das San Francisco Federal Building, das Student Recreation Center der University of Cincinnati, die NOAA Satellitenbetriebseinrichtung in Suitland, Maryland, und – vor der Auswahl Londons – ein Entwurf für die Olympischen Spiele 2012 in New York. Thom Mayne hat 2005 den Pritzker-Preis gewonnen.

Le directeur de **MORPHOSIS**, Thom Mayne, né dans le Connecticut en 1944, est Bachelor of Architecture d'USC de la University of Southern California (1968) et Master of Architecture d'Harvard (1978). Il a créé Morphosis en 1979 avec Michael Rotondi, parti par la suite créer sa propre agence, Roto. Il a enseigné à UCLA, Harvard, Yale et SCI-Arc dont il est un des fondateurs. Parmi ses principales réalisations : Lawrence House (1981); Kati Mantilini Restaurant, Beverly Hills (1986); Cedar's Sinai Comprehensive Cancer Care Center, Beverly Hills (1987); Crawford Residence, Montecito (1987–92); le Yuzen Vintage Car Museum, West Hollywood, projet (1992), ainsi que la Blades Residence, Santa Barbara, Californie (1992–97) et l'International Elementary School, Long Beach, Californie (1997–99). Plus récemment, il s'est consacré au San Francisco Federal Building; à l'University of Cincinnati Student Recreation Center; au centre opérationnel de satellites NOAA à Suitland (Maryland) et à une proposition pour les Jeux olympiques de 2012 à New York, avant le choix de Londres. Thom Mayne a remporté le prix Pritzker 2005.

CALTRANS DISTRICT 7 HEADQUARTERS

Los Angeles, California, USA, 2002–04

*Floor area: 69 677 m². Client: California Department of Transportation.
Cost: $170 million*

This large office building was erected for a cost of 170 million dollars. Located on South Main Street opposite City Hall close to Frank Gehry's Walt Disney Concert Hall and Arata Isozaki's MoCA, it is the new Headquarters for the California Department of Transportation (Caltrans) District 7, and serves 1850 Caltrans employees and 500 employees of the Los Angeles Department of Transportation. Awarded to Morphosis after a competition held in 2001, it is the first building to be commissioned under the State of California's Design Excellence Program. The building is L-shaped in plan, composed of two main volumes. The larger one is 13 stories high, 43 meters wide and 110 meters long, running from north to south. The secondary block is four stories high. The main exterior materials are an exposed galvanized steel structure, and coated perforated aluminum panels. The design features an outdoor lobby and plaza, and a public art installation by Keith Sonnier. A super-graphic sign four stories high features the building's street address, "100." The architects have also been attentive to environmental concerns. As they explain, "The building's south glass façade is entirely screened with sunshade panels incorporating photovoltaic cells, an original system designed by Morphosis, Clark Construction and a team of special consultants. The cells generate approximately 5% of the building's energy while shielding the façade from direct sunlight during peak summer hours, without obstructing the spectacular views towards the city all the way to the ocean."

Das umgerechnet 141 Millionen Euro teure Bürogebäude ist die neue Zentrale der Verkehrsbehörde von Kalifornien (Caltrans). 1850 Mitarbeiter von Caltrans und 500 Mitarbeiter der Verkehrsbehörde von Los Angeles arbeiten hier. Das Gebäude liegt an der South Main Street gegenüber dem Rathaus der Stadt, nicht weit entfernt von Frank Gehrys Walt Disney Concert Hall und Arata Isozakis MoCA. Morphosis wurde nach einem Wettbewerb 2001 mit dem Projekt betraut; das Gebäude ist das erste, das innerhalb des »Programms für herausragende Architektur des Bundesstaates Kalifornien« beauftragt wurde. Das L-förmige Gebäude besteht aus zwei Hauptbaukörpern. Der größere Flügel in Nord-Süd-Richtung hat 13 Geschosse, ist 43 m tief und 110 m lang. Der zweite Flügel ist viergeschossig. Die Außenfassaden sind durch eine sichtbare verzinkte Stahlkonstruktion und beschichtete, perforierte Aluminiumpaneele charakterisiert. Der öffentliche Raum umfasst eine Lobby und eine Plaza, außerdem eine Installation des Künstlers Keith Sonnier; die Hausnummer 100 wurde als vier Geschosse hohe »Supergrafik« gestaltet. Auch auf ökologische Aspekte legten die Architekten Wert. Sie erklären: »Die gesamte Südfassade ist von Sonnenschutzpaneelen mit Fotovoltaikzellen bedeckt. Das neuartige System wurde von Morphosis, Clark Construction und einem Team aus Spezialisten entwickelt. Die Zellen generieren ungefähr fünf Prozent des Energiebedarfs des Gebäudes und schützen die Fassade in der Mittagszeit im Sommer vor direkter Sonneneinstrahlung, ohne die spektakuläre Sicht in Richtung Stadt und bis zum Pazifik zu behindern.«

Ce grand immeuble de bureaux a été construit pour un budget de 141 millions d'euros. Situé South Main Street, face à l'hôtel de ville et proche du Walt Disney Concert Hall de Frank Gehry et le du MoCA d'Arata Isozaki, il est le nouveau siège du Département des transports de Californie (Caltrans), District 7, et accueille 1850 employés de ce département et 500 de celui des transports de Los Angeles. Contrat remporté par Morphosis après un concours organisé en 2001, c'est le premier immeuble commandé dans le cadre du programme d'excellence de l'État de Californie. L'immeuble en L se compose de deux volumes principaux. Le plus grand, orienté nord-sud, mesure 110 m de long, 43 m de large et compte 13 niveaux. Le second en comporte quatre seulement. Les principaux matériaux des façades sont l'acier galvanisé pour la structure, et l'aluminium perforé enduit pour les panneaux de l'habillage. L'ensemble comprend également une plaza, un accueil extérieur et une installation artistique de l'artiste Keith Sonnier. Un signe graphique de quatre niveaux de haut rappelle le numéro de l'adresse de l'immeuble : « 100 ». Les architectes ont également été sensibles aux préoccupations environnementales. Comme ils l'expliquent, « la façade sud de l'immeuble, en verre, est entièrement doublée par des panneaux de protection solaire à cellules photovoltaïques, système original conçu par Morphosis, Clark Construction et une équipe de consultants. Ces cellules génèrent environ 5% de l'énergie consommée par l'immeuble et protègent la façade des rayons solaires directs lors des heures d'ensoleillement maximum, sans obstruer la vue spectaculaire vers la ville jusqu'à l'océan ».

As the program undoubtedly required, the Caltrans building appears to be quite simply massive in its urban context.

Das umfangreiche Raumprogramm führt dazu, dass das Caltrans-Gebäude in seiner städtischen Umgebung sehr massiv wirkt.

Comme le programme l'exigeait sans doute, l'immeuble Caltrans s'inscrit assez massivement dans son contexte urbain.

With its jutting elements and band-
like openings, the building gives
a sense of dynamism that is not
evident when it is viewed from a
greater distance.

Mit seinen Auskragungen und horizontalen Öffnungen in der Fassade
wirkt das Gebäude aus der Nähe
dynamischer als aus größerer Entfer-
nung betrachtet.

Avec ses éléments en saillie et ses
ouvertures en bandeaux, l'immeuble
crée une certaine dynamique, même
si elle devient moins évidente dès
que l'on s'en éloigne.

As has been the case in much of Thom Mayne's work, the Caltrans building takes on a very definitely sculptural aspect through many of its design details.

Wie viele andere Projekte von Thom Mayne wird das Caltrans-Gebäude von einem dezidiert skulpturalen Ansatz geprägt, der sich in zahlreichen Entwurfsdetails zeigt.

Comme la plupart des réalisations de Thom Mayne, le Caltrans prend une allure vraiment sculpturale par le biais de multiples détails de sa conception.

OSCAR NIEMEYER

Oscar Niemeyer
Avenida Atlantica 3940
Rio de Janeiro
Brazil

Tel: +55 215 23 48 90
Fax: +55 212 67 63 88

Caminho Niemeyer

Born in Rio de Janeiro in 1907, **OSCAR NIEMEYER** studied at the Escola Nacional de Belas Artes. He graduated in 1934 and joined a team of Brazilian architects collaborating with Le Corbusier on a new Ministry of Education and Health in Rio de Janeiro. It was Lucio Costa, for whom he worked as an assistant, who introduced Niemeyer to Le Corbusier. Between 1940 and 1954, his work was based in three cities: Rio de Janeiro, São Paulo and Belo Horizonte. In 1956 Niemeyer was appointed architectural adviser to Nova Cap – an organization responsible for implementing Lucio Costa's plans for Brazil's new capital. The following year, he became its chief architect, designing most of the city's important buildings. In 1964 he sought exile in France for political reasons. There, amongst other structures, he designed the building for the French Communist Party in Paris. With the end of the dictatorship he returned to Brazil, immediately resuming his professional activities. He was awarded the Gold Medal of the American Institute of Architecture in 1970 and the 1988 Pritzker Prize. As this book went to press, he was working on at least fourteen new projects, including a huge administrative center for the province of Minas Gerais in Belo Horizonte, and an auditorium completed in 2004 to celebrate the 50th anniversary of his Ibirapuera Park in São Paulo.

OSCAR NIEMEYER wurde 1907 in Rio de Janeiro geboren. Er studierte an der Escola Nacional de Belas Artes, machte 1934 sein Diplom und wurde Mitarbeiter in einem Team brasilianischer Architekten, das mit Le Corbusier zusammen das neue Bildungs- und Gesundheitsministerium in Rio de Janeiro baute. Lucio Costa, für den Niemeyer als Assistent arbeitete, stellte ihn Le Corbusier vor. Zwischen 1940 und 1954 baute er in den drei Städten Rio de Janeiro, São Paulo und Belo Horizonte. 1956 wurde Niemeyer architektonischer Berater von Nova Cap, einem Gremium, das für die Umsetzung von Lucio Costas Planung für Brasiliens neue Hauptstadt verantwortlich war. Im darauf folgenden Jahr wurde er leitender Architekt von Nova Cap und entwarf einen Großteil der wichtigen Gebäude von Brasilia. 1964 ging er aus politischen Gründen ins französische Exil. Dort plante er u. a. das Gebäude für die Kommunistische Partei in Paris. Nach dem Ende der Diktatur in Brasilien ging er dorthin zurück und nahm die Arbeit an seinen Projekten unverzüglich wieder auf. 1970 erhielt er die Goldmedaille des American Institute of Architecture und 1988 den Pritzker-Preis. Zum Zeitpunkt der Drucklegung dieses Buches arbeitete er an mindestens 14 Projekten, darunter ein großes Verwaltungszentrum für die Provinz Minas Gerais in Belo Horizonte. 2004 wurde ein Auditorium für den 50. Geburtstag des Ibirapuera-Park in São Paulo fertig gestellt.

Né à Rio de Janeiro en 1907, **OSCAR NIEMEYER** étudie à la Escola Nacional de Belas Artes. Diplômé en 1934, il fait partie de l'équipe d'architectes brésiliens qui collabore avec Le Corbusier pour le nouveau ministère de l'Éducation et de la Santé à Rio. C'est Lucio Costa, dont il est l'assistant, qui l'introduisit auprès de Le Corbusier. De 1940 à 1954, il intervient essentiellement dans trois villes : Rio de Janeiro, São Paulo et Belo Horizonte. En 1956, il est nommé conseiller pour l'architecture de Nova Cap, organisme chargé de la mise en œuvre des plans de Costa pour la nouvelle capitale. L'année suivante, il devient son architecte en chef, dessinant la plupart des bâtiments importants de Brasilia. En 1964, il s'exile en France pour des raisons politiques. Là, il construit, entre autres, le siège du parti communiste à Paris. À la fin de la dictature, il retourne au Brésil, reprenant immédiatement ses responsabilités professionnelles. Il reçoit la médaille d'or de l'American Institute of Architecture en 1970 et le prix Pritzker en 1988. Au moment de mettre ce livre sous presse, il travaillait sur au moins 14 nouveaux projets, dont un énorme centre administratif pour l'État du Minas Gerais à Belo Horizonte et un auditorium pour célébrer le 50ᵉ anniversaire de son parc d'Ibirapuera à São Paulo.

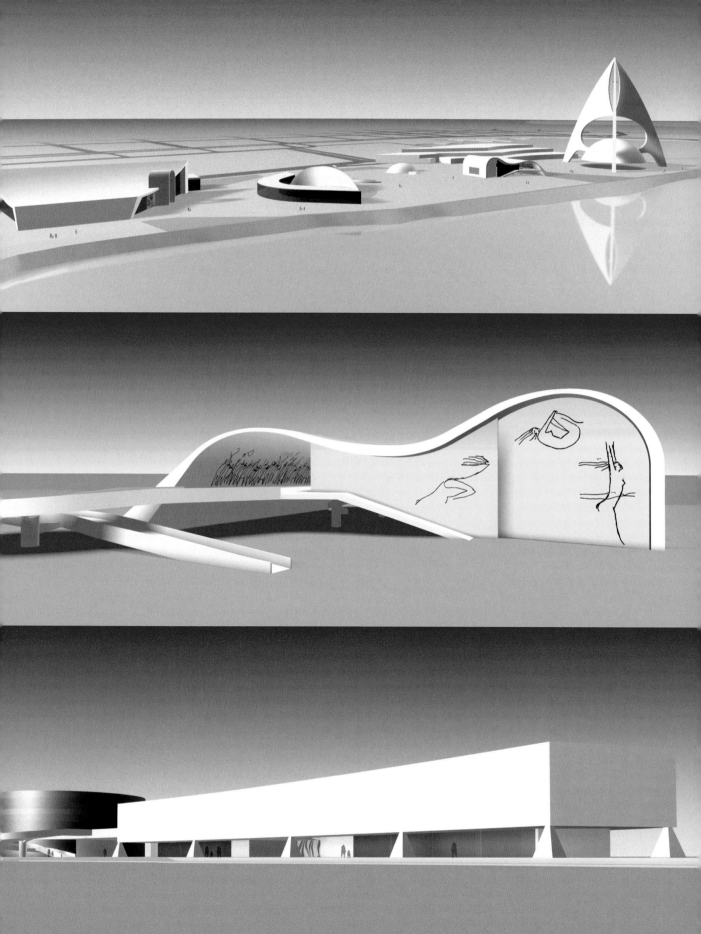

CAMINHO NIEMEYER

Niterói, Brazil, 1997–

Floor area: not disclosed. Client: various clients.
Cost: not disclosed

Oscar Niemeyer built the Museum of Contemporary Art (MAC) in Niterói, across Guanabara Bay from Rio, in 1993. After the completion of the MAC, city authorities approached the architect about creating a series of new buildings in the city in the hope of attracting tourism. Most of these are now nearing completion. Thus the **CAMINHO NIEMEYER**, or Niemeyer Path, came into being. The main group of new buildings in Niterói is located on a concrete platform set at the seaside near the city center. The first structure to actually have been completed is the Roberto Silveira Memorial Center, a 350-square-meter white concrete dome intended as a digital library for the city and a conference room. Silveira was the father of the mayor of Niterói who launched these projects, and a former governor of the state of Rio de Janeiro. A second nearly completed building is a 600-seat theater with a typical undulating concrete design and stunning yellow tile façade decorated with drawings by the architect of dancing figures. Nearby, the impressive concrete shell of the future Oscar Niemeyer Foundation headquarters awaits completion. The main building, set on a large reflecting pond, will be accessed via a spectacular ramp. An annex to the main 1600 m² structure will be a curved building for offices, classrooms and other facilities. Still on the drawing boards are a Baptist Church with a capacity of 5000 people and a Catholic Cathedral in the shape of the Papal Miter, as well as a ferry terminal and parking lot. Niemeyer also plans for a small chapel in the water with a capacity of 40 persons. Down the coast from this site, but still in Niterói, the Juscelino Kubitschek Square, completed in 2002, includes a sinuous concrete canopy similar to the one seen much earlier in the Ibirapuera Park, but on a smaller scale. Two hundred meters further along the coast, the Museum of Brazilian Cinema is taking form. Finally, the light and very successful Charitas Ferry Terminal (completed in October 2004) ends the Niemeyer Path.

Gegenüber von Rio de Janeiro, an der Bucht von Guanabara in Niterói, baute Oscar Niemeyer 1993 das Museum für Zeitgenössische Kunst (MAC). Nach dessen Fertigstellung wandte sich die Stadtverwaltung mit der Bitte an ihn, eine Reihe von neuen Gebäuden zu entwerfen, um damit den Tourismus zu fördern. Viele dieser Gebäude sind bald fertig; sie bilden den **CAMINHO NIEMEYER** (Niemeyerweg). Die meisten der neuen Gebäude in Niterói befinden sich – nicht weit vom Stadtzentrum entfernt – auf einer Betonplattform am Meer. Das erste bezugsfertige Gebäude war das Gedenkzentrum für Roberto Silveira, eine 350 m² große weiße Betonkuppel, die als digitale Bücherei und Konferenzsaal für die Stadt gedacht ist. Silveira ist der verstorbene Vater des Bürgermeisters von Niterói. Er brachte das Projekt auf den Weg und war Gouverneur des Bundesstaates Rio de Janeiro. Ein zweites, fast fertig gestelltes Gebäude ist ein Theater mit 600 Plätzen, das eine für Niemeyer typische wellige Form und eine eindrucksvolle Fassade aus gelben Wandfliesen aufweist, die mit tanzenden Figuren von Niemeyer gestaltet ist. Die imponierende Betonschale daneben, zukünftige Zentrale der Stiftung Oscar Niemeyer, wartet noch auf ihre Vollendung. Der Hauptbaukörper der Zentrale steht in einem großen, reflektierenden Teich und wird über eine spektakuläre Rampe erschlossen werden. Als Annex zum 1600 m² großen Hauptbau wird ein geschwungenes Gebäude mit Büros, Klassenräumen und anderen Einrichtungen errichtet. In der Planung befinden sich ferner eine 5000 Besucher fassende Baptistenkirche, ein katholischer Dom in Form der päpstlichen Mitra, ein Fährterminal und ein Parkplatz. Außerdem plant Niemeyer eine ebenfalls im Wasser stehende Kapelle für 40 Besucher. Südlich dieses Standortes, aber noch zu Niterói gehörend, liegt der 2002 fertig gestellte Platz Juscelino Kubitschek mit einer organisch geformten Überdachung, die ähnlich schon vor vielen Jahren in einem größeren Maßstab im Ibirapuera-Park zu sehen war. 200 m südlich nimmt das Museum für das brasilianische Kino Form an. Das leicht wirkende und sehr gelungene Fährterminal Charitas (2004) bildet den Abschluss des Caminho Niemeyer.

Oscar Niemeyer a construit le Musée d'art contemporain (MAC) de Niterói de l'autre côté de la baie de Guanabara, face à Rio de Janeiro, en 1993. Une fois celui-ci terminé, la municipalité demanda à l'architecte de créer une nouvelle série de bâtiments en espérant ainsi attirer des touristes. La plupart d'entre eux sont aujourd'hui en cours d'achèvement. Ils constituent à leur façon le **CAMINHO NIEMEYER** (ou chemin Niemeyer). Le groupe principal de ces nouvelles constructions se trouve sur une plate-forme de béton au bord de l'océan, près du centre-ville. Le premier bâtiment achevé est le Centre mémorial Roberto Silveira, un dôme en béton blanc de 350 m² qui regroupe une bibliothèque municipale numérique et une salle de conférence dédiés à Silveira, père du maire de Niterói, initiateur de ces projets et ancien gouverneur de l'État de Rio de Janeiro. Un second bâtiment, presque terminé, est un théâtre de 600 places affichant les courbes en béton caractéristiques de l'architecte et une étonnante façade en carrelage jaune étonnante décorée de figures de danseurs dessinées par Niemeyer lui-même. Non loin, l'impressionnante coque de béton du siège de la future Fondation Oscar Niemeyer attend son achèvement. On accèdera au bâtiment principal de 1600 m², implanté au milieu d'un vaste bassin réfléchissant, par une rampe spectaculaire. Une annexe incurvée tout en courbes accueillera notamment les bureaux et des salles de cours et diverses fonctions. Restent encore sur la planche à dessin, une église baptiste de 5000 places et une cathédrale catholique en forme de mitre papale, ainsi qu'un terminal de ferries et un parking. Niemeyer projette également une petite chapelle sur l'eau d'une capacité de 40 personnes. Plus bas sur la côte, mais toujours à Niterói, la place Juscelino Kubitschek, achevée en 2002, comprend un auvent sinueux en béton, semblable à celui du parc d'Ibirapuera, mais à plus petite échelle. Deux cent mètres plus loin au bord de la côte, le Musée du cinéma brésilien prend forme. Le léger et très réussi terminal de ferries de Charitas (achevé en octobre 2004) est le point final de ce « chemin Niemeyer ».

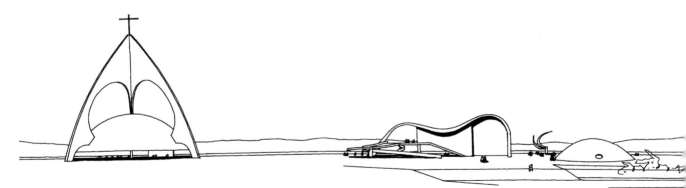

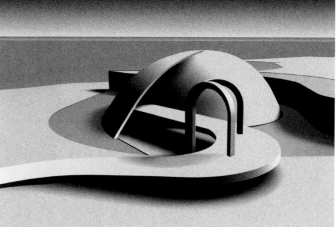

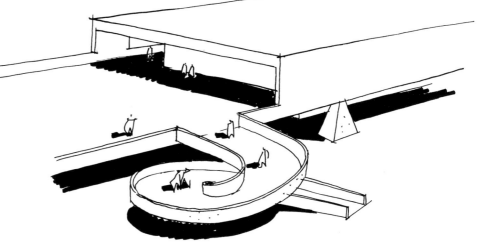

The main area of the Caminho Niemeyer opposite the center of Niteroi is shown below. Above center the new cinema museum on a different site. At the top of the page, the Niemeyer Foundation building, also visible right of center in the main drawing below.

Unten: Der Hauptteil des Caminho Niemeyer gegenüber des Zentrums von Niteroi. Oben: das neue Kino-Museum an einem anderen Abschnitt. Darüber: das Gebäude der Stiftung Oscar Niemeyer, das auch rechts der Mitte in der Hauptzeichnung unten zu sehen ist.

Ci-dessous : la partie principale du Caminho Niemeyer face au centre de Niteroi. Au-dessus au centre, le nouveau musée du cinéma sur un autre site. En haut, l'immeuble de la Fondation Niemeyer, également visible à droite sur le dessin principal, ci-dessous.

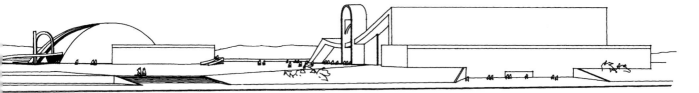

MARCOS NOVAK

Marcos Novak
510 Venice Way
Venice, California 90291
USA

e-mail: marcos@centrifuge.org
Web: www.centrifuge.org/marcos

Born in Caracas, Venezuela, **MARCOS NOVAK** grew up in Greece and received a Bachelor of Science in Architecture, a Master of Architecture and a Certificate of Specialization in Computer-Aided Architecture from Ohio State University (Columbus, Ohio), completing his studies in 1983. He has worked as a Research Fellow at the Center for Advanced Inquiry in the Interactive Arts at the University of Wales, as Co-Director of the Transarchitectures Foundation in Paris (with Paul Virilio). He has numerous publications to his credit. His work has been essentially virtual, and he is regarded as the "pioneer of the architecture of virtuality" according to the organizers of the 7th International Architecture Exhibition in Venice, in which he participated (Greek Pavilion). He is known for such projects as his "Sensor Space," "From Immersion to Eversion," "Transmitting Architecture," "Liquid Architectures," and "Metadata Visualization." Marcos Novak has taught at Ohio State, University of Texas Austin, the Architecture program at UCLA, the Digital Media program at UCLA, Art Center College of Art & Design, Pasadena, and is currently a professor at the University of California Santa Barbara.

MARCOS NOVAK wurde in Caracas geboren und wuchs in Griechenland auf. Er hat einen Bachelor of Science in Architecture, einen Master of Architecture und ein Zertifikat für Spezialwissen im Bereich CAD (Architektur) von der Ohio State University in Columbus, Ohio. 1983 schloss er sein Studium ab. Er war Forschungsstipendiat am Center for Advanced Inquiry in the Interactive Arts der University of Wales und stellvertretender Leiter der Transarchitectures Foundation in Paris (mit Paul Virilio). Ferner hat er zahlreiche Beiträge veröffentlicht. Seine Projekte sind hauptsächlich virtuell. Von den Organisatoren der VII. Architekturbiennale in Venedig, an der er mit dem Griechischen Pavillon teilnahm, wurde er als »Pionier der virtuellen Architektur« bezeichnet. Er ist bekannt durch Projekte wie das »Sensor Space«, »From Immersion to Eversion«, »Transmitting Architectures«, »Liquid Architectures« und »Metadata Visualization«. Marcos Novak hat an der Ohio State University und an der University of Texas, Austin, unterrichtet, und war außerdem beim »Architecture Program« und »Digital Media Program« an der UCLA und am Art Center College of Design in Pasadena tätig. Er ist Professor an der University of California (Santa Barbara).

Né à Caracas, Venezuela, **MARCOS NOVAK** a été élevé en Grèce et a étudié à l'Ohio State University (Columbus, Ohio) où il obtenu son Bachelor of Science in Architecture, son Master of Architecture et un certificat de spécialisation en CAA (conception architecturale assistée par ordinateur, 1983). Il a travaillé comme chercheur au Center for Advanced Inquiry in the Alternative Arts de l'Université du Pays de Galles et a dirigé (avec Paul Virilio) la Fondation Transarchitectures à Paris. Il a beaucoup publié. Ses œuvres sont essentiellement virtuelles et il est considéré comme le « pionnier de l'architecture de la virtualité » selon les organisateurs de la 7e Biennale d'architecture de Venise à laquelle il a participé (pavillon grec). Il est connu pour des projets comme son « Sensor Space », « From Immersion to Eversion », « Transmitting Architecture », « Liquid Architectures » et « Metadata Visualisation ». Marcos Novak a enseigné à l'Ohio State University (Columbus), à l'University of Texas (Austin), l'Architecture Program de UCLA, le Digital Media Program de UCLA, à l'Art Center College of Art & Design de Pasadena. Il est actuellement professeur à l'Université de Californie Santa Barbara.

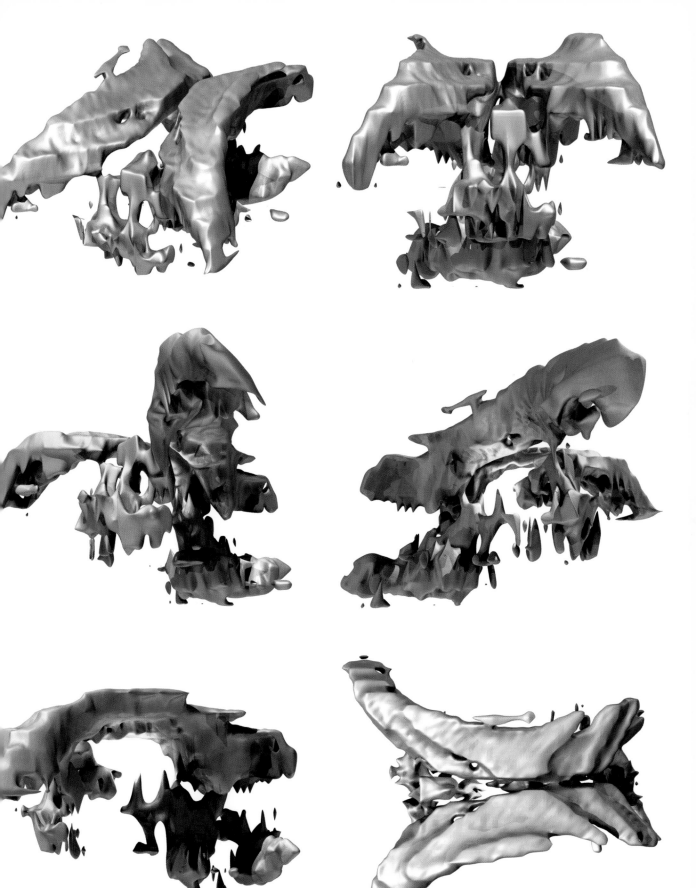

ALLOCORTEX / ALLONEURO

2005

Floor area: 34 000 m². Client: Silken Group. Cost: not disclosed

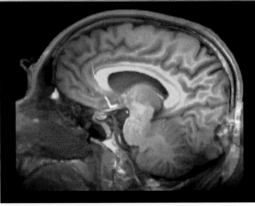

Wahrscheinlich ist es kein Zufall, dass die Formen, die Novak aus Tomografien seines Gehirns entwickelte, einen surrealen Ausdruck annehmen, wenn sie ein Stadium erreicht haben, das man als Präsentation von Architektur im weiteren Sinn bezeichnen könnte (unten).

Ce n'est sans doute pas une coïncidence si des formes dérivées d'images issues du propre cerveau de Novak prennent un aspect surréaliste lorsqu'elles se rapprochent de ce que l'on pourrait qualifier de présentation architecturale (photo ci-dessous).

It may be no coincidence that forms derived from Novak's brain scans seem to take on a Surreal appearance when they approach what might be called an architectural presentation (images below).

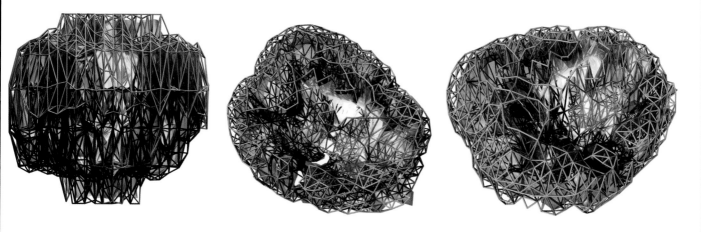

The idea that science, architecture and art can be united, not in a superficial way, but in their most fundamental manifestations, drives the creative impulse of Marcos Novak.

Die Vorstellung, dass Wissenschaft, Architektur und Kunst miteinander verbunden werden können – nicht oberflächlich, sondern in ihren grundlegenden Äußerungen – ist der kreative Antrieb für Novaks Projekte.

L'idée que la science, l'architecture et l'art peuvent s'unir, non de manière superficielle, mais dans leurs manifestations les plus fondamentales, anime la pulsion créative de Marcos Novak.

Working with sMRI and fMRI (structural and functional magnetic resonance imaging) of his own brain, scanned "in the act of observing the algorithmically generated spaces and forms," Novak used the data representing tissue near the corpus callosum to devise "the elements of architectural language." As he points out, the construct thus imagined has a legitimacy because it is literally born of his own brain, in the figurative and literal senses. Nor is the result simply a reproduction of brain structures – it is an interpretation given that the data can be "smoothed and refined" in various ways. Novak says that in related work, "the *AlloNeuroSpace* sequence moves toward a rendition of the brain as a virtual environment, increasingly emphasizing an atmospheric reading of the data and the spatial and formal character implied therein. This work recalls Kazimir Malevich's Suprematist manifesto *The Non-Objective World*, in which he states that while the goal of Suprematist abstraction is pure feeling, even in representational work what is valuable is not the accuracy of resemblance, but rather the feeling that is evoked, in the same abstract sense as that of Suprematist painting. In this case, the attempt is to take literally objective scientific data, but not to yield to that objectivity as far as the experiencing of those data is concerned, but to draw from them the very same kind of abstract feeling that Malevich describes." As unexpected as a reference to Suprematist painting is in this context, it is clear that Novak is above all creating bridges between different disciplines in a process that will surely enrich the future of architecture.

Mithilfe von sMRI und fMRI (strukturelle und funktionelle Kernspintomografie) ließ Marcos Novak Bilder seines eigenen Gehirns erstellen, »um algorithmisch generierte Räume und Formen zu betrachten«. Diese Daten, die das Gewebe in der Nähe des Corpus Callosum darstellen, benutzte er zur Schaffung von »Elementen der architektonischen Sprache«. Er weist darauf hin, dass das so entwickelte Konstrukt legitim ist, da es im übertragenen und im wörtlichen Sinn seinem eigenen Gehirn entstammt. Das Ergebnis ist nicht einfach nur die Reproduktion von Bildern von Gehirnstrukturen, sondern eine Interpretation, da die Daten auf verschiedene Arten »geglättet und verfeinert« werden können. Novak sagt, dass in ähnlichen Projekten »die AlloNeuro-Raumsequenz sich in Richtung einer Interpretation des Gehirns als eine virtuelle Umgebung bewegt und dabei verstärkt ein atmosphärisches Lesen der Daten und der darin implizierten räumlichen und formalen Eigenschaften betont. Dieses Projekt erinnert an Kasimir Malewitschs Suprematistisches Manifest *Die gegenstandslose Welt*, in dem er feststellte, dass neben der suprematistischen Abstraktion, die das reine Gefühl erreichen will, auch in abbildenden Arbeiten das Wichtige nicht die Genauigkeit der Abbildung ist, sondern das Gefühl, das hervorgerufen wird – im gleichen abstrakten Sinn wie in der suprematistischen Malerei. Der Versuch besteht darin, tatsächlich objektive wissenschaftliche Daten zu verwenden, aber nicht um deren Objektivität einzugestehen, was das Erleben dieser Daten betrifft, sondern um mit ihnen genau dasselbe abstrakte Gefühl zu erzeugen, das Malewitsch beschreibt.« Die Referenz zur suprematistischen Malerei kommt in diesem Kontext unerwartet. Klar ist aber, dass es Novak vor allem darum geht, in einen Prozess, der die Zukunft der Architektur sicherlich bereichern wird, Brücken zwischen verschiedenen Disziplinen zu schlagen.

À l'aide d'images de son cerveau obtenues par sMRI et fMRI (imagerie par résonance magnétique structurelle et fonctionnelle) « pendant qu'il observait des volumes et des espaces générés par algorithmes », Novak s'est servi de données représentant le tissu cellulaire proche du corps calleux pour mettre au point « les éléments d'un langage architectural ». Comme il le fait remarquer, la construction ainsi imaginée possède sa légitimité car elle est, littéralement, née de son propre cerveau, au sens tant littéral que figuré. Le résultat n'est pas pour autant une simple reproduction des structures cérébrales, il s'agit d'une interprétation puisque les données obtenues peuvent être « arrangées et affinées » de diverses façons. Marcos Novak explique que, dans sa recherche intitulée *AlloNeuroSpace*, « la séquence s'oriente vers un rendu du cerveau comparable à un environnement virtuel, s'attachant de plus en plus à une lecture atmosphérique des données et du caractère formel et spatial qu'il implique. Ce travail rappelle le manifeste suprématiste de Kazimir Malévitch, *Le Monde non-objectif,* dans lequel il déclarait que, si le but de l'abstraction suprématiste était bien le sentiment pur, ce qui comptait dans le monde de la représentation n'était pas la précision de la ressemblance mais plutôt le sentiment évoqué, dans le même sens abstrait que celui de la peinture suprématiste. Ici, la tentative est de prendre littéralement des données scientifiques objectives mais, au lieu de se contenter de cette objectivité … d'en tirer le type de sentiment abstrait décrit par Malévitch ». Aussi surprenante que soit la référence à ce type de peinture, il est clair que Novak cherche avant tout à créer des passerelles entre différentes disciplines à travers un processus qui enrichira certainement l'architecture de demain.

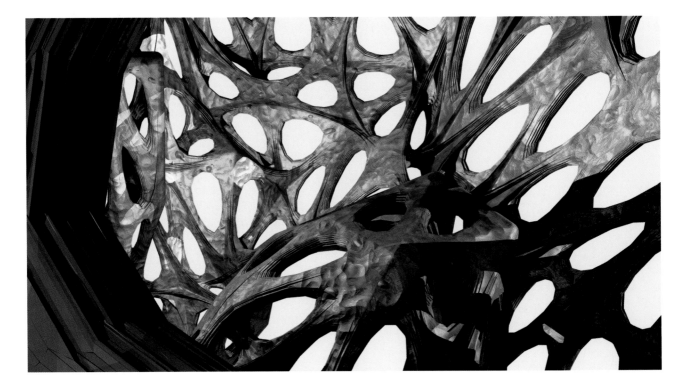

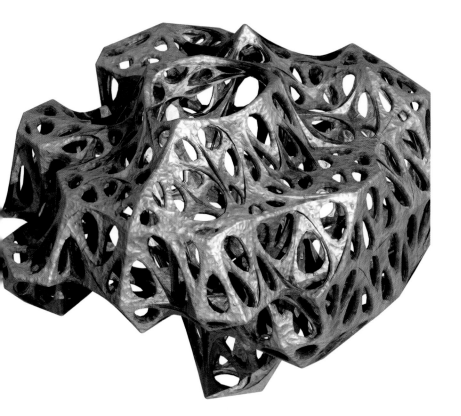

On occasion, Novak's explorations take on shapes that are more readily identifiable as having been derived from the structure of the brain.

Manchmal ist der Ausgangspunkt für Novaks Forschungsarbeit, das menschliche Gehirn, auch leichter zu erkennen.

Parfois, les explorations de Novak prennent des formes dont l'origine cérébrale est plus évidente.

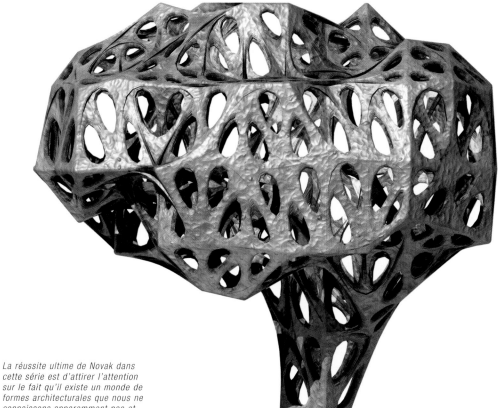

The ultimate achievement of Novak in this series is to call attention to the fact that there is an entire world of architectural form that is unlike any we have ever seen, and yet which has an intimate relationship to the way we are … inside.

Letztlich besteht Novaks Leistung bei dieser Reihe darin, die Aufmerksamkeit darauf zu lenken, dass es eine architektonische Formenwelt gibt, die sich gänzlich von der uns bekannten unterscheidet. Diese Formenwelt steht in enger Beziehung zum Menschen und seinem »Innenleben«.

La réussite ultime de Novak dans cette série est d'attirer l'attention sur le fait qu'il existe un monde de formes architecturales que nous ne connaissons apparemment pas et qui, pourtant, est intimement lié à la façon dont nous sommes … faits.

ONL

ONL [Oosterhuis_Lénárd]
Essenburgsingel 94c
3022 EG Rotterdam
The Netherlands

Tel: +31 102 44 70 39
Fax: +31 102 44 70 41
e-mail: oosterhuis@oosterhuis.nl
Web: www.oosterhuis.nl

ONL [Oosterhuis_Lénárd] is described as a "multidisciplinary architectural firm where architects, visual artists, web designers and programmers work together and join forces." Kas Oosterhuis was born in Amersfoort in 1951. He studied architecture at the Technical University in Delft (1970–79) and was a Unit Master at the AA in London in 1987–89. He has been a Professor at the Technical University in Delft since 2000. He is a member of the board of the Witte de With Museum in Rotterdam. He has built the Multimedia Pavilion, North Holland Floriade (2000–01); Headquarters for True Colors, Utrecht (2000–01) and the Salt Water Pavilion, Neeltje Jans, Zeeland (1994–97). Ilona Lénárd is the other principal of ONL. A visual artist, she was born in Hungary, she worked in the Atelier Theo van Doesburg in Meudon, France (1988–89). She has worked with Kas Oosterhuis on various projects that involve a fusion of art and architecture. One notable recent project is the WTC 9/11 project that proposes a "self-executable and programmable hi-res building which reconfigures its shape, content and character during one year of its life cycle." Other recent work includes: 9 Variomatic catalogue houses, Deventer (2000); TT monument, Assen (2000); and an Acoustic Barrier, Leidsche Rijn, Utrecht (2002). ONL has recently worked on a number of other projects: Their Flyotel (Dubai) is in the design phase and Oosterhuis has also worked on sophisticated projects that use engineering or game software to develop new types of space. ONL's "Protospace" project at the TU Delft involves creating virtual, interactive architecture.

ONL [Oosterhuis_Lénárd] wird als »multidisziplinäres Architekturbüro, in dem Architekten, Grafiker, Webdesigner und Programmierer zusammenarbeiten« beschrieben. Kas Oosterhuis, geboren 1951 in Amersfoort, studierte an der Technischen Universität Delft (1970–79) und lehrte von 1987 bis 1989 als »Unit Master« an der AA in London. Seit 2000 ist er Professor an der Technischen Universität Delft und Mitglied des Rates des Museums Witte de With in Rotterdam. Oosterhuis hat den Multimedia Pavillon für die Nordholland-Floriade (2000–01) gebaut, die Firmenzentrale von True Colors in Utrecht (2000–01) und den Salzwasserpavillon in Neeltje Jans, Zeeland (1994–97). Ilona Lénárd ist die zweite Geschäftsführerin von ONL. Die in Ungarn geborene bildende Künstlerin arbeitete von 1988 bis 1989 bei Theo van Doesburg in Meudon, Frankreich. Mit Kas Oosterhuis hat sie verschiedene Projekte bearbeitet, bei denen es um eine Verbindung von Kunst und Architektur geht. Ein bemerkenswerter Entwurf ist das WTC 9/11. Mit ihm wird ein »sich selbst schaffendes und programmierendes Hochhaus vorgeschlagen, das seine Form, seinen Inhalt und seine charakteristischen Eigenschaften im Verlauf eines Jahres seiner Lebensdauer neu konfiguriert«. Andere Arbeiten der jüngeren Zeit sind u. a. die neun Variomatic-Kataloghäuser in Deventer (2000), das TT Denkmal in Assen (2000) und eine »Schallschutzbarriere« in Leidsche Rijn, Utrecht (2002). Derzeit plant ONL eine Reihe weiterer Projekte: Das Flyotel in Dubai ist in der Entwurfsphase, außerdem beschäftigt sich Oosterhuis mit anspruchsvollen Projekten, bei denen Ingenieur- oder Spielesoftware eingesetzt wird, um neuartige Raumtypen zu entwickeln. Das Projekt »Protospace« an der TU Delft befasst sich mit virtueller, interaktiver Architektur.

ONL [Oosterhuis_Lénárd] est une « agence d'architecture pluridisciplinaire dans laquelle architectes, artistes visuels, web designers et programmeurs se sont réunis pour travailler ensemble ». Kas Oosterhuis, né à Amersfoort en 1951, étudie l'architecture à l'Université technique de Delft (1970–79), puis exerce comme Unit Master à l'Architectural Association de Londres en 1987–89. Il enseigne à l'Université technique de Delft depuis 2000 et fait partie du conseil d'administration du Witte de With Museum de Rotterdam. Il a réalisé le Salt Water Pavilion, Neeltje Jans, Zélande (1994–97), le pavillon multimédia de la Hollande Septentrionale à l'exposition internationale d'horticulture Floriade 2002, Haarlemmermeer (2000–01) et le siège social de True Colors à Utrecht (2000–01). Ilona Lénárd est l'autre responsable d'ONL. Artiste plasticienne née en Hongrie, elle a travaillé dans l'Atelier Theo van Doesburg à Meudon (France, 1988–89). Elle travaille avec Kas Oosterhuis sur des projets variés qui impliquent une fusion d'art et d'architecture. Une de leurs œuvres récentes les plus remarquées est le projet WTC 9/11, un « bâtiment auto-constructible et programmable haute résistance qui reconfigure sa forme, son contenu et son caractère au cours d'une année de son cycle de vie ». Parmi leurs autres réalisations récentes : neuf maisons sur catalogue Variomatic, Deventer (2000) ; le monument TT, Assen (2000) et une barrière acoustique, Leidsche Rijn, Utrecht (2002). ONL travaille également à des projets sophistiqués qui font appel à l'ingénierie ou aux logiciels de jeux pour mettre au point de nouveaux types d'espaces. Le projet « Protospace » à l'Université technique de Delft fait appel à une architecture virtuelle interactive.

FLYOTEL
Dubai, United Arab Emirates, 2004–

Floor area: 66 000 m². Height: 270 m. Client: not disclosed.
Cost: €178.2 million

Part of a wave of new projects planned in Dubai, the **FLYOTEL** is a concept developed by Yasmine Mahmoudieh around the idea of the "passion of flying." As the architects describe the project, a five-star hotel with 600 rooms, "The organic form of the building reminds of a bird, who spreads out its wings and lifts up its head just before starting to fly." Working with the engineers Arup, ONL conceived the building around a three-dimensional computer model permitting "file-to-factory" production of the required materials. This is very much the concept highlighted in the recent "Non-Standard Architecture" held at the Pompidou Center in Paris. According to the architect's calculations, despite its highly unusual shape, the Flyotel should cost "only 10% more than a standard high-rise structure." Restaurants and/or bars are placed every eight floors in the hotel, with one underwater since the building is due to be erected on the ocean bed near shore. Yasmine Mahmoudieh has designed the interiors in harmony with the shapes and colors of the architecture. A lower extension of the building creates a link to the shore while offering marina facilities, or potentially space for seaplanes.

Das **FLYOTEL** gehört zu einer wahren Flut von Projekten, die derzeit für Dubai in Planung sind. Es wurde von Yasmine Mahmoudieh entwickelt und beschäftigt sich mit dem Traum vom Fliegen. Die Architekten beschreiben das Fünf-Sterne-Hotel mit 600 Zimmern so: »Die organische Form des Gebäudes erinnert an einen Vogel, der seine Flügel ausbreitet und seinen Kopf anhebt, bevor er losfliegt.« In Zusammenarbeit mit dem Ingenieurbüro Arup hat ONL das Gebäude mithilfe eines dreidimensionalen Computermodells entwickelt, das eine »file-to-factory«-Produktion erlaubt. Dies entspricht genau dem Konzept, das bei der kürzlich gezeigten Schau »Non-Standard Architecture« im Centre Georges Pompidou in Paris im Mittelpunkt stand. Nach Berechnungen der Architekten wird das Flyotel trotz seiner äußerst ungewöhnlichen Form »nur zehn Prozent mehr kosten als ein gewöhnliches Hochhaus«. Restaurants und/oder Bars sind in jedem achten Geschoss des Hotels vorgesehen, ein Gastronomiebetrieb befindet sich unter Wasser, da das Hotel im Meer, nahe der Küste, gebaut werden soll. Yasmine Mahmoudieh hat die Innenräume in Einklang mit den Formen und Farben der Architektur entworfen. Ein niedriger Anbau verbindet das Flyotel mit der Küste; hier soll ein Jachthafen liegen, oder möglicherweise ein Hafen für Wasserflugzeuge.

Dans le cadre d'une vague de réalisations architecturales qui transforme Dubaï, le **FLYOTEL**, hôtel cinq étoiles de 600 chambres, est un concept développé par Yasmine Mahmoudieh autour de l'idée de « passion du vol ». Pour l'architecte, « la forme organique de l'immeuble rappelle un oiseau qui déploie ses ailes et relève la tête juste avant de s'envoler ». En collaboration avec les ingénieurs d'Ove Arup and Partners, ONL a conçu l'hôtel à partir d'une maquette virtuelle en trois dimensions permettant de transmettre directement les informations de fabrication nécessaires aux fournisseurs de matériaux et de pièces. C'est en grande partie le concept mis en exergue par la récente exposition « Architecture non-standard » organisée par le Centre Pompidou à Paris. Selon les calculs et malgré sa forme qui sort de l'ordinaire, le Flyotel ne devrait coûter que « 10% de plus qu'un immeuble standard de grande hauteur ». Des restaurants ou des bars sont implantés tous les huit niveaux, dont un sous-marin puisque l'immeuble est érigé sur le fond de l'océan près de la côte. Yasmine Mahmoudieh a conçu les aménagements intérieurs en harmonie avec les formes et les couleurs de l'architecture. Une extension, nettement moins haute, crée un lien avec le rivage, tout en offrant un abri pour les bateaux et même pour des hydravions.

ONL's Flyotel is part of the burgeoning world of modern architecture that is taking form in Dubai. The desire to be unusual or up-to-date fuels an openness that might not necessarily be expected of what has not long been a financial or business center.

ONLs Flyotel partizipiert am Bauboom in Dubai. Der Wunsch nach Außergewöhnlichem und Hypermodernem begünstigt eine Offenheit, die an diesem Ort, der noch nicht lange Finanz- und Geschäftszentrum ist, nicht unbedingt zu erwarten ist.

Le Flyotel d'ONL fait partie de cet univers architectural bourgeonnant qui fleurit à Dubaï. Le désir d'être le pionnier nourrit une ouverture d'esprit que l'on n'attendait peut-être pas de ce qui ne fut longtemps qu'un centre financier ou d'affaires.

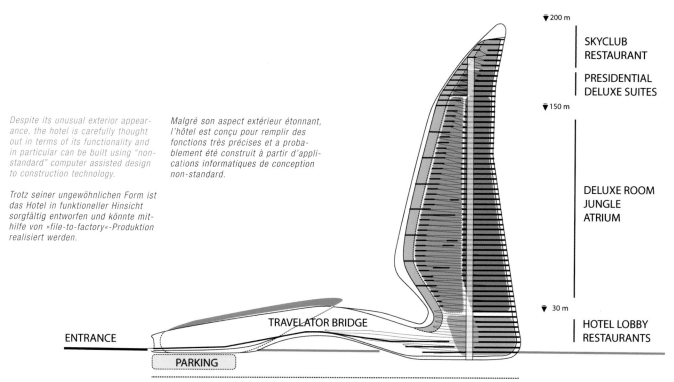

Despite its unusual exterior appearance, the hotel is carefully thought out in terms of its functionality and in particular can be built using "non-standard" computer assisted design to construction technology.

Trotz seiner ungewöhnlichen Form ist das Hotel in funktioneller Hinsicht sorgfältig entworfen und könnte mithilfe von »file-to-factory«-Produktion realisiert werden.

Malgré son aspect extérieur étonnant, l'hôtel est conçu pour remplir des fonctions très précises et a probablement été construit à partir d'applications informatiques de conception non-standard.

200 m · SKYCLUB RESTAURANT
PRESIDENTIAL DELUXE SUITES
150 m ·
DELUXE ROOM JUNGLE ATRIUM
30 m · HOTEL LOBBY RESTAURANTS

TRAVELATOR BRIDGE

ENTRANCE

PARKING

200 m

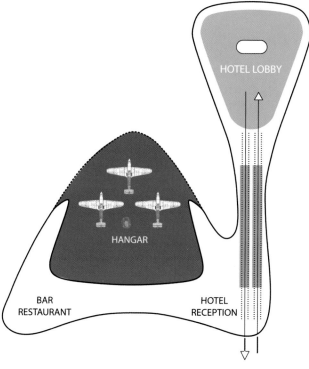

HOTEL LOBBY

HANGAR

BAR RESTAURANT

HOTEL RECEPTION

TRAVELATOR

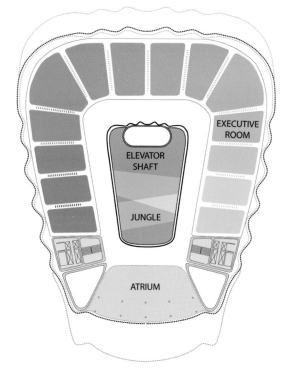

EXECUTIVE ROOM

ELEVATOR SHAFT

JUNGLE

ATRIUM

JOHN PAWSON

John Pawson
Unit B
70–78 York Way
London N1 9AG
UK

Tel: +44 20 78 37 29 29
Fax: +44 20 78 37 49 49
e-mail: email@johnpawson.co.uk
Web: www.johnpawson.com

Monastery of Novy Dv

Born in Halifax in central England in 1949, **JOHN PAWSON** attended Eton and worked in his own family's textile mill before going to Japan for four years. On his return, he studied at the AA in London and set up his own firm in 1981. His has worked on numerous types of project including the flagship store for Calvin Klein in New York, airport lounges for Cathay Pacific airlines at the Chek Lap Kok Airport in Hong Kong, and a small apartment for the author Bruce Chatwin. Pawson may be even better known to the general public because of his 1996 book *Minimum* that focused on such essential subjects as light, structure, ritual, landscape and volume. Because of this book, but also because of his style, Pawson has come to be considered an essential figure in the minimalist style of recent years. Some of his current work includes: Delafontaine House, Knokke, Belgium (2003); Taira House, Okinawa (2003); Lansdowne Lodge Apartments, Grainger Trust, London (2003); Radcliffe Museum, Bury Council, Bury, UK (2004); Calvin Klein Apartment, New York (2003); and The Young Vic Theatre, London (in progress). He also worked on the Hotel Puerta América in Madrid.

JOHN PAWSON, geboren 1949 in Halifax in Mittelengland, war Schüler in Eton und arbeitete in der Textilfabrik seiner Familie, bevor er für vier Jahre nach Japan ging. Danach studierte er an der Architectural Association in London und gründete 1981 sein eigenes Büro. Er hat ganz unterschiedliche Projekte realisiert, so z. B. den Flagship Store für Calvin Klein in New York, Flughafenlounges für Cathay Pacific Airlines im Chek Lap Kok Flughafen in Hongkong sowie ein kleines Apartment für den Autor Bruce Chatwin. Noch bekannter ist Pawson der Öffentlichkeit vielleicht durch sein Buch *Minimum*, das 1996 veröffentlicht wurde und sich mit Grundelementen wie Licht, Struktur, Ritual, Landschaft und Volumen befasst. Wegen dieses Buches, aber auch wegen seines architektonischen Stils, wurde Pawson in den letzten Jahren zu einer Schlüsselfigur des Minimalismus. Neuere Projekte von ihm sind u. a. das Haus Delafontaine in Knokke, Belgien (2003), das Haus Taira in Okinawa (2003), die Lansdowne Lodge Apartments des Grainger Trust in London (2003), das Radcliffe Museum für das Bury Council in Bury, England (2004), ferner ein Apartment für Calvin Klein in New York (2003) und The Young Vic Theatre in London (in Planung). Auch am Hotel Puerta América in Madrid war er beteiligt.

Né à Halifax en Angleterre en 1949, **JOHN PAWSON**, après des études à Eton, a travaillé dans l'usine textile familiale avant de séjourner quatre ans au Japon. À son retour, il a étudié à l'Architectural Association de Londres et créé son agence en 1981. Il a travaillé sur de nombreux types de projets, dont le magasin principal de Calvin Klein à New York (1995), les salons du nouvel aéroport de Hong Kong pour Cathay Pacific (1998) et un petit appartement pour l'écrivain Bruce Chatwin (1982). Le grand public le connaît sans doute plus grâce au succès de son livre, *Minimum* (1996), sur les thèmes de la lumière, de la structure, du rituel, du paysage et du volume. À la suite de ce livre, mais aussi parce que c'est son style, Pawson a été considéré comme une figure essentielle du minimalisme contemporain. Parmi ses réalisations récentes : Maison Delafontaine (Knokke, Belgique, 2003, chantier en cours) ; Taira House (Okinawa, 2003, en cours) ; immeuble d'appartements de Lansdowne Lodge, Grainger Trust, Londres (2004) ; Radcliffe Museum (Bury, Royaume-Uni, 2004, en cours) ; appartement de Calvin Klein, New York (2005) et le Young Vic Theatre (Londres, 2002, en cours). Il a également collaboré aux aménagements de l'Hotel Puerta América à Madrid.

MONASTERY OF NOVY DVÛR

Toužim, Czech Republic, 2004

Floor Area: 70m x 70m (4900 m²) Client: Monastery of Saint Lieu Sept-Fons.
Cost: not disclosed

John Pawson was asked to work on a new monastery by French Cistercian monks in 1999. The site they had selected was a 100-hectare estate located west of Prague, with an 18th century manor house that had been uninhabited for forty years. The monks were familiar with Pawson's book *Minimum* and had seen images of his Calvin Klein store in Manhattan before selecting him. Pawson, who has called the **NOVY DVÛR MONASTERY** "the project of a lifetime," recalls that the "monastic cloister has been likened to an enclosed city, with many sub-programs typically including the functions of church, home, office, school, workshop, guesthouse, hospital and farm." Basing his own 6500 m² scheme on the blueprint drawn up in the 12th century for the Cistercian Order's buildings by Saint Bernard of Clairvaux, which called for simple, pared-down spaces and a respect for light and correct proportions, Pawson restored the baroque manor house and added three wings of new architecture along the lines of pre-existing structures. Pawson was familiar with the Abbaye du Thoronet, a Cistercian abbey located between Draguignan and Brignoles in southern France, but this was the first time he designed a religious building. He explains, "I didn't have to adapt my style particularly. I'd already read Saint Bernard's rules [the Apologia of 1127, against artistic adornment], so the ideas all made sense to me." The challenge of the project as he explains was to design the monastery so that the very precise movements and rituals of the monks could be carried out without hindrance. "The church," he concludes, "had to make praying easier – to bring calm and pleasure – but also to be stimulating without being distracting."

1999 beauftragten französische Zisterziensermönche John Pawson mit der Planung eines neuen Klosters. Als Standort hatten sich die Mönche ein 100 ha großes Grundstück westlich von Prag ausgesucht, mit einem Herrenhaus aus dem 18. Jahrhundert, das 40 Jahre lang nicht bewohnt worden war. Sie kannten Pawsons Buch *Minimum* und hatten Bilder seines Apartments für Calvin Klein in Manhattan gesehen, bevor sie ihn als Architekten auswählten. Pawson, der das **KLOSTER NOVY DVÛR** »das Projekt seines Lebens« nennt, erwähnt, dass ein »Mönchskloster mit einer in sich abgeschlossenen Stadt verglichen wird, mit vielen ›Unterprogrammen‹, die typischerweise Funktionen wie Kirche, Wohnraum, Büro, Schule, Werkstatt, Gästehaus, Krankenhaus und Bauernhof beinhalten.« Pawsons 6500 m² umfassender Entwurf basiert auf einer Zeichnung aus dem 12. Jahrhundert, die der heilige Bernhard von Clairvaux für die Gebäude des Zisterzienserordens anfertigte. Er sah einfache Räume mit natürlicher Beleuchtung und stimmigen Proportionen vor. Pawson setzte das barocke Herrenhaus instand und fügte drei moderne Flügel an, die sich exakt dort befinden, wo bereits früher Gebäude standen. Die Abbaye du Thoronet, eine Zisterzienserabtei zwischen Draguignan und Brignoles in Südfrankreich, war Pawson bekannt; aber zum ersten Mal hat er selbst ein Gebäude mit einer religiösen Funktion entworfen. Er erläutert: »Ich musste meinen Stil nicht besonders anpassen. Ich hatte schon vorher die Regeln des heiligen Bernhard gelesen (die Apologie von 1127 gegen künstlerische Verzierung), daher fand ich die Ideen alle sehr einleuchtend.« Die Herausforderung des Projekts, so Pawson, bestand darin, das Kloster so zu entwerfen, dass die präzisen Ordensregeln und Rituale der Mönche ohne Behinderungen ausgeführt werden können. »Die Kirche«, sagt er abschließend, »sollte das Beten vereinfachen – sie sollte Ruhe und Freude vermitteln – aber sie sollte auch anregend wirken ohne abzulenken.«

C'est en 1999 que des moines cisterciens français ont demandé à John Pawson de les aider à édifier un nouveau monastère dans un domaine de cent hectares à l'ouest de Prague, sur lequel s'élevait un manoir du XVIIIe siècle, inhabité depuis plus de quarante ans. Les religieux connaissaient bien l'ouvrage *Minimum* et avaient vu des photos du magasin Calvin Klein à Manhattan avant de le sélectionner. Pawson, pour lequel cette commande est « le projet de [sa] vie », rappelle que « le monastère a été comparé à une ville fermée, remplissant les multiples fonctions d'église, de foyer, de bureaux, d'école, d'ateliers, de maison d'hôtes, d'hôpital et de ferme ». Appuyant son projet de 6500 m² sur les recommandations établies au XIIe siècle pour les bâtiments de l'Ordre par saint Bernard de Clairvaux, qui voulait des espaces simples et épurés ainsi que le respect de la lumière et de proportions correctes, Pawson a restauré le manoir baroque et lui a ajouté trois ailes sur les traces d'anciennes constructions. Il connaissait bien l'abbaye du Thoronet, ensemble cistercien situé non loin de Draguignan et Brignoles dans le Midi de la France, mais c'était la première fois qu'il devait concevoir un édifice religieux : « Je n'ai pas eu à adapter particulièrement mon style. J'avais déjà lu la règle de saint Bernard [l'Apologie de la vie monastique de 1127 contre l'ornement artistique], aussi toutes ses idées avaient-elles déjà un sens pour moi. » Le défi était dès lors de concevoir un monastère dans lequel les mouvements et les rituels précis des moines pouvaient se dérouler sans la moindre gêne. « L'église, » conclut-il, « devait favoriser la prière – apporter le calme et le plaisir – mais également être stimulante sans pour autant distraire. »

Pawson's careful study of the functions of the Monastery ultimately led him to create simple forms that do not contradict those of the existing buildings on the site.

Pawsons genaue Analyse der funktionalen Abläufe im Kloster führte letztlich zu den einfachen Formen, die mit dem Bestehenden harmonieren.

L'étude approfondie des fonctions du monastère a finalement incité Pawson à créer des formes simples qui ne heurtent pas celles des bâtiments préexistants.

Passageways and patterns of light are the most obvious traces of architecture in these images, where all extraneous intervention has been set aside.

Die Wege und die Lichtführung sind die deutlichsten Spuren einer Architektur, die jede unwesentliche Intervention vermeidet.

Des passages et des effets de lumière sont les traces d'architecture les plus évidentes dans ces images dont toute intervention extérieure semble avoir été exclue.

Pawson's work shows that there is nothing that prohibits centuries-old traditions from being served by contemporary architecture.

Pawsons Projekt zeigt, dass auch zeitgenössische Architektur im Dienst jahrhundertealter Tradition stehen kann.

Le projet de Pawson montre que même l'architecture contemporaine peut être au service d'une tradition séculaire.

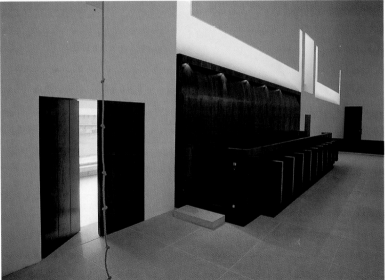

An occasional liturgical object or piece of wooden furniture enters this realm of light and worship. Pawson has sought and surely found something of the quintessence of architecture in Novy Dvůr.

Ein liturgisches Objekt oder ein einzelnes Möbelstück aus Holz findet sich in diesem Reich des Lichtes und der Anbetung. Pawson hat in Novy Dvůr etwas von der Quintessenz von Architektur gesucht und sicher auch gefunden.

De temps à autre, un objet liturgique ou un meuble en bois fait son apparition dans ce lieu de lumière et de prière. À Novy Dvůr, Pawson a cherché et certainement trouvé quelque chose qui se rapproche de la quintessence de l'architecture.

PHILIPPE RAHM

Philippe Rahm architectes
12, rue Chabanais
75002 Paris
France

Tel: +33 149 26 91 55
e-mail: contact@low-architecture.com
Web: www.philipperahm.com

PHILIPPE RAHM was born in 1967 and studied architecture at the EPFL in Lausanne and the ETH in Zurich, graduating in 1993. He created the firm Décosterd & Rahm associés with Gilles Décosterd in 1995 in Lausanne. They won a number of competitions in Switzerland and participated in numerous exhibitions in Europe and the United States and later, in Japan. Amongst these were the 2003 Biennal de Valencia, Spain; and Archilab, Orléans, France, 2000. Their work presented at the CCA Kitakyushu (2004) was called *Ghost Flat*, a three-room apartment "constructed" out of light rather than more conventional materials. All of the rooms occupy the same dimensions of space and time, but each occupies a separate part of the electromagnetic spectrum. Depending on which part of the spectrum you select, you see a different set of furnishings in front of you. The bedroom appears between 400 and 500 nanometers, the living room between 600 and 800 nanometers, etc. Décosterd & Rahm represented Switzerland in the 2002 Venice Architecture Biennale, and then received the Swiss Federal Art Prize in 2003. They worked on an atelier-residence for the artist Fabrice Hybert in the Vendée region of France, and on a project for a park in San Sebastián, Spain with the landscape architects Gilles Clément and Joseph Andeuza. Rahm and Déscosterd ceased direct collaboration in 2005 and Philppe Rahm created his own firm, Philippe Rahm architectes in Paris.

PHILIPPE RAHM wurde 1967 geboren und studierte an der EPFL in Lausanne und an der ETH in Zürich Architektur. 1993 machte er sein Diplom. Zusammen mit Gilles Décosterd gründete er 1995 in Lausanne das Büro Décosterd & Rahm associés. Das Büro hat in der Schweiz eine Reihe von Wettbewerben gewonnen und an zahlreichen Ausstellungen in Europa, den USA und in Japan teilgenommen, 2000 z. B. an der Archilab in Orléans, Frankreich, und 2003 an der Biennale in Valencia. 2004 wurde ihr Projekt *Ghost Flat* auf der CCA Kitakyushu gezeigt: eine Dreizimmerwohnung, die nicht aus konventionellen Materialien, sondern aus Licht »konstruiert« war. Alle Räume sind räumlich und zeitlich gesehen gleich groß, jeder nimmt jedoch einen anderen Teil des elektromagnetischen Spektrums ein. Je nach dem, welchen Teil des Spektrums man auswählt, sieht man ein anderes Mobiliar vor sich. Das Schlafzimmer erscheint zwischen 400 und 500 Nanometern, das Wohnzimmer zwischen 600 und 800 Nanometern usw. Décosterd & Rahm repräsentierten die Schweiz 2002 auf der Architekturbiennale in Venedig und erhielten 2003 den Schweizer Kunstpreis. Sie haben ein Atelier-Wohnhaus für den Künstler Fabrice Hybert im Departement Vendée in Frankreich geplant und, in Zusammenarbeit mit den Landschaftsplanern Gilles Clément und Joseph Andeuza, ein Projekt für einen Park im baskischen San Sebastián. Rahm hat 2005 die Partnerschaft mit Décosterd aufgegeben und ein neues Büro in Paris eröffnet.

Né en 1967, **PHILIPPE RAHM** a fait ses études d'architecture à l'EPFL (Lausanne) et à l'ETH (Zurich). Il a créé l'agence Décosterd & Rahm Associés avec Gilles Décosterd à Lausanne en 1995. Ensemble, ils ont remporté un certain nombre de concours en Suisse et participé à de nombreuses expositions en Europe, dont la Biennale de Valence en Espagne (2003) et Archilab à Orléans, France (2000), aux États-Unis, puis au Japon. Leur œuvre présentée au CCA Kitakyushu en 2004, baptisée *Ghost Flat*, était un appartement de quatre pièces « construit » à partir de la lumière plutôt que de matériaux plus conventionnels. Toutes les pièces occupaient la même surface au même moment, mais chacune n'était visible que dans une fraction précise du spectre électromagnétique. Selon la zone sélectionnée, on pouvait voir ainsi surgir différents types de mobilier. La chambre apparaissait entre 400 et 500 nanomètres, le séjour entre 600 et 800, etc. Décosterd & Rahm ont représenté la Suisse à la Biennale d'architecture de Venise en 2002 et reçu le prix fédéral d'art suisse en 2003. Ils ont conçu un atelier-résidence pour l'artiste Fabrice Hybert en Vendée (France) et un projet de parc à San Sebastian (Espagne) avec les architectes paysagistes Gilles Clément et Joseph Andueza. Rahm et Décosterd ont cessé leur collaboration en 2005 et Philippe Rahm s'est installé à Paris.

VACATION RESIDENCES

Vassivière, Limousin, France, 2005

Floor area: 70 houses, 70 m² each. Client: SYMIVA (Syndicat mixte interdépartemental et régional de Vassivière).
Cost: not disclosed

The basic idea of this project is to create a relationship between interior space and humidity. By pushing this idea to its limit, Philippe Rahm points out that the equipment of the house, and even its form is determined by its relation to internal humidity. The residents themselves of course produce a certain amount of humidity, and their use of warm water for bathing or cooking does as well. Rather than simply accepting the idea that humidity must be dealt with by ventilating interior spaces, Rahm experiments with different degrees of water content in the air, ranging from a desert-like 20% to 100%. Thus the sauna and clothes-drying area has a relative humidity of 0% to 30%; a bedroom and office varies between 30% and 60%; the bathroom, kitchen and living room from 60% to 90%, and the swimming pool area at 100% relative humidity. By recognizing the role of humidity in comfort and the very sensations of a living space, Rahm experiments here with fundamentals that are usually swept aside or ignored, allowing them to actually dictate the shape or appearance of the architecture, as well as its inner workings. He has done the same in other projects by manipulating light or oxygen content in the air, as was the case in the *Hormonorium* (Swiss Pavilion, Architecture Biennale 8, Venice, 2002).

Grundidee des Projekts ist die Schaffung einer Beziehung zwischen Innenraum und Luftfeuchtigkeit. Philippe Rahm treibt diese Idee auf die Spitze und verweist darauf, dass die Ausstattung des Hauses und sogar seine Form durch die Beziehung zur Luftfeuchtigkeit im Innenraum bestimmt werden. Ebenso wie durch ihren Verbrauch von warmem Wasser zum Baden oder Kochen, erzeugen die Bewohner des Hauses natürlich auch selbst eine gewisse Luftfeuchtigkeit. Rahm akzeptiert nicht einfach die Vorstellung, dass man die Feuchtigkeit durch eine Belüftung der Innenräume regulieren muss, sondern experimentiert mit einem unterschiedlichen Feuchtigkeitsgehalt der Luft, der von 20 Prozent – also einem Wüstenklima – bis 100 Prozent reicht. Die Sauna und der Trockenraum für die Wäsche haben eine relative Luftfeuchte von bis zu 30 Prozent, im Schlafzimmer und Büro liegt sie bei 30 bis 60 Prozent, im Badezimmer, in der Küche und im Wohnzimmer bei 60 bis 90 Prozent und im Schwimmbadbereich bei 100 Prozent. Indem er die Bedeutung der Luftfeuchtigkeit für den Komfort sowie die grundlegenden Wahrnehmungen in einem Wohnhaus in den Mittelpunkt stellt, experimentiert Rahm mit Grundlagen, die normalerweise beiseite geschoben oder ignoriert werden und erlaubt ihnen, die Form und das Aussehen der Architektur und ihr inneres Funktionieren zu bestimmen. Bei anderen Projekten ging er ebenso vor: Beim *Hormonorium*, dem Schweizer Pavillon auf der VIII. Architekturbiennale 2002 in Venedig, veränderte er z. B. den Licht- oder Sauerstoffgehalt der Luft.

L'idée de base de ce projet est de créer une relation entre l'espace intérieur et son hygrométrie. En poussant cette idée jusqu'à ses limites, Philippe Rahm est allé jusqu'à déterminer l'équipement de la maison et même sa forme, à partir de leurs relations avec l'humidité interne. Les résidents produisent une certaine quantité d'humidité, en utilisant l'eau chaude pour se laver ou préparer les repas, par exemple. Plutôt que de se contenter de la solution classique – traiter l'humidité par la ventilation – Rahm expérimente divers taux d'hygrométrie, des 20% de l'atmosphère du désert jusqu'à 100%. Ainsi, la zone du sauna et du séchage du linge et des vêtements présente une humidité relative de 0 à 30%, la chambre et le bureau de 30 à 60%, la salle de bains, la cuisine et le séjour de 60 à 90% et la piscine de 100%. En prenant en compte le rôle de l'humidité dans le confort et les sensations que génère un lieu de vie, Rahm joue ici sur des principes essentiels, mais généralement négligés ou ignorés, et leur permet de dicter la forme ou l'aspect de l'architecture et de son aménagement intérieur. Il a fait de même dans d'autres projets où il manipulait la lumière ou l'oxygène, comme dans son *Hormonorium*, Pavillon suisse, Biennale d'architecture de Venise (2002).

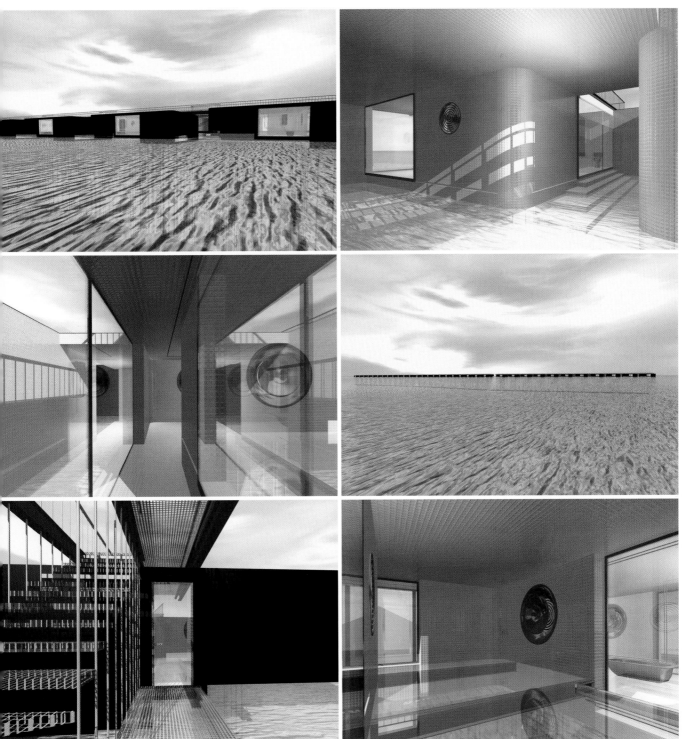

Rahm images a sequence of 70 vacation houses conceived along lines that have as much to do with physiology as with architecture in the more traditional sense of the word. His computer images evoke a world of water, not unlike that which might be found in a video game.

Rahm stellt sich eine Reihe aus 70 Ferienhäusern vor. Die Linie, an der entlang die Häuser angeordnet sind, hat mit Physiologie ebenso viel zu tun wie mit Architektur im klassischen Sinn. Die Computergrafiken zeigen eine Wasserwelt, die der Welt in einem Videospiel ähnelt.

Rahm a imaginé une séquence de 70 maisons de vacances conçues selon des principes qui empruntent autant à la physiologie qu'à l'architecture, au sens le plus traditionnel du terme. Ses images de synthèse évoquent un monde aquatique peu différent d'un jeu vidéo.

REICHEN & ROBERT

Reichen et Robert & Associés
17, rue Brézin
75014 Paris
France

Tel: +33 145 41 47 48
Fax: +33 145 41 47 44
e-mail: architectes-associes@reichen-robert.fr
Web: www.reichen-robert.fr

Bernard Reichen graduated from the École Spéciale d'Architecture in 1965. After spending two years in the Congo, he became a project manager at Arc Practice (Jean-Claude Bernard) in charge of creating large infrastructure projects in mountain regions. He taught for several years at the IFMO (Institut de formation de maitrise d'ouvrage) and was a guest lecturer at the École Spéciale d'Architecture in Paris, where he is now a member of the advisory council. Philippe Robert graduated from the École Spéciale d'Architecture in 1966. He spent two years in the United States, where he completed his training and worked with Paolo Soleri. He held the position of project manager for five years, first with André Bruyères, and then at Ducharme-Larras-Minost, after which he worked in collaboration with Piano and Rogers on the Pompidou Center. **REICHEN & ROBERT** created their office in Paris in 1973. Their major projects include a large number of renovation projects such as the: Pavillon de l'Arsenal, Paris (1988); Halle Tony Garnier, Lyon (1988); Grande Halle at La Villette (1985); Terra Museum of American Art, Giverny (1992); Environmental Technologies Center, Oberhausen (1993–97); the conversion of the former Meunier Chocolate Factory in Nosiel-sur-Marne near Paris into the headquarters of Nestlé France (1996); and the Master Plan for the Faliro Waterfront, Athens, Greece (1999–2004).

Bernard Reichen machte 1965 seinen Abschluss an der Ecole Spéciale d'Architecture in Paris. Nachdem er zwei Jahre im Kongo verbracht hatte, wurde er Projektmanager im Büro Arc Practice von Jean-Claude Bernard und war für umfangreiche Infrastrukturbauten in Bergregionen verantwortlich. Er unterrichtete mehrere Jahre am Institut de Formation de Maitrise d'Ouvrage (IFMO) und war Gastdozent an der Ecole Spéciale d'Architecture in Paris, deren Ratsmitglied er jetzt ist. Philippe Robert machte 1966 sein Diplom ebenfalls an der Ecole Spéciale d'Architecture. Er ging für zwei Jahre in die USA, vervollständigte dort seine Ausbildung und arbeitete bei Paolo Soleri. Er war fünf Jahre lang Projektmanager, erst bei André Bruyères, dann bei Ducharme-Larras-Minost. Anschließend arbeitete er mit Piano und Rogers am Centre Georges Pompidou. **REICHEN & ROBERT** gründeten 1973 in Paris ihr Büro. Zu ihren wichtigsten Bauten gehören zahlreiche Sanierungsprojekte, wie die Grand Halle in La Villette (1985), der Pavillon de l'Arsenal in Paris (1988), die Halle Tony Garnier in Lyon (1988), das Musée d'Art Américain in Giverny (1992), das Umwelt-Technologiezentrum in Oberhausen (1993–97) und der Umbau der ehemaligen Schokoladenfabrik Meunier in Nosiel-sur-Marne in der Nähe von Paris in die neue Firmenzentrale für Nestlé (1996); außerdem haben sie den Masterplan für die Küstenpromenade von Faliro in Athen für die Olympischen Spiele 2004 erstellt (1999–2004).

Bernard Reichen est diplômé de l'École spéciale d'architecture de Paris (1965). Après avoir séjourné deux ans au Congo, il devient gestionnaire de projet chez Arc Practice (Jean-Claude Bernard), en charge de la création de vastes projets d'infrastructures en régions montagneuses. Il a enseigné plusieurs années à l'Institut de formation de maîtrise d'ouvrage (IFMO) et a été conférencier invité à l'École spéciale d'architecture, qui l'a nommé membre de son conseil consultatif. Philippe Robert est diplômé de l'École spéciale d'architecture de Paris (1966). Il a passé deux ans aux États-Unis où il a achevé sa formation et collaboré avec Paolo Soleri. Responsable de projets pendant cinq ans, d'abord pour André Bruyères, puis pour Ducharme-Larras-Minost, il a travaillé avec Piano et Rogers sur le projet du Centre Pompidou. **REICHEN & ROBERT** ont créé leur agence à Paris en 1973. Parmi leurs principaux projets, on note un grand nombre de rénovations : Pavillon de l'Arsenal, Paris (1988) ; Halle Tony Garnier, Lyon (1988) ; Grande Halle de La Villette, Paris (1985) ; musée d'Art américain de la Terra Foundation, Giverny (1992) ; Centre des techniques de l'environnement, Oberhausen, Allemagne (1993–97) ; conversion des anciennes chocolateries Menier en siège social de Nestlé-France (1996) et plan directeur du front de mer de Falaire, Athènes, Grèce (1999–2004).

Vast open spaces, created for the generation of electricity, are retained by the architects to make for convivial interaction. Indeed their project seems to have little of the austere spirit of Herzog & de Meuron's famous conversion of the Bankside Power Station in London into Tate Modern.

Die riesigen offenen Räume, in denen früher Elektrizität hergestellt wurde, ließen die Architekten unverändert. Sie sollen jetzt als soziale Treffpunkte dienen. Mit der herben Strenge von Herzog & de Meurons berühmtem Umbau der Bankside Power Station zur Tate Modern in London hat dieses Projekt nicht viel gemein.

Les vastes volumes conçus pour la production d'électricité ont été conservés par les architectes pour en faire des lieux de travail plus conviviaux. Leur projet semble loin de l'esprit austère d'Herzog & de Meuron lorsqu'ils ont transformé la Bankside Power Station de Londres en Tate Modern.

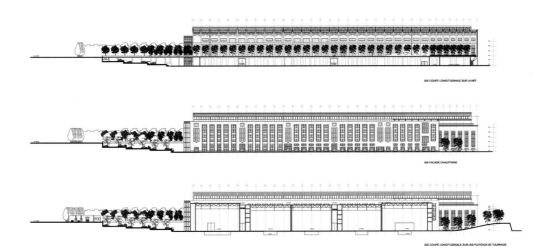

FRANÇOIS ROCHE

R&Sie Architects, 45, rue de Belleville, 75 019 Paris, France
Tel: +33 142 06 06 69, Fax: +33 142 08 27 86, e-mail: rochedsvsie@wanadoo.fr
Web: www.new-territories.com

FRANÇOIS ROCHE was born in 1961 in Paris. He obtained his architecture degree from UPA n°3 in Versailles in 1987. His partner Stéphanie Lavaux was born in 1966 in La Réunion, and she left the French National Fine Arts School (ENSBA) in 1990. They participated in a 2002 show at the ICA in London called "In Many Ways the Exhibition Already Happened" with the artists Pierre Huyghe and Philippe Parreno, as well as the graphic designers M/M (who designed the firm's 2004 monograph *Spoiled Climate*), in a sense summing up much of the most interesting creative work being done in France at the moment. The exhibition catalogue explained that "The architecture of R&Sie François Roche/Stephanie Lavaux is inseparable from the environment; one might speak of a kind of furtive architecture. In his projects, François Roche attempts to refrain from radically modifying the territory, seeking a form of dialogue with it that is entropic and organic. He is currently undertaking a critical exper- iment with new morphing technologies to prompt architectural 'scenarios' of cartographic distortion, substitution, and territorial mutations." They also participated in the innovative "Non-Standard Architecture" exhibition at the Pompidou Center in 2003–04 with Asymptote, dECoi, Greg Lynn, NOX, UN Studio and other equally important firms. François Roche recently collaborated with the conceptual artist Rirkrit Tiravanija and Philippe Parreno on a video called *The Boys from Mars* (2003). Built as part of Tiravanija's "transdisciplinary" collaborative *The Land*, on a site located near Chiang Mai, Thailand, Roche's Hybrid Muscle was a shed combining local and high tech- nology elements. Although R&Sie has not done much actual building until now, their ideas and influence have been of considerable importance.

FRANÇOIS ROCHE, geboren 1961 in Paris, machte 1987 sein Architekturdiplom an der UPA 3 in Versailles. Seine Partnerin, Stéphanie Lavaux, wurde 1966 auf La Réunion geboren und verließ die Ecole Nationale Supérieure des Beaux-Arts (ENSBA) 1990. 2002 nahm das Büro an der Ausstellung »In Many Ways the Exhibition Already Happened« in den ICA Galleries in London teil, die in gewissem Sinn viele der interessantesten und kreativsten Projekte, die derzeit in Frankreich entstehen, zusammenfasste. Der Beitrag von Roche und Lavaux war eine Zusammenarbeit mit den Künstlern Pierre Huyghe und Philippe Parreno und den Graphikern M/M, die die 2004 erschienene Monografie *Spoiled Climate* über das Büro gestalteten. Im Ausstellungskatalog heißt es dazu: »Die Architektur von R&Sie François Roche/Stéphanie Lavaux ist untrennbar mit der Umwelt verbunden; man könnte sie als eine Art ›heimliche‹ Architektur bezeichnen. François Roche möchte mit seinen Projekten nicht das Territorium radikal verändern, sondern sucht eine Form des Dialoges, die man als entropisch und organisch bezeichnen kann. Momentan führt er ein wichtiges Experi- ment mit neuen Techniken des ›Morphing‹ durch, um architektonische ›Szenarien‹ – kartografische Verzerrung, Substitution und territoriale Mutationen – zu schaffen.« Das Büro nahm 2003/04 an der zukunftsweisenden Ausstellung »Non-standard Architecture« im Centre Georges Pompidou teil; weitere Teilnehmer waren Asymptote, dECoi, Greg Lynn, NOX, UN Studio und andere gleichrangige Büros. 2003 hat François Roche zusammen mit den Konzeptkünstlern Rirkrit Tiravanija und Philippe Parreno das Video *The Boys from Mars* produziert. Roches »Hybrid Muscle« war ein Schuppen, der ortstypische und High-Tech-Elemente miteinander verband. Dieser Schuppen war Bestandteil von Tiravanijas »transdisziplinärer« Gemeinschaftsproduktion *The Land* und stand in der Nähe von Chiang Mai in Thailand. R&Sie haben noch nicht viel gebaut, aber ihre Ideen sind wichtig und ihr Einfluss ist beträchtlich.

Né en 1961 à Paris, **FRANÇOIS ROCHE** est diplômé de l'UPA n° 3 de Versailles en 1987. Son associée, Stéphanie Lavaux, née en 1966 à La Réunion, a quitté l'École nationale supérieure des beaux-arts de Paris en 1990. Ils ont participé en 2002 à l'exposition de l'ICA à Londres intitulée « In Many Ways the Exhibition Already Happened », en compagnie des artistes Pierre Huyghe et Philippe Parreno et des graphistes M/M (qui ont conçu la monographie de l'agence parue en 2004, *Spoiled Cli- mate),* qui résumait d'une certaine façon quelques-uns des aspects les plus intéressants de la créativité française du moment. Le catalogue expliquait que « l'architec- ture de R&Sie François Roche/Stéphanie Lavaux est inséparable de l'environnement. On pourrait parler d'une sorte d'architecture furtive. Dans ses projets, François Roche tente d'éviter de modifier radicalement le territoire, cherchant à entretenir avec lui une forme de dialogue entropique et organique. Il expérimente actuellement de nouvelles technologies de ‹ morphing › pour réaliser des scénarii architecturaux de distorsion cartographique, de substitution et de mutations territoriales ». R&Sie a par- ticipé à l'exposition « Architecture non-standard » au Centre Pompidou en 2003–04 avec Asymptote, dECoi, Greg Lynn, NOX, UN Studio et d'autres agences de même catégorie. L'agence a récemment travaillé, avec l'artiste conceptuel Rirkrit Tiravanija et avec Philippe Parreno, à une vidéo intitulée *The Boys from Mars* (2003). Élaboré dans le cadre de l'œuvre collective transdisciplinaire de Tiravanija, *The Land,* sur un terrain proche de Chiang Mai en Thaïlande, Hybrid Muscle (2003) de François Roche était un abri combinant des technologies locales et d'avant-garde. Bien que R&Sie n'ait pas encore beaucoup construit, leurs idées et leur influence sont considérables.

GREEN GORGON
Lausanne, Switzerland, 2004

*Floor area: 7000 m². Client: Ville de Lausanne & Etat de Vaud/Suisse.
Cost: €40 million (approximation)*

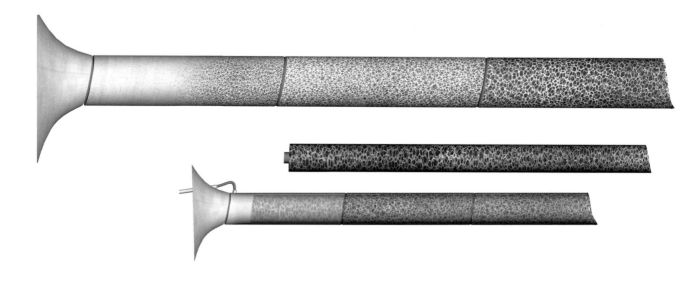

GREEN GORGON was François Roche's entry for the 2004 competition to design a new museum of modern art for the city of Lausanne (nMBA). Roche described it as follows: "The nMBA is the emanation of a lakeside biotope. A reflection in water of branches and undulating gnarled forms was the image that served as the project's starting point. A strange and enchanting dream, Ophelia's hair, or one of Grimm's fairytales that takes place in the middle of a forest… More a landscape than an urbanism; more a forest than architecture. A project that plays with its natures." Almost more surprising is the architect's explanation that the point of departure for this project was the collaboration between Charles Perrault (1628–1703), author of the classic fairy tale book *Histoires ou contes du temps passé* (1697), and the garden designer André Le Nôtre (1613–1700) on the labyrinth at Versailles. Despite a rather unusual appearance, the Green Gorgon was a carefully thought-out and fully "buildable" structure, with a large amount of wood to be used for the complex external forms. The final selection for the nMBA was a much more conventional structure, but Roche's proposal had the advantage of advancing architectural discourse and putting forward his idea that buildings must tell a story, or be based on "fiction" rather than simple utilitarian constraints.

GREEN GORGON nannte François Roche seinen Wettbewerbsbeitrag 2004 für ein neues Museum für moderne Kunst in Lausanne (nMBA). Roche beschreibt ihn folgendermaßen: »Das nMBA ist die ›Ausdünstung‹ eines Seebiotops. Zweige und gewellte, knorrige Formen, die sich im Wasser spiegeln, bestimmten das Bild, das den Ausgangspunkt des Projektes bildete. Ein merkwürdiger und bezaubernder Traum, Ophelias Haar, oder eines der Grimms Märchen, das sich in der Mitte eines Waldes zuträgt… Eher eine Landschaft als etwas Urbanes; eher ein Wald als Architektur. Ein Projekt, das mit seinen eigenen Charakteristika spielt.« Fast am meisten überrascht die Erklärung des Architekten, dass der Impuls für dieses Projekt die Zusammenarbeit von Charles Perrault (1628–1703), Autor des Märchenklassikers *Histoires ou contes du temps passé* von 1697, mit dem Gartenarchitekten André Le Nôtre (1613–1700) am Labyrinth in Versailles war. Trotz seines eher ungewöhnlichen Äußeren war Green Gorgon ein sorgfältig durchdachtes Gebäude, dessen komplexe äußere Form aus sehr vielen Bauteilen aus Holz zu realisieren wäre. Der letztlich ausgewählte Entwurf für das nMBA war sehr viel konventioneller. Ihm gegenüber hatte Roches Vorschlag zudem den Vorteil, den architektonischen Diskurs voranzubringen und seine Idee weiterzuentwickeln, dass Gebäude eine Geschichte erzählen oder auf »Fiktion« anstatt auf einfachen Nutzungsparametern beruhen sollen.

« **GREEN GORGON** » (la Gorgone verte) est la participation de François Roche au concours organisé en 2004 pour la conception d'un nouveau musée d'art moderne à Lausanne (nMBA). Roche présente ainsi son projet : « Le nMBA est l'émanation d'un biotope lacustre. L'image de reflets de branches dans l'eau et de formes noueuses a servi de point de départ au projet. Un rêve étrange et enchanteur, la chevelure d'Ophélie ou l'un des contes de Grimm qui se déroule dans une forêt… Plus paysage qu'urbanisme, plus forêt qu'architecture. Un projet qui joue avec ses natures. » Plus surprenant encore, l'architecte explique que le point de départ de ce projet est aussi la collaboration entre Charles Perrault (1628–1703), auteur des célèbres *Histoires ou contes du temps passé* (1697) et le jardinier André Le Nôtre (1613–1700) pour le labyrinthe de Versailles. En dépit d'un aspect assez curieux, cette « Green Gorgon » est une structure soigneusement pensée et parfaitement constructible. Alors qu'il était prévu de faire largement appel au bois pour le montage de l'enveloppe extérieure, le jury lui préféra une solution beaucoup plus conventionnelle, mais la proposition de Roche a fait avancer la réflexion sur l'architecture et mis en avant son idée d'une architecture qui« raconte des histoires » et repose sur une « fiction » plutôt que sur de simples contraintes utilitaires.

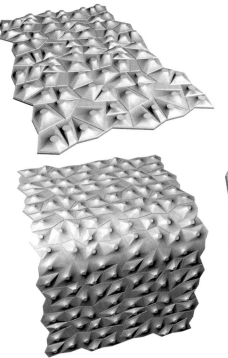

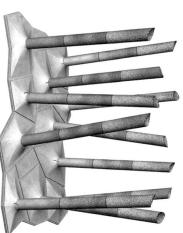

The Green Gorgon is another of the recent buildings to rise up out of its topographical surroundings almost like a biological entity. Roche has carefully thought out the ways in which this apparently complex design could have fulfilled the museum function however.

Auch das Green Gorgon gehört zu den zeitgenössischen Gebäuden, die sich fast wie Lebewesen aus der Topografie erheben. Roche hat genau überlegt, wie dieser komplexe Entwurf die Funktionen eines Museums aufnehmen könnte.

La Green Gorgon est un exemple de ces créations récentes de bâtiments semblant émerger de leur environnement topographique presque comme une entité biologique. Roche a bien réfléchi à la façon dont ce projet apparemment complexe pourrait remplir les fonctions d'un musée.

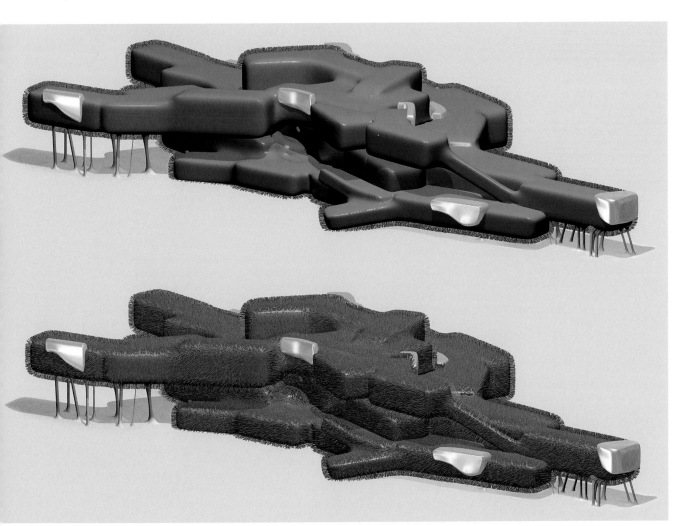

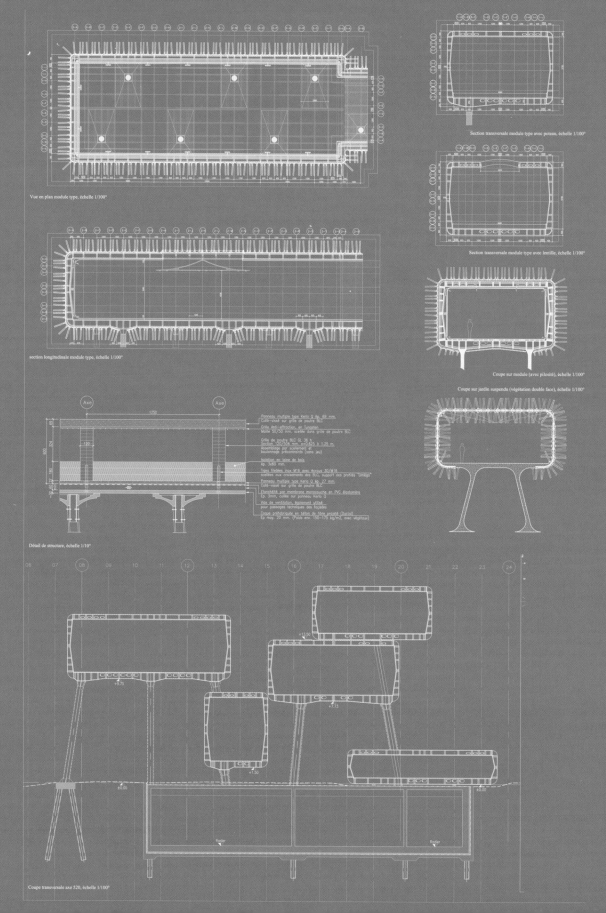

Vue en plan module type, échelle 1/100°

section longitudinale module type, échelle 1/100°

Détail de structure, échelle 1/10°

Section transversale module type avec poteau, échelle 1/100°

Section transversale module type avec lentille, échelle 1/100°

Coupe sur module (avec pilosité), échelle 1/100°

Coupe sur jardin suspendu (végétation double face), échelle 1/100°

Coupe transversale axe 520, échelle 1/100°

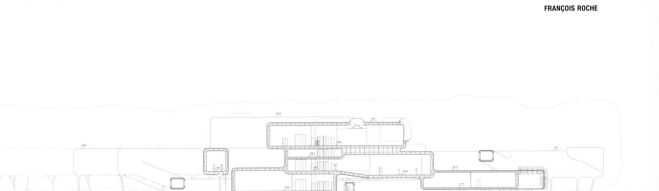

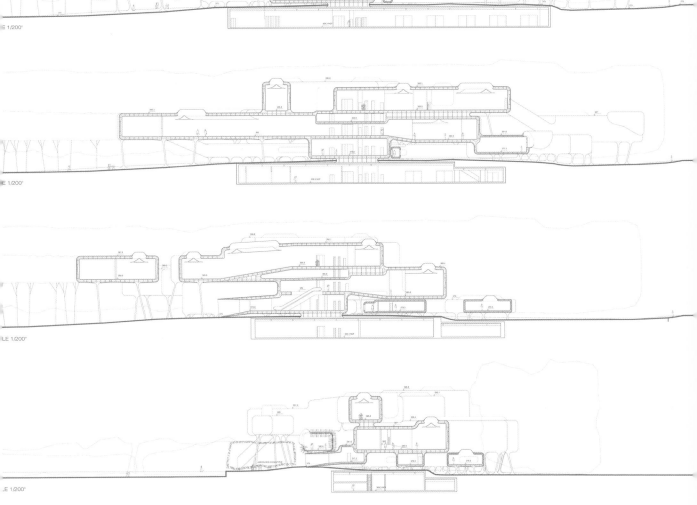

E 1/200°

E 1/200°

LE 1/200°

LE 1/200°

The sections of R&Sie show how the unexpected exterior appearance of the building resolves itself into fully usable spaces below the green outside surface.

Die Schnitte von R&Sie zeigen, dass sich hinter dem ungewöhnlichen Äußeren mit der grünen Oberfläche sinnvoll nutzbare Räume verbergen.

Les coupes de R&Sie démontrent que l'étonnant aspect extérieur de cette construction peut donner naissance à des volumes parfaitement utilisables sous leur surface verte.

THOMAS ROSZAK

Roszak/ADC
1415 Sherman Avenue, Suite 101
Evanston, Illinois 60201
USA

Tel: +1 847 425 7555
Fax: +1 847 425 7540
e-mail: info@roszakadc.com
Web: www.roszakadc.com

Glass Hous

Born in 1967, **THOMAS ROSZAK** graduated from the Illinois Institute of Technology College of Architecture in Chicago in 1989, and went to work for his professor, David Hovey, who had an architectural firm called Optima that developed and built condominiums. He was second in command in Hovey's firm within five years of his arrival. At 29, he left to become vice president of Focus Development, also a condominium developer. He created his own architecture, development, and construction firm, Roszak/ADC, in 1997. Since that date the firm has built over 600 million dollars in condominium and mixed-use projects, as well as commercial design/build and "special projects" like the house Roszak designed for himself (published here). Recent work includes 601 S. Wells, Chicago, Illinois, a 31-story high-rise, 238 unit condominium project including retail space in the South Loop of downtown Chicago (construction to begin spring 2006); and Sienna, Evanston, Illinois, a four-building, 237-unit condominium and town home community in the heart of downtown Evanston (under construction).

THOMAS ROSZAK, geboren 1967, machte 1989 am College of Architecture des Illinois Institute of Technology in Chicago seinen Abschluss. Anschließend arbeitete er für das Architekturbüro Optima seines Professors David Hovey. Bereits nach fünf Jahren war er Leiter des Büros, das sich mit der Entwicklung und dem Bau von Eigentumswohnungen befasste. Mit 29 Jahren wurde er stellvertretender Leiter von Focus Development, ebenfalls ein Bauträger für Eigentumswohnungen. 1997 gründete er Roszak/ADC, Architekturbüro, Entwicklungsträger und Baufirma in einem. Seitdem hat das Büro Eigentumswohnungen und gemischt genutzte Gebäude mit einem Auftragsvolumen von umgerechnet knapp 500 Millionen Euro realisiert. Dazu kommen Geschäftsgebäude und Sonderprojekte wie das hier gezeigte Haus, das Roszak für sich und seine Familie baute. Neue Projekte von ihm sind u. a. 601 S. Wells in Chicago, ein 31-geschossiges Hochhaus mit 238 Eigentumswohnungen und Ladennutzung im South Loop im Zentrum von Chicago (Baubeginn ist im Frühjahr 2006) und Sienna, ein Komplex aus vier Gebäuden mit 237 Eigentumswohnungen im Zentrum von Evanston, Illinois, der 2005 begonnen wurde.

Né en 1967, **THOMAS ROSZAK** est diplômé de l'Illinois Institute of Technology College of Architecture, Chicago (1989) et a débuté en travaillant pour son professeur, David Hover, dont l'agence, Optima, construisait des immeubles de logements dont elle assurait la promotion. Cinq ans après son arrivée, il était directeur adjoint de cette agence et, à 29 ans, devint vice-président de Focus Developement, autre promoteur immobilier. Il a créé en 1997 sa propre agence de promotion immobilière et d'architecture, Roszak/ADC, qui a déjà réalisé pour presque 500 millions d'euros d'immeubles d'appartements, de projets mixtes logements-commerces et de « projets spéciaux » comme la maison que l'architecte s'est construite, publiée ici. Parmi ses récentes réalisations : la maison 601 S. Welles une tour de 30 étages comprenant 238 appartements en copropriété et des commerces dans la South Loop en centre-ville (Chicago, Illinois, 2006-) et un ensemble de 237 appartements et maisons de ville au centre d'Evanston (Illinois, 2005–).

GLASS HOUSE

Northfield, Illinois, USA, 2002

Floor area: 550 m². Client: Thomas and Justyna Roszak.
Cost: $1.5 million

This 550 m² home located on a half-hectare lot contains five bedrooms, four bathrooms, a library, exercise room, yoga room and garage. Surrounded by traditional Tudor-style houses, Roszak's home is entirely clad in glass but surrounded by forty pines and twenty birch trees, planted "according to Chinese and Japanese garden principles." Symmetrical on a north-south axis, the house is aligned on a strict grid, making it look "as though it was constructed with transparent Legos" according to the architect. Most of the rooms are 4.88 meters square. Roszak says, "As a nod to Japanese design; the skeleton of steel support beams glides over the concrete frame. A concrete shear wall in the center of the home bears most of the load." He further emphasizes that the extreme transparency of the house has not kept it from being extremely energy efficient. Passive solar heating and radiant floor heating keep the house comfortable. The Roszak residence may have some points in common with David Hovey's Modular Steel House (Winnetka, Illinois, 1998), but it is certainly a masterful early work by an architect who is not yet forty.

Das 550 m² große Wohnhaus des Architekten auf einem 0,5 ha großen Grundstück hat u. a. fünf Schlafzimmer, vier Badezimmer, eine Bibliothek, einen Trainingsraum, einen Yogaraum und eine Garage. Im Gegensatz zu den Häusern der Nachbarschaft im traditionellen Tudorstil ist Roszaks Haus vollständig verglast, dafür aber von 40 Pinien und 20 Birken umgeben, die »nach chinesischen und japanischen Prinzipien des Gartenbaus gepflanzt wurden«. Ein strenges Raster mit einer Symmetrieachse in Nord-Süd-Richtung bestimmt das Haus, das aussieht »als ob es aus transparenten Legosteinen gebaut wurde«, so der Architekt. Die meisten Räume messen 4,88 x 4,88 m. Roszak erläutert: »Als Verbeugung vor der japanischen Architektur kragen die Stahlträger über die Stahlbetonkonstruktion aus. Eine Wandscheibe in der Mitte des Hauses nimmt den größten Teil der Lasten auf.« Er betont außerdem, dass die extreme Transparenz des Hauses nichts an dem sehr niedrigen Energiebedarf des Hauses ändert. Passive Solarwärme und eine Fußbodenheizung sorgen dafür, dass das Haus angenehm temperiert ist. Das Roszak-Haus mag mit David Hoveys Modular Steel House (Winnetka, Illinois, 1998) einiges gemein haben, für einen noch nicht 40-jährigen Architekten handelt es sich aber zweifellos um ein außerordentliches Frühwerk.

Cette résidence de 550 m² située sur une parcelle d'un demi-hectare comprend, en dehors des pièces de séjour, cinq chambres, quatre salles de bains, une bibliothèque, une salle de gymnastique, une autre de yoga et un garage. Entourée de maisons de style Tudor, elle est entièrement vitrée mais dissimulée par quarante pins et vingt bouleaux plantés « selon les principes des jardins chinois et japonais ». Le plan fait appel à une trame orthogonale symétrique, axée nord-sud, et l'ensemble donne l'impression « d'avoir été construit avec des Lego transparents ». La plupart des pièces mesure 4,88 m de côté. Pour Roszak, « en une sorte de clin d'œil à la conception japonaise traditionnelle, le squelette des poutres de soutien en acier semble planer au-dessus de l'ossature en béton. Un mur de soutènement, au centre de la maison, supporte l'essentiel de la charge ». Il fait remarquer, par ailleurs, que la transparence extrême de la maison ne l'empêche pas d'être très économe en consommation d'énergie. Le chauffage solaire et les sols chauffants radiants garantissent une atmosphère confortable. Si cette maison n'est pas sans points communs avec la Modular Steel House de David Hovey, Winnetka, Illinois (1998), elle représente une œuvre magistrale pour un architecte de moins de 40 ans.

Roszak's house has a stripped down technological appearance with a great deal of glazing offering an open view toward the surrounding greenery.

Roszaks Haus zeigt einen fast industriellen Impetus. Durch den hohen Anteil an verglasten Fassadenflächen bieten sich unverstellte Blicke in die grüne Umgebung.

La maison de Roszak, d'un style « technologique » épuré, s'ouvre toute grande à la verdure environnante par ses immenses baies vitrées.

A relatively simple palette of materials and generous interior space make the Roszak House light and airy.

Relativ einfache Materialien und großzügige Innenräume schaffen ein leichtes und luftiges Ambiente.

Une palette de matériaux relativement simples et de généreux volumes intérieurs rendent cette résidence légère, aérienne.

Holocaust Museum, Yad Vash▪

MOSHE SAFDIE

Moshe Safdie and Associates, Inc., 100 Properzi Way, Somerville, Massachusetts 02143–3740, USA
Tel: +1 617 629 2100, Fax: +1 617 629 2406
e-mail: safdieb@msafdie.com, Web: www.msafdie.com

MOSHE SAFDIE, born in Haifa, Israel, in 1938, later moved to Canada with his family, graduating from McGill University in 1961 with a degree in architecture. After apprenticing with Louis I. Kahn in Philadelphia, he returned to Montreal, taking charge of the master plan for the 1967 World Exhibition, where he also realized an adaptation of his thesis as Habitat '67, the central feature of the World's Fair. In 1970, Safdie established a Jerusalem branch office, commencing an intense involvement with the rebuilding of Jerusalem. He was responsible for major segments of the restoration of the Old City and the reconstruction of the new center, linking the Old and New Cities. Over the years, his involvement expanded and included the new city of Modi'in, the new Yad Vashem Holocaust Museum, and the Rabin Memorial Center. In 1978, following teaching at Yale, McGill, and Ben Gurion Universities, Safdie relocated his principal office to Boston, as he became Director of the Urban Design Program and a Professor of Architecture and Urban Design at the Harvard Graduate School of Design. In the following decade, he was responsible for the design of six of Canada's principal public institutions, including the Quebec Museum of Civilization, and the National Gallery of Canada. In the past decade, Safdie's major cultural and educational commissions in the U. S. have included: the United States Institute of Peace Headquarters, Washington, D. C.; the Skirball Museum and Cultural Center in Los Angeles; and Exploration Place in Wichita; educational facilities such as Eleanor Roosevelt College at the University of California in San Diego; civic buildings such as the Springfield, Massachusetts, and Mobile, Alabama, Federal Courthouses; and performing arts centers such as the Kansas City Performing Arts Center. In addition to major works of urbanism, Safdie's current work includes two airports – Lester B. Pearson International Airport in Toronto and Ben Gurion International Airport in Tel Aviv.

MOSHE SAFDIE wurde 1938 in Haifa in Israel geboren. Seine Familie zog später nach Kanada, wo er 1961 an der McGill University sein Architekturstudium abschloss. Safdie arbeitete als Praktikant im Büro von Louis I. Kahn in Philadelphia und ging dann nach Montreal zurück, um die Umsetzung des Masterplans für die Weltausstellung 1967 zu betreuen. Sein Diplomentwurf bildete in überarbeiteter Form unter dem Namen Habitat '67 den Mittelpunkt dieser Ausstellung. 1970 eröffnete Safdie in Jerusalem eine Zweigstelle und begann intensiv am Wiederaufbau von Jerusalem mitzuarbeiten. Er war für große Teile der Altstadtsanierung und den Wiederaufbau des neuen Zentrums zuständig, wobei die Alt- und Neustadt miteinander verbunden wurden. Im Lauf der Jahre verstärkte sich sein Engagement in Israel und umfasst nun auch die neue Stadt Modi'in, das neue Holocaust-Museum in Yad Vashem und das Rabin Memorial Center. Safdie lehrte in Yale, an der McGill University und an der Universität Ben Gurion. Wegen der Berufung zum Direktor des Urban Design Program und zum Professor für Architektur und Städtebau an der Harvard Graduate School of Design zog er 1978 nach Boston und verlegte auch sein Büro dorthin. In den folgenden zehn Jahren war er für die Planung von sechs der wichtigsten öffentlichen Einrichtungen Kanadas verantwortlich, darunter das Museum für Zivilisation in Quebec und die Nationalgalerie von Kanada. In den letzten zehn Jahren erhielt er Aufträge für zahlreiche Kultur- und Bildungsbauten in den USA, beispielsweise für das United States Institute of Peace Headquarters in Washington, D. C., das Skirball-Museum und -Kulturzentrum in Los Angeles und den Exploration Place in Wichita. Von ihm realisierte Bildungsbauten sind u. a. das Eleanor Roosevelt College der University of California in San Diego. Staatliche Gebäude von Safdie sind u. a. die Bundesgerichtshöfe in Springfield, Massachusetts, und in Mobile, Alabama. Außerdem baute er Schauspielhäuser wie das Kansas City Performing Arts Center. Neben umfassenden Städtebauprojekten plant Safdie derzeit zwei Flughäfen, den Lester B. Pearson International Airport in Toronto und den Internationalen Flughafen Ben Gurion in Tel Aviv.

MOSHE SAFDIE est né à Haïfa (Israël) en 1938 et a émigré avec sa famille au Canada où il a étudié l'architecture à l'Université McGill de Montréal. Après un apprentissage chez Louis Kahn à Philadelphie, il revint à Montréal pour prendre en charge le plan directeur de l'Exposition universelle de 1967 pour laquelle il réalisa également Habitat '67, un projet issu de sa thèse. En 1970, il a créé une agence à Jérusalem et a commencé à s'impliquer dans la restructuration de la ville. Il a été responsable de la restauration d'une bonne part de la vieille ville et de la reconstruction du nouveau centre, faisant le lien entre la ville nouvelle et l'ancienne. Au cours des années, ses interventions en Israël se sont développées et il a conçu la ville nouvelle de Modi'in, le nouveau musée de l'Holocauste de Yad Vashem et le Centre mémorial Ytzhak Rabin. En 1978, après avoir enseigné dans les universités de Yale, McGill et Ben Gurion, il s'installa à Boston avec son agence et devint directeur du programme d'urbanisme et professeur d'architecture et d'urbanisme à la Graduate School of Design de Harvard. Pendant la décennie suivante, il a été responsable de la conception de six grandes institutions canadiennes, notamment le musée des Civilisations du Québec et la Galerie nationale du Canada. Aux États-Unis, il a réalisé, au cours de ces dernières années, le siège du United States Institute of Peace à Washington, D. C. ; le Skirball Museum and Cultural Center à Los Angeles ; Exploration Place à Wichita ; des équipements éducatifs comme le Eleanor Roosevelt College à l'Université de Californie à San Diego ; des bâtiments publics, dont les palais de justice fédéraux de Springfield (Massachusetts) et Mobile (Alabama) et des centres d'arts de la scène, comme le Performing Arts Center de Kansas City. En dehors d'importants chantiers d'urbanisme, Safdie travaille actuellement à des projets pour deux aéroports internationaux, le Lester B. Pearson à Toronto et le Ben Gourion à Tel-Aviv.

HOLOCAUST MUSEUM, YAD VASHEM

Jerusalem, Israel, 2002–05

Floor area: 17 700 m²; Museum complex 9600 m²; Entrance Pavilion complex 4000 m²; Museum exhibits 4000 m².
Client: Yad Vashem Holocaust Martyrs' and Heroes' Remembrance Authority.
Cost: Museum complex $35 million; Entrance Pavilion complex $18 million; Museum exhibits $10 million

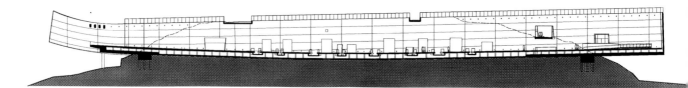

On a hillside overlooking Jerusalem's Ein Kerem Valley, the new **HOLOCAUST MUSEUM** is the culmination of a 10-year, 63 million dollar redevelopment of Yad Vashem, the Holocaust Martyrs' and Heroes' Remembrance Authority. Yad Vashem has been developed as a campus, with buildings including a Holocaust History Museum, Holocaust Art Museum, Exhibition Pavilion, Visual Center, Learning Center, Synagogue and Visitors Center. The central component of the 1.8 hectare campus is the 3800 m² Holocaust History Museum. Safdie has hidden most of the Museum's reinforced concrete "body" within the earth, allowing little more than its elongated, angular spine to convey a sense of its true scale. Inside, among the most important of Safdie's innovations is his placement of the Museum's numerous exhibition spaces. Rather than cluster one after the other as in conventional museums, Safdie concealed the galleries underground, running under the central, 180-meter spine. This path culminates in the Hall of Names. It is surrounded by files containing "Pages of Testimony" listing the names of victims. A suspended cone rises above, with photos of the victims, with a reciprocal cone excavated into the bedrock down to ground water – in memory of those whose names will never be known. As the architects describe the project, "At the north end, the prism bursts out of the mountain, cantilevering over the valley, to light, to the view of the Jerusalem hills, to the vibrant tableau that is modern city of Jerusalem. It is an affirmation of life after an experience of death. The project effectively combines the Holocaust's historical narrative with an appropriate and effective visual experience for the thousands of individuals who visit daily." The museum attracted average of 5000 visitors a day in the three months following its opening in March 2005.

Auf einem Hügel liegend überblickt das neue **HOLOCAUST-MUSEUM** das Ein-Kerem-Tal in Jerusalem. Es bildet den Höhepunkt einer zehnjährigen, umgerechnet 53 Millionen Euro teuren Sanierung von Yad Vashem, der Gedenkstätte für die Opfer des Holocaust und seiner Helden. Das Gelände von Yad Vashem wurde als campusartiges Areal konzipiert und umfasst u. a. das neue Holocaust-Museum, das Museum für Holocaust-Kunst, einen Ausstellungspavillon, ein Visualisierungszentrum, ein Lernzentrum, eine Synagoge und ein Besucherzentrum. Zentrales Element des 1,8 ha großen Campus ist das 3800 m² große Holocaust-Museum. Safdie hat den größten Teil des Stahlbetonbaus in die Erde versenkt, so dass es von außen, abgesehen von dem länglichen, winkligen »Rückgrat«, nur wenige Hinweise auf seine wahre Größe gibt. Im Inneren bildet die Organisation der zahlreichen Ausstellungsräume eine der wichtigsten Neuerungen: Safdie hat sie nicht wie sonst üblich angeordnet, sondern sie entlang des 180 m langen »Rückgrats« in die Erde eingegraben. Sie finden ihren Höhepunkt am Ende in der »Halle der Namen«. Die Halle wird von Regalen eingerahmt, die »Seiten des Zeugnisses« enthalten, auf denen die Namen der Opfer aufgelistet sind. Ein aufgehängter Kegel mit Fotos der Opfer erhebt sich darüber; ein umgekehrter, aus dem Fels gemeißeltes Pendant reicht bis zum Grundwasser – in Erinnerung an all jene, deren Namen niemals bekannt sein werden. Der Architekt beschreibt den Bau folgendermaßen: »Am Nordende bricht das Prisma aus dem Berg hervor, kragt über das Tal aus, hin zum Licht, zum Ausblick auf die Hügel Jerusalems, zum lebhaften ›Tableau‹ der modernen Stadt Jerusalem. Dies ist die Annahme des Lebens nach der Erfahrung des Todes. Das Projekt verbindet sehr effektiv die historischen Erzählungen des Holocaust mit einem angemessenen und wirkungsvollen visuellen Erlebnis für die Tausende Besucher, die täglich kommen.« In den drei Monaten nach seiner Eröffnung im März 2005 besuchten im Durchschnitt täglich 5000 Menschen das Museum.

Au sommet d'une colline dominant la vallée d'Ein Kerem à Jérusalem, le nouveau **MUSÉE DE L'HOLOCAUSTE** est l'aboutissement de dix années d'efforts de la Commission pour le souvenir des martyrs et des héros de l'Holocauste. Ce projet a coûté 53 millions d'euros. Yad Vashem est un campus de 1,8 hectare comprenant plusieurs bâtiments, dont un musée de l'Histoire de l'Holocauste, un musée d'Art de l'Holocauste, un pavillon d'expositions, un centre d'enseignement, une synagogue et un centre d'accueil des visiteurs. La composante principale est le musée de l'Histoire de l'Holocauste de 3800 m². Safdie a dissimulé la plus grande partie du « corps » en béton armé du bâtiment dans le sol, laissant à peine dépasser son arête allongée, seul indice de sa véritable échelle. À l'intérieur, l'un des apports les plus intéressants de l'architecte est la disposition des multiples espaces d'exposition que comprend le musée. Écartant l'idée d'alignement chère aux musées conventionnels, Safdie a dissimulé les galeries sous terre, tout au long des 180m de l'axe central, en un cheminement qui culmine dans la salle des Noms, entourée de classeurs contenant des « Pages de témoignages », listes de noms de victimes. Un immense cône est suspendu dans cette salle, couvert de photos de disparus, et son pendant, un cône symétrique creusé dans la roche jusqu'à la nappe phréatique, rend hommage à ceux dont le nom ne sera jamais connu. Pour Moshe Safdie : « Au nord, le prisme jaillit de la montagne, en porte-à-faux au-dessus de la vallée, vers la lumière, les collines de Jérusalem et le panorama vibrant de la ville moderne de Jérusalem. C'est une affirmation de la vie après cette expérience de la mort. Le projet combine avec efficacité le récit historique de l'Holocauste à une expérience visuelle que découvrent les milliers d'individus qui le visitent chaque jour. » Le musée a attiré en moyenne 5000 visiteurs par jour dans les trois mois qui ont suivi son inauguration en mars 2005.

Slicing through the earth like an inverted knife, the main volume of the Yad Vashem building is buried, with a closed triangular façade emerging at the end of a cantilevered volume on one side, and the other extremity emerging toward views of the hills of Jerusalem.

Wie ein umgedrehtes Messer durchschneidet das Museum in Yad Vashem die Erde. Der Hauptteil liegt im Erdboden. Eine geschlossene dreieckige Fassade markiert das eine Ende des aus dem Erdboden auskragenden Baukörpers; das andere Ende öffnet sich zu den Hügeln von Jerusalem.

Tranchant le sol comme une lame de couteau inversée, le volume principal de Yad Vashem est pratiquement enterré. Il ressort d'un côté sous la forme d'une façade triangulaire en porte-à-faux et, de l'autre, en une baie panoramique sur les collines de Jérusalem.

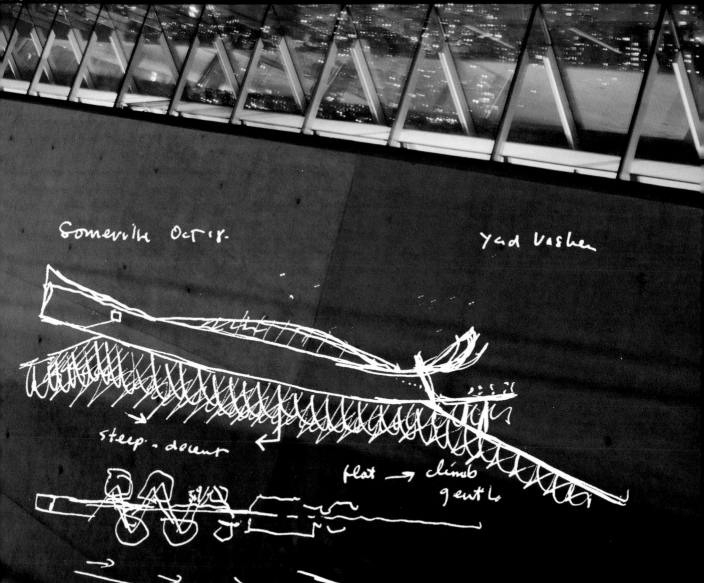

Somerville Oct 19.   Yad Vashem

steep - descent

flat → climb
gently

better!

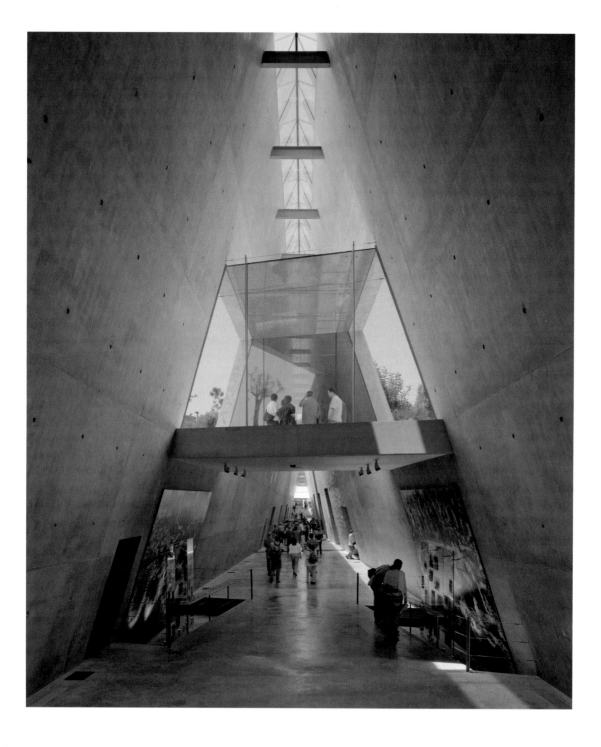

Video screens, books and other arti-
facts define the path through the
180-meter-long interior volume, leav-
ing the powerful, leaning concrete
walls relatively free of displays.

Videobildschirme, Bücher und andere
Gegenstände definieren den Weg
durch den 180 m langen Innenraum.
Die kraftvollen, geneigten Betonwände sind fast frei von Ausstellungs-
stücken.

Des écrans vidéo, des livres et divers
artefacts ponctuent le cheminement
au long des 180 m du parcours intérieur, laissant les solides murs de
béton inclinés relativement exempts
de tout effet d'exposition.

A Hall of Names and portraits of victims of the World War II genocide is a culminating point of the visit of Yad Vashem. Safdie has preserved the austerity or even severity of the architecture, no small feat where the commemoration of such events is the raison d'être of the structure.

Die »Halle der Namen« mit Porträts der Opfer des Genozids im Zweiten Weltkrieg ist ein Höhepunkt des Besuchs von Yad Vashem. Safdie hat eine nüchterne, ernste Architektur geschaffen – eine bemerkenswerte Leistung bei einem Gebäude, dessen »raison d'être« das Gedenken an derartige Ereignisse ist.

La salle des Noms avec les portraits des victimes du génocide de la Seconde Guerre mondiale constituent le point culminant de la visite. Safdie a préservé l'austérité, voire la sévérité de l'architecture – une réelle prouesse dans un édifice dont la raison d'être est la commémoration de tels événements.

AKIRA SAKAMOTO

Akira Sakamoto Architect & Associates
1–14–5, Minamihorie Nishi-ku
Osaka 550–0015
Japan

Tel: +81 06 65 37 11 45
Fax: +81 06 65 37 11 46
e-mail: casa@akirasakamoto.com
Web: www.akirasakamoto.com

Sesami Restaurant

AKIRA SAKAMOTO was born in Fukuoka in 1951. He worked for Kinki Architect Structure Laboratory before establishing his own firm Akira Sakamoto Architect & Associates CASA in 1982. He has won a number of awards in Japan including the 6th Kansai Architect Grand-Prix 2001, the 2001 Architectural Institute of Japan Selected Architectural Design Award, and the 1997 Japan Architects Association Newcomer Prize, all for his Hakuei Residence (Osaka, 1996). His work, always in a minimalist style, includes the House in Tondabayashi (1996); House in Kitakusu (1997); House in Sayama (1998); Hakuu-kan (1999); Atelier in Horie (2000); House in Settsu (2000); House in Tondabayashi (2001); House in Habikigaoka (2002); and the Snow White Dental Clinic (2002, published here).

AKIRA SAKAMOTO, geboren 1951 in Fukuoka, arbeitete im Kinki Architect Structure Laboratory, bevor er 1982 sein eigenes Büro Akira Sakamoto Architect & Associates CASA gründete. In Japan hat er zahlreiche Preise gewonnen, darunter den 6th Kansai Architect Grand Prix 2001, den Architekturpreis des Architectural Institute of Japan 2001 sowie 1997 den Newcomer-Preis des Japanischen Architektenverbands. Alle genannten Preise erhielt Sakamoto für sein Haus Hakuei in Osaka (1996). Seine Bauten sind immer minimalistisch. Er hat u. a. folgende Projekte realisiert: Haus in Tondabayashi (1996), Haus in Kitakusu (1997), Haus in Sayama (1998), Hakuu-kan (1999), Atelier in Horie (2000), Haus in Settsu (2000), ein weiteres Haus in Tondabayashi (2001), Haus in Habikigaoka (2002) und die hier gezeigte Zahnklinik in Toyama (2002).

AKIRA SAKAMOTO, né à Fukuoka en 1951, a travaillé pour Kinki Architectural Structure Laboratory avant de créer son agence, Akira Sakamoto Architect & Associates CASA, en 1982. Il a remporté un certain nombre de prix au Japon, dont le 6e Grand Prix des architectes du Kansai (2001), le prix du projet de l'Institut d'architecture du Japon 2001 et le prix des nouveaux membres de l'Association des architectes japonais 1997, pour sa Résidence Hakuei, Osaka (1996). Son œuvre, toujours de style minimaliste, comprend une maison à Tondabayashi (1996), une maison à Kitakusu (1997) ; une maison à Sayama (1998) ; Hakuu-kan (1999) ; un atelier à Horie (2000) ; une maison à Settsu (2000) ; une seconde maison à Tondabayashi (2001) ; une maison à Habikigaoka (2002) et la clinique dentaire Blanche Neige (2002) présentée ici.

SESAMI

Osaka, Japan, 2004

Floor area: 114 m². Client: Shouzou Wada. Cost: not disclosed

The owners of a traditional sesame store whose creation dates back a century decided to create a restaurant dedicated to their favorite seed. Sakamoto explains that "The construction area is just 86 m² but new spatial opportunities are sought inside. When one enters through the porch, the south side becomes an opening without sashes, providing a space that is contained only by the ceiling and walls, yet still seems open enough to feel the outside elements." The site area is 217 m², and the total floor area of the restaurant built in reinforced concrete is 114 m². The dining room has a large opening on the south side that provides a sense of continuity with the inner courtyard. During the afternoon, sunlight falls through the skylight onto the glass floor on the second level, and casts shadows around the dining room. Sakamoto concludes "Simple designs accentuate carefully chosen and cooked dishes and liquor as well as refined music played. Architecture consists in designing the air that penetrates the atmosphere."

Die Inhaber eines 100-jährigen traditionellen Sesamladens hatten sich dazu entschlossen, ein Restaurant zu eröffnen, in dem Speisen aus oder mit ihrem Lieblingssamen zubereitet werden. Sakamoto erklärt: »Die Grundfläche des Restaurants beträgt nur knapp 86 m², trotzdem werden im Inneren neue räumliche Möglichkeiten ausprobiert. Betritt man den Raum durch den Vorhof, erlebt man die Südseite als Öffnung ohne Schwelle; der Raum wird nur durch die Decke und die Wände gefasst und wirkt offen genug, um ein Gefühl für die Natur zu vermitteln.« Das Grundstück misst 217 m², die Gesamtfläche des Restaurants aus Stahlbeton beträgt 114 m². Durch die große Öffnung nach Süden entsteht ein räumlicher Zusammenhang zwischen Essbereich und Innenhof. Durch ein Oberlicht fallen nachmittags Sonnenstrahlen auf den Glasboden des Obergeschosses und erzeugen im Essbereich Schattenwürfe. Sakamoto sagt: »Wie anspruchsvolle Musik akzentuieren einfache Gebäude sorgfältig ausgesuchte und zubereitete Gerichte und Getränke. Architektur besteht darin, die Luft zu entwerfen, die die Atmosphäre durchdringt.«

Les propriétaires d'une boutique traditionnelle de vente de sésame dont la création remontait à plus d'un siècle, avaient décidé d'ouvrir un restaurant consacré à cette graine. Sakamoto explique que « même si la surface au sol n'est que de 86 m², nous avons recherché de nouvelles possibilités d'occupation intérieure de l'espace. Lorsque l'on pénètre par le porche, le côté sud est perçu comme une ouverture sans châssis, formant un volume qui n'est délimité que par le plafond et les murs, mais semble suffisamment ouvert pour que l'on ressente les éléments extérieurs ». La surface du terrain est de 217 m² et la surface totale utile de ce petit bâtiment en béton armé de 114 m². La salle du restaurant possède une large ouverture sur le sud qui crée un sentiment de continuité avec la cour intérieure. Dans l'après-midi, la lumière naturelle tombe à travers les verrières zénithales sur le sol en verre de l'étage et projette des ombres dans la salle à manger. Pour Sakamoto, « la simplicité du projet met en valeur les plats et les alcools soigneusement choisis et préparés, tout comme une musique raffinée. Ici, l'architecture consiste en quelque sorte à concevoir l'air qui emplit l'atmosphère ».

The poetic sparseness of Sakamoto's architecture can be related to contemporary minimalism, but also to some of the traditional architecture of Japan. A great deal of importance is given to elements such as the single tree near the entrance.

Die poetische Kargheit von Sakamotos Architektur kann mit dem aktuellen Minimalismus, aber auch mit Elementen der traditionellen japanischen Architektur in Verbindung gebracht werden. Dingen wie dem einzelnen Baum neben dem Eingang kommt eine hohe Bedeutung zu.

L'économie poétique de l'architecture de Sakamoto est proche du minimalisme contemporain mais aussi, d'une certaine façon, de l'architecture traditionnelle du Japon. L'architecte a accordé beaucoup d'importance à des éléments comme l'arbre isolé près de l'entrée.

SNOW WHITE DENTAL CLINIC

Toyama, Toyama, Japan, 2002

Floor area: 240 m². Client: Katsuhisa Asada. Cost: not disclosed

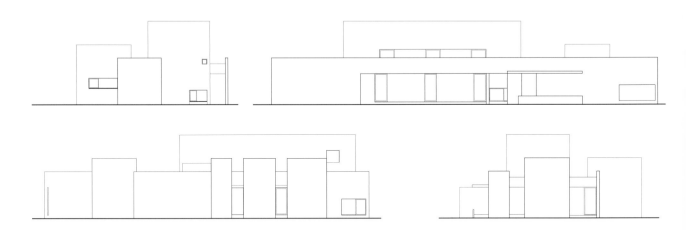

This reinforced concrete building with a total floor area of 240 m² consists of four white volumes centered on an unadorned concrete volume containing the examination area. The dentists' chairs look out onto the landscape, in an unusual approach to what generally is considered to be a very unpleasant visit for most patients. Paying very careful attention to the progression of clients through the space, and to the use of light, Sakamoto explains that in spite of his spare architecture, he is extremely sensitive to the location of this clinic. "Fields that thrive on the clean water and air of this region spread out in all directions;" he says. "Toyama's winters are cold with blankets of snow turning the landscape into majestic silver. The dentist hoped to establish a medical facility that would take advantage of the vast, continuous land, where patients not only come to receive physical treatment but also to seek relaxation and to be cleansed emotionally as well." As is often the case in contemporary Japanese architecture, the presence of nature can be summed up in the penetration of natural light into a space, or in the sound of water in a basin. Sakamoto, in a poetic tone, says, "The place exists quietly, taking in the sky, trees, air, wind, the natural elements of Toyama. The architecture is designed to penetrate and to touch visitors' inner being, in the hope of reaching out to their hearts, like a droplet on the water's surface."

Der Stahlbetonbau mit einer Gesamtfläche von 240 m² besteht aus vier weißen Baukörpern, die um einen puristischen Betonkubus mit den Untersuchungsräumen angeordnet sind. Von den Zahnarztstühlen aus bietet sich ein Blick in die Landschaft der Umgebung – ein ungewöhnlicher Ansatz für den überwiegend als unangenehm empfundenen Besuch einer solchen Praxis. Sakamoto berücksichtigt die Bewegung der Besucher durch das Gebäude und die Belichtung sehr genau. Er erklärt, dass er trotz seiner kargen Architektur extrem sensibel für den Ort ist, an dem sich diese Klinik befindet. »Die Pflanzen auf den Feldern gedeihen aufgrund des sauberen Wassers und der sauberen Luft in dieser Region gut, und die Felder dehnen sich in alle Richtungen aus«, sagt er. »Die Winter in Toyama sind kalt: Schnee deckt die Landschaft zu und verwandelt sie in ein majestätisches Silber. Der Zahnarzt wollte eine medizinische Einrichtung schaffen, die das weite, unbegrenzte Land als Vorteil nutzen würde. Die Patienten sollten nicht nur hierherkommen, um sich physisch behandeln zu lassen, sondern auch, um sich zu entspannen und eine spirituelle Reinigung zu erfahren.« Wie oft in der modernen japanischen Architektur wird die Natur durch eine natürliche Belichtung oder durch das Geräusch von Wasser in einem Bassin vergegenwärtigt. Sakamoto äußert sich auf poetische Weise: »Ruhe prägt diesen Ort. Er nimmt den Himmel, die Bäume, die Luft, den Wind, die natürlichen Elemente von Toyama in sich auf. Die Architektur soll das innere Wesen der Besucher berühren und durchdringen. Ich hoffe, ihre Herzen zu erreichen – wie ein Tropfen, der auf die Wasseroberfläche fällt.«

Cet immeuble en béton armé de 240 m² de surface utile se compose de quatre volumes blancs centrés sur un volume en béton nu contenant la salle d'examen. Les sièges de dentiste sont tournés vers le paysage, façon inhabituelle d'améliorer l'atmosphère d'une visite généralement désagréable. Parce qu'il s'est attaché à étudier l'utilisation de la lumière et la progression des patients à travers l'espace, Sakamoto pense que même si son architecture peut sembler très austère, elle reste extrêmement sensible au lieu. « Les champs qui se nourrissent de l'air et de l'eau purs de cette région s'étendent dans toutes les directions… Les hivers de Toyama sont froids, la neige transforme le paysage en une étendue argentée pleine de majesté. Le dentiste souhaitait une installation qui mette à profit le vaste terrain, il voulait créer un lieu où les patients viennent non seulement pour recevoir un traitement d'ordre physique, mais également pour se relaxer et être libérés de leurs émotions. » Comme c'est souvent le cas dans l'architecture japonaise contemporaine, la présence de la nature peut se résumer à la lumière naturelle qui pénètre dans l'espace ou au son de l'eau dans un bassin. Non sans poésie, Sakamoto précise que « le lieu existe sereinement, absorbant le ciel, les arbres, le vent, tous les éléments naturels de Toyama. L'architecture est conçue pour pénétrer et émouvoir l'être même du visiteur dans l'espoir d'atteindre son cœur, comme une goutte de pluie sur la surface de l'eau ».

The simple architectonic blocks aligned by the architect create a powerful modernity whose function is not readily apparent.

Das Ensemble aus einfachen Kuben ist von einer kraftvollen Modernität. Seine Funktion ist auf den ersten Blick nicht zu erkennen.

Les blocs architectoniques simples ont été alignés par l'architecte pour dégager une modernité pleine de force dont la fonction n'apparaît pas immédiatement.

As is often the case in Japanese interiors, furniture is kept here to a strict minimum, allowing the architecture, space and light to speak as much as any décor.

Wie so oft bei japanischen Interieurs ist die Möblierung auf ein Minimum reduziert. Dadurch wirken die architektonischen Elemente, der Raum und das Licht ebenso stark wie eventuell vorhandenes Dekor.

Comme souvent dans les intérieurs japonais, le mobilier se réduit au strict minimum, ce qui permet à l'architecture, à l'espace et à la lumière de s'exprimer avec plus de présence qu'un simple décor ne pourrait le faire.

SCHMIDT, HAMMER & LASSEN

Schmidt, Hammer & Lassen K/S
Åboulevarden 37, 5.
Clemensborg
Postbox 5117
8000 Århus C
Denmark

Tel: +45 86 20 19 00
Fax: +45 86 18 45 13
e-mail: info@shl.dk
Web: www.shl.dk

ARoS, Århus Museum of Modern Art ▶

MORTEN SCHMIDT was born in 1955. Joint Managing Director of SHL, he graduated from the School of Architecture in Århus (1982). He is in charge of the company's international projects. **BJARNE HAMMER** was born in 1956 and is also a Joint Managing Director of the firm. In charge of projects for the Danish government, municipalities and service businesses, he graduated from the Århus School of Architecture in 1982. **JOHN LASSEN**, born in 1953, also attended the Århus School (1983) and is in charge of housing projects for SHL. The fourth Joint Managing Director is Kim Holst Jensen, born in 1964. Major work includes: Extension of the Royal Danish Library, Copenhagen (1999); Island of Culture, Middelfart, Denmark, (2002–); DGI Building, Århus, Denmark (2002–03); Kolding Technical College, Skovvangen, Kolding, Denmark (2001); Resource and Information Center, Padborg, Denmark (2001); Fjordstokkene Apartments, Holbaek, Denmark (2004), and the 60 000 m² TEDA, Tianjin Exhibition Center in China. One interesting recent project concerns a Cathedral designed for a site 400 km north of the Arctic Circle in Alta, Norway, described as an architectural representation of the *aurora borealis*.

MORTEN SCHMIDT, geboren 1955, und **BJARNE HAMMER**, geboren 1956, machten ihren Abschluss 1982 an der Arkitektenskolen Århus. Beide sind Partner von SHL. Schmidt ist für die Projekte des Büros im Ausland zuständig, Hammer für die staatlichen und kommunalen Gebäude sowie Dienstleistungsgebäude in Dänemark. Auch **JOHN LASSEN**, geboren 1953, studierte an der Arkitektenskolen Århus (Abschluss 1983) und ist als dritter Partner für die Wohnbauten von SHL verantwortlich. Vierter Partner ist der 1964 geborene Kim Holst Jensen. Große realisierte Projekte des Büros sind u. a. die Erweiterung der Königlichen Bibliothek in Kopenhagen (1999), die Kulturinsel in Middelfart, Dänemark (2002–), das DGI Gebäude in Århus (2002–03), die Fachhochschule Kolding in Skovvangen, Kolding (2001), das Ressourcen- und Informationszentrum in Padborg (2001), die Fjordstokkene Apartments in Holbæk (2004) und das 60 000 m² große TEDA (Tianjin Exhibition Center) in Tianjin, China. Eine interessante Planung der jüngeren Zeit ist der Entwurf für eine Kathedrale 400 km nördlich des Polarkreises in Alta, Norwegen, die als architektonische Umsetzung des Polarlichts beschrieben wird.

MORTEN SCHMIDT, né en 1955, est diplômé de l'École d'architecture d'Århus (1982). Codirecteur de l'agence SHL, il est en charge des projets internationaux. **BJARNE HAMMER**, né en 1956, également diplômé de l'École d'architecture d'Århus (1982) est codirecteur, chargé des commandes publiques et des entreprises de services. **JOHN LASSEN**, né en 1953, diplômé de la même école (1983), se consacre aux projets d'immeubles de logements. Le quatrième codirecteur est Kim Holst Jensen, né en 1964. Parmi leurs réalisations les plus importantes : l'extension de la Bibliothèque royale danoise, Copenhague (1999) ; l'Île de la culture (Middelfart, Danemark, 2002–) ; l'immeuble DGI, Århus, Danemark (2002–03) ; le Collège technique de Kolding, Padborg, Danemark (2001) ; le Centre de ressources et d'information de Padborg, Danemark (2001) ; l'immeuble d'appartements Fjordstokkene, Holbaek, Danemark (2004) et un centre d'expositions de 60 000 m² en Tianjin, Chine (concours en 2002). L'un de leurs projets les plus intéressants concerne la Cathédrale des lumières du Nord, conçue pour un site à 400 km au nord du Cercle arctique à Alta (Norvège), décrite comme la représentation architecturale d'une aurore boréale.

AROS, ÅRHUS MUSEUM OF MODERN ART

Århus, Denmark, 2000–04

Floor area: 17 700 m². Client: Municipalty of Århus. Cost: €37.5 million

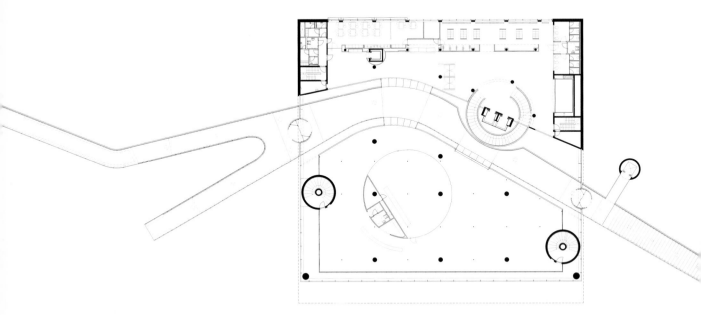

Built for the Municipality of Århus, this 17 700 m² project was the first prize winner in a 1997 international competition with 110 participants. Its construction cost was 37.5 million euros. One of the largest art museums in Northern Europe is located in the center of Århus. It is a ten-story solid cube of red brick, measuring 52 x 52 meters at ground level and almost 50 meters in height. The architects describe it as "a red cube on a green surface with a white interior." In an interesting interpretation of the tendencies of contemporary architecture, Schmidt, Hammer & Lassen declare, "**AROS** is not an Egyptian pyramid, nor is it a typically modern, completely open glasshouse. But in it we have integrated elements borrowed from each of these extremes." They call it a "democratic monument." As they say, "The exhibition area is supplemented by an art bookshop, a café, library, children's museum and workshops and more – a wide range of alternative ways in which people can come face to face with art." One reason for the powerful form of the building is also its proximity to the 1942 Århus Town Hall, Law Courts, the Barracks, Industrial Archives (formerly the State and University Library), the Århus Business College and Kreditforeningen Danmark's head office. In 1979 a Concert Hall was added to this imposing group of buildings, and in the 1990s the Scandinavian Commercial Center was built. The main cube shape of the museum is sliced in two by a curved, glazed section that adds to the surprisingly luminous interior.

1997 ging der Entwurf als Sieger aus einem internationalen Wettbewerb mit 110 Teilnehmern hervor. Der Bau umfasst 17 700 m², die Gesamtkosten betrugen umgerechnet 37,5 Millionen Euro; Bauherr ist die Gemeinde Århus. Das Museum – eines der größten Kunstmuseen in Nordeuropa – liegt im Zentrum der Stadt. Das Gebäude ist ein zehngeschossiger geschlossener Kubus aus rotem Backstein, 52 x 52 m im Grundriss und fast 50 m hoch. Die Architekten beschreiben ihn als »einen roten Würfel mit weißen Innenräumen auf einer grünen Fläche«. Die Tendenzen moderner Architektur auf interessante Weise interpretierend, beschreiben Schmidt, Hammer & Lassen das Museum folgendermaßen: »**AROS** ist weder eine ägyptische Pyramide noch ein typisch modernes, vollständig offenes Glashaus. Wir haben jedoch Elemente beider Extreme in das Gebäude integriert.« Sie nennen es ein »demokratisches Monument« und erläutern: »Der Ausstellungsbereich wird durch einen Kunstbuchladen, ein Café, eine Bibliothek, ein Museum für Kinder mit Räumen für Workshops und andere Einrichtungen ergänzt. Es bietet also eine große Bandbreite von alternativen Möglichkeiten, mit denen Menschen mit Kunst direkt in Berührung kommen können.« Ein Grund für die kraftvolle Gebäudeform ist die Nähe zum Rathaus und zu den Gerichtsgebäuden der Stadt, den Kasernen, den Industriearchiven (ehemals Staatliche und Universitätsbibliothek), der Business-Schule Århus und der Zentrale von Kreditforeningen Danmark. 1979 kam zu dieser imposanten Gebäudegruppe eine Konzerthalle hinzu, in den 1990er Jahren wurde das Skandinavische Einkaufszentrum gebaut. Die dominierende Kubusform des Museums wird durch ein gebogenes, verglastes Element durchschnitten, das zu dem überraschend hellen Inneren beiträgt.

Édifié pour la municipalité d'Århus, ce musée de 17 700 m² a remporté un concours international organisé en 1997, qui avait attiré cent dix participants. Son coût s'est élevé à 37,5 millions d'euros. Ce musée d'art, l'un des plus grands d'Europe du Nord, est situé au centre de la ville et consiste en un cube massif de dix niveaux en brique rouge de 52 x 52 m au sol pour près de 50 m de haut. Dans une intéressante interprétation des tendances de l'architecture contemporaine, les architectes décrivent leur projet comme « un cube rouge sur une surface verte doté d'un intérieur blanc. **AROS** n'est pas une pyramide égyptienne, ni une boîte de verre complètement ouverte et typiquement moderne. Nous avons intégré des éléments empruntés à chacune de ces solutions extrêmes ». Ils parlent également de « monument démocratique…. La partie réservée à l'exposition des œuvres est complétée entre autres par une librairie d'art, un café, une bibliothèque, un musée des enfants et des ateliers… une vaste gamme de propositions pour se confronter à l'art ». L'une des raisons de la puissance voulue pour cette forme est la proximité de l'hôtel de ville de 1942, du palais de justice, des casernes, des Archives industrielles (l'anciennne Bibliothèque nationale et universitaire), de la Bourse et du siège de la banque Kreditforeningen Danmark. En 1979, une salle de concert avait été ajoutée à cet imposant groupe de bâtiments, ainsi que le Centre commercial scandinave dans les années 1990. Le cube du musée est coupé en deux par une section en verre incurvée qui éclabousse de lumière l'intérieur déjà étonnamment lumineux.

The apparently weighty and symmetrical body of the museum is in fact penetrated by a curving rift.

Der nur scheinbar schwere und symmetrische Museumsblock wird von einer gekrümmten »Kerbe« durchschnitten.

Pesante et symétrique au premier coup d'œil, la masse du musée est en fait scindée par une faille intérieure tout en courbes.

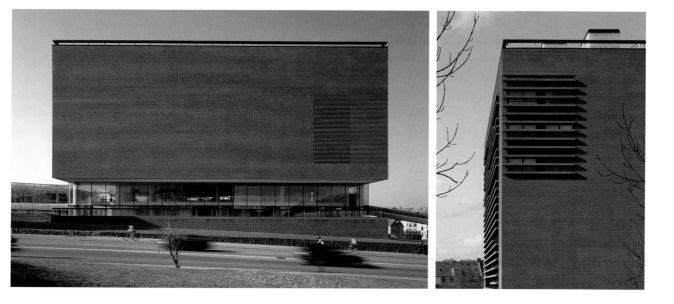

The central passageway and its accompanying band of light becomes the central feature of the museum, adding a variety that is not announced by the austere outside façades.

Der zentrale Weg und das ihm zugeordnete Lichtband sind die wichtigsten architektonischen Merkmale des Museums und führen zu einer räumlichen Vielfalt, die die nüchterne Außenfassade nicht vermuten lässt.

Le passage central, souligné d'un bandeau de lumière zénithale, est devenu l'élément clé de l'identité du musée, l'enrichissant d'un degré de variété que ne laissait pas présager son austérité extérieure.

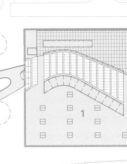

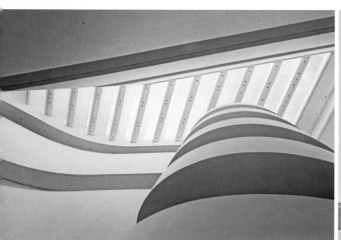

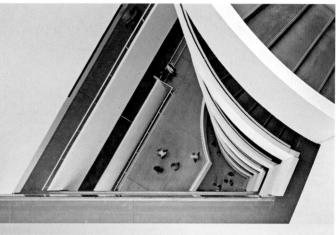

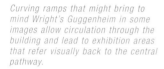

Curving ramps that might bring to mind Wright's Guggenheim in some images allow circulation through the building and lead to exhibition areas that refer visually back to the central pathway.

Die gekurvten Rampen, die auf manchen Abbildungen an Frank Lloyd Wrights Guggenheim Museum erinnern, ermöglichen Rundgänge und erschließen Ausstellungsbereiche, die sich optisch auf den zentralen Weg rückbeziehen.

Des rampes incurvées, qui rappellent parfois celle du Guggenheim de Frank Lloyd Wright, facilitent la circulation dans l'ensemble du bâtiment et mènent aux espaces d'exposition qui se rattachent visuellement au passage central.

SCHWARTZ/SILVER

Schwartz/Silver Architects, Inc.
530 Atlantic Avenue
Boston, Massachusetts 02210
USA

Tel: +1 617 542 6650
Fax: +1 617 951 0779
e-mail: arch@schwartzsilver.com
Web: www.schwartzsilver.com

Shaw Center for the Arts

WARREN SCHWARTZ and **ROBERT SILVER** founded their firm in Boston in 1980. Schwartz was educated at Cornell and Harvard, where he received his degree in Urban Design in 1967. Silver attended Queens College CUNY, Cambridge University and Harvard, where he received his Masters in Architecture in 1970. Recent work includes the Abbe Museum, Bar Harbor, Maine (2001); Farnsworth Art Museum and Wyeth Study Center, Rockland, Maine (1998); Belmont Hill School Prenatt Music Center, Belmont, Massachusetts (2004); Princeton University Anglinger Center for the Humanities, Princeton, New Jersey (2004); and a renovation and expansion of the Boston Atheneum (2002). Schwartz/Silver has received the AIA National Honor Award five times, and they pride themselves in being a "middle-sized firm … organized as an open design studio." Current projects include work for the Maine Historical Society, a master plan for the University of Vermont and buildings for the University of Virginia.

WARREN SCHWARTZ und **ROBERT SILVER** gründeten ihr Büro 1980 in Boston. Schwartz studierte in Cornell und Harvard. 1967 machte er in Harvard seinen Abschluss im Fach Stadtplanung. Silver studierte am Queens College CUNY, an der Cambridge University und in Harvard, wo er 1970 seinen Master of Architecture erlangte. Zu ihren neueren Projekten gehören das Farnsworth Art Museum and Wyeth Study Center in Rockland, Maine (1998), das Abbe Museum in Bar Harbor, Maine (2001), die Instandsetzung und Erweiterung des Boston Atheneum (2002), das Belmont Hill School Prenatt Music Center in Belmont, Massachusetts (2004), und das Princeton University Anglinger Center for the Humanities in Princeton, New Jersey (2004). Schwartz/Silver wurden bereits fünfmal mit dem AIA National Honor Award ausgezeichnet. Sie sind stolz darauf, ein »mittelgroßes Büro zu sein …, das wie ein offenes Entwurfsatelier organisiert ist«. Zur Zeit sind u. a. ein Auftrag von der Maine Historical Society, ein Masterplan für die University of Vermont und Gebäude für die University of Virginia in Arbeit.

WARREN SCHWARTZ et **ROBERT SILVER** ont créé leur agence à Boston en 1980. Schwartz a étudié à Cornell et Harvard dont il est diplômé en urbanisme (1967). Silver a suivi les cours de Queens College City University of New York, de Cambridge University et d'Harvard (Master of Architecture en 1970). Parmi leurs récents travaux : le Abbe Museum, Bar Harbor, Maine (2001) ; le Farnsworth Art Museum et le Wyeth Study Center, Rockland, Maine (1998) ; la rénovation et l'extension du Boston Athenaeum, Boston (2002) ; le Belmont Hill School Prenatt Music Center, Belmont, Massachusetts (2004) ; l'Anglinger Center for the Humanities de Princeton University, Princeton, New Jersey (2004). L'agence a reçu cinq fois le National Honor Award de l'American Institute of Architects et se présente comme «une agence de dimensions moyennes … organisée comme un atelier de conception ouvert ». Elle travaille actuellement pour la Maine Historical Society, sur un plan directeur de l'Université du Vermont et à des bâtiments destinés à l'Université de Virginie.

SHAW CENTER FOR THE ARTS

Baton Rouge, Louisiana, USA, 2003–05

Floor area: 11 613 m². Client: Shaw Center for the Arts, LLC.
Cost: $32.8 million

The very contemporary wrap-around esthetic of the Shaw Center is particularly unusual in that the building sits atop another older structure in a symbiotic relationship that might also be considered indicative of the current interest in extensions and renovations.

Die sehr zeitgemäße, einheitlich umlaufende Fassade des Shaw Center ist besonders bemerkenswert, da das neue Gebäude auf ein bestehendes aufgesattelt wurde. Zwischen den beiden Gebäuden besteht eine symbiotische Verbindung, die typisch für das derzeitige Interesse an Erweiterungen und Instandsetzungen ist.

Très contemporaine, l'esthétique « enveloppante » du Shaw Center est particulièrement surprenante, car le nouveau bâtiment repose sur une structure plus ancienne, dans une relation symbolique assez typique de la tendance actuelle des extensions et des rénovations.

Despite its location near the water in Baton Rouge, the Shaw Center withstood Hurricane Katrina in 2005 without suffering any serious damage.

Obwohl das Shaw Center in Baton Rouge direkt am Wasser liegt, hielt es dem Hurrikan Katrina 2005 ohne nennenswerten Schaden stand.

Malgré sa localisation au bord de l'eau à Baton Rouge, le Shaw Center a résisté à l'ouragan Katrina de 2005, sans souffrir de dommages sérieux.

This 35.7 million dollar center for visual and performing arts has a floor area of approximately 10 000 m². It includes the 322-seat Manship Performing Arts Center at one end and the Louisiana State University Museum of Art at the other. One unusual feature of the building is the 12-meter cantilever over the existing 1930s Auto Hotel. The most visible exterior element of the design is the façade clad in multi-length cast glass channels. The architects explain that "The façade is conceived to evoke many local associations: A paper lantern, glass beading, the meandering Mississippi River. At night the building glows like a 'lantern on the levee,' a ubiquitous feature along the river in antebellum times." A corrugated aluminum wall system is set 15 centimeters behind this glass screen. This type of façade posed a number of technical problems, not least of which is its potential resistance to high winds. "Baton Rouge is only 60 miles inland from the Gulf of Mexico on the southern coast of the United States," they explain. "To test the glazing system against hurricane-force winds, a mock up was produced and placed in front of an old DC-3 airplane propeller to simulate 100-mile-per-hour winds. Further tests were done in Germany by the vendor, Bendheim Wall Systems." Schwartz/Silver worked on this project with local architects Eskew + Dumez + Ripple, and Jerry M. Campbell & Associates.

Das umgerechnet 29,7 Millionen Euro teure Gebäude für bildende und darstellende Künste hat eine Gesamtfläche von mehr als 10 000 m². An einem Ende liegt das Manship Performing Arts Center mit 322 Plätzen, am anderen Ende das Louisiana State University Museum of Art. Eine Besonderheit des Gebäudes ist eine 12 m lange Auskragung über dem »Auto Hotel« aus den 1930er Jahren. Besonders markant ist die Fassade, die aus verschieden langen Glasröhren besteht. Die Architekten erläutern: »Die Fassade soll viele Assoziationen, die mit dem Ort zu tun haben, hervorrufen: eine Papierlaterne, Glasperlenstickerei, den mäandrierenden Mississippi. Nachts leuchtet der Bau wie eine ›Laterne an der Uferböschung‹, früher ein allgegenwärtiges Element am Flussufer.« 15 cm hinter der Glasebene ist ein Wandsystem aus gewellten Aluminiumblechen angeordnet. Aufgrund des Fassadenaufbaus musste eine Reihe von technischen Problemen gelöst werden: Dazu gehörte nicht zuletzt die Aufnahme von hohen Windlasten. »Baton Rouge ist nur 100 km vom Golf von Mexico entfernt, also nicht weit von der Südküste der Vereinigten Staaten«, erklären die Architekten. »Um das Verglasungssystem auch für Windstärken im Bereich von Hurrikans zu testen, wurde ein Fassadenmodell im Maßstab 1:1 gebaut. Eine alte DC-3-Propellermaschine wurde vor das Modell gestellt, um Windstärken mit über 160 km/h zu simulieren. In Deutschland wurden weitere Tests beim Hersteller der Fassade, Bendheim Wandsysteme, durchgeführt. Schwartz/Silver arbeiteten bei diesem Projekt vor Ort mit den Architekten Eskew + Dumez + Ripple sowie Jerry M. Campbell & Associates zusammen.

Ce centre pour les arts visuels et du spectacle occupe une surface de plus de 10 000 m² environ et a coûté 29,7 millions d'euros. Il comprend le Manship Performing Arts Center de 322 places à une extrémité et le Louisana State University Museum of Art à l'autre. L'une de ses caractéristiques est son porte-à-faux de 12 m au-dessus de l'Auto Hotel, un bâtiment des années 1930. La façade extérieure est particulièrement remarquable pour son habillage de panneaux de verre moulé en gouttière de multiples longueurs. Les architectes expliquent : « La façade est dessinée pour évoquer de nombreuses associations d'idées de nature locale : une lanterne en papier, des perles de verre, les méandres du Mississippi. La nuit, le bâtiment luit comme une de ces ‹ lanternes de digue › que l'on trouvait partout le long du fleuve avant la Guerre civile. » Un système de parois en aluminium ondulé est implanté à 15 cm derrière l'écran de verre de la façade. Ce type de montage a posé de nombreux problèmes, celui de la résistance à la force des vents n'étant pas le moindre. « Baton Rouge n'est qu'à 100 km du golfe du Mexique… pour tester le système de vitrage contre les ouragans, une maquette a été construite et placée devant un moteur à hélice de vieux DC3 pour simuler des vents soufflant à 160 km/h. D'autres tests ont été réalisés en Allemagne par le fournisseur, Bendheim Wall Systems. » Schwartz/Silver a travaillé sur ce projet avec les agences locales Eskew + Dumez + Ripple et Jerry M. Campbell & Associates.

The almost ghostly appearance of the
Shaw Center in its nighttime lighting
accentuates its unusual volume and
cantilevered overhang.

Die fast geisterhafte Wirkung des
Shaw Center bei nächtlicher Beleuchtung entsteht durch den ungewöhnlichen Baukörper und die große Auskragung.

Sous l'éclairage nocturne, l'apparence quasi fantomatique du Shaw Center accentue le caractère étrange de
son volume et de son porte-à-faux.

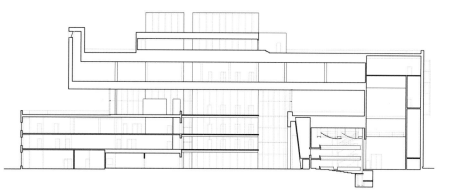

Notes of color render interior spaces warmer than they might have been.

Die Farben lassen die Innenräume wärmer als erwartet wirken.

Des touches de couleur confèrent une certaine chaleur aux intérieurs.

A soaring entrance area and silver, translucent volumes that recall the exterior design of the building greet visitors in the Shaw Center.

Ein hohes Atrium und silbrige, trans-luzente Volumina, die der Außenfas-sade ähneln, begrüßen den Besucher des Shaw Center.

Une entrée aux proportions vertigi-neuses et des volumes argentés et translucides rappelant l'esthétique des façades accueillent les visiteurs du Shaw Center.

ROGER SHERMAN

Roger Sherman Architecture and Urban Design, 713 Ashland Avenue, Santa Monica, California 90405, USA
Tel: +1 310 450 7553, Fax: +1 310 314 1939, email: roger@rsaud.com
Web: www.rsaud.com

ROGER SHERMAN was educated at the University of Pennsylvania and at the Harvard Graduate School of Design, where he received his Masters of Architecture degree in 1985. Located in Santa Monica, Roger Sherman Architecture (RSA) is a partnership that was founded in 1990, and varies in size between four and six persons who work on only two or three projects at any one time. The firm's two principals are Greg Kochanowski and Roger Sherman. Sherman's "interest and research on the politics of property ownership derives from his own practical experience in working on public projects of a controversial nature." These include the West Hollywood Civic Center, a commission won through an international design competition in 1987; and a National Endowment for the Arts-funded development plan for North Hollywood (in the San Fernando Valley) in 1995. Other notable projects by his firm include rePark, a master plan for Fresh Kills Landfill, Staten Island, New York (2001); and Railyard Park, the revitalization of Santa Fe, New Mexico's historic rail yard. In addition to being a practicing architect, Sherman was recently appointed director of the Metropolitan Research and Design (MR+D) program at the Southern California Institute of Architecture (SCIArc), where he has been a studio instructor for 13 years. RSA has concentrated on single family residences, and their projects include: Shanus Residence (new), Cheviot Hills, California (2004–05); Schab Residence (3-in-1 House), Santa Monica, California (2002–03); Gaynor Residence Kitchen Remodel, Brentwood, California (2002); and the Gold Residence Living/Dining Room Remodel/Addition, Los Angeles, California (1997). Current work includes the Flex-Deck-Spec House, Gloucestershire, UK; Johnson/O'Kingston Residence Pleasure Deck, Signal Hill, California; and the Gill/Weg Residence Remodel, Silverlake, California.

ROGER SHERMAN studierte an der University of Pennsylvania und an der Harvard Graduate School of Design, wo er 1985 seinen Master of Architecture machte. Roger Sherman Architects (RSA) wurde 1990 in Santa Monica gegründet. Die Größe des Büros, das von den Partnern Greg Kochanowski und Roger Sherman geführt wird, variiert: Zwischen vier und sechs Personen arbeiten an nur zwei oder drei Projekten gleichzeitig. Shermans »Interesse an politischen Fragen des Grundbesitzes und seine Forschung in diesem Bereich entwickelte sich aus seiner praktischen Erfahrung, die er durch die Planung öffentlicher und umstrittener Projekte machte.« Dazu gehören das West Hollywood Civic Center, ein Auftrag, den er durch den Gewinn eines internationalen Wettbewerbs 1987 erhielt, und der Entwicklungsplan für North Hollywood im San Fernando Valley (1995), der durch Mittel des National Endowment for the Arts (Nationale Kulturstiftung) finanziert wurde. Andere wichtige Projekte des Büros sind rePark, ein Masterplan für die Mülldeponie Fresh Kills in Staten Island, New York, und Railyard Park, die Revitalisierung des historischen Eisenbahngeländes in Santa Fe, New Mexico. Zusätzlich zu seiner Tätigkeit als Architekt ist Sherman seit kurzem Leiter des Metropolitan Research and Design (MR+D) Program am Southern California Institute of Architecture (SCI-Arc), wo er 13 Jahre als Lehrer für verschiedene Entwurfsklassen tätig war. RSA hat bislang hauptsächlich Einfamilienhäuser realisiert. Derzeit in Planung bzw. im Bau sind u. a. das Flex-Deck-Spec House in Gloucestershire, England, die Terrasse der Johnson/O'Kingston Residence in Signal Hill, Kalifornien, und der Umbau der Gill/Weg Residence in Silverlake, Kalifornien. Realisierte Häuser sind u. a. die Shanus Residence in Cheviot Hills, Kalifornien (2004–05), die Schab Residence (3-in-1-Haus) in Santa Monica, Kalifornien (2002–03), der Küchenumbau der Gaynor Residence in Brenntwood, Kalifornien (2002), und der Umbau und die Erweiterung des Wohn- und Esszimmers der Gold Residence in Los Angeles (1997).

ROGER SHERMAN a étudié à l'Université de Pennsylvanie et à la Harvard Graduate School of Design (Master of Architecture en 1985). Installée à Santa Monica, l'agence Roger Sherman Architecture (RSA) a été fondée en 1990 et compte de quatre à six collaborateurs qui ne travaillent que sur deux ou trois projets à la fois. Ses deux dirigeants sont Greg Kochanowski et Roger Sherman. «L'intérêt [de Sherman] pour la politique de la propriété vient de son expérience personnelle de projets publics de nature controversée», tels que le West Hollywood Civic Center, commande remportée à l'issue d'un concours international en 1987, et un plan d'urbanisme pour North Hollywood (vallée de San Fernando) bénéficiaire d'une aide du National Endowment for the Arts en 1995. Parmi les autres projets notables de l'agence : rePark, plan directeur pour Fresh Kills Landfill, Staten Island, New York (2001) ; Railyard Park, réhabilitation de friches ferroviaires à Santa Fe au Nouveau-Mexique. En dehors de ses activités d'architecte, Sherman a été récemment nommé directeur du Metropolitan Research and Design (MR+D) Program du Southern California Institute of Architecture (SCI-arc), où il enseigne depuis 13 ans. RSA se concentre sur les maisons individuelles : Shanus Residence, Cheviot Hills, Californie (2004–05) ; Schab Residence (3-in-1 House, Santa Monica, 2002–03) ; restructuration de la cuisine de la Gaynor Residence, Brentwood (2002) ; extension et restructuration du séjour-salle à manger de la Gold Residence, Los Angeles (1997). Actuellement, l'équipe travaille aux projets de la Flex-Deck-Spec House (Gloucestershire, Grande-Bretagne), à une terrasse pour la Johnson/O'Kingston Residence (Signal Hill, Californie) et à la restructuration de la Gill/Weg Residence (Silverlake, Los Angeles).

3-IN-1 HOUSE

Santa Monica, California, USA, 2002–03

Floor area: 254 m². Client: Jennifer Schab.
Cost: $610 000

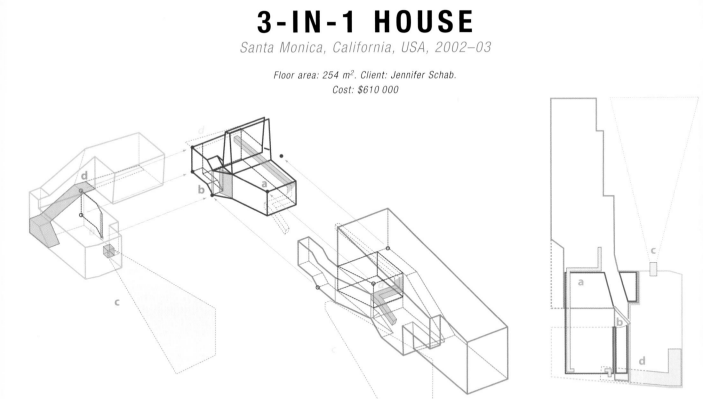

The **3-IN-1 HOUSE** built for a professional couple with one child, is a 254 m² residence located on a 15 x 35 meter lot with a 10% grade. It has a steel super-structure with wood stud infill, stucco and bonderized metal-panel exterior finish, concrete slab and birch veneer plywood floors, and birch veneer and wallpapered walls. Located just seven blocks from the Pacific Ocean, the site offers views of the Santa Monica Mountains toward the rear (north). The structure consists in a single-family residence, studio/office and attached rental unit. The studio and home share a common entry. Roger Sherman comments "With the cost of both steel and wood sky-rocketing, the use of inexpensive materials is no longer enough to keep things affordable. The recent emphasis on home-as-lifestyle instead of home-as-form may be one symptom of this paradox. In such a climate, this project is intended to serve as a model and method by which architecture can still be achievable, if not affordable through a series of design strategies whose aim is to more compactly but creatively accommodate the ordinary residential program, in order to allocate and preserve a sufficient portion of the budget to create a strong overall architectural statement and experience." A great deal of importance was given by the architect to the flexibil-ity and compactness of the design. Given the warm climate of Los Angeles, some frequently usable space is external. Terraces extend from the house at three levels down the hillside, "allowing the accoutrements of daily life to be left outside rather than building additional square footage to accommodate them."

Das 254 m² große **3-IN-1-HAUS** für ein Paar mit einem Kind steht auf einem Grundstück mit einer Fläche von 15 x 35 m und einem Gefälle von zehn Prozent. Die Stahlkonstruktion des Gebäudes ist mit Holz ausgefacht und außen mit beschichteten Metallpaneelen verkleidet. Die Stahlbetonböden haben einen Belag aus Sperr-holz mit Birkenfurnier, die Wände sind mit Birkenholzfurnier und Tapete verkleidet. Das Grundstück liegt sieben Straßenblöcke vom Pazifik entfernt. Nach Norden bietet sich ein Blick auf die Santa Monica Mountains. Das Haus besteht aus einem Einfamilienhaus, einem Studio/Büro und einem Anbau mit einer Mietwohnung. Büro und Privathaus teilen sich einen Eingang. Roger Sherman kommentiert: »Heutzutage, wo die Preise für Stahl und Holz in den Himmel schießen, reicht es nicht mehr aus, preis-werte Materialien beim Bauen zu verwenden, um die Kosten niedrig zu halten. Das Motto ›die Form bestimmt das Haus‹ hat sich in letzter Zeit in Richtung ›der Lebens-stil bestimmt das Haus‹ verändert. In diesem Kontext soll das 3-in-1-Haus als Modell und Methode dienen, wie Architektur machbar und finanzierbar sein kann. Dies wird durch eine Entwurfsstrategie erreicht, die darauf abzielt, auf kompaktere, aber kreative Weise das typische Einfamilienhausprogramm unterzubringen und dadurch einen ausreichenden Teil des Budgets dafür zu benutzen, eine insgesamt starke architektonische Aussage zu schaffen.« Die Architekten legten großen Wert auf Flexibilität und Kompaktheit. In Anbetracht des warmen Klimas befinden sich einige der häufig genutzten Räume im Außenbereich. Terrassen auf drei Ebenen vergrößern das Haus in Richtung Hangseite, »so dass das Equipment des täglichen Lebens draußen gelassen werden kann, anstatt dass man größere Räume baut, um es aufzubewahren«.

Cette maison de 254 m² construite pour un couple et son enfant est située sur un terrain de 15 x 35 m incliné à 10%. La structure est en acier à remplissage de panneaux de bois, l'extérieur est revêtu de panneaux de stuc à finitions en métal bondérisé, l'intérieur est en dalles de béton et sols en placage de bouleau, les murs sont habillés de bouleau ou de papier peint. Situé à sept blocs seulement du Pacifique, le terrain donne, au nord, sur les Santa Monica Mountains. La maison comprend à la fois la résidence de la famille, un bureau/studio et un appartement à louer. Le studio et la maison partagent la même entrée. Pour Roger Sherman, «avec les aug-mentations faramineuses du prix du bois et de l'acier, le recours à des matériaux bon marché n'est plus une solution suffisante. La mode récente de la ‹maison-style de vie› au détriment de la ‹maison-objet› est peut-être un symptôme de ce paradoxe. Dans un tel contexte, ce projet entend être un modèle et une méthode grâce aux-quels on peut encore faire de l'architecture, ou du moins la rendre accessible. La stratégie de conception a pour but de répondre de façon créative mais plus resserrée aux contraintes d'un programme résidentiel classique, afin de pouvoir consacrer une part suffisante du budget à cette aventure qu'est la création architecturale propre-ment dite». Une grande attention a été accordée à la souplesse et à la compacité du projet. Compte tenu du climat de Los Angeles, une partie des activités peut se dérouler en plein air. Les terrasses prolongent la maison et se déploient sur trois niveaux à flanc de colline, «permettant de laisser à l'extérieur les accessoires de la vie quotidienne au lieu de construire des mètres carrés supplémentaires pour les recevoir».

Wrapping surfaces with different colors and textures form the exterior of the house, which does not show a predictable sequence of doors and windows.

Umlaufende Fassaden mit unterschiedlichen Farben und Texturen bestimmen das Äußere des Hauses, das ohne eine vorhersehbare Anordnung von Türen und Fenstern auskommt.

L'extérieur de la maison est caractérisé par des surfaces enveloppantes de différentes textures et couleurs, en l'absence de toute séquence attendue de portes et de fenêtres.

The choice of furniture is less the object of interest in these images than the interesting use of wrapping surfaces and materials.

Nicht die Auswahl der Möbelstücke steht hier im Vordergrund, sondern der reizvolle Einsatz von hüllenden Oberflächen und Materialien.

Le choix du mobilier est ici moins intéressant que l'utilisation des surfaces et des matériaux de revêtement.

SITE

SITE
25 Maiden Lane
New York, New York 10038
USA

Tel: +1 212 285 0120
Fax: +1 212 285 0125
e-mail: info@siteenvirodesign.com
Web: www.siteenvirodesign.com

Private Residential Tower, Mumbai

James Wines, founding principal of **SITE** (Sculpture in the Environment) was born in Chicago, Illinois in 1932 and studied art and art history at Syracuse University (B. A. 1956). Between 1965 and 1967, he was a sculptor. He created SITE with Alison Sky and Michelle Stone in 1970. Notable buildings include: Indeterminate Facade Showroom, Houston, Texas (1975); Ghost Parking Lot, Hamden, Connecticut (1978); Highway 86, World Exposition, Vancouver, British Columbia, Canada (1986); Four Continents Bridge, Hiroshima, Japan (1989); Avenida 5, Universal Exhibition, Seville, Spain (1992) and Ross's Landing Plaza and Park, Chattanooga, Tennessee (1992); landscape design and promenades for MCA Garden – Universal Studios, Orlando, Florida (1996); Brinker International Chili's Restaurant, prototype restaurant design, Denver, Colorado, (1998). More recent projects include the Shake Shack in Madison Square Park, Manhattan (2004); interior design for Xerion Capital Partners, New York (2003); and the work in Mumbai published here.

James Wines, Gründungspartner von **SITE** (Sculpture in the Environment), wurde 1932 in Chicago geboren und studierte Kunst und Kunstgeschichte an der Syracuse University (B. A. 1956). Von 1965 bis 1967 war er als Bildhauer tätig. 1970 gründete er zusammen mit Alison Sky und Michelle Stone SITE. Wichtige Projekte des Büros sind: Indeterminate Façade Showroom in Houston, Texas (1975), Ghost Parking Lot in Hamden, Connecticut (1978), Highway 68 auf der Weltausstellung in Vancouver, Kanada (1986), Four Continents Bridge in Hiroshima (1989), Avenida 5 auf der Weltausstellung 1992 in Sevilla und Ross's Landing Plaza und Park in Chattanooga, Tennessee (1992). Ferner hat das Büro u. a. für MCA Garden – Universal Studios in Orlando, Florida, Außenanlagen und Wandelhallen geplant (1996) und das Brinker International Chili's Restaurant in Denver, Colorado (Prototyp eines Restaurants, 1998). Zu den neueren Projekten des Büros gehören der Shake Shack im Madison Square Park in Manhattan (2004) sowie Innenraumplanungen für Xerion Capital Partners, New York (2003), und der hier gezeigte Mumbai Tower.

James Wine, associé fondateur de **SITE** (Sculpture in Environment) est né à Chicago en 1932 et a étudié l'art et l'histoire de l'art à Syracuse University, Bachelor of Art (1956) avant de devenir sculpteur (1965–67). Il a créé SITE avec Alison Sky et Michelle Stone en 1970. Parmi leurs réalisations les plus notables : Indeterminate Facade Showroom, Houston, Texas (1975); Ghost Parking Lot, Hamden, Connecticut (1986); Highway 68, Exposition universelle, Vancouver, Canada (1986); Four Continents Bridge, Hiroshima, Japon (1989); Avenida 5, Exposition universelle, Séville, Espagne (1992); Ross's Landing Plaza and Park, Chattanooga, Tennesse (1992); aménagement paysager et promenades pour le MCA Garden, Universal Studios, Orlando, Floride (1996); Brinker International Chili's Restaurant, prototype de chaîne de restaurants, Denver, Colorado (1998). Plus récemment, le Shake Shack, Madison Square Park, Manhattan (2004), des aménagements intérieurs pour Xerion Capital Partners, New York (2003) et l'intervention à Mumbai (Bombay) publiée ici.

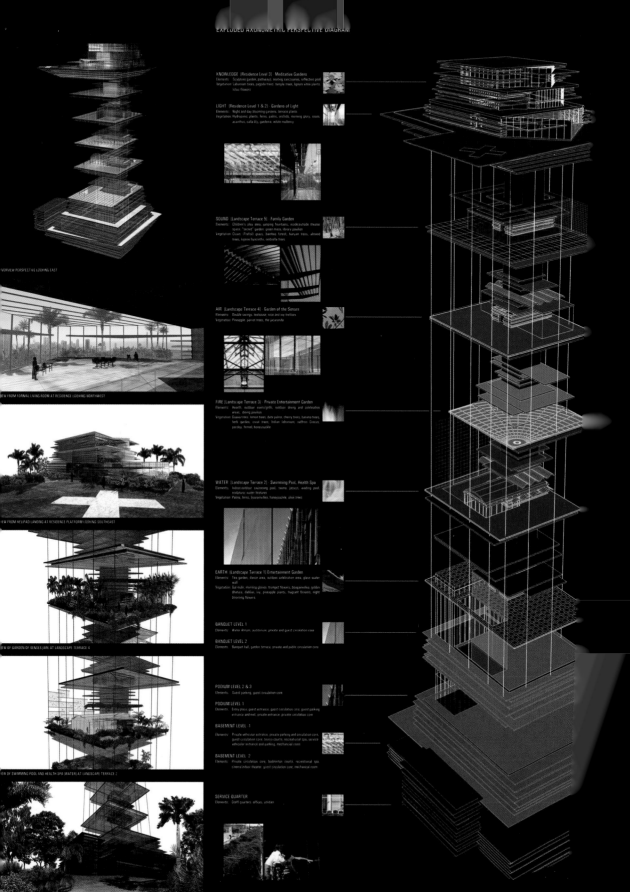

EXPLODED AXONOMETRIC PERSPECTIVE DIAGRAM

KNOWLEDGE (Residence Level 3) Meditative Gardens
Elements: Sculpture garden, pathways, seating sanctuaries, reflection pool
Vegetation: Laburnum trees, pagoda trees, temple trees, lignum vitae plants, lotus flowers

LIGHT (Residence Level 1 & 2) Gardens of Light
Elements: Night and day blooming gardens, terrace plants
Vegetation: Hydroponic plants, ferns, palms, orchids, morning glory, roses, acanthus, calla lily, gardenia, white mulberry

SOUND (Landscape Terrace 5) Family Garden
Elements: Children's play area, jumping fountains, inside/outside theater space, "secret" garden, green maze, library pavilion
Vegetation: Clover (Trefoil) grass, bamboo forest, banyan trees, almond trees, hyacinths, umbrella trees

AIR (Landscape Terrace 4) Garden of the Senses
Elements: Double swings, teahouse, rose and ivy trellises
Vegetation: Pineapple, parrot trees, the jacaranda

FIRE (Landscape Terrace 3) Private Entertainment Garden
Elements: Hearth, outdoor events/grills, outdoor dining and celebration areas, dining pavilion
Vegetation: Guava trees, lemon trees, date palms, cherry trees, banana trees, herb garden, coral trees, Indian laburnum, saffron Crocus, parsley, fennel, honeysuckle

WATER (Landscape Terrace 2) Swimming Pool, Health Spa
Elements: Indoor/outdoor swimming pool, sauna, jacuzzi, wading pool, sculptural water features
Vegetation: Palms, ferns, bougainvilles, honeysuckle, olive trees

EARTH (Landscape Terrace 1) Entertainment Garden
Elements: Tea garden, dance area, outdoor celebration area, glass water wall
Vegetation: Gul mohr, morning glories, trumpet flowers, bougainvillea, golden dhatura, dahlias, ivy, pineapple plants, fragrant flowers, night blooming flowers

BANQUET LEVEL 1
Elements: Water Atrium, auditorium, private and guest circulation core

BANQUET LEVEL 2
Elements: Banquet hall, garden terrace, private and public circulation core

PODIUM LEVEL 2 & 3
Elements: Guest parking, guest circulation core

PODIUM LEVEL 1
Elements: Entry plaza, guest entrance, guest circulation core, guest parking entrance and exit, private entrance, private circulation core

BASEMENT LEVEL -1
Elements: Private vehicular entrance, private parking and circulation core, guest circulation core, bocce courts, recreational spa, service vehicular entrance and parking, mechanical room

BASEMENT LEVEL -2
Elements: Private circulation core, badminton courts, recreational spa, cinema/indoor theater, guest circulation core, mechanical room

SERVICE QUARTER
Elements: Staff quarters, offices, utilities

OVERVIEW PERSPECTIVE LOOKING EAST

VIEW FROM FORMAL LIVING ROOM AT RESIDENCE LOOKING NORTHWEST

VIEW FROM HELIPAD LANDING AT RESIDENCE PLATFORM LOOKING SOUTHEAST

VIEW OF GARDEN OF SENSES (AIR) AT LANDSCAPE TERRACE 4

VIEW OF SWIMMING POOL AND HEALTH SPA (WATER) AT LANDSCAPE TERRACE 2

PRIVATE RESIDENTIAL TOWER

Mumbai, India, 2004

Floor area: 26 942 m². Client: not disclosed. Cost: $145 million

This project, to be built on a 4325 m² hilltop site overlooking Mumbai, would be 110 meters tall and include a total of 26 942 m² of floor area with a probable building cost of 145 million dollars. The appearance of the building is described by SITE in the following terms: "The concept responds to the client's desire to have a multi-tiered, heavily landscaped structure, similar to the ancient Hanging Gardens of Babylon. For this reason the entire building is conceived as a garden in the sky, freeing landscape from its normal earthbound confinement. The philosophical foundations for this structure respond to Vastu principles in Hinduism, wherein the spine is regarded as the main source of support, leading upward to enlightenment." A stratified structural spine reinforced by steel cables holds up seven levels of residence space. The terrace levels "emerge from a core structure similar to the role played by vertebrae in the spine." The main residence is located on the top platform, covering an area of 4000 m² that includes a helipad and a garden. A precisely oriented (north/south/east/west axis) central, sky-lit atrium brings light to all floors from the inside of the building. SITE worked with the New York structural engineers Weidlinger Associates Inc., specialists in blast-resistant buildings, for this design.

Das Gebäude mit Blick auf Bombay, das auf einem 4325 m² großen Grundstück auf einer Bergkuppe gebaut werden soll, wäre 110 m hoch, hätte eine Gesamtfläche von 26 942 m² und würde umgerechnet etwa 120 Millionen Euro kosten. Die Architekten beschreiben es folgendermaßen: »Das Konzept antwortet auf den Wunsch des Bauherren, ein gestaffeltes, stark landschaftsplanerisch gestaltetes Gebäude zu bauen, das den Hängenden Gärten des Altertums in Babylon ähnelt. Das gesamte Gebäude ist daher als ein Garten im Himmel entworfen und befreit so die Landschaft von ihren üblichen erdgebundenen Beschränkungen. Die philosophische Begründung für die Konstruktion entspricht Prinzipien des hinduistischen Vastu, worin das Rückgrat als die wesentliche Quelle des Stützens angesehen wird und nach oben, hin zur Erleuchtung, führt.« Ein geschichtetes, durch Stahlseile verstärktes konstruktives Rückgrat trägt sieben Ebenen mit Wohnnutzung. Die Terrassenebenen »entwickeln sich aus dem Kern, der den Wirbeln der Wirbelsäule gleicht.« Die größte Wohneinheit befindet sich auf der obersten Ebene und umfasst 4000 m² (inklusive Helikopterlandeplatz und Garten). Ein präzise orientiertes, von oben belichtetes zentrales Atrium (Nord/Süd- und Ost/West-Achsen) lenkt zusätzlich Tageslicht auf alle Geschosse. SITE plante den Entwurf in Zusammenarbeit mit dem Ingenieurbüro Weidlinger Associates, Inc., Spezialisten für detonationssichere Gebäude.

Cette tour de 110 m de haut et 26 942 m² de surface devrait être édifiée pour un budget estimé à 120 millions d'euros sur un terrain de 4325 m² situé au sommet d'une colline dominant Mumbai (Bombay). Son aspect est décrit par SITE en ces termes : « Le concept répond au désir du client d'une construction fortement paysagée en gradins, similaire aux anciens Jardins suspendus de Babylone … l'immeuble est conçu comme un jardin dans le ciel, un paysage libéré de son lien avec le sol. Ses fondations philosophiques répondent aux principes de *vastu* de l'hindouisme qui considèrent la colonne vertébrale comme le principal support de l'homme, ce qui le pousse vers l'illumination. » Une colonne structurelle stratifiée renforcée de câbles d'acier soutient les sept niveaux d'espaces résidentiels. Les niveaux des terrasses « émergent d'une structure de noyau similaire jouant un rôle proche de celui des vertèbres dans la colonne vertébrale ». Le principal espace résidentiel est situé sur la dernière plate-forme. Ses 4000 m² comprennent un héliport et un jardin. Tout en haut, un atrium à éclairage zénithal central, orienté nord/sud/est/ouest, apporte de la lumière à tous les niveaux inférieurs. SITE a travaillé pour ce projet avec les ingénieurs structurels new-yorkais Weidlinger Associates Inc., spécialistes en constructions résistantes aux explosions.

suspension cables

Residence Antilia

Designed for a well-known personality, the residence tower would have not only to be ecologically sound but also structurally solid enough to withstand possible bombs.

Der Wohnturm für eine bekannte Persönlichkeit sollte sowohl umweltverträglich als auch detonationssicher konstruiert sein.

Conçue pour une personnalité célèbre, cette tour résidentielle devait être non seulement écologique mais aussi capable de résister aux explosions.

SIZA/SOUTO DE MOURA

Álvaro Siza Arquitecto Lda, Rua do Aleixo, 53–2, 4150–043 Porto, Portugal
Tel: +351 226 16 72 70, Fax: +351 226 16 72 79, e-mail: siza@mail.telepac.pt, Web: www.alvarosiza.com
Souto Moura Arquitectos Lda, R. do Aleixo, 531° A, 4150–043 Porto, Portugal
Tel: +351 226 18 75 47, Fax: +351 226 10 80 92, e-mail: souto.moura@mail.telepac.pt

Born in Matosinhos, Portugal in 1933, **ÁLVARO SIZA** studied at the University of Porto School of Architecture (1949–55). He created his own practice in 1954, and worked with Fernando Tavora from 1955 to 1958. He has been a Professor of Construction at the University of Porto since 1976. He received the European Community's Mies van der Rohe Prize in 1988 and the Pritzker Prize in 1992. He built a large number of small-scale projects in Portugal, and more recently, he has worked on the restructuring of the Chiado, Lisbon, Portugal (1989-); the Meteorology Center, Barcelona, Spain (1989–92); the Vitra Furniture Factory, Weil-am-Rhein, Germany (1991–94); the Porto School of Architecture, Porto University (1986–95); and the University of Aveiro Library, Aveiro, Portugal (1988–95). He has also completed the Portuguese Pavilion for the 1998 Lisbon World's Fair (with Souto de Moura); the Serralves Foundation, Porto (1996–99); or the Portuguese Pavilion for the Expo Hanover (1998–2000, also with Souto de Moura). **EDUARDO SOUTO DE MOURA** was born in Porto, Portugal in 1952. He graduated from the School of Architecture of Porto (ESBAP) in 1980. He was an Assistant Professor at the Faculty of Architecture in Porto (FAUP) from 1981 to 1991. He worked in the office of Alvaro Siza from 1974 to 1979 and created his own office the following year. Recent work includes Row houses in the Rua Lugarinho, Porto, Portugal (1996); Renovation of the Municipal Market in Braga (1997); the Silo Norte Shopping building; and a house and wine cellar, Valladolid, Spain (1999). More recent work includes the conversion of the building of the Carvoeira da Foz, Porto, and the Braga Stadium (2004). He completed Two Houses at Ponte de Lima (2002).

ÁLVARO SIZA, geboren 1933 in Matosinhos, Portugal, studierte von 1949 bis 1955 an der Escola Superior de Belas Artes der Universität Porto. 1954 gründete er sein eigenes Büro und arbeitete von 1955 bis 1958 mit Fernando Tavora zusammen. Ab 1976 war er Professor für Konstruktionslehre an der Universität Porto. 1988 wurde er mit dem Mies-van-der-Rohe-Preis der Europäischen Union ausgezeichnet, 1992 erhielt er den Pritzker-Preis. Er hat zahlreiche kleinere Projekte in Portugal realisiert. In jüngerer Zeit plante er die Neustrukturierung der Altstadt Chiado in Lissabon (1989–), das Meteorologische Zentrum in Barcelona (1989–92), ein Fabrikgebäude für Vitra in Weil am Rhein (1991–94) und die Architekturfakultät der Universität Porto (1986–95) sowie eine Bücherei in Aveiro, Portugal (1988–95). Er realisierte ebenfalls den Portugiesischen Pavillon auf der Weltausstellung 1998 in Lissabon (mit Souto de Moura), die Stiftung Serralves in Porto (1996–99) und den Portugiesischen Pavillon auf der Expo Hannover (1998–2000, ebenfalls mit Souto de Moura). **EDUARDO SOUTO DE MOURA** wurde 1952 in Porto geboren. 1980 machte er an der Escola Superior de Belas Artes der Universität Porto seinen Abschluss. Von 1981 bis 1991 war er Wissenschaftlicher Mitarbeiter an der Architekturfakultät (FAUP) in Porto. Von 1974 bis 1979 arbeitete er im Büro von Alvaro Siza, ein Jahr darauf gründete er sein eigenes Büro. Zu seinen Bauten gehören die Reihenhäuser in der Rua Lugarinho in Porto (1996), die Sanierung der Markthalle in Braga (1997), das Einkaufszentrum Silo Norte in Matosinhos (1999) und ein Haus mit Weinkeller in Valladolid (1999). Gebäude jüngeren Datums sind der Umbau des Gebäudes der Carvoeira da Foz in Porto und das Braga-Stadion (2004). Zwei Häuser in Ponte de Lima wurden 2002 fertig gestellt.

Né à Matosinhos, au Portugal, en 1933, **ÁLVARO SIZA** a fait ses études à l'École d'architecture de l'Université de Porto (1949–55). Il crée son agence en 1954 et travaille avec Fernando Távora de 1955 à 1958 et enseigne la construction à l'Université de Porto depuis 1976. Il a reçu le prix Mies van der Rohe de la Communauté Européenne en 1988 et le prix Pritzker en 1992. Il a réalisé un grand nombre de petits projets au Portugal et, plus récemment, est intervenu sur la restructuration du quartier du Chiado à Lisbonne (1989-) ; le Centre de météorologie, Barcelone, Espagn (1989–92) ; un bâtiment pour l'usine de meubles Vitra, Weil-am-Rhein, Allemagne (1991–94) ; l'École d'architecture de Porto, Université de Porto (1986–95), la bibliothèque de l'Université d'Aveiro, Aveiro (1988–95) ; le pavillon portugais d'Expo 98 à Lisbonne (1998), avec Souto de Moura, la Fondation Serralves (Porto, 1996–99) et le pavillon portugais d'Expo à Hanovre (1998–2000, également avec Souto de Moura). Né à Porto, au Portugal, en 1952, **EDUARDO SOUTO DE MOURA** est diplômé de l'École d'architecture de Porto, ESBAP (1980). Il a été Professeur assistant à la faculté d'architecture de Porto (FAUP) de 1981 à 1991. Après avoir travaillé auprès d'Álvaro Siza de 1974 à 1979, il a fondé sa propre agence en 1980. Parmi ses réalisations récentes : une série de maisons Rua Lugarinho, Porto (1996), la rénovation du marché municipal de Braga (1997) ; le centre commercial de Silo Norte, une maison et un chai, Valladolid, Espagne (1999) ; deux maisons à Ponte de Lima (2002) ; la reconversion de l'immeuble de la Carvoeira da Foz (Porto) et le stade de Braga (2004).

SERPENTINE GALLERY PAVILION 2005

Kensington Gardens, London, UK, 2005

Floor area: 380 m². Client: The Serpentine Gallery. Cost: not disclosed

Built between the 11th of April and the 30th of June 2005, this 380 m² temporary pavilion is the fifth of its kind to be built in Kensington Gardens next to the Serpentine Gallery, a contemporary art showplace originally built as a tea pavilion in 1934. Previous projects were designed by Zaha Hadid (2000), Daniel Libeskind (2001); Toyo Ito (2002); and Oscar Niemeyer (2003). An ambitious project originally scheduled for 2004 with the Dutch firm MvRdV had been delayed, and Álvaro Siza was called on, working with Eduardo Souto de Moura and Cecil Balmond (Arup), to design the 2005 pavilion by Gallery director Julia Peyton-Jones. The architects had previously worked together on the Portuguese Pavilion, Expo 1998 Lisbon (1995–98) and the Portuguese Pavilion, Expo 2000 (Hanover, Germany). With its 22 x 17 meter footprint and maximum height of 5.4 meters, the pavilion is a timber framed column-free structure with semi-transparent 5 mm thick polycarbonate roofing. Tables and chairs designed by the architects adorned the interior of the building, which was dismantled during October 2005. Some 427 unique timber beams were placed in a complex interlocking pattern that started in one corner and "radiated out to finish at the opposite extreme." As Hamish Nevile from the engineer's firm Arup explains, "It was created as an evolution of the 'lamella' barrel-vault roofs developed in Germany in the early 1920s. While traditional lamellas were built from identical elements, however, each element of the Pavilion is unique, having a different length and inclination. This geometric freedom enables the precise expression of the complex form demanded by the architects. The reciprocal beam system creates a continuous structure that runs from the roof down to form the walls of the Pavilion."

Der 380 m² große, fünfte temporäre Pavillon wurde vom 11. April bis 30. Juni 2005 neben der Serpentine Gallery, einer Galerie für Kunst in Kensington Gardens, errichtet. Das Gebäude der Serpentine Gallery war ursprünglich als Teepavillon gedacht und stammt aus dem Jahr 1934. Die früheren temporären Pavillons wurden von Zaha Hadid (2000), Daniel Libeskind (2001), Toyo Ito (2002) und Oscar Niemeyer (2003) entworfen. Ein ehrgeiziges Projekt, das 2004 mit dem niederländischen Büro MvRdV realisiert werden sollte, musste verschoben werden. Daraufhin wendete sich die Leiterin der Galerie, Julia Peyton-Jones, an Álvaro Siza, der mit Eduardo Souto de Moura und Cecil Balmond (Arup) den Pavillon für 2005 entwarf. Die Architekten hatten bereits am Portugiesischen Pavillon für die Expo 1998 in Lissabon (1995–98) und am Portugiesischen Pavillon für die Expo 2000 in Hannover zusammengearbeitet. Der Pavillon mit einer Grundfläche von 22 x 17 m und einer maximalen Höhe von 5,4 m war eine stützenfreie Holzkonstruktion, die mit halbtransparenten, 5 mm dicken Polykarbonatplatten eingedeckt war. Von den Architekten entworfene Tische und Stühle komplettierten den Innenraum des Pavillons, der im Oktober 2005 abgebaut wurde. 427 verschiedene Holzbinder bildeten das komplexe, ineinander greifende Konstruktionssystem. Beginnend auf einer Seite, »strahlte dieses System aus, um den gegenüberliegenden Punkt zu erreichen«. Hamish Nevile vom Ingenieurbüro Arup erläutert: »Das Dach ist eine Weiterentwicklung des Lamellen-Tonnendaches, das in Deutschland in den frühen 1920ern entwickelt wurde. Die traditionellen Lamellen waren identische Konstruktionselemente, bei dem Pavillon hingegen hat jedes Element eine unterschiedliche Länge und Neigung. Mit dieser geometrischen Freiheit konnte die komplexe Form, die die Architekten wünschten, ihren präzisen Ausdruck finden. Das wechselständige Trägersystem schafft eine durchgehende Struktur, die vom Dach hinunter die Wände des Pavillons bildet.«

Edifié du 11 avril au 30 juin 2005, ce pavillon temporaire de 380 m² est le cinquième à être construit dans les jardins de Kensington, près de la Serpentine Gallery, ancien pavillon de thé datant de 1934 et lieu d'exposition d'art contemporain. Les précédents projets avaient été conçus par Zaha Hadid (2000), Daniel Libeskind (2001), Toyo Ito (2002) et Oscar Niemeyer (2003). Un ambitieux projet programmé pour 2004 par l'agence néerlandaise MvRdV a été retardé. Álvaro Siza a été appelé par la directrice de la galerie, Julia Peyton Jones, pour réaliser la version 2005 en collaboration avec Eduardo Souto de Moura et Cecil Balmond (Arup). Les architectes avaient déjà travaillé ensemble sur le pavillon portugais de l'Expo 1998 à Lisbonne (1995–98) et à l'Expo 2000 à Hanovre. D'une emprise au sol de 22 x 17 m et d'une hauteur maximum de 5,4 m, le pavillon est une structure en bois, sans colonnes porteuses, à couverture en polycarbonate semi-transparent de 5 mm d'épaisseur. Des tables et des chaises dessinées par les architectes équipent l'intérieur. Quelque 427 poutres en bois d'un dessin unique ont été montées, selon un système complexe qui part d'un angle et « irradie jusqu'à l'extrémité opposée ». Comme l'explique Hamish Nevile, de l'agence d'ingénierie Arup, « c'est une évolution de la voûte en berceau à lamelles mise au point en Allemagne au début des années 1920. Alors que les lamelles traditionnelles étaient faites d'éléments identiques, chaque élément de ce pavillon est unique puisqu'il présente une longueur et une inclinaison différentes. Cette liberté géométrique permet une expression précise de la forme complexe demandée par les architectes. Le système réciproque des poutres génère une structure continue qui court du toit jusqu'au sol pour former les murs du pavillon ». L'ensemble a été démonté en octobre 2005.

Architecture fans might well have had a difficult time identifying the designer(s) of the 2005 Serpentine Pavilion, since it looks nothing much like the earlier work of either Álvaro Siza or Eduardo Souto de Moura.

Architekturfans hatten es vielleicht nicht leicht, den/die Architekten des Serpentine Pavilions 2005 zu benennen, da der Bau weder den früheren Gebäuden von Siza noch denen von Souto de Moura besonders ähnelt.

Les amateurs d'architecture ont pu avoir quelques difficultés à identifier les auteurs du pavillon de la Serpentine 2005, tant il diffère des œuvres antérieures aussi bien d'Álvaro Siza que d'Eduardo Souto de Moura.

A sketch by Siza below shows the flowing, almost organic concept of the Pavilion. The nature and spacing of its armature gives rise to unexpected visual effects under certain angles.

Sizas Skizze zeigt das fließende, fast organische Konzept des Pavillons. Die Art der Konstruktion und die Abstände zwischen den Elementen des Gerüsts führen aus bestimmten Perspektiven zu unerwarteten optischen Effekten.

Un croquis de Siza, ci-dessous, montre la conception en flux, presque organique du pavillon. La nature et l'espacement de l'armature génèrent des effets visuels inattendus sous certains angles.

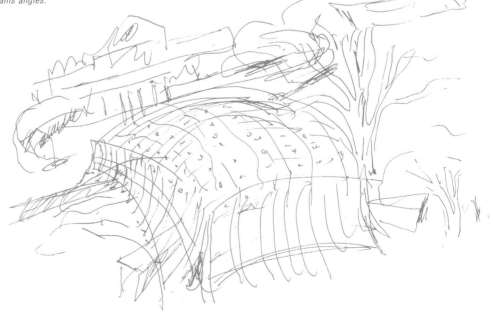

FRANK STELLA

Paul Kasmin Gallery
293 Tenth Avenue
New York, New York 10001
USA

Tel: +1 212 563 4474
Fax: +1 212 563 4494
e-mail: inquiry@paulkasmingallery.com
Web: www.paulkasmingallery.com

FRANK STELLA was born in Maiden, Massachusetts in 1936 and studied at Phillips Academy, Andover, and at Princeton University. One year after his graduation in 1959, he moved to New York and was included in an exhibit entitled *Sixteen Americans,* at the Museum of Modern Art. His works exhibited there, the *Black Paintings* executed with ordinary house paint, are seen as the beginning of the minimalist movement in the United States. The same year, at the age of 23, his work was shown at the Castelli Gallery. In New York, Stella became friendly with Jasper Johns, Robert Rauschenberg, and also with Richard Meier and Philip Johnson. Frank Stella is of course known as one of the foremost American painters and sculptors, although he has long been interested in architecture. It was in 1983 that he gave the Charles Eliot Norton lectures at Harvard, and in 1990 he began conceiving architectural projects, including a wing of Alessandro Mendini's Groningen Museum. In 1991 he conceived an arts center for the city of Dresden. Stella is one of the few artists to be featured in two major retrospectives at MoMA, in 1970 and in 1987. Frank Stella did not actually create his first work of architecture until 2000, a 10.4-meter-high, 15-meter-long band shell called *Broken Jug*, which was intended for a location in front of Arquitectonica's American Airlines Arena (Miami, Florida), although it was not put in place. More recently, he participated in an architectural competition for the Malba – Colección Costantini, Museum of Latin American Art of Buenos Aires, which he did not win.

FRANK STELLA wurde 1936 in Maiden, Massachusetts, geboren und studierte an der Phillips Academy in Andover und an der Princeton University. 1960, ein Jahr nach seinem Abschluss, zog er nach New York und nahm an der Ausstellung *Sixteen Americans* im Museum of Modern Art teil. Für seine dort ausgestellten Arbeiten, die *Black Paintings*, benutzte Stella gewöhnliche Wandfarbe; sie werden als Beginn des Minimalismus in den USA angesehen. Im selben Jahr – Stella war 23 Jahre alt – wurden seine Bilder in der Galerie von Leo Castelli gezeigt. In New York freundete er sich mit Jasper Johns und Robert Rauschenberg und auch mit Richard Meier und Philip Johnson an. Frank Stella ist einer der berühmtesten amerikanischen Maler und Bildhauer, gleichzeitig ist er aber auch seit langem an Architektur interessiert. 1983 hielt er in Harvard die Charles-Eliot-Norton-Vorträge, und seit 1990 befasst er sich mit architektonischen Entwürfen, z. B. für einen Anbau an das Groningen Museum von Alessandro Mendini; 1991 entwarf er ein Kunstzentrum für Dresden. Stella ist einer der wenigen Künstler, dem das MoMA bereits zwei große Retrospektiven, 1970 und 1987, widmete. Erst 2000 konnte Stella sein erstes architektonisches Projekt realisieren: den 10,4 m hohen, 15 m langen muschelförmigen Musikpavillon *Broken Jug*, der vor Arquitectonicas American Airlines Arena in Miami aufgestellt werden sollte, wozu es allerdings nicht kam. In jüngerer Zeit nahm er an einem Wettbewerb für das Malba – Colección Costantini, ein Museum für Lateinamerikanische Kunst in Buenos Aires teil, den er jedoch nicht gewann.

Né à Maiden, Massachusetts, en 1936, **FRANK STELLA** a étudié à la Phillips Academy à Andover et à Princeton University. Diplômé en 1959, il part un an plus tard pour New York, où il participe à une exposition intitulée *Sixteen Americans* au Museum of Modern Art. Ses œuvres, les *Black Paintings* exécutées à la peinture de décoration ordinaire, sont considérées comme le début du mouvement minimaliste aux États-Unis. La même année, à 23 ans, il est exposé à la galerie Castelli. Il se lie d'amitié avec Jasper Johns, Robert Rauschenberg, Richard Meier et Philip Johnson. Frank Stella est l'un des plus célèbres peintres et sculpteurs américains, l'un des rares à avoir bénéficié de deux rétrospectives majeures au MoMA, en 1970 et 1987. Il s'intéresse depuis longtemps à l'architecture. En 1983, il participe aux « Charles Eliot Norton Lectures » à Harvard et, en 1990, commence à concevoir des projets architecturaux, dont une aile du musée de Groningue (Pays-Bas) d'Alessandro Mendini. En 1991, il conçoit un centre artistique pour la ville de Dresde. Sa première réalisation ne date cependant que de 2000. Il s'agit de *Broken Jug,* une coque faite d'un bandeau de 10,4 m x 15 m, destinée à être implantée devant l'American Airlines Arena d'Arquitectonica (Miami, Floride), mais qui n'a pas encore été mise en place. Plus récemment, il a participé à un concours d'architecture pour le Malba-Colección Costantini, le musée d'Art latino-américain de Buenos-Aires (Argentine).

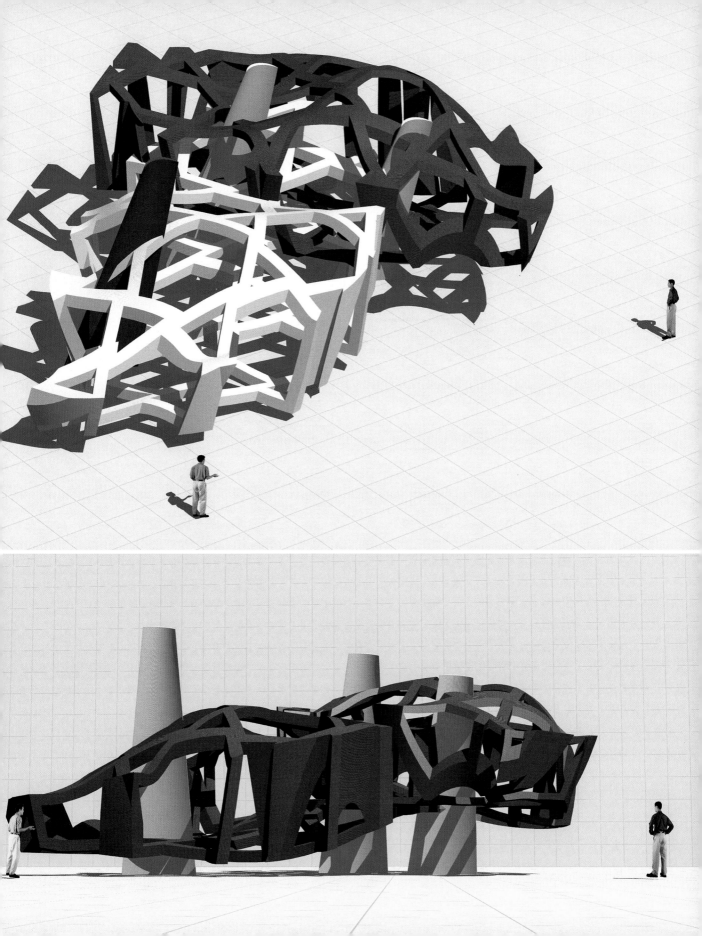

CHINESE LEAVES PAVILION

2005

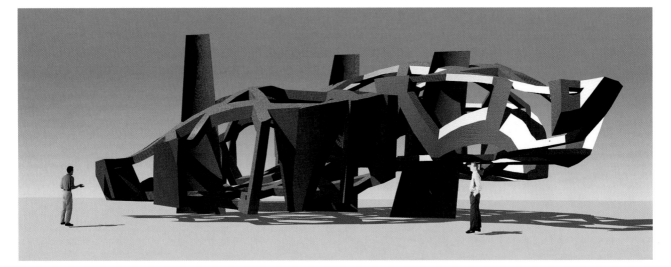

Frank Stella has long been fascinated by architectural form, but in this instance he does not claim to be designing a building – more a sculpture on an architectural scale. Though it is meant to be walked through, the Chinese Leaves Pavilion will serve no particular purpose.

Architektonische Formen faszinieren Frank Stella schon lange. Bei diesem Projekt behauptet er nicht, ein Gebäude zu entwerfen – eher eine Skulptur in einem architektonischen Maßstab. Man soll durch den Chinese Leaves Pavilion hindurchgehen; sonst hat er keinen bestimmten Zweck.

Frank Stella, longtemps fasciné par la forme architecturale, ne prétend pas ici concevoir un bâtiment. Il s'agit plus d'une sculpture à l'échelle architecturale. Bien qu'il soit pénétrable, ce pavillon ne possède pas de fonction précise.

Currently being built in a factory space being used by the artist in Fishkill in Dutchess County, New York, this Pavilion is made of carved foam covered in fibre glass and then in black carbon fiber. The red, white and blue images shown here do not correspond to the final color selection, since the carbon fiber coating apparently favors black. The artist explains that the form of this work is directly related to his earlier designs for a wing of the Groningen Museum, but that he has chosen in this instance to build it with much lighter materials. Although the models and drawings show a walkway going through the work, Stella says, "Let's just call it a sculpture," in particular because he does not wish to get involved in the more stringent requirements of building codes. Weighing approximately 6350 kilos, the **CHINESE LEAVES PAVILION** is inscribed within a 15-meter circle and is 7 meters high. The structure is suspended from three pylons that rest on the ground and project above the structure. The engineering of the design was done in collaboration with Arup. With something of the humor that characterizes him, Stella has written, "Architecture is really about the physicality of the forms, making things that seemed three dimensional – at a certain point, you make something big enough, it's potentially habitable. If it's a habitable sculpture, why isn't it architecture? Because it doesn't have a toilet in it?"

Der Pavillon, der derzeit in von Stella genutzten Fabrikräumen in Fishkill im Staat New York gebaut wird, besteht aus ausgehöhltem Hartschaum, der erst mit Fiberglas und dann mit schwarzer Kohlefaser ummantelt wird. Die hier gezeigten roten, weißen und blauen Farben entsprechen also nicht der endgültigen Farbgebung – für die Kohlefaserschicht bietet sich natürlich schwarz an. Der Künstler erläutert, dass die Form des Pavillons sich direkt auf seine früheren Entwürfe für einen Anbau an das Groningen Museum bezieht, er sich jetzt aber für ein sehr viel leichteres Material entschieden hat. Obwohl die Modelle und Zeichnungen einen Weg durch den Pavillon zeigen, sagt Stella: »Nennt es einfach eine Skulptur.« Vor allem sagt er dies, weil er nichts mit den strengeren Auflagen der Baubehörde zu tun haben will. Der 6350 kg schwere **CHINESE LEAVES PAVILLON** ist in einen Kreis mit einem Durchmesser von 15 m eingeschrieben und 7 m hoch. Er wird von drei auf dem Boden stehenden, über ihn hinausragende Pylonen abgehängt. Die Statik wurde in Zusammenarbeit mit Arup erarbeitet. Mit dem ihm eigenen Humor schreibt Stella: »Architektur hat im Grunde etwas mit der Physis von Formen zu tun; sie macht Dinge, die dreidimensional erschienen. Wenn man etwas groß genug macht, ist es ab einem gewissen Punkt potenziell bewohnbar. Wenn es eine bewohnbare Skulptur ist, warum ist es nicht Architektur? Weil es keine Toilette gibt?«

Actuellement en chantier dans une ancienne usine utilisée par l'artiste à Fishkill dans le Dutchess County (New York), ce pavillon est en mousse sculptée recouverte de fibre de verre et de fibre de carbone. Les images en rouge, blanc et bleu présentées ici ne correspondent pas à la sélection finale des couleurs, puisque la fibre de carbone est plutôt noire. Frank Stella explique que cette forme est directement liée à de précédents dessins pour une aile du Musée de Groningue, et qu'il a décidé de la construire en matériaux beaucoup plus légers. Bien que les maquettes et les dessins montrent une passerelle qui permet de pénétrer dans l'œuvre, il s'agit plutôt pour Stella « d'une sculpture », en particulier parce qu'il ne veut pas s'impliquer dans les contraintes des codes de construction. Ce Pavillon chinois de 6350 kg environ s'inscrit dans un cercle de 15 m de diamètre et de 7 m de haut. La structure est suspendue à trois pylônes reposant sur le sol et se projetant au-dessus d'elle. L'ingénierie du projet a été menée en collaboration avec Arup. Avec l'humour qui le caractérise, Stella a écrit : « L'architecture traite en fait de la matérialité des formes ; en faisant des choses qui semblent tridimensionnelles – jusqu'à un certain point – vous réalisez quelque chose d'assez grand, qui devient potentiellement habitable. Si c'est une sculpture habitable, pourquoi ne serait-ce pas de l'architecture ? Parce qu'il n'y a pas de toilettes ? »

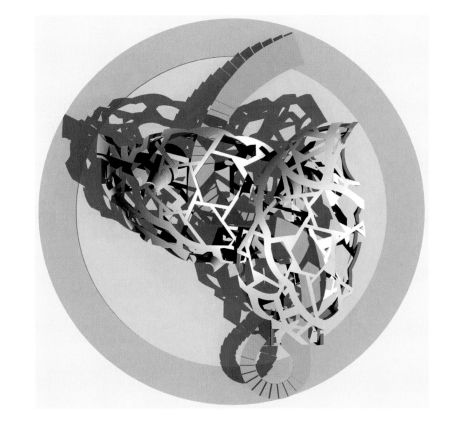

Stella's models and drawings for the Pavilion sometimes make use of color (this page) but the sculpture is intended to be black. Despite its apparently complex form, the design is neatly inscribed in a 15-meter-diameter circle.

Für die Modelle und Zeichnungen des Pavillons verwendet Stella auch Farbe (diese Seite); die Skulptur soll jedoch schwarz sein. Die komplexe Form ist in einen Kreis mit einem Durchmesser von 15 m eingeschrieben.

Les maquettes et les dessins de Stella font parfois appel à la couleur, mais la sculpture devrait être noire. Malgré sa forme apparemment complexe, l'ensemble s'inscrit avec netteté dans un cercle de quinze mètres de diamètre.

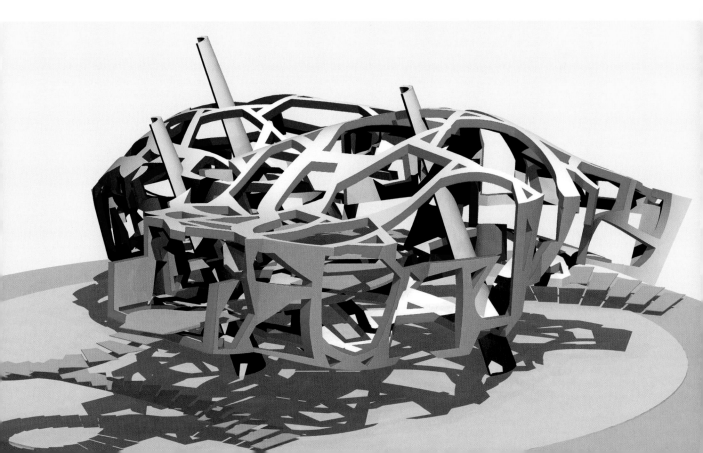

PETER STUTCHBURY

Stutchbury & Pape Pty Ltd.
4/364 Barrenjoey Road
Newport Beach NSW 2106
Australia

Tel: +61 299 79 50 30
Fax +61 299 79 53 67
e-mail: snpala@ozemail.com.au

A graduate of the University of Newcastle, Australia in 1978, **PETER STUTCHBURY** lived "on the land" as a child and with aborigines on the banks of the Darling River and with tribes in the highlands of New Guinea. He works with his wife and business partner Phoebe Pape, who is a landscape architect, on houses "that nurture their occupants and celebrate a palpable spirit of place." The firm has been given 24 awards by the Royal Australian Institute of Architects (RAIA) since 1999. In 2003 Peter Stutchbury was the first architect ever to win both the top National Architecture Awards from the RAIA for residential and non-residential projects with the Robin Boyd Award for houses for the Bay House at Watson's Bay, Sydney, and the Sir Zelman Cowan Award for Public Buildings for Birabahn, the Aboriginal Cultural Center at the University of Newcastle. Architect of the Sydney 2000 Olympics Archery Pavilion, he has also built several structures on the University of Newcastle campus, including the Design Building and the Nursing Building (with EJE Architecture), the Aboriginal Center (with Richard Leplastrier and Sue Harper), and the Life Sciences Building (with Suters Architects). His built work includes: Israel House, Paradise Beach (1982–92); Treetop House, Clareville (1991); McMaster Residence, Hawk's Nest, (1995–98); Kangaroo Valleys Pavilion (1996–98); Reeves House, Claireville Beach (1997–99); and the Wedge House (2001).

PETER STUTCHBURY machte 1978 an der University of Newcastle in Australien seinen Abschluss. Als Kind lebte er »auf dem Land«, genauer gesagt mit den Aborigines am Ufer des Darling River und mit Naturvölkern im Hochland von Neuguinea. Er arbeitet mit seiner Frau und Geschäftspartnerin Phoebe Pape, einer Landschaftsplanerin, zusammen. Die von ihnen geplanten Häuser »nähren ihre Bewohner und zelebrieren den spürbaren Geist des Ortes«. Seit 1999 erhielt das Büro 24 Preise des Royal Australian Institute of Architects (RAIA). 2003 war Peter Stutchbury der erste Architekt, der je mit den beiden höchsten National Architecture Awards des RAIA in den Kategorien »Wohnbauten« und »Gewerbebauten/Öffentliche Bauten« ausgezeichnet wurde: Für das Bay House an der Watson's Bay in Sydney erhielt er den Robin Boyd Award für ein Privathaus und für Birabahn, das Kulturzentrum der Aborigines der University of Newcastle, den Sir Zelman Cowan Award für ein öffentliches Gebäude. Er hat den Pavillon für das Bogenschießen bei den Olympischen Spielen 2000 in Sydney entworfen, ferner diverse Campusbauten der University of Newcastle, darunter das Design Building und das Nursing Building (mit EJE Architecture), das Kulturzentrum der Aborigines (mit Richard Leplastrier und Sue Harper) und das Naturwissenschaftliche Gebäude (mit Suters Architects). Weitere Bauten des Büros sind u. a. das Israel House, Paradise Beach (1982–92), das Treetop House in Clareville (1991), die McMaster Residence in Hawk's Nest (1995–98), der Kangaroo Valleys Pavilion (1996–98), das Reeves House, Claireville Beach (1997–99) und das Wedge House (2001).

Diplômé de l'Université de Newcastle (Australie) en 1978, **PETER STUTCHBURY** a passé son enfance « dans les terres » avec les Aborigènes des rives de la Darling River et des tribus des hautes terres de Nouvelle-Guinée. Il travaille avec son épouse et associée, l'architecte-paysagiste Phoebe Pape, à des projets de maisons « qui enrichissent leurs occupants et célèbrent un esprit du lieu palpable ». L'agence a reçu vingt-quatre prix du Royal Australian Institute of Architects (RAIA) depuis 1999. En 2003, Stutchbury a été le premier architecte à remporter les principaux prix du RAIA à la fois pour les projets résidentiels et pour les non-résidentiels : le Robin Boyd Award (maisons individuelles) pour sa Bay House à Watson's Bay et le Sir Zelman Cowan Award (bâtiments publics) pour Birabahn, le Centre culturel aborigène de l'Université de Newcastle. Architecte du pavillon des archers des Jeux olympiques de Sydney en 2000, il a également réalisé plusieurs bâtiments pour le campus de l'Université de Newcastle, dont le Design Building et le Nursing Building (en collaboration avec EJE Architecture), le Aboriginal Center (avec Richard Leplastrier et Sue Harper) et le Life Sciences Building (avec Suters Architects). Parmi ses autres réalisations : Israel House, Paradise Beach (1982–92) ; Treetop House, Clareville (1991) ; McMaster Residence, Hawk's Nest (1995–98) ; Kangaroo Valleys Pavilion (1996–98) ; Reeves House, Clareville Beach (1997–99) et la Wedge House (2001).

SPRINGWATER

Seaforth, Sydney, New South Wales, Australia, 1999–2002

Floor area: 514 m² (including terraces). Client: not disclosed. Cost: not disclosed

Built on a 1478 m² site on Sydney Harbor "foreshore", the **SPRINGWATER** house has a floor area of 514 m² (including terraces, decks and lap pool). Stutchbury says that the house is "Conceived as a reliable camp, the frame is concrete on stone." Galvanized steel frames are bolted onto the structure, and "long building fingers down the site toward the harbor allow the land a conscious freedom." Set on three levels, with ceiling heights adjusted according to their position on site, "the building is skinned simply allowing the user to operate walls, adjusting to views and cooling breezes as required." The architect says that "the house sits as only a veil within the landscape" allowing constant views of the landscape, or alternatively a certain amount of shelter as required by the inhabitants. Built for a relatively low cost, in part because of "systematic and repetitive structure/formwork and similar door window systems," Springwater is entered "deliberately down, toward the view, onto an open courtyard … North."

Das **SPRINGWATER**-Haus wurde auf einem 1478 m² großen Grundstück im Küstenvorland des Hafens von Sydney gebaut. Die Terrassen, Decks und den Bahnenpool eingerechnet beträgt die Grundfläche des Hauses 514 m². Stutchbury sagt: »Das Haus ist als ein ›verlässlicher Ruheplatz‹ entworfen. Die Konstruktion ist aus Beton, der Untergrund aus Stein.« An das Haus sind verzinkte Stahlkonstruktionen angeschraubt, und lange ›Gebäudefinger‹ in Richtung Hang und Hafen lassen dem Grundstück bewusst seine Freiheit«. Das Haus hat drei Ebenen. Die Deckenhöhen richten sich nach der Position der Ebenen auf dem Grundstück. Das Gebäude »ist einfach gebaut, damit die Nutzer auf einfache Weise Wände verschieben können, je nach dem, welche Aussicht sie wünschen oder wo sie eine kühlende Brise benötigen«. Der Architekt kommentiert: »Das Haus liegt wie ein Schleier auf der Landschaft« und bietet den Bewohnern, je nach ihren Bedürfnissen, Blicke in die Natur oder aber auch ein bestimmtes Maß an Schutz. Die Baukosten waren relativ niedrig, z. T. aufgrund »einer systematischen und sich wiederholenden Konstruktion bzw. Schalung und ähnlicher Tür- und Fenstersysteme«. Springwater wird absichtlich in Richtung des Hangs, also nach unten, betreten, zum Ausblick hin, auf einen offenen Hof … nach Norden.«

Édifiée sur un terrain de 1478 m² sur le port même de Sydney, la maison **SPRINGWATER** a une superficie de 514 m² (y compris ses terrasses, ses plates-formes et le bassin). Pour Stutchbury, cette maison est « conçue comme un camp dans lequel on se sentirait en sécurité… l'ossature en béton est posée sur la pierre ». Les cadres d'acier galvanisé sont boulonnés sur l'ossature et « les ailes qui s'avancent comme des doigts vers le port créent un sentiment de liberté ». Comptant deux étages, avec des hauteurs sous plafond variant en fonction de la position sur le terrain, « la maison a été habillée d'une peau simple qui permet à l'occupant de modifier les murs, de les adapter au panorama et aux brises rafraîchissantes à volonté… elle est comme un voile dans le paysage » et le propriétaire peut soit profiter de la vue, soit recréer une certaine protection, en fonction de ses désirs. Construite pour un budget relativement réduit grâce, notamment, à des « coffrages d'ossature systématisés et répétitifs et à des systèmes de portes et fenêtres similaires », la maison s'ouvre au visiteur « délibérément par le bas, vers la vue, sur une cour ouverte … vers le nord ».

Springwater is a spectacular juxtaposition of strong architectural elements with an equally powerful natural setting.

Springwater ist eine spektakuläre Gegenüberstellung von kraftvollen architektonischen Elementen und einer ebenso kraftvollen Naturkulisse.

Springwater est une juxtaposition spectaculaire d'éléments architecturaux puissants dans un cadre naturel tout aussi fort.

The twisting form of tree trunks
does not seem to be contradictory
to the sharply defined verticals and
horizontals of the house. Gaps and
openings allow the natural setting
to be admired while creating a
dynamism in the architecture itself.

*Die verschlungenen Formen der
Baumstämme wirken den klar defi-
nierten Vertikalen und Horizontalen
des Hauses nicht entgegen. Lücken
und Öffnungen erlauben es, die
natürliche Umgebung zu genießen
und lassen die Architektur dynamisch
wirken.*

Les silhouettes tordues des troncs
d'arbres ne contrarient nullement
les verticales et les horizontales très
nettes de la maison. Les ouvertures
et les failles permettent d'admirer
la nature tout en dynamisant
l'architecture.

YOSHIO TANIGUCHI

Yoshio Taniguchi
Yanakatsu Building 7F
4–1–40 Toranomon
Minato-ku, Tokyo 105–0001
Japan

Tel: +81 334 38 12 47
Fax: +81 334 38 12 48

Museum of Modern Art

YOSHIO TANIGUCHI was born in Tokyo in 1937. He received a Bachelor's degree in Mechanical Engineering from Keio University in 1960 and a Master of Architecture degree from the Harvard Graduate School of Design in 1964. He worked in the office Kenzo Tange from 1964 to 1972. He created Taniguchi, Takamiya and Associates in 1975, and Taniguchi and Associates in 1979. His built work includes the Tokyo Sea Life Park, Tokyo (1989); Marugame Genichiro-Inokuma Museum of Contemporary Art and Marugame City Library, Marugame (1991); Toyota Municipal Museum of Art, Toyota City (1995); the Tokyo Kasai Rinkai Park View Point Visitors Center, Tokyo (1995); the Tokyo National Museum Gallery of Horyuji Treasures, Tokyo (1997–99), and the complete renovation and expansion of the Museum of Modern Art in New York published here. He won the project after a 1997 invited competition against Wiel Arets, Steven Holl, Rem Koolhaas, Herzog & de Meuron, Toyo Ito, Dominique Perrault, Bernard Tschumi, Rafael Viñoly, and Williams & Tsien. He is completing the Kyoto National Museum, Centennial Hall (2006), and beginning work on Asia House in Houston.

YOSHIO TANIGUCHI wurde 1937 in Tokio geboren. Er machte seinen Bachelor in Maschinenbau 1960 an der Keio University und seinen Master of Architecture an der Harvard Graduate School of Design 1964. Von 1964 bis 1972 arbeitete er im Büro von Kenzo Tange. 1975 gründete er Taniguchi, Takamiya and Associates, 1979 Taniguchi and Associates. Das Büro hat u. a. folgende Gebäude realisiert: den Tokyo Sea Life Park in Tokio (1989), das Marugame Genichiro-Inokuma Museum für moderne Kunst und die Stadtbibliothek in Marugame (1991), das Städtische Toyota Museum für Kunst in Toyota City (1995), das Aussichts- und Besucherzentrum im Kasai Rinkai Park in Tokio (1995) und die Galerie für Horyuji Schätze im Tokioer Nationalmuseum (1997–99) sowie die hier gezeigte umfassende Sanierung und Erweiterung des Museum of Modern Art in New York, für die Taniguchi 1997 einen eingeladenen Wettbewerb gewonnen hatte, an dem außer ihm Wiel Arets, Steven Holl, Rem Koolhaas, Herzog & de Meuron, Toyo Ito, Dominique Perrault, Bernard Tschumi, Rafael Viñoly und Williams & Tsien teilnahmen. Die Hundertjahrhalle des Nationalmuseums in Kioto wird derzeit fertig gestellt (2006), danach beginnen die Arbeiten am Asia House in Houston.

Né à Tokyo en 1937, **YOSHIO TANIGUCHI** est diplômé en ingénierie mécanique de l'Université Keio (1960) et Master of Architecture de la Harvard Graduate School of Design (1964). Il a travaillé pour Kenzo Tange de 1964 à 1972 et a créé Taniguchi, Takamiya and Associates en 1975, puis Taniguchi and Associates en 1979. Parmi ses réalisations : le Parc de la vie sous-marine de Tokyo (1989) ; Le musée d'Art contemporain et la bibliothèque de la ville de Marugame, Marugame (1991) ; le Musée d'art municipal Toyota, Toyota-City (1995) ; le Belvédère du centre des visiteurs du Kasai Rinkai Park, Tokyo (1995) ; la galerie des Trésors Horuji du Musée national de Tokyo, Tokyo (1997–98) et la rénovation et l'extension du Museum of Modern Art de New York. Il en avait remporté le concours sur invitation face à Wiel Arets, Steven Holl, Rem Koolhaas, Herzog & de Meuron, Toyo Ito, Dominique Perrault, Bernard Tschumi, Rafael Viñoly et Williams & Tsien. Il achève actuellement le Musée national de Kyoto, Centennial Hall (2006) et travaille sur un projet de Maison de l'Asie à Houston.

THE MUSEUM OF MODERN ART EXPANSION AND RENOVATION

New York, New York, USA, 2002–04

Floor area: 24 000 m² (new space). Client: The Trustees of the Museum of Modern Art.
Cost: $315 million (construction)

A mere twenty years after the 1984 expansion of New York's **MUSEUM OF MODERN ART** by Cesar Pelli that created the greenhouse-like rear of the museum and its single place escalators, the institution has reemerged in a surprising new form, laid out, at least in its major components, by Tokyo architect Yoshio Taniguchi. The total budget for the project was 425 million dollars, with construction alone costing 315 million dollars, yet even these figures understate total expenses that rise to 858 million dollars when the costs of MoMA Queens and moving back and forth are added to some acquisitions. Although some say that MoMA lost its original spirit when Pelli added a 55-story residential tower to the premises, the Taniguchi-led expansion creates vast spaces that the curators have clearly had difficulty filling, as is the case in the monumental 33.5-meter high second-floor atrium. Adding roughly 24 000 square meters to the institution, and doubling its available exhibition space, Taniguchi achieved a remarkable degree of refinement and detailing on this project, considering that he was not familiar with American building methods. As early as the schematic design phase, the Museum of Modern Art proposed that Taniguchi work with a firm that had local building experience. Kohn Pedersen Fox (KPF) was selected and ultimately became the executive architect for the project, with Gregory Clement and Steven Rustow heading their effort. Rustow had considerable museum experience, having worked actively on I. M. Pei's Grand Louvre project and in particular the Richelieu Wing phase. KPF was also called to supervise the renovation of the original 1939 building by Phillip Goodwin and Edward Durell Stone as well as Philip Johnson's 1964 east wing addition. Philip Johnson's 1953 sculpture garden, in an expanded version, emerges as the real center of the new MoMA, where much of the new construction can be admired in a peaceful atmosphere.

Nur 20 Jahre nach der Erweiterung des **MUSEUM OF MODERN ART** durch Cesar Pelli im Jahr 1984 hat sich die Institution in einer überraschenden Form neu erfunden. Pelli hatte das Museum mit einem rückwärtigen wintergartenähnlichen Anbau versehen und es mit Rolltreppen in diesem Bereich ausgestattet. Der anspruchsvolle Entwurf für die neuerliche Erweiterung stammt zum größten Teil von dem Tokioer Architekten Yoshio Taniguchi. Die Kosten für das Projekt beliefen sich auf umgerechnet 353 Millionen Euro, davon waren allein 261 Millionen Euro reine Baukosten. Aber selbst diese hohen Zahlen entsprechen nicht den Gesamtkosten, die etwa 713 Millionen Euro betragen, wenn man den Umzug des MoMA nach Queens und wieder zurück und einige Ankäufe hinzurechnet. Pelli hatte 1984 dem Museum zusätzlich einen 55-geschossigen Wohnturm angefügt (manche meinen, das MoMA hätte dadurch seinen ursprünglichen Charakter verloren). Taniguchi ist es trotzdem gelungen, das Gebäude um Räume mit beträchtlichen Ausmaßen zu erweitern. Offensichtlich hatten die Kuratoren aber einige Probleme, diese zu füllen – deutlich wird dies im 33,5 m hohen monumentalen Atrium im 1. Obergeschoss. Die Erweiterung umfasst 24 000 m² und verdoppelt die bisher vorhandene Ausstellungsfläche. Taniguchi hat einen bemerkenswerten Grad der Verfeinerung und Qualität der Ausführung erreicht und dies, obwohl er mit der amerikanischen Praxis der Bauausführung nicht vertraut war. Schon in der Phase der Entwurfsplanung schlug das Museum of Modern Art Taniguchi vor, mit einem Büro mit Bauerfahrung in den USA zusammenzuarbeiten. Kohn Pedersen Fox (KPF) wurde als Projektpartner ausgewählt und war für die Ausführung zuständig. Gregory Clement und Steven Rustow waren die Projektleiter. Rustow, ein im Museumsbau sehr erfahrener Architekt, hatte vorher im Büro von I. M. Pei an der Erweiterung des Grand Louvre mitgewirkt, und hier besonders am Richelieu-Flügel. KPF wurde auch beauftragt, die Sanierung des ursprünglichen MoMA-Gebäudes von Phillip Goodwin und Edward Durell Stone aus dem Jahr 1939 und des Ostflügels von Philip Johnson aus dem Jahr 1964 zu leiten. Philip Johnsons 1953 geschaffener Skulpturgarten wurde erweitert und entpuppt sich als wahres Zentrum des neuen Museums, von dem aus man einen Großteil des neuen MoMA sehen und in einer friedlichen Atmosphäre bewundern kann.

Vingt ans après l'intervention de Cesar Pelli sur le **MUSEUM OF MODERN ART** de New York, qui avait créé l'extension en forme de serre à l'arrière du musée et posé d'étroits escaliers mécaniques, l'institution connaît aujourd'hui une mutation formelle conçue, pour sa majeure partie, par l'architecte tokyoïte Yoshio Taniguchi. Le budget total de l'opération s'est élevé à 353 millions d'euros, dont 261 pour la seule construction. Cependant, l'investissement s'élèvera à 713 millions lorsque les coûts du MoMA Queens et des différents déménagements auront été intégrés. Si certains ont pu dire que le musée avait déjà perdu son esprit originel lorsque Pelli lui ajouta une tour d'appartements de 55 étages, l'extension de Taniguchi a créé de vastes espaces que les conservateurs semblent avoir quelques difficultés à maîtriser, en particulier les 33,5 m de haut du monumental atrium du premier étage. Tout en ajoutant 24 000 m² et en doublant les espaces d'exposition, Taniguchi a atteint un remarquable niveau de raffinement, surtout quand on sait qu'il n'était pas familier des méthodes de construction américaines. Dès la phase des plans, le MoMA a proposé que l'architecte collabore avec une agence dotée d'une expérience locale. Kohn Pedersen Fox (KPF) fut sélectionné et finit par devenir l'architecte exécutif de l'ensemble du projet, sous la direction de Gregory Clement et Steven Rustow. Rustow possède une longue expérience des musées puisqu'il a travaillé activement au Grand Louvre de I. M. Pei, en particulier sur l'aile Richelieu. KPF a également été invitée à superviser la rénovation du bâtiment d'origine de Philip Goodwin et Edward Durell Stone (1939) et de l'aile est, ajoutée en 1964 par Philip Johnson. Le Jardin de sculptures de Johnson (1953) est devenu, après agrandissement, le vrai centre du musée, d'où la plus grande partie du nouveau bâtiment peut être admirée dans une atmosphère paisible.

A new building by Taniguchi looks over the slightly extended area of MoMA's Sculpture Garden. Within, design reclaims the place of honor it had in the museum's earlier incarnations.

Das neue Museumsgebäude von Taniguchi überblickt den etwas vergrößerten Skulpturengarten des MoMA. Innen erobert sich die Designabteilung den Rang zurück, den sie früher im Museum hatte.

Le nouveau bâtiment de Taniguchi donne sur le Jardin de sculptures du MoMA, légèrement agrandi. L'intérieur a été totalement repensé, comme lors des précédentes interventions sur ce musée.

Some of the museum space seems to be too large for the art that is exhibited there, and overall, the massive expansion seems to rob MoMA of the intimacy which remained part of its character even after the most recent expansion by Cesar Pelli.

Einige der neuen Museumsräume scheinen zu groß für die in ihnen ausgestellte Kunst zu sein. Insgesamt verliert das MoMA durch die umfangreiche Erweiterung an Intimität, die – auch nach der vorletzten Erweiterung durch Cesar Pelli – einen Teil seines Charmes ausmachte.

Certains volumes sont, semble-t-il, trop grands pour les œuvres qu'ils accueillent. Cette brutale expansion prive peut-être le MoMA de l'intimité qui le caractérisait, même après les dernières interventions de Cesar Pelli.

TEZUKA ARCHITECTS

Tezuka Architects
1–19–9–3F Todoroki
Setagaya Tokyo 158–0082
Japan

Tel: +81 03 37 03 70 56
Fax: +81 03 37 03 70 38
e-mail: tez@sepia.ocn.ne.jp

Matsunoyama Natural Science Museum

TAKAHARU TEZUKA, born in Tokyo in 1964, received his degrees from the Musashi Institute of Technology (1987), and from the University of Pennsylvania (1990). He worked with Richard Rogers Partnership Ltd (1994) and established Tezuka Architects the same year. Born in Kanagawa in 1964, Yui Tezuka was educated at the Musashi Institute of Technology and the Bartlett School of Architecture, University College, London. The practice has completed more than 20 private houses, and won the competition for the Matsunoyama Museum of Natural Sciences in 2000. Since then it has been based in Tokyo. Their work includes the Soejima Hospital; Jyubako House; Shoe Box House; Big Window House; Observatory House; Forest House; Clipping Corner House; Floating House; Engawa House; House to Catch the Sky III; Saw Roof House; Skylight House; Canopy House; Thin Wall House; Thin Roof House; Anthill House; Step House; The House To Catch The Sky 2; The House To Catch The Sky 1; Wall-less House; Roof House; Megaphone House; Machiya House; Light Gauge Steel House and the Wood Deck House.

TAKAHARU TEZUKA, 1964 in Tokio geboren, machte seine Abschlüsse 1987 am Technischen Institut Musashi und 1990 an der University of Pennsylvania. 1994 arbeitete er bei Richard Rogers Partnership Ltd und gründete im selben Jahr Tezuka Architects. Yui Tezuka, geboren 1964 in Kanagawa, studierte ebenfalls am Technischen Institut Musashi und an der Bartlett School of Architecture am University College of London. Das Büro hat mehr als 20 Privathäuser gebaut und 2000 den Wettbewerb für das Naturwissenschaftliche Museum Matsunoyama gewonnen. Seit dem Gewinn des Wettbewerbs befindet sich das Büro in Tokio. Tezuka Architects haben u. a. folgende Projekte realisiert: das Krankenhaus Soejima, das Jyubako Haus, das Schuhschachtel-Haus, das Haus »Großes Fenster«, das Sternwarten-Haus, das Waldhaus, das Haus »Abgeschnittene Ecke«, das schwebende Haus und das Engawa Haus, ferner das »Fang-den-Himmel-Haus III«, das Sägedach-Haus, das Oberlicht-Haus, das Vordach-Haus, das Haus »Dünne Wand«, das Haus »Dünnes Dach«, das Ameisenhügel-Haus, das Stufen-Haus, das »Fang-den-Himmel-Haus II«, das »Fang-den-Himmel-Haus I«, das »Haus ohne Wände«, das Dach-Haus, das Megafon-Haus, das Machiya Haus, das »Lichtfühler-Stahlhaus« und das Holzterrassen-Haus.

TAKAHARU TEZUKA, né à Tokyo en 1964, est diplômé de l'Institut de technologie Musashi (1987) et de l'Université de Pennsylvanie (1990). Il a travaillé pour Richard Rogers Partnership Ltd (1994) et fondé l'agence Tezuka Architects la même année. Né à Kanagawa en 1964, Yui Tezuka est diplômé de l'Institut de technologie Musashi et de la Bartlett School of Architecture, University College, Londres. Installée aujourd'hui à Tokyo, l'agence a déjà réalisé l'hôpital de Soejima, Japon (1996) et plus de 20 résidences privées : Jyubako House ; Shoe Box House ; Big Window House ; Observatory House ; Forest House ; Clipping Corner House ; Floating House ; Engawa House ; House to Catch the Sky III ; Saw Roof House ; Skylight House ; Canopy House ; Thin Wall House ; Thin Roof House ; Anthill House ; Step House ; The House to Catch The Sky II ; The House To Catch The Sky 1 ; Wall-less House ; Roof House ; Megaphone House ; Machiya House ; Light Gauge Steel House and the Wood Deck House. Tezuka Architects a remporté le concours pour le Musée des sciences naturelles de Matsunoyama en 2000.

MATSUNOYAMA NATURAL SCIENCE MUSEUM

Matsunoyama, Niigata, Japan, 2002–04

Floor area: 1248 m². Client: Matsunoyama-machi/Secretariat of Tokamachi Regionwide Area Municipal Corporation.
Cost: €5.4 million

Located approximately 200 km to the north of Tokyo in a region that has the heaviest snowfalls of Japan (up to five meters), the **MATSUNOYAMA NATURAL SCIENCE MUSEUM** was built without firm foundations because the building expands 20 cm in summer. A Corten steel tube designed to resist snow loads of up to 2000 tons meanders over a length of 111 meters, following the topography and allowing visitors to "experience the light and colors under the different depths of snow from 4 m deep to 30 m above the ground." Steel plates 6 mm thick weighing 500 tons were welded in place to the load-bearing steel structure, and four large windows made of 75 mm-thick Perspex and located at the turning points in the museum space permit direct observation of life under the snow. A 34-meter-high observation tower, the only element with a normal foundation, completes the project. Tezuka Architects describe the structure as a "submarine, with the tower its periscope," in a willful effort to contrast with the white natural winter landscape.

Das **NATURWISSENSCHAFTLICHE MUSEUM MATSUNOYAMA** liegt etwa 200 km nördlich von Tokio. In dieser Region gibt es die stärksten Schneefälle in Japan – der Schnee kann hier bis zu 5 m hoch liegen. Das Gebäude dehnt sich im Sommer 20 cm aus und hat daher keine festen Fundamente. Eine 111 m lange, mäandrierende Röhre aus Corten-Stahl, die Schneelasten bis 2000 t abfangen kann, folgt der Topografie und ermöglicht es dem Besucher »das Licht und die Farben unter dem Schnee, der sich hier 4 bis 30 m hoch auftürmt, zu erleben«. 6 mm dicke Stahlplatten mit einem Gesamtgewicht von 500 t wurden vor Ort an die tragende Stahlkonstruktion geschweißt. Vier große Fenster mit 75 mm dicken Perspex-Scheiben sind an den Stellen angeordnet, an denen sich die Richtung des Museumsraums ändert. Hier kann das Leben im Schnee direkt beobachtet werden. Ein 34 m hoher Aussichtsturm, der einzige Teil des Museums mit normalen Fundamenten, komplettiert die Anlage. Tezuka Architects beschreiben das Gebäude als »ein U-Boot – mit dem Turm als Periskop«. Der Turm stellt dabei einen gewollten Kontrast zur weißen Winterlandschaft her.

Situé à environ 200 km au nord de Tokyo dans une région qui connaît les plus importantes chutes de neige du Japon (jusqu'à 5 m), ce **MUSÉE DES SCIENCES NATURELLES** a été construit sans fondations fixes car il se dilate de 20 cm en été… Il s'agit essentiellement d'un tube en acier Corten conçu pour résister à une charge de neige de 2000 tonnes, qui se fond dans la topographie sur une longueur de 111 m et permet aux visiteurs « de faire l'expérience de la lumière et des couleurs sous différentes épaisseurs de neige, de 4 m de profondeur jusqu'à 30 m au-dessus du niveau du sol ». Les 500 tonnes de tôles d'acier de 6 mm d'épaisseur ont été soudées sur place sur la structure porteuse en acier et quatre grandes baies fermées d'un panneau de Perspex de 75 mm d'épaisseur positionnées aux angles de la structure pour faciliter l'observation directe de la vie sous la neige. Une tour d'observation de 34 m de haut, seul élément à posséder des fondations normales, complète l'ensemble. Tezuka Architects décrit ce musée comme « un sous-marin, dont la tour serait le périscope », volontairement conçu pour contraster avec le paysage hivernal enneigé.

The rusted Corten steel exterior of the museum gives it something of the appearance of a curious industrial artifact, lost in the woods.

Die rostige Fassade aus Corten-Stahl gibt dem Museum etwas von einem sonderbaren industriellen Relikt, das im Wald vergessen wurde.

Sa peau en acier Corten patiné donne au musée l'apparence d'un objet industriel bizarre perdu dans les bois.

*A café offers an outside view, while
exhibitions concentrate on the unique
ecosystems of this region which is
prone to very heavy snow in winter.*

*Das Café bietet einen Ausblick nach
draußen. Die Ausstellungen konzentrieren sich auf die einzigartigen
Ökosysteme der Region, die im Winter heftigen Schneefällen ausgesetzt
ist.*

*Le café bénéficie d'une vue sur
l'extérieur tandis que les expositions
se concentrent sur les écosystèmes
spécifiques à cette région sujette
à d'importantes chutes de neige en
hiver.*

TRAHAN ARCHITECTS

Trahan Architects
445 North Boulevard, Suite 570
Baton Rouge, Louisiana 70802
USA

Tel: +1 225 924 6333
Fax: +1 225 924 6398
e-mail: ttrahan@trahanarchitects.com
Web: www.trahanarchitects.com

Holy Rosary Catholic Church Complex

VICTOR TRAHAN was born in Crowley, Louisiana. He received a Bachelor of Architecture degree from Louisiana State University in 1983. His work includes: the First National Bank Of Crowley, Crowley, Louisiana (1997); St. Jean Vianney Catholic Church, Baton Rouge, Louisiana (1999); LSU Academic Center For Student Athletes, Baton Rouge, Louisiana (2002); and the Holy Rosary Catholic Church Complex, St. Amant, Louisiana published here, which won a National AIA Honor Award For Excellence In Architectural Design (2005). Recent and current work includes: LSU Tiger Stadium East and West Side Expansion, Baton Rouge, Louisiana (2005); (MSEAR) Institute of Medicine Science Experience and Research, Beijing, China (completion date 2007); and an office tower in Baton Rouge, Louisiana (due for 2007 completion). He also participated in the 2002 World Trade Center Memorial competition.

VICTOR TRAHAN, geboren in Crowley, Louisiana, machte seinen Bachelor of Architecture 1983 an der Louisiana State University. Bauten des Büros sind u. a. die First National Bank of Crowley in Crowley, Louisiana (1997), die katholische Kirche St. Jean Vianney in Baton Rouge, Louisiana (1999), das LSU Academic Center for Student Athletes, ebenfalls in Baton Rouge (2002), und der Holy Rosary Catholic Church Complex in St. Amant, Louisiana (hier gezeigt), der 2005 mit dem National AIA Honor Award für die besondere Qualität des architektonischen Entwurfs ausgezeichnet wurde. Zu den neuesten Projekten des Büros gehören die östliche und westliche Erweiterung des LSU Tiger Stadium in Baton Rouge, (2005), das Institute of Medicine Science Experience and Research (MSEAR) in Peking (Fertigstellung 2007) und ein Bürohochhaus in Baton Rouge, das 2007 vollendet sein soll. 2002 nahmen Trahan Architects am Wettbewerb für das Mahnmal für das World Trade Center in New York teil.

VICTOR TRAHAN, né à Crowley (Louisiane), est Bachelor of Architecture de la Louisiana State University (1983). Parmi ses réalisations : First National Bank of Crowley, Crowley (1997) ; église catholique de Saint-Jean Vianney, Baton Rouge, Louisiane (1999) ; LSU Academic Center for Student Athletes, Baton Rouge (2002) ; complexe de l'église catholique du Saint-Rosaire de Saint Amant (Louisiane) publié ici, qui lui a valu un prix d'honneur pour l'excellence de la conception architecturale de l'AIA (2005). Récemment construit: l'extension du LSU Tiger Stadium à Baton Rouge (2005). Il a participé en 2002 au concours pour le Mémorial du World Trade Center à New York et travaille actuellement au projet de l'Institut des sciences, de l'expérimentation et de la recherche médicale de Pékin qui sera livré en 2007 et à celui d'une tour de bureaux à Baton Rouge, également prévue pour 2007.

HOLY ROSARY CATHOLIC CHURCH COMPLEX

St. Amant, Louisiana, USA, 2000–04

*Floor area: 1586 m². Client: Holy Rosary Catholic Church, St. Amant, Lousiana.
Cost: $2.4 million*

Trahan's strong, simple architecture honors the religious function of this small complex. The lack of color and the subtle landscaping participate in the creation of a religious mood.

Eine kraftvolle, klare Architektur unterstreicht die religiöse Funktion dieses kleinen Komplexes. Durch den Verzicht auf Farbe und die subtile landschaftsplanerische Gestaltung entsteht eine religiöse Stimmung.

L'architecture de Trahan, puissante et simple, est un hommage à la fonction religieuse de ce petit complexe. L'absence de couleur et un subtil aménagement paysager contribuent à créer une atmosphère de recueillement.

This 1586 m² complex was built on a seven-hectare site for a cost of 2.4 million dollars. As the architect explains the program, "The client is a rural Catholic Parish in South Louisiana with strong French influence. There are three buildings in the first phase of the Holy Rosary Complex – a structure housing the administrative functions of the parish; the religious education building; and the oratory, or chapel for the celebration of the rites. The oratory is intended for the daily use of small assemblies, less than 50 congregants. The parish desired a relationship between the oratory, the existing church and for there to be a place of prominence for this chapel in the new complex of buildings. The client also required the new complex to play an important role in the community life of the predominantly Catholic residents." Trahan was careful to separate the secular and sacred components of the complex. Inspiration for the cubic oratory comes from the womb and from the Japanese four-and-a-half tatami configuration. The architect explains that "This non-hierarchical system accommodates the numerous seating configurations for liturgical purposes." Intentionally limiting the use of costly or rare materials, the complex is built essentially of concrete and glass. Construction began on the Religious Education and Administration Building in 2000 and was completed in 2002. Construction began on the Chapel in 2003 and was completed in 2004. Trahan concludes "Neither opulent nor austere, the Chapel presents a thoughtful meditation on sacred spaces and the spatial embodiment of spiritual experience."

Die 1586 m² große Anlage wurde für umgerechnet fast 2 Millionen Euro auf einem 7 ha großen Grundstück errichtet. Die Architekten erklären das Programm wie folgt: »Der Bauherr ist ein ländlicher, katholischer, stark an Frankreich orientierter Pfarrbezirk im Süden Louisianas. Während des ersten Bauabschnitts wurden drei Bauten realisiert: ein Verwaltungsgebäude, eine Religionsschule und ein Andachtsraum bzw. eine Kapelle, in der die religiösen Rituale zelebriert werden. Die Kapelle wird täglich genutzt, weniger als 50 Gläubige versammeln sich hier. Die Gemeinde wünschte einen Bezug zwischen der Kapelle und der bereits vorhandenen Kirche; die Kapelle sollte innerhalb der neuen Anlage einen besonderen Platz einnehmen. Der Bauherr wollte außerdem, dass die Gebäudegruppe im Gemeindeleben der hauptsächlich katholischen Bewohner eine wichtige Rolle spielt.« Trahan hat die säkularen und die sakralen Elemente der Anlage sorgfältig voneinander getrennt. Inspirationen für den kubischen Andachtsraum waren der Mutterleib und das japanische Grundmuster aus viereinhalb Tatami-Matten. Dazu der Architekt: »Dieses nicht hierarchische System erlaubt verschiedene Sitzanordnungen, passend zu dem jeweiligen liturgischen Zweck.« Die Verwendung von kostbaren oder seltenen Materialien wurde bewusst eingeschränkt, im Wesentlichen besteht der Bau aus Beton und Glas. 2000 wurde mit dem Bau des Schulgebäudes und des Verwaltungsbaus begonnen, die 2002 fertiggestellt waren. Die Bauzeit der Kapelle dauerte von 2003 bis 2004. Trahan: »Die Kapelle ist weder opulent noch erhaben. Sie stellt eine Meditation über heilige Räume und die räumliche Verkörperung des spirituellen Erlebnisses dar.«

Ce complexe de 1586 m² a été construit sur un terrain de sept hectares pour un budget de presque 2 millions d'euros. Comme l'explique l'architecte, « le client est une paroisse catholique rurale de la Louisiane du Sud, à forte influence française. Trois bâtiments ont été édifiés lors de la première phase : un pour les fonctions administratives de la paroisse, un autre pour l'enseignement religieux et enfin l'oratoire, ou chapelle, pour la célébration des offices. L'oratoire est conçu pour un usage quotidien par de petites assemblées de moins de 50 personnes. La paroisse souhaitait établir une relation entre ce lieu et l'église existante et qu'il occupe une position éminente dans le nouvel ensemble de bâtiments. Elle voulait également que l'ensemble joue un rôle important dans la vie de cette communauté rurale essentiellement catholique ». Trahan a séparé avec soin les composantes sacrées et séculières. La forme cubique de l'oratoire tire son inspiration de l'idée de matrice et de la configuration classique du tatami japonais. « Ce système non hiérarchique s'adapte à la disposition des sièges qui varie en fonction de la liturgie. » Le recours aux matériaux rares ou coûteux a été volontairement limité et le complexe est bâti essentiellement en béton et en verre. La construction a commencé en 2000 par les bâtiments administratifs et d'enseignement et s'est achevée en 2002. La chapelle, dont le chantier a débuté en 2003, a été livrée en 2004. Pour Trahan : « Ni opulente ni austère, cette chapelle est une méditation sur l'espace sacré et la matérialisation spatiale de l'expérience spirituelle. »

Although it is less ambitious than Pawson's Novy Dvûr, the Holy Rosary Church shares something of the bright austerity of its European counterpart.

Die Holy Rosary Church ist weniger ehrgeizig angelegt als Pawsons Novy-Dvûr-Projekt. Mit ihrem europäischen Gegenstück verbindet sie aber ihre helle Kargheit.

Bien que moins ambitieux que le monastère de Novy Dvûr par Pawson, le projet de l'église du Saint-Rosaire partage l'austérité lumineuse de l'exemple européen.

The play of light on concrete gives a more powerful message of religion than might a whole battery of outmoded objects. This is not the strict geometry of Ando, but the influence of Japanese architecture seems to have reached this place.

Das Spiel des Lichtes auf dem Beton vermittelt die religiöse Botschaft stärker als eine ganze Batterie unzeitgemäßer Objekte. Dies ist zwar nicht die strenge Geometrie eines Tadao Ando, aber der Einfluss der japanischen Architektur scheint auch diesen Ort erreicht zu haben.

Le jeu de la lumière sur le béton porte un message religieux beaucoup plus fort que la présence de quelques objets démodés. Il ne s'agit pas là de la stricte géométrie de Ando, mais l'influence de l'architecture japonaise semble néanmoins avoir touché ce lieu.

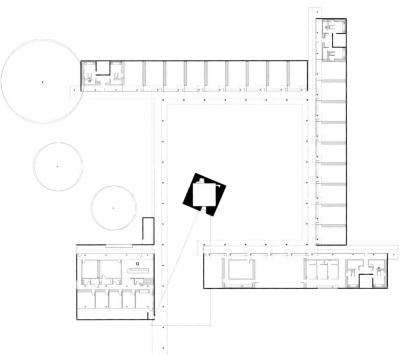

Water, light and stone combine to open the spirit of those willing to pause and think in such a place. Perhaps unexpected in Louisiana, which is not necessarily known for its contemporary architecture, Trahan's Holy Rosary has a universality about it that reveals no particular geographical origin.

Wasser, Licht und Stein verbinden sich, um die Sinne derjenigen anzusprechen, die an einem solchen Ort innehalten und nachdenken möchten. Louisiana ist nicht unbedingt für seine zeitgenössische Architektur bekannt und ein solches Projekt überrascht hier vielleicht. Trahans Holy Rosary Church ist von einer Universalität, die keinen Hinweis auf geografische Ursprünge gibt.

L'eau, la lumière et la pierre, assemblées, peuvent favoriser l'ouverture d'esprit de ceux qui viennent méditer dans un tel lieu. Un peu inattendue en Louisiane, qui n'est pas spécialement réputée pour son architecture contemporaine, l'église de Trahan revêt un caractère universel.

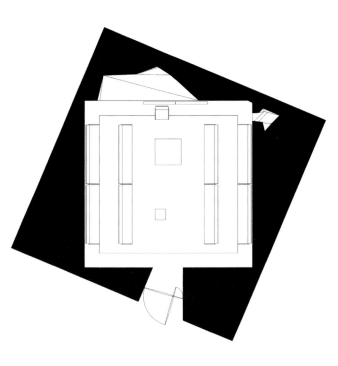

VARIOUS ARCHITECTS

Jean Nouvel, Zaha Hadid, Norman Foster, David Chipperfield,
Eva Castro and Holger Kehne, Vitorio & Lucchino, Marc Newson,
Ron Arad, Kathryn Findlay, Richard Gluckman, Arata Isozaki,
John Pawson, Christian Liaigre

Hotel Puerta América, Avenida de América 41, 28002 Madrid, Spain
Web: www.hotelpuertamerica.com

HOTEL PUERTA AMÉRICA

Madrid, Spain, 2002–05

Floor area: 34 000 m². Client: Silken Group.
Cost: not disclosed

Jean Nouvel designed the façade and the twelfth floor of this very unusual collaborative project, which brought together the talents of no less than nineteen internationally recognized architects and designers. With its 12 floors, 342 rooms and a floor area of 34 000 m², the project is relatively large on the scale of the fashionable "designer" hotels that have sprung up all over the world in the past 15 years. Run by the Silken Group that manages 4600 rooms and 30 hotels in various Spanish cities, the Puerta América does pose some questions about the nature of the collaboration of so many well-known figures. As the promotional material for the hotel declares, "At the **HOTEL PUERTA AMÉRICA**, the guest discovers the finest cutting-edge design and architecture almost without even realizing it." This may or may not be flattering for the talents involved. In any case, Nouvel's colorful façade gives way inside to a large variety of approaches to interior design. The first floor "characterized by the fluidity of the spaces based on new developments in digital design" is the work of Zaha Hadid. The second floor is the result of Norman Foster's desire to evoke the inspiration of the late Basque sculptor Eduardo Chillida, who was a personal friend and client of the architect, while on the third floor, David Chipperfield called on a minimalist vocabulary of "hand-made floorings, upholstered walls, and white marble." Plasma Studio (Eva Castro and Holger Kehne) was commissioned to create the 4th floor. Their aim was to "move away from the stereotype of a hotel as an anodyne and homogenous place, experimenting with the differentiation of space by developing the surface areas." Seville architects Vitorio & Lucchino were given the responsibility of the fifth floor, while one level up, and in the hotel bar, Marc Newson was in charge. With Ron Arad on the seventh floor, Kathryn Findlay (Ushida Findlay) and Richard Gluckman of Chelsea gallery fame, fans of international design are certainly spoiled in this new Madrid Hotel. Arata Isozaki designed the 10th floor, John Pawson the foyer and reception rooms, and Christian Liaigre the hotel restaurant. Although the promotion of the hotel evokes the idea of "liberty" in this large choice of designers – the liberty given to the architects and to the clients to select the ambiance that best suits them – it would seem that the all-star list of collaborators on the project might be its most salient feature.

Jean Nouvel entwarf die Fassade und das 12. Obergeschoss des Hotels, das als sehr ungewöhnliches Gemeinschaftsprojekt realisiert wurde, bei dem nicht weniger als 19 international anerkannte Architekten und Designer zusammenarbeiteten. Mit seinen 12 Geschossen, 342 Hotelzimmern und einer Gesamtfläche von 34 000 m² ist das Hotel im Vergleich zu anderen Design-Hotels, die in den letzten 15 Jahren überall auf der Welt entstanden sind, relativ groß. Das Puerta América gehört zur Silken-Gruppe, die 4600 Zimmer bzw. 30 Hotels in verschiedenen spanischen Städten führt. Die Zusammenarbeit so vieler bekannter Persönlichkeiten wirft einige Fragen auf. »Im **HOTEL PUERTA AMÉRICA** entdeckt der Gast das beste, modernste Design (bzw. entsprechende Architektur), fast ohne es zu bemerken«, verspricht die Werbung des Hotels. Ist das für die Beteiligten ein Kompliment? Jedenfalls verbirgt sich hinter Nouvels Fassade eine große Bandbreite unterschiedlich gestalteter Innenräume. Das 1. OG entwarf Zaha Hadid: Es »wird durch fließende Räume bestimmt, die auf neuen Entwicklungen des digitalen Designs basieren«. Norman Fosters 2. OG ist durch das Spätwerk des baskischen Bildhauers Eduardo Chillida inspiriert; dieser war ein persönlicher Freund und Bauherr Fosters. Im 3. OG verließ sich David Chipperfield auf ein minimalistisches Vokabular aus »handgemachten Fußbodenbelägen, gepolsterten Wänden und weißem Marmor«. Plasma Studio (Eva Castro und Holger Kehne) wurde mit der Gestaltung des 4. OG betraut. Ziel war es, »sich vom Stereotyp des Hotels als einem ›schmerzlindernden‹ und homogenen Ort zu lösen und mit der Differenzierung von Raum durch verschiedenartige Oberflächen zu experimentieren.« Die Architekten Vitorio & Lucchino aus Sevilla zeichnen für das 5. OG. verantwortlich, Marc Newson plante das darüberliegende Geschoss und die Hotelbar. Mit Ron Arad (7. OG), Kathryn Findlay (Ushida Findlay) und dem für seine Galerieplanungen in Chelsea bekannten Robert Gluckman kommen Fans des internationalen Designs in Madrids neuem Hotel sicherlich auf ihre Kosten. Arata Isozaki plante das 10. OG, John Pawson das Foyer und die Rezeption, Christian Liaigre das Restaurant. Obwohl die Werbung des Hotels durch die große Auswahl von Designern die Vorstellung von »Freiheit« hervorruft – die Freiheit, die den Architekten gegeben wurde und die Freiheit der Gäste, sich das Ambiente auszusuchen, das ihnen am besten gefällt – hat es doch den Anschein, als ob die »Starbesetzung« die herausragendste Eigenschaft des Projektes ist.

Jean Nouvel a conçu la façade et le douzième étage de cette très intéressante réalisation, fruit d'une collaboration entre 19 architectes et designers de réputation internationale. Avec ses 12 étages, ses 342 chambres et suites et une surface de 34 000 m², ce projet est relativement important à l'aune des « design hotels » très en vogue qui ont surgi un peu partout dans le monde au cours de ces quinze dernières années. Géré par le groupe Silken, qui contrôle 4600 chambres et 30 établissements en Espagne, l'**HÔTEL PUERTA AMÉRICA** soulève quelques questions sur la nature de la collaboration entre des personnalités aussi connues. Comme on peut le lire dans les documents de promotion de l'hôtel, « … le client découvre le design et l'architecture d'avant-garde les plus raffinés, presque sans le réaliser ». Ceci peut être jugé flatteur, ou non, par les talents concernés. La façade colorée de Nouvel cache une grande diversité d'approches dans les aménagements intérieurs. Le premier étage, « caractérisé par la fluidité des espaces inspirée des développements les plus récents de la conception numérique », est l'œuvre de Zaha Hadid. Le deuxième niveau est la traduction du désir de Norman Foster d'évoquer celui qui fut son ami et client, le sculpteur basque Eduardo Chillida, tandis qu'au troisième, David Chipperfield a opté pour le vocabulaire minimaliste de « sols réalisés à la main, de murs tapissés et de marbre blanc ». Plasma Studio (Eva Castro et Holger Kehne) a reçu commande du quatrième étage. Leur but était de « s'écarter du stéréotype de l'hôtel, lieu anodin et uniforme, pour expérimenter une différenciation de l'espace par le traitement des surfaces ». Les architectes sévillans Victorio & Lucchino ont été chargés du cinquième, Marc Newson du sixième et du bar. Du septième étage au neuvième, avec Ron Arad, Kathryn Findlay (Ushida Findlay) et Richard Gluckman, connu par la Chelsea Gallery, les amateurs de design international sont gâtés. Arata Isozaki a conçu le dixième, John Pawson le hall d'accueil et les salons, Christian Liaigre le restaurant. Bien que la promotion de l'hôtel évoque l'idée de « liberté » dans ce large choix d'intervenants – liberté donnée aux architectes et aux clients de choisir l'ambiance qui leur convient le mieux – il se pourrait que cette liste de stars en soit le principal intérêt.

Marc Newson was given the responsibility of the 6th floor passageway seen opposite.

Marc Newson zeichnet für den Flur im sechsten Obergeschoss (gegenüber) verantwortlich.

Marc Newson a été chargé du couloir du sixième étage (page ci-contre).

John Pawson designed "communal" areas in the hotel including this typically minimalist space (above left). The façade was conceived by the Paris architect Jean Nouvel.

John Pawson entwarf die »öffentlichen« Bereiche wie z. B. diesen für ihn typischen minimalistischen Raum (oben links). Die Fassade stammt von dem Pariser Architekten Jean Nouvel.

John Pawson a conçu les parties communes, notamment ce volume typiquement minimaliste (en haut, à gauche). La façade de l'hôtel a été dessinée par Jean Nouvel.

On the preceding double-page, the 7th floor vestibule by Ron Arad. On the left-hand page, a 4th floor space by Eva Castro & Holger Kehne (Plasma Studio). Below, a 1st floor room and passageway by Zaha Hadid, and right, a 3rd floor room by David Chipperfield.

Vorhergehende Doppelseite: Vestibül im siebten Obergeschoss von Ron Arad. Linke Seite: Flur im vierten Obergeschoss von Eva Castro und Holger Kehne (Plasma Studio). Unten: Hotelzimmer und Flur im ersten Obergeschoss von Zaha Hadid; rechts: Flurbereich im dritten Obergeschoss von David Chipperfield.

Double page précédente : le vestibule du septième niveau, par Ron Arad. Page de gauche, un espace du quatrième, dû à Eva Castro et Holger Kehne (Plasma Studio). Ci-dessous, une chambre du premier étage et un couloir par Zaha Hadid et, ci-contre, une chambre du troisième signée David Chipperfield.

VHP

VHP stedebouwkundigen + architekten + landschapsarchitekten BV
Prins Hendrikkade 14, 3071 KB Rotterdam, The Netherlands
Tel: +31 104 52 07 44, Fax: +31 104 53 24 54
e-mail: vhp@vhp.nl, Web: www.vhp.nl

NIO architecten
Schiedamse Vest 95-A, 3012 BG Rotterdam, The Netherlands
Tel: +31 104 12 23 18, Fax: +31 104 12 60 75
e-mail: nio@nio.nl, Web: www.nio.nl

Soundbarrier Houses

Maurice Nio, architect of the Soundbarrier Houses, was born in 1959 and studied at the Faculty of Architecture of Delft University of Technology (1988). He was a founder, with Lars Spuybroeck, of NOX Architects. He also worked on larger architectural projects for BDG Architects and Engineers (1991–96). His best-known work from this period is the enormous aviTwente Waste Incineration Plant. From 1997 to 1999 he worked at **VHP** urban developers + architects + landscape architects on both architectural and urban development projects. The Soundbarrier Houses published here were undertaken when he was working at VHP. In 2000, Maurice Nio created his own design firm, NIO architecten. Nio has also designed books, made seven video productions and published more than seventy articles about architecture, film, video, television, photography, dance and culture in general. His work realized since creating NIO includes: Residential and accessory building, Waverveen (2003–05); and Extension of the office building for Twence Waste Incineration, Hengelo (2000–02).

Maurice Nio, Architekt der »Schallschutzhäuser«, wurde 1959 geboren und studierte an der Architekturfakultät der Technischen Universität Delft, wo er 1988 seinen Abschluss machte. Zusammen mit Lars Spuybroeck gründete er NOX Architects. Von 1991 bis 1996 arbeitete er für BDG Architekten und Ingenieure an größeren Hochbauten. Sein bekanntestes Projekt aus dieser Zeit ist die riesige Müllverbrennungsanlage aviTwente. Von 1997 bis 1999 war Nio bei **VHP** tätig und arbeitete an Hochbau- und Städtebauprojekten. Die hier gezeigten Schallschutzhäuser plante er während seiner Tätigkeit bei VHP. 2000 gründete Maurice Nio sein eigenes Büro, NIO architecten. Darüber hinaus hat Nio Bücher entworfen, sieben Videos produziert und mehr als 70 Artikel über Architektur, Film, Video, Fernsehen, Fotografie, Tanz und allgemeine kulturelle Themen geschrieben. Zu den Gebäuden, die er mit seinem eigenen Büro realisierte, gehören das Wohn- und Nebengebäude in Waverveen (2003–05) und die Erweiterung des Bürogebäudes für Twence Müllverbrennung in Hengelo (2000–02).

Maurice Nio, né en 1959, a fait ses études à la Faculté d'architecture de l'Université de technologie de Delft (1988). Avec Lars Spuybroeck, il a été l'un des fondateurs de NOX Architects et a également collaboré à d'importants projets pour BDG Architects and Engineers (1991–96). Son œuvre la plus importante pour cette période est l'énorme usine d'incinération aviTwence. De 1997 à 1999, il a travaillé pour **VHP** sur des projets à la fois architecturaux et d'urbanisme. Les Soundbarrier Houses publiées ici ont été réalisées pour cette agence. En 2000, il crée sa propre agence, NIO architecten. Il a également conçu des livres, réalisé des vidéos et publié plus de soixante-dix articles sur l'architecture, le cinéma, la vidéo, la télévision, la photographie, la danse et la culture. Les réalisations de NIO comprennent un immeuble résidentiel, Waterveen (2003–05) et l'extension de l'immeuble de bureaux de l'entreprise d'incinération Twence, Hengelo (2000–02).

SOUNDBARRIER HOUSES

Diependaal, Hilversum, The Netherlands, 2001

Floor area: 207 m² per house, 12 houses = 2484 m². Client: Slokker Vastgoed BV.
Cost: €3.29 million

Cyclopean and repetitive, the Soundbarrier Houses offer dignified and
unusual homes while they solve noise
problems in an efficient way.

Die zyklopischen, gleichartigen
Schallschutzhäuser bieten anspruchs-
volles, ungewöhnliches Wohnen
und sorgen für einen wirksamen
Lärmschutz.

Cyclopéennes et répétitives, les
maisons de la « Barrière sonore » sont
des résidences pleines de dignité
mais d'apparence inhabituelle, qui
résolvent, par ailleurs, avec efficacité
le problème du bruit de la circulation.

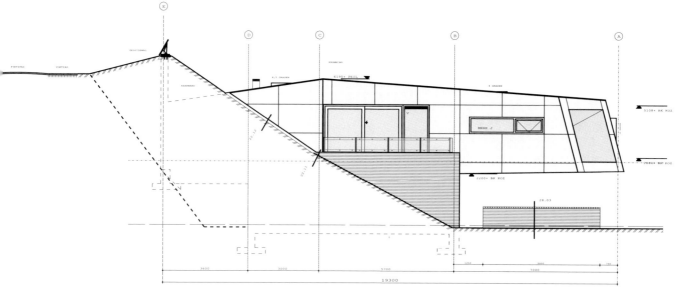

This design, commenced in 1997, was completed in 2001 for a cost of 3.29 million euros. The project architect was Maurice Nio, who at that time worked with the firm VHP. As the writer François Thiry explains, "The twelve houses form an integral part of a soundproof embankment along a secondary road from Diependaal, an exclusive residential district in the woods of Hilversum. Despite its inhospitable setting and the clients' initial skepticism, the futuristic, not to say fantastic, design of the houses attracted users who bought their houses off the drawing board, several years before delivery." Each house measures 207 m^2 (ground floor 87 m^2, upper floor 120 m^2), or a total of 2484 m^2 for the twelve residences. The considerable cantilevered area of the upper floor allows cars to be parked beneath the top level. Aligned with identical forms and cyclopean upper story windows, the construction of these houses, and the attendant reduction of ambient noise within acceptable levels, allowed the overall urban design plan for Diependaal to advance.

Die 1997 begonnenen Gebäude wurden 2001 fertig gestellt und kosteten 3,29 Millionen Euro. Projektleiter war Maurice Nio, der in dieser Zeit für das Büro VHP arbeitete. Der Architekturkritiker François Thiry erläutert: »Die zwölf Häuser sind integraler Bestandteil einer Schallschutzwand entlang einer Bundesstraße nach Diependaal, ein exklusiver Wohnbezirk in den Wäldern von Hilversum. Trotz seines unwirtlichen Standortes und der anfänglichen Skepsis der Bauherren, sprach der futuristische – um nicht zu sagen fantastische – Entwurf der Häuser Nutzer an, die ihre Häuser vom Bildschirm weg kauften, einige Jahre bevor diese gebaut wurden.« Jedes Haus ist 207 m^2 groß (Erdgeschoss 87 m^2, Obergeschoss 120 m^2); die Gesamtfläche der zwölf Häuser beträgt 2484 m^2. Das erheblich auskragende Obergeschoss überdeckt die Stellplätze. Durch den Bau der aneinander gereihten, identischen Häuser mit Zyklopenfenstern im Obergeschoss konnten die Geräuschemissionen auf ein akzeptables Maß gesenkt werden, so dass die Umsetzung des Bebauungsplans für Diependaal weiter fortschreiten konnte.

Lancé en 1997, ce projet a été achevé en 2001 pour un budget de 3,29 millions d'euros. L'architecte de projet était Maurice Nio, qui travaillait alors pour VHP. Comme l'explique l'auteur François Thiry, «les douze maisons sont partie intégrante d'un talus anti-bruit édifié le long d'une voie secondaire de Diependaal, quartier résidentiel élégant dans les bois d'Hilversum. Malgré ce cadre inhospitalier et le scepticisme initial du client, la conception futuriste, pour ne pas dire fantastique, des maisons, a attiré des amateurs qui ont acheté sur plans, plusieurs années avant la livraison». La superficie de chaque maison est de 207 m^2 (rez-de-chaussée 87 m^2, étage 120 m^2), soit un total de 2484 m^2 pour les douze résidences. Le porte-à-faux considérable de l'étage permet de garer des voitures à l'abri. Cet alignement de formes identiques et de baies cyclopéennes et la réduction du bruit ambiant à des niveaux acceptables ont donné un nouvel essor au plan directeur d'urbanisme de Diependaal.

Systematically cantilevered, allowing for car parking space below, and angled away from neighboring residences, these designs give new life to the idea of the row house.

Unter den Auskragungen befinden sich die Stellplätze. Die Häuser orientieren sich nicht zu den Gebäuden in der Umgebung; der Typus des Reihenhauses wird um eine neue Variante bereichert.

Avec ses porte-à-faux systématiques qui ménagent des places où garer les voitures et avec ses façades inclinées pour isoler du voisinage, ce projet redonne vie au concept de maisons en bande.

As plans and images show, the main windows of each house afford residents a view to the outside world and not on the activities of neighbors. Simple and powerful, they are the defining architectural gestures of the sequence.

Wie die Grundrisse und Abbildungen zeigen, bieten die großen Panoramafenster den Bewohnern einen Ausblick in die Umgebung und nicht auf die Aktivitäten der Nachbarn. Diese einfachen und kraftvollen Elemente sind die definierenden architektonischen Gesten dieser Sequenz.

Comme le montrent les plans et les photographies, les baies principales de chaque maison donnent sur l'extérieur et non sur les activités des voisins. Il s'agit d'un geste architectural simple et puissant qui participe à la définition de cette intéressante séquence de résidences.

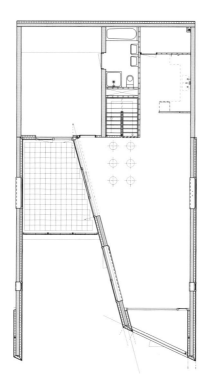

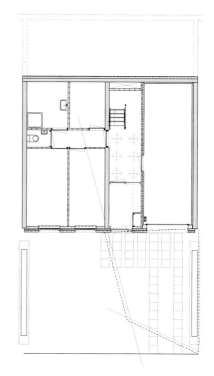

BILL VIOLA

Haunch of Venison, 6 Haunch of Venison Yard
Off Brook Street, London W1K 5ES, UK
Tel: +44 20 74 95 50 50, Fax: +44 20 74 95 40 50
e-mail: info@haunchofvenison.com, Web: www.haunchofvenison.com

BILL VIOLA is recognized as a real pioneer of video art. Born in 1951, he lives and works in Long Beach, California with his wife Kira Perov who is the Executive Director of the studio. After graduating from Syracuse University in 1973, Viola studied and worked with the composer David Tudor, and under Tudor's direction, he participated in the Rainforest group, experimenting with music and sonic sculpture. As Viola's own biography states, his videos "explore the spiritual and perceptual side of human experience, focusing on universal human themes – birth, death, the unfolding of consciousness – and have roots in both Eastern and Western art as well as the spiritual traditions of Zen Buddhism, Islamic Sufism and Christian mysticism." Inevitably, this exploration of the fundamentals of life and death has brought Viola into a frequent dialogue with architectural space, either within the videos themselves, or in terms of the places in which they are presented. Major exhibitions of his work include *Bill Viola: Installations and Videotapes*, the Museum of Modern Art, New York (1987); *Unseen Images*, organized by Kunsthalle Düsseldorf (1992); *Buried Secrets* at the U.S. Pavilion, 46th Venice Biennale (1995); and *Bill Viola: A 25-Year Survey*, organized in 1997 by the Whitney Museum of American Art. In 2002, Viola completed *Going Forth By Day*, commissioned by the Guggenheim Museum, New York and Deutsche Guggenheim Berlin. It was recently on view in *Bill Viola: Visions* at the ARoS Århus Kunstmuseum in Denmark. In 2000 Viola created a suite of three video pieces for the rock group Nine Inch Nails' *Fragility* world tour. In 2003 the J. Paul Getty Museum, Los Angeles organized *Bill Viola: The Passions*; other venues included the National Gallery, London, and the Fundación "La Caixa", Madrid, in 2005.

BILL VIOLA, geboren 1951, ist ein echter Pionier der Videokunst. Mit seiner Frau Kira Perov, Geschäftsführerin seines Studios, arbeitet und lebt er in Long Beach, Kalifornien. 1973 erwarb er seinen Abschluss an der Syracuse University, anschließend studierte und arbeitete er bei dem Komponisten David Tudor. Unter Tudors Leitung war er Mitglied der Gruppe Rainforest, die mit Musik und Klangskulpturen experimentierte. Laut eigenen Angaben zu seiner Biografie erforscht Viola mit seinen Videos »die spirituelle und wahrnehmende Seite der menschlichen Erfahrung, [sie] konzentrieren sich auf die den Menschen betreffenden universellen Themen – Geburt, Tod, die Entwicklung des Bewusstseins – und haben ihre Wurzeln in der östlichen und westlichen Kunst und im Zen-Buddhismus, im islamischen Sufismus und im christlichen Mystizismus.« Zwangsläufig brachte die Erforschung der Grundlagen von Leben und Tod Viola immer wieder in einen Dialog mit architektonischem Raum, entweder in den Videos selbst oder durch die Orte, an denen sie präsentiert werden. Violas Arbeiten wurden u. a. in folgenden wichtigen Ausstellungen gezeigt: *Bill Viola: Installations and Videotapes* im Museum of Modern Art in New York (1987), *Unseen Images*, organisiert durch die Kunsthalle Düsseldorf (1992), *Buried Secrets* im Amerikanischen Pavillon auf der 46. Biennale in Venedig (1995) und *Bill Viola: A 25-Year Survey*, organisiert 1997 vom Whitney Museum of American Art. 2000 schuf Viola eine Serie aus drei Videos für die *Fragility*-Welttournee der Rockgruppe Nine Inch Nails. 2002 beendete Viola *Going Forth By Day*, ein Auftragswerk für das Guggenheim Museum New York und das Deutsche Guggenheim Berlin, das kürzlich in *Bill Viola: Visions* im ARoS Kunstmuseum in Århus, Dänemark, zu sehen war. 2003 organisierte das J. Paul Getty Museum in Los Angeles die Ausstellung *Bill Viola: The Passions*, die außerdem u. a. in der National Gallery in London und 2005 in der Fundación »La Caixa« in Madrid gezeigt wurde.

BILL VIOLA est connu pour être l'un des pionniers de l'art vidéo. Né en 1951, il vit et travaille à Long Beach (Californie) avec son épouse, Kira Perov, qui dirige son studio. Diplômé de Syracuse University en 1973, il a ensuite étudié et travaillé avec le compositeur David Tudor et, sous la direction de celui-ci, a participé au sein du groupe « Rainforest » à des expérimentations sur des sculptures musicales et sonores. Comme sa biographie le précise, ses vidéos « explorent le côté spirituel et sensoriel de l'expérience humaine et s'attachent à des thèmes universels – naissance, mort, déploiement de la conscience. Elles puisent aux sources de l'art aussi bien occidental qu'oriental et des traditions spirituelles du bouddhisme zen, du soufisme islamique et du mysticisme chrétien ». Inévitablement, cette exploration des principes fondamentaux de la vie et la mort a amené Viola à dialoguer fréquemment avec l'espace architectural, que ce soit dans ses vidéos ou par le biais des lieux dans lesquelles elles étaient présentées. Parmi ses expositions les plus importantes : *Bill Viola, Installations and Video Tapes*, the Museum of Modern Art,, New York (1987) ; *Unseen Images*, Kunsthalle, Düsseldorf (1992) ; *Buried Secrets*, Pavillon américain de la 46e Biennale de Venise (1995) et *Bill Viola : A 25 Year Survey*, Whitney Museum of American Art, New York (1997). En 2002, il a achevé l'œuvre *Going Forth By Day*, commande du Guggenheim Museum de New York et du Deutsche Guggenheim berlinois. Elle avait été récemment vue lors de *Bill Viola : Visions* au ARoS, musée d'Art contemporain de Århus (Århus, Danemark). En 2000, il a créé trois vidéos pour *Fragility*, la tournée mondiale du groupe de rock Nine Inch Nails. En 2003, le J. Paul Getty Museum de Los Angeles a monté l'exposition *Bill Viola : The Passions,* présentée également à la National Gallery de Londres et à la Fundación « La Caixa » à Madrid en 2005.

TRISTAN AND ISOLDE

Paris, France, 2005

In 2004 Bill Viola began work on a 4-hour video/film to accompany Richard Wagner's opera **TRISTAN AND ISOLDE**. The artist collaborated with opera/theater director Peter Sellars and conductor Esa-Pekka Salonen on the work that premiered as the *Tristan Project* at Frank Gehry's Walt Disney Concert Hall in Los Angeles, presenting one act per night. This new production of the complete opera received its world premiere at the Paris Opera Bastille in April 2005. As Viola says, "The images are intended to function as symbolic, inner representations that become, to echo the words of Seyyed Hossein Nasr, 'reflections of the spiritual world in the mirror of the material and the temporal.' They trace the movement of human consciousness through one of its most delicate, poignant states: the surrender to an absolute, all-consuming love." The representation of this opera clearly places the artist in a position of having to deal with the singers, the music, and with the physical space of the stage. As Bill Viola explains, "Moving images live in a domain somewhere between the temporal urgency of music and the material certainty of painting, and so are well suited to link the practical elements of stage design with the living dynamics of performance. I knew from the start that I did not want the images to illustrate or represent the story directly. Instead, I wanted to create an image world that existed in parallel to the action on the stage, in the same way that a more subtle poetic voice narrates the hidden dimensions of our inner lives." The sublimation of the story line and the emergence of Viola's "image world" represent the kind pure creation of space that many architects can only dream of, given the constraints implied by the use of buildings, however, the ideas of fiction, changing states and the representation of emotion, life and death are at the heart of contemporary architecture. In this sense, an artist like Bill Viola can be considered a source of inspiration and change in architecture. *Tristan and Isolde* was produced by the Paris National Opera in collaboration with the Los Angeles Philharmonic Association and Lincoln Center for the Performing Arts, with assistance from James Cohan Gallery, New York, Haunch of Venison, London, and the Bill Viola Studio.

2004 begann Bill Viola die Arbeit an einem vierstündigen Video bzw. Film zu Richard Wagners Oper **TRISTAN UND ISOLDE**. Viola arbeitete bei diesem Projekt mit dem Opern-und Theaterregisseur Peter Sellars und dem Dirigenten Esa-Pekka Salonen zusammen. Das Video wurde als *Tristan Project* erstmals in Frank Gehrys Walt Disney Concert Hall in Los Angeles gezeigt, wobei jeweils ein Akt pro Nacht zu sehen war. Die Neuinszenierung der Oper erlebte im April 2005 an der Pariser Opéra Bastille ihre Welturaufführung. Viola sagt: »Die Bilder sollen als Symbole und Darstellung des Inneren funktionieren. Sie werden, um die Worte von Seyyed Hossein Nasr zu gebrauchen, zu ›Reflexionen der spirituellen Welt im Spiegel des Materiellen und des Temporären‹. Sie zeichnen die Bewegung des menschlichen Bewusstseins in einem seiner sensibelsten, ergreifendsten Momente nach: dem Moment der Aufgabe einer absoluten, alles verschlingenden Liebe.« Die Visualisierung der Oper erforderte vom Künstler die Auseinandersetzung mit den Sängern, der Musik und dem physischen Bühnenraum. Bill Viola sagt dazu: »Bewegte Bilder leben in einem Bereich irgendwo zwischen der temporären Dringlichkeit der Musik und der materialhaften Sicherheit der Malerei, sind also gut geeignet, die greifbaren Elemente des Bühnenbildes mit der lebendigen Dynamik der Aufführung zu verbinden. Mir war von Anfang an klar, dass ich mit den Bildern nicht die Geschichte direkt illustrieren, sondern eine Bilderwelt schaffen wollte, die parallel zum Geschehen auf der Bühne existiert, so wie eine subtilere poetische Stimme die verborgenen Dimensionen unseres Innenlebens erzählt.« Die Sublimierung der Geschichte und die Entstehung der Bilderwelt von Viola sind die Art der reinen Schaffung von Raum, von der viele Architekten nur träumen können. Trotz der durch die Nutzung von Gebäuden vorgegebenen Bedingungen sind doch die Ideen von Fiktion, veränderlichen Zuständen und die Darstellung von Emotionen, Leben und Tod zentrale Bestandteile der heutigen Architektur. In diesem Sinn kann ein Künstler wie Bill Viola als Quelle der Inspiration für Architektur und Veränderung in der Architektur betrachtet werden. *Tristan und Isolde* wurde von der Nationaloper Paris in Zusammenarbeit mit der Los Angeles Philharmonic Association und dem Lincoln Center for the Performing Arts produziert. Die James Cohan Gallery in New York sowie Haunch of Venison in London und das Bill Viola Studio waren an der Produktion unterstützend beteiligt.

En 2004, Viola a commencé à travailler sur un programme vidéo/cinéma de quatre heures en accompagnement du **TRISTAN ET ISOLDE** de Richard Wagner. Pour cette œuvre donnée pour la première fois, (avec un acte par soirée) sous le titre de *Tristan Project* au Walt Disney Concert Hall de Frank Gehry à Los Angeles, il a collaboré avec le metteur en scène d'opéra et de théâtre Peter Sellars et le chef d'orchestre Esa-Pekka Salonen. Une nouvelle production de l'opéra complet fut donnée à l'Opéra de Paris Bastille en avril 2005. Comme l'explique Viola, « les images fonctionnent comme des représentations intérieures symboliques qui deviennent, pour faire écho aux termes de Seyyed Hossein Nasr, ‹des reflets du monde spirituel dans le miroir du matériel et du temporel›. Elles retracent le mouvement de la conscience humaine à travers l'un de ses états les plus délicats et les plus poignants : l'abandon à un amour absolu et dévastateur ». La représentation de cet opéra confronte l'artiste aux chanteurs, à la musique et à l'espace physique de la scène. « L'image animée existe dans un domaine qui se situe entre l'urgence temporelle de la musique et la certitude matérielle de la peinture, aussi est-elle tout indiquée pour faire le lien entre les éléments pratiques de la scénographie et la dynamique vivante de la représentation. Je savais dès le départ que je ne voulais pas d'images qui illustrent ou représentent directement l'histoire. Je voulais plutôt créer un monde d'images qui existe en parallèle à l'action se déroulant sur la scène, de la même façon qu'une voix poétique plus subtile raconterait les dimensions cachées de nos vies intérieures ». La sublimation de l'histoire et l'émergence du « monde imagé » de Viola illustrent cette pure création d'espace dont beaucoup d'artistes ne peuvent que rêver, au regard des contraintes qu'impliquent l'utilisation du bâti. Cependant, les idées de fiction, d'états changeants et de représentation des émotions, de la vie et de la mort, sont au cœur de l'architecture contemporaine. En ce sens, un artiste comme Bill Viola peut être considéré comme une source d'inspiration et de changement en architecture. *Tristan et Isolde* a été produit par l'Opéra national de Paris en collaboration avec la Los Angeles Philarmonic Association et le Lincoln Centre for the Performing Arts, avec l'assistance de la James Cohan Gallery, New York, de Haunch of Venison, Londres et du Bill Viola Studio.

And what if architecture were ultimately to be made of nothing more than water and fire, from the floating security of the unborn child to the fires of incineration.

Was wäre, wenn Architektur in letzter Konsequenz nur aus Wasser und Feuer bestünde – von der schwerelosen Sicherheit des ungeborenen Kindes bis zum Feuer der Einäscherung?

Et si finalement l'architecture n'était faite que d'eau et de feu, du flottement confiant de l'enfant à naître aux feux de l'incinération ?

Not the fires of hell, nor necessarily the candles of prayer in any one religion, but the fire that cleanses and consumes.

Dieses Feuer ist nicht unbedingt das Höllenfeuer, auch nicht das der in jeder Religion verwendeten Gebetskerzen, sondern das Feuer, das reinigt und verzehrt.

Non pas les feux de l'enfer, ni la flamme des cierges, mais le feu qui purifie et consume.

MAKOTO SEI WATANABE

Makoto Sei Watanabe Architects' Office
#2806 Azumabashi 1–23–30
Sumida-ku, Tokyo, 130
Japan

Tel: +81 338 29 32 21
Fax: +81 338 29 38 37
e-mail: msw@makoto-architect.com
Web: www.makoto-architect.com

InOut/Shanghai House

Born in 1952 in Yokohama, **MAKOTO SEI WATANABE** attended Yokohama National University from which he graduated with a Master's Degree in Architecture in 1976. He worked from 1979 to 1984 in the office of Arata Isozaki before creating his own firm. His first built work, the Aoyama Technical College (Shibuya, Tokyo, 1989), created considerable controversy because of its unusual forms inspired by cartoon graphics. Since that time Watanabe has worked more and more with computer-generated designs. His work includes: Chronospace, Minato-ku, Tokyo (1991); Mura-no-Terrace gallery, information office and cafe, Sakauchi Village, Ibi-gun, Gifu (1995); *Fiber Wave*, environmental art, Gifu and Tokyo (1995–96); Atlas, housing, Suginami-ku, Tokyo (1996); K-Museum, Koto-ku, Tokyo (1996); *Fiber Wave*, environmental art, The Chicago Athenaeum, Chicago (1998); and the Iidabashi Subway Station, Tokyo (2000), and the Shin-Minamata *Shinkansen* station (2004). He has also participated extensively in international exhibitions.

MAKOTO SEI WATANABE wurde 1952 in Yokohama geboren. Er studierte an der Nationaluniversität Yokohama, wo er 1976 seinen Abschluss erwarb. Bevor er sein eigenes Büro gründete, arbeitete er von 1979 bis 1984 bei Arata Isozaki. Sein erstes Gebäude, die Fachhochschule Aoyama in Shibuya, Tokio (1989), führte aufgrund der ungewöhnlichen, von Comiczeichnungen inspirierten Formen zu beträchtlichen Kontroversen. Seitdem arbeitet Watanabe zunehmend mit computergenerierten Formen. Zu den von ihm realisierten Projekten gehören das Chronospace in Minato-ku, Tokio (1991), die Mura-no-Terrasse: Galerie, Informationsbüro und Café im Dorf Sakauchi (Ibi-gun, Gifu, 1995), und die *Faserwelle*, ein Kunst-Environment in Gifu und Tokio (1995–96, gezeigt auch 1998 im Athenaeum in Chicago). Ferner entwarf er die Wohnbauten Atlas in Suginami-ku, Tokio (1996), das K-Museum in Koto-ku, Tokio (1996), die Iidabashi U-Bahnstation in Tokio (2000) und die *Shinkansen*-Station Minamata (2004). Watanabes Projekte waren schon vielfach in internationalen Ausstellungen zu sehen.

Né en 1952 à Yokohama, **MAKOTO SEI WATANABE** a étudié à l'Université nationale de Yokohama dont il est sorti diplômé en 1976. Il a travaillé de 1979 à 1984 dans l'agence d'Arata Isozaki avant de créer sa propre structure. Sa première réalisation, le Collège technique d'Aoyama, Shibuya, Tokyo (1989), a soulevé une importante controverse à cause de ses formes étonnantes inspirées de la bande dessinée. Depuis cette époque, il utilise de plus en plus l'ordinateur pour concevoir ses bâtiments. Parmi ses réalisations : Chronospace, Minato-ku, Tokyo (1991) ; la galerie Mura-no-Terrace, bureau d'information et café, Sakauchi Village, Ibi-gun, Gifu (1995) ; *Fiber Wave*, œuvre d'art environnemental, Gifu et Tokyo (1995–96) ; logements Atlas, Suginami-ku, Tokyop (1996) ; le K-Museum, Koto-ku, Tokyo (1996) ; *Fiber Wave*, au Chicago Athenaeum, Chicago (1998), la station de métro Iidabashi (Tokyo) et la gare du train rapide *Shinkansen*, Shin-Minamata (2004). Il a également participé à de nombreuses expositions internationales.

INOUT/SHANGHAI HOUSE

Shanghai, China, 2005

Floor area: 565 m². Client: Lin Mei.
Cost: not disclosed

The site of this house is in central Shanghai near other residences dating from the colonial period. The street side was designed to respond to the appearance of the surroundings. The height and depth are about the same as those of neighboring buildings. The slanted roof, window placement and use of color are also comparable. As Watanabe says, "In other words, it could be said that this architecture has no façade. Since the whole is never visible from any one point, more emphasis was placed on blending into the neighborhood as an accumulation of parts that functions as an element in the streetscape." An elliptical inner court paved in black granite and surrounded by a glass screen forms the heart of the house. Because the granite continues inside, the architect says, "Interior and interior are continuous, severed, and overlapping." The glass screen rises directly from the granite surface of the courtyard which can be covered with water, bringing varied reflections into the house. The furnishings of the first floor are in black lacquer with either relief work in gold dust, or inlaid mother of pearl. Watanabe explains, "Both are simple in form, but make special use of traditional Chinese technology and designs. Lacquer is sometimes referred to as 'japan' but it is also part of traditional Chinese culture… These designs are not simply a resurrection of traditional styles. They are an attempt to apply genetic engineering to elements in Chinese tradition that should be passed down." Makoto Sei Watanabe seeks to blend his own culture with that, more ancient, of China, and to highlight local craftsmanship.

Das Grundstück des Hauses befindet sich im Zentrum Shanghais. In der Umgebung stehen Wohnhäuser aus der Kolonialzeit. Die Straßenfront des Hauses soll auf die Gestaltung der Umgebung antworten; Höhe und Tiefe des Gebäudes entsprechen denen der Nachbarhäuser. Das geneigte Dach, die Anordnung der Fenster und die Farbgebung sind ebenfalls vergleichbar. Watanabe sagt: »Mit anderen Worten: Man könnte sagen, das Haus hat keine Fassade. Da man von keiner Stelle das ganze Haus sehen kann, haben wir mehr Wert darauf gelegt, es in die Nachbarschaft einzufügen. Das Haus ist eine ›Anhäufung von Teilen‹ und funktioniert als Element in der Straßenlandschaft.« Ein elliptischer Innenhof mit einem schwarzen Granitboden und einer filterartigen, umlaufenden Glasfassade bildet das Zentrum des Hauses. Der Granitboden setzt sich im Inneren des Hauses fort. »Außen und Innen sind eine Einheit, voneinander getrennt und sich überlappend«, sagt der Architekt daher. Die Glasfassade ist direkt in den Granitboden des Innenhofes eingelassen. Der Hof kann mit Wasser geflutet werden, wodurch vielfältige Reflexionen im Haus entstehen. Die Möbel des Erdgeschosses sind aus schwarz lackiertem Holz mit Reliefarbeiten aus Goldstaub oder Intarsien aus Perlmutt. Watanabe erklärt: »Beide Möbelarten sind einfach in der Form, benutzen aber auf spezielle Weise traditionelle chinesische Techniken und Gestaltungsmuster. Lack wird manchmal als typisch japanisch bezeichnet, er ist aber auch Teil der traditionellen chinesischen Kultur. Diese Entwürfe sind nicht einfach eine Wiederaufnahme der traditionellen Stile. Sie sind der Versuch, ›Genmanipulationen‹ auf Elemente der chinesischen Tradition, die weitergegeben werden sollten, anzuwenden.« Insgesamt gesehen will Makoto Sei Watanabe seine eigene Kultur mit der älteren chinesischen Kultur mischen und das ortsspezifische Handwerk stärken.

Le site de cette maison se trouve dans le centre de Shanghai, à proximité d'autres résidences datant de la période coloniale. La façade sur rue a été dessinée en fonction de cet environnement. La hauteur et la profondeur sont à peu près les mêmes que celles des bâtiments voisins. Le toit incliné, la disposition des fenêtres et l'utilisation de la couleur sont également comparables. Pour Watanabe, « … en d'autres termes, on pourrait dire que cette architecture n'a pas de façade. Comme l'ensemble n'est jamais visible en totalité quel que soit le point de vue, l'accent a été mis sur l'intégration au voisinage par une accumulation de pièces qui fonctionnent comme un élément dans le paysage urbain ». Une cour intérieure en ellipse, pavée de granit noir et entourée d'un écran de verre, forme le cœur de la maison. Le granit se poursuivant à l'intérieur, l'architecte explique que « … l'intérieur et l'extérieur sont en continu, disjoints et superposés ». L'écran de verre s'élève directement depuis le granit de la cour, qui peut être noyé d'eau pour créer de multiples reflets. Le mobilier de l'étage est en laque noire à reliefs de poussière d'or ou incrustations de nacre. « Ces deux techniques simples utilisent de façon particulière les styles et les savoir-faire chinois traditionnels … Ces dessins ne sont pas seulement une résurrection de styles anciens. Ils représentent une tentative d'appliquer une ingénierie génétique à des éléments de la tradition chinoise qui pourraient disparaître. » Makoto Sei Watanabe cherche à fusionner sa propre culture à celle, plus ancienne, de la Chine, et à mettre en valeur l'artisanat local.

With the InOut House, Makoto Sei Watanabe substantially broadens the field of his work, known more until now for its relation to computer-driven design, and projects such as museums, or subway and railroad stations.

Mit dem InOut-Haus erweitert Makoto Sei Watanabe sein Spektrum beträchtlich. Bislang war er eher für seine computergrafisch aufbereiteten Entwürfe für Museen, U-Bahnstationen und Bahnhöfe bekannt.

La InOut House de Makoto Sei Watanabe marque une évolution dans l'œuvre de cet architecte, connu surtout pour ses recherches sur la conception par ordinateur pour des musées, des gares ou des stations de métro.

Sensitive to the spirit of the times, Watanabe has not hesitated to call on some of the imagery or techniques of traditional China in the décor and furniture of the house.

Watanabe, dem Zeitgeist gegenüber aufgeschlossen, zögert nicht, die Bilderwelt und Techniken des alten Chinas für das Dekor und die Möblierung zu verwenden.

Sensible à l'esprit du temps, Watanabe n'a pas hésité à employer les styles et les techniques traditionnels chinois pour le décor et le mobilier de la maison.

The shallow central reflecting pool gives light and creates an impression of constant movement to the house.

Der flache, reflektierende zentrale Pool spendet Licht und erweckt im Haus den Eindruck permanenter Bewegung.

Le bassin réfléchissant central est une source supplémentaire de lumiè- re qui crée une impression de mou- vement constant dans la maison.

ISAY WEINFELD

Isay Weinfeld Arquiteto
R.André Fernandes,175
CEP04 536–020
São Paulo SP
Brasil

Tel: +55 11 30 79 75 81
Fax: +55 11 30 79 56 56
e-mail: iwarq@uol.com.br
Web: www.isayweinfeld.com

Fasano Hotel

ISAY WEINFELD was born in 1952 in São Paulo, Brazil. He graduated from the School of Architecture at Mackenzie University in 1975. In an unusual mixture of careers, Weinfeld has also worked in cinema since 1974, making fourteen short films that have received numerous international awards. In 1988, he wrote and directed his first full-length movie, *Fogo e Paixão,* considered in Switzerland to be one of the ten best comedies produced that year worldwide. In 1989, the São Paulo Art Critics' Association awarded him the Prize for Best New Director. He has taught the Theory of Architecture courses at the School of Architecture of Mackenzie University and was a professor of Kinetic Expression at the School of Communications of the Fundação Armando Álvares Penteado. Weinfeld has completed dozens of private homes, commercial projects, banks, advertising agencies, discotheques, a bar, a restaurant, an art gallery and the Fasano Hotel and Restaurant published here. He has worked with Marcio Kogan on numerous projects, including the 2001 exhibit *Umore and Architektur*, at the Casa Brasileira Museum.

ISAY WEINFELD, geboren 1952 in São Paulo, Brasilien, machte seinen Abschluss an der Architekturfakultät der Mackenzie University 1975. Sein Werdegang ist eine ungewöhnliche Mischung: Ab 1974 arbeitete er auch beim Film und drehte 14 Kurzfilme, die mehrfach mit internationalen Preisen ausgezeichnet wurden. 1988 schrieb er das Drehbuch und führte Regie für seinen ersten Spielfilm *Fogo e Paixão,* der in der Schweiz auf der Liste der weltweit besten zehn Komödien des Jahres stand. 1989 zeichnete ihn der Kritikerverband von São Paulo als besten Newcomer-Regisseur aus. Er hat Architekturtheorie an der Architekturfakultät der Mackenzie University unterrichtet und war Professor für Kinetischer Ausdruck an der Schule für Kommunikation der Fundação Armando Álvares Penteado. Weinfeld hat mehrere Dutzend Privathäuser gebaut, ferner kommerzielle Gebäude, Banken, Werbeagenturen, Diskotheken, eine Bar, ein Restaurant, eine Kunstgalerie und das hier gezeigte Hotel Fasano. Zahlreiche Projekte hat Weinfeld zusammen mit Marcio Kogan bearbeitet, darunter 2001 die Ausstellung *Umore and Architektur* im Museum Casa Brasileira.

Né en 1952 à São Paulo, **ISAY WEINFELD** est diplômé de l'École d'architecture de Mackenzie University en 1975. Conjuguant deux carrières, il travaille également dans le cinéma depuis 1974 et a réalisé 14 courts-métrages qui ont reçu de nombreux prix internationaux. En 1988, il a écrit et dirigé son premier long-métrage, *Fogo e Paixaõ,* considéré comme l'une des meilleures comédies de l'année par un festival suisse. En 1989, l'Association des critiques d'art de São Paulo lui a décerné le prix du meilleur nouveau réalisateur. Il a enseigné la théorie de l'architecture à Mackenzie University et l'expression cinétique à l'École de communication de la Fondation Armando Álvares Penteado. Il a réalisé de nombreuses résidences privées, projets commerciaux, banques, agences de publicité, discothèques, un bar, un restaurant, une galerie d'art et l'hôtel Fasano publié ici. Il a collaboré avec Marcio Kogan sur de nombreux projets, notamment l'exposition *Umore and Architektur* au musée de la Casa Brasileira (2001).

FASANO HOTEL AND RESTAURANT

São Paulo, Brazil, 2001–03

Floor area: 10 300 m². Client: Rogerio Fasano, João Paulo Diniz. Cost: not disclosed

Isay Weinfeld worked on the 10 300 m² **FASANO HOTEL** with Marcio Kogan, and designed the spectacular attached 810 m² restaurant on his own. As Weinfeld describes the project, "The Fasano family is the best-known traditional family in the field of gastronomy in Brazil. One day, Rogerio Fasano came to our office with an English brick in his hand and a dream on his mind. We tried to make the dream come true by designing a hotel that would, above all, translate the character of the Fasano family. The project is at once contemporary and classic. It is not a boutique hotel or a design hotel. Rather, it is a hotel that, right at its opening, already seemed to have existed for many years. It was made to last, not to tire. One of the strongest ideas of the project was moving the reception desk to the back of the lobby. Thus, when you come into the main lobby, you find a pleasant bar, and the reception desk is behind it. The hotel has 64 rooms. The suites have different sizes but they all overlook Jardim Europa, a residential neighborhood of São Paulo that is registered as historical heritage of the city. The hotel facilities include a pool on the roof, saunas, spa, fitness center, business center and a small restaurant for light meals, Nonno Ruggero. On the ground floor are Baretto, a bar featuring live jazz and bossa nova, and Fasano Restaurant, long considered the best restaurant in Brazil." Sophisticated and modern, the Fasano has been called a "reinterpretation of 1930s style," but it is above all comfortable and coherent.

Isay Weinfeld plante das 10 300 m² große **HOTEL FASANO** in Zusammenarbeit mit Marcio Kogan; der Entwurf des spektakulären Restaurantanbaus stammt von Weinfeld. Er beschreibt das Projekt folgendermaßen: »Die Fasano-Familie ist die bekannteste Familie in der traditionellen brasilianischen Gastronomie. Eines Tages kam Rogerio Fasano in unser Büro, einen englischen Ziegelstein in der Hand und einen Traum in seinem Kopf. Wir haben versucht, diesen Traum Wirklichkeit werden zu lassen, indem wir ein Hotel entwarfen, das vor allem den Charakter der Fasano-Familie vermitteln sollte. Das Gebäude ist gleichzeitig modern und klassisch. Es ist kein ›Boutique-Hotel‹ und kein Design-Hotel, eher eines, das von Anfang an so wirkte, als existiere es seit vielen Jahren. Es wurde gebaut, um die Zeit zu überdauern, nicht um zu ermüden. Eine der stärksten Ideen des Entwurfs war die Verlegung der Rezeption in den hinteren Bereich der Lobby. Betritt man die Lobby, findet man daher eine angenehme Bar vor; die Rezeption liegt dahinter. Das Hotel hat 64 Zimmer. Die Suiten sind unterschiedlich groß, haben aber alle einen Ausblick auf den Jardim Europa, einen unter Denkmalschutz stehenden Wohnbezirk São Paulos. Zu den Einrichtungen des Hotels gehören ein Pool auf dem Dach des Gebäudes, mehrere Saunen, ein Spa, ein Fitnesscenter, ein Businesscenter und das kleine Restaurant Nonno Ruggero für leichte Mahlzeiten. Im Erdgeschoss liegen die Bar Baretto – hier werden Live Jazz und Bossa Nova geboten – und das Restaurant Fasano, das lange als bestes Restaurant Brasiliens galt.« Anspruchsvoll und modern, wurde das Restaurant Fasano eine »Neuinterpretation des Stils der 1930er Jahre« genannt, in erster Linie aber ist es komfortabel und in sich schlüssig.

Isay Weinfeld a conçu l'**HÔTEL FASANO** de 10 300 m² en collaboration avec Marcio Kogan et réalisé seul son spectaculaire restaurant (810 m²). Il décrit ainsi son projet : « Les Fasano sont une grande famille, la plus célèbre dans le domaine de la restauration gastronomique du Brésil. Un jour, Rogerio Fasano est venu à notre agence, une brique anglaise à la main et une idée en tête. Nous avons essayé de concrétiser celle-ci en lui dessinant un hôtel qui traduirait avant tout le caractère de cette famille. C'est un projet à la fois contemporain et classique. Ce n'est pas un « boutique hotel » ni un « design hotel ». C'est plutôt un établissement qui, dès son ouverture, semblait avoir existé depuis de longues années. Il a été fait pour durer, non pour lasser. L'une des idées fortes est d'avoir déplacé la réception au fond du lobby. Ainsi, lorsque vous entrez, vous trouvez d'abord un bar agréable, avant la réception même. L'hôtel possède 64 chambres ; les suites sont de différentes tailles, mais donnent toutes sur le Jardim Europa, un quartier résidentiel de São Paulo qui fait partie du patrimoine culturel de la ville. Il possède une piscine sur le toit, des saunas, un spa, un centre de remise en forme, un centre d'affaires et un petit restaurant pour des repas légers, « Nonno Ruggero ». Au rez-de-chaussée se trouvent le Baretto, un bar avec orchestre de jazz ou de bossa-nova, et le Fasano Restaurant considéré depuis longtemps comme le meilleur du Brésil. » Sophistiqué et moderne, le Fasano a pu être qualifié de « réinterprétation du style des années 1930 », mais il est avant tout confortable et cohérent.

The entrance to the hotel, rather than containing the usual lobby, is a bar (right), and visitors encounter the check-in desk only in a second sequence of spaces (lower left).

Im Eingangsbereich des Hotels liegt nicht wie sonst üblich die Lobby, sondern eine Bar (rechts). Die Rezeption findet der Gast erst in einer zweiten Raumfolge (unten rechts).

L'entrée de l'hôtel n'est pas l'habituel comptoir d'accueil mais un bar (à droite). Les visiteurs ne découvrent la réception que dans une seconde séquence de volumes (à l'extrême droite).

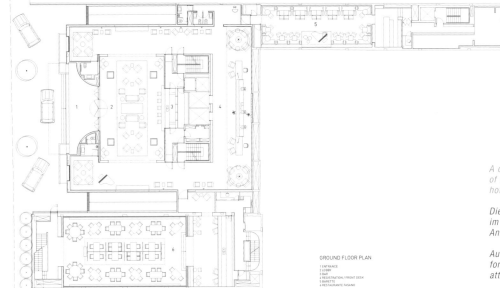

A dark and comfortable bar is one of the ground floor amenities of the hotel.

Die dunkle und komfortable Bar im Erdgeschoss gehört zu den Annehmlichkeiten des Hotels.

Au rez-de-chaussée, le bar, confortable et sombre, est l'une des attractions de l'hôtel.

A guest room (below), and the
restaurant (following double-page).

Unten: ein Hotelzimmer. Nächste
Doppelseite: das Restaurant.

Une chambre (ci-dessous) et le
restaurant (double page suivante).

INDEX OF PLACES

CREDITS

PHOTO CREDITS

52 © David Adjaye / **53–59** © Timothy Soar / **60** © Asymptote Architecture / **66** © Auer + Weber + Architekten / **67–71** © Roland Halbe/artur / **72** © Shigeru Ban Architects / **73–77** © Michael Moran / **79–81** © Didier Boy de la Tour / **82** © Barclay & Crousse Architecture / **83, 85–89** © Jean Pierre Crousse / **90–95** © baumraum Andreas Wenning / **96–99, 101** © "Booster" Bekkering & Adams Arch / **102** © Caramel Architekten / **103–105** © Hertha Hurnaus / **106** © Casey Brown Architecture / **108** right, **109** bottom, **111** top © Patrick Bingham-Hall / **107, 108** left, **109** top left to right, **110, 111** bottom, **112, 113** top right and bottom © Anthony Browell / **114** © David Chipperfield / **115–119** © Hélène Binet / **120–123** © Hisao Suzuki / **124** © Cox Richardson Architects / **125–129** © Patrick Bingham-Hall / **130** © G. Darugar / **136** © Diller + Scofidio + Renfro / **139** top © George A. Fuller, builder, courtesy of archiveofindustry.com / **139** bottom © Joel Sternfeld 2000 / **140** © Dennis Dollens / **144–151** © Yutaka Suzuki / **152, 157** bottom right © Stefan Eberstadt / **153–154** © Silke Koch / **155–156, 157** bottom left © Claus Bach / **158** © Udo Hesse/akg-images / **159–162** © Werner Huthmacher/artur / **163** top © Klaus Frahm/artur / **163** bottom © Roland Halbe/artur / **164** © Eric Morin / **165–173** © Christian Richters / **174** © Yoshiharu Matsumura / **175–179** © Edmund Sumner/VIEW / **180** © FLAnk / **184, 186–188, 191** top right © Fuksas Office / **185, 189** top and bottom left © Paolo Riolzi / **189** bottom right, **190, 191** top left and bottom © Philippe Ruault / **192** © Ga.A Architects / **193, 195–197** © Kim Yong Kwan / **198** © Gehry Partners, LLP / **199–203** © andreas secci/architekturphoto / **204** © GRAFT / **205–211** © hiepler brunier architekturfotografie / **212–219** © Groep Delta / **220** © Zaha Hadid / **221, 224–227** © Hélène Binet/artur / **222–223** © Roland Halbe/artur / **228** © Herrmann + Bosch / **229, 231–233** © Roland Halbe/artur / **234** © Hertl.Architekten / **235–239** © Paul Ott, Graz / **240** © Herzog & de Meuron / **241–249** © Duccio Malagamba / **250–251, 252** top left to right, **253, 254** top left and bottom left © Roland Halbe/artur / **252** bottom, **254** top right and bottom right © Tim Griffith/Esto / **256** © Mark Heitoff / **257–261** © Margherita Spiluttini / **263–267** © Andy Ryan / **268** © Joan Costes / **269–275** © Jean Marie Monthiers / **278** © Agence Patrick Jouin / **279, 281–285, 290–292** bottom left and right, **293** © Thomas Duval / **286–289, 292** top, **294, 295** Eric Laignel / **296** © Nader Khalili / **297, 299** top right, **301** © Virginia Sanchis / **299** top left and bottom left to right, **300, 301** top left and bottom left © Khalili/Cal-Earth, courtesy of Aga Khan Award for Architecture / **302** © Anselm Kiefer / **303–309** © Philippe Chancel 2005 / **310** © Klein Dytham architecture / **311–313** © Kozo Takayama / **314–317** © Katsuhisa Kida / **318** © Mathias Klotz / **319–323** © Roland Halbe/artur / **324** © Marcio Kogan / **325–331** © Nelson Kon / **332** © Rem Koolhaas/OMA / **333–341** © Timothy Hursley / **342** © Kengo Kuma & Associates / **343–351** © Daici Ano / **352** © Henning Larsens Tegnestue / **353–359** © Adam Mørk / **360** © Maya Lin Studio / **361–365** © Timothy Hursley / **366–373** © LLPS Arquitectos S. L. / **374** © LTL Architects / **375–377** © Michael Moran / **378, 380, 381** top left to right © Michael Moran / **379, 381** bottom © Rudolph Janu / **382** © Michael Maltzan Architecture / **384–385** © Joshua White / **386–387, 389** top, **390, 392–394** top, **395** © Mansilla + Tuñón / **389** bottom, **391** top, **394** bottom © Roland Halbe/artur / **396** © Corinne Trang Photographer / **400** © Richard Phibbs / **401, 403–405** © Roland Halbe/artur / **406** © Morphosis / **407–411** © Roland Halbe/artur / **412** © Oscar Niemeyer / **416** © Marcos Novak / **422** © ONL / **426** © John Pawson / **427–433** © Stepan Bartoš, fotostudio* / **434** © Pierre Fantys / **436** © Philippe Rahm architectes / **438** © Gaston F. Bergeret / **439** bottom © IGN 2005 / **440** © Plaine Commune / **444** © François Roche / **450** © Thomas Roszak / **451–455** © Jon Miller, Hedrich Blessing / **456** © Moshe Safdie / **457, 459–465** © Timothy Hursley / **466** © Akira Sakamoto / **467–469** © Hiroyuki Hirai / **471–473** © Yoshiharu Matsumura / **474** © Schmidt, Hammer & Lassen / **475, 477–479** © Adam Mørk / **480, 486** bottom © Schwartz/Silver Architects / **481–486** top right, **487** © Timothy Hursley / **488** © Roger Sherman / **489, 491–493** © Tom Bonner / **494** © SITE / **498** left © Tereza Siza / **498** right © Luis Ferreira Alves / **499–503** © Duccio Malagamba / **504** © Nathan Benn/CORBIS / **508** © Peter Stutchbury / **509–513** © Michael Nicholson / **514** © Yoshio Taniguchi / **515–519** © Timothy Hursley / **520** © Tezuka Architects / **521–525** © Katsuhisa Kida / **526** © Trahan Architects / **527–535** © Timothy Hursley / **536** © various architects / **537–543** © Hisao Suzuki / **544** © VHP / **545–549** © Ralph Richter/architekturphoto / **550–555** © Kira Perov, courtesy Bill Viola Studio** / **556–563** © Makoto Sei Watanabe/Architects' Office / **564** © Isay Weinfeld / **565–571** © Tuca Reinés

CREDITS PLANS / DRAWINGS / CAD DOCUMENTS

*The community of monks at Novy Dvur tries to lead a life of prayer in silence and a great solitude. They inform their possible visitors that visiting or taking photos of the monastery is not allowed, inside as well as outside. The conditions of reception are specified on the web site www.novydvur.cz

**Tristan and Isolde is produced by the Paris National Opéra in collaboration with the Los Angeles Philharmonic Association and Lincoln Center for the Performing Arts, with assistance from James Cohan Gallery, New York, Haunch of Venison, London, and the Bill Viola Studio.

Architecture

Philip Jodidio / pj002@dial.oleane.com

Contemporary architecture by country

TASCHEN's new architecture series brings a unique perspective to world architecture, highlighting architectural trends by country. Each book features 15 to 20 architects—from the firmly established to the up-and-coming—with the focus on how they have contributed to the current face of architecture in the chosen nation. Entries include contact information and short biographies in addition to copiously illustrated descriptions of the architects' or firms' most significant recent projects. Traversing the globe from country to country, this new series celebrates the richly hued architectural personality of each nation featured.

Series author: **Philip Jodidio** studied art history and economics at Harvard University, and was Editor-in-Chief of the leading French art journal *Connaissance des Arts* for over two decades. He has published numerous articles and books, including TASCHEN's *Architecture Now* series, *Building a New Millennium*, and monographs on Norman Foster, Richard Meier, Alvaro Siza, Tadao Ando, and Renzo Piano.

ARCHITECTURE IN JAPAN
Philip Jodidio / Hardcover, format:
Hardcover, 23.1 x 28.9 cm (9.1 x 11.4 in.), 192 pp.
English/German/French edition
3–8228–3988–4
€ 19.99 / $ 24.99 / £ 14.99 / ¥ 3.900

ARCHITECTURE IN THE NETHERLANDS
Philip Jodidio / Hardcover, format:
Hardcover, 23.1 x 28.9 cm (9.1 x 11.4 in.), 192 pp.
English/German/French edition
3–8228–3971–X
€ 19.99 / $ 24.99 / £ 14.99 / ¥ 3.900

ARCHITECTURE IN SWITZERLAND
Philip Jodidio / Hardcover, format:
Hardcover, 23.1 x 28.9 cm (9.1 x 11.4 in.), 192 pp.
English/German/French edition
3–8228–3973–6
€ 19.99 / $ 24.99 / £ 14.99 / ¥ 3.900

ARCHITECTURE IN THE UNITED KINGDOM
Philip Jodidio / Hardcover, format:
Hardcover, 23.1 x 28.9 cm (9.1 x 11.4 in.), 192 pp.
English/German/French edition
3–8228–3972–8
€ 19.99 / $ 24.99 / £ 14.99 / ¥ 3.900

TADAO ANDO. COMPLETE WORKS
Philip Jodidio / Hardcover, **XXL-format**: 30.8 x 39 cm
(12.1 x 15.3 in.), 504 pp. / English/German/French edition
3–8228–2164–0
€ 99.99 / $ 125 / £ 69.99 / ¥ 15.000

RENZO PIANO. WORKS 1966–2004
Philip Jodidio / Hardcover, **XXL-format**: 30.8 x 39 cm
(12.1 x 15.3 in.), 496 pp. / English/German/French edition
3–8228–5768–8
€ 99.99 / $ 125 / £ 69.99 / ¥ 15.000

ARCHITECTURE NOW!
Philip Jodidio / Flexi-cover, format:
19.6 x 24.9 cm (7.7 x 9.8 in.), 576 pp. /
English/German/French edition
3–8228–6065–4
€ 29.99 / $ 39.99 / £ 19.99 / ¥ 5.900

ARCHITECTURE NOW! VOL. II
Philip Jodidio / Flexi-cover, format:
19.6 x 24.9 cm (7.7 x 9.8 in.), 576 pp. /
English/German/French edition
3–8228–1594–2
€ 29.99 / $ 39.99 / £ 19.99 / ¥ 5.900

ARCHITECTURE NOW! VOL. III
Philip Jodidio / Flexi-cover, format:
19.6 x 24.9 cm (7.7 x 9.8 in.), 576 pp. /
English/German/French edition
3–8228–3989–2
€ 29.99 / $ 39.99 / £ 19.99 / ¥ 5.900

"A cross-section of existing projects, plus some truly experimental ideas still only alive in cyberspace."
—*TIME OUT*, London